CHRISTIAN ETHICKS

BY THOMAS TRAHERNE

General Introduction and Commentary
by CAROL L. MARKS
Cornell University

Textual Introduction and Text Prepared
by GEORGE ROBERT GUFFEY
University of California, Los Angeles

Cornell University Press

ITHACA, NEW YORK

CORNELL UNIVERSITY PRESS

First published 1968

This book has been published with the aid of a grant from the Hull Memorial Publication Fund of Cornell University.

Library of Congress Catalog Card Number: 66-20015

PRINTED IN THE UNITED STATES OF AMERICA

BY THE MAPLE PRESS COMPANY

CORNELL STUDIES IN ENGLISH

EDITED BY

M. H. ABRAMS

FRANCIS E. MINEKA

WILLIAM M. SALE, JR.

VOLUME XLIII

CHRISTIAN ETHICKS

BY THOMAS TRAHERNE

Preface

PUBLISHED in 1675, *Christian Ethicks* was ignored for some two hundred and fifty years. Interest in the book developed after the discovery of Traherne's manuscripts and the publication of their literary content (1903, 1908, 1910). Since then students of Traherne have urged the republication of the *Ethicks,* copies of which are still relatively scarce. The poems interspersed in the latter part of the volume were printed in the editions of Traherne's poetry edited by Bertram Dobell, Gladys Wade, and H. M. Margoliouth; and two chapters (XIX and XXVIII) were published in 1942 under the title *Of Magnanimity and Charity,* with an introduction by John Rothwell Slater. In 1962 a modernized version of the *Ethicks* appeared under the title *The Way to Blessedness,* prepared by Margaret Bottrall for the Faith Press of London; it is unfortunately marred by errors of transcription. While making a text available to the lay reader, Mrs. Bottrall's edition does not aim to satisfy the scholar's need for an accurate text and for an *apparatus criticus* which explains the obsolete aspects of the treatise and places it both historically and generically. The purpose of the present edition is to satisfy that need.

In structure and terminology *Christian Ethicks* reminds us of the persistence through the seventeenth century of medieval forms of thought, of the continued influence in academic curricula of Aristotle and his expositors. But although the mold was Aristotle's, the metal was Plato's; Traherne was temperamentally akin not to Aristotelianism but to Renaissance Neoplatonism, in particular to that version developed at Cambridge during his lifetime. His lonely analysis—nothing

v

like it was published in English in the thirty years after the Restoration—really belongs to no "school," however; Traherne wished simply to draw a picture of virtue so engaging as to attract men of good will almost irresistibly. He appealed to religious and humane feelings more than to the intellect. Neither a manual of behavior nor a comprehensive outline of ethics, *Christian Ethicks* in its writing required—and in its reading still requires—resources of heart even more than of mind; it is felt thought.

The feeling remains vivid today, thanks partly to Traherne's persuasive style; the thought, though easy enough in 1675, may now need clarification. The Commentary of the present edition attempts to elucidate *Christian Ethicks* largely by means of quotations from Traherne's contemporaries, giving preference to works that we know Traherne read. When an idea was part of the intellectual atmosphere of the seventeenth century, the Commentary does not always point to the ultimate source. Commonplaces have no "source": it would falsify intellectual history to cite Aristotle in reference to statements which actually represent Aristotle transformed through centuries of commentary.

The scholar investigating Traherne's intellectual interests now has at his disposal a wealth of manuscript evidence scarcely tapped in published scholarship. The opening section of the General Introduction surveys the manuscript material pertinent to *Christian Ethicks*. The other principal source of factual knowledge about Traherne is H. M. Margoliouth's introduction to Traherne's *Centuries, Poems, and Thanksgivings* (Oxford, 1958); the present editors assume familiarity with the information assembled there.

The critical, old-spelling text of this edition was established after a collation of six copies of the 1675 edition of *Christian Ethicks*. All press-variants discovered in the collation of these copies are listed in Press-Variants by Formes. Emendations have been held to a minimum, and all corrections have been recorded in Corrections of the Text. Specific reasons for emending or not emending apparently corrupt passages and for choosing certain press-variants over others are stated in Textual Notes.

The Selected Bibliography lists all the works of Traherne—both published and unpublished—which this edition cites. In references to the *Centuries* (C) and Select Meditations (SM) the roman numeral indicates the century and the arabic numeral the meditation, thus: *C* II.46. The poems and *Thanksgivings,* which constitute Volume II of Margoliouth's edition, are referred to by individual title, volume, and page, thus: "Wonder," II, 6. Other abbreviations are as follows: CB, Commonplace Book (references are to folio and column, thus: f. 64.1); *CE, Christian Ethicks,* in the present edition; CYB, Church's Year-Book; EN, Early Notebook; FN, Ficino Notebook.

This edition is based on doctoral dissertations written at the universities of Wisconsin (Marks) and Illinois (Guffey); the editors are grateful for the supervisory advice of Professor Helen C. White of Wisconsin and Professor Gwynne B. Evans of Illinois. Professor David Novarr of Cornell University read the entire manuscript and commented most helpfully. Special thanks are due to Mr. James M. Osborn of Yale for his extraordinary kindness in giving permission to read and quote from the Select Meditations, which he will edit as Volume III of the Oxford Traherne. The General Introduction could not have been written without the generosity of the Union Theological Seminary Library (New York) and especially of Mrs. Sue M. Foster, the then Curator of Rare Books. Miss Imogen Forster checked minutiae in England, and Harry J. Marks read and improved the General Introduction. The Grant-in-Aid Fund of the Cornell Department of English made possible a summer in Oxford. For permission to examine their copies of *Christian Ethicks,* the editors are indebted to Union Theological Seminary, the Bodleian Library, the British Museum, Parker and Son (copy sold to Syracuse University), B. H. Blackwell and Son (copy sold to the University of Waterloo), Mr. H. Bradley Martin, and the libraries of the universities of Cambridge, Illinois, Princeton, Rochester, and Yale. The Clarendon Press has kindly given permission to quote from Traherne's *Centuries, Poems, and Thanksgivings,* ed. H. M. Margoliouth, 2 vols.

C. L. M.

G. R. G.

April 1967

Contents

x Contents

General Introduction

I   The Traherne Manuscripts

THE student of Traherne's thought is fortunate in the abundance of both manuscript and printed works. In the latter category appear not only the *Centuries, Poems, and Thanksgivings,* edited by H. M. Margoliouth, but also *Christian Ethicks* (1675), *Roman Forgeries* (1673), and the *Meditations on the Six Days of the Creation* (1717).[1] Five manuscripts include a large amount of unpublished writings. One, discovered in 1964 by James M. Osborn, consists of "Select Meditations" of the sort contained in the *Centuries.*[2] In his introduction (I, xii–xiv, xvii–xxii) Dr. Margoliouth describes three of the four other manuscripts (all three in the Bodleian Library, Oxford): the Commonplace Book, which forms the largest part of the so-called Dobell Manuscript; the Church's Year-Book; and the Early Notebook, which Dr. Margoliouth inaccurately entitles "Philip Traherne's Notebook." The last unpublished manuscript is the Ficino Notebook in the British Museum.

Although none but the Osborn manuscript has more than an occasional flash of literary interest, all the manuscripts are pertinent to the study of Traherne's thought. We must wait until Mr. Osborn edits

---

[1] Formerly ascribed to Susanna Hopton, the *Meditations* have been shown definitively to be Traherne's work; see Catherine A. Owen, "The Authorship of the 'Meditations on the Six Days of Creation' . . . ," *Modern Language Review,* LVI (1961), 1–5; and George Robert Guffey, Intro. to the reprint of the *Meditations* by the Augustan Reprint Society (Los Angeles, 1966), pp. i–vii.

[2] On this manuscript see James M. Osborn, "A New Traherne Manuscript," *The Times Literary Supplement,* Oct. 8, 1964, p. 928. There are at least two precise links between the Select Meditations and the *Ethicks;* see *CE,* pp. 41:18, 171:31, and Commentary.

the Select Meditations to assess the full import of that work; it is possible now to give brief accounts of the other manuscripts.

The Early Notebook originally belonged to Traherne's brother, but Philip Traherne ceased writing on page five (he added some notes on pp. 237–240 when he reacquired the notebook after Thomas's death). Hence it was Thomas Traherne who wrote the Latin epitomes of Eustache de Saint-Paul's ethics textbook, of an unidentified Renaissance geometry textbook, and of Justin's *History*, all of which Dr. Margoliouth ascribed to Philip. The three epitomes date from Traherne's undergraduate days at Brasenose College, Oxford (1653–1656); of this material only the summary of ethics (discussed Part II, Section A) is of much relevance, though an anecdote from Justin made its way into the chapter on meekness in *Christian Ethicks* (Chap. XXV).

In the central section of the Early Notebook, Traherne excerpted voluminously from Francis Bacon's *De augmentis scientiarum,* with one quotation each from Bacon's *Apophthegmes* and *Essays* (EN, pp. 69–170, with twenty-five blank pages interspersed). Scattered throughout these pages are various short passages from other authors, identified and unidentified, in Latin and in English. Edward Reynolds, later Bishop of Norwich, is the most significant author cited; Traherne referred three times to Reynolds' youthful and verbose *Treatise of the Passions and Faculties of the Soule of Man* (1640), a self-styled (sig. a1) "Phylosophicall Miscellany" stressing man's dignity and his natural and commendable thirst for knowledge. Although the quotations from Bacon and Reynolds may have been made by 1656, internal evidence indicates a slightly later date—shortly after Traherne had gone down from Oxford, while he was pursuing private studies as the incumbent of St. Mary's, Credinhill, in Herefordshire. The same temporal hypothesis applies to the material which follows the Bacon section—extracts from an unidentified Latin work on religion and early poems (two of which are epitaphs for members of Traherne's Credinhill parish). The Early Notebook, in short, suggests Traherne's intellectual interests both during his student days and during the period immediately following, when he "resolved to Spend" all his time "in Search of Happiness, and to Satiat that burning Thirst which Nature had Enkindled, in me from my Youth" (*C* III.46).

The Church's Year-Book depicts Traherne as an orthodox, dutiful clergyman, an aspect of his character often submerged in his other works. The manuscript was most probably begun in 1669 and the extant portion written during April–November, 1670. A product of Traherne's London period (1669–1672), it seems to reflect in part his duties as chaplain to Sir Orlando Bridgeman.[3]

The Church's Year-Book forms a valuable adjunct to a study of *Christian Ethicks,* in part because it is Traherne's most clerical work, in part because the authorities Traherne cited indicate his reading just prior to the composition of the *Ethicks.* His debts in the Year-Book were almost all to seventeenth-century theologians and devotional writers of a distinctly orthodox Anglican cast. Sermons by Andrewes and Donne, devotions by Andrewes (*Institutiones Piae* as well as the *Private Devotions*), George Herbert's poem "To All Angels and Saints"—these are works we still read. The other known sources, now largely forgotten, were by no means obscure in their day: Daniel Featley's *Ancilla Pietatis,* John Gerard's *Meditations,* Edward Sparke's *Scintilla-Altaris,* Anthony Sparrow's *Rationale upon the Book of Common-Prayer,* Jeremy Taylor's *Great Exemplar,* William Austin's *Devotionis Augustinianae Flamma,* Meredith Hanmer's translation of *The Auncient Ecclesiasticall Histories* by Eusebius and others, and the pseudo-Augustinian *Meditations.* One source, obscure at any time, was "Leontius a father in the Nicene Counsel" (f. 51). Behind the entire Year-Book lie the Bible and the Book of Common Prayer.

Since Traherne, aided by an amanuensis, compiled the Commonplace Book[4] during the last four years of his life, it is particularly relevant to *Christian Ethicks;* twice he drew on it directly for the *Ethicks* (see pp. 126:31, 225:21, and Commentary). The five known sources

---

[3] On the dating, debts, and content of this manuscript, see Carol L. Marks, "Traherne's Church's Year-Book," *Papers of the Bibliographical Society of America,* LX (1966), 31–72.

The *Centuries,* the *Ethicks,* and the *Meditations* provide additional evidence of Traherne's reading. In the *Centuries* (*c.* 1670) he referred to Plato, Aristotle, Plutarch, St. Anselm, Eusebius, St. Gregory Nazianzen, St. Gregory the Great, Pico della Mirandola, Luther, Philippe de Mornay, Seneca, Thomas à Kempis, and Varro. In *C* III.41 he cited Albertus Magnus as an authority on "the Secrets of Nature"; Galileo on astronomy; Hevelius on the moon; Galen on human anatomy; Hippocrates on diseases; Orpheus on music; Homer on poetry; Lilly on Latin grammar. The mixed bag of the *Ethicks* includes Aristotle, Plato, Seneca, Cicero, Hermes Trismegistus, St. John Chrysostom, Pierre Charron, *The Whole Duty of Man,* and (perhaps) Henry Hammond. In the *Meditations* he referred to Ambrose and Lactantius.

[4] See Carol Marks, "Thomas Traherne's Commonplace Book," *Papers of the Bibliographical Society of America,* LVIII (1964), 458–465.

of the Commonplace Book account for most of its contents. Traherne opened the book with extracts from Theophilus Gale's *Court of the Gentiles*, Part II (Oxford, 1670), an ungainly summary of civilization consisting in good part of précis of the principal Semitic and Western philosophers; Gale's theme is the ultimate derivation of all thought and expression from Hebrew culture. The other four identified sources are more obviously congenial to Traherne's thought. Four volumes of the *Commentaries on the Creed* (1625, 1628, 1629, 1657) by Thomas Jackson, an Arminian Oxonian who expressed attitudes akin to Traherne's, constitute the largest source for the Commonplace Book. He incorporated into the *Ethicks* (Chap. XXVIII) part of his quotations in the Commonplace Book from the *Divine Pymander* of Hermes Trismegistus, translated by John Everard (1657). The inclusion of extracts from the first of Henry More's *Divine Dialogues* (1668) gives evidence of Traherne's indebtedness to Cambridge Platonism. From Isaac Barrow's sermon *On the Duty and Reward of Bounty to the Poor* (1671) Traherne copied six long passages exhibiting striking affinities with his own thought and style.

All but one of the unidentified passages in the Commonplace Book are in Traherne's own hand; some are almost certainly original, among them scientific notes on "Cold" which incorporate a quotation from Robert Boyle's *Experimental History of Cold* (1665). The unidentified sources include a devotional work from which came four entries consisting of somewhat disjointed penitential reflections; a work discussing technical theology; and one or more general religious treatises. In the last category is a passage headed "Preparation," which Traherne also incorporated into *Christian Ethicks* (p. 126:31 and Commentary).

Linked with the Commonplace Book by the presence of two passages from Gale transcribed by Traherne's amanuensis (ff. 57ᵛ, 59ᵛ), the Ficino Notebook—otherwise in Traherne's own hand—consists largely of extracts from Marsilio Ficino's Latin epitomes and translations of Plato. Probably dating from the late 1660's, this manuscript also includes the first part of Ficino's "Argumentum" to his translation of Hermes Trismegistus; notes on a work called "Stoicismus Christianus"; and a long Latin life of Socrates from an unidentified source. Of great importance for its documentation of Traherne's philosophical leanings, the Ficino Notebook is also the source of two Platonic references in the *Centuries* (I.40 and III.60, neither noted by Dr. Margoliouth) and of one in the *Ethicks* (see p. 95:32 and Commentary).

II   Ethical Thought and Its Students at Mid-Century

A.   *Ethics as an Academic Subject*

In approaching seventeenth-century writing on ethics one must distinguish between ethical teaching and the teaching of ethics. The divergence could be considerable. Though Neoplatonic in philosophy, Traherne's *Christian Ethicks* owes all of its technical language and many of its assumptions to the formal training in Aristotelianism he received as a student. For evidence of his education we have the manuscript epitome made in Traherne's last year at Oxford (1655–1656), an epitome derived from a popular textbook by Eustache de Saint-Paul.

Before describing Traherne's epitome and its source we should examine briefly the nature of the ethics curriculum at the mid-seventeenth-century English university. The next few paragraphs must be construed as suggestions rather than as conclusions, for few scholars have dealt in any thorough way with the subject.[5]

The Laudian Statutes required Oxford undergraduates in their second and third years to attend the semi-weekly lectures of the professor of moral philosophy. The professor's subject, the Statutes decreed, must be "Aristotelis Ethica ad Nicomachum, Politica, necnon Oeconomica."[6]

[5] See, however, the admirable works of William T. Costello (*The Scholastic Curriculum in Early Seventeenth-Century Cambridge* [Cambridge, Mass., 1958]) and Mark H. Curtis (*Oxford and Cambridge in Transition, 1558–1640* [Oxford, 1959]). An invaluable source for the study of the curriculum at mid-century is '*A Library for Younger Schollers*,' ed. Alma DeJordy and Harris Francis Fletcher, ("Illinois Studies in Language and Literature," XLVIII [Urbana, 1961]). Compiled at the time of Traherne's undergraduate studies, this list is possibly the work of Thomas Barlow (see '*A Library*,' Foreword, p. x), whom Traherne knew at least slightly (see *Roman Forgeries*, p. 90). Two other seventeenth-century curricula are Barlow's Αὐτοσχεδιάσματα, *De Studio Theologiae: or, Directions for the Choice of Books in the Study of Divinity*, ed. William Offley (Oxford, 1699), and Henry Dodwell's *Two Letters of Advice: I, For the Susception of Holy Orders; II, For Studies Theological, especially such as are Rational* (Dublin, 1672). Neither of these books, however, has been of use in the present study.

[6] *Statutes of the University of Oxford Codified in the Year 1636*, ed. John Griffiths (Oxford, 1888), p. 35 (Tit. IV, sec. 1, par. 5). The chair of moral philosophy had been founded in 1621 by Thomas White; the statutes—which do not prescribe texts—appear in Griffiths (pp. 255–257) and in *Statuta Antiqua Universitatis Oxoniensis*, ed. Strickland Gibson (Oxford, 1931), pp. 540–544. During Traherne's last two years at Brasenose, when the Statutes required his attendance at the moral philosophy lectures, the professor was Francis Howell, who published little or nothing at this or any other period of his career: see Anthony Wood, *The History and Antiquities of the University of Oxford*, ed. John Gutch,

Until the time of Descartes and Hobbes, systematic ethics consisted of a series of footnotes to Aristotle, the most thorough and influential annotation of all being the Second Part of the First Part of Thomas Aquinas's *Summa Theologica*. Because Hobbes was anathema to the academic establishment and Descartes's followers had not yet codified his scattered ethical thought,[7] Aristotle as modified by the Schoolmen continued to dominate the curriculum at mid-century.

The Aristotelian hegemony resulted not merely from the antiquity of the *Nicomachean Ethics,* but also (and indeed primarily) from Aristotle's intellectual clarity. "This is all the Moral Philosophy of *Aristotle,*" said Rapin: "the most exact, the most regular and compleat of all other Moralities."[8] Because of this "regularity" all subsequent moral philosophy devolved from Aristotle—even though his morality is "too humane, and too much confin'd within the bounds of this life"; whereas Plato's ethics, grievously deficient in method, "are more noble and elevated; they are a preparation to a life more pure and perfect. . . ."[9] Not surprisingly, *Christian Ethicks* employs Aristotle's language to convey Plato's truths: Traherne could not do otherwise, given his education, for every manual of ethics followed Aristotle. These textbooks, nearly all by Continental scholars, were often reprinted in England. They were of several kinds.

A basic type was the commentary dealing with the *Nicomachean Ethics* book by book, frequently in the form of questions and answers. The student could choose from numerous authors, among them the

---

II (Oxford, 1796), 874; and also the *Dictionary of National Biography* (hereafter *DNB*).

[7] Henry More's *Enchiridion Ethicum* (1667; tr. 1690 by Edward Southwell as *An Account of Virtue*) expounded Descartes's treatise on the passions. The *Institutio Philosophiae* of Antoine Le Grand, a leading Cartesian propagandist, was published in London in 1672, reaching a fourth edition in 1680; it was translated by Richard Blome as Part I of *A Body of Philosophy* (1694) and includes many elements of the traditional scheme. (Unless otherwise noted, all works cited in the Introductions were published in London.)

[8] René Rapin, *Reflexions upon Ancient and Modern Philosophy,* tr. A. L. (1678), p. 135.

[9] René Rapin, *The Comparison of Plato and Aristotle,* tr. John Dancer (1673), p. 97. The same point was made by Alessandro Piccolomini: "Di quella felicita poi che puo convenire a l'huomo vivendo, non ha molto cura Platone," whereas Aristotle restricts himself to practical rather than contemplative (or speculative) philosophy (*De la institutione di tutta la vita de l'homo nato nobile e in citta libera* [Venice, 1545], ff. 23–23ᵛ).

thirteenth-century Frenchman, Jean Buridan (*Quaestiones in decem libros ethicorum Aristotelis ad Nicomachum,* Oxford, 1637); the sixteenth-century German, Theophilus Golius (*Epitome doctrinae moralis,* Cambridge, 1634); the sixteenth-century Englishman, John Case (*Speculum quaestionum moralium, in universam Aristotelis philosophi summi ethicen,* Oxford, 1585); and the Portuguese Jesuit Collegium Conimbricensis,[10] which issued a volume entitled *In libros ethicorum Aristotelis ad Nicomachum, aliquot . . . disputationes* (4th ed., Cologne, 1612). Latin translations of Aristotle generally came provided with a copious commentary; Cambridge students were directed to the edition by Johannes Magirus,[11] which with its Greek-Latin parallel texts and commentary ran to more than a thousand pages (*Corona virtutum moralium universam Aristotelis ethica enucleans,* Frankfort, 1601). Students who had already mastered an intermediate textbook would use a commentary like that of Magirus as a reference work to aid their investigation of special problems.[12]

Other textbooks, while adhering to Aristotle's general approach and depending upon him for definitions, departed in varying degrees from the scheme and emphases of the *Nicomachean Ethics.* One of the most popular of these texts was Traherne's source, the *Ethica* of Eustache de Saint-Paul, to be considered shortly. Bartholomaeus Keckermann, writing his *Systema ethica* (1607) for students at the Danzig Academy, began with a "Praecognitio Generalia" introducing the subject and defining terms; devoted the opening chapters to the general characteristics of moral virtue; then took up the cardinal virtues and their subdivisions; next considered the "imperfect" and "semi-virtues"; went on to analyze heroic virtue; and in the final three chapters discussed friendship. The professor of ethics and logic at the University of Leyden, Franco Burgersdijck, produced a textbook which went through seven English editions (*Idea philosophiae tum moralis, tum naturalis,* Oxford, 1631). In the preliminary chapters Burgersdijck treated moral philosophy broadly (the good, happiness, kinds of actions, the passions, pleasure and pain), then dealt with the intellectual and moral virtues in general, and finally examined the individual virtues in turn. These

---

[10] I.e., the Academy of Coimbra. This work and the commentaries by Buridan and Case were recommended in 'A Library,' p. 2. Note also that Golius's *Epitome* was prepared for students of the Strasbourg Academy, whereas Case's work was designed for students at the English universities.

[11] 'A Library,' p. 2.

[12] Curtis, p. 111.

works of Eustache, Keckermann, and Burgersdijck helped the student to deepen his understanding of the elements of ethics: they offered a *systema majus*.[13]

Lastly there were compendia or "summes," intended as elementary texts providing a *systema brevius*. An example in the vernacular was William Pemble's *Summe of Moral Philosophy* (1632). Closely adhering to Aristotle,[14] Pemble wrote a sketchy outline proliferating in brackets; he discussed the nature and scope of ethics and of happiness, the passions, the faculties of the soul governing virtuous actions, and the Aristotelian virtues themselves.

Ethical compendia, usually in Latin, often formed part of a manual providing a conspectus of the principal subjects of academic study. For ethics, Richard Holdsworth directed his Cambridge pupils to Johann Stier's *Praecepta doctrinae logicae, ethicae, physicae, metaphysicae, sphaericaeque* (Cambridge, 1647),[15] in its eighth edition in England by 1678. Stier dealt with ethics in twenty-one diagrammatic pages; in Part I he considered the *summum bonum*, and in Part II (after preliminary remarks on the moral virtues, the principles of human actions, and the passions) he dispatched the Aristotelian moral virtues and appended three chapters on the intellectual virtues. Stier borrowed most of his definitions from the *Nicomachean Ethics*, providing the reader with both the original Greek and its Latin translation. Each virtue was set out in Synoptic Tables, analyzed according to standard categories—"Nomen," "Quid sit," "Objectum," "Actus," "Extrema," and so on.

Another German author popular in England was Christoph Scheibler, whose *Philosophia compendiosa* (Oxford, 1628) achieved its tenth English edition by 1685.[16] Book VII, "De Ethica," occupies

---

[13] Curtis, pp. 110–111. The fourth edition of Burgersdijck's *Idea* appeared in 1637; three others are listed in Wing: 1641, 1654, 1667. Richard Holdsworth recommended this work to his pupils at Cambridge (Curtis, p. 110, n. 79).

[14] S[imon] P[atrick] stigmatized Pemble, Calvinist divinity reader of Magdalen Hall (Oxford) from 1618 until his early death in 1623, as representative of seventeenth-century scholasticism (*A Brief Account of the New Sect of Latitude-men* [1662], p. 18). The *Summe* was included in Pemble's *Works* (3d ed., 1635; 4th ed., Oxford, 1659) and published separately in 1635; according to the *DNB* there was an edition in 1630 (not listed in the *STC*).

[15] Curtis, p. 110, n. 79. The description here refers to the eighth edition, published in London (the 6th ed. appeared in Oxford in 1667). The *Praecepta Ethicae* was also printed separately in 1666.

[16] Scheibler's *Metaphysica* (Oxford, 1637) was recommended in 'A Library,' p. 4. The *Philosophia compendiosa* included, besides ethics: logic, metaphysics,

some eight or nine pages divided into eighteen chapters; each chapter consists of conventionally Aristotelian one-sentence definitions listed in one-two-three fashion. Excellent material for rote learning, Schiebler's compendium—like most contemporary texts—from any other point of view remains dry bones.

Traherne's epitome, being a skeletal analysis, resembles Scheibler's work, but Eustache's *Ethica,* from which it largely derives, was an advanced textbook.[17] With no indication of his source, Traherne entitled his fifteen-page summary "Totius Moralis Philosophiae Perfecta Epitome et concisa per Quaestiones et responsiones Tradita" (EN, pp. 7–21). The first twelve pages of the epitome condense the first 115 pages of the *Ethica* of Eustache; Traherne omitted Eustache's final section of fifteen pages on the vices (as he omitted discussion of the vices from *Christian Ethicks*) and appended a series of definitions of the virtues similar to the account given by Scheibler.

A French monk, Eustache de Saint-Paul taught at the Sorbonne and wrote texts on philosophy and theology intended to reform (not to revolutionize) the prevalent arid scholasticism. His *Summa philosophiae quadripartita, de rebus dialecticis, moralibus, physicis, & metaphysicis* was first published in Paris in 1609 and went through some thirty editions; three editions were printed in Cambridge (1640, 1648, 1649), where the *Ethica* also appeared by itself in three editions (1654, 1677, 1693). There was also a London edition of the *Ethica* (1658).[18]

For all his intention to reform the curriculum, Eustache nonetheless poured Thomistic wine into Thomistic bottles, although admittedly

---

physics, geometry, astronomy, optics, politics, and economics. John Locke complained that "the Burgursdicus's [*sic*] and the Scheiblers" that "swarm[ed]" in his day perverted true learning, which should be concerned with the "most necessary" and useful subjects ("Some Thoughts Concerning Education," in *On Politics and Education,* ed. Howard Penniman [New York, 1947], p. 282).

[17] Richard Holdsworth suggested Eustache for intensive work in ethics (Curtis, p. 111, n. 80).

[18] On Eustache (Eustachius à Sancto Paulo), born Eustache Asseline (1573–1640), see the articles by Maur Standaert in the *Dictionnaire de spiritualité,* ed. Marcel Viller *et al.,* IV, Part II (Paris, 1961), cols. 1701–1705, and by Pierre Pourrat in *Catholicisme hier, aujourd'hui, demain,* ed. G. Jacquemet, IV, fascicule 14 (Paris, 1954), cols. 713–714. Eustache was a prominent member of the *Feuillants,* an offshoot of the Cistercian order, and a friend of François de Sales, Bérulle, and Mme Acarie. He published several spiritual works in French, as well as a textbook entitled *Summa theologica tripartita* (2 vols.; Paris, 1613, 1616).

he strained out much accumulated scholastic sediment. After some "Quaestiones procemiales" defining the scope of moral philosophy, Eustache in his lesser *Summa* followed the topical order of St. Thomas in his greater. The table of contents indicates the possibly Procrustean arrangement as well as the thoroughly orthodox selection of topics:

PART I. *Happiness*

A. The good and the end
  1. The good
  2. The end
B. Happiness itself
  1. The objective happiness of man
  2. The formal happiness of man

PART II. *The principles of human actions*

A. The internal principles of human actions
  1. The innate internal principles of human actions—i.e., intellect, will, appetite
  2. The acquired internal principles of human actions—i.e., habits
B. The external principles of human actions
  1. The external principle of human actions as it is their efficient cause—i.e., God
  2. The other external principles of human actions—i.e., angels

PART III. *Human actions, hence a treatment of the passions, whence follow the virtues and vices*

A. Human actions themselves
  1. Human actions in general
  2. Human actions in particular
B. The passions of the soul
  1. The passions in general
  2. The different passions in particular
C. The virtues and vices
  1. The virtues in general
  2. The cardinal virtues
    a. Prudence
    b. Justice
    c. Fortitude

    d. Temperance
   3. The vices and sins[19]

Traherne's epitome radically simplified and in some cases considerably distorted the measured presentation of Eustache. Traherne's method was to quote, with greater or lesser fidelity, a "Quaestio" (or occasionally a marginal gloss posing a subsidiary problem), then either to summarize the conclusions or to extrapolate one of several answers from Eustache's discussion. A true scholastic, Eustache took pains to set forth the leading and sometimes contradictory arguments on each subject; at times Traherne noted not Eustache's answer but that of another (usually unnamed) moral philosopher. In a few instances Traherne departed from Eustache, but in the main he kept close to the *Summa;* up to the passions he made notes on every topic. He summarized Eustache's general account of the passions but omitted the detailed chapters dealing with each in turn; for—as he observed parenthetically (EN, p. 16)—further investigations could easily be made on the basis of what was already given. With the analysis of justice Traherne concluded his condensed version of Eustache's manual, turning elsewhere for his definitions of the two remaining cardinal virtues and of all the lesser virtues.

The rest of Traherne's epitome is simplified Aristotelianism of the kind purveyed in elementary textbooks. Each virtue is defined with extreme brevity in terms of its mean, excess, and defect; there is no expansion whatsoever. After fortitude and temperance,[20] the epitome proceeds to the "*less Principal* Vertues" almost exactly as listed in *Christian Ethicks:* liberality, magnificence, modesty, magnanimity, honor, mansuetude (*"Courtesie"* or *"Gentleness of behaviour"*), comity (*"Affability"*), urbanity, truth, and taciturnity (*CE,* p. 24:21 and Commentary). The epitome ends with definitions of the "semi-virtues" of continence and tolerance. Sometime later Traherne had an afterthought and below "Finis" he wrote the query: "Quomodo differunt

[19] Sigs. A2–A4 of the 1658 London ed. of the *Ethica.* Each part is divided into a "prior" and a "posterior tractatus" (in the case of Part III, "primus," "secundus," "tertius tractatus"), each of which consists of a "prior" and a "posterior disputatio" (with the obvious variations in the third treatise of Part III). The treatises are here indicated by upper-case letters and the disputations by arabic numerals; III.C.2 is further divided into "sections," indicated by lower-case letters. Each of the subdivisions given here is treated by means of "questions," which are the basic units of the *Summa.*

[20] The two kinds of temperance—frugality and chastity—are similarly analyzed according to the mean-excess-defect scheme. Traherne appended to the Eustachian definition of justice a paragraph on its extremes (EN, p. 19).

Ars et prudentia? item praxis et poesis?" (EN, p. 21). There is no answer.

Traherne's epitome suggests admirably the stultifying traditional academic training to which Englishmen were still being subjected in 1650—and indeed for some decades thereafter. Scorned by Glanvill as "an huddle of *words* and *terms insignificant*,"[21] Aristotelian scholasticism had become obsolete; yet its terminology, engraved in the adult mind by schoolboy rote learning, strait-jacketed original reconsiderations of philosophical issues. In *Christian Ethicks* Traherne only partly escaped the restrictions imposed by the old language—the opening chapters are particularly heavy with outworn terms—and as a consequence failed to set forth a new ethical theory.

B. *New Approaches to Ethics*

Even as Traherne wrote, new ideas in ethics were being voiced. Ten years after Traherne died, a keen young Oxford don mentioned in a letter to Henry More "the more Modern Masters of Morality (such as *Grotius*, Dr. *Cumberland*, *Puffendorf* with many others)."[22] It is noteworthy that two members of this modern trio—Hugo Grotius and Samuel von Pufendorf—were eminent European jurists and political philosophers, and all three gained fame for their studies of natural law: the trend was toward secularism.

Grotius, whose works began appearing in England in the 1630's, reached the zenith of his English renown after his death in 1645. Dramatist, historian, and biblical scholar, he attained a permanent place in history with his *De jure belli et pacis*, written in 1625. *De jure* was twice translated into English, in 1654 (another ed. 1655) and in 1682. His *De veritate religionis Christianae* achieved fourteen

[21] Joseph Glanvill, *The Vanity of Dogmatizing*, ed. Moody E. Prior (New York, 1931), p. 150. Glanvill devoted pp. 148–188 to a censure of Aristotelianism, which of course included scholasticism: "A *School-man* is the Ghost of the *Stagirite*, in a Body of condensed Air: and *Thomas* but *Aristotle* sainted" (p. 152).

[22] John Norris, letter dated 28 January 1684, in *The Theory and Regulation of Love* (Oxford, 1688), p. 166. Norris was Fellow of All Souls from 1680 (when he graduated B.A. at Exeter) to 1689. With his recommendations cf. those of John Locke (Traherne's contemporary at Oxford), who proposed that the young student of *"virtue,"* having started with the Bible and "Tully's *Offices*," should go on to Pufendorf's *De officio hominis* and finally to "Grotius, *de Jure Belli et Pacis*, or, which perhaps is the better of the two, Puffendorf, *de Jure naturali et Gentium*" ("Some Thoughts Concerning Education," p. 362). (*Tully's Offices*, complained its translator, Sir Roger L'Estrange, was generally made "a *Lesson*, to the Boys, rather of *Syntax*, then *Morality*" [1680, sig. A6ᵛ].) On Norris's trio, see Maximilian E. Novak, *Defoe and the Nature of Man* (Oxford, 1963).

English editions by 1700, and was twice translated into English (anonymously in 1669; by Simon Patrick in 1680, 5th ed., 1700). Grotius's
Catechisme was also translated into English (1668; another ed. 1682).
A three-volume Latin edition of his theological works was published
in London in 1679; his annotations upon the Bible early became standard fare for English theologians. Grotius was not, in short, a professional moral philosopher, but rather a brilliant intellectual of
polymathic achievements whose works contained much moral philosophy without being explicitly devoted to that subject. That he ranked
among "the more Modern Masters of Morality" suggests the inade-
quacy of scholastic ethics for Restoration England and the need for
a new formulation.

Pufendorf's immensely influential works came forth at the very time
Traherne was preparing to write *Christian Ethicks.* The vast *De jure
naturae et gentium* was published in Lund in 1672; *De officio hominis
et civis prout ipsi praescribuntur lege naturali*—essentially an abridgment of *De jure naturae*—appeared a year later in Lund, ten years
later in Cambridge (8th ed., 1715). Andrew Tooke's English version
of *De officio* followed in 1691, under the catchy title *The Whole
Duty of Man* (the title continues: *According to the Laws of Nature*).
Tooke wanted to cash in on the popularity of the earlier *Whole Duty
of Man* (1658); his translation reached a fourth edition in 1716. Book
I, dealing with the duties of the individual, begins with a traditional
discussion of human actions; progresses to natural law and man's duties
to God, neighbor, and self; and ends with the ethics of business. Book
II considers the duties of the individual in society, discussing first the
natural state of man and then the duties of men in their various civic
relationships. Pufendorf wrote as a Christian, but as a Christian
civilian.

Bishop of Peterborough from 1691 to 1718, Richard Cumberland
published his anti-Hobbist *De legibus naturae* in 1672, the year of
Pufendorf's magnum opus. Cumberland dedicated *De legibus* to his
friend Sir Orlando Bridgeman, Traherne's patron.[23] "In its ethical matter thoroughly modern,"[24] although dully scholastic in form, the treatise

---

[23] One of Bridgeman's first acts on becoming Lord Keeper in 1667 was to
give Cumberland a living in Stamford. Another of Cumberland's friends was Traherne's predecessor as Bridgeman's chaplain, Hezekiah Burton, who contributed
a preface to *De legibus.* Like Bridgeman, and like Traherne, Cumberland was
strongly anti-Catholic. See Leslie Stephen's article in the *DNB* on Cumberland.

[24] Henry Sidgwick, *Outlines of the History of Ethics* (1922), p. 174. *De
legibus* appeared in 1692 in J. Tyrell's abridged translation, approved by Cumberland.

assumes "that the Whole of *moral Philosophy,* and of the Laws of Nature, is ultimately resolv'd into *natural Observations* known by the Experience of all Men, or into Conclusions of true *Natural Philosophy.*"[25] As the basis of his analysis Cumberland posited the proposition—which he was the first to enunciate—that *"the common Good is the supreme Law."*[26] For a churchman this is secular ethics indeed, and it reveals the shape of things to come. Cumberland pointed to future developments; Traherne summarized past achievements.

Although the last thirty years of the century witnessed the emergence of new ethical thought, tradition died hard. In 1684 Daniel Whitby published in Oxford his *Ethices compendium, in usum academicae juventutis,* in which William Ames, who died in 1633, was the sole modern authority mentioned. Full of exemplary allusions to the New Testament, adorned with the stock scholastic formulas, Whitby's *Compendium* was reprinted three times by 1724: demand evidently existed. Thomas Hobbes, the most original and excoriated of all English seventeenth-century commentators on moral philosophy, explained why:

Those Men who have written concerning the Faculties, Passions, and Manners of Men, that is to say; of *Moral Philosophy,* and of *Policy, Government,* and *Laws,* whereof there be infinite Volumes, have been so *far from removing Doubt* and Controversie . . . *that* they have very much *multiplied the same: Nor* doth any Man at this day so much as pretend to *know* more than hath been delivered Two thousand Years ago by *Aristotle.* . . . The Reason whereof is . . . that in their Writings and Discourses they take for Principles those Opinions which are already vulgarly received; whether true or false, being for the most part false.[27]

Popular as well as academic writers perpetuated the reign of the old clichés. John Scott's five-volume *Christian Life* (1681–1699) taught Londoners "the blessed art how to live happily in a distracted world"[28] in the conventional language Scott learned while at Oxford in the same decade as Traherne. Another old-fashioned ethical guide for the

[25] Richard Cumberland, *A Treatise of the Laws of Nature,* tr. John Maxwell (1727), p. 41. Cumberland explains in the next sentence that he includes under natural philosophy the study of the human soul and of God as the First Mover.

[26] Cumberland, *Treatise,* p. 41. Cumberland was not, of course, the first to stress the importance of the common good: he was the first to make the common good the cornerstone of an ethical structure (Sidgwick, *History of Ethics,* p. 174).

[27] Thomas Hobbes, *Humane Nature,* in *Hobb's Tripos* (3d ed., 1684), pp. 85–86.

[28] John Scott, *Works* (Oxford, 1826), I, viii.

common reader was Giovanni Cardinal Bona's *Manuductio ad coelum* (1658), which in Sir Roger L'Estrange's Anglican translation (*A Guide to Eternity*) went through six editions between 1672 and 1712.[29] The old standby of the first part of the century, Lewis Bayly's *Practice of Piety* (1612), continued to proliferate in edition after edition, and was joined in 1658 by the surpassingly successful *Whole Duty of Man.* Attributed to Richard Allestree, Regius Professor of Divinity at Oxford, *The Whole Duty* offered "a *short* and *plain direction to the very meanest readers,* to behave themselves so in this world, that they may be happy for ever in the next."[30] These common-sense precepts pronounced on the eve of the Restoration suited the pious needs of ordinary Englishmen until the end of the next century.

Besides such guides to morality, other genres of religious writing offered moral instruction: for England, the seventeenth was "the Century of Ethics."[31] A plethora of little books, advertised variously as "short," "plain," or "profitable," inculcated Christian morality by means of expositions of the Catechism or one of its constituent parts. There were as well doctrinal treatises directed to a more professional audience and devotional manuals on various levels of complexity. Casuists applied ethical principles to practical affairs; among the best-known later Protestant practitioners of this Roman Catholic art were Jeremy Taylor (*Ductor Dubitantium,* 1660) and Richard Baxter (*A Christian Directory,* 1675).[32] There was, furthermore, a huge literature dealing with moral problems in the form of essays, meditations, and aphorisms.

Popular religious works cannot be expected to set forth new moral philosophies; they tend rather to maintain the status quo. It would be incorrect, however, to assume that beneath the traditional terminology ethical attitudes remained static. Indeed, the change in attitudes

[29] A Roman Catholic translation (*A Guide to Heaven*) by James Price appeared in 1672, with another edition—published in Rouen—the following year. "L. B." translated another of Bona's works, *Precepts and Practical Rules for a Truly Christian Life* (1678), which bore Archbishop Sheldon's imprimatur, a dedication to Bishop Ken, and the translator's assurance that the book was worthy of the Church of England, "this purest of Churches" (sig. A8).

[30] *The Whole Duty of Man* (1731), Preface, p. i. See C. J. Stranks, *Anglican Devotion* (1961), pp. 123–148. On Traherne's use of *The Whole Duty,* see CE, p. 3:10 and Commentary, as well as Stranks, p. 124.

[31] So suggests Costello, *Scholastic Curriculum,* p. 64.

[32] On English casuistry in this period, see H. R. McAdoo, *The Structure of Caroline Moral Theology* (1949); Thomas Wood, *English Casuistical Divinity in the Seventeenth Century . . .* (1952); and George L. Mosse, *The Holy Pretence* (Oxford, 1957).

may well be the main factor responsible for the perpetuation of the old language: rejecting the theoretical, the "practical Christian"[33] of the Restoration demanded not a philosophy of morals thought out anew, but rather a guide to conduct. Utilitarianism was to become the touchstone for ethics in a secular period, and the earlier vocabulary was adapted to newer uses.

C. *Traherne's Audience and His Patron*

To discern the features of Traherne's audience we must extrapolate from the internal evidence of *Christian Ethicks,* since no contemporary reactions are known. Traherne designed his *Ethicks* not for professional philosophers but "for vulgar Apprehensions" (*CE,* p. 23): that is, for laymen unconcerned with technical minutiae. Yet his were not *"the very meanest readers"* who relished *The Whole Duty of Man* but, rather, high-minded men of the world. As chaplain to Sir Orlando Bridgeman from 1669 to 1674, Traherne learned the ways of "high-born Souls in Courts and Palaces" (*CE,* p. 260) and was himself "admitted to the society and friendship of Great men" (*CE,* p. 173). He "often experienced" the trust of these men, who confided "their Wives and Children in his hands . . . their Gold, their Bonds, their Souls, their Affairs, their Lives, their Secrets, Houses, Liberties, and Lands" (*CE,* p. 200). Revelatory of Traherne's acquaintance with the ruling class, this passage probably describes as well his position in Bridgeman's household. Though Henry More complained that "great houses commonly have a chaplain rather for fashion sake then private devotion,"[34] Bridgeman was clearly an exception to More's rule. In a tone of admiration but not of adulation Traherne commended Bridgeman's "many Charitable and Pious works, perhaps surmounting his Estate, though concealed from the notice and knowledge of the World" (*CE,* p. 239). Chaplain and patron were well matched.

Strong in personal virtue, Bridgeman nonetheless failed by all accounts in his greatest public trust, the office of Lord Keeper. Bridgeman was born about 1606, educated at Cambridge, and called to the bar in 1632; he quickly attained a high professional reputation, winning several offices and a knighthood (1640). The Civil War interrupted his

---

[33] At least two books were published with that title, one by John Bartlet (1670), another by Richard Sherlock (1673).

[34] More to Lady Conway, 14 July 1671, in *Conway Letters,* ed. Marjorie Hope Nicolson (New Haven, 1930), p. 340. As Miss Nicolson observes (p. 340, n. 5), "More's words offer an interesting parallel to Macaulay's famous passage about the state of the clergy in 1685, in his *History of England,* chap. iii. . . ."

public career: to *"his Royal Master, King* CHARLES *the First . . .
he intirely adhered . . . and* [was] *often imployed . . . as a Com-
missioner in the Negotiations then on foot."* During this period, his
clerk went on to explain, he led *"a Sedentary kind of Life in his
Chamber,"* becoming *"the great Oracle, not only of his Fellow
Sufferers, but of the whole Nation in Matters of Law"*[35]—particularly
property law. Upon Charles's return Bridgeman's advancement was
immediate: awarded the first baronetcy of the Restoration, he presided
over the trial of the regicides and soon after received several other
offices. As Lord Chief Justice of the Common Pleas he evinced a "love
of legal exactitude" which, according to Osmund Airy, became
"proverbial."[36] But his elevation, as Clarendon's successor, to the office
of Lord Keeper "did not at all contribute any increase to his fame,
but rather the contrary. . . ."[37] That scrupulosity which served Bridgeman well as a common lawyer served him ill as Charles's chief minister:
fairness, North observed with unconscious irony, "is a temper of ill
consequence in a judge."[38] Refusing to compromise his principles,
Bridgeman lost his office to Shaftesbury on November 17, 1672, retiring
to his country home in Teddington.

It is difficult to arrive at a just estimation of Bridgeman's character,
for two of the main authorities—North and Campbell—are blatantly

[35] Thomas Page Johnson (Bridgeman's clerk), "To the Reader," *Sir Orl. Bridgman's Conveyances* (1682), sig. a2. The *Conveyances,* published posthumously,
attained a sixth edition by 1725.

[36] See Osmund Airy's article on Bridgeman in the *DNB,* a fair assessment,
from which the foregoing facts were derived.

[37] Roger North, *The Lives . . . ,* new ed. (1826), I, 179; see also p. 421.
Cf. Gilbert Burnet's statement that as a Common Pleas judge Bridgeman enjoyed
"great esteem, which he did not maintain long after his advancement" (*History
of My Own Time,* ed. Osmund Airy, I [Oxford, 1897], 454). Bridgeman was
given the Great Seal "at first merely as a temporary arrangement, till another
Lord Keeper could be fixed upon" (John Campbell, *Lives of the Lord Chancellors*
[5th ed., 1868], IV, 139), as one may infer from the fact that he held the
title not of Lord Chancellor but of Lord Keeper. "The *Lord Chancellour* and
the *Lord Keeper* are the same in Authority and Power and Precedence, yet they
differ in Patent, in Height and Favor of the King . . ."; the main duty of the
position was "to keep the Kings Great Seal, to judge, not according to the *Common
Law,* as other Civil Courts do, but to moderate the rigor of the Law, and to
judge according to Equity, Conscience, or Reason" (Edward Chamberlayne, *Angliae
Notitiae; or The Present State of England,* Part I [8th ed., 1674], pp. 152,
151).

[38] North, *Lives,* p. 179; North means by "judge" Bridgeman's position as Lord
Keeper, which required a decisiveness he did not possess. "His study and practice
lay so entirely in the common law, that he never seemed to apprehend what
equity was: nor had he a head made for business or for such a court" (Burnet,
History, I, 454).

tendentious.[39] Although complaining in his *Lives* of the Norths about Bridgeman's niggling over details, North in his *Examen* attributed to him a readiness to compliance "for the Sake of his Family, that gathered like a Snow-ball while he had the Seal. . . ."[40] North further accused him of lacking "the vigour of mind, and strength to coerce" his family into decorous behavior, his sons being unruly and his wife "a most violent intriguess in business."[41] Yet Burnet credited Bridgeman with "a courage . . . that could stand against a current";[42] and Heneage Finch, Lord Chancellor after Shaftesbury, spoke warmly of him: "It is due to the memory of so great a man, . . . to mention him with reverence, and with veneration for his learning and integrity."[43] A broadsheet "Congratulatory Poem" (1667) commemorating Bridgeman's acquisition of the Seal acclaimed him with a pun: "A sober piety in a Virtuoso / And an *Orlando* without a *Furioso*."

Bridgeman's legal and political activities have attracted the attention of historians, yet his interests as a churchman have been virtually ignored. Son and brother of bishops, he "had very serious impressions of religion on his mind."[44] We have already noted his connection with Richard Cumberland, a member of his college (Magdalene).[45] His chaplain from 1667 to 1669, Hezekiah Burton, was a Latitudinarian divine and like Bridgeman a fellow of Magdalene; Leslie Stephen calls him Bridgeman's "college friend."[46] Burton's successor, Traherne was

---

[39] As James Crossley points out in a note in his edition of John Worthington's *Diary and Correspondence*, Chetham Society, XIII (1847), 107 n. According to Crossley, "Roger North had a grudge against [Bridgeman] on his brother Lord Guildford's account." It might be added that Campbell's account in his *Lives of the Chancellors* (pp. 139–153) abounds in factual errors.

[40] Roger North, *Examen: or, An Enquiry into the Credit and Veracity of a Pretended Complete History* (1740), pp. 38–39.

[41] North, *Lives*, pp. 180–181.

[42] Burnet, *History*, I, 455.

[43] Quoted in Campbell, *Lives of the Chancellors*, p. 152. Lady Conway's brother, Heneage Finch—later first Earl of Nottingham—probably met Bridgeman first through the Conway circle (see below, n. 49). His wife belonged to the Harvey family of Herefordshire, of which Traherne's friend Mrs. Hopton was a member; Gladys Wade reasonably supposes that Traherne owed his chaplaincy to the recommendation of Finch, a friend of Bridgeman's and "patron and friend" of Philip Traherne (*Thomas Traherne* [Princeton, 1944], p. 87).

[44] Burnet, *History*, I, 454. Bridgeman's father, John, was Bishop of Chester (1619–1652) and his brother Henry succeeded Isaac Barrow as Bishop of Sodor and Man (1671–1682). See *DNB, s.v.* John Bridgeman and Henry Bridgeman.

[45] Campbell, observing that Bridgeman "favoured men of learning," incorrectly says that Cumberland was his chaplain (*Lives of the Chancellors*, p. 153).

[46] Leslie Stephen in the *DNB, s.v.* Hezekiah Burton. Tillotson edited Burton's posthumous *Discourses* (1684).

fortunate to be summoned from his rural parsonage in Herefordshire to serve Bridgeman in London, for worldly contact stimulated Traherne's mind, as we see in *Christian Ethicks,* and his patron evidently allowed him ample time for his own pursuits.[47] In the five years of his association with Bridgeman Traherne wrote and prepared for publication two books, *Roman Forgeries* and *Christian Ethicks,* wrote the *Centuries* for Mrs. Susanna Hopton in Herefordshire (see Margoliouth's notes on *C* I.80 and *C* IV.55), and very probably composed the Church's Year-Book: a list of accomplishments testifying to Bridgeman's generosity as well as to Traherne's industry. In gratitude Traherne dedicated *Roman Forgeries* to his anti-Catholic patron.[48]

Besides being Fellow of Magdalene, Bridgeman had other means of keeping in close touch with English religious life. Serving during the Interregnum as legal adviser to the Conway family,[49] he presumably came into contact with the Cambridge divines they patronized. We know he took an interest in religious scholarship: John Worthington wrote to Henry More, Lady Conway's great friend, that "Lord Chief Justice Bridgman (upon Mr. Zanchy's his chaplain's commendation) and Lord Chief Baron [Sir Matthew] Hales read your book [*A Modest Inquiry into the Mystery of Iniquity,* 1664] with diligence; and the noise perhaps of such great men reading it might make for your advantage at Cambridge."[50]

Such stray facts, indicative of Bridgeman's religious concerns, do not exhaust the extant evidence. One of his early projects as Lord Keeper was to erase the evil effects of the Ejection of 1662; Bridgeman, though "always on the side of the church, . . . had great tenderness for the nonconformists. . . ."[51] His objective accorded with the promises Charles made immediately after the Restoration: "a *Comprehension* for the *Presbyterians,* and an *Indulgence* for the *Independents* and the rest."[52] His chief associates in discussions on this subject were

[47] Note that in addition to his duties as chaplain Traherne served as parish curate when at Teddington (Wade, p. 91).

[48] The dedication reads: "To the Right Honorable Sʳ Orlando Bridgeman Knight and Baronet One of His Majesties Most Honourable Privy Council; The Author Devoteth his best Services and Dedicateth The Use and Benefit of his Ensuing Labors."

[49] Majorie Nicolson, *Conway Letters,* p. 128, n. 4: Bridgeman "seems to have been at this time [1655] the Conway family solicitor."

[50] Letter dated 2 December 1664, in Worthington, *Diary and Correspondence,* ed. Crossley, Chetham Society, XXXVI (1855), 155.

[51] Burnet, *History,* I, 454.

[52] Unidentified Presbyterian source quoted by White Kennett, *A Complete History of England,* III (2d ed., 1719), 295. The project got under way in January, 1668.

Sir Matthew Hale (another distinguished lawyer) and the leading Latitudinarian divines: John Wilkins (chief negotiator, aided by Burton[53]),
John Tillotson, and Edward Stillingfleet. The Nonconformists were
represented by William Bates, Thomas Manton, and Richard Baxter.[54]
Wilkins and Tillotson were chidden for their efforts by their ecclesiastical superiors, but they persevered nonetheless, meeting—recounted the
venomous Wood—"in the chamber of that great trimmer and latitudinarian Dr. Hezekiah Burton in Essex house, without the Temple barr,
being then the habitation of sir Orl. Bridgman, to whome Burton was
chaplayne then [1668]. . . ."[55] The negotiations failed with crashing
finality, in Baxter's prejudiced estimation because of Bridgeman's in-
vincibly indecisive nature: the Nonconformists lost faith in his "seeming
moderation to the Nonconformists," and the "Ruling Prelates" looked
askance at his liberalism; both sides concluded him "an uncertain,
timerous man," in Baxter's words. "High Places, great Businesses and
Difficulties," continued Baxter resentfully, "do so try Mens Abilities
and their Morals, that many who in a low or middle station, obtained
and kept up a great Name, do quickly lose it, and grow despised and
reproached Persons, when Exaltation and Trial hath made them
known."[56]

Unfair, obviously; yet it is easy enough to understand Baxter's
annoyance. In advocating comprehension, Bridgeman publicly an-
tagonized the High Church establishment; yet in choosing men like
Burton and Traherne for chaplains, he allied himself privately with
that establishment. But he was not so muddled as it might seem, for
while his Latitudinarian friends urged a return to High Church order,
they also preached toleration. Bridgeman may have been weak, but
he was neither stupid nor immoral, as Baxter insinuated. Considered
sympathetically, he seems to have suffered from overdeveloped intellec-

[53] Richard Baxter, *Reliquiae Baxterianae*, ed. Matthew Sylvester (1696), Part
III, p. 24.

[54] Burnet, *History*, I, 466.

[55] Anthony Wood, *Athenae Oxonienses*, ed. Philip Bliss, IV (1820), col. 513.

[56] Baxter, *Reliquiae*, Part III, p. 22. The nastiness of Baxter's innuendo becomes
understandable when we read William Sherlock's report of his interview with
Burton; the conference ended, Burton recalled, with Bridgeman addressing Baxter
"in the greatest Passion that he [Burton] ever saw him in" (Sherlock, *Vindication
of the Rights of Ecclesiastical Authority* [1685], p. 188). For an account of the
abortive scheme for comprehension in 1667–1668, see Roger Thomas, "Comprehension and Indulgence," in *From Uniformity to Unity, 1662–1962*, ed. Geoffrey
F. Nuttall and Owen Chadwick (1962), pp. 196–205; and Walter G. Simon,
"Comprehension in the Age of Charles II," *Church History*, XXXI (1962),
440–448.

tual and moral sensibilities. And if we abstract his dominant personal qualities from his political circumstances, we find a picture of what was probably the typical reader of *Christian Ethicks:* an educated, intelligent person playing an active role in an increasingly secular world, a thoughtful person seeking a pragmatic ethic based upon eternal and immutable morality.

As for the author, Traherne's humble provincial origin, university education, rural ministry and urban chaplaincy provided him with the varied experience necessary for the composition of a treatise on practical morality. But qualifications other than these made *Christian Ethicks* a work of lasting value: Traherne's eclectic philosophy built upon childhood intuitions, his affirmation of the positive joy of life in an age still possessed by a negative stress on sin, and a rhythmic and varied style better suited to conveying intuited truths than academic facts.

III Traherne's *Ethicks:* Thought and Expression

A. *The Method of* Christian Ethicks

The title *Christian Ethicks* is inaccurate (and, it might be noted, possibly the responsibility of the printer or publisher rather than the deceased author): Traherne's subject was *Christian Virtue.* Comparison with the contents of his university ethics textbook, the *Ethica* of Eustache, shows immediately the omissions in *Christian Ethicks:* Traherne mentioned either cursorily or not at all the principles of human actions, human actions themselves, the passions, and the vices. He made no pretense of writing a comprehensive philosophical dissertation; but what he wrote, he wrote systematically. Inspired by his "many years earnest and diligent study" of felicity, he wished

not to stroak and tickle the *Fancy,* but to elevate the *Soul,* and refine its Apprehensions, to inform the Judgment, and polish it for Conversation, to purifie and enflame the Heart, to enrich the Mind, and guide Men (that stand in need of help) in the way of *Vertue;* to excite their Desire, to encourage them to Travel, to comfort them in the Journey, and so at last to lead them to true Felicity, both here and hereafter. [*CE,* p. 3]

This was no casually conceived program. Traherne had indeed begun early the "earnest and diligent study" of his topic, as many passages in his Select Meditations prove. "In the Study of felicity," he wrote in that work, "we haue been brought to vertues. to see their original Nature offices Effects & Consequences" (SM III.53). He devoted seven meditations (SM IV.55–61) to the cardinal virtues, and there are, as references in the Commentary suggest, a great many more likenesses between the Meditations and the *Ethicks*.

Full analysis of these relationships must of course await publication of the Select Meditations. At present two observations must suffice. First, Traherne voiced repeatedly in the Meditations that insistence on a practical, as opposed to a rigidly dogmatic, religion which characterizes *Christian Ethicks;* he declared that "the Things included in Religion" were "the 10 Commandments, the Lords Prayer, the Two Sacrements, & the Articles of o[u]r faith" (SM III.58). Second, the Meditations include a putative embryo of the *Ethicks,* a list of twelve "Instructions Teaching us how to Liv the Life of Happieness" (SM III.31). Announcing one of Traherne's abiding themes, these "Instructions" take the form of reminders that through God's love all the world was made for man—and this world included human as well as divine creation, along with the Incarnation and the Redemption; man's business, and his best return for this bounty, should be to love God and his gifts. Traherne's final comment expresses the prophet-autobiographer: "The seeds of all wisdom Happines & Glory are here Included. And these Instructions so Great, that I would haue given in my childhood Millions of worlds to haue met with one teaching them, so earnestly did I Long after them."

Besides the "Instructions" there is another possible germ of *Christian Ethicks,* somewhat later in date, somewhat more dubious as a source. The Bodleian manuscript of the *Centuries* contains a list which may relate either to the *Ethicks* or the *Thanksgivings* (cf. the "Thanksgivings for the Blessedness of his LAWS," II, 271). Not printed by Dr. Margoliouth, it appears on f. 2ᵛ, the verso of the dedicatory page, and reads:

> Of the Signes of Blessedness
> Of the Objects of Blessedness
> Of the Causes of Blesse[dness]
> Of the Laws of Bless[edness]
> Of the Qualifications of a Blessed man
> Of the Effects of Blessedness
> Of the Maner how Blessedness is to be enjoyed
>   God
> Of the Blessedness of Angels
>   Men.

                           Magistrates
                           Ministers
Of the Blessedness of   Physicians
                           Lawyers
                           Soldiers
                           Marriners
                           Artificers
                                    Rich
                                     &
                                    Poor.

So, in a time when everyone wrote ethics, he wanted to write about *virtue.*"

Both this passage and the "Instructions" are related to *Christian Ethicks* insofar as all three works evince Traherne's central concern with felicity. Declining futher conjecture, we may rest for the moment on the anticlimactic but incontrovertible fact that the *Ethicks* and the manuscripts differ vastly.

When Traherne collected in print his thoughts on virtue, he performed a real service, albeit apparently to a very small audience, for until then no such work existed. Unaware of *Christian Ethicks,* John Norris mused some thirty-five years later *"that if the whole System of* Christian Vertues *were distinctly treated of, it would be a very great, useful, and noble Work."*[57] Traherne's contribution was the only systematic treatise on ethics intended for the educated layman to appear in English during the thirty years after the Restoration. Henry More produced his *Enchiridion Ethicum* (1668) at the instigation of friends who felt that the "captious" age would follow virtue only if persuaded by "Right Reason": but More wrote in Latin and his "honest Intention to excite the Minds of Men unto Virtue"[58] remained unenglished until 1690. Archetypally academic, More wrote with studious rationality, only occasionally revealing his enthusiastic temperament; although he, like Traherne, wished to demonstrate "the reality, force, and efficacy of *Vertue*" (*CE,* p. 3), he composed a manual rather than an appeal or exhortation. Still more academic, the Principal of Edinburgh University, William Colvill, wrote a Latin treatise entitled *Philosophia Moralis Christiana* (Edinburgh, 1670), in which he reproduced tradi-

---

[57] Norris, *A Treatise Concerning Christian Prudence,* Preface (1710), sig. A3. Norris regarded his *Practical Treatise Concerning Humility* (1707) as the *"first link of this Golden Chain,"* and his work on prudence as a second contribution (*Prudence,* sig. A3).

[58] More, *An Account of Virtue,* tr. Edward Southwell (1690), "Epistle to the Reader," sigs. A3, A4.

tional material while taking into account recent writings, such as More's *Enchiridon*. Colvill's work was intended for professional students of divinity. John Hartcliffe, a Cambridge don, wrote his old-fashioned *Treatise of Moral and Intellectual Virtues* (1691) for the layman; feeble admixtures of Cambridge Platonism leavened only slightly his conventionally Aristotelian discussion. Hartcliffe's pallid platitudes do not begin to rival Traherne's work, although there is some similarity in their philosophy.

In designing his treatise Traherne had to choose among several ethical schemes codified—or fossilized—by centuries of use. The ultimate debt of all these systems was to classical philosophy, the formulas of which had early been incorporated into Christian philosophy.

Virtue is one, writers agreed for two millenia; but it bears different names according to its aspects, and on this the philosophers disagreed. Colvill reported some common classifications: the three main categories proposed by the Platonists (civil, purgatorial, heroic); the four cardinal virtues espoused by the Peripatetics (prudence, justice, temperance, fortitude); the three heads of virtue distinguished by Christian theologians (temperance, justice, piety).[59] These last distinctions, derived from Titus 2:12 and popularized by Calvin, were also translated as duties to self, neighbor, and God[60] and as such formed the framework of the immensely influential *Whole Duty of Man*. Colvill himself followed the "two-tables" system introduced by St. Augustine and adopted by Luther and Melanchthon,[61] and after them by Milton in *De doctrina christiana* (Book II); this arrangement divided the Decalogue into our duties to God (the first table, comprising the first four Commandments) and our duties to our neighbor (the second table, including the rest).

Whether tripartite or bipartite, Christian ethical schemes rested finally upon classical prototypes, in particular upon the distinction of four principal virtues (a classification reaching back at least as far as Plato). Introduced by St. Ambrose, the cardinal virtues were integrated into Christian philosophy by St. Augustine.[62] Other medieval

[59] Colvill, *Philosophia Moralis Christiana* (Edinburgh, 1670), p. 31.

[60] Otto Zöckler, *Die Tugundlehre des Christentums* (Gütersloh, 1904), pp. 316–317. The General Confession in the Anglican Morning and Evening Prayer also quotes Titus 2:12.

[61] Zöckler, *Tugundlehre*, pp. 305, 310. The "Zweitafelteilung" was illustrated by the words of Jesus in Matt. 22:37–39 (and Mark 12:30–31), as well as by the Anglican Catechism.

[62] Zöckler, p. 83. Augustine explained the cardinal virtues as aspects of love (Zöckler, pp. 83–84).

philosophers adopted and further adapted the cardinal virtues and much else in ancient ethics, endowing Renaissance philosophers with a fully developed scholastic-Aristotelian terminology.

Traherne used the scholastic scheme for the structure of *Christian Ethicks*.[63] Like every textbook of the time, the *Ethicks* begins with general chapters which explain the nature and end of felicity and virtue and outline the facts of psychology basic to the subsequent discussion. Traherne then discusses the divine virtues (Chaps. V-XIV), among which he includes justice, normally a cardinal virtue (*CE*, p. 94). Next he treats the theological virtues of faith, hope, and love; to this traditional triad Traherne adds a fourth virtue, repentance (Chaps. XV–XIX). Having dealt with the more spiritual virtues, Traherne proceeds to the cardinal or "principal moral" virtues (Chaps. XX–XXIII). He then places meekness and humility (Christian virtues) between patience (implicitly a Christian virtue) and contentment (which was not in his original plan). The most important of the "less principal" virtues follow: magnanimity, modesty, liberality, and magnificence. The work concludes with two chapters on gratitude, consolidating Traherne's teaching by describing the love man owes God. An appendix discusses the practice of virtue in hostile circumstances.

Aside from the introductory chapters, marred by an archaic terminology and arid schematization, *Christian Ethicks* displays a commendable clarity of thought. Because of the concatenation of the virtues—all were links in a single golden chain—Traherne, like all moral philosophers, experienced occasional difficulties in differentiating closely related virtues. Several attempts to explain the relationship of one virtue to the rest result in little essays on virtue in general, as in the chapters on prudence, temperance and magnificence. Furthermore, Traherne felt the pull of another system of classification, dividing human history into the four "estates" of innocence, misery, grace, and glory, and assigning to each estate appropriate virtues (see p. 4:37 and Commentary). To develop these categories as instruments of ethical theory would have demanded far greater concentration on psychology than Traherne allowed, but he recurred to them throughout the *Ethicks* and to some extent they supplement the scholastic classification.[64]

[63] Traherne lays out his categories in Chap. III, pp. 23–28, and gives a preview of the contents in the address "To the Reader."

[64] Note also that Traherne mentions the Neoplatonic categorization of the purgative and perfective virtues (see p. 126:14 and Commentary), but he does not follow up the idea, which is alien to his ethics of activity.

Traherne kept to the point rather more severely than the casual reader might realize. By refusing to discuss vice he eliminated a division of moral philosophy that "would require a distinct and intire Volume to unfold" fully (*CE,* p. 207); of course, sin does on occasion intrude, revenge being subsumed under meekness, pride under humility, and original sin under mercy. Another possible subject Traherne declined to treat is the passions, often a point of departure for moral philosophers. This omission would be seriously detrimental to any rigorous philosophical treatise, for it deprives ethical theory of its psychological underpinnings; but for his purposes in *Christian Ethicks* Traherne was justified in assuming, rather than extensively describing, the conventional psychology. Finally, he dispensed with certain of the *"less Principal"* virtues: *"Gentleness of behaviour, Affability, Courtesie, . . . Urbanitie"* (*CE,* p. 24), veracity, taciturnity, and honor; nor did he discuss the "semi-virtues" of continence and tolerance.[65] Friendship, often the subject of elaborate commentary by moral philosophers, received only tangential attention. Aware of the dangers of inflation, Traherne selected for detailed treatment the essential features of virtue, so as best to display "its *Beauty, Dignity,* and *Glory*" (*CE,* p. 3).

B. *The Philosophy of* Christian Ethicks

Traherne wished not to convey information but to persuade his reader of the existence of intangibles, to reveal to the inward eye the landscape of the spirit. Like the Cambridge Platonists, he "affirm[ed] values where orthodoxy affirmed facts."[66] Because this stress on values, interweaving the farther reaches of theology with the practical concerns of ethics, marks the thought of both the Oxford-trained Traherne and his Cambridge contemporaries, the relationship between his philosophy and theirs merits close study if one wishes to understand Traherne in his intellectual context, to hear him at times speaking with his own voice, at others joining with the voices of his fellows.[67]

[65] All these virtues and "semi-virtues" are included in EN, pp. 20–21.

[66] Basil Willey, *The Seventeenth Century Background* (1934), p. 138.

[67] For a fuller discussion of the matters dealt with in the following pages, see Carol L. Marks, "Thomas Traherne and Cambridge Platonism," *PMLA,* LXXXI (1966), 521–534. The only previous study of any length is Frances L. Colby, "Traherne and the Cambridge Platonists: An Analytical Comparison" (unpublished Ph.D. diss., Johns Hopkins University, 1947). K. W. Salter discusses Traherne and the Platonists—mainly Smith—in *Thomas Traherne: Mystic and Poet* (1964), pp. 80–88. Affinities between More and Traherne have been observed by Marjorie Hope Nicolson in *The Breaking of the Circle* (Evanston, 1950; 2d ed., New York, 1960), and between Sterry and Traherne by Vivian de Sola Pinto in *Peter*

The Platonic revival at Cambridge commenced in the 1630's under the impetus of Benjamin Whichcote. Arguing that "Morals . . . are nineteen parts in twenty, of all Religion,"[68] Whichcote spoke for his colleagues in urging the rejection of dogmatism and the cultivation instead of a tolerant, rational, and effective love of God and neighbor. Their mild message achieved wide circulation when, a decade after the Restoration, Latitudinarian divines became more prominent in the Church of England. These "Men of Latitude"—led by Edward Stillingfleet, John Tillotson, and Simon Patrick—had all been educated at Cambridge under Whichcote and his Platonist associates, principally Ralph Cudworth, Henry More, John Smith, and Nathanael Culverwel. The Cambridge Platonists thus were responsible[69] for the tolerant, undogmatic tone characteristic of the Church during the Restoration and eighteenth century—though not directly responsible for the concomitant diminution of emotional fervor and the increasingly utilitarian bent.

Traherne, while Bridgeman's chaplain, certainly met the Latitudinarian divines; as we have seen, Bridgeman allied himself overtly with the Latitudinarian cause and before Traherne's advent employed one of their number as his chaplain. Indications of Traherne's acquaintance with Cambridge Platonism go beyond conjecture, however, since we know from the Commonplace Book that he devoted much attention to Henry More's popular *Divine Dialogues* shortly after their publication. Further proof that Traherne made an intensive study of Platonism rests solidly upon the Ficino Notebook, consisting as it does largely of notes from Ficino's analyses of the Platonic dialogues; and also upon the Commonplace Book excerpts from Gale and Jackson. Under thirty different rubrics in the latter manuscript Traherne included material from Gale's section on Platonic philosophy. Jackson, too, afforded Traherne contact with Platonism, for Platonic elements strongly tincture Jackson's Arminianism. Student, fellow, then President of Corpus Christi College (Oxford) during most of his life, Jackson in his treatises challenges the assumption that Cambridge was the sole academic fount

---

Sterry (Cambridge, Eng., 1934). On the Cambridge Platonists see John Tulloch, *Rational Theology and Christian Philosophy in England in the Seventeenth Century* (1872), II; for their place in the history of philosophy, see Ernst Cassirer, *The Platonic Renaissance in England,* tr. James P. Pettegrove (Austin, Texas, 1953), *passim;* and G. R. Cragg, *From Puritanism to the Age of Reason* (Cambridge, Eng., 1950), pp. 37–39, 54–60.

[68] Benjamin Whichcote, *Moral and Religious Aphorisms,* intro. W. R. Inge (1930), no. 586, p. 68.

[69] Such was the judgment of Burnet, *History,* I, 330–331.

of Platonism in England. Further research may well reveal deeper
and more spreading Oxonian roots of Platonism, but our present knowledge suggests that while Cambridge tutors actively fostered Platonic
studies, at Oxford students were left largely on their own in acquiring
familiarity with the Divine Plato. Traherne, according to the evidence
of the Ficino Notebook, did not study Platonism systematically until
some years after graduating B.A.

Yet another indication of Traherne's Platonic leanings exists in the
Commonplace Book: the more than two hundred paragraphs copied
from the *Divine Pymander* of Hermes Trismegistus, translated into
biblically rhythmic English by the eccentric divine John Everard. Although Traherne knew Ficino's Latin version of Hermes, the Commonplace Book extracts testify to his renewed fascination on meeting
Hermes in English. Despite disputes as to the authenticity of the Hermetic texts, the *Divine Pymander* was still considered by most a mainly
Platonic work, and Traherne's selective quotations emphasize this aspect of the mysterious Hermes. The main reason in Traherne's mind
for questioning "whether there were any such Hermes or no" was
in fact the Platonic insights evinced by the *Pymander:* "The Mysteries
seem too clear & Perspicuous & Divine for any Heathen." Such doubts
notwithstanding, Hermes remained for Traherne, as for most of his
contemporaries, "a venerable & Learned Author of great Esteem &
Authority in the World," the next link after Moses himself in the
chain of wisdom passing through Zoroaster, Pythagoras, Plato,
Orpheus, and yet more obscure philosophers.[70]

Although Traherne's fascination with Platonism and Neoplatonism
is obvious, it is more difficult to determine how these influences mingled
with other philosophical attitudes and interacted with his intuited beliefs. Analysis of the major tenets distinguishing *Christian Ethicks* will
at least suggest the affinities between Traherne's thought and the major
expressions of Platonic Christianity in seventeenth-century England.

Traherne's philosophy is radically positive; from this trait derives
the exuberantly optimistic tone characteristic of his prose and poetry.
In stressing man's potential, in proclaiming what man *could* do, Traherne made assumptions different from those held by many of his con-

[70] Traherne, CB, ff. 48bᵛ.2–49.1. See *CE*, p. 230:14 and Commentary. Robert
Ellrodt discusses the influence of the hermetic texts on Traherne in *L'Inspiration
personnelle et l'esprit du temps chez les poètes métaphysiques anglais*, Pt. I, vol. II
(*Poètes de transition, poètes mystiques*) (Paris, 1960), 267–275, 333–334. See also
Carol Marks, "Thomas Traherne and Hermes Trismegistus," *Renaissance News*, XIX
(1966), 118–131.

[handwritten annotation: This is my basic thesis of the difference of Traherne's Milton, Augustine]

temporaries, who expressed in negative terms their views on man's place in the universe. Theories of natural law and moral philosophy were predicated upon the Fall—as that "Modern Master of Morality" Samuel Pufendorf observed—and "even the greatest part of the Precepts of the *Decalogue,* as they are deliver'd in Negative Terms, do manifestly presuppose the *deprav'd State* of Man."[71] Most men still agreed with Sir Matthew Hale's endorsement of Solomon's contention (Prov. 15:33) that fear of God produces wisdom; [72] but the Cambridge Platonists maintained that "love is a sweeter and surer and stronger principle of obedience then feare" and based their ethics on love alone:

'Tis love that glews and fastens the whole Creation together. Those seeds of love which God himself, (who is love,) has scatter'd amongst Beings; those sparks of love which God himself, (who is love) has kindled amongst Beings, and those indeleble prints of love which God himself, (who is love,) has stampt upon Beings, maintain the whole fabrick of the world in its just beauty and proportion. The harmonious composure of Beings, the tuning of the several strings, makes them sound out his praise more melodiously. O how comely is it to see the sweet context and coherence of Beings, the loving connexion and concatenation of causes: one being espous'd to another in faithfulnesse and truth; the mutual claspings and twinings, the *due benevolence* of entities. . . . Glorious things are spoken of thee, thou Lady and Queen of Affection! thou art the first-borne of the soul, and the beginning of its strength.[73]

Optimism or pessimism about man's prospects for earthly felicity depended upon the philosopher's ideas concerning the stain created by Adam's lapse. Traherne, instead of squinting at the stain, gazed at the whole fabric, and in gazing found a Christian hope. For, as Louis L. Martz observes, "there is nothing heretical or occult in Traherne's conviction that he came into the world with the illumination

[71] Pufendorf, *The Whole Duty of Man According to the Law of Nature,* tr. Andrew Tooke (4th ed., 1716), Preface, sig. c1.

[72] See Hale's essays "Of Wisdom and the Fear of God, That that is True Wisdom" and "An Inquiry touching Happiness," respectively in the first and second parts of his *Contemplations* (1676).

[73] Nathanael Culverwel, "The White Stone," in *Discourse of the Light of Nature,* ed. William Dillingham (1652), pp. 143–144. It should be noted, however, that Culverwel manifested in addition to his Cambridge Platonism a strong Calvinist strain, and he added to his praise of love the warning that "God, though he be of vast and boundlesse love, . . . yet he has chose to concentricate it all in a few pickt out of the world: that he might thus engage them the more to himself" (p. 152).

of the Divine Light."[74] Because of this belief, Traherne deserves mention in the history of ethics along with Henry More "as one of the earliest English thinkers to state clearly a position in opposition to the conventional view [of fallen man] which generation had offered to generation."[75] Traherne, More, and most of More's Cambridge friends, while acknowledging human imperfections, affirmed the dignity of man, stressing above all the powers of the human mind.

Certain presuppositions underlay the Platonists' championship of human reason. Their reaction to Hobbes's moral relativism brought out clearly their assumption (which only Cudworth took pains to "prove") of an eternal and immutable morality—a morality grounded in turn upon a Platonic belief in innate moral ideas from which reason, like a heavenly hen "warming and brooding upon these first and oval [i.e., *ab ovo*] Principles of her own laying, . . . does thus hatch the Law of Nature." Innocent Adam could read these "first and Alphabetical Notions"[76] unaided, but postlapsarian man required help from above. God therefore supplemented the *"Truth of Natural Inscription"* with the *"Truth of Divine Revelation."*[77] All things except Christian redemption "are evident in themselves by the Light of Nature," according to Traherne, "because they may either be clearly deduced from the principles of Reason, or certainly discerned by plain Experience"; God republishes all truths either because they lie buried "under the Rubbish of our Fall," or because he wishes to emphasize certain aspects or to "confirm all by the Seal of his Authority" (*CE*, p. 119). Such views did not go unchallenged by the opposition: "I find that some men take offence," Whichcote remarked in a sermon, "to hear *reason* spoken of out of a pulpit, or to hear those great words of *natural light, of principles of reason, and conscience."*[78] But, replied the liberals, reason and faith do not conflict: *"Faith* is by *Reason* confirmed, and *Reason* is by *Faith* Perfected"* (*CE*, p. 112:29 and Commentary). Indeed, said More proudly, it is the *"special Prerogative"* of Christianity "that it dares appeal unto Reason."[79]

[74] Martz, *The Paradise Within* (New Haven and London, 1964), p. 87. See also William H. Marshall, "Thomas Traherne and the Doctrine of Original Sin," *Modern Language Notes*, LXXIII (1958), 161–165. K. W. Salter, however, sees Traherne as a crypto-Pelagian (*Traherne*, pp. 132–134).

[75] Marjorie Nicolson in *Conway Letters*, p. 380 (referring to More alone).

[76] Culverwel, *Light of Nature*, pp. 55, 54.

[77] John Smith, *Select Discourses*, ed. John Worthington (1660), p. 383.

[78] Benjamin Whichcote, *Works* (Aberdeen, 1751), I, Discourse XXIII, 370.

[79] Henry More, *A Collection of Several Philosophical Writings* (1662), p. vi.

This "reason" of the Platonists was by no means simply logical thinking, or, as More put it, *"dry Reason."*[80] True reason for the Platonists
was, in its most important aspect, a perception of the relationship of
an object to God, and it was effective only when allied with *"a good
and holy man, throughly sanctified in Spirit, Soul and body."*[81] "Holy
Sagacity," said More, combined both reason and "a discerning Spirit,"
and enabled a man to "feel and smell out . . . what is right and
true, and what false and perverse. . . ."[82] Traherne's understanding
of "reason" accorded with the Platonists' description of a faculty employing intuition more than logical deduction, and like them he insisted
that felicity could be attained only by living "the Life of Clear Reason"
(*C* II.99).

In the opinion of the Platonists, we need only apply reason, which
is the "Light of Nature,"[83] to the visible world in order to infer from
its manifest beauty and intricacy the essential truths about God,
"since . . . this visible World is the Body of GOD, not his Natural
Body, but which He hath assumed" (*C* II.21). Although the Platonists
(and particularly Traherne) drew the deduction, others did not succed
so well in the practice of natural religion. Both Christians and "the
better sort of Heathens" (*CE*, p. 63), though intellectually capable,
failed to perceive the obvious. For Latitudinarian divines, blind assertion of the superior insights of Christianity no longer sufficed to explain
away heathen ignorance; nor did the conventional hypotheses of original sin account for persistent Christian imperception. Traherne confessed himself baffled (*CE*, p. 59).

To man's past and present allegiance to sin Traherne and his philo-
sophic compeers accorded but a moment's reflection. Incorrigible optimism swept them on to lofty considerations of human possibilities.
Inspired by the telescopic and microscopic revelations of the new science, the Platonists—who were closely allied in thought and amity

[80] Henry More, *Divine Dialogues* (1668), 5th Dialogue, p. 403. More wrote
to Lady Conway: "The thirst after knowledge is ever dangerous till the divine
life has its birth in a man" (*Conway Letters,* p. 54).

[81] More, *Collection,* p. viii. Cf. Smith: *"Reason* in a Good man sits in the
Throne, & governs all the Powers of his Soul in a sweet harmony and agreement
with it self" (*Discourses,* p. 388).

[82] More, *Divine Dialogues,* 5th Dialogue, p. 404.

[83] The phrase was commonly applied to reason, e.g. by Traherne in CB, f.
64.1, and by Theophilus Gale in a passage from *The Court of the Gentiles,*
Part II (1670), p. 293, quoted in CB, *s.v.* "Reason," f. 82ᵛ.1. On Traherne's
idea of reason, see Salter, *Traherne,* pp. 34–37.

with the Royal Society—projected infinite vistas of intellectual and spiritual achievement.

Coincidentally proving man's mental prowess, scientific discoveries confirmed older theories of God's immanence and eternity. New spatial conceptions of the universe provoked renewed examination of the percipient soul, divinely fitted, proclaimed Traherne, "to be filled with infinite Objects. For by the Indwelling of GOD all Objects are infused, and contained within. The Spiritual Room of the Mind . . . is the Greatest Miracle perhaps in Nature" (*CE*, p. 73). Not only the New Philosophy but Renaissance Platonism informs these words. Compare them with the utterances of the most Platonizing of all the Cambridge men, Peter Sterry, who early abandoned a promising academic career to become one of Cromwell's religious advisers. In an essay "Of the Nature of a Spirit" Sterry dilated upon the infinite capacity of man's soul, which can contain not only its own body, but also "the world with all Varietie of things in it," and indeed "in the supreame, & inward part of itselfe it conteineth all Formes of things in their Originall, Eternall, Glorious Truths, & substance."[84]

Man's "capacity" for infinity was the subject of frequent comment by the Cambridge Platonists. The soul, said More, was "thirsty still in all estates," for nothing can "satisfie/Her hungry self, nor fill her vast capacity."[85] But Traherne was indebted to no one, not even to More, for his perceptions of infinity.[86] The autobiographical material in his poems and the *Centuries* makes it clear that his grasp of the great metaphysical abstractions of time and space went back to childhood intuitions.

Hermes Trismegistus was even closer than More to Traherne's ideas. In his Commonplace Book under the headings "Capacity" and "Man" Traherne included extracts from the *Divine Pymander* which he later incorporated into *Christian Ethicks,* and Hermes it was who fired his imagination, reinforcing his infant intuition. Not a "source," the *Pymander* offered confirmation of Traherne's own beliefs, abundantly and strikingly affirming ideas which years previously Traherne had developed independently. Both Hermes and Traherne celebrated the far-reaching extent of man's *"intellectual Operation"*: *"Command thy Soul to go into* India," said Hermes, *"and sooner than thou canst*

---

[84] Quoted from an unpublished MS. by Vivian de Sola Pinto, *Sterry,* pp. 161–162.

[85] More, "Psychathanasia," II.iii.28, in *The Complete Poems,* ed. Alexander B. Grosart (Edinburgh, 1878), p. 65.

[86] See Ellrodt's analysis of Traherne's "passion de l'infini" in *Les Poètes métaphysiques,* Pt. I, vol. II, 334–343.

bid it, it will be there. . . . Command it to flie into Heaven, and it will need no wings. . . Behold how great Power, how great swiftness thou hast!" (*CE,* p. 226). A house, a kingdom, the world itself were for Traherne a mere "confinement to the power, that is able to see Eternity, and conceive the Immensity of Almighty GOD!" (*CE,* p. 276).

That man—"the Golden clasp whereby Things Material and Spiritual are United" (*CE,* p. 104)—that man, this miracle of creation, possessed such marvelous powers filled Traherne with grateful exaltation. But the stupendous capacity of man's imagination was only an auxiliary to his potential moral greatness. The fundamental power intrinsic in man's nature was the power to choose the good, "to dare to be Good" (*CE,* p. 169). In man's choice lay his glory, and not merely his glory, but his essence: for, as Whichcote said, "a man ceaseth to be a man, if divested of . . . intelligence and liberty."[87]

Whichcote's definition of man was by no means universally accepted, and in fact in the early days of his career it would have aroused violent antagonism. When, in 1628, Thomas Jackson dedicated his *Treatise of the Divine Essence and Attributes* to the Earl of Pembroke, he felt obliged to warn Pembroke that the book was likely "to be censured for . . . *Arminian,"* even though he maintained no more than *"that the Almightie Creator hath a true freedome in doing good; and Adams off spring a true freedome of doing evill. . . ."*[88]

By mid-century the debate between the extremes of Calvinist predestination and Arminian free will had become wearisome. "*Free-will,* which we so much contend for," Whichcote observed, "is no absolute perfection, and we need not be so proud of it. For free-will, as it includes a power to do wrong, as well as right, is not to be found in God himself; and therefore it is no perfection in us."[89] In general the Cambridge theologians, though repelled by the doctrine of absolute reprobation and obviously committed to free will, avoided enthusiastic endorsement of complete spiritual liberty. Philosophy told them that man must act in accordance with his rational nature, and that right reason will always counsel complete obedience to God. As More, echo-

---

[87] Whichcote, *Works,* I, Discourse XXI, 337.

[88] Thomas Jackson, *Divine Essence,* Part I (1628), sigs. *3-*3ᵛ.

[89] Whichcote, *Works,* I, Discourse XV, 251. The freewill connotation of the word "liberty" gave way to the political after 1660. When, at the end of the century, Jeremy Collier (a clergyman) wrote an essay "Of Liberty," he defined his subject in civil terms, as "a Latitude of Practice within the compass of Law, and Religion" (*Miscellanies upon Moral Subjects,* Part II [1695], p. 141).

ing the Book of Common Prayer, advised Lady Conway: "We are not servants to any thing but Him whose service is indeed perfect Freedome."[90]

Cromwell's chaplain, Sterry, alone of the Cambridge Platonists, developed the paradox of freedom in servitude, arriving at the uncomfortable conclusion in his *Discourse of the Freedom of the Will* (1675) that sinful man, meant by God for the beatific vision, had instead become a nothing in the dust. Not so for Traherne. Whereas for Sterry and the Puritans the human drama lay in the infinite disparity between God and man, for Traherne dramatic tension sprang from God's having made "the most Sublime and Sovereign Creatures all *Free*" (*CE*, p. 149). As man could fall, so could he rise; the choice thrilled Traherne, and he hymned free will with more vigor and less equivocation than the other Platonists. God's gift of liberty was "one of the Best of all Possible Things" (*CE*, p. 90). " O Adorable and Eternal GOD! hast thou made me a free Agent!" he wrote, adding: "Of all Exaltations in all Worlds this is the Greatest" (*C* IV.43).

In Traherne's philosophy the *raison d'être* of the whole material universe depends on man's appreciation: he is the significant hinge on which the entire meaning of creation turns. The "one singular End" of man's own creation, More concurred, is "that he may be a *Priest* in this magnificent *Temple* of the *Universe,* and send up Prayers and Praises to the great Creator of all things on behalf of the rest of the Creatures."[91] Hence Traherne concluded *Christian Ethicks* with a rhapsody on God's loving preparation of the universe for man and man's loving enjoyment, which makes meaningful God's gift.

By his love God gave man the universe, establishing "an exact and pleasant Harmony between us and all the Creatures" (*CE*, p. 53). It was a music to which Traherne's ear was peculiarly attuned. For all his Platonism he avoided the spirit-matter duality and more than most Neoplatonists he truly felt that the world was God's body. He never opposed the physical to the spiritual world, but rather distinguished between "the works of GOD, and the works of men" (*CE*, p. 53). Physical creation, especially the human body, was a source of infinite wonder to him. Whereas his contemporaries anatomized man to counter atheism, Traherne praised man's "Organized Joynts, and Azure Veins" ("The Salutation," II, 4) as manifestations of God's overflowing love. Even in heaven, Traherne daringly predicted, we

---

[90] More, in *Conway Letters,* p. 76 (4 April 1653). Cf. also Smith, *Discourses,* pp. 393–395.

[91] More, *Antidote against Atheism,* in *Collection,* p. 85.

shall be "ravished with Sensible Pleasures in all our Members, not inconsistent with, but springing from these high and Superior Delights" (*CE,* p. 123). Meanwhile, here on earth, "Men are Images of GOD carefully put into a Beautiful Case," spirits endowed with bodies "certainly for unspeakable and most Glorious Ends" (*CE,* p. 104).

The universal spectacle devised by the Great Dramatist to delight the embodied soul lacked not a single part. God, being infinitely good, created all possible beings: like all good Platonists, Traherne believed in that plentitude of creation first described in the *Timaeus,* powerfully re-emphasized by Plotinus, and reaffirmed by Renaissance humanists. Employing a popular aquatic metaphor much used by Traherne, Theophilus Gale Platonically explained that the "*Grandeur* and sovereign *Perfection* of God consists principally in his being the *first principle* and *last end* of all things: from whom all things at first flow as from the *Plentitude of Being:* to whom they again have their *refluxe,* as rivers to the Ocean."[92]

The most common metaphor for plentitude was that of a "long chain of life and Being propagated from the highest to the lowest of all, from the most *incorporeal* Deity to *Matter* it self. . . ."[93] Because all were interconnected, each link in the chain possessed inherent value: "Every creature is a line leading to God."[94] God exhibited his wisdom "by making every the smallest Thing in his Kingdome infinitely serviceable in its Place" (*CE,* p. 69). Plenitude, Traherne stressed in prose and verse, was arranged with divine neatness, "so that every thing is best in its proper place" (*CE,* p. 182).

Yet God's exquisite distributive propriety did not produce a world of passive calm. Rather, productive agitation pervaded Traherne's universe: "All Life consists in Motion and Change" (*CE,* p. 211). Continuously creating, God's "Essence is his Act, and his Act his Pleasure. . . . Act is the Top and Perfection of Nature" (*CE,* pp. 67–68). Mere potentiality will not do, in Traherne's view, for "*PERFECT life* is the full exertion of perfect power" (*CE,* p. 20). "All Glorious Things have a Height of *Intensness* in them; and owe most of their Beauty to the Motion of their Strength and Activity" (*CE,* p. 89).

Traherne's stress on activity is a natural correlative of his paeans

---

[92] Theophilus Gale, *The Court of the Gentiles,* Part I (Oxford, 1669), p. 2. For a subtle analysis of the metaphor, see Arthur O. Lovejoy, *The Great Chain of Being* (New York, 1960; first published 1936), especially pp. 49–50, 62.

[93] [George Rust], *A Letter of Resolution Concerning Origen and the Chief of His Opinions,* ed. Marjorie Hope Nicolson (New York, 1933), p. 46. Rust was one of the lesser Cambridge Platonists.

[94] Whichcote, *Works,* III, Discourse LVIII, 176.

to free will, his embrace of infinity. In the moral realm, too, the keynote is activity, as man's insatiable soul instinctively searches the universe for felicity. "IT is the Glory of man," said Traherne with bold intent to shock, "that his *Avarice* is insatiable, and his *Ambition* infinite" (*CE,* p. 54). Benjamin Whichcote explained: "God Created Man with a Vast *Capacity* of Receiving, and (answerably hereunto) with a Restless *Desire* of Greater Good; than the Creature [i.e., physical creation] can afford."[95] Nothing but full knowledge of God can quench the innate thirst for happiness, and even the attainment of felicity results in activity.

Repeatedly and with passion Traherne denied that happiness consisted in the Stoics' "meer Apathy, or conceited 'Αυτάρκεια, a self-sufficiency" (*CE,* p. 60); true felicity lay instead in "an activity of life, reaching through all Immensity, to all Objects whatsoever" (*CE,* p. 20). Like Traherne, Smith reiterated attacks upon Stoic "autarchy,"[96] supporting his opposition by reference to the Platonists' belief that, as Traherne put it, we are "led by Instinct eagerly to thirst after" felicity (*CE,* p. 16). "*Lukewarmness,*" being a repression of man's striving nature, crossed the very purpose of human existence, and was "infinitely Base and Dishonourable, . . . Odious and Distastful" (*CE,* pp. 88–89).

Traherne's, then, was an ethics of activity: "Philosophers are not those that speak, but Do great Things" (*C* IV.2): "The reality of Religion consists in the solid practice of it among the Sons of men that are daily with us" (*CE,* p. 246). With Traherne's Protestant insistence that faith manifests itself in works the Cambridge Platonists concurred. "A Good man," said Smith, "hath a Spring of perpetual motion within,"[97] and he realizes himself in God's similitude by doing good to his neighbors. For God's joy is to "communicate" his blessings to appreciative recipients, and God is man's model. As Thomas Jackson observed in a passage copied in Traherne's Commonplace Book: "All the goodnesse man is capable of, doth but expresse Gods goodness communicative."[98] Of course deficient man, unlike God, must first receive before he can give; but having received, "we are in danger of bursting, till we can communicate all to some fit and amiable Recipient,

[95] Whichcote, *Aphorisms,* no. 860, p. 97.

[96] Smith, *Discourses,* pp. 136, 420, 445, 470. The Greek term was more commonly used than the anglicized version; the *Oxford English Dictionary* lists only two illustrations for "autarchy" in this meaning, one in 1643, the other in 1863.

[97] Smith, *Discourses,* p. 470.

[98] Jackson, *Divine Essence,* Part I, p. 189; quoted CB, *s.v.* "Liberty," f. 62ᵛ.1.

and more delight in the Communication than we did in the Reception"
(*CE,* p. 258). For, as Traherne wrote in the Church's Year-Book:
"By Communicating our selvs we are united to others, give others
the Benefit of our selvs, & Enjoy our selvs in being Enjoyed. . . . for
all the Joy even of Living in Heaven, is the Twofold Joy of Communicating & Receiving."[99] We can receive only by perceiving the
gift: "He, that conceits Nothing in the World to be his own but his
low Cottage and course diet, will think it needless to praise his Maker,
and will deny himself to be happy in those narrow and Mean enjoyments" (*CE,* p. 71).

"*TRUE Contentment,*" Traherne proclaimed aphoristically, "*is the
full satisfaction of a Knowing Mind.*" His persistently positive spirit
abhorred "that Negative Contentment, which past of Old for so great
a Vertue" (*CE,* pp. 216–217), and he declared with absolute assurance:

> *Life! Life is all: in its most full extent*
> *Stretch out to all things, and with all Content!*   [*CE,* p. 218]

It is this persuasive emotion, rather than intellectual originality, which
distinguishes *Christian Ethicks.* Traherne was a philosopher in the root
sense of the word; his love of wisdom was ardent and fundamental.
"He thought that to be a Philosopher a Christian and a Divine, was
to be one of the most Illustrious Creatures in the World" (*C* IV.3):
Christian Ethicks shows that he was indeed such a miracle of three in
one.

C.   *Intuition and Style*

Traherne's prose exactly embodies his thought. An urgent need to
communicate intuited truths endowed his ideas and the prose that
clothed them with concentration and directness. In his philosophy he
played variations upon a very few themes; in his prose he modulated
a few basic patterns. The product of emotional rather than
abstractly intellectual experience, Traherne's philosophy demanded a
controlled yet responsive prose. He wrote well only when conveying
felt ideas; the flatness of the early expository chapters of *Christian
Ethicks* results from their being an explanation of other men's ideas,
rather than a revelation of Traherne's own insights and beliefs. His
best prose reflects not Traherne the Oxford graduate familiar with

---

[99] CYB, f. 51. Cf. Edward Sparke's *Scintilla-Altaris,* a source of CYB: "Yet
Passive Communion is not enough for Saints, it must be active, too, by communicating of good" ([4th ed., 1666], p. 527).

textbook language, but Traherne the clergyman intimate with the cadences of the Bible.

In the private *Centuries* Traherne favored brief sentences; in the public *Ethicks* he showed his mastery of the long sentence. Loose rather than periodic, his sentences flow in elastic rhythms created by subtle variations upon a basic structure. Traherne could sustain a long series of short phrases without becoming monotonous and could build anaphoric patterns with finesse. He understood, too, the construction of approximate parallelisms which suggest symmetry without obtruding stylized balance. The paragraph more than the sentence was his medium in the *Ethicks,* for it gave him the necessary amplitude for broad rhythmic modulations. These characteristics are best illustrated by Traherne's expositions of love (see *CE,* pp. 56–57), for love lies at the heart of his philosophy. In explaining the variant meanings of "love," he exemplified not only his comprehensive ethics but his ability to manipulate a pattern to superb effect; he took his departure from the Bible (1 Pet. 3:10): "We can Love Life, and desire to see Good Days; we can Love the Sun, and Wine, and Oyl, and Gold; Love our Dogs and Horses, fine Clothes and Jewels, Pleasures, Honours, Recreations, Houses, Riches, and as well as Love Men and Women, Souls and Angels" (*CE,* p. 134).

Like most Restoration prose, Traherne's style is relatively unadorned. His rhythms are functional, the outgrowth of thought. There is, however, a curious feature of his style which harks back to the prose of the previous generation: like Browne he was fond of yoking together approximately synonymous terms: "Mechanical fitness, and Dead convenience" (p. 80), "Oyl and Fuel" (p. 145), "springs and sources" (p. 190), "disbursments and effusions" (p. 259), "alienate and estrange" (p. 266), "imagination and fancy" (p. 275). Aside from this tendency, Traherne endorsed if he did not always realize the contemporary ideal of the plain style.

Functionalism in the elements of the sentence extended into the realm of exemplum and metaphor. Suspicious of the delusive effects of decoration in poetry,[100] Traherne made his analogies integral parts of his exposition:

ALL inferiour felicities are but Miseries compared with the Highest. A farthing is *good* and pleaseth a Beggar in time of distress: but a piece

---

[100] See "The Author to the Critical Peruser," II, 2–3; "The Person," ll. 25–26, II, 76; and "Thanksgivings for the Body," ll. 339–340, II, 223.

of Gold is *Better*. An Estate of a thousand pounds a year is better than a Piece of Gold; but our Ambition carries us to Principalities and Empires. An Empire is more desirable than a Province; and the Wider, the Richer, the Better it is, the more Desirable. But the Empire of all the Earth is a Bubble compared to the Heavens: And the Heavens themselves less than nothing to an infinite Dominion.

PERFECT Felicity is not Dominion, nor Pleasure, nor Riches alone, nor Learning, nor Virtue, nor Honour; but all in Perfection. [*CE,* p. 15]

Predominantly Neoplatonic in origin, Traherne's metaphors nearly all relate to God and, analogously, to the soul and to love. His metaphors tend to fall into clusters. One group—more common in his poetry than in his prose—associates the ocean, rivers, and fountains. The most important cluster in *Christian Ethicks* focuses on the sun and abounds in images of visual perception; such solar and visual metaphors were frequent in seventeenth-century literature, particularly so in the works of the Cambridge Platonists (pre-eminently Sterry in prose and More in poetry). Frequent mirror images belong to this cluster as well as to another principal group; this second configuration seems peculiar to Traherne, involving as it does not only mirrors but reflections in water (occurring in the poems especially), abysses, and the antipodes—all based on the paradox that by looking down man sees above. The most extraordinary instance of this group of images is the extended metaphor describing humility:

It is like a Mirror lying on the ground with its face upwards: All the height above increaseth the depth of its Beauty within, nay turneth into a new depth, an inferiour Heaven is in the glass it self . . . A man would little think, that by sinking into the Earth he should come to Heaven. He doth not, but is buried, that fixeth and abideth there. But if he pierceth through all the Rocks and Minerals of the inferiour World, and passeth on to the end of his Journey in a strait line downward, in the middle of his way he will find the Centre of Nature, and by going downward still begin to ascend, when he is past the Centre; through many Obstacles full of gross and subterraneous Darkness, which seem to affright and stifle the Soul, he will arrive at last to a new Light and Glory, room and liberty, breathing-place and fresh-air among the *Antipodes,* and by passing on still through those inferiour Regions that are under his feet, but over the head of those that are beneath him, finally come to another Skie, penetrate that, and leaving it behind him sink down into the depth of all Immensity. [*CE,* pp. 209–210]

As a man of the Restoration, Traherne was devoted to right reason, but in his response to paradox he reminds us of an earlier age.[101] His relish for antitheses appears not only in his account of humility but throughout the *Ethicks,* and it appears as well in the *Centuries.* His great purpose in writing the *Centuries,* he announced at the outset, was to make apparent "Things Strange, yet Common; Incredible, yet Known; Most High, yet Plain; infinitely Profitable, but not esteemed" (*C* I.3). Riddles entranced him: he liked to propose "a strange Paradox" which was nevertheless "infinitely true," then to astound his reader with "a stranger Paradox yet," and finally to provide an answer "which solveth the Riddle" (*CE,* pp. 178–179). Patience and humility delighted him by their union of conflicting elements, and he dwelt similarly upon the oxymoronic virtues of modesty ("the most friendly strife, and kind Contention," *CE,* p. 237) and repentance (likened to "a Child so Black and so Beautiful," *CE,* p. 125).

Although Traherne's love of paradox belongs to the age of Donne, it does not clash with the other characteristics of his style and thought. For religious philosophers the post-war years were a period of transition, juxtaposing relics of the past with harbingers of the future. Emblematic of his time, Traherne in his ethics combined scholastic jargon with intuited perceptions, in his style harmonized the plainness of the Royal Society with the richer rhythms of the Jacobean Bible.

[101] On paradox in Traherne's works, see Rosalie L. Colie, "Thomas Traherne and the Infinite," *Huntington Library Quarterly,* XXI (1957), 69–82; and A. L. Clements, "On the Mode and Meaning of Traherne's Mystical Poetry: 'The Preparative,' " *Studies in Philology,* LXI (1964), 500–521.

Textual Introduction

I Printing and Publication of *Christian Ethicks*

THOMAS TRAHERNE'S *Christian Ethicks* was entered in the Stationers' Register on August 6, 1674; the publisher, as in the case of Traherne's earlier *Roman Forgeries* (1673), was Jonathan Edwin. A note inserted by the printer immediately following the table of contents implies that since Traherne had recently died he had had no opportunity to correct the proofs of *Christian Ethicks:* "The Author's much lamented Death hapning immediately after this Copy came to the Press, may reasonably move the Readers charity, to pardon those few Errata's which have escaped in the Printing by so sad an occasion." Traherne was buried in October, 1674, two months after the work was entered in the Stationers' Register. The *Term Catalogue* for Michaelmas, 1674, noted the publication of the book, "Christian Ethicks, or Divine Morality opening the way to blessedness by the Rules of Virtue and Reason. By Tho. Traherne, B. D., Author of the 'Roman Forgeries.' In Octavo. Price, bound, 5s. Printed for Jon. Edwin at the Three Roses in *Ludgate street.*"[1] The title-page of *Christian Ethicks*, however, bears the date 1675.

It is well known that Philip Traherne, Thomas's brother, revised some of the manuscripts of Thomas's poems;[2] and it is thought that he was readying an edition of the poems for publication. No such edition ever appeared. Since Thomas died just after *Christian Ethicks* went to the printer, one might expect Philip to have seen the book through the press. Fortunately (for "corrections" would have

[1] *The Term Catalogues,* I, ed. Edward Arber (1903), 184–185.
[2] See, for example, H. M. Margoliouth, ed., Thomas Traherne's *Centuries, Poems, and Thanksgivings* (Oxford, 1958), I, xii–xvii.

abounded), such was not the case; Philip had recently been appointed chaplain to an expedition which was in Smyrna at the time of Thomas's death;[3] and he was, it can be assumed, not responsible for the stop-press "corrections" that were made while the book was being printed.

The printer's note about the "few Errata's" notwithstanding, *Christian Ethicks* was badly printed. Or perhaps one should say that part of the book was badly printed (sigs. B–Z). All evidence indicates that two compositors worked on the book. One compositor (Compositor A) set sigs. A, a, Aa–Qq; the other (Compositor B) set sigs. B–Z. Obvious errors (misprints, turned letters, dropped letters, omitted words, repeated words, misplaced words, and other such weaknesses) are frequent in the part of the book set by B; but the parts set by A are, in general, relatively free of such errors. As a result, the number of emendations required in the text is far lower in the section set by A.[4]

Each compositor set approximately half of the book. Compositor B's work ended on Z8^v, the last page of Chapter XXI; even a casual comparison of Z8^v with Aa1 reveals striking differences. Although those pages appear to use the same type font, the types used to print Aa1 were in much better condition than those used to print Z8^v. Many of the types employed in printing sigs. B–Z were broken, bent, chipped, or otherwise distinctively mutilated. On the other hand, those used in setting Aa–Qq were relatively undamaged.

The same distinctively mutilated types can be traced through sheet after sheet of sigs. B–Z; they never appear, however, in sigs. A, a, Aa–Qq. Obviously different type cases were being used by the two compositors. The chipped *P*'s, broken *l*'s, squashed *n*'s and *O*'s found in the work of Compositor B often appear in successive sheets of signatures B–Z. These same mutilated types, however, do not appear in both the inner and outer formes of any sheet. Casting off was, therefore, not a factor in the printing of the book.

Even a casual observer of Z8^v and Aa1 also immediately notes an error in pagination. Z8^v is numbered "352," but Aa1 is numbered "323." It is possible that the two compositors worked on the book at the same time. If so, they may have agreed that B would finish setting his part of the text on Z8^v, which would be numbered "352." Compositor A was to begin on Aa1, which would then be numbered "353."

---

[3] Margoliouth, I, xxxiii–xxxiv.

[4] Two hundred and nineteen emendations were necessary in the section set by Compositor B, but only twenty-nine in the parts set by A.

Compositor A, however, erroneously numbered Aa1 as "323." It is less likely, but still possible, that only one compositor was working at a time. Compositor B would have set B–Z; Compositor A would then have taken over, setting Aa–Qq and misnumbering his first page "323" rather than "353." In any case, page numbers "323" to "352" appear twice in the book (sigs. Y2 to Z8^v, Aa1 to Bb7^v). Signature Bb8 is finally numbered "353," and from that point on no other pagination anomalies occur.

It was a quite normal practice to set introductory matter after the body of the text had been printed. The collational formula of *Christian Ethicks* (A^8, a^8, B–Z^8, Aa–Qq^8) suggests that such was the case here; sigs. A1–A8^v and a1–a8^v contain all the introductory matter, and the text begins on B1.

That two compositors divided the work, as suggested, is certain. There are, for example, distinctive spelling differences between the portions set by Compositor B (B–Z) and Compositor A (A, a, Aa–Qq). In spelling "than," "only," and "truly," Compositor B was not very consistent. He spelled "than" as "then" 67% of the time, "only" as "onely" 16%, and "truly" as "truely" 50% of the time. Compositor A, on the other hand, was quite consistent; he used "then" 3%, "onely" and "truely" not at all. Similarly, if Compositor B spelled "though" as "tho" 99%, Compositor A spelled "though" 98%. Compositor B favored "hazzard" (100%) over "hazard"; Compositor A always spelled the word "hazard," never "hazzard."

The two compositors had other distinctive mannerisms. At least thirty times, Compositor B used "&" for "and"; Compositor A never made this substitution. Compositor A did, more often than B, use apostrophes in words like "Author's" and "remov'd." Excluding verse passages, there are thirty-eight such apostrophes in A's work, and only nine in B's. Also Compositor B was often guilty of using italic initial capitals in words otherwise in roman. On V5 alone are found "*L*ove," "*L*ove," "*L*ight," "*E*asie," "*E*asie," "*E*xcellency," "*P*art," "*P*urity, and "*P*erversness." In the part of the book here attributed to Compositor B, one hundred and eighty-six such substitutions occur; in the parts attributed to Compositor A, only five such erroneously italicized initial capitals appear. At first thought one might attribute these substitutions in B's work to a shortage of capital letters in his type case. But as we have seen, distinctively mutilated types can be traced through sheet after sheet set by B; therefore the types must have been distributed after each sheet was printed. This being so, it is improbable that the substitutions were the result of a shortage of roman capitals; as further proof, the first page of a sheet sometimes contains a mixture of these italicized initial capitals and regular roman initial capitals. Thus one finds on V1 "*Felicity*," "*End*," and "*Essence*," together with "For," "Eternal," and "Eye." In other words, these italicized initial capitals are likely to occur anywhere in a forme.[5]

It is likely that the firm of Bennet Griffin (also spelled "Griffith") printed *Christian Ethics*. The imprint of Traherne's *Roman Forgeries* says in part that *Roman Forgeries* was "printed by *S*. and *B*. *Griffin*." Unlike *Christian Ethicks, Roman Forgeries* has an errata page; but that book too is badly printed, and the errata page really notes only a small portion of the errors in the work. As in *Christian Ethicks*, the pagination is erratic; the numbering of the pages on the entire inner forme of sheet. R is particularly badly handled. More important, one finds in *Roman Forgeries*, as in various other books printed by the Griffins, the tendency of a compositor, possibly Compositor B of *Christian Ethicks*, to substitute italic initial capitals for roman capitals. On A3 of *Roman Forgeries* he set "*Rome*" and "*Nice*"; on A3ᵛ, "*Roman*," "*Nice*," "*Bishops*," "*Metropolitan*," "*Councils*," "*Person*," and "*Province*." Similar examples also occur on sigs. A4, A4ᵛ, A5, A5ᵛ, A6, A6ᵛ, and A7.

Other books printed by the Griffins contain sections in which italic initial capitals have been erroneously substituted for roman capitals. In *The Antiquity of the Protestant Religion*, printed by Bennet Griffin in 1687, there are seven italic initial capital *C*'s on B1ᵛ; on D1, three italic *C*'s and four italic *B*'s. Signatures C3, C4, and C4ᵛ also abound with such letters. Closer to the time of publication of *Christian Ethicks* (1675), Thomas Flatman's *Poems and Songs* (London, 1674) reveals some of the same characteristics; for example, the prefatory matter contains erroneously italicized capitals. Like Traherne's *Christian Ethicks*, this book has numerous misprints, frequent ragged lines, and many spacing errors. The type font is similar to that used in *Christian Ethicks*, and many of the mutilated types were very much like correspondingly mutilated types used in the printing of sigs. B–Z of *Christian Ethicks*. It is true that the types used to print part of *Christian*

---

[5] In sheet Y, for example, all but four (Y1, Y3ᵛ, Y5, Y6ᵛ) of the sixteen pages of that sheet include at least one erroneously italicized initial capital. Compare the frequency of other kinds of errors. In his running-titles, Compositor A made only five errors; Compositor B made forty-eight. Compositor A made only one error in pagination; Compositor B made nineteen. Compositor A left no leaves unsigned; Compositor B failed to sign seven. Compositor A made two catchword errors; Compositor B made forty-three (see Textual Introduction, Part II).

Ethicks (B–Z) were in generally worse condition than those used in setting Flatman's poems. But Charlton Hinman has demonstrated that individual types can undergo considerable change during the printing of a single work.[6] If the Griffins printed Traherne's *Christian Ethicks,* they may have printed numerous other works with the same types during the time between the printing of Flatman's book and the printing of Traherne's,[7] enough time to allow considerable change in the types.

The Griffin printing house was an old, established one. Started by John Jackson, Ninian Newton, Edmond Bollifant, and Arnold Hatfield in 1590, it was acquired by Edward Griffin I in 1613. He ran it until his death in 1621, when it passed into the hands of his widow, Anne Griffin. By 1637 Edward Griffin II, son of Anne and Edward Griffin I, was helping Anne Griffin run the business. On July 11, 1637, the Star Chamber Decree noted that a great many "libellous, seditious, and mutinous" books were currently being published; henceforth, all books were to be licensed. In an effort to control the situation, the Star Chamber decreed that the number of master printers was to be limited to twenty; listed among the twenty so authorized was Edward Griffin II.[8] He proceeded to run the business until his death in 1652.[9]

On Edward's death, Sarah Griffin, his wife, took over the business. She ran it (located in the Old Bailey, St. Sepulchre's Parish) over twenty years.[10] In 1671 Bennet Griffin's name began to appear with Sarah's in the imprints of some of the books printed by the Griffin establishment. Bennet was probably the son of Sarah and Edward Griffin II. He printed and sold books in the Old Bailey until 1700, when "nothing more is heard of him."[11]

Although the Griffin printing house was an old one, it was not a

---

[6] *The Printing and Proof-Reading of the First Folio of Shakespeare,* I (Oxford, 1963), 52–69.

[7] Donald Wing (*Short-title Catalogue of Books Printed in England, Scotland, Ireland, Wales, and British America and of English Books in Other Countries, 1641–1700* [New York, 1945–1951]) listed only one book definitely printed by the Griffins during that period, but they may have printed others anonymously. In addition, the types in question may have been used to print matter of an entirely ephemeral nature, matter long since passed into oblivion.

[8] Henry R. Plomer, *A Short History of English Printing* (1900), pp. 178–179.

[9] Henry R. Plomer, *A Dictionary of the Booksellers and Printers Who Were at Work in England, Scotland and Ireland from 1641 to 1667* (1907), p. 86.

[10] Plomer, *A Dictionary . . . from 1641 to 1667,* p. 87.

[11] Henry R. Plomer, *A Dictionary of the Printers and Booksellers Who Were at Work in England, Scotland and Ireland from 1668 to 1725* (Oxford, 1922), p. 134.

particularly large operation as Restoration printing houses went. In 1668 a rather large firm, Mr. Flesher's, for example, had five presses and employed two apprentices and thirteen workmen. Mrs. Griffin at that time had only two presses, and she employed one apprentice and six workmen.[12]

Jonathan Edwin, who required the services of the Griffins a number of times during the years he published and sold books (1671–1679), "dealt in all kinds of literature, from sixpenny pamphlets dealing with the lives of pirates and murderers, to folio histories and classics." He "was a staunch Royalist and Churchman, issuing several books against the Presbyterians and Dissenters."[13] Miss Wade believes that another staunch Royalist and member of the Church of England, Mrs. Susanna Hopton, was instrumental in Sir Orlando Bridgeman's offering the position of Chaplain to Thomas Traherne. Perhaps Traherne returned the favor later by finding a publisher for a book by Mrs. Hopton.[14] Significantly, Jonathan Edwin published Mrs. Hopton's *Daily Devotions, consisting of Thanksgivings, Confessions, and Prayers.* For that work, the Stationers' Register reads, "Entred . . . under the hand of Master Warden MEARNE a coppy or booke intituled *Dayly devotions consisting of thanksgiving confessions and prayers. . . .*" The very next work entered in the Register was Traherne's *Roman Forgeries.* Like *Daily Devotions,* it was entered on September 25, 1673; and like *Daily Devotions,* it was "entred . . . under the hand of Master Warden MEARNE."[15]

II   Bibliographical Description of *Christian Ethicks*

[within double rules] Chriſtian | ETHICKS: | OR, | Divine MORALITY. | Opening the WAY to | BLESSEDNESS, | By the RULES of | VERTUE | AND | REASON. | [rule] | By *THO. TRAHERNE,* B.D. | Author of the *Roman* Forgeries. | [rule] | *LONDON,* | Printed for *Jonathan Edwin,* at the *Three* | *Roſes* in *Ludgate-ſtreet,* 1675.

[12] Plomer, *A Short History of English Printing,* pp. 225, 227.
[13] Plomer, *A Dictionary . . . from 1668 to 1725,* p. 111.
[14] Gladys I. Wade, *Thomas Traherne* (Princeton, 1944), pp. 87, 132.
[15] *A Transcript of the Registers of the Worshipful Company of Stationers; from 1640–1708 A.D.,* II, eds. G. E. Briscoe Eyre and Charles Robert Rivington (1913), 471–472.

Collation: 8⁰: A⁸, a⁸, B–Z⁸, Aa–Qq⁸, 320 leaves; pp [32] 1–78 59 80–
135 135–136 138–139 139–140 142–171 171 173–175 [176] 177–
188 198 911 190 192–275 376 277–290 292 292–293 295 279 296–
297 282 299–318 316 320–330 313 332–333 336 325 336–352
323–577 [578] [= 608]. In headline and outer margin. (*Variants:*
omitting 243 and misprinting 84 as 49, 89 as 99, 350 as 351, 351 as
350, and 352 as 350.)

HT, sig. B1] CHRISTIAN | ETHICKS | OR | DIVINE MOR-
ALITIE. | Opening | 𝕿𝖍𝖊 𝖂𝖆𝖞 𝖙𝖔 𝕭𝖑𝖊𝖋𝖋𝖊𝖉𝖓𝖊𝖋𝖘 | By | The rules of
Virtue and Reaſon. | [rule]

Contents: A1 : Title (verso blank). A2 : [orn: leaves and flowers,
with naked figure in center facing front, holding branches in both
hands; two satyrs leaping away from center figure on either side;
goats leaping toward satyrs] | 'TO THE | READER.' | 'T⁴[init.]*HE
deſign of this . . . .*' a3ᵛ: [blank]. a4: [double row of type orn.; top
row pointing up, bottom row pointing down] | 'The Contents.' |
'CHAP.I.' | 'O²*F the End, for . . . .*' [description of contents ending
on a8]. a8ᵛ: 'To the Reader.' [note on errata]. B1:HT with text
(cap⁵) headed 'CHAP..I. | *Of the End, for the ſake of which, Vir-|
tue is deſired.*' Pp6: [text ends] || 'An APPENDIX.| *Of Enmity and
Triumph: Of Schiſm and | Hereſie, Fidelity, Devotion, Godlineſs. |
Wherein is declared, how Gratitude and | Felicity inſpire and perfect
all the Vertues.*' [with text of appendix (cap²)]. Qq8: [appendix
ends] || 'FINIS.' Qq8ᵛ: .blank.

Running-titles: To the Reader. \$A2ᵛ–a3; The Contents. \$a4ᵛ–a8;
𝕺𝖋 𝖙𝖍𝖊 𝕰𝖓𝖉|𝖔𝖋 𝖁𝖎𝖗𝖙𝖚𝖊. B1ᵛ–B6 [*excepting*[16]*:* 𝖔𝖋 𝖁𝖎𝖗𝖙𝖚𝖊, B2, B3]; 𝕺𝖋
𝖙𝖍𝖊 𝕹𝖆𝖙𝖚𝖗𝖊 𝖔𝖋 𝕱𝖊𝖑𝖎𝖈𝖎𝖙𝖞,|𝖎𝖙𝖘 𝕰𝖝𝖈𝖊𝖑𝖑𝖊𝖓𝖈𝖞 𝖆𝖓𝖉 𝕻𝖊𝖗𝖋𝖊𝖈𝖙𝖎𝖔𝖓. B6ᵛ–C3 [*except-
ing:* 𝕺𝖋 𝖙𝖍𝖊 𝖓𝖆𝖙𝖚𝖗𝖊 𝖔𝖋 𝕱𝖊𝖑𝖎𝖈𝖎𝖙𝖞. B8ᵛ; 𝕺𝖋 𝖙𝖍𝖊 𝕹𝖆𝖙𝖚𝖗𝖊 𝖔𝖋 𝕱𝖊𝖑𝖎𝖈𝖎𝖙𝖞. C2ᵛ];
𝖎𝖙𝖘 𝕰𝖝𝖈𝖊𝖑𝖑𝖊𝖓𝖈𝖞 𝖆𝖓𝖉 𝕻𝖊𝖗𝖋𝖊𝖈𝖙𝖎𝖔𝖓. C3ᵛ; 𝕺𝖋 𝖁𝖎𝖗𝖙𝖚𝖊. | 𝖎𝖓 𝕲𝖊𝖓𝖊𝖗𝖆𝖑. C4ᵛ–C5;
𝕺𝖋 𝖁𝖎𝖗𝖙𝖚𝖊|𝖎𝖓 𝕲𝖊𝖓𝖊𝖗𝖆𝖑. C5ᵛ–D1 [*excepting:* 𝕺𝖋 𝖁𝖎𝖗𝖙𝖓𝖊 C8ᵛ]; 𝕺𝖋
𝖁𝖎𝖗𝖙𝖚𝖊, &c. D1ᵛ; 𝕺𝖋 𝖙𝖍𝖊 𝕻𝖔𝖜𝖊𝖗𝖘 𝖆𝖓𝖉, &c. D2; 𝕺𝖋 𝖙𝖍𝖊 𝕻𝖔𝖜𝖊𝖗𝖘 𝖆𝖓𝖉
|𝕬𝖋𝖋𝖊𝖈𝖙𝖎𝖔𝖓𝖘 𝖔𝖋 𝖙𝖍𝖊 𝕾𝖔𝖚𝖑. D2ᵛ–E1ᵛ [*excepting:* 𝕺𝖋 𝖙𝖍𝖊 𝕻𝖔𝖜𝖊𝖗 𝖆𝖓𝖉|

---

[16] The two compositors, B far more often than A, were inconsistent in setting
the periods and commas of the running-titles. They tended to use black-letter and
roman punctuation marks interchangeably. A description of the running-titles
reflecting fully these anomalies would necessitate several pages of exceptions;
consequently, the editors have decided, only as far as *style* of pointing is concerned,
to present a normalized listing.

Affections of the Soul. D7ᵛ–D8; Of the Powers and | Affections of the
Soul. D8ᵛ–E1]; Of Knowledge. $E2–F2ᵛ [*excepting:* Of Knowledge.
E3]; Of Love and Hatred. $F3ᵛ–F8ᵛ [*excepting:* Of Love and Hatred,
F6; Of Love and Hatred F8]; Of Eternal Love. G1; Of Eteenal Love.
G2; Of Eternal Love. $G2ᵛ–H2 [*excepting:* Of Eternal Love H1ᵛ];
Of the Excellency | of Truth. H3–H8ᵛ; Of the Excellency I1; Of Eter=
nal Love I1ᵛ, Of Eternal Love. I2; Of Wisdome. I2ᵛ, I3, I7, I7ᵛ, I8ᵛ;
Of the Excellency I3ᵛ; Of Wisdom. I4, $I5–I6ᵛ; Of Wisdom I4ᵛ; Of
Wisdome I8; Of Righteousnefs. $K1–K7ᵛ [*excepting:* Of Righteouf-
nefs. K3; Of Righteous. K4]; Of Goodnefs. K8; Of Righteousnefs.
K8ᵛ; Of Goodnefs. $L1–M2ᵛ, M3ᵛ; Of Holinefs. $M4–N2ᵛ; Of
Juftice | in General. N3ᵛ–N6; in General. | Of Juftice N6ᵛ–N8; Of
Mercy. $N8ᵛ–O8ᵛ; Of Faith. $P1ᵛ–Q5; Of Hope. $Q6–R6 [*excepting:*
Of Hope.. Q7ᵛ, R2]; Of Repentance. $R7–S6ᵛ, S8; Of Repentnce. S7;
Of Charity $S8ᵛ– T1; Of Repentance. | towards God. T1ᵛ–T2; Of
Charity | towards God. T2ᵛ–V3ᵛ [*excepting:* Of Charity V1]; Of
Charity | to our Neighbour. V4–X5 [*excepting:* Of Charity. V5ᵛ;
Of Charity. | to our Neighbonr. X1ᵛ–X2ᵛ]; Of Prudence. $X6–Y7;
Of Courage. $Y8–Z8ᵛ [*excepting:* Of Cauroge. Y8ᵛ; Of Conrage.
Z6ᵛ; Of Courage Z7ᵛ]; Of Temperance | in matters of Art. Aa1ᵛ–Bb1;
Of Temperance | in GOD. Bb1ᵛ–Cc1; Of Temperance in GOD.
Cc1ᵛ; Of Patience. $Cc2ᵛ–Dd3ᵛ; Of Meeknefs. $Dd4ᵛ–Ee7; Of
Humility. $Ee7ᵛ–Gg2 [*excepting:* Of Humilty. Ff4]; Of Contentment.
$Gg3–Hh3 [*excepting:* Of Magnanimity. Hh1ᵛ]; Of Magnanimity.
$Hh3ᵛ–Ii7 [*excepting:* Of Contentment. Hh4]; Of Modefty. $Ii8–
Kk1ᵛ; Of Liberality. $Kk2–Ll3ᵛ; Of Magnificence. $Ll4–Mm7ᵛ
[*excepting:* Of Magnificeuce. Mm3ᵛ]; Of Gratitude. $Mm8ᵛ–Pp6;
An Appendix. $Pp6ᵛ–Qq8 [*excepting:* An Appendix. Qq5].

Catchwords (only catchword anomalies are recorded) : B1ᵛ vain [vain,]
B3ᵛ (Operati-)ons [ons;] B5 assurance [Assurance] C2 (en-)joyed
[joyed,] C5ᵛ *Truth* [*Truth,*] C7 (Care-) lesseness [lesseness,] E3 himself [himself,] E5 Dam- [mage,] F5ᵛ (Be-)haviour [haviour,] G5ᵛ
Divine [Divine:] I5ᵛ self [self,] I6ᵛ (prepa-)red [red,] K1 (Hea-)-
vens [vens,] K4ᵛ Omnipresent [Omnipresent:] L2ᵛ Stars [Stars,] L4
Decrees [Decrees,] L7 Excellencies. [Excellences.] M8ᵛ By [by] N6
the [they] N8ᵛ (concern-)ed [ed,] P2 present [present,] P4 extended
[extendeth] P5 (Em-)pires [pires,] P6ᵛ Types [Types,] Q1 (De-)light-
ful [lightful;] Q1ᵛ *Time* [*Time,*] Q6ᵛ Image [Image,] Q8ᵛ suitable

[suitably] R7 attended [attended,] R7^v But [But,] T2^v (suffer-)ings [ings,] T8 World, [world,] V1^v Earnestly [*Earnestly,*] V7^v admired [admired,] V8 IF [If] X5^v (Cha-)rity [rity.] X7^v Hazzards [Hazzards,] Y1^v Graces [Graces,] Y3^v It [IT] Z2^v (Tray-)tor [tor,] Z4 (*with-*)*in* [*in.*] Z4^v To [*To*] Z7 *FOR* [*For*] Mm6^v sphere; [sphere:] Oo5 Vertue [Vertue,]

Signatures: \$4(–FKLRZ3,BM4) signed; letters and numerals employed are of the same type font used in the principal matter of each signed page. All signatures are printed on the same lines as the catchwords.

Type: A2–a3: 18 ll. 130 (146) x 72 mm. (A4), italic (some roman), 146 mm. for 20 ll.; B1–Qq8: 29 (26–31) ll. 135 (146) x 72 (68–74) mm. (K2^v), roman (frequently italic), 94 mm. for 20 ll. Italic verse in B–Z8: 82 mm. for 20 ll. (Z5); italic verse for Aa–Qq: 94 mm. for 20 ll. (Bb5^v).

Notes: Running-titles. In many cases the running-titles are erroneously placed: Sig. C3^v should read "𝕺𝖋 𝖙𝖍𝖊 𝕹𝖆𝖙𝖚𝖗𝖊 𝖔𝖋 𝕱𝖊𝖑𝖎𝖈𝖎𝖙𝖞," rather than "𝖎𝖙𝖘 𝕰𝖝𝖈𝖊𝖑𝖑𝖊𝖓𝖈𝖞 𝖆𝖓𝖉 𝕻𝖊𝖗𝖋𝖊𝖈𝖙𝖎𝖔𝖓.". Sig. G1: "𝕺𝖋 𝕷𝖔𝖇𝖊 𝖆𝖓𝖉 𝕳𝖆𝖙𝖗𝖊𝖉." rather than "𝕺𝖋 𝕰𝖙𝖊𝖗𝖓𝖆𝖑 𝕷𝖔𝖇𝖊."; Sig. I1: "𝖔𝖋 𝕿𝖗𝖚𝖙𝖍." rather than "𝕺𝖋 𝖙𝖍𝖊 𝕰𝖝𝖈𝖊𝖑𝖑𝖊𝖓𝖈𝖞"; Sig. I1^v: "𝕺𝖋 𝖂𝖎𝖘𝖉𝖔𝖒𝖊." rather than "𝕺𝖋 𝕰𝖙𝖊𝖗𝖓𝖆𝖑 𝕷𝖔𝖇𝖊". Sig. I2: "𝕺𝖋 𝖂𝖎𝖘𝖉𝖔𝖒𝖊." rather than "𝕺𝖋 𝕰𝖙𝖊𝖗𝖓𝖆𝖑 𝕷𝖔𝖇𝖊."; Sig. I3^v: "𝕺𝖋 𝖂𝖎𝖘𝖉𝖔𝖒𝖊." rather than "𝕺𝖋 𝖙𝖍𝖊 𝕰𝖝𝖈𝖊𝖑𝖑𝖊𝖓𝖈𝖞"; Sig. I8^v: "𝕺𝖋 𝕽𝖎𝖌𝖍𝖙𝖊𝖔𝖚𝖘𝖓𝖊𝖘." rather than "𝕺𝖋 𝖂𝖎𝖘𝖉𝖔𝖒𝖊."; Sig. K8^v: "𝕺𝖋 𝕲𝖔𝖔𝖉𝖓𝖊𝖘." rather than "𝕺𝖋 𝕽𝖎𝖌𝖍𝖙𝖊𝖔𝖚𝖘𝖓𝖊𝖘."; Sig. M3^v: "𝕺𝖋 𝕳𝖔𝖑𝖎𝖓𝖊𝖘." rather than "𝕺𝖋 𝕲𝖔𝖔𝖉𝖓𝖊𝖘."; Sigs. N6^v–N8: "𝕺𝖋 𝕵𝖚𝖘𝖙𝖎𝖈𝖊|𝖎𝖓 𝕲𝖊𝖓𝖊𝖗𝖆𝖑." rather than "𝖎𝖓 𝕲𝖊𝖓𝖊𝖗𝖆𝖑.|𝕺𝖋 𝕵𝖚𝖘𝖙𝖎𝖈𝖊"; Sig. S8: "𝕺𝖋 𝕮𝖍𝖆𝖗𝖎𝖙𝖞" or "𝖙𝖔𝖜𝖆𝖗𝖉𝖘 GOD." rather than "𝕺𝖋 𝕽𝖊𝖕𝖊𝖓𝖙𝖆𝖓𝖈𝖊."; Sig. T1: "𝖙𝖔𝖜𝖆𝖗𝖉𝖘 GOD." rather than "𝕺𝖋 𝕮𝖍𝖆𝖗𝖎𝖙𝖞"; Sig. T1^v: "𝕺𝖋 𝕮𝖍𝖆𝖗𝖎𝖙𝖞" rather than "𝕺𝖋 𝕽𝖊𝖕𝖊𝖓𝖙𝖆𝖓𝖈𝖊."; Sig. V1: "𝖙𝖔𝖜𝖆𝖗𝖉𝖘 GOD." rather than "𝕺𝖋 𝕮𝖍𝖆𝖗𝖎𝖙𝖞"; Sig. Hh1^v: "𝕺𝖋 𝕮𝖔𝖓𝖙𝖊𝖓𝖙𝖒𝖊𝖓𝖙." rather than "𝕺𝖋 𝕸𝖆𝖌𝖓𝖆𝖓𝖎𝖒𝖎𝖙𝖞."; Sig. Hh4: "𝕺𝖋 𝕸𝖆𝖌𝖓𝖆𝖓𝖎𝖒𝖎𝖙𝖞." rather than "𝕺𝖋 𝕮𝖔𝖓𝖙𝖊𝖓𝖙𝖒𝖊𝖓𝖙.".

Type. The smallest number of lines for a full page is twenty-six; this number occurs only once (Hh4^v). Sheet Hh underwent at least two stages of correction; perhaps this short page shows the results of early changes or deletions not apparent in the copies collated. The number of lines per page generally becomes greater near Z8^v as Compositor B lengthens his page in order to finish on Z8^v.

III   Rationale of the Text

If a manuscript of Traherne's *Christian Ethicks* still exists, it has not come to light. Twenty-five years ago, few copies of the 1675 edition were available to scholars. When John Rothwell Slater considered editing *Christian Ethicks* in 1942, he wrote, "So far as can be discovered, the only copies in the United States are those in the McAlpin Collection at Union Theological Seminary, New York, and the University of Rochester Library, the latter recently acquired after several years' search."[17] Wing listed five copies—in the Union Theological Seminary Library, the Yale University Library, the British Museum, the Bodleian Library, and the Cambridge University Library. During the last fifteen years, twenty-eight other copies have been located. In Great Britain, the following institutions possess copies: Brasenose College, Oxford; Worcester College, Oxford; Christ Church College, Oxford; Trinity College, Cambridge; Reigate Public Library; Plume Library, Maldon; Sion College; Newcastle-upon-Tyne Public Library; Durham Cathedral Library; City of Cardiff Public Libraries; Brotherton Library, University of Leeds; National Library of Scotland, Edinburgh (two copies); Theological College of the Episcopal Church in Scotland Library, Edinburgh; and the Glasgow University Library. In addition, there are copies in two private collections, those of Mr. George Goyder (Henley-on-Thames) and Sir Geoffrey Keynes (London). Ten institutions in North America have copies: Princeton University; Harvard University; Syracuse University; University of Minnesota; University of Illinois; Tusculum College, Greenville, Tennessee; Olin Memorial Library, Wesleyan University (Connecticut); Folger Library; the Detroit Public Library; and the University of Waterloo, Canada. Finally, Mr. H. Bradley Martin (New York), owns a copy.[18]

The five copies listed by Wing were collated against the University of Illinois copy. The result is the following critical, old-spelling text. Punctuation and capitalization of the 1675 edition have been retained except where they definitely obscure the meaning. Perhaps Slater was partially correct when he wrote in 1942, "Traherne's capitals in prose, as Miss Wade observes of capitals in his verse, are a key to the emphasis and rhythm of the sentence. He undertook to record by his apparently

---

[17] *Of Magnanimity and Charity* (New York, 1942), p. v. Slater eventually decided to reprint only two chapters of *Christian Ethicks*—"Of Magnanimity" and "Of Charity to Our Neighbour."

[18] The editors are indebted to Mr. Donald G. Wing and Mr. Richard L. Sauls for much of this information.

capricious capitals the intonations of the voice, by his colons and semi-colons the pauses of oral interpretation."[19] But in a text so riddled with errors, so prone to reflect the peculiarities of spelling, punctuation, and capitalization of the individual compositors, all such "caprices" cannot be attributed to Traherne. Some of the more flagrant examples (such as ending the last sentence of a paragraph with a comma) were almost certainly introduced by the compositors, particularly Compositor B.[20] Emendations have nonetheless been held to a minimum, and all emendations of the 1675 text are recorded in Corrections of the Text, following the Textual Notes.

The readings of corrected formes have not always been chosen. Specific reasons for emending or not emending particular passages are given in Textual Notes immediately following the text itself.

All marginal notes of the 1675 edition are recorded in footnotes to the text. The eight marginal notes elucidating or amplifying points made in the text may be Traherne's. The forty-six marginal notes identifying Biblical quotations are perhaps the work of someone else. These latter notes are probably too infrequent and too incomplete or inaccurate to be Traherne's.

In some sections of this critical edition—such as *"TO THE READER"* (pp. 3–6), *"The Contents"* (pp. 7–11), and *"To the Reader"* (p. 12) —type fonts (italic and roman) have been reversed. But in the text of *Christian Ethicks* here reproduced (pp. 13–286), all italic words remain italic and all roman words remain roman (except for emendations as noted in Corrections of the Text).

Although the 1675 edition of *Christian Ethicks* did not include chapter short-titles, it did contain running-titles. The chapter short-titles (p. x) and the running-titles of this new edition are based on the running-titles of the 1675 edition. But readers wishing a fuller description of the running-titles of the 1675 edition should consult the Textual Introduction, Part II. Readers will also find a full description of the title-page and the head-title of the 1675 edition in Part II of the Textual Introduction.

---

[19] P. vii.

[20] Another example: a description of the contents of each of the chapters appears twice within the book—once in "The Contents" (sigs. a4–a8) and once immediately preceding the text of each chapter. Compositor A set "The Contents." If A's setting of the description of Chap. XVIII (p. 8) is compared with B's (p. 133), distinctive differences in spelling, punctuation, and (especially) capitalization are readily apparent. A comparison of other similar passages will yield much the same results.

A number of silent alterations were deemed necessary. All long *s*'s have been replaced by modern *s*'s, and all turned letters have been silently righted. Words with erroneously italicized initial capitals have been corrected. Wherever "VV" and "vv" occurred, they have been replaced with "W" and "w." No distinction has been made between double hyphens and single hyphens, which were used indiscriminately. The misuse of italicized colons for roman colons has been corrected.

IV   Apparatus

The textual apparatus includes (a) Textual Notes, (b) Corrections of the Text, and (c) Press-Variants by Formes. The Textual Notes section contains statements explaining why certain portions of the text were or were not emended. Corrections of the Text records all emendations as well as those readings chosen from among press-variants. Rejected press-variants in corrected (*c*) and uncorrected (*u*) states are indicated. A wavy dash (~) is substituted for a repeated word associated with pointing, and an inferior caret (ᴧ) is used to emphasize pointing absent in the text of this edition or in a copy or copies of the 1675 edition. The page and line numbers preceding each entry in Corrections of the Text refer to page and line numbers of this edition, not the 1675 edition.

In order to keep the text of *Christian Ethicks* unencumbered by notations, the Textual Notes and the Commentary have been printed as separate parts of the book. Page and line numbers in the notes and commentary refer to this edition; the reader, in using the apparatus, is asked to find the lines himself.

Press-variants are arranged by formes and recorded in Press-Variants by Formes. In a few cases two states of correction are recorded.

Christian Ethicks

TO THE READER.

THE design of this Treatise is, not to stroak and tickle the *Fancy,* but to elevate the *Soul,* and refine its Apprehensions, to inform the Judgment, and polish it for Conversation, to purifie and enflame the Heart, to enrich the Mind, and guide Men (that stand in need of help) in the way of *Vertue;* to excite their Desire, to encourage them to Travel, to comfort them in the Journey, and so at last to lead them to true Felicity, both here and hereafter.

I need not treat of Vertues in the ordinary way, as they are *Duties* enjoyned by the Law of GOD; *that* the Author of *The whole Duty of Man* hath excellently done: nor as they are *Prudential Expedients* and *Means* for a mans Peace and Honour on Earth; *that* is in some measure done by the *French Charron* of Wisdom. My purpose is to satisfie the Curious and Unbelieving Soul, concerning the reality, force, and efficacy of *Vertue;* and having some advantages from the knowledge I gained in the nature of *Felicity* (by many years earnest and diligent study) my business is to make as *visible,* as it is possible for me, the lustre of its *Beauty, Dignity,* and *Glory:* By shewing what a necessary Means *Vertue* is, how sweet, how full of Reason, how desirable in it self, how just and amiable, how delightful, and how powerfully conducive also to Glory: how naturally Vertue carries us to the *Temple* of *Bliss,* and how immeasurably transcendent it is in all kinds of *Excellency.*

And (if I may speak freely) my Office is, to carry and enhance *Vertue* to its utmost height, to open the Beauty of all the Prospect, and to make the *Glory* of *GOD* appear, in the Blessedness of Man, by setting forth its infinite Excellency: Taking out of the *Treasuries* of *Humanity* those Arguments that will discover the great perfection of the *End* of Man, which he may atchieve by the capacity of his *Nature:* As also by opening the Nature of *Vertue* it self, thereby to display the marvellous Beauty of Religion, and light the Soul to the sight of its Perfection.

I do not speak much of *Vice,* which is far the more easie Theme, because I am intirely taken up with the abundance of Worth and Beauty in *Vertue,* and have so much to say of the positive and intrinsick Goodness of its Nature. But besides, since a strait Line is the measure

3

both of it self, and of a crooked one, I conclude, That the very Glory
of *Vertue* well understood, will make all *Vice* appear like *dirt* before
a *Jewel,* when they are compared together. Nay, *Vice* as soon as it
is named in the presence of these Vertues, will look like Poyson and
a Contagion, or if you will, as black as *Malice* and *Ingratitude:* so
that there will need no other Exposition of its Nature, to dehort Men
from the love of it, than the Illustration of its Contrary.

Vertues are listed in the rank of *Invisible things;* of which kind,
some are so blind as to deny there are any existent in Nature: But
yet it may, and will be made easily apparent, that all the *Peace* and
Beauty in the World proceedeth from *them,* all *Honour* and *Security*
is founded in them, all *Glory* and *Esteem* is acquired by them. For
the *Prosperity* of all Kingdoms is *laid* in the *Goodness* of GOD and
of Men. Were there nothing in the World but the *Works* of *Amity,*
which proceed from the *highest Vertue,* they alone would testifie of
its Excellency. For there can be no *Safety* where there is any *Treach-
ery:* But were all *Truth* and *Courtesie* exercis'd with *Fidelity* and
Love, there could be no *Injustice* or *Complaint* in the World; no
Strife, nor *Violence:* but all *Bounty, Joy* and *Complacency.* Were
there no *Blindness,* every Soul would be full of Light, and the *face*
of *Felicity* be seen, and the *Earth* be turned into *Heaven.*

The things we treat of are great and mighty; they touch the Essence
of every Soul, and are of infinite *Concernment,* because the Felicity
is eternal that is acquired by them: I do not mean *Immortal* only
but *worthy* to be *Eternal:* and it is impossible to be happy without
them. We treat of Mans great and *soveraign End,* of the Nature of
Blessedness, of the *Means* to attain it: Of *Knowledge* and *Love,* of
Wisdom and *Goodness,* of *Righteousness* and *Holiness,* of *Justice* and
Mercy, of *Prudence* and *Courage,* of *Temperance* and *Patience,* of
Meekness and *Humility,* of *Contentment,* of *Magnanimity* and *Modesty,* of *Liberality* and *Magnificence,* of the *waies* by which *Love* is
begotten in the Soul, of *Gratitude,* of *Faith, Hope,* and *Charity,* of
Repentance, Devotion, Fidelity, and *Godliness.* In all which we shew
what *sublime* and *mysterious Creatures* they are, which depend upon
the Operations of Mans Soul; their great *extent,* their *use* and *value,*
their *Original* and their *End,* their *Objects* and their *Times:* What
Vertues belong to the Estate of *Innocency,* what to the Estate of *Misery*
and *Grace,* and what to the Estate of *Glory.* Which are the *food* of
the *Soul,* and the *works* of *Nature;* which were occasioned by Sin,
as *Medicines* and *Expedients* only: which are *Essential* to Felicity,

and which *Accidental;* which *Temporal,* and which *Eternal:* with the true *Reason* of their Imposition; why they all are commanded, and how *wise* and *gracious* GOD is in enjoyning them. By which means all *Atheism* is put to flight, and all *Infidelity:* The Soul is reconciled to the *Lawgiver* of the World, and taught to delight in his *Commandements:* All *Enmity* and *Discontentment* must vanish as Clouds and Darkness before the Sun, when the *Beauty* of *Vertue* appeareth in its *brightness* and *glory.* It is impossible that the *splendour* of its *Nature* should be seen, but all *Religion* and *Felicity* will be manifest.

Perhaps you will meet some *New* Notions: but yet when they are examined, he hopes it will appear to the Reader, that it was the actual knowledge of true *Felicity* that taught him to speak of *Vertue;* and moreover, that there is not the least *tittle* pertaining to the *Catholick Faith* contradicted or altered in his Papers. For he firmly retains all that was established in the Ancient Councels, nay and sees Cause to do so, even *in the highest and most transcendent Mysteries:* only he enriches all, by farther opening the *grandeur* and *glory* of Religion, with the interiour depths and Beauties of *Faith.* Yet indeed it is not he, but GOD that hath enriched the Nature of it: he only brings the Wealth of *Vertue* to light, which the infinite Wisdom, and Goodness, and Power of GOD have seated there. Which though Learned Men know perhaps far better than he, yet he humbly craves pardon for casting in his *Mite* to the *vulgar Exchequer.* He hath nothing more to say, but that the Glory of GOD, and the sublime Perfection of *Humane Nature* are united in Vertue. By Vertue the Creation is made *useful,* and the *Universe* delightful. All the Works of GOD are crowned with their End, by the Glory of Vertue. For whatsoever is good and profitable for Men is made Sacred; because it is delightful and well-pleasing to GOD: Who being LOVE by Nature, delighteth in his Creatures welfare.

There are two sorts of concurrent Actions necessary to Bliss: Actions in GOD, and Actions in Men, nay and Actions too in all the Creatures. The *Sun* must warm, but it must not burn; the *Earth* must bring forth, but not swallow up; the *Air* must cool without starving, and the *Sea* moisten without drowning: *Meats* must feed but not poyson: *Rain* must fall, but not oppress: Thus in the inferiour Creatures you see Actions are of several kinds. But these may be reduced to the Actions of GOD, from whom they spring; for he prepares all these Creatures for us. And it is necessary to the felicity of his Sons, that he should make all things healing and amiable, not odious and destructive: that he should Love, and not Hate: And the Actions of Men must concur aright with these of GOD, and his Creatures. They must not *despise* Blessings because they are given, but *esteem* them; not *trample them under feet,* because they have the benefit of them, but *magnifie* and extol them: They too must *Love,* and not *Hate:* They must not *kill* and *murther,* but *serve* and *pleasure* one another: they must not *scorn* great and inestimable Gifts, because they are *common,* for so the Angels would lose all the happiness of *Heaven.* If GOD should do the most *great* and *glorious* things that infinite *Wisdom* could devise; if Men will resolve to be *blind,* and *perverse,* and *sensless,* all will be in *vain:* the most High and Sacred things will *increase* their Misery. This may give you some little *glimpse* of the excellency of *Vertue.*

You may easily discern that my Design is to reconcile Men to GOD, and make them fit to delight in him: and that my last End is to celebrate his Praises, in communion with the Angels. Wherein I beg the Concurrence of the Reader, for we can never praise him enough; nor be fit enough to praise him: No other man (at least) can make us so, without our own willingness, and endeavour to do it.

Above all, pray to be sensible of the Excellency of the Creation, for upon the due sense of its Excellency the life of *Felicity* wholly dependeth. Pray to be sensible of the Excellency of *Divine Laws,* and of all the Goodness which your Soul comprehendeth. Covet a *lively* sense of all you know, of the Excellency of GOD, and of Eternal Love; of your own Excellency, and of the worth and value of all Objects whatsoever. For to *feel* is as necessary, as to *see* their *Glory.*

The Contents.

7

Christian Ethicks

Chap. XI.

Of Goodness natural, moral, and divine; its Nature described. The benefits and Works of Goodness.

Chap. XII.

Of Holiness: Its nature, violence and pleasure. Its beauty consisteth in the infinite love of Righteousness and Perfection.

Chap. XIII.

Of Justice in general, and particular. The great good it doth in Empires and Kingdoms; a token of the more retired good it doth in the Soul. Its several kinds. That Gods punitive Justice springs from his Goodness.

Chap. XIV.

Of Mercy. The indelible stain and guilt of Sin. Of the Kingdom which God recovered by Mercy. The transcendent nature of that duty; with its effects and benefits.

Chap. XV.

Of Faith. The faculty of Believing implanted in the Soul. Of what Nature its Objects are. The necessity of Faith: Its end; its use and excellency. It is the Mother and fountain of all the Vertues.

Chap. XVI.

Of Hope. Its foundation: its distinction from Faith; its extents and dimensions; its life and vigour; its several kinds; its sweetness and excellency.

Chap. XVII.

Of Repentance. Its original; its nature; it is a purgative Vertue; its necessity; its excellencies. The measure of that sorrow which is due to Sin is intollerable to Sence; confessed by Reason, and dispensed with by Mercy.

Chap. XVIII.

Of Charity towards God. It sanctifieth Repentance, makes it a Vertue, and turns it to a part of our true Felicity. Our Love to all other objects is to begin and end in God. Our Love of God hath an excellency in it, that makes it worthy to be desired by his eternal Majesty. He is the only supream and perfect Friend; by Loving we enjoy him.

Chap. XIX.

Charity to our Neighbour most natural and easie in the estate of Innocency: *Adams* Love to *Eve,* and his Children, a great exemplar of our Love to all the World. The sweetness of Loving. The benefits of being Beloved. To love all the World, and to be beloved by all the World, is perfect security and felicity. Were the Law fulfilled, all the World would be turned into Heaven.

Chap. XX.

Of Prudence. Its foundation is Charity, its end tranquility and prosperity on Earth; its office to reconcile Duty and Convenience, and to make Vertue subservient to Temporal welfare. Of Prudence in Religion; Friendship, and Empire. The end of Prudence is perfect Charity.

Chap. XXI.

Encouragements to Courage. Its Nature, cause, and end. Its greatness and renown. Its ornaments and Companions. Its objects, circumstances, effects, and disadvantages: how Difficulties increase its vertue. Its Victories and Triumphs. How subservient it is to Blessedness and Glory.

Chap. XXII.

Of Temperance in matters of Art, as Musick, Dancing, Painting, Cookery, Physick, *&c.* In the works of Nature; Eating, drinking, sports and recreations: In occasions of passion, in our lives and Conversations. Its exercise in Self-denial, measure, mixture and proportion. Its effects and atchievments.

Chap. XXIII.

Of Temperance in God. How the Moderation of Almighty Power, guided in his Works by Wisdom, perfecteth the Creation. How it hath raised its own Glory and our Felicity beyond all that simple Power could effect by its Infiniteness.

Chap. XXIV.

Of Patience. Its original. How God was the first patient Person in the World. The nature, and the glory, and the blessed effects of his eternal Patience. The Reason and design of all Calamities. Of Patience in Martyrdom. The extraordinary reward of ordinary Patience in its meanest obscurity.

Chap. XXV.

The cause of Meekness is Love. It respects the future beauty and perfection of its object. It is the most supernatural of all the Vertues. The reasons and grounds of this Vertue in the estate of Grace and Misery. Its manifold effects and excellencies. Of the Meekness of *Moses* and *Joseph.*

Chap. XXVI.

Humility is the basis of all Vertue and Felicity, in all estates, and for ever to be exercised. As Pride does alienate the Soul from God, Humility unites it to him in adoration and amity. It maketh infinite Blessedness infinitely greater, is agreeable to the truth of our condition, and leads us through a dark and mysterious way to Glory.

Chap. XXVII.

That Contentment is a Vertue. Its causes, and its ends: Its Impediments, Effects, and Advantages. The way to attain and secure Contentment.

Chap. XXVIII.

Of Magnanimity, or greatness of Soul. Its nature. Its foundation in the vast Capacity of the Understanding. Its desire. Its objects are infinite and eternal. Its enquiries are most profound and earnest. It disdaineth all feeble Honours, Pleasures and Treasures. A Magnanimous Man is the only Great and undaunted Creature.

Chap. XXIX.

Of Modesty. Its nature. Its original. Its effects and consequences.

Chap. XXX.

The excellent nature of Liberality. Rules to be observed in the practice of it. Regard to our Servants, Relations, Friends and Neighbours must be had in our Liberality, as well as to the Poor and Needy. How our external acts of Charity ought to be improved for the benefit of mens Souls. Liberality maketh Religion real and substantial.

Chap. XXXI.

Of Magnificence in God. Its resemblance in Man. The chief Magnificence of the Soul is Spiritual. It is perfectly expressed in the outward life, when the whole is made perfect, and presented to God. God gives all his Life to us: and we should give ours all to him. How fair and glorious it may be.

Chap. XXXII.

Of Gratitude. It feeds upon Benefits, and is in height and fervour answerable to their Greatness. The Question stated, Whether we are able to love GOD more than our selves. It is impossible to be grateful to GOD without it. A hint of the glorious Consequences of so doing.

Chap. XXXIII.

The Beauty of Gratitude. Its principal Causes. Amity and Communion are the great effect of its Nature. The true Character of a grateful

Person. Gods incommunicable Attributes enjoyed by Gratitude. All Angels and Men are a grateful Persons Treasures, as they assist him in Praises. He sacrifices all Worlds to the Deity, and supreamly delighteth to see him sitting in the Throne of Glory.

An APPENDIX.

Of Enmity and Triumph: Of Schism and Heresie, Fidelity, Devotion, Godliness. Wherein is declared, how Gratitude and Felicity inspire and perfect all the Vertues.

To the Reader.

The Author's much lamented Death hapning immediately after this Copy came to the Press, may reasonably move the Readers charity, to pardon those few Errata's which have escaped in the Printing by so sad an occasion.

CHAP. I.

Of the End, for the sake of which, Virtue is desired.

[handwritten: Nature (Aristotelian) and Telos = fosoe]

IT is the Prerogative of Humane Nature to understand it self, and guide its Operations to a Known End: which he doth wholly forfeit, that lives at random, without considering what is worthy of his Endeavors, or fit for his Desires. *[handwritten: → not on purpose]*

THE End is that which crowns the Work; that which inspires the Soul with Desire, and Desire with a quick and vigorous Industry. It is last attained, but first intended in every Operation. All Means which can be used in the Acquisition of it, derive their value from its Excellency and we are encouraged to use them only on the Account of that End which is attained by them.

IT is the Office of *Morality* to teach Men the *Nature* of *Virtue*, and to encourage them in the Practice of it, by explaining its use and Efficacy.

THE Excellence of Virtue, is the Necessity and Efficacy thereof in the Way to Felicity. It consisteth in this, Virtue is the only Means by which Happiness can be obtained.

SINCE the Consideration of the End is that alone, which does animate a Man, to the use of the Means, they that treat of Virtue do worthily propose the End in the beginning, and first shew the Excellency of Bliss before they open the Nature of Virtue. For it is a vain thing to discover the Means, unless the End be desired by those to whom the Nature and use of them, in their tendency to that End, is taught and commended; for if the End be despised, all endeavors are but fruitless, which instruct us in the Means; and the Knowledge of them vain, if they never be used or improved. *[handwritten: → Seeing]*

THAT Reason, whereby Man is able to Contemplate his End, is a singular Advantage, wherein he is priviledged above a Beast. It enables him not only to examine the Nature and perfection of his End, but the Equity and fitness of the Means in Order thereunto, and the singular Excellency of his first Cause, as its Glory and Goodness appeareth in the Design and Contrivance: Especially in making mans Happiness so compleat and perfect.

[handwritten: This is a contemplative means]

THE Heathens, who invented the name of *Ethicks,* were very short in the Knowledge of Mans End: But they are worse then Heathens, that never consider it.

THE more Excellent the End is, the more prone by nature we are to pursue it, and all the Means conducive thereunto are the more Desirable.

REASON, which is the formal Essence of the Soul of Man, guides Him to desire those Things, which are absolutely supreme. For it is an Eternal Property in Reason to prefer the Better, above the Worse: He that prefers the worse above the Better acts against Nature, and Swervs from the Rule of Right Reason.

WHATEVER Varieties of Opinion there are concerning Happiness, all conclude and agree in this, that Mans last End is his perfect Happiness: And the more Excellent his Happiness is, the more ought his Soul to be enflamed with the Desire of it, and inspired with the greater Industry.

THE more perfect his Bliss is, the greater is the Crime of despising it. To pursue an infinite and Eternal Happiness is Divine and *Angelical;* to pursue a Terrene and Sensual Felicity, is *Brutish;* but to place Felicity in Anger and Envy is *Diabolical:* the pleasures of Malice being Bitter and Destructive.

TO live by Accident, and never to pursue any Felicity at all, is neither Angelical, nor Brutish, nor Diabolical: but *Worse* then any Thing in some respect in the World: It is to act against our *own* Principles, and to wage war with our very *Selves.* They that place their Ease in such a Carelessness, are of all others, the greatest Enemies and Disturbers of themselves.

IT is Madness and folly to pursue the first object that presents it self, under the Notion of felicity: And it is base to content ones self in the Enjoyment of a mean estate, upon a suspicion there is no true happiness, because the nature thereof is so much doubted in the World. The Disputations concerning its nature argue its existance. And we must cease to be Men, before we can extinguish the desire of being Happy. He only is truely Generous, that aspires to the most perfect Blessedness of which God and Nature have made him Capable.

BY how much Greater the Uncertainty is, by so much the more Heedful ought we to be, lest we should be seduced and deceived, in the Choice of Happiness: For the Danger is the Greater. And by how much the more Eager Men are in their Disputations, concerning it, by so much the more weighty is the Nature of the Theme to be presumed.

HASTINESS in catching at an unexamined Felicity, is the great Occasion of all the Error about it, among the Vulgar: who are led, like Beasts, by their *Sense* and Appetite, without discerning or improving any other faculty. The lip of the Cup is annointed with Hony, which, as soon as they taste, they drink it up, tho the liquor be nothing but Gall and Poyson. Being deluded with a shew, instead of *Pleasure*, they rush hand over head on their own *Destruction*.

IT is as natural to Man to desire happiness, as to live and breath: Sence and Instinct carry him to Happyness, as well as Reason: onely *Reason* should rectifie and direct his *Instinct*, inform his *Sence*, and compleat his *Essence*, by inducing those perfections of which it is capable.

THINGS Good in themselves, when they stand in Competition with those that are better, have the notion of Evil: Better Things are Evil, if compared with the Best; especially where the Choice of the one hinders the Acquisition of the other. For where Good, Better, and Best, are subservient to each other, the one is the better for the others sake; but where they interfere, and oppose each other, the Good are bad in comparison of the Better, and the Better worse than the Best of all. This is the Cause why Reason cannot acquiesce in any Felicity less than the Supreme: which must needs be infinite, because Almighty Power, which made Reason active, is illimited in its Operations; and never rests, but in the production of a Glorious Act, that is infinite in Perfection.

IF Felicity be infinite, the Loss is as great, that attends our Miscarriage, and the misery intolerable, that follows our Loss. For (our eyes being open) a Loss that is incomprehensible must needs produce a Greif unmeasurable, an Anguish as infinite as our Damage.

ALL inferiour felicities are but Miseries compared with the Highest. A farthing is *good* and pleaseth a Beggar in time of distress: but a piece of Gold is *Better*. An Estate of a thousand pounds a year is better than a Piece of Gold; but our Ambition carries us to Principalities and Empires. An Empire is more desirable than a Province; and the Wider, the Richer, the Better it is, the more Desirable. But the Empire of all the Earth is a Bubble compared to the Heavens: And the Heavens themselves less than nothing to an infinite Dominion.

PERFECT Felicity is not Dominion, nor Pleasure, nor Riches alone, nor Learning, nor Virtue, nor Honour; but all in Perfection. It requires that every Soul should be capable of infinite Dominion, Pleasure, Learning, and Honor for the full and perfect attainment of it.

IF all these be infinite and Eternal in that Felicity which is prepared for Man, those Actions are of inestimable Value, by Virtue of which his Felicity is gained; and it becomes his Wisdom and Courage to suffer many Things for so noble an End: Especially if in this Life it may in any measure be thereby acquired and enjoyed.

THE Great Reason why GOD has concealed Felicity from the Knowledge of man, is the enhancement of its nature and value: but that which most conceals it, is the Corruption of Nature. For as we have corrupted, so have we blinded our selves. Yet are we led by Instinct eagerly to thirst after things unknown, remote and forbidden. The truth is, our Palates are vitiated and our Digestion so Corrupted, that till our Nature be purified by a little Industry, to make felicity Known, is but to Expose it to Contempt and Censure. It is too Great and Pure for perverted Nature.

THE Concealment of an object whets our Appetite, and puts an Edge upon our endeavours, and this carries some thing of Mystery in it; For whereas the Maxime is *Ignoti nulla Cupido, All Love comes in at the Eye,* we affect an Object to which we are Blind, and the more Blind we are, the more restless. We are touched with an unknown Beauty which we never saw, and in the midst of our Ignorance are actuated with a Tendency, which does not abate the value of our Virtues, but puts Life and Energy into our Actions.

THO Felicity cannot perfectly be understood, because it is incomprehensible to Men on Earth, yet so much of it may be discerned, as will serve to meet our Instinct, and feed our Capacity, animate our Endeavour, encourage our Expectation (to hope for more then we enjoy) enable us to subdue our Lusts, support us in temptations, and assist us in overcoming all obstacles whatsoever.

INFINITE Honors and Pleasures, were there no more in Felicity, are enough to allure us: but the fruition of all in the Best of Manners, in Communion with God, being full of Life, and Beauty, and Perfection in himself, and having the certain Assurance that all shall be included in his Bliss, that can be thought on; it is a Thing so Divine, that the very Hope of it fills us with Comfort here, and the Attainment with perfect Satisfaction hereafter.

HE that can enjoy all Things in the Image of GOD, needs not covet their fruition in a Baser Manner: Man was made in GODS Image, that he might live in his Similitude.

I am not so Stoical, as to make all Felicity consist in a meer Apathy, or freedom from Passion, nor yet so Dissolute, as to give the Passions all their Liberty. Neither do I perswade you to renounce the Advantages of Wealth and Honor, any more then those of Beauty and Wit: for as a Man may be Happy without all these, so may he make a Happy use of them when he has them. He may be happy with Difficulty without them, but Easily with them. If not in Heaven, yet certainly on Earth, the Goods of fortune concur to the Compleating of *Temporal Felicity,* and therefore where they are freely given, are not to be despised.

THAT which I desire to teach a man is, How to make a Good use of all the Advantages of his Birth and Breeding; How in the Increase of Riches and Honors, to be Happy in their Enjoyment: How to secure himself in the temptations of Affluence, and to make a man glorious in himself, and delightful to others in Abundance: Or else if Affliction should arise, and the State of Affairs change, how to triumph over *adverse* Fortune, and to be Happy notwithstanding his Calamities. How to govern himself in all Estates so as to turn them to his own advantage.

FOR tho felicitie be not absolutely perfect in this World, nor so compleat in Poverty, as in a great and plentiful Estate; you are not to believe that wealth is absolutely necessary; because sometimes it is requisite to forfeit all for the sake of Felicity. Nothing is absolutely necessary to Bliss, but Grace and vertue, tho to *perfect* Bliss, Ease and Honour be absolutely necessary.

THERE are many degrees of Blessedness beneath the most Supream, that are transcendently Sweet and delightful: And it sometimes happens, that what is most bitter to *Sence,* is pleasant to *Reason.*

RATHER then make Shipwrack of a good Conscience, we must do as Mariners in a storm, cast our riches over board for our *own* Preservation. It is better losing *them,* then *our selves.*

VERTUE is Desirable and Glorious, because it teacheth us through many Difficulties in this Tempestuous World to Sail Smoothly, and attain the Haven.

CHAP. II.

Of the Nature of Felicity,
its Excellence and Perfection.

How different is this from Wither? wou...

interesting Liberty bodily

THE *Peripateticks,* so far forth as they contemplated the Nature and Estate of man *in this World,* were Wise, in defining the Goods of the Body, Soul and Fortune to concur to Mans perfect Happiness. For Difficulties and Conflicts are not Essential to the Nature of Bliss, nor consistent with the fruition of its fulness and Perfection.

THERE is the Way, and the journeyes end.

IN the Way to Felicity many things are to be *endured,* that are not to be *desired.* And therefore is it necessary, to make a Distinction between the way to Felicity, and the Rest which we attain in the end of our Journey.

THE Goods of the Soul, are absolutely necessary in the Way to Happiness; the Goods of the Body are very convenient, and those of Fortune Commodious enough. But the latter of these are not with too much eagerness to be pursued.

THE Goods of the soul are wisdom, Knowledg, Courage, all the Virtues, all the Passions, Affections, Powers and faculties. And these you know are absolutely necessary.

THE Goods of the Body are Health, Agility, Beauty, Vivacity, Strength and Libertie: and these shall in Heaven it self, together with those of the Soul, be enjoyed. By which you may discern that the Goods of the Body are real Parts and Ingredients of Happiness.

THE Goods of Fortune are food and Rayment, Houses and Lands, Riches, Honours, Relations and Friends, with all those convenient Circumstances without the Body, that are subject to chance. By which vertue is assisted, and of which a noble use may be made, in Works of Justice, Hospitality, Courtesie and Charity, which may redound to our greater Felicity here and in heaven.

THE more Honor and pleasure we enjoy, the Greater and more Perfect is our present Happiness: Tho many times in the Way to Felicity, we are forced to quit all these, for the Preservation of our Innocence.

GALLANT Behavior in slighting all Transitory things for the Preservation of our Virtue, is more conducive to our future Perfection, then the greatest ease imaginable in our present condition.

IT is incumbent upon us, as a special part of our Care, to take heed, that we be not ensnared by the easiness of Prosperity, and that we do not set up our Rest in the *Way* to Happiness, nor deceive our selves in thinking the Goods of Fortune Essential: nor discourage our selves, by thinking it impossible to be Happy without them. Our Thoughts and Affections must be always disentangled, that we may run, with Alacritie the Race set before us, and close with the Sublimest Perfection of Bliss, as our only portion and Desire.

This is a very, very balanced

FELICITY is rightly defined, to be *the Perfect fruition of a Perfect Soul, acting in perfect Life by Perfect Virtue.* For the Attainment of which Perfection, we must, in the Way to Felicity, endure all Afflictions that can befall us. For tho they are not Parts of Felicity themselves, yet we may acknowledge them great Advantages for the Exercise of Virtue, and reckon our Calamities among our *Joys,* when we bear and overcome them in a virtuous Manner, because they add to our *Honor,* and contribute much to our Perfection, both here, and hereafter.

Inge's thesis?

FOR this purpose we are to remember, that our present Estate is not that of Reward, but Labour: It is an Estate of Trial, not of Fruition: A Condition wherein we are to Toyl, and Sweat, and travail hard, for the promised Wages; an Appointed Seed Time, for a future Harvest; a real Warfare, in order to a Glorious Victory: In which we must expect some Blows, and delight in the Hazzards and Encounters we meet with, because they will be crowned with a Glorious and joyful Triumph; and attended with ornaments and trophies far surpassing the bare Tranquillity of idle peace.

strong doctrine of sin!

WHEN we can cheerfully look on an Army of Misfortunes, without Amazement we may then freely and Delightfully contemplate the Nature of the Highest Felicity.

That's realism

ARISTOTLE never heard of our Ascension into Heaven, nor of sitting down in the Throne of GOD, yet by a lucky Hit (if I may so say) fell in point blanck upon the Nature of Blessedness. For a perfect fruition by perfect virtue, is all that can be thought of: It implies our *Objective,* and our *formal* Happiness.

OBJECTIVE Happiness is all the Goodness that is fit to be enjoyed either in GOD or in his Creatures: while *Formal Happiness* is an active Enjoyment of all Objects by Contemplation and Love, attended with full Complacency in all their Perfections.

the Formal or this, is related to contemplation

PERFECT Fruition implies the Perfection of all its Objects. Among which GOD himself is one, Angels and Saints are next, the World also with all the variety of Creatures in it, the Laws of GOD, and his wayes in all Ages, his Eternal Counsels and Divine Attributes are other Objects of our Content and Pleasure. Unless all these be perfect in their Nature, Variety, Number, Extent, Relation, Use and Value, our fruition cannot be simply perfect, because a Greater and more perfect fruition might, upon the production of better Objects, be contrived, and no fruition can be truly perfect, that is not conversant about the highest things. The more Beautiful the Object is, the more pleasant is the enjoyment. But where Delight may be increased, the Fruition is imperfect.

A *Perfect Soul* is a Transcendent Mystery. As GOD could not be Perfect, were it possible there could be any Better Essence then he; so neither would the Soul be perfect, could any more Perfect Soul be created.

IT is a Soul in which no Defect, or Blemish can be discerned; perfect in the variety and Number of its Powers, in the fitness and Measure of every power, in the use and value of every Endowment. A perfect Soul is that whereunto nothing can be added to please our Desire. As all its Objects are perfect, so is it self. It is able to see all that is to be seen, to love all that is Lovely, to hate all that is Hateful, to desire all that is Desirable, to honour all that is Honorable, to esteem all that can be valued, to delight in all that is Delightful, and to enjoy all that is Good and fit to be enjoyed. If its Power did fall short of any one Object, or of any one Perfection in any Object, or of any Degree in any Perfection, it would be imperfect, it would not be the Master piece of Eternal Power.

PERFECT life is the full exertion of perfect power. It implies two things, Perfection of Vigour, and perfection of intelligence, an activity of life, reaching through all Immensity, to all Objects whatsoever; and a freedome from all Dulness in apprehending: An exquisite Tenderness of perception in feeling the least Object, and a *Sphere of activity* that runs parallel with the Omnipresence of the Godhead. For if any Soul lives so imperfectly, as to see and know but some Objects, or to love them remisly, and less then they deserve, its Life is imperfect, because either it is remisse, or, if never so fervent, confined.

PERFECT Fruition, (as it implies the Perfection of all objects) more nearly imports the intrinsick Perfection of its own Operations. For if its Objects be never so many, and perfect in themselves, a Blemish lies upon the Enjoyment, if it does not reach unto all their Excellence. If the Enjoyment of one Object be lost, or one Degree of the enjoyment abated, it is imperfect.

PERFECT Vertue may best be understood by a consideration of its Particulars. Perfect *Knowledg* is a thorow, compleat understanding of all that may be Known. Perfect *Righteousness* is a full and adequate Esteem of all the value that is in Things. It is a Kind of Spiritual Justice, whereby we do Right to our selves, and to all other Beings. If we render to any Object less than it deserves, we are not *Just* thereunto. Perfect *Wisdome* is that whereby we chuse a most perfect end, actualy pursue it by most perfect Means, acquire and enjoy it in most perfect manner: If we pitch upon an inferiour end, our Wisdom is imperfect; and so it is, if we pursue it by feeble and inferior Means, or neglect any one of those Advantages, whereby we may attain it. And the same may be said of all the Vertues.

NOW if all Objects be infinitely Glorious, and all Worlds fit to be enjoyed, if GOD has filled Heaven and earth, and all the Spaces above the Heavens with innumerable pleasures, if his infinite Wisdome, Goodness, and Power be fully Glorified in every Being, and the Soul be created to enjoy all these in most perfect Manner; we may well conclude with the Holy Apostle, that we are *the children of GOD, and if Children, then Heirs, Heirs of GOD, and joynt heirs with Christ, if so be that we suffer with him, that we may also be glorified together. That our light Affliction, that is but for a Moment, worketh out for us, a far more exceeding and eternal Weight of Glory: That beholding as in a Glass the Glory of the Lord, we shall at last be transformed into the same Image from Glory to Glory, even as by the Spirit of the Lord.* For all his Works, of which the Psalmist saith, *They are worthy to be had in remembrance, and are sought out of all them that have pleasure therein,* are like a Mirror, wherein his Glory appeareth, as the face of the Sun doth in a clear fountain. We may conclude further that Vertue, by force of which we attain so great a Kingdome, is infinitely better then Rubies, all the Things thou canst desire, are not to be compared to her: So that with unspeakable comfort we may take Courage to go on, not only in the study, but the Practice of all Kind of Vertues, concerning which we are to treat in the ensuing Pages. For as the Apostle *Peter* telleth us, *He hath given to us all things that pertain to Life and Godliness, through the Knowledge of him that hath called us to Glory and virtue: whereby are given unto us exceeding great and precious Promises; that by these you might be Partakers of the Divine Nature, having escaped the Corruption that is in the World through Lust. And besides this,* saith he, *giving all diligence, adde to your Faith vertue: and to vertue, knowledge; and to knowledge, temperance; and to temperance, patience; and to patience, godliness; and to godliness, brotherly kindness; and to brotherly kindness, Charity. For so an Entrance shall be Ministred to you abundantly into the everlasting Kingdome of our Lord and Saviour Jesus Christ.* Which Kingdom being so Divine and Glorious as it is, we have need to bow our Knees, *to the GOD and father of our Lord Jesus Christ, of whom the whole Family in Heaven and Earth is named, that he would grant us according to the Riches of his Glory, to be strengthened with might, by his Spirit in the inward Man, that Christ may dwell in our Hearts by Faith, that we being rooted and grounded in Love, may be able to comprehend with all Saints, what is the Breadth, and Length, and Depth, and Height, and to know the love of Christ which passeth Knowledg, that we may be filled with all the fulness of GOD.*

TO be Partaker of the Divine nature, to be filled with all the Fulness of GOD, to enter into his Kingdom and Glory, to be transformed into his Image, and made an Heir of GOD, and a joynt Heir with Christ, to live in Union and Communion with GOD, and to be made a Temple of the Holy Ghost; these are Divine and transcendent things that accompany our Souls in the Perfection of their Bliss and Happiness: the Hope and Belief of all which is justified, and made apparent by the explanation of the very nature of the Soul, its Inclinations and Capacities, the reality, and greatness of those Vertues of which we are capable, and all those objects which the Univers affordeth to our Contemplation.

CHAP. III.

Of Vertue in General. The Distribution of it into its several Kinds, its Definition.

BEFORE we come to treat of particular *Vertues,* it is very fit that we speak something of *VERTUE* in General.

VERTUE is a comprehensive Word, by explaining which we shall make the way more easy to the right Understanding of all those particular Vertues, into which it is divided. Forasmuch as the Nature of Vertue enters into knowledge, Faith, Hope, Charity, Prudence, Courage, Meekness, Humility, Temperance, Justice, Liberality, *&c.* Every one of these hath its *essence* opened in part, by the explication of that which entreth its Nature, which is *VERTUE* in General.

THE Predicament of *Quality* contains within it either Natural *Dispositions* or *Habits:* Habits may be either *Vertuous* or *Vicious;* Virtuous Habits are either *Theological, Intellectual, Moral,* or *Divine.* And these are branched into so many Kinds of Vertue, as followeth.

THE *Theological Vertues* are generally divided into Three, *Faith, Hope,* and *Charity:* which are called *Theological,* because they have GOD for their Principal Object, and are, in a peculiar manner, taught by his Word among the Mysteries of Religion. To which we may add *Repentance;* forasmuch as this Virtue, tho it be occasioned by sin, is chiefly taught by the Word of GOD, and respects GOD as its Principal Object. For which reason we shall account the Theological Virtues to be four, Faith, Hope, Charity and Repentance, to which, if we are making them more, we may add *Obedience,* Devotion, Godliness.

THE *Intellectual Vertues* are generally reckoned to be five, *Intelligence, Wisdome, Science, Prudence, Art.* Which, forasmuch as the Distinction between them is over-nice and curious (at least too obscure for vulgar Apprehensions) we shall reduce them perhaps to a fewer number.

INTELLIGENCE is the Knowledg of Principles; *Science* the Knowledg of Conclusions. *Wisdom,* that knowledg, which results from the Union of both *Prudence* and *Art,* has been more darkly explained. The Objects of Wisdom are always *Stable; Prudence* is that knowledge, by which we guide our selves in Thorny and *uncertain* Affairs; *Art* is that Habit, by which we are assisted in composing Tracts and Systems, rather then in regulating our Lives, and more frequently appears in Fiddling and Dancing, then in noble Deeds: were it not useful in Teachers for the Instruction of others, we should scarce reckon it in the number of Vertues.

ALL these are called *Intellectual* Vertues, because they are Seated in the Understanding, and chiefly exercised in Contemplation. The Vertues that are brought down into action, are called *Practical,* and at other times *Moral,** Because they help us in perfecting our Manners, as they relate to our Conversation with Men.

THE *Moral Vertues* are either Principal, or less Principal. The *Principal* are four: *Prudence, Justice, Temperance,* and *Fortitude.* Which, because they are the Hinges upon which our whole Lives do turn, are called *Cardinal,*† and are commonly known by the name of *The four Cardinal Vertues.* They are called *Principal,* not onely because they are the *chief* of all Moral Virtues, but because they enter into every *Vertue,* as the four *Elements* of which it is compounded.

THE *less Principal* Vertues are *Magnificence* and *Liberality, Modesty* and *Magnanimity, Gentleness of behaviour, Affability, Courtesie, Truth* and *Urbanitie,* all these are called *less Principal,* not because they are indifferent, or may be accounted useless, for then they would not be Vertues: but because, tho their Practice be of extraordinary Importance in their places, they are more remote, and less Avail in the Way to Felicity, and are more confined in their Operations.

DIVINE Vertues (which we put instead of the Heathenish *Heroical,*) are such as have not only GOD for their Object and End, but their Pattern and Example. They are Vertues which are seen in his eternal Life, by Practicing which we also are changed into the same Image, and are made partakers of the Divine Nature. *Wisdome, Knowledge* and *Truth,* in the Sublimest Height we confess to be Three: but we shall Chiefly insist upon *Goodness,* and *Righteousness,* and *Holiness.* All which will appear in *Divine Love,* in more peculiar manner to be handled.

BESIDES all these, there are some Vertues, which may more properly be called *Christian:* because they are no where Else taught but in the Christian Religion, are founded on the Love of Christ, and

---

* Manners *in Latine are called* Mores *whence the English word* Moral *is derived.*
† *Cardo* is a Hinge.

the only Vertues distinguishing a *Christian* from the rest of the World, of which sort are *Love to Enemies, Meekness* and *Humility.*

ALL these Virtues are shut up under one common Head, because they meet in one common Nature; which bears the name of *Vertue.* The Essence of which being well understood will conduce much to the clear Knowledge of every one in particular.

VERTUE (in General) *is that habit of Soul by force of which we attain our Happiness.* Or if you please, *it is a Right and well order'd Habit of mind, which Facilitates the Soul in all its operations, in order to its Blessedness.* These Terms are to be unfolded.

1. *VERTUE is a Habit:* All Habits are either Acquired, or Infused. By calling it a Habit, we distinguish it from *a Natural Disposition,* or *Power* of the Soul. For a *Natural disposition* is an inbred Inclination, which attended our Birth, and began with our beings: not chosen by our Wills, nor acquired by Industrie. These Dispositions, because they do not flow from our Choise and industry, cannot be accounted Virtues. Tis true indeed that vertuous Habits are sometimes *infused* in a Miraculous Manner, but then they are rather called *Graces* then *Vertues:* and are *ours,* only as they are Consented to by our Wills, not ours by choise and acquisition, but only by Improvement and exercise. Tho they agree with Virtues in their Matter and their end, yet they differ in their Original and form. For as all Humane Actions flow from the Will and the Understanding, so do all Vertues, when they are rightly understood; whereas we are Passive in the reception of these, and they flow immediately from Heaven.

AND it is far more conducive to our Felicity, that we should conquer Difficulties in the attainment of Vertue, study, chuse, desire, pursue, and labour after it, acquire it finally by our own Care and Industry, with Gods Blessing upon it; then that we should be Dead and Idle, while virtue is given us in our Sleep. For which cause GOD ordered our state and Condition so, that by our own Labour we should seek after it; that we might be as well pleasing in his Eys, and as Honorable and Admirable in the *Acquisition* of vertue, as in the *Exercise* and Practice of it. And for these reasons GOD does not so often infuse it, and is more desirous that we should by many repeated Actions of our own attain it.

GOD does sometimes upon the General Sloth of mankind inspire it, raising up some persons thereby to be like salt among corrupted men, least all should putrifie and perish: Yet is there little reason why he should delight in that way, without some such uncouth and Ungrateful necessity to compel him thereunto.

FOR any man to expect that GOD should break the General Order and Course of Nature, to make him Vertuous without his own Endeavours, is to Tempt GOD by a presumptuous Carelesseness, and by a Slothful abuse of his Faculties to fulfil the parable of the unprofitable Servant.

THE Powers of the Soul, are not vertues themselves, but when they are clothed with vertuous Operations, they are transformed into Vertues. For Powers are in the Soul, just as Limbs and Members in the Body, which may indifferently be applied to Vertues and Vices, alike be busied and exercised in either.

AS the Members are capable of Various Motions, either comely, or Deformed, and are one thing when they are naked, another when attired, and capable of being modified with several Habits: so are the Powers and Faculties of the Soul. As they are in the Nature of Man without Exercise, they are void and Naked: But by many acts of Vice or Vertue, they put on a Habit, which seems chiefly to consist in an Inclination and Tendency to such Actions, a Facility of Working, an Aquaintance with them, a Love to them, and a Delight in them; For by long Custome it turns to a second Nature, and becomes at last as Necessary as Life it self; a confirmed Habit being taken in and incorporated with the Powers of the Soul by frequent exercise.

2. IN the second Definition we add, that *Vertue is a right and well ordered Habit.* A *Habit* is something added to that which wears it, and every Power of the Soul is naked, without the Quality wherewith long Custom cloaths it. Much of the *Formal Reason* of Vertue is shut up in those Words, *Right and well ordered.* For confused, irregular, and careless Habits will be alwayes erroneous and Deformed, and must consequently end in Dishonor and Miseries. He must aim at the Mark, that hits it, for only those actions that are well guided, produce right and well order'd Habits, which right and well order'd Habits alone can carry us to our Sovereign end.

A Mind in Frame is a Soul clothed with Right Apprehensions: Thoughts and affections well ordered, Principles and Contrivances well proposed, Means and Ends rationaly consulted, all considered, and the Best chosen. [Long Custom inuring us to the Benefit and Excellence of these, disposes the Soul into *a right and well ordered Habit, or Frame of spirit,* which regards that Glorious End for which we were created.]

BY *force of which we attain our Happiness.* Idleness and vertue are as Destructive to each other, as fire and water. In all vertue there is some force, and in all Force much action. A vertuous Habit ceaseth to be virtuous unless it actually incline us to virtuous Operations. As the Powers of the Soul when they are well exerted turn into Vertues, so is it by that *Exertion* that we attain our Happiness. *Vertue is that right and well ordered Habit by force of which we attain our Happiness.*

ITS force is never expressed but in exercise and operation. Yet even when we are asleep, it may tacitely incline us and make us ready, when we awake, to be Vertuous. Perhaps the *Habit* Sleeps and awakes with the Body: But if the Habit and its Energie be the same thing; it still sleepeth when its energie ceaseth: if they be Divers, the Habit may continue for some time without the force of its Operation.

BUT not to Divert into Blind and Obscure Corners: Whether the Soul of a man asleep may be stiled Vertuous or no; Whether the Habits continue in him at that time without their Acts, is nothing to our purpose. It is Sufficient, that when he is awake, he, that hath a Vertuous Habit, is in all his Actions inclined and Carried to his own Felicity, unless he falls into an oblivion worse than Sleep, because without some such Damnable and vicious Lethargy, he is always mind-ful of his Last End, and tends towards it in a Direct Line.

ALL his Actions derive a Tincture from the first Principle, *that Habit of Soul by which he is carried toward his own Felicity.* All those Actions, that Spring from that Habit tend to Bliss, and by force of that Habit are made Vertuous, and with facility performed.

ALL the Difficulty is in the Beginning. Vertues in the beginning are like green fruits, sour and imperfect, but their Maturity is accom-panied with sweetness and delight. It is hard to acquire a vertuous Habit at first, but when it is once gotten; it makes all Virtue exceeding Easie, nor Easie alone, but Happy and delightful. For a virtuous Habit as certainly acts according to its own nature, as the Sun shines, which is light by Constitution. It acts freely, yet when it does Act, it must needs act Vertuous, and can do nothing else. For it is no vertuous Habit; but some other Principle that exerteth vicious and bad Operations.

HAPPINESSE is with so much Necessity the end of Vertue, that we cannot take a Due Estimate of the Excellence of Vertue without considering the tendency which it has to Felicity. For as the Means are extravagant (and indeed no means) that have no Relation nor Proportion to their End: so would all the Vertues be inept and Worth-less (no Vertues) if they did not in some Sort conduce to our Happiness. For Happiness is the adequate End, which by nature we seek: Whether it be Glory, or pleasure, or Honor that we design, or wealth, or Learning; all that is Delightful, and Grateful to our reason, is comprehended in our Happiness. If we desire to glorifie GOD, or to please the Angels, or be grateful to men, it is because we love our selves and delight in our own Happiness, and conceit all those actions whereby we so do, either a Means, or a part of it. So that in the Partition and Distribution of Vertues we must take another Course to display their Glory, by exhibiting them in such a prospect, as that is, wherein their Place and office will appear in their Tendency towards mans last End, his Blessedness and Glory.

Of the Powers and Affections of the Soul; What virtues pertain to the Estate of Innocency; what to the Estate of Grace; what to the estate of Glory.

TWO things in Felicity are apparent to the Eye, Glory and Treasure; and the Faculties of the soul do in a several manner affect both. The *Understanding* was made to see the value of our Treasure; and the freedome of *Will,* to atcheive Glory to our actions; *Anger,* to stir us up against all Difficulty, and opposition, that might stand in our way; *Appetite,* to pursue the Pleasure in either; *Fear,* to heighten our concernment, that we might more dread the danger of losing that Happiness, wherein no less then Glory and Treasure are infinitely united: *Reason* it self, to compare Felicities and weigh which is the most perfect. *Desire,* to covet it; *Hope,* to encourage us in the pursuit of it; *Aversion,* for the avoiding of all Temptations and Impediments; *Love,* to the goodness of it; *Joy,* for its fruition; *Hatred,* to keep us from the Misery which is contrary thereunto; *Boldness,* to attempt it; *Sorrow* and *Despair,* to punish and torment us, if we fail to attain it. For these two, being unpleasant affections, serve to engage us in the pursuit of Happiness, because we are loath to experience the Sence of such Troublesome passions.

AMBITION and *Covetousness* are Inclinations of the Soul, by the one of which we are carried to *Glory,* by the other to *Treasure.* And as all the rest, so may these be made either Vertues, or Vices: *Vertues* when they are Means conducive to the Highest end; *Vices* when they distract and entangle us with inferior Objects.

THE Inclinations and affections of the Soul may be Defective or excessive in their exercise towards Objects. In relation to the Highest Object there is no danger of excess. We can never too violently either *love* or *desire* our Supream Happiness; our *Hope* can never exceed its greatness, we can never too much *rejoyce* in the fruition of it; Nor can we exceed in *Anger* or *Hatred* against those Things, that would bereave us of it; or too much *fear* the Misery of that Life, which will be ever without it; or be affected with too much *Sorrow* and *Despair* at the Losse of it. But if we look upon inferior Things, which are meerly Accidental to the nature of Felicity, such as the Favour of men, Injuries, Crosses, Temporal successes, the Beauty of the Body, the goods of Fortune, and such like; our affections and passions may be too excessive, because the good or evil of these is but finite; whereas the Good of Sovereign Bliss is altogether infinite, and so is the evil of Eternal Misery.

WHEN our own Actions are Regular, there is nothing in the World but may be made conducive to our highest Happiness: Nor is there any value in any Object, or Creature in the World, but as it is Subservient to our Bliss. No member of the Body, no sence or endowment of any Member, no Inclination or Faculty of the Soul, no passion or affection, no Vertue, no Grace, no Spiritual Gift, no Assistance, no Means of Grace, nothing (how great or Precious soever) can be of any Value, but in order to Felicity. In real truth, nothing without this can be Great or Estimable. Every Vertue therefore must have this, in common with all the Laws and Ordinances, and Works of GOD, they must all directly or Obliquely tend to our supreme Happiness; upon this dependeth all their Excellency.

SOME Vertues are necessary in the Estate of Innocency, some in the Estate of Grace, some in the Estate of Glory.

WITHOUT *seeing,* it is impossible to enjoy our Happiness, or find out the Way unto it; therefore is *Knowledge* necessary in all estates: without *Loving* it is impossible to Delight in its Goodness. The Office of *Righteousness* is to render to every Thing a Due esteem; And without this it is apparent that no Treasure can be to us, (tho in it self never so great) of any value. *Holiness* is the conscience that we make of discharging our duty, and the Zeal wherewith we avoid the Prophaness of its Contrary. *Goodness* is necessary, because we our selves cannot without that be Amiable, nor unless we be Delightful to others, enjoy our selves, or acquire Glory. The office of *Wisdom* is to chuse, and pursue the Highest end, by the Best of all means that can be chosen.

THESE are Transcendent Vertues, whereby even GOD himself doth enjoy his Felicity. They are incumbent on us by the Law of nature, and so essentially united to our Formal Happiness, that no Blessedness or Glory can be enjoyed without them. Therefore are we to look upon them as the Life and Soul of Religion, as *Eternal* Duties in all Estates for ever to be exercised. They are all Exercised in the very fruition it selfe, as will more apparently be seen, when we come to every one of these Vertues in particular. They were enjoyed in the Estate of Innocency, without any need of a positive Law, by the very nature of GOD and the Soul, and of things themselves, and must be exercised in the state of Grace and will abide for ever in the State of Glory.

THAT Vertues might be *ours,* in being wrought by *our selves;* and be Vertues *indeed,* in being wrought with *Difficulty;* that we might be so much the more Laudable and Glorious in our eternal Condition, GOD gave us Liberty, in the beginning, that we might chuse what we would, and placed us in such an Estate; that, having in us only the Seeds and Principles of all Vertue, we might exercise our natural Powers of our own Accord, for the Attainment of that actual Knowledge, Wisdom and Righteousness, wherein the Perfection of our soul consisteth, and by which the Perfection of our Bliss is to be enjoyed. That being Naked by Nature, tho Pure and clean, we might cloath our selves with our own *Habits,* attain the Glory of those Ornaments, in our own Acts, for which we were created; And work our *own* Righteousness, in such a Way as GOD had appointed.

FOR the Glory which we were to attain, is that Goodness which we are to shew in our own voluntary Care and obedience; and that Goodness is chiefly expressed in the kind and Genuine Exercise of our own Liberty, while we are tender of Displeasing him, to whom we are Obliged, and so Good as to gratifie his Desires, tho we had no restraint upon us.

TO make our selves amiable and beautiful, by the Exercise of our own Power, produces another kind of Beauty and Glory, than if we were compelled to be good by all his preventing Power. All Goodness is spoiled by Compulsion. Our own Actions, springing from an interiour Fountain, deep within the Soul, when voluntarily and freely exerted, are more acceptable; and the Will, whence they spring, is more excellent and perfect. This I would have you to note well, for the intrinsick Goodness and Glory of the Soul consists in the Perfection of an excellent Will, and without this it might be a piece of Dirt surrounded with Gold; but no imputed or annexed value could make it a Jewel.

THE Actions of GOD, or of the Angels, or of other men towards it, add no value to the Soul, if it will do nothing of it self. If it be Idle or unactive, the more excellent the Actions of GOD, and of all other Creatures are towards it, so much the more deformed and perverse is the Soul: nor will all the Glory of its Powers and Inclinations excuse it, but the more Great and Divine they are, the more abominable will it make it self by abusing them, in frustrating their Inclinations.

FOR the removing of all Constraint, and the infusing of greater Excellency and Beauty into these holy Actions; which he required from them, it pleased GOD to make *Men* obnoxious to Temptations, that having obstacles to overcome, and disadvantages to strugle with, Mans Righteousness might be more full of Vertue, and himself made capable of Victory and Triumph. For this End he seated him in a low Estate; even in an Estate of Trial: wherein was the Occasion of Exercising Faith and Hope, because his Felicity was distant from him: Faith in believing the Promises of God, and Hope in waiting for the Accomplishment of his Bliss: He had Occasions for Fear also, in relation to Gods Power and Justice, who was able to remove his Happiness, upon the least offence, and to bring upon him that Misery that was denounced for his Transgression. In this Estate of Trial, Prudence, which is conversant in nice Affairs, was to watch, and consider, and direct his Behaviour, in the midst of those Dangers and Temptations, that might possibly be expected: His *Temperance* was to be exercised in the Government of his Appetite; so that all inferiour satisfactions, and sensual Pleasures might be limited and ordered, as it most consists with his highest Happiness: *Humility,* in the acknowledgement of his own Unworthyness, who was taken out of Nothing; and Gratitude in a kind of just Retribution to his Benefactor, for all the Glory to which he was advanced.

ALL these Vertues are in themselves Delightful, and Easie in their Exercise; they immediately respect Felicity, and are by nature necessary to Mans enjoyment of it, they are consonant to Reason, and agreeable to the Circumstances of his Happy Condition: His Fear and Humility, which were in Paradise the severest, were aided and comforted, with a Transcendent Hope and Assurance, that upon his Diligent Care, he might be Eternally Blessed; and with the Sweet Sence of his Happy Change, and a Glorious Admiration resulting from the Comparison between his present Estate, and the Estate to which by his Creator he was to be exalted.

I will not say but there were more Vertues than these to be Exercised in *Eden:* But by these you may discern of what nature they all are, and conjecture they must be such as obedience to God, and Charity to one another.

ALL *Harsh* and *Sour* Virtues came in by Sin: and we are to look upon them, not as Vertues intended by God and Nature, but occasioned afterwards, because their Use and Existence is accidental.

WHEN we fell into Sin, we let Death and Misery into the World, contracted shame and guilt upon our selves, defiled our Nature with Deformities and Diseases, and made many Things upon that Occasion, necessary to our Happiness, that before were not so: And whereas they have a Mixture of *Bitterness* and *Advantage* in them, we may thank our selves for the *Bitterness,* and GOD for the *Advantage:* For as we by Sin forfeited our *Happiness,* so a new Obedience, consisting in the practice of proper Vertues, was necessary to recover it. Vertues, whose Names and Natures were of another kind, and never heard of before: All which we must look upon, not as Food, but Physick, and considering them under the notion of Remedies, not admire that there should be something in them Distasteful to Sence, tho they are now, when their Occasions are known, infinitely agreeable to Reason.

THEY are but an *Æquivocal* Offspring of the Fall: Sin could never beget such beautiful Children, as Meekness, Repentance, Patience, Alms-Deeds, Self Denyal, Submission and Resignation to the Divine Will, Fortitude, Contentment in all Estates, &c.

WHILE there was no Sin, there was no need of *Penitence;* while there was no *Pain* or Misery, no *Patience;* Without wrongs and Injuries there is no use of *Meekness;* nor place for *Alms-Deeds,* where there is no *Poverty:* no Courage, where are no Enemies. In *Eden* there was no ignorance, nor any Supernatural Verities to be confirmed by Miracles; Apostles therefore and Prophets, Ministers and Doctors were superfluous there, and so were Tythes and Temples, Schools of Learning, Masters and Tutors, together with the unsavoury Duty incumbent on Parents to chastise their Children. For as all would have been instructed by the Light of Nature, so had all been Innocent, and Just, and Regular: Whereupon no Magistrate had been needful to put any to Shame, no Courts of Judicature, nor Lawyers in the World. No Buying and Selling, and thereupon no commutative Justice, because the Blessed Earth had naturally been fertile, and abounded with rich and Glorious Provisions: Nakedness had been the Splendor and Ornament of Men, as it will be in Heaven: the Glorious Universe had been their common House and Temple, their Bodies fited for all Seasons, no Alien or Stranger, no Want, Distress, or War, but all Peace, and Plenty, and Prosperity; all Pleasure, and all Fellow Citizens throughout the World. Masters and Servants had been unknown, had we continued in that Estate, all had enjoyed the Liberty of Kings, and there had been no Dominion, but that of Husbands and Fathers,

a Dominion as full of sweetness, as so gentle and free a Relation importeth. I can see no Use that there had been of *Trades* and Occupations, onely the pleasant Diversion that *Adam* had in dressing the Garden, and the consequents of that: I am sure there had been no Funeral
Pomps, no *Sickness, Physick,* or *Physician.* There had been no *Faith*
in the *Incarnation* of the Son of God, because no occasion for that
Incarnation; no Ceremonial *Law of Moses,* no *Baptism,* nor *Lords
Supper,* because there were no supernatural Mysteries to be Typified,
but the clear Light of a Diviner Reason, and a free Communion with
God in the Right discharge of those Vertues, Divine and Moral, which
naturally belong to the Estate of Innocency. All which Original and
Primitive Vertues ought now to continue, as it were the Face of Religion beneath that *Mask* or *Vizor* of Ordinances and new Duties,
which Sin and Corruption hath put upon it; Tho we have forgotten
the Vertues of our first Estate, and are apt now to terrifie our selves
with that *Disguise,* wherewith we have concealed their Beauty, by regarding only the Vertues, that were occasioned by Sin and Misery.

IT is a great Error to mistake the *Vizor* for the *Face,* and no less
to stick in the outward *Kind* and Appearance of things; mistaking
the Alterations and Additions that are made upon the Fall of Man,
for the whole Business of Religion. And yet this new Constellation
of Vertues, that appeareth aboveboard, is almost the only thing talked
of and understood in the World. Whence it is that the other Duties,
which are the *Soul* of Piety, being unknown, and the *Reason* of these
together with their Original and Occasion, unseen; Religion appears
like a sour and ungratefull Thing to the World, impertinent to bliss,
and void of Reason; Whereupon GOD is suspected and hated, Enmity
against GOD and *Atheism* being brought into, and entertained in the
World.

FOR it is an *Idea* connatural to the Notion of GOD, to conceive
him *Wise* and *Good:* And, if we cannot see some *Reason* in his Ways,
we are apt to suspect there is no *Deity,* or if there be, that he is
Malevolent and *Tyrannical,* which is worse then none. For all Wisdom
and Goodness are contained in Love: And if it be true that GOD
is Love, he will shew it in our Beings, by making us Great and Excellent
Creatures; in his Gifts and Bounties, by surrounding us with real and
serviceable Treasures, in all his Laws, as well as in all his Works,
by consulting our Welfare in the one and in the other. And as he
makes the World Glorious and Beautiful for us to dwell in, so will
he make such Actions and Vertues only needful to be exercised by

us as are excellent and Divine: he will impose no Duties but such as are full of reason, and lead us more Advantageously to Bliss and Glory.

We are apt to charge our own Faults on God, by confounding all things: and because we see not how *Penitence,* and *Meekness,* and *Acts* of *Charity,* in relieving the Poor, directly and immediately bring us unto Bliss, are apt to repine at their Imposition. But when we see all these Virtues in their several Places and Offices, their Objects and their Uses, the Ends for which, and the occasions on which they were introduced, all are Delightful to the Reason of mans Soul, and highly Eligible, while GOD is adored and admired for the depth of his Wisdom and Goodness, and beloved for the Equity and Excellency of his Proceedings. For all these Occasional Vertues are but Temporary, when our Life, and this present World are past and gone as a Dream, Love, and Joy, and Gratitude will be all that will continue for ever, in which Estate, Wisdom and Knowledge, Goodness and Righteousness, and True Holiness shall abide, as the Life and Glory into which the Souls of all that are Blessed will be transformed. Repentance shall be gone, and Patience cease, Faith and Hope be swallowed up in fruition, Right Reason be extended to all Objects in all Worlds, and Eternity in all its Beauties and Treasures, seen, desired, esteemed, enjoyed.

Let it be your Care to dive to the Bottom of true Religion, and not suffer your Eyes to be Dazled with its Superficial Appearance. Rest not in the *Helps* and *Remedies* that it bringeth, but search for the Hidden Manna, the substantial Food underneath, the Satisfaction of all Wishes and Desires, the true and Cœlestial Pleasures, the Causes of Love, and Praise, and Thanksgiving founded in the Manifestations of Gods Eternal favour, especially in the Ends, for the sake of which all Helps and Remedies are prepared. For it is exceeding true, that *his Laws are Sweeter then the Hony and the Hony Comb, and far more precious then thousands of Gold and Silver.*

Of the Necessity, Excellency, and Use of Knowledge; its Depths and Extents, its Objects and its End.

KNOWLEDGE and Love are so necessary to Felicity, that there can be no Enjoyment or Delight without them. Heaven and Earth would be Dark and obscure, Angels and Men vain and unprofitable, all the Creatures base and unserviceable, Felicity impossible, were there no Knowledge. Nay GOD himself, without Knowledge and Love, could not well exist; for his very Essence is seated in infinite Knowledge.

GOD is Light, and in him is no Darkness at all; He is Love by nature and there is no hatred in his Essence. His very Godhead is all Perfection, by the infinite Knowledge and Love in his Nature.

THE Original of our Knowledge is his Godhead, His Essence and his will are the Fountain of it; and the stream so excellent, that in all Estates it is for ever to be continued, as the Light and Glory of the whole Creation.

THE understanding Power, which is seated in the Soul, is the Matter of that Act wherein the Essence of Knowledge consisteth: Its form is the Act it self, whereby that Power of knowing apprehendeth its Object.

ITS nature is invisible, like that of all other Spirits, so simple and uncompounded, that its form and matter are the same. For all Powers, when transformed into Act, are Acts themselves. And the faculty of understanding, in a Compleat and Perfect Act of Knowledge attains its Perfection, and is Power exerted, or an Act in its Exercise. For every Act is Power exerted.

THE Power of Knowing is vain if not reduced into Act; and the Soul a melancholly and Dreadful Cave, or Dungeon of Darkness, if void of Knowledge. Had GOD himself a Power of Knowing Distinct from its Operation, if he never exercised that Power, it would be useless to him. His Glory and Blessedness are seated in the Light of that Knowledge, which to us upon Earth appeareth *Inaccessible*.

IF we would *be perfect, as our Father which is in Heaven is perfect,* our Power of Knowing must be transformed (into *Act,*) and all Objects appear in the interior Light of our *own* understanding. For tho all Eternity were full of Treasures, and the Whole World, and all the Creatures in it transformed into Joys and our Interest to all never so perfect; yet if we are Ignorant of them, we shall continue as poor and Empty, as if there were nothing but Vacuity and Space. For not to *be,* and not to *appear,* are the same thing to the understanding.

WERE a Man a Seraphim by his Essence, or something by nature more Glorious and Divine then the Highest Order of the most Blessed Angels, nay the greatest Creature that Almighty Power was able to produce, his Soul and Body would signifie nothing, if he were unknown to himself, and were not aware of his Excellence.

IF you would have a solid Prospect of any Vertue, you must understand, that Vertues are Powers transformed into right, wise, and regular Acts, avoiding all extremes of *remissness* on the one hand, and *excess* on the other. The Extreams of Knowledge are Ignorance and Error.

FOR ought you know Heaven and Earth are as full of Treasures, as Almighty Power was able to create them, and you by Nature, the best and highest of all possible Creatures, made like GOD, for the highest and best of all possible Ends, and called to live in Communion with him, in all his fruitions: but being vilely corrupted, you have lost the sence of all these Realities, and are ignorant of the Excellences of your own Estate and Nature.

I am sure that GOD is infinite in Wisedom, Goodness and Power, and nothing is wanting on his Part, to perfect your Desires: But yet you may be blind, and idle, and ignorant, and dead in a manner, while you are wanting to your self, and have need of nothing, but clear and perfect apprehensions, but because they are Sottish and Erroneous at present, they may make you miserable, and Poor, and Blind, and Naked.

IF Sin had been like *Circe*'s Cup, and changed the shape of Mans Body, to that of a *Swine* or *Dragon,* the Depravation of his Nature had been plain and visible; yet without knowing what kind of Form he had before, it would not appear, because we should be unsensible of his first Form, and unable to compare the one with the other: But Sin is a *Moral Obliquity,* and the change it produceth in the Soul is *Spiritual.* It makes a man to differ far more from himself, than any alteration of Body can do; but withal so blinds his Understanding, that he does not remember what he was in his first Parent; Tho the first Man (who had experience of both Estates) was able to compare them, because in his Corruption, he might possibly retain a Sence of that Nature, and Life which he enjoyed in his integrity: Yet all his Posterity, that are born Sinners, never were sensible of the Light and Glory of an Innocent Estate, and for that cause may be wholy ignorant both of GOD and themselves, utterly unable to conceive the Glory of the World, or of that Relation, wherein they should by Nature have stood towards all the Creatures.

IT is impossible to conceive, how great a change a slight Action may produce. It is but pressing the Wiek a little with ones Finger, and a Lamp is extinguished, and Darkness immediately made to overspread the Room. The Glory and Splendor of the whole World would vanish upon the Extinction of the Sun: And one Instants Cessation from the Emission of its Beams would be its Extinction. A Soul is a more Glorious Thing than the Sun: The Sphear of its Activity is far Greater, and its *Light* more *Precious*. All the World may be filled with the splendor of its Beams; Eternity it self was prepared for it! Were there but one Soul, to see and enjoy all the Creatures, upon the suspension of its Light all the Creation would be rendred vain. Light it self is but *Darkness* without the Understanding.

THE Existence of many Souls is so far from abating the value of one, that it is by reason of their multitude more useful and Excellent. For the value of the Objects, imputes a Lustre and *Higher* value to the Light wherein they are enjoyed. And if Souls themselves are more excellent than all other Creatures, and are with, and above all other, to be enjoyed, that Power, whereby this Soul is able to enjoy them, is more to be esteemed, upon the account of those Souls, than for all the other Creatures, which are made for the same: GOD himself and his holy Angels are Objects of the Understanding. Those Felicities and Glories, which the Sun cannot extend to, the Soul can comprehend. All which, since their Fruition depends upon that Act of the Understanding by which they are *considered,* reflect a Lustre, and add a value to that Knowledge by which the Soul does attain them. Whereupon it follows that the infinite value of all these is seated in the intellect; and as the Power, so the Act of Knowledg, on which their Fruition dependeth, is of infinite use and Excellency. As the loss is infinite, when the Soul is bereaved of them, so is the Dammage, which it suffers by failing of its Light, whether that Defect be voluntary, or imposed by some outward Impediment.

AS for the *Use* of Knowledge, it is apparent enough. For the Relation between the Use and Excellency of things is so near and intimate, that as nothing Useless can be at all excellent, so is every Excellence in every Being founded in its usefulness. The use of Souls is as great as their Excellency: The use of Knowledge as endless in Variety, as in Extent, and Value.

KNOWLEDGE is that which does illuminate the Soul, enkindle Love, excite our Care, inspire the mind with Joy, inform the Will, enlarge the Heart, regulate the Passions, unite all the Powers of the Soul to their Objects, see their Beauty, understand their Goodness, discern our Interest in them, form our Apprehensions of them, consider and enjoy their Excellences. All Contentments, Raptures, and Extasies are conceived in the Soul, and begotten by Knowledge, all Laws, Obligations and Rewards are understood by Knowledg: All Vertues and Graces of the Mind are framed by Knowledge, all Advantages are by it improved, all Temptations discerned, all Dangers avoided, all Affairs ordered, all Endowments acquired; all the Ornaments of Life, all the Beauties of the inward Man, all the Works of Piety are affected by Knowledge. In the Light of knowledge all Pleasures arise, and as Fruits and Flowers are begotten in the Earth by the Beams of the Sun, so do all kinds of Joy spring from the Creatures, and are made ours, by the help of that Knowledge, that shineth on them; its last Off-spring are Eternal Thanksgivings and Praises. The Divine Image and the Perfection of Bliss are founded in Knowledge, GOD himself dwelleth in the Soul, with all his Attributes and Perfections, by Knowledge: By it we are made Temples of the Holy Ghost, and Partakers of the Divine Nature, And for this cause it is that St. *Paul* prayeth,* *That we might be filled with the Knowledge of his Will, in all Wisedome and Spiritual Understanding, that we might walk worthy of the Lord unto all pleasing, being fruitful in every Good Work, and increasing in the Knowledge of GOD, strengthened with all Might according to his glorious Power, unto all Patience and long-suffering, with Joyfulness giving Thanks to the Father, who hath made us meet to be Partakers of the Inheritance of the Saints in Light: who hath delivered us from the Power of Darkness, and translated us into the Kingdom of his Dear Son.*

THE Sun is a glorious Creature, and its Beams extend to the utmost Stars, by shining on them it cloaths them with light, and by its Rayes exciteth all their influences. It enlightens the Eyes of all the Creatures: It shineth on forty Kingdomes at the same time, on Seas and Continents in a general manner; yet so particularly regardeth all, that every Mote

* Col. 1.9, 10, 11, 12.

in the Air, every Grain of Dust, every Sand, every Spire of Grass is wholly illuminated thereby, as if it did entirely shine upon that alone. Nor does it onely illuminate all these Objects in an idle manner, its Beams are Operative, enter in, fill the Pores of Things with Spirits, and impregnate them with Powers, cause all their Emanations, Odors, Vertues and Operations; Springs, Rivers, Minerals and Vegetables are all perfected by the Sun, all the Motion, Life and sense of Birds, Beasts and Fishes dependeth on the same. Yet the Sun is but a little spark, among all the Creatures, that are made for the Soul; the Soul, being the most High and Noble of all, is capable of far higher Perfections, far more full of Life and Vigour in its uses. The Sphere of its Activity is illimited, its Energy is endless upon all its Objects. It can exceed the Heavens in its Operations, and run out into infinite spaces. Such is the extent of Knowledge, that it seemeth to be the Light of all Eternity. All Objects are equally near to the splendor of its Beams: As innumerable millions may be conceived in its Light, with a ready capacity for millions more; so can it penetrate all Abysses, reach to the Centre of all Nature, converse with all Beings, visible and invisible, Corporeal and Spiritual, Temporal and Eternal, Created and Increated, Finite and Infinite, Substantial and Accidental, Actual and Possible, Imaginary and Real; All the Mysteries of Bliss and Misery, all the Secrets of Heaven and Hell are Objects of the Souls Capacity here, and shall be actually seen and known hereafter.

WERE Almighty Power Magnified by filling Eternity with created objects, and were all the Omnipresence of God full of Joys, it is able, when assisted by his Divine Knowledge, to look upon all: and tho every one of them should have an infinite Depth within, an Endless variety of Uses, a Relation to all the rest of the World, the Soul, as if it were able to contract all its strengths from all the expansions of Eternity and space, and fix them upon this Moment, or on this Centre, intirely beholding this alone, in all its fulness, can see its Original, its End, its Operations, Effects and Properties, as if it had nothing to consider but this alone, in a most exquisite and perfect manner.

IT is not to be denied, that every Being in all Worlds is an Object of the Understanding: nor can that of the Psalmist be doubted, *In his Presence there is fulness of Joy, and at his right hand there are Pleasures for evermore:* that is, his Omnipresence is full of Joys, and his Eternity of Riches and Pleasures: nor is it to be denied, that the Soul is by its Creation intended for the *Throne of GOD.* For it is made capable of his Omnipresence and Eternity, and, as the Apostle speaketh, *may be filled with all the fulness of GOD,* which fulness is adequate to the Immensity of his Eternal Power (of which you will see more in the Vertues of Love, Wisdom, Righteousness and Holiness:) This only is here to be noted, that Nature never made any Power in vain, but ever intendeth the Perfection of what it produceth; and prepareth objects for the understanding, the Perfection of which Power is the actual attainment of that Knowledge of which it is capable.

THE principal objects of our Knowledge are GOD, and a Mans self: The Kingdom of GOD, his Laws and Works, his Ways in all Ages, his Counsels and his Attributes, Mans Interest and Duty, Transactions of the World, the Thoughts and Actions of Angels and Men are considerable; which tho they may be stiled less material Objects of the understanding, yet in relation to GOD and a Mans self, are of great Importance.

GOD as he is the Life and fountain of all Felicity, the End of all Perfection, and the Creator of our Being, Almighty in Power, infinite in Wisdom and Goodness, Author of the universe, and Lord of all the Creatures, is most fit to be Known. *Plato* makes him the very *Light* of the understanding, and affirms, that as three Things are necessary to *Vision,* the Eye rightly prepared, the object conveniently seated, and Light to convey the *Idea* to the Eye; so there are three things required to compleat and perfect Intelligence, an understanding Eye, an Intelligible Object, and a Light intelligible in which to conceive it: Which last is GOD. Nor is the Royal Psalmist and Divine Philosopher *David* far from the Notion, while he saith, *In thy Light we shall see Light.* For GOD is the Light of the understanding. His Nature is the Light of all the Creation. Therefore it is said by Christ himself that the *Knowledge of GOD is Life Eternal.* For his Light is the Life of men, and without him we can do nothing. Till we Know his Nature, we cannot apprehend the Excellency of his Works: For all their Goodness is derived from him, and ends in him. His Love moved him to create the World, and the principal End for which it was made, is the Glory of the Creator in the Felicity of his Creatures. The Glory of the Creatures is seen in his. By his Wisdom and Goodness we are guided to the Hope, and Investigation of their Excellence. His infinite bounty made them all our *Treasures,* that for the Perfection of their Beauty and Worth we might celebrate his Praises.

HE that would not be a stranger to the Universe, an Alien to Felicity, and a foreiner to himself, must Know GOD to be an infinite Benefactor, all Eternity, full of Treasures, the World it self, the Beginning of Gifts, and his own Soul the Possessor of all, in Communion with the Deity. That the Business of Religion is Complacency in GOD, and that GOD never laid aside his Wisdom in any Operation of his Power, never forgot to make the least of his Works agreeable to his Goodness. Nay rather he is so perfect, that his infinite Goodness, Wisdom, and Power, are exerted wholy and wholy Conspicuous in every Operation. It is the Beauty of Truth that maketh Knowledge of such infinite Value. For if all the Treasures of Wisdom and Knowing be ordained for a Wise and Knowing Man, if all Objects in the clear Light of Heaven and Eternity be laudable and Glorious, if Divine Wisdome hath so far obtained, that the number and Value of GODS Gifts is accurate, and exactly answerable to the nature of its causes; if every Soul, that will live in his Image, may be the friend of GOD, and acquire the Empire of the World, and be Beloved of Angels, and admired of Men; if fruition be the End of Knowledge, and all Things made that they may be enjoyed: Knowledge is the only Thing that enriches the Soul, and *the Knowing Man is the friend of GOD.* The Exercise and Pleasure of this Divine Amity is the End of the Creation, and the Perfection of the Soul.

The Knowledge of a Mans self is highly conducive to his Happiness, not only as it gives him Power to rejoyce in his Excellencies, but as it shews him his End, for which he was created. For by Knowing what Inclinations and Powers are in his Soul, he discerns what is agreeable with, and fit for his Essence; what objects and what Operations are conducive to his Welfare, what means he is to use for the Attainment of his End, and what that is, wherein his Perfection consisteth. If the Powers of his Soul are illimited, his Desire infinite, and his Reach Eternal, if he be able to see and enjoy all Worlds, and all that is above all Worlds in the Image of GOD: If his Ambition carry him to be Pleasing to all Angels and Men, and to be Glorious in the Eyes of all Kingdoms and Ages; if his Abilities are indeficient for the fruition of all that is Excellent in eternity it self, it is a token that he is ordained for GOD, and the enjoyment of his Kingdom: and a wicked folly to restrain himself to the miserable Contentment of a Cell, or Cottage, and to delight in nothing but some fragments of the Creation, that in Comparison of the whole are infinitely Defective.

OF all other things I would have this most deeply engraven in the mind, that GOD hath exceeded all Imagination in the Works of his Hands, that he that overcometh shall be the Son of GOD and inherit all Things, that there is an infinite end why the secrets of all hearts shall at last be revealed, that in Heaven all Thoughts and Things shall be Known, that the Kingdome of Heaven is so Glorious, that all the blessed are Perfect Sovereigns, every one the Possessor and End of it all: that all Things proceeding immediately from GOD, are the Best that are possible: that the best and the worst things as ordered by him, are perfectly amiable, and subservient to Felicity, that he him-self alone hath a Proper Right to all that is excellent, and that GOD is in every Thing to be enjoyed, that he is enjoyed only when his essence and his Works satisfie the Desires of perfect reason, and exceed all Wishes in filling and delighting the soul: That having filled the soul with infinite Wisdome, he has laid infinite Obligations upon us, and set infinite Rewards before us, made Laws infinitely amiable, and given us Duties infinitely Desirable: for which he deserves eternal Adorations and Thanksgivings.

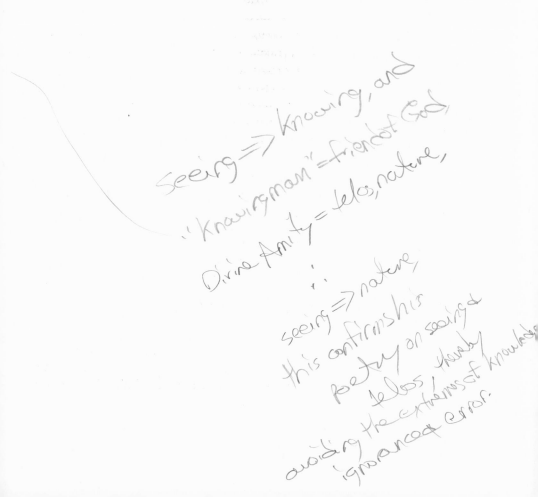

Of Love and Hatred. The necessity and sweetness of Love. Its General use and efficacy. The several kinds of love. Of the Power, Inclination and act of Love. Its extent and capacity.

BECAUSE Love is the most Desirable Employment of the Soul, the Power of Loving is to be accounted the most High and Noble of the Faculties. It is not seated by it self in the mind, but attended with a mighty Proneness and Inclination.

THERE is no Creature so unsociable and furious but it is capable of loving something or other. Wolves and Tygres live at peace among themselves, Lions have an Inclination to their Grim Mistresses, and Deformed Bears a natural Affection to their Whelps, expressed in their Rage, when they are bereaved of them. Things must either be absolutely Dead, or live in misery, that are void of love. Whatsoever is endued with Life and sence delights in easie and grateful Operations. Love is a necessary Affection of their Souls, because it is impossible to apprehend any thing Delightful, but it must be pleasing; and what is Pleasing must be Lovely. For to be Pleased, and to love are the same thing. If there be any difference, the pleasure we take in any Object is the root of that Desire, which we call Love; and the affection, whereby we pursue the pleasure that is apprehended in it, is part of the Love that we bear unto it; the end of which is the Completion of that pleasure which it first perceives: All is Love variously modified, according to the Circumstances wherein the Object is represented.

AS Love is the only Easie and Delightful Operation, so is Hatred of all other the most troublesom and tormenting. Displeasure and Enmity are the Ingredients of its nature; and the fruits of it (allyed to their Root) as Bitter as Gall, and Wormwood. Murder, and Vexation, and Grief are the off-spring of the one, with Separation, Contention, and Horror; Peace and Embraces are the Fruit of the other,

with Praises and Complacencies, Honors, Services, Benefits and Pleasures. These are the little *Cupids* that flie about this cœlestial *Venus,*
when it is, what it ought to be, the Mother of Felicity, and the Daughter of GOD.

ALL Creatures that are sensible of Pain or pleasure, must of necessity
be addicted to Love and Hatred; to the Love of what is pleasing,
to the Hatred of what is Painful. And if any Question be made, which
of these Twins is the First born? the answer is; that they may seem
Twins in respect of Time, but in nature Love is the first born, and
the Mother of Hatred. For where nothing to be hated does at all
appear, pleasant Things are Beloved for their own sake: whereas if
there were no pleasant thing to be beloved, nothing could be hated,
because nothing could be Hurtful, which appeareth by this, because
where there is no Love, there is no Interest, and where there is no
concernment, there can be no Affection, no Fear, or Hope, or Joy,
or sorrow.

AS Fire begets Water by melting Ice, so does Love beget contrary
passions in the soul of a living creature, Anger, Malice, Envy, Grief
and Jealousie: not by its own nature, but by the accidental Interposure
of some Obstacle, that hinders or endangers the fruition of its Object.
Were there no Love of Ease and Pleasure, there could be no Anger
or Quarrel between Competitors; no Emulation or Desire, no Aversion
or Endeavour. All Enmity and Hostility Springs from a Contention,
who shall enjoy what is Desirable; or from some other Principle of
Envy or Revenge, in relation to what is Good: as is Obvious to Daily
Experience.

LIFE and Love are so individualy united, that to live without Loving
something is impossible. Even in Hell, where their whole Life seemeth
to be spent in Detestation and Hatred, and actual Love is, like fire
under those Embers, covered and continued, Could they put off self
Love, all Love of Felicity, and Interest, their Torments would be gone:
Punishments and Rewards are things impossible, where there is not
self-Love: For without Love to something, Pains and Joys are equally
Grateful.

AS *Love* is the Root of Endeavor, so is it the Spring of all the
Passions: They all depend upon Love alone. We are *Angry* at that
which stands in our Way, between our Love and its object: We *Desire*
an absent Good, because we Love it: We *Hope* for it, when we conceive
its Attainment feasible: We *rejoyce* in it, when we have it: We *fear*
to lose it: we *grieve* when it is gone: we *despair,* if we cannot get,

or recover it: We *hate* all that is opposite to it. And for this Cause is our Love, when well regulated, the greatest Vertue, because upon the right Choise of its Object, and true Goverment of it self, all the Powers and Affections of the Soul are well employed; and when we Love all that we ought as we ought to do, we fulfil all Laws, Hope and Fear, and Hate, and Grieve, and Desire, and Rejoyce, and do every thing in a regular Manner.

THERE is a Sensual and Brutish Love, there is a Humane and Divine: Brutish Love is of two sorts, the one Springs from a Harmony of Complexions and a Sympathy of Bodies, the other from the Consideration of Pleasure abstracted. The First of these is occasioned by a secret and unexpressible Agreement of Tempers, by which upon the presence of each other, the Senses are delighted, we know not why; it being a mystery in nature; and perhaps founded in a grateful Transpiration of Spirits from one to the other.

THE Consideration of Beauty seemeth peculiar to the Love of Men; because no Beast is observed to make any Distinction between Lineaments and Features, nor upon any account of shape and Colours to be delighted with each other. Wherein Man exceeds the Capacity of Beasts, in being able to note and admire the Workmanship of GOD in the decent Order of Symmetry and Proportion.

HUMANE Affection and Divine Love are near allyed, yet of several Kinds. If you take the Love of Reason in its utmost Height, it is always Divine. For it is conformable to the Love of GOD in its measures and Degrees, in its Effects and Causes. For the Love of GOD is it self the Love of perfect Reason. And as the Reason of his Love is Infinite and Eternal, so is its Operation. But in a lower Acceptation Humane Love differs from Divine; it being founded upon Temporal Causes, Vivacity, Wit, Learning, Beauty, Behaviour, Moral Honesty, Fidelity, Kindness, Goodness, Power, Majesty, Wealth, Nobility, Worth, Vertue, and the like. But all these may be exalted, when they are Sanctified, and made Divine by the superadded concurrence of Cœlestial Causes. For when a Man loves another, because he is made in the Image of GOD, and by the Beauty of his Soul is something more than Humane, this Love is made Sacred, and receives a Grace from the Influences of Religion.

DIVINE Love strictly so called, is founded on Eternal Causes, agreeable to the Life of Heaven, Delightful to GOD, and Pleasing to the Angels.

IF Divine Love be taken in the *highest* Sense, there is none but in GOD. For it is his Peculiar Prerogative to Love without Obligation or Reward, to be the Sole Author of all Felicity, and to over-flow with Goodness of himself freely, without any Motive, to prevent the Beauty and Existence of his Object, and to Love from all Eternity in an immutable manner: And this is the nature of Divine Love. Howbeit even here, are infinite Ends and Causes of his Love, tho they are all in Himself: For he Loves, that he may Love, and begets that Love which is his Essence. His Love is the foundation of all his Treasures, the Cause and End of the whole Creation, and that alone by which he proceeds from himself (to all his Creatures, and by those) to himself again for ever. All his Kingdome and Greatness and Pleasure, all his Wisdome and Goodness, all his Life and Perfection is seated in Love, which is his Beauty and his Holiness, his Bounty and his Godhead. He Loves therefore that he may be all Beauty and Goodness, and Holiness, and that he may enjoy himself and the Eternal Pleasure of his Essence in Glory and Blessedness for ever.

IT is GOD alone that Loves by his Essence, Angels and Men may Love by Inclination, but their Affection is Accidental to their nature, begins in time, may alter and cease. It is subject to Chance, Obligation and Reward, and ought to be guided according to the Pleasure of an Higher Agent. In this it differs from the Love of God, but in many things there is a great Agreement and proportion between them. For GOD has made the love of Angels and men so like his own, by extending their Knowledge to all objects, that infinite Perfections are contained in their love. It is as GODLIKE as any Thing created is capable of being; for Almighty Power and infinite Wisdome are employed in the production of it.

FOR the better understanding of this Love, we will consider it in the power of Loving, in the inclination to Love, in its act and Perfection. It may seem a surprizing verity; but the Power of Loving is as necessary to Blessedness and Glory as life it selfe; an inclination to love as necessary as the Power; and the act of Love as necessary as the Inclination. The world is useless without Life, and Life without Love, the Body without the Soul, the Soul without the Power of Loving, the Power of Loving without the Inclination, the Inclination without the Act.

IN the Power of Loving I shall note nothing at present, but its Extent and Capacity. In Beasts it is confined, but in Men it is Endless. As a Beast is unable to examine what spaces are above the Heavens, so is it unable to extend its Affections beyond the memory of things perceived, for a Beast cannot represent to it self the Idea's of its Progenitors; nor see into Ages that are before its birth, nor contemplate Objects that will be after it is Dead. But man can see, and know, and love any object, in any Age or Kingdom in the World. He can look into any Region, tho it be never so far removed and be as familiarly conversant with any Person or Transaction there, when represented once in a clear Light, as with any Object in his own country. He can look into *Eden,* consider *Adams* Dust in its first Creation, survey the Procedure of God in his Six Dayes Works, pass out of Time into Eternity it self, run up to the Original and fountain Head of all existence, ponder the nature of GOD, search in his Bosom for his Eternal Counsels, pierce into the Centre of the Earth, and survey the Circumference of all Immensity. His Love can follow his Knowledg in all its flights, while in spirit he can be present with all the Angels. He is able to Love not only his Family and Relations, but all the City and Country where he liveth, all the Kingdom, all the Cities and Kingdoms in the world, all the Generations in all Kingdoms, all the Spirits of Just men made perfect, all the Cherubims and Seraphins, and GOD blessed for ever. This is the extent: The capacity of Love is so alsufficient, that his Affection is not diminished, but the more he loves one, the more he is able, and the more inclined to love all that are united to him. As in ordinary friendship, the more we love the Father, the more we love his Wife and all his children. For the more we love any Person, the more we love all that love him, or are beloved by him. As the reasons of our Love increase, so may our Love it selfe; the capacity of Love being so indeficient, that it never can be exceeded, or surmounted by its Object.

THE Capacity of Love being so exceeding vast, multiplies and heightens in the Soul of man, that is apt to overflow of its own Accord. For nothing is so prone to communicate it self as that Active Principle of Love; that Soul which is Generous and Divine, being disposed to the exercise of Love, because therein it findeth its Proper Element. The very Sun is not more inclined to communicate its Beams, then the Soul to love. For the Soul being made in the Image of GOD, who is Love by his Essence, must needs be like him in Power and Inclination, and is made for nothing else but the Attainment of its perfection, so that it can never rest, till it actually love after his similitude. Some Operation it must of Necessity have. For as all Life, so all pleasure is founded in Action.

IF Love in its Perfection be considered, all that is lovely is Beloved by the soul; all the Capacity of Love is filled with its objects, and all the Goodness of the Creator and his Creatures, at once enjoyed. It is the Life and pleasure and enlargment of the Soul, it is the Wisdom, and Goodness, and Glory of the Soul. I confess there be many Errors and Diseases in Love; and that Love is alwayes miserable, in its Effects, that is *vicious:* yet it so bewitches the Sences, that the Soul being captivated by the Force of present Delight is violently carried in an irresistible appetite to those Things which Reason condemnes, and advises to shun as Evil. *Medea's* faction most prevails in the World.

———*Video meliora proboque,*
Deteriora Sequor.

LOVE is *then* a vice, when it is irrational and illegal, rebellious and Sensual, Blind, Defective, Unjust, Absurd. When Evil things are beloved, when Good things are preferred above the Better, and the Best neglected.

VERTUOUS Love is that which proceedeth from a well governed understanding, and is seated in a Will that is guided by Reason. It renders to all things their just Due, and is the Powerful Parent of all Kind of Vertues. This Love may be considered either in its Properties, or Effects, the last of which relate to the Soul it self, to the Conversation of the whole man, to all its Objects; when it is well understood, it will be found the proper and immediate Means by which we attain our Perfection and Felicity.

*What Benefit GOD himself does receive by his
Eternal Love. That when our Love is made
compleat and Perfect, it will be like his, and
the Benefit of it will be Eternal.*

BEFORE we can fully discern the Benefit of Love, or see the Glory
of it in all its high and admirable Effects, we must consider what
Love is and doth in GOD. For as we have said, *The Life of GOD
is Love;* nay the Apostle saith, *GOD is Love:* By Loving he begot
his Love. And if his Love be his Godhead, his Essence is an infinite
and Eternal Act of Love, by extending which through all infinity,
and by Loving Eternally, he begot his infinite and Eternal Essence:
which is the Love that filleth all Worlds with Beauty and Glory. When
you consider it well, An Act of Love is begotten by *Loving:* And
if his Wisdome, and Goodness, and Blessedness, and Glory be seated
in Love, his Love is his Wisdome which is the Son of GOD, and
his Goodness, and his Glory, and his Blessedness. For all these, tho
we conceive them diversly, are the same Thing: and of the Son of
GOD it is said, that *he is the Wisdom of the Father, and the Brightness
of his Fathers Glory.* He is the Life of the Father, *by whom also he
made the Worlds,* and the Love of the Father *for whom all Things
were created, that are in Heaven, and that are in Earth, visible and
invisible, whether they be Thrones, or Dominions, or Principalities,
or Powers: all Things were created by him, and for him.** For GOD
enjoyeth all Things by his Love, which is his Eternal Son; and made
them as perfect and delightful as it was possible for things created
to be, that he might take Pleasure in them. As he himself is made
Glorious and Delightful in the Eyes of all Angels and Men *by* Love,
so doth his whole Kingdom arise and Spring *from* Love; the Beauty
and felicity of all his Creatures, their Joys and Praises, their Uses and

* Col. 1.16.

Perfections are founded in his Love, by his Love he begetteth all his pleasures in himself, by his Love he made his Treasures infinite, and by that alone doth he take infinite Pleasure and Delight in himself and his Kingdome. Thus useful is the Love of GOD.

Had not GOD from all Eternity Loved, had he never desired, nor delighted in any thing; he had never exerted his Almighty Power, never communicated his Goodness, or begot his Wisdom, never enjoyed Himself, never applyed himself to the Production of his Works, never appeared in his Glory to any eie whatsoever. Removing his Love we remove all the Properties and Effects of his Essence, and are utterly unable to conceive any Idea of his Godhead. For his Power, tho it be Almighty, yet if it be Dead and idle, is fruitless and Deformed. Idle Power is not the Essence of the Deity, but a meer Privation and Vacuity; or at least a positive Being as ignoble as it is unactive. The Reason of his Works is founded in Love, so are all the Obligations, that are laid upon his Creatures to adore him. All their Rewards are founded in Love, and by Love prepared: All his Laws are the Laws of Love, all his Attributes and Counsels are Love, in several formes, acting upon several occasions. When his Love communicates it self in Joys to innocent Creatures, it is *Goodness;* when it attains the most perfect End by the most perfect means, it is *Wisdome;* when it rescues guilty Creatures from Hell, it is *Mercy;* when it punishes the Rebellious it is *Justice;* when it inspires Obedience into any obstinate Person, it is *Grace;* when it delights in the Beauty of all its Works, it is *Blessedness;* when it appears in the perfection of its works, it is glory. For Glory is the perfection of Beauty, that ariseth from, and is seated in the lustre of excellent Actions, discovering the internal Properties of an excellent Agent, which is by those his Properties and Actions made Delightful to all *Judicious* Spectators.

NOR is it onely in GOD, but in us also that the fruits and Benefits of *Love* are ineffable. For by loving, as it ought to do, the Soul acquires its own Perfection, and is united to all its Objects. By loving as it ought to do, it is made Holy, and Wise, and Good, and Amiable. Onely by Loving does it embrace the Delights of which it is capable. Love is the root and Soul of those Actions for which a Creature is desired, and praised by others.

IT is an infinite Advantage, that we are able to live in GODS Image, if we please: For if GOD alone be infinitely Glorious and Blessed, there is no way for us to become Glorious and Blessed, but by being made, either by our selves, or some other, like unto him.

BY nature he hath implanted the Similitude of his power: which we are to improve by Grace, turning it into Act after his Similitude. To be able to Love is neither Grace nor vertue, but a meer Gift of GOD, a natural Endowment, which may be Blasted, or compleated. Actually to love is the Work of vertue; for by that Act we enjoy our Felicity.

HAD GOD limited and confined our understanding, our power of Loving had been shut up in Bounds. Had he made it infinite, but not prepared objects for the same, our Love had been deluded, and had lost its force. Had he made some Objects, but not so many as it was capable of Loving, it had been Superfluous and dissatisfied; Had he prepared Objects innumerable and Endless, but made them evil, our Love had been irrational, had he commanded us to Love them; Had he made more Objects then we were able to love, we had been discontented: But having made all Objects infinitely Amiable and Glorious, and filled his Immensity and Eternity with himselfe, and with the Lustre of his Actions, Love is an infinite Vertue, because nothing is wanting, but an Act of Love to enjoy them.

IF they are all Amiable in all Respects, they are all according to our Hearts desire, in their Natures, Places, Durations, Ends, Occasions, Causes, Uses, Services, Relations, Properties, Operations, &c. All things, as they immediatly proceed from him, are in all respects most perfectly pleasing. And if we have an Eye to see and discern this, and a Soul able to resent the Benefit; if our nature be so vast and perfect, as to see and take pleasure in all their Circumstances; it is the most unreasonable and *bruitish* thing in the world to withdraw our Affection from them, nay it is worse then *Diabolical.* For we Kill our selves, we blast our Felicity, we offend GOD, we slight the Beauty of all his Creatures, we break his Laws, we act against nature, we darken the Light and Splendor of our Souls, we deface his Image, we grieve his Love, we do the most vicious and abominable thing that is imaginable. But if we excite and awaken our Power, we take in the Glory of all objects, we live unto them, we are sensible of them, we delight in them, we transform our souls into Acts of Love and Knowledge, we proceed out of our selves into all Immensities and Eternities, we render all Things their Due, we reap the Benefit of all, we are Just, and Wise, and Holy, we are Grateful to GOD, and Amiable in being so: We are not divided from, but united to him, in all his Appearances, Thoughts, Counsels, Operations; we adorn our souls with the Beauty of all objects whatsoever, are transformed into the Image of GOD, live in communion with him, nay live in him, and he in us, are made Kings and Priests unto GOD, and his sons forever; There is an exact and pleasant Harmony between us and all the Creatures: We are in a Divine and spiritual Manner made as it were Omnipresent with all Objects (for the Soul is present only by an Act of the understanding) and the Temple of all Eternity does it then becom, when the Kingdom of GOD is seated within it, as the world is in the Eye; while it lives, and feels, and sees, and enjoyes, in every object to which it is extended, its own & its objects Perfection.

IF by our voluntary Remisness, or Mistake, or Disorder, we dote upon one Object, or suffer some few things to engage our Souls so intirely, as to forget and neglect all the rest, we rob all those we desert, of their due Esteem, and abridge our selves of that Liberty and Extent, wherein the greatness of our soul consisteth. As if the Sun, that is made to shine upon all the World, should withdraw its Beams from the Stars and the Heavens, and chuse to shine upon nothing else but a Spire of Grasse, a grain of Dust, or a little sand. We lose innumerable Objects, and confine our selves to the Love of one; by sacrificing all our Affection to that, become guilty of *Idolatry* in one respect, of *Atheism* in another. For we elevate that Creature which we love alone, into the place of GOD, and we rob the Creator of that supream affection which is due unto him: And in so doing bereave our selves of the Sovereign Object, in the fruition of which all the rest are happily enjoyed. Thus when a man so Loveth his Wife, or Children, as to despise all mankind, he forfeits his Interest in all Kingdoms, and the Beauty of all Ages is taken from his Eys, his Treasures are contracted, and his Felicity is maimed, and made Defective. When a Covetous man doteth on his Bags of Gold, the Ambitious on Titles of Honor, the Drunkard on his Wine, the Lustful Goat on his Women, the foolish Hector on his Dice and Duels, they banish all other Objects, and live as absurdly, as if a King should relinquish his Crown, and confine his Thoughts and Care to a Country Mannor.

I will not deny, but that there are many Disorders and Evils in the World, many Deformities, Sins, and Miseries: but I say two things; first that in the Estate of innocency, wherein all things proceeded purely from GOD, there was no Sin, nor sickness, nor Death, nor Occasion of Complaint or Calamity. Secondly, that all the Evils that are now in the world, men brought on themselves by the Fall: And there is great need of distinguishing between the works of GOD, and the works of men. For all that GOD did is Lovely and Divine: nothing is bitter and distasteful, but what we have done: himself surveyed the whole Creation, and pronounced concerning every Thing, that it *was exceeding Good*. So that *he* was in all his Works an Object of Complacency. To these we add two Considerations more; That of all the Evils and Mischeifs which men have introduced, there is not one left *uncorrected* in his Kingdome. Secondly, that GOD bringeth Order out of Confusion, Light out of Darkness, Good out of Evil, and by a Providence irresistable, and a Power infinite, so limiteth and divideth all, that even *Evils* themselves become the Matter of his Victory, the Ground of his Triumph: They are all improved; and he makes the Greatest Evils Objects of Joy and Glory.

NOW if all Things before GOD are fit to be enjoyed, all Good Things perfect, all Evil overcome; if without any Change of Place or Scituation, all Things are naked and open before his Eyes, and there be no Walls to exclude, or Skreens to hide, no Gulph to pass, nor Distance to over come, but all things equally neer and fair; there is some Hope, that the same Felicity is prepared for the soul which is made in his Image, and that every thing, being fit for GOD, is full of infinite Depth and Beauty. For which Cause St. *John* being in the Spirit saw all the Kingdomes of the World, become the Kingdomes of the Lord and of his Christ, and heard *every Creature which is in Heaven, and on the Earth, and under the Earth, and such as are in the Sea, and all that is in them, saying Blessing, and Honor, and Glory, and Power, be unto him that Sitteth upon the Throne, and to the Lamb for evermore.* This we are the rather induced to believe, because *the Faithful Servant* is commanded to *enter into the Joy of his Lord,* and our *Masters Joys* are the Rewards of Believers. Our Saviour telleth us his *Lord will make his Wise Servant Ruler over all his Goods,* in one place, *and over all that he hath,* in another.

TO see beyond all Seas, and through all interposing Skreens and Darknesses, is the Gift of the Understanding, and to be able to Love any Object beyond the Skies, any Thing that is Good from the Centre of the Earth to the Highest Heavens, is the Property of the Soul; which it exerciseth here by Parts, and Degrees, but shall at once exert at the Day of Consummation. The Infinity of the Father in the Son, & the Godhead of the Son in the Holy Ghost will entirely be enjoyed.

IT is the Glory of man, that his *Avarice* is insatiable, and his *Ambition* infinite, that his *Appetite* carries him to innumerable Pleasures, and that his Curiosity is so Endless, that were he Monarch of the World, it could not satisfie his Soul, but he would be curiously inquisi-

tive into the original and End of Things, and be concerned in the
Nature of those that are beyond the Heavens. For having met with
an infinite Benefactor, he would not be fit for his Bounty, could any
finite Object satisfie his Desire: and for this Cause is his Reason so
inquisitive, to see whether every thing be Delightful to his Essence;
which, when he findeth agreable to his Wish, and to exceed his Imagination, it is impossible to declare how his Avarice and Ambition will
both rejoyce, how much his Appetite will be satisfied, and his Curiosity
delighted. To sit in the Throne of GOD and to enjoy Communion
with him, in those Things which neither Eye hath seen, nor Ear heard,
nor hath it entered into the Heart of Man to conceive, is no mean
thing: the Advancement is infinitely Greater then we are able to understand. No young man can gaze upon a Beauteous face with greater
Pleasure, no Epicures Sence be ravished with more Delight, than that
which he apprehends in so Glorious a fruition.

THE very sight of other mens Souls, shining in the Acts of their
Understanding throughout all Eternity, and extending themselves in
the Beams of Love through all Immensity, and thereby transformed
(every one of them) into a Sphear of Light comprehending the
Heavens, every Angel and every Spirit being a Temple of GODS Omnipresence and Perfection; this alone will be a ravishing Spectacle
to that Goodness, which delights to see innumerable Possessors of the
Same Kingdome: Much more will the Perfection of the Kingdome
it self, which by infinite Wisdome is so constituted, that every one
is the Sovereign Object, the First born, and Sole heir, and End of
the Kingdome; Every one the Bride of GOD, every one there a King,
yet without Confusion, or Diminution, every one distinctly, enjoying
all, and adding to each others fruition.

TO understand all this, and not to delight in it, is more miserable
then not to understand it. To see it, without being able to enjoy it,
is to pine away in a prison, from whence we see the Glory of a Palace,
and repine in our misery at the Pleasures of those that are about it:
To delight in these Things, without being affected with them; is impossible. Nor is there any Affection but that of Love, whereby we can
enjoy them.

THE Angels see the Glory of GODS Kingdom and delight in it;
the Damned see the Joys of the Blessed, and are tortured by them;
the Wicked upon Earth neither see, nor are affected with them; the
Saints on Earth apprehend them in part, and believe them, desire
and endeavour after them; they wait with Expectation for the whole,

and by certain degrees, as it were in a Glass, enjoy the Image and Reflection of them: As many as they comprehend, they actually delight in: for their love is awakened, and extended to the goodness of all they understand, which it feeds upon by meditation, and turnes into Nourishment, for the Beneffit of their Souls, which are made more Great, and Strong, and Vigorous by their Fruitions. But without Love, it is easie to see, that no Goodness can be at all enjoyed.

GOD does desire Love from us, because his *Wisdom* very well knows, that without Love the World would be in vain, and the End of the Creation frustrated: his *Goodness* is diffusive and infinitly desires to communicate it self, which it cannot do, unless it be Beloved. To receive it, is the highest service we can do unto it, nothing being more agreeable to the Nature of his *Goodness,* then that it should be enjoyed. His *Blessedness* consisteth in the pleasure he taketh in the Felicity of others, and brancheth it self out into two Parts, the Pleasure of Communicating all to others, and the pleasure of receiving all from others, in the satisfaction which he taketh to see others Blessed, in the Returns of those joys and Praises, which are offered up to his Goodness and Glory. His *Glory* desires to be seen, and delighted in: To be esteemed and beloved: to be honored and admired, is natural to *Glory,* the Brightness of whose splendor is more Sensibly Pleasant in the Reflection of its face, and in the Joy that it makes in anothers Soul. His *Holiness* takes Pleasure in pure and upright Actions, of all which Love is the fountain. There is an *Objective fitness* and Excellency in Love, for which it is infinitely valued by him. It is one of the first and immediate Properties of Love to desire to be beloved, to make its object most Amiable and Beautiful, as well as Blessed; to be united to it, to have its own Goodness acknowledged, its Essence approved, its excellency desired, admired and delighted in; to see all its Actions, Appearances, Gifts and Tokens esteemed; and to feel its own Efficacy, in the Grateful Acceptance it finds, in the Raptures it occasions, in the flames it enkindles in anothers Soul. Now Love is the fountain of all Honour, Gratitude, Praise and Esteem: By Love the Soul is transformed into the Similitude of God, by love made Bright and Beautiful, all its Blessedness and Glory are founded in its Love, it is by Love it self made Communicative and Diffusive, and Great, and Rich, and as the Scripture speaketh, *fit for Delights.* All Obedience and service are founded in Love; And if a Creature, that is Beloved, must freely give up it self to anothers Pleasure, before it can shew its Love, or intirely be enjoyed; Love is of all other things in the World most fit to answer

Love, because the very heart and Soul is given thereby to the Person that desires it.

LOVE is the Fountain of all Benefits and Pleasures. House, Estate, and Lands, Authority, Wealth, and Power, Life it self is consecrated and Devoted by a Lover to his Object. So that on our side all is given to GOD by Love, as well as by Love it is received from him. The Heavens and the Earth and all the Creatures are Gifts and Tokens of his Love, Men and Angels are a Present of his Love, which he hath infinitely adorned, and made endlessly serviceable to every Soul that is Beloved. All these his Love would have us to receive with a due Esteem, and therefore is it that of his Love he will have us to exercise our reason aright, and Love them as much as their Goodness deserveth. When we see and understand their Excellence, and Esteem them according to the transcendent value that appeareth in them, we adorn our selves with their fair Ideas, we enlarge and beautifie our Souls with Bright and clear Apprehensions, and which is much more, with regular and well ordered Affections, we enrich our selves, and increase our Greatness (in the fruition of his Gifts), we are lively, and pleasant, and vigorous Creatures, full of Knowledge, and Wisdome, and Goodness, and fit to offer up all these things unto him *again,* while we empty them as Helps and Advantages in that Service which we pay unto him: For our Love to himself is enkindled by these Incentives, and while we sacrifice our selves and them unto him, we delight in nothing more then to see him, that is so Great in Love and Bounty, the Author and Possessor of all his Glories.

CHAP. VIII.

Of the Excellency of Truth, as it is the Object and Cause of Vertue. The Matter and form of Vertuous Actions. That their form is infinitely more Excellent then their Matter, and the Heathen Morality infinitely defective and short of the Christian.

I do not see that *Aristotle* made the End of Vertue any other then a finite and temporal Felicity, which is infinitely short of that felicity which is here begun, and enjoyed for ever. He did not make GOD the Object and End of the Soul, and if all Acts are distinguished into their Kinds by their Objects and their Ends, those Vertues must be infinitely base, that have no other Objects or Ends, but Creatures; and those only Divine and Noble, that flow from an infinite and Eternal Original, respect an infinite and Eternal Object, rest in an Infinite and Eternal End. His Difinition of Felicity importeth all this, but his Behavior makes me to fear he did not understand it: As *Seneca* luckily hit upon that saying, *Deus me solum dedit toti mundo, totum Mundum mihi soli,* GOD gave me alone to all the World, and all the World to me alone; yet could not understand it. For had he Known what it was he said, he would have made a better use of it, and been more copious and explicite in the Illustration. An actual Respect had to infinite Obligations and Rewards, a Desire in every action to please an infinite and eternal Lover, to Glorifie a Divine and Endless Benefactor, to bring forth the fruits of infinite Benefits, and to be truely Grateful for all the Advantages of a mans Creation, that is made to have Dominion over all the World; these are higher and better Qualifications of those Vertuous Actions which Christians perform, than Heathens understood: And yet if nature were divested of its Corruption, the Natural Man, that is, no Christian, might, by the Light of Nature, be fitted to understand them. And the Truth is, I wonder much, (the World being so Beautiful and Glorious in every Eye, so really deep and valuable in Worth, so peculiarly applied to the use and service of every person;) that the Heathens did miss the fruition of it, and fail to measure themselves and their Felicity, by the Greatness of its Beauty, and the Joy which all the Creatures ought to produce in the mind of Man by their real Services. For the Earth is really better than if all its Globe were of beaten Gold, the Seas are better than if all their Abysses were full of Diamonds, the Air is better, than if all the space between us and the Skys were full of Scepters, and the Sun alone a greater Treasure then all the wealthy Mines in the Indies: every man is surrounded with all the Light of their Advantages, and so much served by them, as if no man but himself were alive in the World. So that it is a natural and easie Investigation, even for Heathens themselves, to discern the mystery of Bliss, and to discover the misery of Humane Nature to be founded in some Disease of the Will, or Understanding: And to return from Inadvertency and Sloth, to Truth and Right Reason, which was the ready Way to true Felicity. For they Knew not the *Arcanum* or Hidden mystery of Divine Laws, nor the Excellency and Perfection of immortal Souls, which make every one a Soveraign and Transcendent Creature; yet they might easily observe the miserable Effects of Eternal Solitude, and in external Services, how useful and comfortable men were ordained by Nature to be to one another.

EVERY man Loves to have many Eys fixt on his Beauty, and to have many Delightful Objects and Transactions for his own. Be the Theatre never so Magnificent, the Actions and the Actors are more Delightful to the Spectators than the Gildings, and Dead Engravings. Were all other men removed out of the World to make room for one, the empty Theatre would remain, but the Spectacle be lost, all the Cities, and Kingdoms, and Ages would be removed, with all that was lively, and rare, and Miraculous in all their Occurrences. Palaces, and Temples had been prevented, Houses and Villages, Fields and Vineyards! The World had been a Wilderness overgrown with Thorns, and Wild Beasts, and Serpents: Which now by the Labor of many hands, is reduced to the Beauty and Order of *Eden*. It is by Trades and Occupations that a man gets him Corn, and Wine, and Oyl, &c. all which he would have been without had he never seen any Company but himself; condemned to Idleness and melancholly. Vertues and Praises had been things unknown, Admiration and Honor, Love and Knowledge, the mysteries of Religion and Piety, all the speculations of Wisdom, for want of Education had been lost, at least the Sence and Exercise of these Bright and Glorious Things, for want of Conversation: Corrupted Nature being prone to afford no other fruits but Barbarism and Ignorance in that Solitary Condition. For the Powers of the Soul are improved by Tradition: and it is by the Information of others that our minds are awakened to perceive the Dignity of our own Nature, the Value of all the Creatures, and our Interest unto them.

But Religion teaches us far more, the Beginning and the End of the World, how highly we are honored, and beloved of GOD, the Manner wherein we are to converse with him, the transcendent Excellency of Souls, and the Divine Perfections of the Deity, What his Omnipresence and Eternity is, how we are to be enlarged in our Apprehensions and Desires, and prepared for infinite and Eternal fruitions; in what Quality, and Capacity, we are to live in the world, and Exercise Vertue, how we are to spend our Time, and employ our Powers on all Objects, every one as Lord of the Creation and the friend of GOD! How all Angels and Men are commanded to Love us as themselves, and by that Love to serve and delight us more, than by all other Actions and Offices whatsoever: That every Soul is a more excellent Being than the visible World, more nearly allyed to God, and more precious in it self than any Treasure whatsoever: That it is endued with Powers, Inclinations and Principles so fitly subservient and conducive to Blessedness, that any one of these is more Delightful then all inanimate Things; in the Contemplation and Enjoyment of which we may justly be lost in Wonder and Extasie. All this by the Light of Nature is asserted, but covered with so Gross a vail, that we discern it not, till it is newly revealed by the Ministery of Men. And upon all these Accounts are Men themselves, (which are generally mistaken to be Impediments) Means & Assistances of our Happy living.

BUT however familiar, and near, and easie these Great and evident Truths appear, it so happened, that the Heathen Philosophers were Blind unto them, and in the midst of their Searches after Felicity, failed of the Discovery; they became vain in their Imaginations, placing felicity in a meer Apathy, or conceited 'Αυτάρκεια, a self-sufficiency, or in a brave Contempt of all misfortunes, in a forced Contentment Dark and empty, or in Sensual Pleasures, or in the Goods of fortune, either alone, or conjoyned with those of the Soul and Body, which they lamely enumerated, and knew not how to imploy; as if the Dis-

covery of the highest and best Truths in nature, had been reserved
for him that redeemed Nature, and the Plainest Truths had been appointed to honor and attend that Religion which brought supernatural
Mysteries to Light, by the Preaching of the Gospel.

BY this last the Qualifications of an humble and pious Soul, a Penitent and Grateful Person, sensible (at once) of his infinite Guilt and
Grandure, were introduced: Another foundation laid upon the Meritorious Death and Passion of GOD, the Son of GOD, a Second Love
continued in the Deity to the miserable after an infinite forfeiture;
all the Oracles, and Visions, and Miracles, by which the Nature of
Man is magnified, and Ages enlightned, the Ministry of Angels, and
the Dispensations of Providence, by which the Care and Tenderness
of GOD is shewn, the infinite measures and Violences of his Love,
the infinite Variety and Number of Obligations, the present Advantages
and Benefits, the Eternal Rewards, the Relation of GOD to Man as
a Father and a friend, a Bridegroom and a King, a Light and Example,
the sweetness of our Union and Communion with him, and the Gift
of the Holy Ghost sent down from Heaven; all these Things, which
the Angels desire to look into, were by the Christian Religion (with
the rest before mentioned) plainly revealed, with our victory over
Death, the Resurrection of our Bodies, and Life Eternal.

IN the Light of these Circumstances the Interior form of Vertuous
Acts more evidently appears. For to exercise Vertue in the Quality
and Capacity of a Son of GOD, is another sort of Business, than to
exercise Vertue as an ordinary Mechanick: and to do all things being
clothed with a Sence of our Cœlestial Grandeur, as we are Heirs of
the World, infinitely Beloved of GOD, ordained for his Throne, Delightful in the Eyes of all, Angels and Men, Beloved and honored
by all the Creatures, made Partakers of the Divine Nature, intending
and designing to Please all Spectators in Heaven and Earth (by the
excellency of our Actions). This makes every little Deed as it were
infinite within; while the *Matter* of the Action seemeth nothing; it renders the *Form* Divine and Blessed.

THE best Actions of the prophaner Heathen fell under the notion
of *Dead Works:* By which name the Apostle calleth all wicked Deeds,
to intimate the Privation of all that excellency that ought to be in
Humane Actions. Every Deed and Thought of ours ought to be *Inspired*
with Life from Heaven. The Light of the Understanding, and the
vigor of the Will is the *Soul* that informes it. When it is void of Knowledge, and springs not from that series of GODS infinite Love, that

ought to animate it, nor regardeth those Eternal Joys that are set before us, nor at all considers those Obligations that are laid upon us, it is bereaved of its *Vital* and *Essential* form, it is like a fair Carcase without a Soul, *unsensible* of those Interests and Concerns, that ought chiefly to be valued and promoted. And by this you may see clearly, that the Matter of a Good act falles infinitely short of that Perfection wherewith it ought to be inspired, if this *Soul,* or *Form* be wanting; which tho less visible to the Eye of flesh, is of as much greater Excellence and Importance, as the Soul in nature is above Body.

THUS when a Heathen giveth to the Poor, the matter of the Act is the very self same which a Christian man does: So is an Act of Courage, or Patience, in encountring Death; the subduing of the Appetite, and the Denial of a Lust, a piece of Justice against Interest and friendship, an Act of Prudence, Temperance, or Fidelity: In all these, if we respect the Matter of them, Heathens have acted (in a manner) as high as any Christian, and consequently appear to vulgar Apprehensions as Heroick and Stupendious. But consider the *inside,* the Heathen did it that he might satisfie his Conscience and please the GODS, that he might acquire honor and immortal fame, or please the generous Inclination of his own Soul, which delighted in Honor and Worth, or assert his own Principles, or save his friends, or preserve his Country. And doubtless these are Great and brave considerations, but they are *limited* and *finite:* and Sick of two Defects, (for the most part) that are incurable. They were Sacrifices of Obedience to false Gods, plain Idolatry, and attended with an ignorant Loftiness and Height of Mind, that confided in them: and besides this, they aspired to little more then a Glorious name in following Ages.

WHEREAS the Christian makes all Kind of Graces to meet and concentre in every Action, Wisdom, Goodness, Justice, Courage, Temperance, Prudence, Humility, Penitence, Patience, Meekness, Liberality, Cheerfulness, Gratitude, Joy in the Holy Ghost, Devotion, Piety, Faith, Hope, Charity, all Kind of Holiness; And his Action extends to all the Objects of these Graces, and includes their Causes. He remembers the infinite Obligations that are laid upon him by that Deity, which infinitely Loves him; the Benefit of the Creation, and the Glory of the Divine Image, the Guilt of the fall, and that blot and misery that lyes upon him, the Wonder of his Redemption, and the Love of Christ, his Death and Passion, the Miraculous Pains and Endeavors of GOD in all Ages, to reclaim him, the Giving of the Holy Ghost, and his holy Baptism, the New Covenant which he is in with GOD, the Height and Glory of his Place and station, the Beauty of the World, and his Dominion over all the Living Creatures, the Joy and Amity of all the Angels, the Benefit and Welfare of all his Neighbours, the Joy and Prosperity of future Ages; the Glory of GOD, the Honour of his Church, and the Propagation of Religion, the Salvation of others Souls, and the Eternal State and condition of his own, the Acquisition of a Cœlestial and Eternal Kingdom, and the Delight he taketh in an infinite Sphere of Eternal Joys, the fervent Desire he has to be Grateful to the Almighty; all these by the Light of his Divine and Cœlestial Knowledge enter into the Act, for want of which the other work, that is wrought by an Ignorant Heathen, is in a Manner rightly called *a Work of Darkness*.

I do not speak this, as if I would discourage a Heathen from doing the Best that he is able; or condemn those reasons upon which he proceedeth in his Vertuous Deeds; No, nor as if all this were necessary to the Acceptance of an Action. But to shew how highly Christianity does ennoble the Soul of Man, how far more sublime its Principles are, and how far more perfect it makes his Actions: When they are what they may be: And withal to provoke Christians to a more Intelligent and lofty Practice of Christian Vertues, lest they differ not in their Morals from the better sort of Heathens. All these things are necessary to the perfection of an Action, tho not to its Acceptance; And GODS Omnipresence, and Power, and Wisdom, and Love ought to be considered in all places, among all Persons, upon all occasions; And the Blood of Christ, and the infinite Glory of Eternal Bliss. But that which above all I chiefly intend, is to shew what influence the great Perfection of Felicity hath upon all our Vertues: not only to stir us up to do them, but by entering their Constitution, to inspire them with their Beauty and form for their fuller Lustre, Glory and Perfection: That we may see also, how Great and Transcendent that Life must be, wherein every Act is capable of so much Majesty and Magnificence, if I may so speak, by reason of the variety of its Ends and Causes. And how abominable and absurd they are all that exclude GOD out of their Thoughts and Considerations; Who is alone the Fountain of all the Beauty in every Vertuous Deed, and the proper fulness, Cause and End of all its Perfection!

HOW Ambitious we ought to be of Knowledge, which is the Light wherein we are to adorn and compleat our selves, we may learn and collect from all that is said. It is rightly called *the Key of Knowledge;* it admits us into the spacious Recesses of every Vertue, openeth the

Gate by which we enter into the Paths of Righteousness, that lead to the Temple and Palace of Bliss. Where all the Treasuries of Wisdome are exposed to the Eye of the Soul, tho hidden from the World. How Great and Amiable every Vertue is, how Great and Perfect it may be made, is only discerned by *the Eye of Knowledge;* It is by this alone that men come to discern how full of Reason Religion is, and with what Joy and Security and Sweetness it may be practised.

CHAP. IX.

Wisdom is seated in the Will, it attaineth
the best of all possible Ends by the
best of all possible Means.

KNOWLEDGE, how excellent soever it may be conceived, is without Wisdome like skill without Practice; which whether it be in Musick, or Painting, or in any other Art, as Government, Navigation, Preaching, Judicature, is altogether vain and fruitless, if it be not reduced into Act and Exercise. For Wisdome is that Excellent Habit of Soul by which we chuse the most Excellent End of all those which may be Known, and actually prosecute it, by the best Means that are conducive thereunto.

TO Know the best of all possible Ends and not to embrace it, is the greatest folly in the World. To chuse and embrace it, without Endeavouring after it, is a folly contending with the other for Eminence. To chuse any means less then the best in Order thereunto, is a new piece of folly, even then when we pursue what Wisdom requires. For no less than the best of all possible Means is requisite to the Acquisition of the best of all possible Ends. And by all this we discern, that Wisdome is not a meer Speculation of Excellent Things, but a Practical Habit, by Vertue of which we actually atchieve and compleat our Happiness. For it is impossible for the best of Means (when they are well used) to fail; we may grow remiss, and suspend our Endeavor, which is another Kind of folly, and so be diverted from the best of all possible Means by some strong Temptation, or cease from using them through our own Inconstancy, or yield to some Light and easie Allurement, or be discouraged by some terrible Danger, and thus may abandon the Best of all Ends, but without some such folly it can never be lost.

POSSIBILITIES are innumerable, so that nothing less than infinite Wisdome can find out that which is absolutely the Best. But when the best of all possible Ends is by infinite Wisdome found out, it is an Easie thing for Wisdome to discover that End to the Knowledge of others, to whom it is able to communicate it self by way of Gift and Participation.

WHAT the best of all possible Ends is, only GOD fully comprehendeth. But in General it is such, that it includeth all Kind of Goods in the highest Perfection, infinite varieties and Degrees of Possibility *turned into Act*, all Sweetness and Beauty, Empire, Dominion, and Power, all Riches, Pleasures, and Honors, Victories, and Triumphs, and Possessions, will be in it, and nothing possible or Desirable be wanting to it. GOD alone is the Best of all possible Ends, who includeth all things in himself as their Cause, and End: the Perfection of his Will is his Blessedness and Glory, and his Essence the only Means by which he can attain unto it. By himself it is that we come unto him in a manner afterward more fully to be explained. His Essence is the Best of all possible Means, by which he attains himself, and by which he is enjoyed. Our Conformity to his Essence is our Way, by a Wise Application of our Souls to that Eternal Act which is his End.

THAT Sweetness and Beauty are Attributes of the best of all possible Ends, is evident and clear: As it is also that these must be infinite in their Degree and Measure, because nothing but what is infinitely convenient, is absolutely Eligible. Now what is infinitely convenient is infinitely Sweet and Beautiful. What is infinitely Desirable is infinitely Good, because it is Agreeable to that Love wherewith every Existence intends it self, and pursues its own sublime Happiness.

IT is easie to conceive how GOD should be the End of his Creatures, but how he should really be his own End is difficult to understand: Because his Creatures are Defective, and have something besides themselves to aspire after: but GOD from all Eternity is infinitely perfect, and being all that he can be, needeth nothing that he can endeavor to attain. But if we consider the nature of Wisdome, which is a voluntary Act, we may be freed from the Despair of understanding the Mystery. For Wisdome must of necessity intend it self in its Operations, because it becometh Wisdome by doing the Best of all Excellent Things, and doth them all that it may be Wisdome, or Wise in doing them. It implies Deliberation and Freedome; being a Vertue seated in the Will and Understanding, It implies a Power of Knowing, and Chusing, and Doing all Things, it consisteth not in the Power of Knowing only, nor in Power of Chusing, nor in the Power of Doing. Nothing else is Wisdome, but to chuse and do what we Know is absolutely most

Excellent. Wisdome then is founded in the Act of Doing, nay it is the Act of Doing all that is Excellent. And if it be a free and voluntary Act, as it must needs be, because nothing is Wisdome, but that which guideth it self by Counsel freely, to a Known End, which it discerneth to be most Excellent, it implies an Ability to forbear, in him that is wise, by chusing to do what he might forbear. Had it forborn to do what is most Excellent, it had turned into folly, because it had by that means lost the most Excellent End: but by chusing to do all that was best, it became an act of Wisdome; which being most Lovely, it chiefly desired to be. And so by Chusing and Doing the most Excellent of Things, begot it self; and by it self proceeded to all its Operations, which must needs be infinite, if Wisdome be so, because any thing less would (if rested in) be infinitely Defective.

THAT Riches and Pleasures may be infinite, is evident from the Nature and extent of space, which is illimited and Endless, from the Omnipresence and Eternity of GOD, in which there is infinite Room for innumerable varieties, especially from his Wisdom and Goodness which are *Infinite Treasures.* It appears also from his Almighty Power, which is able in all Parts of his Omnipresence and Eternity, to work without any Bound or Period, without cessation at once to work in all Places of his Dominion, and throughout all his Immensity to act, and do what he will. So that in one Instant he can fill both Eternity and Time with enjoyments, Every Part and Particle of which shall be infinitely Delightful, because of the vigor of his Eternal Power in every Operation. Thus is he intirely Acting in Heaven, and Earth, and Hell, at the same time, and at all conceivable Distances beyond all Heavens ever Acting, because he is Willing, Decreeing, seeing and ruling there, and every where accomplishing his Counsel and Pleasure. His Essence and his Will are both the same, his Essence is his Act, and his Act his Pleasure.

BY exerting his Almighty Power he begot that Act, which is the Means and End of all his Endeavors. An Act of Wisdome infinite and Eternal is his Blessedness and Glory. We must take heed of conceiving GOD to be one Thing, and his Act another, for all his Wisdom and Goodness, all his Blessedness, and Life, and Glory are in the Act, by which he became the Fountain and the End of all Things. He became so freely, and yet was so by his Essence from everlasting, for Eternity is an infinite Length of Duration, altogether present in all its parts in a Stable manner. To fill one part of space with Treasures, and leave another Empty, was not Wise. Common Reason will instruct us, that it is better to have all spaces full of Delights, than some few or none. And by his infinite Wisdome it is that he Knows how to enjoy, what he never needed, and to improve his Enjoyments by giving them away.

INFINITE and Eternal Wisdom does not onely imply the Possibility, but the certain Reality and Existence of Eternal Treasures. Where least you should wonder how such should be infinite, you must needs be informed that God is his own best and most perfect Treasure. For if Treasures are by nature those precious Things, which are Means whereby we acquire our Ends, or those Things which we most Esteem, as the Sovereign Objects of our Joy; GOD is in both those respects his own *Wealth,* because his Essence is the *Means* by which he atchieveth all his ends, and the Sovereign End of all those Means which he by his Wisdom useth for his Ends. *For of him, and by him, and to him are all things:* As the Scripture witnesseth. Matter is the Dreg of Nature, and Dead without Power; Power is the Abyss of Nature, but void without act: Act is the Top and Perfection of Nature, it is the fulness of Power, the fountain and the means of all that is; for Power by transforming it self into Act, becometh an act, and by that Act produceth and perfecteth all its Works both outward and inward; so is it the Means of all its Productions: being so infinitely Simple and various together, that nothing but Power exerting it self is in the Nature of the Act by which it is exerted. All the Essence of that Act is the compleat Exertion of Eternal Power, and yet to it alone we ascribe the Original and Means of all: it is the Cause, and Means and End of it self, as well as of other Things, which for its own sake, are produced by it. For idle Power can do nothing: Meer Power is neither the Cause, nor the Means, nor the End of any thing. Power not Idle, but exerted, and throughly employed, is all Act: And this is the Cause of all its Productions, because of this Power exerting it self they spring: and the Means of all, because by this Power exerting it self, they are; and the End of all, because it did all, that it might be not *Idle,* but Power *Exerting* it self, or a Glorious Act in its full Perfection.

IT was an effect of infinite Wisdom, wherein GOD by one Act acquired himself, and all his Dominion, prepared his own, and his Creatures blessedness, made himself and all his Kingdome Glorious. But this is scarcely intelligible, because the manner of his Life is incomprehensible: we cannot tell how to conceive, what the Learned constantly affirm, that all Eternity is at one Time. All I shall observe in Order to the explaining of this Mystery, is onely this, that tho the World begins and Ends with Time, yet Eternity does immutably include Time, and the Operations of Divine Wisdom are various, and exactly fitted to their several Seasons, yet all the parts of Eternity are filled with Operations, which, tho they are one in GOD, like that of shining in the Sun, are manifold in Effects, as the Beams of the Sun in their different Works among all the Creatures.

IT is a natural Effect of infinite Wisdom to make every of its Treasures suitable to its own excellence. And that the Wisdom of GOD has done, by making every the smallest Thing in his Kingdome infinitely serviceable in its Place, and station, for the manifesting of his Wisdom, Goodness, and Glory to the Eye of a clear Beholder. And this he hath done by making all his Kingdome one Intire Object, and every Thing in it a Part of that Whole, Relating to all the innumerable Parts, receiving a Beauty from all, & communicating a Beauty to all, even to all objects throughout all Eternity. While every one among Millions of Spectators, is endued with an Endless Understanding to see all, and enjoy all in its Relations, Beauties, and Services.

I cannot stand to enlarge on this, otherwise I might illustrate it by a familiar Example. No single Part of a stately Monument is so Beautiful out of its Place, as it is in its Place: because if it be seen alone, it is not understood; for the Beauty that results from all, consists in Order and Symmetry, which by any Division is broken to pieces. He Knoweth nothing as he ought to Know, who thinks he Knoweth any thing, without seeing its Place, and the Manner how it relateth to GOD, Angels and Men, and to all the Creatures in Earth, Heaven, and Hell, Time, and Eternity.

IT is an Act of Wisdome to prize and enjoy, what is by Wisdome prepared, and Because infinite Wisdome includeth all Wisdome, infinite Wisdome at once Knoweth, Chuseth, Doth, Esteemeth, and Enjoyeth, all that is Excellent. It is an Act of Wisdome to make ones self Good and Delightful to others, because Honor, and Peace, and Amity, are founded therein. It is infinite Wisdome to become infinitely Good and Delightful to others, and for that cause to be infinite in Bounty. For what is infinitely Good is infinitely *Glorious*. And therefore is it, that GOD needing Nothing in himself, gives all Things to others, Gives them in enjoying them, enjoys in Giving them, while his Goodness delights in the Felicity of others, and in being the Felicity of others. For by making them Great and Blessed he magnifieth himself; and by replenishing them increaseth his Treasures.

HOW little soever of this you are able to conceive, you may understand, that to be like GOD is the way to be Happy: And that if
GOD hath put it in your Power to be like him, it is the extremest
Madness in the World to abuse your Power, and to neglect his Treasures, but it is infinite Wisdome by the best of all possible Means
to embrace and enjoy them, Because an infinite End is thereby attained,
even GOD himself, who is thereby made the portion of the Soul, and
its Reward forever.

THE best of all possible Means whereby we can acquire his Eternal
Treasures, is to imitate GOD in our Thoughts and Actions; to exert
our Powers after his Similitude, and to attain his Image, which is
after GOD in *Knowledg, Righteousness,* and *true Holiness.* For by
Knowing all Things, as GOD Knoweth them, we transform our Souls
into an Act of Knowledge, most Bright and Glorious: By Loving all
Things as GOD Loveth them, we transform our Wills into an Act
of Love, which is most Sweet and Blessed. We enrich and Beautifie
our selves with the Image of his Goodness, while we communicate
our Souls (in our Powers) to all Objects in his whole Eternity. We
magnifie our selves by magnifying Him in all his Works: We do right
to our selves by doing right to GOD, and all other Things. Which
for as much as we must here on Earth learn by Degrees, and can
never perfectly accomplish the Work, till it is given us in Heaven,
it is Wisdome to walk in the Paths of Righteousness as far as we
are able, and to do those Things here, tho small and defective, which
he will recompence with a Reward so perfect hereafter.

IF ever we be so happy as to come to Heaven, his Wisdome shall
be our Wisdom, his Greatness our Greatness, his Blessedness our Blessedness, his Glory our Glory, All his Joys and Treasures shall be ours,
his Life and Love ours, and Himself ours for evermore.

HIS Wisdome is made ours because it is the Light in which we
shall see Light, and learn thereby to inherit all Things: the Exemplar
and Original of our Wisdome; the Fountain and Patern of all our
Joys, the Author and Inventor of all our Delights, the End and Sum
of all our Desires, the Means of all our Felicity, our very Blessedness
and Glory.

Of Righteousness. How Wisdome, Justice, and Right Reason are shut up in its Nature. What GOD doth, and what we acquire, by the Exercise of this Vertue.

RIGHTEOUSNESS and Wisdome are neer allyed. For to be Just towards all Objects is to render them their spiritual Due, their *Due Esteem*. It is Wisdome, because thereby we attain our End, and enjoy their Excellency. It is Right Reason, because to value all Things just as they are, rendering to them neither more nor less then they deserve, is to do Right to our selves and them, it is a Vertue, because by force thereof we attain our Happiness.

For the better understanding of this Vertue we must Know that there is a Righteousness of Apprehension, a Righteousness of Esteem, a Righteousness of Choise, and a Righteousness of Action. Righteousness of Thought is that Habit by Vertue of which we think aright; forming and framing within our selves aright Apprehensions of all Objects whatsoever. This, tho it be the First and smallest Part of Righteousness, is of Great importance; because no man can use that aright, the Nature of which he does not apprehend. He that mistakes his Hand for his Meat, will rise hungry from Table. He that mistakes a Fiddle for an Axe, will neither cut Wood well, nor make good Musick. The Misapprehension of Great and Transcendent Objects, whether visible or Spiritual, is not perhaps so Gross, but more pernicious and Destructive. He that apprehends GOD to be a Tyrant, can neither honour GOD, nor Love him, nor enjoy him. He that takes Vertues to be vices, and apprehends all the Actions of Religion unpleasant will loath and avoid them. He, that conceits Nothing in the World to be his own but his low Cottage and course diet, will think it needless to praise his Maker, and will deny himself to be happy in those narrow and Mean enjoyments. He that thinks all the wealth is shut up in a Trunk of Gold, will little regard the Magnificence of the Heavens, the Light of the Sun, or the Beauty of the Universe.

RIGHTEOUSNESS in esteem is that Habit, by Vertue of which we value all things according as their Worth and Merit requires. It presupposes a right Apprehension of their Goodness, a clear Knowledge of all their excellencies. It is a Virtue by which we give to every thing that place in our Soul which they hold in Nature. It is wonderful both for its extent, and Value. For there is Room enough for all Objects in the esteem of the Soul, and it is by esteem that they are honored, perfected and enjoyed.

A wise man will actually Extend his Thoughts to all Objects in Heaven and Earth, for fear of losing the Pleasure they afford him, which must necessarily spring from his esteem of their excellency.

HONOUR and Esteem are neer akin. How the Creatures are honoured by esteem, needeth not to be unfolded: but how they are perfected by it, is a little Misterious. A thing is then perfected when it attains its End. Now the End for which all things were made is that they may be seen and enjoyed. They are seen that they may be esteemed, and by an intelligent and right esteem are all enjoyed. In our esteem therefore they find and attain their end, and by attaining that are consequently perfected. The Application of *Actives* to *Passives* is a mystery in Nature of very great and General Importance; In all Pleasures, Cures, and Productions. All satisfactions, Joys, and Praises are the happy off-spring of Powers and Objects well united. Both the one and the other would lie void and barren if they never met together: and when they meet their Union must be regular, wise and holy.

GOD is an Object of Mans Esteem: Which unless it were able to render him his Due and Quadrat with his Excellencies, a man could never be *Righteous* towards GOD. For that Esteem is void of Righteousness, that either exceeds, or falles short of its Object. If it becometh us *to fulfil all Righteousness,* it becometh GOD, to endue us with the Power of Esteeming all, that is Good and Excellent, according to the Worth and Value thereof. For which cause he enables us to Esteem all that we can see in Heaven and Earth, and in the Heaven of Heavens. For this Esteem is the Foundation of that choise which is the Original Spring of all excellent Actions. Even GOD himself meeteth his Honour in the esteem of our Souls. He is injured by the Sacrilegious Impiety that robs him of his Esteem; being infinitely Quick and Tender in apprehending, he is more jealous of his Honour, and more grieved when he loseth it then any other. His Wisdom and his

Love are infinitly offended, when they are slighted and profaned; but pleased extreamly when they are sanctified and honored: and that they are by a just Esteem. And for this cause he hath made us able to attend him in all his Works, and in all his ways, and to have Communion with him in all his Counsels and Perfections that as our Saviour saith,* *The Father loveth the Son, and hath given all things into his hand,* And again,† *The Father loveth the Son, and sheweth him all things that himself doth:* so we might become the Sons of GOD and see his Love and to delight in all that he hath done for us. For which cause he afterwards saith,‡ *Henceforth I call you not Servants, for the Servant Knoweth not what his Lord doth. But I have called you friends, for all Things that I have heard of my Father, I have made Known unto you.*

THE Omnipresence and Eternity of GOD are so far from filling the Soul, that they fit it only to be filled with infinite Objects. For by the Indwelling of GOD all Objects are infused, and contained within. The Spiritual Room of the Mind is Transcendent to Time and Place, because all Time and Place are contained therein: There is a Room in the Knowledge for all Intelligible Objects: A Room in our Esteem for all that is worthy of our Care and Desire. I confess this Room is strange and Mysterious. It is the Greatest Miracle perhaps in Nature. For it is an infinite Sphere in a Point, an Immensity in a Centre, an Eternity in a Moment. We feel it, tho we cannot understand it.

WHATEVER we close our Eye against, we exclude out of our Knowledge. Whatsoever we Hate, we reject, tho we Know it. We give a Place in our Heart only to that, which we receive and embrace with a Kind Affection.

ETERNITY it self is an Object of Esteem, and so it is the infinity of Almighty GOD: there are infinite Causes for which they ought to be Esteemed. Our Esteem of these cannot be abridged, for upon the least substraction of the smallest Part, Infinity is lost, and so is Eternity. We must be able to esteem the utmost Extent of every Perfection of GOD, or our *Righteousness* in relation to that will be infinitely Defective. The Proportion, between our Esteem and its Object, is that wherein Righteousness is seated, if our Esteem be finite, it is utterly destroyed: for where the Object is infinite, instead of Proportion, there is infinite Disproportion.

FROM Righteousness in Esteem we proceed to Righteousness in Choice. We weigh and consider what is fittest to be valued, and what

* Joh. 3.35.　　† Joh. 5.20.　　‡ Joh. 15.15.

we find of greatest Esteem, we most desire. To prefer the Better above the worse is a righteous Choise; but to prefer the Worse, is abominable Impiety. The Election of GOD may be more strictly, or Generally conceived. His Election of perticular persons from the Rebellious Mass of Mankind to be employed, as Ministers, in restoring the residue, is a matter of Grace; which as Arbitrary and free, is occasioned by the Accident of their General Rebellion, and his Mercy thereupon. Howbeit it is Righteous: for he does Right to himself, and to all his Creatures, and Perfections therein. For thereby notwithstanding the universal Apostasie of the World, he upholdeth and continueth his Righteous Kingdome. But the *Primitive Election* (by which, when he had considered the nature of all Possible Things, he chose the fittest and the Best) was wholy Natural. For according to the Merit of all Objects he chose them, which Merit nevertheless was to be infused by himself, in their first Creation. Whether a star were a Thing fit to be made, whether the Sun should be limited, whether his Image should be infinite, whether naked Spirits, or Bodies should be created, or Bodies and Spirits personally united: Whether Men should at first Instant be placed in Glory, or in an Estate of Trial, whether when they fell into Sin they should be redeemed or no, what Laws were most fitting under the Covenant of Works, what conditions were most proper for the Covenant of Grace; What Helps and Assistances Men should have, what Impediments and Obstacles; all these and many Millions of Objects more passed his Examination, in order to the Perfection of his Kingdome: as it did also whether he should *Create* a Kingdome or no? and look what surpassed in Esteem, as best and most Eligible, that he chose to create, and Perform. To fail in a Tittle had been an infinite fault, because had he in any one perticular preferred the Worse above the better he had contracted a Blot upon his own Wisdome and Goodness, and made the whole Creation deformed. For there is such a Love to Righteousness implanted in our Natures, that should GOD be unjust to a poor Indian beyond the Seas, we should be grieved at the Blemish, and any Blemish in him would blast our Felicity. For the Justice of the Soul is an impartial Thing, and its Severity Greatest, where its Expectation is the Highest. It is more easie with GOD to be infinitely Wise then with Man to be any thing; He may be Exact and perfect in every action with Greater Ease, then any other of his Creatures can, because he is Almighty, Omniscient, and Omnipresent: all the Advantages of his Wisdom, and Knowledge, and Goodness, and Power, would be Aggravations of his fault should he Sin against himself. The least offence would be an infinite Blot in him because committed against all Wisdom, Goodness, and Power, and a misery to us, because it would tend to the Ruine of his Creatures: The Accurate Perfection which he acquires in all his Ways, (having to do with so many millions of Objects) becomes our infinite Joy, our Amazement and Wonder, a Transcendent Cause of Complacency and Adoration, it fills Eternity with Delights and Praises. The possibility of doing otherwise, in him that is Subject to no Laws awakens our Concernment: But the prevention of our fear, by the establishment of our Security, supplies our contentment; he is an Absolute and free Agent, and therefore we may fear a miscarriage in his Choise: but as from all Eternity he hath determined himself, and is by his Essence an Eternal Act of Wisdom and Righteousness, he secures our Felicity and makes it more Great, because he is not imposed on by another, but freely of himself, delights in the most Excellent things.

THIS relateth to the Righteousness of action, whereby GOD did execute all his Decrees, and *does* Eternally. For Nothing is past, but all things in him are immediately neer and present for ever. If you desire further Information, concerning the Nature of Righteous Actions, Those Actions are properly called Righteous, that are adequately fitted to their ends and Causes. And in this respect there is in every being under several Circumstances a several Righteousness.

THE Effect of Righteousness with men is Peace and Assurance for ever: because Righteous men are Agreable to GOD and all his Creatures: rightly answer all their Natures, and assist in the Harmony of the whole Creation. It is Fruition and Blessedness, because all the perfection and Goodness of GOD is, with his Kingdome, received into the Soul, by the Righteous esteem of all Objects. It is the Beauty and Glory of the Inward Man, because a voluntary Agent, that does incline himself to such excellent Actions, is highly Amiable and Delightful to be seen; Not only because his soul is transformed into an *Intelligible World*, transcendent to all that is created, by the *Ideas* of GOD, and his Works erected in the mind, but his *Affections* are framed in a living and incomparable Order, according as every Cause and Object requires. There is something in the Soul of a Righteous man, that fitly answers all Obligations and Rewards, It is transformed into the Image of GOD in such a sort, that in the *Righteous Act,* which it becomes, GOD for ever dwelleth and appeareth.

THE Effect of Righteousness in GOD is so Great, that whereas all Impossibles are stark naught, all things which it is possible for

GOD to do, are fair and excellent, all the Best are made actual, by the execution of his Righteous Decree. By this the Son of GOD is in the bosom of the Father, and the Spirit of GOD proceedeth throughout all Eternities to his own perfection. For the Righteousness of GOD is not like the Righteousness of Men, that may be permitted to sleep, and intermit their Operations, an Accidental Habit, distinct from their Essence, which may sometimes exist, when it doth not work; but it is Quick and Powerful, and ever in action and is indeed the Act it self which is his eternal Essence and his Son begotten of it self for ever. *For Wisdom* is more moving then any motion, she passeth and goeth through all things by reason of her Pureness, It is the Breath of the Power of GOD, and a pure Influence flowing from the Glory of the Almighty, the Brightness of the Everlasting Light, the unspotted Mirror of the Power of GOD, and the Image of his Goodness. Being One it can do all things, and remaining in it self, maketh all things new, and in all Ages entering into holy Souls, she maketh them Friends of GOD, and Prophets.* GODS Righteousness is the end and effect of it self. His Essence is an infinite and Eternal Act of Righteousness and Wisdome, which filleth his Kingdom with the Majesty of its Glory, and by coming into Being in a voluntary Manner giveth to all Things their Essence, and Perfection. Because it cometh into Being in a voluntary manner it is mysterious and incomprehensible.

THE Glory of this Act is derived from himself, and springeth purely from the Perfection of its pleasure. Of its Pleasure it is what it is, and as the Son of GOD is LIGHT of LIGHT, so he is Wisdome of Wisdome, Righteousness of Righteousness, Life of Life, and Goodness of Goodness. For it is infinite Wisdome that found out the Perfection of this Act, and Eternal Righteousness that first atcheived it. The Righteousness atcheived could not spring from any but Eternal Righteousness in it self atcheiving it, which is unbegotten in the Person of the Father, Begotten in the Person of the Son, and Proceeding in the Person of the Holy Ghost to all its Creatures and Operations, in its Actions, existing and abiding Perfect for ever.

IN GOD, to *Act* and to *Be*, are the same Thing. Upon the suspension of his act, his Essence would be gone; whereas our Essence may without its Act, or Operation, remain. And if his Act existeth, by Acting, his Righteousness is, and existeth of it self, and by it self compleateth its Essence forever. It is not the Power of being Righteous, but the Exertion of that Power, which is the Parent of Eternal Righteousness.

* *Wis.* 7.

GOD, having such an infinite Delight in the Righteous Act, which *himself,* is, designed to make *us* such Righteous Acts as *himself* is. And when we perfectly do what we ought, we shall in Operation and Extent be like unto him, being *perfect, as our Father which is in Heaven is perfect,* for *we shall see as we are seen, and Know as we are Known.* In the mean time GOD hath taken care to endue us with Power, to make our perticular Actions compleatly Righteous. Every little Act we perform is a fruit & Off-spring of the whole Creation, infinite Love is delighted by it, infinite Glory and Blessedness acquired. A Creature of infinite Value is preserved, the Crown is put upon all GODS Works, and all the Spectators, Angels and Men, are Eternally pleased. For being done it is admitted into Eternity, and shall remain in its Place, and be visible forever. *For the Lord* will Come, who both will bring to Light the hidden Things of Darkness, and will make manifest the Counsels of the Hearts: And then shall every man have Praise of GOD.* All that was done shall be remembred forever, and be praised and admired by the Holy Angels, Esteemed by all Saints, and Crowned with Acceptance by GOD Almighty. Which will turn to the Joy of the Righteous, because of the innate Goodness of their Souls, which moveth them to delight in nothing more then in becoming (in all their Righteous Actions) Objects of Complacency to GOD and his Creatures.

* 1 Cor. 4.5.

Of Goodness Natural, Moral and Divine; its Nature described, The Benefits and Works of Goodness.

GOODNESS is a vertue of the first Estate, a Divine Perfection in GOD by which he is, and enjoys his Blessedness. In Men it is an Habit or an Act of the Soul, by force of which they Love, and delight in all that is Blessed. Tis that by which all Creatures Communicate themselves to others Benefit, all Living Creatures affect others, and delight in doing Good unto them. In GOD it is that infinite and Eternal Act from which all other Goodnesses spring, and on which they depend. The Nature of Goodness is founded in a *Convenience,* between that which is Good, and that to which it is profitable. If we consult its several Kinds, there is a *Natural* Goodness, a *Moral,* and a *Divine.*

NATURAL Goodness is the Aptitude of Corporeal Beings, to produce such profitable and healing Effects as the enjoyer desires. The Nutritive Power in Aliment, the Medicinal Vertue in Herbs, the Pleasing Quality in Perfumes, the Grateful Lustre in Precious Stones, the Comfortable Heat in fire, the Beautiful splendor in the Sun, the Refreshing Moisture in the Sea, the Reviving Nature of the Air, the solid Convenience and fertility of the Ground, all these are *Physically* Good. But this is Goodness in the meanest Degree, being no more then the natural fitness of Dead Agents that are made to act by a *Fatal* Necessity, without sence or Desire; tho their Action be answerable to the several Exigencies of other Creatures.

MORAL Goodness includeth all the Perfections of the former, and something more. For *Life* and *Liberty* enter its Existence; and it is *Wisely* exercised in *Love* and *Vertue.* A clear Understanding and a free will are the principles of those Actions that are *Morally* Good: they must flow from *Ingenuity* and *Desire;* tho the Person doing them be subject to anothers Empire, and made to give Account of his Actions. The Nature of its Excellence is very deep and retired, because it consists more in the *Principal* and *Manner* of its Operation, than the *Thing* that is *Done;* and is measured more by the *Intention,* then the *Benefit.* A mad man, or a fool, may by accident save a mans

78

Life, or preserve an Empire, yet be far from that Goodness which is seated in the Will and Understanding. Which plainly shews, that the *Goodness* chiefly regarded is in the *Soul* of him that does any thing convenient, not in the *Benefit* received, but in the *Mind* of the Benefactor. And the Truth is that the *External Benefit,* tho it saves the Lives, and Souls, and Estates, and Liberties, and Riches, and Pleasures, and Honors, of all mankind, acts but *Physically* by a Dead or passive Application, the root of its influence and value is seated in another place, in the Soul of him whose Goodness was so Great as to sacrifice his Honor, and Felicity for the Preservation and Welfare of those whom he *intended* to save. It is seated in the *Counsel* and *Design* of the Actor. It is a hard matter to define it, but it is something like *a willing Conformity to the Interests and Affections of his fellow Creatures,* attended with a voluntary Convenience in a person Obliged and subject to Laws, to all those Obligations that are laid upon him, & to all the Rewards that are set before him, but especially to the Desires and Commands of his Superior, to whom he Naturally owes himself and desires to be pleasing. To Act upon Great and Mighty Principles, in a vigorous free and Generous Manner, for the sake of those that obliged him, and for the sake of those to whom his Kindness is shewn, increases the *Measure* of Moral Goodness: but its Perfection is seated in a Loyal Respect, and Perfect Gratitude to GOD Almighty. Who, by being infinitely Good to us, has infused and created such a Goodness in the Soul, that its principal Joy and Delight is to please him. For tho all Creatures consult themselves & their own Preservation, yet the force of Gratitude upon an Ingenuous Soul is very powerful. Moral Goodness is an Alacrity and Readiness of the Will, to sacrifice it self, upon consideration of the Benefits a Man hath received, to anothers Benefit, Enjoyment, Comfort, Satisfaction.

DIVINE Goodness is an Active and Eternal Principle, stirring up it self without Obligation or reward, to do the best and most excellent Things in an Eternal manner. It is proper only to GOD; Its Excellency is Supreme, its Beauty infinite, its Measure endless, its Nature ineffable, its Perfection unconceiveable. It hath no Cause, but it is the Cause of all other Things whatsoever. It is a *Living* and *Eternal Act* of free and undeserved Love, an indeficient Ocean of Bounty, which can never be fathomed, or (by finite Degrees be) wholy received. It is *Invisible* in its Essence, but *Apparent* in its effects; Incomprehensible, but manifest enough, to be *believed* and *adored*. It is an infinite and Eternal Essence, which is Good to it self, by being Good to all, infinitely Good to it self, by being without Bound or Measure Good to all its Objects. It is an infinite and Eternal Act, which continually ponders, and intirely intends the Welfare of others, and establishes its own (in a voluntary manner) by that intention: An Act whose Essence is seated in the Preparation of all Delights and the Communication of all its Glories. Its Felicity is Eternal and Infinite, yet seated intirely in the Felicity of others. It doth infinite Good, to all its Recipients Meerly for the sake of the Excellency of the Act of *Doing Good*. It delighteth in the Excellency of that Act, and useth all its power in doing Good, that the Act in which it delighteth might be infinitely perfect. And the perfect Act in which it finally resteth is the Goodness which all adore and desire. Its Sovereign Joy and Pleasure, is to be delightful to others. All its Creatures are Delightful to it self, only as they imitate, and receive its Goodness. Should we run into its Properties, they are innumerable and Endless; but as infinite in Beauty, as variety and greatness. It is the utmost Height of all Goodness as well as the Original, and end of all. It exceedeth Moral Goodness, as much as that exceedeth Natural, and infinitely more. In Physical Goodness there is a Mechanical fitness, and Dead convenience: but all it can pretend to, is the Benefit and Pleasure of Moral Agents. For the Sun, and Moon, and Stars, and Trees, and Seas, and Minerals are made for Men. Whereas Moral Goodness is made to enjoy all Physical Goodness, that in a higher sphere it might be pleasing to GOD and is immediately subservient to his Divine & Essential Goodness.

THIS *Divine* Goodness is the first Perfection of the efficient Cause of the Worlds Creation, which of necessity derives an immediate Excellency into all the Creatures, because it is the most Communicative and active Principle that is. But the Necessity is attended with a Liberty no less then infinite. For it freely pleaseth it self in all its operations, and its Pleasure is to delight it self in the Acquisition of Felicity for others. Its freedom is a necessary Circumstance of its operation. For the Glory of its inclination and Kindness could not be, much less be seen, did it act by Necessity of Nature, Imposition, Chance or Accident. When the Act is in Being it worketh Physically, and it is no Wonder that such an Act should produce such Effects, and be so Beneficial. For when it is done it cannot be otherwise, but that such and such Effects must follow its Existence; They are as Natural as if they were Essential to it: All the Wonder is, what should determine the Liberty of the Agent at first to do such Great and Mighty Things for others sake, and all that can be said, is his own Goodness and the Excellency of the Action. For it is not with GOD as it is with Men: few men will be at the expence of Doing, what all admire: all that receive the Benefit, applaud and delight in the Action; and so much the more by how much the more *Hazzardous,* and great, and Painful it was; but scarcely one will endure the Difficulty of an Heroick Deed for the sake of others. GOD on the contrary takes infinite Delight in the Action which all admire, and because it is infinitly great and Heroick, and perfectly Divine, finds his Liberty and Ease in that Act, and is so taken with the Beauty of the Work, that his infinite Pleasure exceeds all the necessity and fate in Nature.

THAT Pleasure, which he taketh in promoting the Happiness of all Existences created and increated, is his Goodness. It is the infinite use of Perfect Liberty freely Delighted in: as Pleasant to himself as to all Intelligent Spectators and all Enjoyers. It is easie to discern that this goodness is the Foundation and Essence of his Happiness and glory.

BY it he becomes Delightful to himself, by it he becomes Delightful to others. By it he communicates all his Powers and Perfections with pleasure, and receives the Services of all the Creatures with high Satisfaction. By it he is concerned in the Joy of others, and enjoys their Blessedness. By it he is capable of all their Affections, and of the Services which his Laws require. By it all Angels and Cherubims are moved to admire and adore his Glory. By it all Creatures visible and invisible are made his Treasures. By it he is multiplied and magnified in every Soul, as the same Object is in several Mirrors, being intirely represented in every living Temple of his Eternal essence. By it he becometh his own end, and the Glorious Author, and the King of Heaven. By it he liveth a Divine and a Blessed Life, and by it he is what he is for ever. By it all the Graces, Exaltations, and Vertues of all his Creatures are made his Joys and their Persons and Praisers are Delightful to him. Of all his Laws and Decrees, and Counsels his Goodness is the fountain. It is the Original and final Cause of all our Thanksgivings. Our ease, and repose, and Satisfaction, our Bliss and enjoyment are founded in it, and caused by it. For its own Pleasure all our Delights are made exquisite in their place, and the most of them Eternal. For its own Glory it maketh all its Creatures Glorious, and prizeth its own Glory, because it is the Sovereign Delight of all its Creatures. It is every way compleat and perfect, as infinitely Convenient, as it is Great in Bounty, as Good to it self as to all others. There is no End of all its Perfection, and for that Cause it is *Incomprehensible.*

TO be made Partaker of the Divine Nature, without having the Goodness of Almighty GOD is impossible. Nor can we enjoy his Goodness, or bear the similitude of his Glory, unless we are good in like Manner. We enjoy the Goodness of GOD, and may be said to have it, either when we have its *Similitude* in our selves, or the *Pleasure* of it in others. Since the Goodness of GOD is the great Object of our Joy, its Enlargment is our Interest; and the more there are to whom he is Good, and the more he communicates his Felicity to every one the Greater Pleasures he prepares for us, and the more is our goodness therein delighted. To see innumerable Millions in Communion with him, and all of them made Glorious and Blessed, and every one seated in his throne, is the greatest Elevation of our Souls, and the highest Satisfaction in the World. When our Goodness meeteth his in all Places, and congratulates the Felicity of every person, we may then use the Words of our Saviour, because we are endued with the same *Mind* and Affection: And as he accepts all the Good that is done to his Members as done to himself, saying *Inasmuch as ye have done it to the least of these my Brethren, ye have done it to me:* Our Souls will reply, *Inasmuch as thou hast done all this to the least of these my Brethren, thou hast done it to me,* for loving our Neighbours as our selves, all Angels and Men will be our fellow Members, our Brethren, our other selves! As we delight in all Acts of Goodness for their own sakes, that are done to us, so shall we delight in all the Bounties of GOD for theirs, who are the partakers of them, and in GOD for this very reason, *Because he is good to all.* We shall be as Happy in others, as in our selves; and Esteem the Goodness of GOD our Felicity, because it hath prevented our Goodness, and done all for them, which were it undone, we should desire to do our selves; because our Goodness is a principle that carries us to delight in their perfect Felicity. Which that we may do the more Sweetly, and with more full Satisfaction and perfect Reason, his Goodness to all others is but the Perfection of Goodness to us, for they are all made Blessed for our fuller and greater Felicity.

HAD GOD withheld, or withdrawn his Goodness from all others, it had not been Greater to us, but less. The Stars are no hindrance to our Enjoyment of the Skie, but the Light and Beauty of the place which we contemplate. Were they all annihilated, the Heavens would be obscure. They do us many Services, of which we should be bereaved, by their Absence and Destruction. GOD by giving Beams and influences to them, made our Treasures more rich and fair, which are increased and multiplied by their Beauty and Number. Did the Sun shine upon us, and upon Nothing else, it would be less beneficial to us, than now it is. Its Beams that are scattered, seem to be lost; yet were they contracted upon one, his Body would be consumed, and all the rest of the World be dark about him; those Rays which fly from the Sun to the utmost parts of the World, illuminate all Objects, and from them more conveniently return to the Eye with their Beauty and Glory, which by those Rayes that are dispersed become visible and Profitable. They fall not all upon every single man, but work for him in other places, begetting Herbs, and Fruits, and Flowers, and Minerals, and Springs, and Trees, and Jewels, with all that is rich and delectable in the World for his fruition. It serves Beasts, and Fowles, and Fishes, for my sake, and for my sake does it serve even Men and Angels: That they, being more Divine and Glorious Creatures, might adorn Heaven and Earth with their Persons, which without them would be void and Empty. For we all desire to be seen, and Known, and Beloved, and for that Cause, without Living Agents, should be very Desolate and discontented.

THUS you see, if GOD had given all Eternity and Immensity to a man, if he had made no other Creatures but him alone, his Bounty had been defective: Whereas by the Creation of these he hath filled Eternity and Immensity with Treasures. All which he hath made ours by commanding them to Love us as themselves; fit to be enjoyed, and beloved by us, by filling them with his Goodness, and making them in his Image. For every one of them is to Love all his Creatures as he does, and to delight in the Beauty and Felicity of all, and to be the joy and Delight of all, as he is: And the Greater, and the Richer, and the fairer they are, the more Great and Happy are we, because they are made our Lovers and Friends, our Brides and Brethren, our Sons and Daughters, our Fathers, and our Servants, which the more Honourable and Excellent they are, the more Delightful: the more Glorious and Blessed these are, their Love is the more precious and Acceptable. True Goodness removes all Envy and Contention out of the World, and introduces nothing but Peace, and Bounty, and Joy, unspeakeable and full of Glory.

WE Love nothing more then to be Delightful to others, and to have our Glory seen is a natural Desire, which our Saviour has countenanced by his own Petition. It is our Interests, that the Eys should be innumerable, that see and admire the Glory which we had with the Father in some Sense before the World was; that they should see (I mean) how much we are Beloved of GOD from all Eternity; that there should be Millions of Blessed Persons to whom we may communicate our selves, concerns our Glory, as it doth also that they should be Great and Perfect, that are made to Admire and Delight in us. If we enter *Into his Eternal Glory,* as the Scripture saith, and our Bliss be individually one with his, or so perfectly like his, as is promised, it is no fault to desire Glory, for it is *Goodness* it self that desires Glory and Esteemeth all those its Best and Sovereign Treasures, that are capable of Loving and Delighting in it.

THERE is in the Goodness of GOD, and Men, and Angels, a Living Power, that is exquisitely tender in Sence and feeling, which as it feels and apprehends it self, doth also feel its Object, and apprehend both its own, and its Objects Excellences. By Vertue of which *Living Power,* it is able to delight in its own Goodness, and its Objects Glory. The Apple of its Eye is not more tenderly regarded, than the Person which it Loveth. It is afflicted in all our Afflictions, and crowned and delighted in all our Prosperities. It tendeth by its nature to the Benefit of others, and cannot endure the least Damage or Detriment to any. It infinitely hates the least Defect in it self, or in its Creatures. Nothing can be Evil to it, but what is Evil to another. Its Interests, and its Objects are so united, that it intirely lives, and sees, and feels, and enjoys, in others. All its inclination is to be doing Good, and it has no other Element than the Felicity of its Creatures. In friendship it appeareth, and from Love it proceedeth, it endeth in felicity. It hath many Great and Glorious Designes, all contending with each other for Supremacy. It cloths it self with Glory, and adornes its Essence with all Kind of Beauties. It endures all Afflictions and Hazzards, It undertakes all Labors, It builds a Palace, and provides a Kingdome for its Beloved. And yet when all is done nothing can exceed the Delight which it taketh in the Person of its Beloved. All the Honour, and Esteem, and Glory it desires, it findeth there, the Use and Value of all its Treasures consists in the Benefit they do to its Beloved. Infinite Goodness can be seated no where but in Love alone, for that onely is capable of infinite Benevolence and Complacency.

THE Liberal Soul deviseth Liberal Things, and by Liberal Things shall he stand. The more Good it doth, the more Good it is, and the more Good, the more Great and Honourable, the more perfect and Happy. There can be no Excess in Goodness; because the more Delightful it is to its Object, and the more Divine and Glorious its Object is, the more abundant Pleasure it taketh in communicating all Felicities to its Object, & the more Great and manifold its Treasures are, the more Sweet and Precious the Things are which it giveth away, and the more its Beloved delighteth in them; by so much the more Admirable and Divine it is, its Goodness and its Blessedness are both the Greater. There is no Inconvenience which it can possibly meet, but a stop or Impediment. It cannot be hurt by it self, because its Essence is always overflowing, and the only Evil it can fear from others is the unkindness of its Object, or the Wrong that it may receive from free Agents. For Angels and Men being made free, that they may Love, and Honour, and Praise in a voluntary manner, and be, and become Good of their own Accord, (because they cannot be made *Morally* or *Divinely* Good, without the Liberty of their Concurrence, and their own Consent) there is some fear, that they may abuse their Power, because for the more Illustrious use of it, they are left in the Hand of their own Counsel. Howbeit he has endeavoured as much as is possible, without prejudicing their Excellence, to secure their Duty; he hath infused into them the greatest Inclinations to goodness imaginable, and the Greatest principles of Honour, he hath shewn them the Glory and felicity of Goodness by his one Example, he hath commanded them by the Severest Laws that are possible, to be Good, he hath founded their Peace and Pleasure in Goodness, he hath made the suspension of Goodness uncouth and unnatural, all evil Actions Dark and disagreeable, he has laid infinite Obligations upon them to excerise Goodness, and set Eternal Rewards before them. He hath made the Object unto which they must shew it extremly amiable, he hath given them all Advantages, Helps and Assistances. He hath prepared the Severest Penalties and Torments to punish the Ommission of it. And for a Complement of all, will extremely be grieved, if they fail to shew it. This in the Estate of Innocency. Since the fall indeed we must be kind and Good to injurious Persons: but this is founded in his own Goodness toward us Sinners, and tho it be a difficult Work in the first Appearance, Carries us to higher and more Perfect Glory.

THAT such a Goodness as this should be, cannot be incredible to them that are acquainted with the Nature of the Universe: tho it seemeth hard at least, if not impossible to them that converse with peevish men. Being corrupt in their Understandings, they are narrow and base and servile in their Affections. They start at a shadow, and boggle at a feather. Sin hath transformed them into slaves and Cowards. They misapprehend the Nature of their Duty like *Fools;* that were made to be great and Mighty as *Kings.* They think they shall be undone, if they become too Great and Good: they fear they shall grow weak and Contemptible by Goodness: whereas nothing makes them so Amiable and Glorious as Excess of Goodness.

TO shew that there is such a Goodness as that, which infinitely delights in powring out its Glory upon all Creatures, the Sun was made: Which continues Night and Day powring out its Streams of Light and Heat upon all Ages, yet is as Glorious this day as it was the first Moment of its Creation. To shew this the Stars were made, that shine in their Watches and Glitter in their Motions only to serve us. The Moon was made to shew this Goodness, which runs her race for ever to serve us. The Earth was made to support us, Springs and Rivers expend their Streams to revive us. Fruits, and Flowers, and Herbs, and Trees delight us. All corruptible Things wast and consume away, that they may sacrifice their Essence to our Benefit. For if they were made Stiffe and unalterable they could not feed us, nor communicate their Essence and Perfection to us. The Emanations and Effusions of Minerals are unknown, but that of Spicies and Odours is well understood. And if these by Disbursing their proper sweetness, become more sweet and enlarge themselves, if they are made Bright and fair for our sake, if they enjoy any Light and Pleasure in their Service, as the Sun and Stars do, as Herbs and Flowers do, as Beasts, and Birds, and Fishes do; the Goodness of the Creator is abundantly more clear and apparent herein, for in all those Creatures that perfect themselves by the Service which they do, the Service it self is a sufficient Recompence: while those upon which we feed, being more Corruptible, are exalted in their Beings, by being turned into ours. And the Trade of Bees, in the Hony they make for us, and the Warmth of sheep, in the fleeces they bear for us, the Comfort of Birds in the feathers they wear, and the Nests they build for us, and the pleasures of Beasts in the off-spring they beget and bring up for us, these things shew that *GOD is Good to all, and that his mercy is over all his Works.* And if any perish in our Service, the Bloody Characters of his Love and Goodness are the more Stupendious. All Nature is sacrificed to our Welfare, and all that we have *By pure Nature* to do (till Sin marres all) is to admire and enjoy that Goodness, to the Delight of which we sacrifice our selves in our own Complacency.* And in real truth, if it be a great Wonder that any Goodness should be thus infinite, the Goodness of all other Things without that Goodness, is a far Greater. If it be Wonderful, admire and adore it.

* *Note, All this is spoken for Encouragement and Imitation.*

CHAP. XII.

Of Holiness: Its Nature, Violence, and Pleasure.
Its Beauty consisteth in the infinite Love of
Righteousness and Perfection.

THE infinite Love of his own Goodness is the Holiness of GOD. There are infinite Pleasures and perfections in its Nature, that Merit an infinite Esteem and Desire. His Goodness is all Beauty, and his Holiness all Fire and flame in pursuing it. His Holiness is all Beauty, and his Goodness all Fire and flame to enkindle it. The infinite Excess of his Eternal Goodness is its own Holiness, and the Beauty of Holiness is Excess of Goodness. For if Righteousness and Holiness be well distinguished, Righteousness is that Vertue by which GOD doth apprehend, affect and Esteem all Excellent Things according to their value, and chuse and do always the Best and most Excellent: Holiness is the Love which he beareth to his own Righteousness: Which being infinite, makes him infinitely enflamed with the Love of the most perfect Actions; and carries him with an infinite Ardor to the performance of them. For tho it be a Righteous Thing to esteem the Righteousness of GOD in an infinite manner, yet there is as much difference between Righteousness and the Love of Righteousness, as between an Object and the Affection embracing it. Tho here also the Affection & the Object are the same Thing: For this Holy Esteem and Love of Righteousness is Righteousness it self: for it does but render Righteousness its due, tho the Affection be infinite which it bears unto it.

HOLINESS (if it be strictly defined) is that Vertue in GOD, by which he Loveth the most Perfect Things, and infinitely delighteth in them. For by Vertue of this Affection he shunneth and hateth all that is profane, pursuing and delighting in all that is Holy. For the Object of Holiness may be Holy, as well as the Affection, Whereupon it followeth, that Holiness is of two kinds, either the Holiness of the Affection, or the Holiness of the Object. They bear a Relation to each other, yet are absolute Perfections in themselves. For the Hatred of all Defects, Imperfections, Blemishes and Errors is a Glorious thing in it self, yet relates to the Perfection of those Objects from which it would remove those odious Imperfections. The Perfection of all Objects when they are free from all Blemishes is a Glorious Thing in it self too, yet is Acceptable to that Affection, that desires to see a Compleatness and Perfection in every Object. And all is resolved into the same Goodness of which we have been speaking.

FOR infinite Goodness must needs desire with an infinite violence, that all Goodness should be compleat and Perfect: and that Desire, which makes to the Perfection of all Goodness, must infinitely avoid every slur and Miscarriage as unclean: and infinitely aim at every Grace and Beauty, that tends to make the Object infinitely perfect, which it would enjoy. It cannot desire less then infinite Perfection, nor less then hate all Imperfection, in an infinite Manner. All Objects are made, and Sanctified by the Holiness of GOD. It is the measure and strength and Perfection of Goodness.

THE Holiness of GOD is sometimes, called in his Oracle, *The Beauty of Holiness.* As if all the Beauty of GOD were in this. It extends to all Objects in Heaven and Earth, from the Highest to the Lowest, from the Greatest to the Meanest, from the most Pure to the most profane, with a Goodness and Wisdome so infinitely perfect disposing all, that some way or other every Thing might answer its infinite Affection. It infinitely hates all that is Bad, and as infinitely desires to Correct the same. The Influence of that Affection, by which GOD abhorreth the least Spot in his Kingdome, reaches to the Perfection of every Object, and is the real & proper fountain of all the Perfection of Life & Glory. And for this Cause in all Probability, do the Angels so continually cry, *Holy, Holy, Holy, Lord GOD of Hosts;* because the Brightness of his Infinite Glory and Perfection appeareth in his *Holiness,* the violence of his Eternal Love, and the Excess of Goodness. It may be, also because all the Heights of Created Perfection owe themselves to this Holiness, all the Raptures and Extasies of Heaven depending on the Zeal wherewith GOD is carried to perfect Blessedness. All which are occasioned by those pure and Quintessential Joys, those most sublime and Perfect Beauties, which they see and feel every where effected by the irresistible Strength of that Eternal *Ardor.*

SINS of Omission have an unknown Guilt and Demerit in them. They unsensibly bereave us of infinite Beauty. To let alone that Perfection which might have been infinite, to pass by, or neglect it, to exert Almighty Power in a remiss and lazy manner, is infinitely Base and

Dishonourable, and therefore unclean because so Odious and Distastful. *Lukewarmness* is Profane, as well as *Malice*. And it hath pleased GOD to brand it with a worse and more fatal Censure. No folly or iniquity can dwell with him; Omission is both. To be hated is to be rejected; but to be beloved Lukewarmly is to be embraced with polluted and filthy Armes. And for this Cause, the fire of his Jealousie burns most *devouringly* about the Altar. He will be sanctified in all them that draw nigh unto him, and but to touch his Ark irregularly, is to be consumed. Nor is this any other then a concomitant of his Holiness, and an evident Testimony of his Love to perfection, For it First shews, that on his own Part, he maketh our Powers Perfect, that we may be able to see and adore him worthily; and next that he delights in no Adoration but the most Worthy. It moreover shews that he infinitely delights in the Perfection of his own Actions, for otherwise he would not be so severe against the Imperfection of ours.

NOR is the reason of his Love to the utmost Perfection less then infinite: You Know that all impure Things upon Earth are dull and Obscure; as Vile in Esteem, as Base and faint in their Operations. Neither will a Lump of Dirt shine like the Sun, nor a Mudwall be Resplendent like polisht Marble. All Glorious Things have a Height of *Intensness* in them; and owe most of their Beauty to the Motion of their Strength and Activity. But GOD is a more High and Necessary Thing than these. Perfection is his Essence, and he could not be himself upon any Abatement. It is a great Wonder! But the smallest Thing in the world may spare somewhat of it self rather than that which is infinite. Upon the least substraction, that which is infinite is made finite, and the Loss is infinite. We cannot be at all Beloved by Almighty GOD unless we are infinitely Beloved. For to Love and neglect us at the same time is impossible, and to be able to do infinite Things for us, and yet to do but some of them, is to Love and neglect us at the same time. Tis Love in what it does, & neglect in what it leaveth undone. The Reason why it is our duty to Love him infinitely, is because he infinitely Loved us. Did he not exert all his Power himself, he would never command us to exert ours. The Love of all Perfection is his Essence and must be infinite for its own Perfection. The least flaw in a Diamond abates its Price: one Tooth awry, or wanting in a Clock, doth make it useless. *Dead flies corrupt the Apothecaries Oyntment, so doth a little folly him that is in Reputation for Wisdome and Honour.* The Greater his Reputation and Wisdome is, the more Grievous a Disparagement is any Stain. Nor is GOD above these

Rules, for his Essence it self is the Ruler of ours: and the Higher his Divinity is the more Exquisite is its *Care* of its own Perfection. There is no Danger of being Severe in our Expectations, for GOD does infinitely hate any Defect in himself, more then we, tho we infinitely hate it; and enjoys himself only as he is an Object Worthy of his own infinite Love and Honour.

FROM GODS Love of Righteous Action it proceedeth, that he made ours so compleatly capable of becoming Righteous, and that he adventured a Power into our Hands of offending. It is a strange thing, that the Excess of the Hatred of all Sin should make Sin possible, and that the most perfect Righteousness should be the Accidental Cause of Unrighteousness. But yet it is so, an infinite Love to the Best of all Possible Things made the worst of all things that could be possible, excepting those that are impossible, which yet we need not except.

TO read these Riddles aright, you must understand, that even *Impossibles* themselves are conceiveable Things, and may be compared with *Possible,* and *Actual.* That the Highest and Best of all that are Possible, are the most Easie with GOD, and most near to his Nature; that inferior Possibles are more remote, and only thought on in the second place; that Things Impossible are the worst of *Evils,* and Things Actual the *Best* of GOODS. For nothing is impossible but that GOD should lye, or Dishonour, or displease, or deny himself, or abuse his Power, or suspend his Goodness, or injure his Creatures, or do some such thing, which is contrary to his Nature, yet very conceiveable, because he is a free Agent; and has a kind of Power, were it not prevented by his Eternal Act, whereby he is able to do these Impossible things. Nothing is Eternally Actual, but the Goodness, and Wisdome, and Holiness of GOD, or some such Thing; as his Righteousness, and Blessedness, and Perfection. All which spring from his Will, and are Eternally his pleasure, as well as his Essence. In the idle Power of being, and doing all Excellent Things, there is much Hazzard and danger; but he freely and voluntarily became all these from all Eternity. He wrought all Righteousness, and Wisdom, and Goodness from everlasting, and by so doing became the fountain of all that is Glorious from all Eternity. The Worst of all *Possible* Evils are the Sins of Men: Which have an infinite Demerit and Vileness in them, yet are truely possible. And the reason of their Possibility is thus accounted. Impossible, which are worst of all, are Sins in GOD.

TO make Creatures infinitely free and leave them to their Liberty is one of the Best of all Possible Things; and so necessary that no

Kingdome of Righteousness could be without it. For in every Kingdome there are subjects capable of Laws, and Rewards, and Punishments. And these must be free Agents. There is no Kingdome of Stones nor of Trees, nor of Stars; only a Kingdome of Men and Angels. Who were they divested of their Liberty would be reduced to the Estate of Stones and Trees; neither capable of Righteous Actions, nor able to Honor, or to Love, or praise: without which Operations all inferior Creatures and meer Natural Agents would be totally Useless. So that all the Glory of the World depends on the Liberty of Men and Angels: and therefore GOD gave it to them, because he delighted in the Perfection of his Creatures: tho he very well knew there would be the Hazzard of their abusing it, (and of Sin in that abuse) when they had received it. The abuse of it he infinitely hated yet could not prevent it, without being Guilty of a Greater Evil. He infinitely hated it, because those Actions of Love and Honor which should spring from the right use of it, were the onely fair off-spring, for the sake of which the whole World was made, and without the right use of their Liberty all Creatures, Angels and Souls would be in vain: he could not Prevent it without being himself Guilty of what in them he abhorred.

FOR himself to be Guilty, was the worst of Evils, and absolutely impossible. Twas better let them make their Power vain themselves, then do so himself. For the Author of that vanity, be it who it will, is the Author of the Sin. If *they* would make it vain, *He* could not help it, for him to divest them of the use of Liberty after he had given it, was as inconsistent with himself, as it was with their Beauty to abuse it: the Act of giving it by taking it away being made vain. He infinitely hated that the Liberty should be frustrated, which he gave unto men, for their more perfect Glory: he laid all Obligations upon them to use it well, and deterred them (as much as was possible) from abusing it, but would not transfer their fault upon himself, because he fore saw they were about to do it; which he certainly had done, had he made their Power vain *himself,* after he had given it. Either to refuse to give the Power, or Having given it, to interpose and determine it without their Consent, was alike detrimental to the whole Creation. For indeed it is impossible, that he by determining their Wills, should make them the Authors of Righteous Actions, which of all things in the World he most desired. There is as much Difference between a Willing Act of the Soul it self, and an Action forced on the Will, determined by another, as there is between a man that is dragged to the Altar, whether he will or no, and the man that comes with all his Heart with musick and Dancing to offer sacrifice. There is Joy, and Honour, and Love in the one, fear and constraint, and shame in the other. That GOD should not be able to deserve our Love, unless he himself made us to Love him by violence, is the Greatest Dishonour to him in the World: Nor is it any Glory or Reputation for us, who are such sorry Stewards, that we cannot be entrusted with a little Liberty, but we must needs abuse it.

GOD adventured the possibility of sinning into our hands, which he infinitely hated, that he might have the Possibility of Righteous Actions, which he infinitely Loved. Being a voluntary and free Agent, he did without any Constraint Love and desire all that was most high and Supreamly Excellent of all Objects that are possible to be thought on, his own Essence which is a *Righteous Act* is the Best: and the Righteous Acts of Saints and Angels are the Highest and Best next that which Creatures could perform: The very utmost Excellence of the most noble Created Beings, consisted in Actions of piety freely wrought: which GOD so Loved, that for their sake alone, he made Angels and Souls, and all Worlds. These Righteous Actions he so Loved, that for their sake he prepared infinite Rewards and Punishments. All the Business of his Laws and Obligations are these *Righteous Actions*. That we might do these in a Righteous Manner he placed us in a mean Estate of Liberty and Tryal, not like that of Liberty in *Heaven* where the Object will determine our Wills by its Amiableness, but in the Liberty of *Eden,* where we had absolute Power to do as we pleased, and might determine our Wills our selves infinitely, desiring and Delighting in the Righteous use of it, hating and avoiding by infinite Cautions and Provisions all the unjust Actions that could spring from it. If we Love Righteous Actions as he does, and are holy as he is holy, in all manner of Wisdome and Righteousness; then shall we delight in all Righteous Actions as he doth, shall Love Vertue and Wisdome as he doth, and prefer the Works of Piety and Holiness above all the Miracles, Crowns and Scepters in the World, every Righteous and Holy Deed will be as pleasing to us, as it is to him: all Angels and Men will be as so many Trees of Righteousness bearing the fruit of Good Works, on which we shall feast in Communion with GOD; Or if our Righteous Souls be vexed, as *Lots* Soul in *Sodom* was, in seeing and hearing the unlawful Deeds of the wicked, they shall be recreated and revived with the sight of GODS most Righteous Judgments, and with the Beauty of his holy Ways, by which he rectifies the Malignity of the Wicked, overcomes the evil of their Deeds, and

turnes all the vices of men into his own Glory, and ours, in the Kingdome of Heaven. The Delights of Wisdome, and Righteousness, and
Holiness are suitable to their Nature as those of Goodness are to the
nature of Goodness: Which no man can enjoy, but he that is qualified
for them, by the Principles of Goodness and Holiness implanted in
his Nature. For as he that has no Eys, wanteth all the Pleasures of
sight, so he that has no Knowledge wanteth all the pleasures of Knowledge, he that is void of Holiness, is void of the Sence which Holiness
inspires, and he that is without Goodness must needs be without the
Pleasures of Goodness, for he cannot delight in the Goodness of GOD
towards other Creatures. To be Good, to be Holy, to be Righteous
is freely to delight in Excellent Actions, which unless we do of our
own Accord no External Power whatsoever can make us, Good, or
Holy, or Righteous: because no force of External Power can make
us free; whatever it is that invades our Liberty, destroys it. GOD therefore may be infinitely Holy, and infinitely desire our Righteous Actions,
tho he doth not intermeddle with our Liberty, but leaves us to our
selves; having no Reserve but his Justice to punish our ofences.

Of Justice in General, and Particular. The Great Good it doth in Empires and Kingdoms, a Token of the more retired Good it doth in the Soul. Its several Kinds. That GODS Punitive Justice Springs from his Goodness.

THO following the common Course of Moralists, in our Distribution of Vertues, we have seated *Justice* among the Cardinal *Moral;* yet upon second Thoughts we find reason to reduce it to the number of *Divine* Vertues, because upon a more neer and particular Inspection, we find it to be one of the Perfections of GOD, and under that notion shall discover its Excellence far more compleatly, then if we did contemplate its Nature, as it is limited and bounded among the Actions of Men.

THE Universal Justice of Angels and Men regards all Moral Actions and Vertues whatever: It is that Vertue by which we yield Obedience to all righteous and Holy Laws, upon the Account of the Obligations that lye upon us, for the Publick Welfare of the whole World. Because we Love to do that which is Right, and desire the fruition of Eternal Rewards. There is much Wisdome and Goodness, as well as Courage and Prudence necessary to the Exercise of this Vertue, and as much need of Temperance in it, as any. For he that will be thus just must of necessity be Heroical, in despising all Pleasure and Allurements that may soften his Spirit, all fears and dangers that may discourage and divert him, all inferior Obligations and Concernes that may intangle and ensnare him, he must trample under foot all his Relations and friends and particular Affections so far as they incline him to partiality and sloth; he must be endued with Great Wisdome to discern his End, great Constancy to pursue it, great Prudence to see into Temptations and Impediments, and to lay hold on all Advantages and Means that may be improved, he must have a Great Activity and Vigor in using them, a Lively sence of his Obligations, a transcendent Love to GOD and felicity, a mighty Patience and Long-suffering, because his Enemies are many, his Condition low, his Mark afar off, his Business manifold, his Life tho short in it self, yet long to him, his undertaking Weighty, and his nature corrupted.

THEY otherwise define Justice to be that Vertue by which we render unto all their Due. Which is of large Extent if the Apostles Commentary comes in for Explication, *For this Cause pay you Tribute also, for they are GODS Ministers attending continually on this very thing: Render therefore to all their Dues, Tribute to whom Tribute is Due, Custom to whom Custom, Fear to whom Fear, Honour to whom Honour: Owe no man any thing, but to Love one another, for he that Loveth another hath fulfilled the Law.* Kings, and Magistrates, and Ministers, and Parents, and Children, must have all their *Due,* and so must GOD, Blessed for ever: Adoration, to whom Adoration is due, and Obedience, to whom Obedience. In strict Justice we must render Hatred to whom Hatred is Due, and Love to whom Love. Hope is due to certain Grounds of Encouragement, and Sorrow to certain sorrowful Objects. But all our Passions must still be guided by the Rule of the Law, and all our Actions as Honour and Equity require.

PARTICULAR Justice is conversant in the Distribution of Rewards and Punishments, or else it observes the Rules of Equity and Reason in Buying and Selling. It is called particular, because the Excercise of it is not allotted to all, the Power of rendring Rewards and Punishments being committed to a few, namely to the Magistrates: and among Private persons many not at all accustomed to Buying and Selling. This Vertue, being to be exercised by some particular men, is particular Justice. However it has occasioned a Distinction in the Thing, whereby *Justice* is divided into *Distributive* and *Commutative:* the one being used in Courts of Judicature, the other in the Market.

IT was a notable Observation of *Plato,* that by reason of our Dim Eyes we are not able to see immediately what Vertue does in Secret in the Soul. And therefore he sayes, that as an Old man that is blear-ey'd if he hath something given him to read in little Characters, finds it necessary first to see the same in Capital Letters; so to observe first what Vertue doth in a Commonwealth, is expedient to him, that would understand what it doth in his own Soul. The Throne is upholden by Justice; the Majesty of Kings, and the Glory of Kingdomes is preserved by Justice. When Vertue is rewarded, and Vice supprest, the

City flourisheth; as the Laws are the Rampart of Mens Estates, Justice is the Rampart of the Law, the Guardian Angels of every family, State and Kingdome. Kings and Counsellors, and Priests, and Soldiers, and Tradesmen, have all their several Office, and proper Duty in a Kingdome: and that Nation is blessed (with order and Beauty) where every one contains himself in his proper Duty. But where Tradesmen invade the Priests office and defile the Altar, the Soldiers turn Counsellors, and every Consellor deposes the King, nothing but Confusion can follow in such a State. The Senses and Members of the Body are like Tradesmen, they traffick with sensible Objects, the Irascible passions of the Soul are Soldiers, and very apt to rebel and Mutiny; the Conscience is the Priest in the Temple of the Mind; Right Reason is the King, and the Concupiscible Affections or smoother Passions, especially *Avarice* and *Ambition* may pass for Counsellors. They may do well to put a man in mind of his Interest, but when they depose Right Reason, and usurp the Throne, Ruine must follow in the Soul, the Passions will turn Consellors, the Trades-men invade the Temple, and all Rights (Sacred and Profane) be blended together. To sell offices of Trust and Places of Judicature, is for a King to do that himself which Rebels attempt in violence; to put unworthy men in places of Trust promiscuously, that will sell Justice by Retail, as they bought it by Whole Sale. Justice is a Severe Vertue, and will keep up all the Faculties of the Soul upon hard Duty. For otherwise it would not pay to Felicity its Due: But where its Care is remiss in taking an Account, and solid Goods are barterd away to counterfeit false Commodities, the Soul will grow loose and poor in a moment: All its Powers subordinate and Superior will forget their Duty, and the Healthy Estate of the Mind fall into Anarchy and Confusion. All its Hopes and Felicities will be lost, for want of that Justice which Distributes to every Power its proper office.

THERE are two passages that I mightily desire to be imprinted in the Memory of all the World: and they are both of our Saviour. The one is, *He that is faithful in a little, shall be Ruler over much:* The other is this, *Who then is that faithful and Wise Servant, whom his Lord hath made Ruler over his Houshold, to give them meat in due season: Blessed is that Servant, whom his Lord when he cometh shall find so doing. He that is faithful in a little, is faithful also in much.* To be Just in a little Silver and Gold, and accurate in deciding Causes between a Man and his Neighbour, are Actions that in their own Nature seem to have little tendency to Bliss and Glory. But when we consider that we are Servants for a time, entrusted by a Lord, that will come and examine what we have done, we are not to measure our Hopes by those little Acts, as they determine in a Moment, but in relation to the Recompences which our Lord will give when he cometh. For our Saviour hath added, *Blessed is that Servant &c. Verily I say unto you that he shall make him Ruler over all his Goods. But and if that evil Servant shall say in his Heart my Lord delayeth his Coming; and shall begin to smite his fellow Servants, and to eat and drink with the Drunken, the Lord of that Servant shall come in a day when he looketh not for him, and in an hour that he is not ware of, and shall cut him asunder, and appoint him his portion with Hypocrites, there shall be Weeping and gnashing of Teeth.*

IF GOD should be loose and careless in his Kingdome, as it is infinitely Greater then all other Dominions, so would it quickly be more full of confusions: Especially Since the King would then himself be so loose and Careless. For Licence and profaness are of a spreading Nature, and such as the King is, such is the people. The vices of Kings do always punish themselves in the Imitation of their subjects, especially where the Distinction between Profane and Holy is lost, and there is no Hope and Fear of Punishments or Rewards. If GOD should declare it by any Act of his, to be a Thing indifferent whether men did well or ill; it would mightily abate the Rectitude of his nature, and Eclipse his Majesty. His Sovereignty would be slighted, and his Will despised, which ought infinitely to be dreaded. While Justice is infinite and there is an infinite difference put between Good and Evil, his Creatures we see are apt to abuse their Liberty, and Rebel, and become Apostates; tho they have an infinite pleasure to aspire after, and an infinite destruction, or Wrath to fear. What would they do, if the Divine Will were feeble and remiss, and exacted no reverence to its Law and Pleasure? It is the Height and Glory of GOD, that he sets an infinite Rate upon Excellent Deeds, and infinitely detests and abhors the Wicked. Their last ends are not more distant then their first Beginnings; in his Esteem, and Displeasure. Because he is infinitely Offended and displeased at Evil Deeds, he guards and fortifies his Law, deterres men from displeasing him by the fear of infinite Punishments; Encourages men to please him by proposing infinite Rewards, and the Truth is the infinite Approbation and Esteem which he hath for Wise and Holy Deeds, produceth a Delight and Complacency in them, which is the principal Part of the Reward. Nothing is more honourable then to be Praised and honoured by the King of Kings; The infinite Hatred of Evil Deeds is the very Torment it self, that afflicts the Wicked. Tis but to see how much we are hated of GOD, and how base the Action is, no other fire is needful to Hell: The Devils chiefest Hell is in the Conscience. They are obdurate and seared that cannot discern and feel the Wound which they inflict on themselves, who grieve and offend their Creator. It is easie to see, the Necessity of that Justice which springs from Holiness, and that GOD could not be infinitely Holy, were he not infinitely Just in like manner.

THAT his *Punitive Justice* springs from his Goodness, is next to be observed. He punishes them that are hurtfull to others. He is most severe in pleading the Cause of the Fatherless and the Widow. Himself is persecuted when his Saints are molested: and the faults for which the untoward servant was punished, are particularly those of *beating his fellow Servants*. A good man by how much the more tender and compassionate he is, by so much the more is he provoked at any gross Affront or abuse of the Innocent. Every soul is the Bride of GOD: and his own infinite Goodness, which deserves infinite Love, is infinitely Beloved by him. He infinitely tenders it and avoids its least Displeasure: but its Displeasure is infinite at every Sin, and consequently his Anger, when such a Sovereign Beauty as his infinite Goodness, is offended by it.

THE foundation of his Righteous Kingdome, and of the Room prepared for his Eternal Justice to act in, is infinitely deeper, and must in other Discourses more full and copious (on that Theme) be shewn. And to those we refer you. All we shall observe here is, that this Punitive Justice being GODS infinite Zeal whereby he vindicates his abused Goodness: His Goodness must of necessity proceed it, and be abused, before he can be Angry, and before his Anger can be accounted Justice. His Dominion is infinite, but cannot be Arbitrary (in a loose Construction) because it is infinitely *Divine* and Glorious.

Of Mercy, The indelible Stain and Guilt of Sin.
Of the Kingdom which GOD recovered by Mercy,
The transcendent Nature of that Duty,
with its Effects and Benefits.

SUCH is the infinite Justice of God, and the Severity of his Displeasure at Sin, his Holiness so Pure, and his Nature so irreconcilable, his Hatred so real and infinite against it, that when a Sin is committed, his Soul is alienated from the Author of the Crime, and his infinite Displeasure will ever see the Obliquity, and ever loath the Deformity therein.

THE Person of a man is concerned, in (and always represented in the Glass of) his Action. Union between him and his Deeds is Marvellous. Tis so close, that his Soul it self is hated or Beloved in his Actions. As long as it appeareth in that deed which is Odious and Deformed, he can never be Beloved.

HOW slight soever our Thoughts of Sin are, the least Sin is of infinite Demerit, because it breaketh the Union between God and the Soul, bereaveth him of his Desire, blasteth his Image, corrupteth the Nature of the Soul, is committed against infinite Goodness and Majesty, being as the Scripture speaketh *Exceeding sinful*, because it is committed against infinite Obligations and Rewards, displeasing to all the Glorious Angels, abominable to all the Wise and Holy, utterly against all the Rules of Reason, and infinitely Opposite to the Holiness of God, who is of purer Eys then to behold the least Iniquity. So that unless there be some way found out to deliver the Soul from the Guilt of Sin, to blot out the Act and to purifie it from the Stain, there can be no Reconciliation between GOD and a Sinner. That an offence so infinite should be Eternally punished, is the most reasonable thing in the World.

NOTHING but infinite power and Wisdom is able to wash away Leprosie of guilt, and to restore the Soul to its former Beauty and

Perfection. Without which all Pardon is vain, and the Soul dishonourable, and sick unto Death, as long as the shame and Confusion of its Guilt does lie upon it. Which cannot be removed by feeble Tears, nor by Acts of Indignation against our selves, nor by any Penitence or Sorrow of ours. For if these could prevail, the Divels might repent, and be cleared of their Trespasses; long agoe.

THAT no Law of Works can justifie Sinners is evident enough from that of the Apostle,* *For if there had been a Law given which could have given Life, verily Righteousness should have been by the Law.* GOD was not so prodigal, as without an infinite Cause to expend the Blood of his Son. And the principal Cause for which he came, was that he might *be made a Curse* and *Sin* for us, that we might be delivered from the Curse of the Law, and be made *the Righteousness of GOD in him.*†

THE reason why the Devils can not be saved, is because the Son of GOD *took not upon him the Nature of Angels, but the seed of Abraham.* And there is no other name given under Heaven among men whereby we may be saved, but only the name of Jesus, who offered up himself a sacrifice for us, that he might purifie to himself a peculiar people Zealous of Good Work. He pacified the Wrath of God by his Death, and satisfied his Justice in our nature, and washed us in his Blood, and made us Kings and Priests unto GOD. To him be Glory and Dominion forever. Amen.

IT was the Design of Christ, and it became the Mercy of GOD in our redemption, to take away all the filth and Deformity of Guilt, in which the Perfection of his Love and Power appeareth. *Even as Christ also Loved his Church, and gave himself for it, that he might Sanctifie and cleanse it with the washing of Water, by the Word, That he might present it to himself a Glorious Church, not having Spot, or Wrinkle, or any such thing, but that it might be holy and without Blemish.*‡ For the Church of GOD being his *Bride,* and we *Members of his Body, and of his Flesh, and of his Bones;*§ it was meet that we should be restored to the Perfection of Beauty, and if not recover the same, enjoy a Better Righteousness than we had before.

THE Light of Nature could discover nothing of all this, and therefore it was taught by Revelations, and Miracles, and Oracles from Heaven.

AS all things before his fall were subservient to mans Glory and blessedness, so all things after his fall became opposite to him; all

* Gal. 3.21.   † 2 Cor. 5.21.   ‡ Eph. 5.25, 26, 27.   § Eph. 5.30.

creatures up braided him with his Guilt, every thing aggravated his Sin and increased his Damnation. The glory and Blessedness which he lost was his Torment, the Honour which he had before, was turned into shame; the Love of GOD which he had offended, increased his Guilt, Eternity was a Horror to him, his Conscience a Tormentor, and his Life a Burden; Nothing but shame and Despair could follow his Sin, the Light of nature it selfe condemned him, and all that he could see was, that he was deformed, and hated of God. For that of the Psalmist is an Eternal verity,* *Thou art not a GOD that hath pleasure in Wickedness, neither shall Evil dwell with thee: The Foolish shall not stand in thy sight, thou hatest all Workers of iniquity: Thou shalt destroy them that speak leasing: The Lord will abhor the Bloody and Deceitful man.*

THE Express Declaration of GOD assured *Adam,* that his Recovery was impossible, *In the Day that thou eatest thereof thou shalt die the Death.* For not being able to dive into the Secret Reservation, which depended absolutely upon Gods holy Will and pleasure, as an Act of Sovereignty above the Tenor of the Law, all that he could see was, that he must *die the Death,* because the Veracity of GOD (as well as his nature) obliged him to fulfil the Denunciation of the Sentence: at least as *Adam* conceived.

IN the midst of this Black and Horrid Condition, the Mercy of GOD appeared like a Morning Star, and the Redeeming Love of GOD was that alone which was able by its Discovery to dispell the Mystes of Darkness that were round about him.

AS all things were before turned into Evil, by the force of Sin, and conspired to sink him lower into the Bottomless Pit; so all the Evils of his present condition were, by this infinite Mercy, turned to his Advantage, and his Condition in many Respects far better than before.

IT is fit to see how Sin enfeebled his Soul, and made him unable to serve GOD; that we might the better understand the Manner of his Recovery, and how his Spiritual Life and Power is restored, in the new strength which he received in his Saviour.

THE Account of it is this: By his *self Love* he was prone to desire all that was Profitable and Delightful to him: While therefore GOD infinitely Loved him, being apparently the fountain of all his Happiness, he could not chuse, (as long as he considered it) but Love GOD and Delight in him, it was natural and Easie to celebrate his Praises.

* Psal. 5.4,5,6.

But when he was hated of GOD, tho he could not chuse but acknowledge that hatred *Just;* yet his Self Love made him to look upon GOD in a Malevolent manner, as his Greatest Enemy and his Eternal Tormentor. All that was in GOD was a Terror to him. His power, his Eternity, his Justice, his Holiness, his Goodness, his Wisdome, his Unalterable Blessedness, all was a grief and Terror to his Soul, as long as the Hatred of GOD continued against him it made him desperate to think it would continue forever, and reduced him to the miserable slavery of hating GOD even to all Eternity.

BUT when the Love of GOD towards Man appeared, the Joy wherewith he was surprized, was, in all Likelyhood, so far beyond his Expectation, and his Redemption so far above the Powers of Nature, that his very Guilt and Despair enflamed him with Love. GOD appeared now so Welcome to him, and so Lovely above all that was before, that it was impossible for him to look upon GOD, and not to Love him with Greater Emazement and Ardor then ever. Self Love, that Before compelled him to hate GOD, carried him now most violently to the Love of GOD; and the Truth is, the Love of GOD in the Eye of the Understanding, is the influence of the Holy Ghost proceeding from the Father by the Son into the Soul of the Spectator. For GOD is Love, and we therefore Love him, because he first Loved us. A faln man is Still a reasonable Creature, and having more reason to Love GOD then he had before, is by the pure Nature of his Essence infinitely more prone to Love GOD, and delight in him, and praise him for ever, because he is so mercifully and so Strangely restored. Thus are we in Christ restored to the Exercise of that Power which we lost by Sin: But without him we can do Nothing.

WHEN all the Kingdom of GOD was at an End by the fall of man, and all the Labor of the Creation lost, by the Perversness of him for whom the whole World was made; GOD by his Mercy recovered it, and raised it out of the Rubbish of its Ruines, more Glorious than before. Which is the chief reason for the sake for which we introduce the Mercy of GOD, as our best pattern. For when a man has injured us, by Nature there is an End of all the Lovely Exercises of Peace and Amity. If natural Justice should be strictly observed; but then the Season of Grace arrives, and the Excellencie of Mercy shews it self in the Lustre of its Wisdome, and so our Empire is continued, our loss retrived: For by shewing Mercy we often recover the Love of an Enemy, and restore a Criminal to the Joy of our freindship. We lengthenout our Goodness, and Heighten its measure; we make it victorious, and cloath it with a Glory above the course of Nature.

And all this we are enabled to do by the Coming of *Jesus Christ,* who hath restored us to the Hope of Salvation, and taught us a Way to increase our own Goodness by other mens Evils, to turn the vices of others into our own Vertues, and to Live a Miraculous Life of Worth and Excellency in the midst of Enemies, Dealing with men better than they deserve, adorning our selves with Trophies by the Advantages of their vileness, making our selves more Honourable by the Ignominy they cast upon us, more Lovely and Desirable by the Hatred which they bear towards us.

THE foundations upon which we Exercise this Vertue, are wholy Supernatural. To be kind to the innocent is but Justice and Goodness, but to be Kind to the Malevolent is Grace and Mercy. And this we must do, *because our Father which is in Heaven Causeth his Sun to rise on the Just and the unjust and his Rain to descend on the Righteous and the Wicked.* Because Mercy is the Head Spring of all our Felicities, therefore should we shew Mercy, as we have obtained Mercy. As the Blood was sprinkled upon the Tabernacle and all its Utensils; so is the Blood of Christ upon the Heathens, and the Earth, and all our Enjoyments. They are Daily Monitors of Mercy to us, because they are purchased by the Blood of Christ. For of him it is, that the Heavens declare the Glory of GOD, and the firmament sheweth his Handy work to us sinners at this day. The Salvation of Sinners being the only End for the sake of which we can be permitted now to enjoy them.

THE Incarnation of our Lord Jesus Christ is an incredible mystery to them, that do not consider the Love of GOD towards Men, in the Creation of the World. But they that measure it by his Laws and works, and see it in the value of their own Souls, would think it very Strange, if that Love which appeareth so infinite in all other things, should be defective only in its Ways of Providence. They easily believe, it may express it self in the Incarnation. Especially Since all Ages are Beautified with the Effects and Demonstrations of this verity, that *GOD so Loved the World, that he gave his only begotten Son, that whosoever believeth in him should not perish but have Everlasting Life.* For Love is apt to transform it self into all shapes, that the necessity of its Object requires; and as prone to suffer as rejoyce with it, as apt to suffer for it, as with it. Many fathers have died for their Children, many for their Country, but the Love of GOD exceedeth them all. To be beloved in our Guilt is exceeding Wonderful: but this also is in the Nature of Love, it may be provoked with the Guilt, or moved with Compassion at the misery of a Sinner.

WHERE the Love is extreamly violent, and the weak Estate of
the Object fit for Compassion, it is more inclined to Pity than Revenge:
Tho where the Object is strong, and endued with all advantages, it
is more offended at the Outrage of its Rebellion.

WHETHER we consider the Nature of Man, or his Estate before
the Fall, we have some reason to believe that he was more Beloved
then the Holy Angels for there was more exquisite Care and Art manifested in the Creation of his *Person,* and his *Condition* was fitted for
a more curious Tenderness and Compassion, if he offended.

IF you look into the *Nature* of Angels and Men you will find this
mighty Difference between them, Angels are more Simple Spirits, Men
are Images of GOD carefully put into a Beautiful Case. Their Souls
would seem equal to the Angels were they not to live in Humane
Bodies, and those Bodies are Superadded, certainly for unspeakable
and most Glorious Ends; the visible World was made for the sake
of these Bodies, and without such persons as men are, it would be
utterly useless. The Hypostatical Union of two Natures so unspeakable
different as the Soul and Body are, is of all things in the World most
mysterious and Miraculous. Man seems to be the Head of all Things
visible, and invisible, and the Golden clasp whereby Things Material
and Spiritual are United. He alone is able to beget the Divine Image,
and to multiply himself into Millions. His Body may be the Temple
of GOD, and when it pleased GOD to become a Creature, he assumed
the Nature of Man. Angels are made Ministring Spirits for the sake
of Man, and by him alone GOD and his works are United.

IF you respect his *Condition* he was made a little lower than the
Angels, that he might be crowned with Glory and Honour; *Lower* for a
Time, that he might be *Higher* for ever. The Angels were placed in such
an Estate, that if they fell, it would be with more shame; yet if they
stood, it would be with less Glory: For having the Advantages of
Greater Light and strength, to Sin against them was more Odious,
and to stand in them less Wonderful. While man, being more remote
from GOD, was more Obnoxious to Dangers, and more Weak to resist
them; His Want of Clear Light if he fell, would lessen his offence;
And the Difficulties wherewith he was surrounded, if he stood, would
increase his Vertue, which by consequence would make his Obedience
more pleasing, and much augment his Eternal Glory. All which put
together, when Angels and Men both fell, fitted Man rather to be
chosen and redeemed; he being the Greater Object of Compassion
and Mercy.

THE Degrees and measures of that Mercy which was shewn to Man in his Redemption, are very considerable. When he was Weak and unable to help himself, when he was Guilty, when he was an Enemy, when he was Leprous and deformed, when he was Miserable and Dead, before he desired, or Thought of such a Thing, God freely gave his Son to die for his Salvation, and condescended to propose a reconciliation. Which should teach us, tho higher then the Cherubims, and more pure then the Light, tho our Enemies are never so base, and injurious, and ingrateful, nay Obstinate and Rebellious, to seek a reconciliation by the most Laborious and Expensive Endeavors, to manifest all our Care and kindness toward them, pursuing their Amendment and Recovery. For the same Mind ought to be in us that was in Christ Jesus: who being in the form of GOD thought it no Robbery to be Equal with GOD, yet took upon him the Form of a Servant, and being found in fashion as a man, humbled himself to the Death, of the Cross: Wherefore GOD also hath highly exalted him, and given him a Name above every Name that at the Name of Jesus every Knee might bow. The very reason why we so infinitely adore him, being the incomparable Height and Perfection of his Mercy, expressed in his Humiliation and Abasement for us. If we would enter into his Glory, we must walk in the Way which he hath trod before us, for that only will lead us into it.

THO GOD hath in his infinite Mercy redeemed us from the unavoidable Necessity of being Damned, yet hath he with infinite Prudence ordered the Way and Manner of our Redemption: in such sort that we are not immediately translated into Heaven, but restored to a *new Estate of Trial,* and endued with Power to do new Duties, as pleasing to him, as those which he required from us in *Eden.* For he Loved a Righteous Kingdome from the Beginning, wherein his Laws were to be obeyed, Rewards and Punishments expected, and administred in a Righteous manner.

THE Great and necessary Duties in this second Kingdome are Faith and Repentance introduced by his Wisdom, and occasioned by Sin, necessary for our Justification, and Sanctification, and Superadded to the former.

THIS Kingdome of Evangelical Righteousness, being founded on the Blood of Christ, is by Death and Sin, and by the Supernatural Secrets of Love and Mercy, made infinitely more Deep and mysterious than the former.

Of Faith. The Faculty of Believing implanted in the Soul. Of what Nature its Objects are. The Necessity of Faith; Its End, Its Use and Excellency. It is the Mother and Fountain of all the Vertues.

FAITH and Repentance are the Principal Vertues, which we ought to exercise in the Kingdome of *Evangelical Righteousness:* because by them alone a Sinner is restored to the Capacity and Power of living in the Similitude of GOD, in the Practice of his Divine and Eternal Vertues. For *without Faith it is impossible to please GOD,* because we can never believe that he is the Rewarder of all those that diligently seek him, without that Credit which is necessary to be given to the Discovery of his Love to them that are defiled by the Guilt of Sin. For as long as we think GOD to be an infinite and Eternal Enemy to all Offenders, we cannot use any Endeavor to please him, because we Know there is no Hope of Reconciliation, and the vanity of the Attempt appears like a Ghost that always haunts us, and stands in our Way to oppose and discourage us, in the Atchievment we would undertake. For to Fight with *Impossibility* is so Foolish a thing that Nature it self keeps us back from doing it. Till therefore we believe our Reconciliation possible, we have no Strength at all to endeavour our Salvation. Our Despair oppresseth and frustrates our Desires, with the inevitable Necessity of our Eternal shame, and Guilt, and misery.

TO believe that GOD will be so Gracious, as to pardon our horrible Apostacy and Rebellion, is a Work so Great, that GOD accepteth it instead of all other Works of Innocence and Piety: to believe that he hath given his Eternal Son to dy for us, and that he so Loved us as to come down from Heaven to suffer the wrath of GOD in our stead, is so much against the Dictates of Nature and reason, that GOD *imputeth this Faith alone for Righteousness,* not as if there were no Good Works necessary beside, but by this alone we are justified in his Sight, and our Justification cannot be ascribed to any other Work of ours whatsoever. Howbeit that which maketh Faith it self so Great a Vertue, is that we thereby receive a Power and an Inclination with all, to do those Works of Love and Piety, the Performance and the Reward of which was the very End of our Saviours Coming.

THAT there is implanted in Man a Faculty of *believing,* is as certain as that his Eys are endued with the Faculty of *seeing,* or his Soul with *Knowledge,* or any other Faculty. And that this Power implanted is of some *Use* in Nature, is as sure, as any Thing in the World. For nature never gave to any thing a Power in vain, this therefore being one of the Powers of the Soul, must have a certain *End* ordained for it: And its use is the Exercise of *Faith,* in order to that End.

OBJECTS of Faith are those Things which cannot be discovered but by the Testimony of others. For some things are known by Sence, some by Reason, and some by Testimony. Things that are Known by Sence, are present, some time or other, to the Senses themselves. Those Things which Reason discovers, are Known, as Effects are by Causes, or as Causes by Effects; a Good and rational Demonstration being made by the Concatenation of Causes and Effects depending upon each other, whereby Things remote from Sence are evident to Reason, because the one is necessarily implied by the existence of the other. But some Things there are, which have no such necessary Dependance at all: such are the fortuitous Occurences that have been in the World, with all those Actions of free Agents that flow meerly from their Will and pleasure. For of these, there can be no certain Knowledge when they are past, but by History and Tradition. That the World was made so many years ago, that Man was created in an estate of Innocency, that he fell into Sin, that GOD appeared, and promised the seed of the Woman to break the Serpents Head, that there was a Flood, that *Sodom* and *Gomorrah* was burnt by fire, that all the World spake one Language till the Confusion at *Babel,* that there were such men as *Julius Cæsar,* or *Alexander the Great,* or such as *Abraham,* and *Moses,* and *David;* that the children of *Israel* were in *Egypt,* and were delivered from thence by Miracles; that they received the *Law* in the *Wilderness,* and were afterwards setled in the Land of *Canaan,* that they had such and such *Prophets,* and *Priests,* and *Kings:* that *Jesus Christ* was born of the Virgin *Mary,* that he was GOD and Man, that he died and rose again, that he ascended into Heaven, and sent the *Holy Ghost* down upon his

Apostles. Nay that there is such a City as *Jerusalem;* all these things can no other Way be understood but only by Faith, for no Light of Nature nor principle of Reason can declare such verities as these, among which we may reckon these, that all the Nations in the World, except that of the Jews, were *Pagans* and Idolatrous, till the *Gospel* began to come forth from *Jury;* that by the Miracles, and Perswasions, and Faith, and Patience, and Persecutions, and Deaths of the *Martyrs,* they were converted, and forsook their Dumb Idols, and erected Temples to the GOD of Heaven; that his Eternal Son was crucified in *Judea;* that such *Emperors* made such Laws, that such *Councils* were held in such Ages, that such and such *Fathers* sprung up in the Church; that there is such a Place as *Rome,* and *Constantinople:* these and many Millions of the like Objects, to them that live in this Age, and never stirred any further then the English Coast, are revealed only by the Light of History, and received upon Trust from the Testimony of others. Nevertheless there is as great a Certainty of these Things, as if they had been made out, by Mathematical Demonstration, or had been seen with our Eys.

FOR tho there are some *false* and some *Doubtful* Testimonies, yet there are also some that are *True* and *Certain.* And least all Faith should be utterly blind, and vain, and uncertain, there are External Circumstances and inward Properties, by which those Testimonies which are true and infallible are distinguished from others.

ALL those Things that are absolutely necessary to the Welfare of Mankind, the Knowledge of which is of general Importance, that are unanimously attested by all that mention them, and universally believed throughout all the World, being as firm and certain, as the Earth, or the Sun, or the Skye it self. We are not more Sure that we have Eys in our Heads, then that there are Stars in the Heavens: tho the Distance of those Stars are many Millions of Leagues from our Bodily Organs.

THE Objects and Transactions which in former Ages occur to our Eys, (I mean the Spiritual Eys of the intelligible Soul, that are seated within) are by Faith received, and brought to the understanding. When they are transmitted to our Knowledge, their Nature is apprehended immediately by the Soul, and their existence examined by Reason. There being certain clear and infallible Rules, by which their Truth or falshood may be discerned. And for this Cause is it that we are commanded, to *Try all Things, and hold fast that which is Good;* It is our Duty, to be *ready always to give a reason of the Hope that is in us.* For Reason is a transcendent faculty, which extendeth to all Objects, and penetrates into all misteries, so far as to enquire what probability may be in them; what Agreement or repugnance there is in the Nature of the Things revealed; what Harmony or Contradiction there is in the Things themselves, what Correspondence in all the Circumstances, what consistence between those Things which we certainly *Know,* and those which we are perswaded to *believe,* what Authority the Relation is of, what is the Design and integrity of the Relators, what is the Use and End of the things revealed, whether they are important or frivolous, absolutely necessary, meerly convenient, or wholy Superfluous, things to be abhorred, or things to be desired, Absurd or Amiable, what Preparations went before, what Causes preceded their Existence, what Effects followed, what Concomitants they had, what Monuments of them are now left in the world, How the Wise and Learned judge of them, what Consent and Unity there is in all the Relations, and Histories, and Traditions, of the Things reported.

WHERE there is no Repugnance between the Objects offered to our Faith and the Things we already know, no Inconsistance in the Things themselvs, no difference, no Contention between the Relators, no fraud in promoting, nor folly (discernable) in the first Embracing of the Things that are published, no Want of Care in Sifting and examining their Reality, nor any want (in the Hearers) of Industry, Skill and Power to detect the Imposture, there is a fair Way laid open to the Credible of such Objects attested and revealed with such Circumstances. But if the Things attested were openly transacted in the face of the World and had Millions of Spectators at the first, if they were so publick as to be taken notice of in all Kind of Histories of those times and places, if they were founded on great and weighty causes, if they were pursued by a constant Series, and succession of affairs, for many Ages, if they produced great and publick alterations in the World, if they overcame all suspicious oppositions, obstacles, and impediments, if they changed the state of Kingdoms and Empires, if old Records, and Monuments and Magnificent Buildings are left behind, which those Occurrences occasioned; our Reason it self assists our Belief, and our Faith is founded upon *Grounds,* that cannot be removed: Much more if the Things be agreeable to the Nature of GOD, and tend to the Perfection of Created Nature, if many Prophesies and long Expectations have preceded their Accomplishment, if

* I Pet. 3.15.

the misteries revealed are attested by Miracles, and painted out many
Ages before, by Types and Ceremonies, that can bear no other Explication in Nature, nor have any Rational use besides; if all the Beauty
of former Ages is founded in, and compounded by their Harmony,
if they fitly answer the Exigencies of Humane Nature, and unfold
the True Originals of all the Disorder and Corruption in the world,
if the Greatest and Best Part of Learning it self consists in the Knowledge of such affairs; if the Doctrines on which they attend, be the
most pure, and Holy, and Divine, and Heavenly; if the most of them
are rooted in Nature it self, when they are examined and considered,
but were not discerned nor Known before; if they supply the Defects
of our Understanding and lead us directly to felicity, if they take off
our Guilt, and are proper Remedies to heal the Distempers and
Maladies of our Corruption; if they direct and quiet the passions of
Men and purifie their Hearts, and make men Blessings to one another;
if they exterminate their vices, and Naturally tend to the Perfection
of their Manners, if they lead them to Communion with GOD, and
raise up their Souls to the fruition of Eternity, enlarge their Minds
with a Delightful Contemplation of his Omnipresence, enrich them
with infinite varieties of Glorious Objects fit to be enjoyed, if they
perfect all the Powers of the Soul, and Crown it with the End for
which it was prepared: Where all these Things meet together, they
make a Foundation like that of the Great Mountains which can never
be moved. But if there be any flaw, or Defect, in these Things, if
any of them be wanting, our Faith will be so far forth lame and uncertain, as our Reason shall discern its Cause to be failing.

NOW of all the Things that the World doth afford, the Christian
Religion is that alone wherein all these Causes of Faith perfectly concur.
Insomuch that no Object of Faith in all the World is for *Certainty*
Comparable to that of Religion. Never had any Truth so many Witnesses, never any Faith so many Evidences, they that first taught and
published it, despised all the Grandeurs and Pleasures in the World,
designed nothing but their Eternal Felicity, and the Benefit of men,
trampled all Honours and Riches under feet, attested the Truths they
taught and revealed, by Miracles wrought, not in obscure Corners,
but in the Eye of the Sun, many Nations far distant from each other
were in a Moment reduced, and changed at a time. Millions of Martyrs
were so certain of the Truth of these Things, that they laught at Persecutions, and Flames, and Torments. The Jews that are the great
enemies of Christianity, confess those Histories, and Prophesies, and

Miracles, and Types, and Figures upon which it is founded. They reverence the Book wherein they are recorded above all the Writings in the World, confess that they had it before our Saviour was born, and glory that it was theirs, before it was ours. Their whole Faith and Religion is made up of Such Materials, which being granted, it is impossible the Christian Religion should be false, Turks acknowledge the Historical Part. The Artifices of Corruptors have been all detected, and must of necessity so be as long as there are inquisitive Men in the World: All Schismaticks and Hereticks have cavilled and disputed about the true Interpretation of certain Texts, but never so much as Doubted, much less shaken the foundation. Nay when you look into Matters well, the very Certainty of the one was the occasion of the other. The great Moment of what they took for granted made the strife the more Eager.

THIS Advantage our Faith has above all, it is suspected only by Lazy and Profane, half witted men that are as Empty as self conceited, as rash as Wanton, and as much Enemies to Felicity and Vertue, as to Truth and Godliness. But the more you search into it, the more Light and Beauty you shall discern in the *Christian Religion*, the Evidences of it will appear still more deep and abundant, as endless in Number, force, and Value, as they are unexpected.

AMONG other Objects of Felicity to be enjoyed, *the Ways of GOD* in all Ages are not the least considerable and Illustrious. Eternity is as much Beautified with them, as his Omnipresence is with the Works of the Creation. For Time is in Eternity, as the World is in Immensity: Reason expects that the one should be Beautiful, as well as the other. For Since all *Time* may be Objected to the Eye of Knowledge altogether, and Faith is prepared in the Soul on purpose, that all the Things in Time may be admitted into the Eye of the Soul, it is very Displeasing to Humane Reason, that *Time* should be horrid, and Dark, and empty, or that he that has expressed so much Love in the *Creation* of the World, should be Unmindful of our Concerns in the Dispensations of his *Providence*. Especially Since the World, how Glorious soever it is, is but the Theatre of more Glorious Actions, and the Capacity of *Time* as Great and Large as that of the *Universe*, Ages are as long and as Wide as Kingdoms. Now if GOD have altogether neglected the Government of the World, all Time will be Dark and vain, and innumerable Bright and Delightful Objects, which were possible to be desired, denied to the Soul, and the better half of GODS Love be removed. But if GODS Will and Pleasure be Uniform in his Operations, and Time it self Beautified by this Wisdome, Goodness, and Power, as well as the World, our *Faith* will have a peculiar Excellency because, it is that by which all the Beauties in *Time* and *Providence* are enjoyed: Especially if it be able to see and feel them in clear Light, and in as lively a manner as the *Reason* of the Soul can do, when most fully informed. It is evident that without this *Faith,* the Greater half of our Felicity can never be enjoyed.

TO Know that we are Men, encompassed with the Skies, and that the Sun and Moon, and Stars are about us, with all the Elements and Terrestrial Creatures, is matter of Sence and *Reason;* as it is also, that we have the Dominion and use of them; and that such Excellencies and Degrees of Goodness are Connatural to them: But their utmost Perfection is discovered only by the Truth of Religion; that alone discloses their first Cause, and their last End, without which all their Intermediate uses are *Extremely* Defective: It is far more Pleasant to see the Infinite and Eternal GODHEAD from the incomprehensible Height of his Glory, stooping down to the abyss of Nothing, and actually making all these Transcendent Things out of Nothing for our sakes, then to see our selves at present surrounded with them. This is the first Act of all the Ornaments of *Time* and *Nature.* Which tho it be founded on clear Reason, yet is it an Object of our Highest Faith, as it is revealed by the Word of GOD: and therefore it is said, *Through faith we understand that the Worlds were made.* For Faith and Reason are not so divided, but that (tho formally Distinct) they may enter into each others Nature, and Materially be the same. The very same Object (I mean) that is Known to Reason, may by Faith be believed: *Reason* not destroying but confirming *Faith,* while it is *Known* upon one account, and *believed* on another. For there is a Mutual Convenience between these two, *Faith* is by *Reason* confirmed, and *Reason* is by *Faith* Perfected.

TO see GOD stooping down to Create the World, and Nothing follow, is not so Beautiful, as to see him afterward in the Act of making Man, and Giving him Dominion over all the Creatures. It is more pleasant to see Man made in GODS Image, then to see the World made for the use of Man. For the End of the Creation is that, upon which all the Perfection of its Glory does depend, and the more Noble *Man* is, for whose use the *World* was made, the more sublime and Glorious its *End* is. To see him placed in the Estate of Innocency, Light, and Glory, wherein he was secure from Death, and Sin, and Sickness, and Infelicity, if himself pleased, is very Delightful; so it is to see, that Nature never intended any of those Abortive Errors, that now so confound us: But to see the *End* why man was placed in such an Estate, to be his *Trial,* and the End of that his *freindship with GOD,* whose Exercise consisteth in voluntary Acts of *Gratitude* and *Amity;* and the End of those the Beauty of his Life, and his fuller Exaltation to Bliss and Glory; this is far more Pleasant then the other. To see him fall is infinitely Displeasing, but the fault is intirely charged on himself: And had GOD Eternally destroyed him, tho we perhaps had never lived to see it, yet we confess it would have been just in it self, and the Justice Adorable. But to see GOD exalting his mercy in pardoning the offence, and for all our sakes redeeming Man by the Death of his Son is sweeter still: as it is also to see his infinite Justice and Holiness in the *Manner* of our Redemption. To see him lay the foundation of our Hope on a certain Promise, seconded with his Long-suffering, yet defer the Accomplishment of it for our greater Benefit, wisely forbearing to send his Son till *the fulness of Time,* is very transporting, but the Reason of it is very Difficult to understand. His foresight of our Obstinate *Blindness* and *Incredulity* was the Cause of his Delay. That he might gain Time, before our *Saviour* came, to speak of him, to paint him forth, to make him the expectation of the World, and the Hope of all Nations; To see him for that End reveal himself to *Abraham, Isaac,* and *Jacob,* and bringing down their Posterity into the Land of *Egypt,* that he might make that Nation, out of which our Saviour was to spring, *Famous* by *Miracles,* and by his Conduct and Government of them, more *Glorious* then all Nations, to appear himself among them, and give his Oracles unto them, and to make them conspicuous to the Eye of all the World, by mighty Signes, and Wonders, and Judgments, punishing them for their offences, yet Graciously continuing a Seed among them, that *Christ* might be raised up according to the *Prophesies,* that went before concerning him. To see all the Mysteries of the Gospel painted out in so *Lively* a Manner, in all the Types and Figures of the *Ceremonial Law,* and that Service with so much splendor and Glory continued, before he came by the Space of two thousand years, wherein all the mysteries of his Kingdome are exhibited; to see *the Volumne of the Book in which it was written of him,* so highly magnified and exalted, by them that crucified him after it was written, and that now continue so much to oppose him as the *Jews* do; To see the *Prophets* at various Times, and in Divers manners, so clearly to describe all the particulars of his Life and Doctrine, his Eternity, his Godhead, the Hypostatical Union, his Incarnation in the Virgins Womb, his Poverty, his Meekness, his Miraculous Life, his Death and Passion, his Resurrection and Ascension into Heaven, the Sudden and Miraculous Conversion of the Gentiles, compared to a *Nation's being born at once,* the very *Town* where he should be born, and the *City* from whence the Law should go forth into all the World, and the *Temple* in which the Gospel should begin to be preached. To see the Accomplishment of all these Things attended with so many Glorious and Transcendent Wonders, and the utter subversion of that Nation, for their Incredulity when they had slain him; To see Kings and Queens become the *Nursing Fathers* and *Mothers* of the Church, and so many Glorious Empires receive his Law that was *hanged* on a Tree; To see Temples erected over all the World to a Crucified GOD, and Nations upon Earth adoring his Glory in the Highest Heavens; Especially to see the manner of his satisfaction, by way of *Sacrifice* in our stead, the laying of our Sins upon his Head, & the sprinkling of his Blood upon all Nations so lively represented, the Necessity of such a Saviour exhibited by the Rigor and Severity of the Law, his Person and his Office being pointed out in so particular a Manner; all this as it is sweet & Heavenly, so does it enrich the Contemplation of the Soul, & make it meet to walk in Communion with GOD in all *Ages,* adoring his Wisdome, and Goodness, and Power, admiring & delighting in the *fulness* of his Love, And all these most Great & Transporting Things we receive into our souls by *Faith* alone.

BUT that which above all other Things is most satisfactory is to see Jesus Christ *the end of the Law,* and the centre of time, the main Business of all the Dispensations of GODS Providence, and the only Hinge upon which all mysteries both of the Law and Gospel Principally turn.

HAD he come in the Beginning of the World, there had been no *Room* nor *Place* for all these Prophesies, and Figures, and Expectations, and Miracles, Precedeing his Birth, we had had nothing but a *bare* and *naked* Tradition, that he had been in the world, which by the carelesness of men had passed away like a Dream, and died unprofitably; As we may plainly see by their Backwardness to believe these Things, notwithstanding their strength and Beauty, and the reiterated Appearances of GOD to excite and awaken Man-kind, notwithstanding his care to erect a Ministery among us, for this very end, *that Jesus Christ might be Known.*

HAD he not been GOD and MAN in one Person, had no satisfaction been necessary for our sins, had he not made satisfaction for us; there had been no Necessity of believing on his name. The light of nature had been sufficient to guid us to sorrow and Obedience; all this trouble and care might have been spared, all this Oeconomy might have been changed into a Government of less expence, and the most of these proceedings had been impertinent and superfluous. For they all receive their Attainment and Perfection in *Jesus Christ,* who is the fulness, and substance, and Glory of them.

NOR is it, the excellency of Faith alone, that it looks back upon Ages past: it takes in the Influences of all these, that it may bring forth fruit, in our Lives for the time to come. For what is it but the Faith of these things, attended with the Glory which is intimated by them, that made so many Divine and Heavenly persons, so many Wise and Holy Heroes, so many Saints and Martyrs! What can enflame us with the love of GOD, inspire us with Courage, or fill us with Joy, but the Sence of them! A true and lively Faith is among Sinners the only Root of Grace and Virtue, the only Foundation of Hope, the only Fountain of excellent Actions. And therefore it is observed by the Apostle *Paul,** that *by Faith* Abel *offered a more Excellent sacrifice than* Cain, *by Faith Enoch* walked with GOD, *by Faith Noah* prepared an Ark, in which being warned of GOD, he saved himself from the general Deluge; *by Faith Abraham* did such Things, as made his Seed to multiply above the Stars of Heaven; *by Faith Moses* despised the Honours and Treasures of Egypt, and endured, as seeing him that was invisible; *What should I say more* (saith the Apostle) *For the time would fail me to tell of* Gideon, *and of* Barak, *and of* Sampson, *and of* Jeptha, *of* David *also, and of* Samuel, *and of the Prophets: who through Faith subdued Kingdoms, wrought Righteousness, obtained Promises, Stopped the mouths of Lions, Quenched the violence of fire, escaped the Edge of the Sword, out of Weakness were made strong, waxed valiant in fight, turned to flight the Armies of the Aliens. Women received their Dead raised to Life again; and others were tortured, not accepting Deliverance, that they might obtain a better Resurrection. And others had tryal of cruel Mocking and Scourges, yea moreover of Bonds and Imprisonments. They were stoned, they were sawn asunder, were tempted, were slain with the sword, they wandred about in Sheep-skins and Goat-skins, being desti-*

* Heb. 11.

tute, afflicted, tormented; of whom the World was not worthy, they wandered in Deserts and Mountains, and in Dens and Caves of the earth. All these things were done through *Faith,* while yet there were but a few Things seen to encourage them. But the whole Accomplishment of mysteries and myracles is far more fair, and vigorous, and enflaming; the Beauty of the whole Body of GODS Dispensations fitly united in all its Parts, being an eternal *Monument* of his Wisdom and Power, declaring the Glory of his Love, and Kingdom in a more Eminent manner, and making us *more then conquerors in and thorrow Jesus Christ, who loved us, and gave himself for us.*

Of Hope. Its foundation, its Distinction from Faith,
its Extents and Dimensions, its Life and Vigor,
its Several Kinds, its Sweetness and Excellency.

JANUS with his two Faces, looking backward and forward, seems to be a fit Emblem of the Soul, which is able to look on all Objects in the Eternity past, and in all Objects before, in Eternity to come. Faith and Hope are the two Faces of this Soul. By its Faith it beholdeth Things that are past, and by its Hope regardeth Things that are to come. Or if you please to take Faith in a more large and Comprehensive Sence, Faith hath both these Faces, being that Vertue by which we give Credit to all Testimonies which we believe to be true concerning Things past, present and to come: Hope is a Vertue mixt of Belief and Desire, by which we conceive the Possibility of attaining the Ends we would enjoy, and are stirred up to endeavour after them. Faith respects the *Credibility* of Things believed to be *True;* Hope, the *Possibility* and *Goodness* of their *Enjoyment.* The Simple Reality of Things believed is the Object of the one, the facility of their attainment, and our Interest united are the Object of the other.

HOPE presupposes a Belief of the Certainty of what we desire. It is an Affection of the Soul of very general Importance. Which forasmuch as it is founded on Faith, and derives its strength from the Sure Belief of what we hope to attain, and there can be no fruition of that which is not really *existent,* to lay the foundation of our Hope more firmly, we will again consider the Objects of Faith in the best Light wherein their apparent certainty may be discerned.

THE Objects of Divine Faith revealed in the holy Scripture may fitly be ranked into three Orders. For the *Matter* of the Bible being partly *Historical,* and partly *Prophetical,* and partly *Doctrinal,* the Objects of *Divine Faith* fall under these three Heads, of *Doctrine, History,* and *Prophesie.*

THE *Doctrine* of the Scripture is of two sorts: for some Doctrines

are *Natural,* some are *Supernatural.* The Natural are again divided
into two. For some of them are *Laws* that teach us our Duty, some
of them *Propositions* only, or bare and Simple *Affirmations,* which
we call Articles guiding our Apprehensions in the Truth of those Things
which are meet to be Known. *Speculation* is intended in the one,
and Practice in the other.

NATURAL Doctrines are Objects of Divine Faith, only as they
are revealed by the Word of GOD. For the Authority of the Witness
is that which maketh our Faith *Divine.* They are called *Natural,* because how ever Blind any man is, in his present condition; upon a
diligent Search, those Things may be clearly discerned by the Light
of Nature. Those Doctrines which are Objects of Divine *Faith,* and
yet may be found out by the Investigation of *Reason,* are such as
these. That there is a GOD, that the World was made, that man
was created in GODS Image, that he hath Dominion over the works
of his Hands, that he is or ought to be tenderly Beloved of all mankind,
that he is to be good, and full of Love to others: that he is to render
all Objects their Due Esteem, and to be Grateful for the Benefits he
hath received of his great Creator: that the first Estate of the Worlds
Creation was pure and perfect, that Sin came in by the Accidental
abuse of the Creatures Liberty, that Nature is Corrupted, that Death
was introduced as the Punishment of Sin, that the Soul is Immortal,
that GOD is infinitely Just, and Wise, and Holy; that he will distribute
Rewards, and Punishments according to Right; that there is such
a Thing as Eternity and Immensity; that the Body is frail and subject
to Diseases; that we receive all Things from GOD, and depend in
the fruition of all upon his Power and Providence; that it is Wise
to please him, and foolish to displease him; that Punishment is due
to Sin, and that GOD hateth it; that Reward is due to Vertue, and
GOD delighteth in it; that there is a Conscience in the Soul, by which
it feels and discovers the Difference between Guilt and Innocence.
That man is a Sinner, that he is prone to Evil, and Obnoxious to
GODS Wrath, that nevertheless he is spared by the Long-suffering
of GOD, and that GOD Loveth him, and desireth his Salvation. That
there is a felicity and a Supream Felicity appointed for man: that
he is a free Agent, and may lose it, if he pleases: that misery is the
Consequent of the Loss of Felicity: that GOD delighteth in all those
that Love and practice Vertue: that he hateth all those that drown
their Excellencies in any Vice: that Sorrow and Repentance are necessary for all those that have offended GOD: that there is Hope to

escape the Punishment of Sin, if we endeavour to live as piously as we ought. All these things are evident in themselves by the Light of Nature, because they may either be clearly deduced from the principles of Reason, or certainly discerned by plain Experience: And are therefore taught by the Word of GOD, either because they had need to be revived and raised up to light from under the Rubbish of our Fall, or because GOD would sanctifie Nature by his express Consent, or make its Dictates more remarkable and Valid by his Approbation, and confirm all by the Seal of his Authority: or because a fair Way is laid open by these to more retired and Cœlestial Mysteries.

FOR when we know these Things we are prone to enquire what GOD hath done, what Way there is to recover our ancient Happiness, what Remedies are prepared for the corruption of Nature, how the Guilt of Sin may be removed, how we may be aided and assisted in the works of Virtue, by what Means our Reconciliation with GOD is wrought, and in what manner we ought to demean our selves that we may be accepted of him? For the knowledge of our former health is necessary for the clear apprehension of our present Sickness, and the sense of our Infirmitie fits us for the Physician. When we know all that *Nature* can teach, and see something needful, that Nature cannot unfold; when we are condemned by our Conscience yet feel our selves beloved, find that we have forfeited all, yet see the Glory of the creation continued (for our use and service,) stand in need of an Atonement, yet Know not where to get it; our Exigency meeting with the grace of GOD, the sence of our Misery and Hope united, our own Guilt and GODS Mercy (of both which we have the feeling and experience,) adapts us for the Reception of the Holy Gospel, wherein those things are revealed that come in *most fitly* to answer our Expectations. Satisfaction for Sin by the Death of Christ, and the Incarnation of his GODHEAD above the course of Nature, for that End; His active and passive Obedience in our Stead, our Justification thereby, the application of his Merits to our souls by faith, the Glory which we owe him for so great an undertaking, the coming down of the Holy Ghost to Sanctifie our Nature, and the dignity of Both these Persons by reason of their Unity in the eternal Essence; for the manifestation of which the Mysterie of the Trinitie is largly revealed, these supernatural Points come in so suitably and are so agreeable to Nature, so perfectly fit in their places, so marvellously conducive to the perfection of the Residue, that the very Harmony and sweetness of altogether is enough to perswade us of their *Credibility;* and then the *Matter of fact* comes in with the Testimony and Authority of GODS Word, assuring us that these Things are so, by History and Prophesie. The Miracles at our Saviours Birth alone one would think enough to clear the business: much more if we take in all the Miracles of his life; wherein his Glory appeared, as of the only begotten of the Father; more fully yet, if we take in the Miracles of his Death; and abundantly more, if the Glory of his Resurrection and Ascension be added. But especially the *Coming down of the Holy Ghost,* and the Power the Apostles received from heaven, all the Prophesies that went before, and all the successes that followed after, all the Faith and Learning of the Fathers, all the Canons and Decrees of Councils, all the Transactions of the World drawn down to our own Age in a continued series, illustrate and confirm all that is revealed.

BUT you will say, How shall we know such Histories to be true, and that such Prophesies and Prophets were in their several Ages; Since we never saw the same with our eyes, and there are many sleights and Fables in the World: How dost thou know there are any Antipodies? Thou didst never see them! Or that there is any Sea, which thou didst never behold! Or that the next River has a Fountain Head? Is not the Universal Tradition of all the world (wherein the Church of *Rome,* nay the Catholick Church, is but a little Part) a clear Light for a *matter of Antiquitie,* attended with a *Stream* of Effects and clear *Monuments* concurring together, without any Dissonancy in the Things themselves, or Contention of Parties? How dost thou know that there was such a man as King *James,* or *William* the Conqueror. Is he not a mad man that will doubt, or Dispute it? All that thou hast to confirm thee in the certainty of these, and infinitely more, conspires together, to confirm thee in the certainty of the other. The History of the Bible is confest by Turks, and Jews, and Infidels, and which is far more, by the Testimony of the Church, which deserves to be believed above them all. And if the History be true, there were such Persons as *Adam, Enoch, Noah, Abraham, Joseph, Moses, Samuel, David, Solomon, Elias, Elisha, Josiah, Isaiah, Jeremiah, Ezekiel, Daniel,* and the rest of the Prophets; such persons as Jesus Christ, and his Apostles in such Ages; such Prophesies, and such Accomplishments at vast Distances; such Acts, and such Miracles, and such Doctrines upon such occasions: And if all this *Matter of fact* be true, tis impossible but these Doctrines must be Divine, which the Devil and wicked men so much Oppose and Blaspheme in the World. And if these Doctrines are true, then all the Promises of GOD are true, and there is a large foundation of Eternal *Hope* prepared for the Soul: because if all these Preparations be not Eternally disgraced by the feebleness of their End, the Glory and Felicity which is designed by them, is infinite and Eternal.

THAT all these Things are intended for thy Benefit, thou mayst clearly see, by thy very Power to see them, and by the Natural Influence which they have upon thy Estate and condition. For tho it may happen by some succeeding Accident, that thy Power to see and enjoy all may be bereaved of its Objects, when thine *Interest* is Eclipsed and forfeited by thy Rebellion, and the *Influence* of all may at last through thine own Default be *ineffectual* and *Malevolent* to Thee; yet thou art assured by the Nature of GOD, and of thy own Soul, that it could not be intended Evil from the Beginning; nay the very Order and disposition of the Things themselves importeth the Design to be Felicity and Glory. For all these Things were written for our Admonition, upon whom the Ends of the world are come: And the Apostle expresly saith, that* *whatsoever Things were written aforetime, were written for our Learning, that we through Patience and Comfort of the Scriptures might have Hope.* This Hope maketh not ashamed, because the Love of GOD is shed abroad in our Hearts. We Delight in Beauty, and by that very Inclination that we have unto it, are apt to Delight in any Thing that is Amiable. We delight to see the Order and Perfection of GODS Ways, and GOD himself taketh Pleasure in manifesting his Wisdome and Goodness, for the Behoof of our Souls, because he is Great in Bounty, and infinite in Love by his very Essence: Nay further we are every one Capable of all the Benefit that accrueth thereby, and by Nature fitted to celebrate his Praises for all the Advantages that by any of his Dispensations are imparted to us, and have Liberty to improve them all for the Acquisition of that Glorious End to which we are ordained. The Nature of GOD, which is hereby manifested to be Love to his Creatures, is that which enableth thee by this very means to honour and adore him, and by so doing to enter into his Kingdome, where he, that did all these Things for a farther End, will appear in Glory, and shew thee a Perfection of Life and Bliss, that is worthy of all this Care and Providence, being as great as thy Heart can Wish or desire.

HOPE is for its Extent and Dimensions vast and wonderful. All the Honour, Advancement, Exaltation, Glory, Treasure, and Delight, that is concievable in Time or Eternity, may be hoped for: all that

* Rom. 15.4.

the Length, and Breadth, and Depth, and Height, of the Love of
GOD, which passeth Knowledge, is able to perform; All that Ambition
or Avarice can desire, all that Appetite and Self-Love can pursue,
all that Fancy can imagine Possible and Delightful; Nay *more then
we are able to ask or think;* we are able to desire, and aspire after
(if it be promised to us) the very throne of GOD, and all the Joys
of his Eternal Kingdom. And the more Sublime its Objects are, the
more Eagerly & violently does our Hope pursue them, because there
is more Goodness in them to ravish our Desire.

TO fall from the Height of ones Hopes, where the Kingdome and
Glory was infinite, to which we aspire, is to fall from the Height of
Heaven into the Depth of Hell, it produceth a misery and Anxiety
in the Soul, an Indignation and Sorrow, answerable to all the Greatness
of our Objects, and the expectancies of our Hopes: Especially where
the Hope is *Lively* and *Tender,* and *Strong,* and *Sensible* of all it
conceiveth.

FOR it is the property of a true and lively Hope to Elevate the
Soul, to the Height of its Object: tho dull and drowzy Hopes make
no Impression or Alteration in the Mind. The Soul extends it self
with a kind of Pleasure in its Wishes and in touching the Possibility
of such Goodnesses, as it proposes to its self in its own Imagination.
Love and Beauty even in *Romances* are Delightful: the very Dreams
and *Ideas* of the Perfections of Bliss, have a Pleasure as well as their
Reallity. The Desires of it are something more Rich and Sacred then
the fancy or Imagination: but to Hope for such a Thing with a clear
and joyful expectation, is to grasp at its fruition, with a faint Kind
of Promise, that it shall at last be ours. Had our Hopes in *Spiritual*
Things, as much *Sence* as they have in *Temporal,* those Beams of
Assurance that enlighten our Hope and fill it with Glory, would infuse
a solid Strength into our Desire and our pleasures would be so Great
that we should not exchange them for all the Empires in the World.
Especially if it ascended so high as to be founded on infinite and Eternal
Causes, and the only fears that did chequer our Hope, sprung from
Nothing but the Danger of being Wanting to our selves. For who
would think, That when our Lives and Liberties are at stake, we should
be false to our selves, that infinite Love and Power should be tendered
to us, infinite Beauty and Goodness be before us, infinite Honour and
Pleasure be offered us, Eternal Delights, inestimable Riches, Ever flour-
ishing Joys, an infinite Empire be without fraud attainable, and we
be so Treacherous and false to our selves, as to sleight it all! It is

an Absurdity so incredible, that we should lose all these Enjoyments by our own Default, and bare Remissness that we shall hate our selves Eternally if we lose so fair an Advantage. Yet this is our Case, we daily do that which in point of Reason is impossible to be done, and for doing which we judge our selves Guilty of Eternal Tortures. All the Misery that is lodged in infinite Despair has comfort and refreshment answerable to it in infinite Hope. Tis the present food and Support of our Lives, 'tis the Anchor of our Souls in the midst of all the Storms and Tempests in the World, 'tis the foretaste of Bliss and Cœlestial Glory, a Glympse and Appearence of the Beatifick Vision, without which to Live is to Dye, and to Dye is to perish for evermore.

THE Great Reason for which a right Hope is accounted so Great a Vertue, is because its Objects do really surpass all Imagination. The fulness of the GODHEAD in the Soul of Man, the Perfection of the Divine Image, a Transformation for Glory, to Glory, even as by the Spirit of the Lord, Communion with the Father, Son and Holy Ghost, infinite Love and Bounty, the Estate of a Bride in Communion with GOD, the Possession of his Throne, with another Kind of sweetness then the Bridegroom himself enjoys, the Resurrection of the Body, and Life Eternal, in a Kingdome where all Occasions of Tears and Fears shall ever be removed, Where all Regions, and Ages, and Spaces, and Times, and Eternities, shall be before our Eys, and all Objects in all Worlds at once Visible, and infinitely Rich, and Beautiful, and *Ours!* Our very Appetites also being ravished with Sensible Pleasures in all our Members, not inconsistent with, but springing from these high and Superior Delights, not distracting or confounding our Spiritual Joys, but purely Superadded, and increasing the same; while our Bodies *are made like to his most Glorious Body, by that Almighty Power whereby he is able to subdue All Things to himself,* all these infuse their Value; and the Hope that is exercised about these Things is a Vertue so great, that all inferior Hopes, which this doth Sanctifie, are made Vertues by it, but without this all other Hopes are Debasements and Abuses of the Soul, meer Distractions and delusions, and therefore *Vices.*

I Know very well that Presumption and Despair are generally accounted the Extreams of Hope, and the only vices that are Opposite thereunto. But I Know as well, that there may be many Kinds and Degrees of Hope, of which some may be *vicious,* and some *Vertuous:* and that some sorts of Hope themselves are Vices. When ever we make an inferior Desire the Sovereign Object of our Hope, our Hope is abominable, Idolatrous and Atheistical. We forget GOD, and magnifie an inferior Object above all that is Divine. To Sacrifice all our *Hopes* to Things unworthy of them, or to be Remiss and sluggish in *Hoping* for Things of infinite Importance, is apparently *Vicious:* But to be just to all our Encouragements, and to lift up our Eys to the Eternal GOD, with an humble Expectation; to wait upon him, and to hope for all that from his Bounty, which his Goodness has promised, to desire the most high and perfect *Proofs* of his Love, is the Property of a most Great and Noble Soul, by which it is carried above all the World, and fitted for the Life of the most high and perfect Vertue.

Of Repentance. Its Original, its Nature, it is a
Purgative Vertue. Its necessity, its Excellencies.
The measure of that sorrow which is due to
Sin is intollerable to Sense, confessed by
Reason, and dispensed with by mercy.

REPENTANCE is a Sowre and austere Kind of Vertue, that was
not created nor intended by GOD, but introduced by Sin, made fair
by Mercy, in remitting the offence, and pardoning the Sin. It is a
Strange Kind of off-spring, which flows from Parents so infinitely different, and has a mixture in its Nature, answerable to either an *Evil*
which it derives from *Sin,* and a *Goodness* which flows from *Mercy.*
Its Evil is that of Sorrow, Indignation and Shame, Its Goodness is
the usefulness, and necessity of the thing, considering the Condition
we are now in. It is highly ingrateful to Sence, but transcendently
convenient and amiable to *Reason;* for it is impossible for him that
has once been defiled with sin, ever to be cleansed, or to live after
in a Vertuous manner, unless he be so ingenious as to lament his Crime,
as to loath, acknowledge, and detest his Error.

THE Union of the Soul and Body is mysterious, but that Sin and
Mercy should be united, as Causes so infinitely different, for the production of a Child so Black and so Beautiful, is the Greatest Wonder
which the Soul can contemplate on this side Heaven; and will continue
to be remembred for ever, and appear more Wonderful than before
when the perfect Disparity and Opposition between them is clearly
seen, in the Light of Glory.

THE *Efficient Cause* of Repentance is either Remote, or Immediate:
Its immediate Efficient Cause is the Gracious Inclination, or the Will
of the Penitent, its remote Efficient is GOD, the Father of Lights from
which every Good and Perfect Gift descended. Its *Material Cause*

is Sorrow. Its *Formal Cause,* which makes it a Vertue, is the Reason and Manner of that Sorrow, the Equity and Piety wherewith it is attended, containing many ingredients in its Nature too long a particular to be described here. Its *Final Cause* is either immediate, or ultimate, the first is Amendment, the last Salvation.

BEING thus bounded by its Causes, its Definition is Easie, Repentance is a Grace, or Christian Vertue, wherein a man confesses, hates and forsakes his Sin, with Grief that he hath been Guilty of it, and purposes of Amendment of Life in Order to His Peace and Reconciliation with GOD, that he may answer the Obligations that lye upon him, discharge his Duty, lay hold on the Advantages of GODS Mercy, escape everlasting Damnation, and be made a Partaker of Eternal Glory.

AMONG the Vertues some are *Purgative,* and some are *Perfective.* The Purgative Vertues are all Preparatory to Bliss, and are occasioned only by the Disorder of the Soul: the perfective are Essential to our formal Happiness, and Eternally necessary by the Law of Nature. Repentance is not in its own Nature, (If Simply and absolutely considered) necessary to Bliss: But, in Relation to Sinners, it is as necessary as Physick to the Recovery of Health, or as the *Change* it self is, by which we pass from the Distemper we are Sick of, to the right and Sound Estate which we had lost by the Disease. As the malady is accidental, so is the Cure. For the Nature of Man may be *well,* and perfect, without either this, or the other. He that is originally pure, has no need of a Purgative Vertue: but he that is faln defiled must needs rise, and wash away the filth, before he can be clean.

FOR this Cause, even among the Heathens themselves, the more Knowing and Learned have a Conscience of Sin; their Priests and Philosophers, devised several Rites and Manners of Purgation, which they taught, and imposed on their Disciples with much Circumstance and Ceremony, in order to their Reception. Nor was there any Temple, or Religion in the World, that pretended not something to Diviner Mysteries: Which were graced & beautified with Preparatory Washings, Humiliations, Fashions, Attirs, Watchings, Retirements, Shavings, Sprinklings, Anoyntings, Consecrations, Sacrifices, or some other Disciplines like unto these, to be endured and past thorow, before their Votaries could be admitted to their mysteries. All which Rites as they made a great shew, because they were sensible, so were they apt to put a magnificent face on their Religion to dispose the Persons *exercised* by them to a more complying Obedience, and to beget a Reverence mixt with Awful Admiration in their ignorant Spectators. All which nevertheless were but *Emblematical Ordinances,* signifying something invisible that was necessary to be done, of which the Priests themselves knew not the meaning. They had the name of *Pœnitentia* in their Common Conversation, but applied it to profane and Trivial occasions: But *Repentance* in Religion, which is the Soul and substance of those mystical Observations, a broken and Contrite Heart, an internal Sorrow for their sin, was a thing unknown; so that all their Appearances, how magnificent soever, were but Empty shells.

REPENTANCE alone though never so simple and short in its name, being of such value, that GOD accepts one contrite Groan above all the Ceremonies, even of his own Law. And therefore he saith,* *Thou desirest not sacrifice else would I give it; thou delightest not in Burnt offering. The Sacrifices of GOD are a Broken Spirit: A broken and a contrite Heart, O God, thou wilt not despise.*

FOR tho Repentance be not in it selfe a desirable Vertue, nor so much as a *Vertue,* till there be a sphere and Occasion for it, wherein to be exercised, tho Repentance in it selfe be far worse then obedience, yet upon the Account of our Saviours Merits, and GODS Love to Sinners, it is preferred above the Greatest Innocency and Purity whatsoever. For *there is more Joy in Heaven over one sinner that repenteth, then over Ninety and nine Just persons that need no Repentance.*† If the Soul be of greater value than the whole World, if the loss of any Thing we esteem, increaseth the sence of its excellency; if our Saviour justly and rationally compareth himself to a Shepheard, that leaveth Ninety and nine sheep in the wilderness, to seek one that is gone astray; if he rejoyceth when he hath found it, more for that one that was lost, then for the ninety and nine which he had in safety; if his Delight in the success of his Labours be answerable to their Greatness; if the frustration of all his Desires, and painful endeavours in seeking it, be infinitely Grievious; and the Vertues more Amiable and Wonderful, which sinners exercise after their Redemption; if their Love, and their joy, and their praise be increased, by the extreamity of their Distress and the multitude of the sins that are forgiven them; if their Communion with GOD be more sweet, and their Happiness more exalted, and the Kingdom of GOD it selfe made more sublime and Glorious thereby; *Repentance* hath something more in it then Perfection had before the fall, and as sinners have made themselves more infinitly Indebted, so are they infinitly more subject to the Arbitrary Disposal

* *Psal.* 51.16, 17.   † *Luke* 15.

of Almighty Power, infinitly more Capable of Obligations and Rewards, infinitely more Obliged for Pardon and deliverance, as well as infinitly more Obnoxious to Divine Justice, their Fear and Danger is infinitly Greater, they stand in need of infinite Grace, and Mercy, which when they receive and enjoy, their Love and Gratitude are proportionably greater, their Delights are more quick, and vigorous, and full, and so are their praises.

BUT before a sinner can atchieve all this, or GOD enjoy the fruit of his Salvation, he must needs *repent,* for Repentance is the true and substantial Preparation of the Soul, the only Purgative Vertue, by which it is fitted for these Divine Attainments. It is, we confess in outward Appearance a slight invisible Act, but as Great within, as Wide and Comprehensive as the Heavens. It receiveth the Vertue of the Divine Essence of the whole Creation, of infinite Mercy, of the Blood of Christ, of his Humiliation, Merit, Exaltation, Intercession, and glory, of all the Work of Redemption into it self; and having fed it self, digested them, it receiveth strength by the Influence of these to dispence all their Vertue again, in the Production of those Fruits, for the sake of which GOD hath filled all the World with miracles, the Verdure, and Maturity, and Perfection of which shall with their beauty and sweetness continue in life and Florish for ever.

IF we respect Man alone, and the things that are done in himself by Repentance, it seemeth a Vertue of infinite value: It divests him of all his Rebellion, Pride, and vain Glory, strips him of all his Lust and Impiety, purges him of all his corruption, Anger, and Malice, pares off all his Superfluities, and excesses, cleanseth his Soul of all its filthiness and pollution, removeth all that is so infinitly Odious to GOD, and makes him amiable and Beautiful to the holy Angels. It fits and prepares him for all the exercises of Grace and Piety, introduces Humility and Obedience into his Soul, makes him capable of a Divine Knowledge, and makes way for the Beauty of his Love and Gratitude, inspires Fortitude, and Prudence, and Temperance, and Justice into his soul; renues his Nature, and makes him a meek and patient Person, restores him to that Wisdom and Goodness he had lost, cloaths him with righteousness and true Holiness, and seats him again in the Favour of GOD. By Repentance he recovers the Divine Image, and by Consequence it extends to all that Blessedness and Glory which is for ever to be enjoyed.

REPENTANCE is the Beginning of that Life, wherein all the sweat and Labour of the Martyrs, all the Persecutions and Endeavours of the Apostles, all the Revelations of the Prophets, all the examples of the *Patriarchs,* all the Miracles of old Time, all the Mysteries of the Law, all the Means of Grace, all the Verities of the Gospel begin to take full force and Effect, in obtaining that for which they were intended. Which sufficiently intimates the value of the Grace, and how highly well pleasing it must be to GOD: It is the *Conception* of Felicity, and the *New Birth* of the *Inward Man,* the Dereliction of the Old, and the Assumption of a New, and more cœlestial Nature. It is the Gate of the Heavenly Kingdome which they that refuse to enter at, can never enjoy. It is one of the Keys of Death and Hell, by which the Gate of the Prison is unlockt, nay the very knocking off the Chains, and Manacles of Satan; the very Act wherein we regain our Liberty, and become the Sons of GOD, and Citizens of Heaven. It was fitly Typified in the old Law, by the Laver that was set at the Door of the Tabernacle for the Priests to wash in, before they entred into the Sanctuary, to walk in the Light of the Golden Candlesticks, to offer their Devotions at the Incense Altar, and to partake of the shew-bread on the Golden Table. In the Outward Court they enjoyed the society of the visible Church, the sight of the Bloody Altar, (which answers our Saviors Cross erected in the World) and the Benefit of their Outward Profession, which consisted in their Admission to the Visible Ordinances, and exterior Rites of Religion: But that Court was open over head, obnoxious to showers, in Token that a bare *Profession* is not Enough to shelter us from the Dangers and Incommodities that may be rained down in Judgments upon us from the wrath of GOD: whence the face of Heaven is overcast with Clouds, and Covered with black and Heavy Displeasure, till we wash and be clean, and enter by penitence into the Invisible Church, of which the *Second Court* is a Figure, wherein we are illuminated by the Holy Ghost, and offer up the sweet Perfumes of our Thanksgivings and Praises, being admitted to feed upon the Heavenly Feast represented by the Shew-bread-Table; we are never received into the Society of the Saints and Angels, painted out in the *Cherubims* and *Palm Trees* round about on the inside of its *Walls,* nor Covered over head with a vail to protect us: A vail of *Blew* to represent the inferior Heaven, wherein *Cherubims* were interwoven to represent the *Angels* looking down upon us, a vail of *Goats-hair* concealed and unseen above that of Blew, to signifie the fruits of our Saviours Life, and another of *Rams-skins* died *Red,* to signifie the Blood of Christ, by which we are secured from all the Displeasure which otherwise for Sin, was due to us. The Goats hair fitly resembles the Active Obedience, or the Righteousness of Christ; for as much as *Hair* may be clipped off, and a Covering made of it, while the Beast is *alive:* For so might Christ have been perfectly Righteous, tho his Life had never been Taken away: But *red* is the Color of *blood,* the *Skin* importeth Death for as much as it cannot be fleyed off, without the destruction of the Creature. These vails therefore as they were above the other, were of higher and more mysterious importance: And spread over the inclosed, and invisible Court, into which none but *Priests* and *Levites* entered, that *washed* at the *Laver,* to intimate the security only of those, that are washed in the Laver of Regeneration, and made *Kings* and *Priests* unto God, being purged from their old sins, and sanctified and illuminated, in a secret Spiritual manner. For as they only that tarried in their Houses, were under the protection of the *Paschal Lamb,* whose *Blood* was sprinkled on the *Lintils* of their *Gates* and *Doors,* when the destroying Angel past through the Land of *Egypt* to kill the First-born of Man and Beast: So onely they that keep within the *Pale* of the *Invisible Church,* are under the *Shaddow* of the Almighty, because they only dwell in the secret place of the most High, and they alone are under the Coverture of that Powerful *Blood,* which speaketh better things than the Blood of *Abel,* but pleads for the preservation of them onely, that repent and believe, and is therefore effectually spread over the *Invisible Church* alone. Which in another Type is exhibited by the mixture of the *Blood* and *Oyl,* which was sprinkled upon the Priests and Lepers that were cleansed: *Sanctification* and *Justification* moving alwayes together hand in hand, the Unction of the Holy One, or the Oyl of Love and Gladness annointing all those that are washed, and only those are washed in clean and pure water, they alone being effectually sprinkled with the *Blood* of Christ, *who of GOD is made unto us Wisdome, and Righteousness, and Sanctification, and Redemption.*

FOR if God should take Pleasure in us before we were *pure,* his Complacency would be *false,* and his Delight unrighteous. Till we are Delightful to him we can never be *Honorable* nor *Glorious* before him: Nor ever be pleasing to that *Goodness,* which is indelible (tho latent) in our *own* Souls, till we feel our selves clean and Beautiful.

IF any thing in the World can commend the value of Repentance, or discover the infinite use and necessity of it, this will certainly be a consideration Effectual: That tho GOD love us with an infinite and eternal Love, tho he magnifies his Mercy infinitely over all our Deservings, tho Jesus Christ loved us so, as to sacrifice himself in our places, tho he made infinite satisfaction to the Justice of God for our Sins, tho the Holy Ghost came down from Heaven for our sakes, nay tho we ourselves were taken up into Heaven, all this would be of little avail, and we should quickly be tumbled down again, if only Sin were Delightful to us, and our Wills so obstinate, that there was no place for Repentance in our Hearts, no sorrow, nor Contrition for the Offences we had committed. It is not the Love of GOD to us, so much as our love to him, that maketh Heaven. It may surprize you perhaps, but shall certainly instruct you, for the Love of GOD may be infinite, yet if it be unseen, breed no delight in the Soul: if it be sleighted and despised, it shall increase our Guilt, Shame, and Deformity, and make us the more Odious; which it must needs do, when we are impenitent. For so long, it is manifest that we are neither *Sensible* of his Love, nor *Just* unto it. The taste of its sweetness, and the Pleasure we take in his infinite Love, is the *Life* of Blessedness, and the *Soul* of Heaven. It is the *Concurrence* of our Love and His, when they meet together, that maketh Heaven.

HERE upon Earth we ought actually to grieve, and repent for our Sins:—But should GOD require a measure in our *Grief* answerable to its Causes, our Repentance it self would be an *Hell* unto us: For the Grief would be Endless and insupportable. Right Reason requires that we should be *infinitely* afflicted for the infinite folly and madness of Sin. But the Mercy of GOD dispenseth with our Grief so far, that it takes off the Pain, which its *infinite Measure* would inflict upon our sense, and accepts of an Acknowledgement made by our Reason that it ought to be infinite, if strict Justice were exacted at our Hands. Our intention is (in the Course of Reason,) to be infinitely and Eternally grieved for the Baseness of the Act, and the Vileness we have contracted, and so we should be, did its Effects continue and abide forever; for then we should be hated of GOD and become his Enemies World without End. But the Removal of that Hatred, and the infinite Mercy whereby we are forgiven, hath a kindly Operation on the Soul of every Penitent, and the Joy it infuseth restrains and limits the Excess of our Sorrow, it leaves the Intension of Grief, and its inclination in the Mind, yet stops the persecution, and relieves our Reason, by diverting the stream of its Operations and Exercises; it engageth its actual Resentments upon other Objects, which turn it all into Love and Adoration, Praise and Thanksgiving, Joy and Complacency. For the Love of God continued after our fall, and the Felicity to which we are called out of the Depth of our misery, all the Advantages we receive upon our Redemption, the Improvements of our miserable Estate, the Degrees and Ornaments that are added to the Beauty and perfection of Gods Kingdome upon so sad an occasion as Sin is, all these things take up our Thoughts in such a manner that while we are actually and fully Just to these, and Loving GOD, for his Eternal Love, infinitely more than we Love our selves, we live in him, and are all in raptures of Blessedness. Yet is there a *Vertual Sorrow* which Reason conceives as most due to Sin, which being expressed only in the Humility of our Souls, and seen as it were underneath the fruition of our Joys, in the lowly Conceit we retain of our selves (in the confession of our vileness and the deep Sence of our own unworthiness;) is far Greater, now we are restored to the favour and Love of GOD, far sweeter to be seen, and deeper to be understood; than the Grief for Sin would have been, had we been not redeemed, but Damned forever.

Of Charity towards GOD. It Sanctifieth Repentance, makes it a Vertue, and turns it to a Part of our true Felicity. Our Love to all other Objects is to begin and End in GOD. Our Love of GOD hath an Excellency in it that makes it worthy to be desired by his Eternal Majesty. He is the only Supreme and Perfect friend. By Loving we enjoy him.

REPENTANCE without Love is so far from seating us in the Felicity of Heaven, that it is one of the Ingredients of the Torments in Hell, a natural Effect of Sin, and a great Part of the Misery of Devils. Love is a genuine Affection of the Soul, and so powerfully Sweet, when it is Satisfied and pleased, that it communicates the Relish of its own *Delightfulness* to every Thing near it, and Transformes the most *Virulent* Affections into *Smooth,* Healing, *Perfective* Pleasures. Insomuch that in Heaven our Sorrow for Sin shall perhaps be infinite, yet the malignity of it so perfectly corrected, that tho we continue Eternally *Just,* in rendring our Sins that grief which is their due, it shall not discompose our peace, nor corrode our Delights, but increase our Repose in the Beauty of our souls, and make our Joys more full of Extasie, by those Melting, Lively, Bleeding, Resentments, which our Love will occasion in the very Grief, wherewith it perfects our Felicity. For as the falling out of Lovers is the Renewing of Love, so is the Mercy and Kindness of the one, even of him that was injured; and the calm and secure Indignation wherewith the other hates himself, for being guilty of so vile a miscarriage, the very Grace and Beauty of the Reconciliation; it is a great means of their mutual Endearment and Tenderness ever after: the Compassion of him that is Innocent, and the humble grief of the Guilty making the Joy of their future Correspondence more Deep and Serious, more Vigorous and Enflaming, more lasting.

LOVE is that which Sanctifies Repentance, and makes it pleasant both to him that is Beloved, and to him that is adored; Acceptable and Delightful to him that repenteth, as well as to him that had been injured. For the Sinners Restauration makes it as *Natural* to grieve for his *Fault* as to rejoyce in his *Felicity,* his sad and humble Resentments are his own Satisfaction, because he sees himself *Just* and *Rational* in them; he delights in his Sorrow, because it is *Honourable,* and finds a new Kind of pleasure in his *Abasement,* because it is relieved by the Wonder of his Happy condition; and what he hath lost in himself is regained in the perfection and Goodness of his Object.

THAT GOD is the sovereign Object of Love I scarcely need to mention; all I shall observe upon this occasion, is; that we are more to Love him for his *Mercy* and *Compassion* towards us as *Sinners,* then for his *Goodness* and *Bounty* expressed at the first, as we were *Innocent Creatures.* The Bleeding Spectacle of his *Incarnate* Deity, and the Perseverance of his Miraculous and *Transcendent* Love after all our Offences, is another Kind of Motive to heighten our Charity of, and gives it another form, as much more Mysterious, so much more perfect and Delightful then ever. Our Sorrow for Sin infuses a New *Sense* into Nature, a New Beauty into Love, and gives as much unto it, as it receiveth from it. But this being better known by Experience, then by description I shall refer you to the Life of Heaven and Grace, for more ample satisfaction.

LOVE, as we have shewed, may be extended to all Objects in Heaven and Earth; all that is Goodly and Amiable being capable of that Affection. Hereupon the Word *Love* is generally used for that Liking and Esteem we have for any thing, whether *Dead* or *alive.* We can Love Life, and desire to see Good Days; we can Love the Sun, and Wine, and Oyl, and Gold; Love our Dogs and Horses, fine Clothes and Jewels, Pleasures, Honours, Recreations, Houses, Riches, and as well as Love Men and Women, Souls and Angels. And evermore our Love expresseth it self in Tenderness and Care for the Preservation of what we Love, in Esteem of its Worth, and Delight in its Beauty, in endeavours also to promote its Welfare as far as it is capable. But there is another sort of Love towards *Living Objects,* Divine and reasonable, which we call *Charity.* This is that Vertue of which the Apostle saith, (after he had spoken of all the Miracles, Helps, Governments, Prophesies, Tongues, and other Gifts of the Holy Ghost, that were then in the Church) *And Yet shew I unto you a more Excellent Way.* 1 *Cor.* 12. ult. And in the next Chapter.* *Tho I speak with the Tongues of Men and of Angels, and have not Charity, I am become as sounding Brass, or a tinkling Cymbal. And tho I have the Gift of Prophesie, and understand all mysteries, and all Knowledge, and tho I have all Faith, so that I could remove Mountains, and have no Charity, I am nothing, and tho I bestow all my Goods to feed the poor, and tho I give my Body to be burned, and have not Charity it profiteth me nothing.* It is that concerning which our Saviour speaketh,† *The first of all the Commandements is, Hear O Israel, the Lord our GOD is one Lord, and thou shalt Love the Lord thy GOD with all thy heart, and with all thy Soul, and with all thy Mind, and with all thy Strength: This is the first Commandement: And the Second is like, namely this, Thou shalt Love thy Neighbour as thy self: There is none other Commandement greater then those.* Nay perhaps it is that of which he saith to his Apostles, when they had admired at his Miracles. *He that believeth on me, the works that I do shall he do also, and greater Works then these shall he do, because I go to the Father.* For Faith worketh by Love, Love is the Life of Faith, and without the Works of the one the other is Dead: The Works of Love are the End of all Miracles, and more Blessed then they. Nay Love is the End of *Faith* as well as it is of the *Law:* for the Apostle saith, *The End of the Commandment is Charity, out of a pure Heart, and of a good conscience, and of Faith unfeigned.* It is the End of the very Creation of the World, of all Gods Labors and Endeavours, of all his Ways in all Ages, all the faculties and powers of the Soul, the very End of the Redemption of Mankind, the End of the Jewish Oeconomy under the Law, the End of all the Dispensations of Grace and Mercy under the Gospel; the End of our Saviours coming down into the World, the End of all his Miracles, Tears, and Blood, the End of the Holy Ghosts appearing upon Earth, the End of all the Means of Grace, and in some sort the very last End of all Rewards and Punishments whatsoever. The everlasting Continuance of this Love is the End of Eternity it self in a manner, and if our Love be not the End of GODS Love, his is of ours. And if the Truth be deeply inquired into, the *Intermixture* is so sweet, that his is the End of ours, ours of his. For he Loveth us with the Love

---

* 1 Cor. 13.1.   † Mark. 12.30, 31.

of *Benevolence,* that we may Love him; and he desires to be beloved
of us, that he may Love us, with another Kind of Love, distinct from
the former, even that of *Complacency.* Which Love of Complacency
is the Crown of ours, and so Delightful to us, that it is the very End
of our Desire, and begetteth in us a new Love of Complacency fitly
answering his unto us.

NOW if Love be the End of all the Laws, Works, and Ways of
GOD, of all our Saviours Labours and sufferings, of our souls and
Bodies, of the whole Creation, of all the Endeavours and Desires of
the Deity, in all the Dispensations of his Grace and Providence, there
must be something in its Nature Equivalent to all these Transcendent
Undertakings, to justifie the *Wisdom* that selected Love for its Sovereign Object, for it is the office of Wisdome to suit the means and
their End together, so that the Excellency of the one may be worthy
of all the Cost and Difficulty of the other. For it is a foolish thing
to pursue a base and feeble End by Glorious and Wonderful Methods,
because its Vileness will Disgrace the Design, and with it their Beauty,
their very Grandure will be absurd, where their Issue is but contemptible. The Apostle therefore telleth us that *Love is the fulfilling of the
Law,* and that it is *the Bond of Perfectness.* And pursuing its properties
a little more Ample, he saith,* *Charity suffereth long, and is kind,
Charity envyeth not, Charity Vaunteth not it self, is not puffed up,
doth not behave it self unseemly, seeketh not her own, is not easily
provoked, thinketh no evil, rejoyceth not in iniquity, but rejoyceth
in the Truth, beareth all Things, believeth all things, hopeth all things,
endureth all things. Charity never faileth,* &c.

IT is one noble Effect of Charity, that it suffereth afflictions cheerfully and patiently for the sake of its Beloved: Another is its Kindness
to its Object; its sweet and Courteous inclination to do all manner
of Good: Another, for which it is highly valuable, is, that it envieth
not the Felicity or Glory of its Beloved but taketh Pleasure to see
it far higher and greater then its own: is not apt to vaunt and brag
of its Perfections, but hath an humble Esteem of all its Atchievments:
doth not behave it self in a distasteful manner, but studies and designes
the Honour, Benefit and satisfaction of its Object. But that which of
all other is its greatest Perfection, is, that *it seeketh not its own:* it
is not Mercenary or self ended, but truly Generous and Heroick in
its Performances. It Sacrificeth it self, and all its interests, to the Advantage of its Object; it preferreth the Person it Loveth above it self,

* 1 Cor. 13.4, 5, *&c.*

desires its Exhaltation, and delights in its Glory more then its own, It *is not easily provoked,* because it puts the best sence upon all that is done by its Object: *Thinketh no evil,* is not suspicious, or malevolent, or censorious, but frameth honourable and fair *Ideas* of all that is thought or done by its Beloved: Hateth all Impurity that may displease its Object, all black and crooked Apprehensions, that may wrang and disguise it; *beareth all* with Hope and Equanimity, because it *believeth* its Object to be Good, and Wise, till it must of necessity change its Opinion, and entertain a Judgement tending to its condemnation. It is no longer Charity then, but dislike and aversion, when it ceaseth to think well of its Object: for it is another *Principle* or is as distinct in Nature from *Love,* as its Actions are from the Actions of Love; the diversity of the Effects evidently proving a Difference in their Causes.

THE Quality, by which Charity *rejoyceth in the Truth,* is an incomparable excellence and commendation of its Nature. Because the Truth is GODS infinite Goodness, and Love, and Providence, which are exercised in preparing Delights and Treasures for his Beloved. The truth is the Felicity and Glory of the Soul. And if it be *true* that all Eternity is full of Joys, and all the World enriched with Delights, that a man is infinitely beloved of GOD, and made in his Image on purpose, that he might enjoy all the Best of all possible Treasures in his similitude, he may well *rejoyce in the Truth:* because no Truth can be greater or more delightful, than that himself is exalted to the Throne of GOD, and ordained to live in Communion with him.

BUT that Quality, by which the Soul *believeth,* and *hopeth all things,* that concern the Honour and Fidelity of its Beloved, is yet more acceptable and delightful than the former. For a good opinion of the Nature and Intention of the Person with whom we are united, is the *Basis* and Foundation of all our Respect, the Cement of our Peace, and the Life and Soul of all that Honour that is paid unto him. The very Grace and Beauty of all our Conversation dependeth upon it, and if it be true, that we are more to love GOD for the intrinsick Perfections of his Essence, then for all his Gifts, the chief Business of our Knowledge is to Frame glorious Apprehensions of his Nature, and to Believe him in all things so Kind and Wise, that he is True and Faithful in all his Declarations, and most fit to be Honoured in all the Dispensations of his Providence, because he is ever mindful of his Protestations and Promises. For then we can believe, that all things shall work together for our Good, can safely trust our selves, and all that is ours in his hands; resign our selves up to his Disposal with Joy, and say *Thy Will be done,* for it is *Holy, Good, and acceptable.* Thy Will alone is of all other Wills most Perfect and Desirable. There are on Earth indeed more nice Emergencies, many Obscurities and Riddles, in the midst of all which to think so well of GOD as he deserveth, is the most acceptable thing in the World; for it argues a great confidence of his Worth, and a Love that is founded on *Substantial Causes* never to be removed. It feedeth the Soul with a lively hope, and fair Expectation of great Things from him: by which alone we do right to His GODHEAD, in acknowledging the Perfection of his Love and Goodness, and by which alone we are made able to adore him and to live in Union and Communion with him.

THERE is great Talk of Friendship, it is accounted the only Plea-sure, in the World; Its Offices are highly magnified of all: Kindness of Behaviour, a through and clear communication of Souls, a secure Reliance upon each others Fidelity, a perfect Discovery of all our Thoughts, Intentions, and Resentments, an ardent willingness to impart Lives and Estate for the Benefit of our Friend, the Reposing of all our Secrets in each others Bosomes, to do all services, and suffer all afflictions, for each others sakes, to prefer the Concerns of our Friend upon all Occasions above our own, these are the *Magnalia Amicitiæ, & Arcana mutuæ Benevolentiæ,* the Great and mighty Effects for which Friendship is admired: But all these, without a good Opinion of our Friend, are nothing worth, they are but Externals of Friendship, the greatest Secret in its Nature is, the mutual agreement of Souls and Spirits, the Delight which either taketh in the other, the honour and esteem they give and receive, the Approbation and Love of each others Dispositions, the Sence and Admiration of each others Vertues, the continual Desire of being alwayes together, peculiar Extasie, which the Beauty of either occasioneth in the other, when of all other Trea-sures in the World their Persons are the greatest to one another. Either is the proper Element and *Refrigerium* of the others Soul. Their Bosomes are the mutual Receptacles and Temples of each others ac-complishments, whereinto they are received in all their Desert, and have *Justice* done to every degree and Perfection in their Nature; their Hearts are the Thrones where they are exalted, and magnified, and live at Ease, are honoured and worshipped, extolled, and reign as absolute in each others Souls. There are some slight aims and Adum-brations of this Friendship on Earth; but the best and highest Degree of it here beneath is but a rude and imperfect shadow, only GOD is the *Sovereign friend,* all Adoration paid to any one beside is meer Idolatry. Our Hearts can be absolutely Sacrificed to none, but him; because he alone is immutable in Goodness. We cannot infinitely honour and delight in any but Him; it is he alone that can infinitely honour, and delight in us. All our Lives, Estates, and Services are Due to him, his Will alone is to be wholly ours, because no other Will is infallibly Right, Wise, Holy, but his alone.

THE Union of our Wills is a Perfection of Love: but that at which he aimeth by all his Labours, and Gifts, and Benefits, is our Right and Good Opinion of his Excellencies and Perfections. That we should see and discern his interior Properties, admire his Graces, adore his Perfections, adore and magnifie his Beauty and Glory, this is the End for which he communicates himself in all his Works and Ways unto us; it is the End of the whole Creation, and of all the Excellent Things in the universe: for by this he establisheth his Empire in our souls and makes us Pleasing to himself in all our Operations. And for this Cause it is, that the Apostle plainly tells us that tho we give our Body to be burned, and all our Goods to feed the poor, without Charity it profiteth nothing. To render to GOD the Honour that is due to his Name, to receive and admire all his Bounties, to rejoyce in all his Operations, to adore him in all his Ways, to take pleasure in all his Works, to fill Heaven and Earth with our Joys and Praises, is a Work which cannot but be agreeable by its Nature, to his Eternal Essence. And if this be the Work of Love, it is that which is most Excellent, because he is therein both pleased and enjoyed. GOD and all his Creatures are united together by Love alone, and in the Eternal Exercise of pure and perfect Love all Blessedness and Glory consisteth.

IF you require what it is to love GOD, you will find it worthy of his Highest desire, because thereby all our souls, nay all his Creatures, and his whole Kingdome are perfected, for to Love GOD as we ought to do, is to Honour him as our Father, Benefactor, Bridegroom, and King, to contemplate him as our Cause with Complacency, and to rest in him as our End, to delight in him as our Creator, Preserver, Lawgiver, and Redeemer, to dedicate our selves, wholly to that Service, whatever it be, wherein he is chiefly pleased and delighted. It is to love him in himself, in all his Works, in all his Ways, in all his Laws, in all his Attributes, in all his Thoughts and Counsels, in all his Perfections; It implies the Knowledge of all Objects, the Use of all Means, the Attainment of all Ends: all Wisdome and Goodness, all Obedience and Gratitude, all Righteousness and Holiness, all Joy and Praise, all Honour and Esteem, all Blessedness and Glory. For it is to Love him with all our Heart, and with all our Soul, with all our Strength, and with all our Might, with all our Understanding, with all our Will, with all our Affection, with all the Powers of our soul, with all our Inclinations and Faculties, in all his Creatures, in all his Appearances, in Heaven and Earth, in Angels and Men, in all Kingdoms and Ages. It is to see and desire, to Esteem and delight in his Omnipresence and Eternity, and in every Thing by which he manifesteth himself in either of these, so that all Enlargement, and Greatness, and Light, and Perfection, and Beauty, and Pleasure, are founded in it, and to Love him to Perfection implies all Learning and Attainment, because we must necessarily be acquainted with all Things in all Worlds, before we can thorowly and compleatly do it. Which here upon Earth to do by Inclination and Endeavour to the utmost of our Power, is all that is required of us; And if we do it to our utmost, it shall be rewarded in the Beatifick Vision, with a full and Blessed Perfection, with an actual Love exactly resembling his, and fully answerable to it in the Highest Heavens.

THERE are two common Motives of Love among Men, the one the Goodness and Excellency of the Person, the other his particular Kindness and Love to us: And both these are in the Highest Degree in GOD. He is of infinite Goodness and Excellency in himself, for there is nothing Good in the world, but what hath received all its Goodness from Him. His Goodness is the Ocean, and all the Goodnesses of Creatures little Streams flowing from that Ocean. Now you would think him a Madman that should say the Sea were not greater then a trifling Brook: and certainly it is no less folly to suppose that the Goodness of GOD doth not as much (nay infinitely more) exceed that of all the Creatures. The Sun is a lively Mirror of that Eternal Act of Love which is the Glory of his Essence, but it is infinitely less prone to communicate its Beams, and doth less Good to it self, and infinitely less to all other Creatures. It shines for their sakes nevertheless, and clothes it self with Glory, by the splendor of its Beams and is an Emblem of GOD, who exerteth his Power with infinite Pleasure, and by communicating his Essence in an infinite Manner, propagates his Felicity, and Glory, to the utmost Height and Perfection. By proceeding from himself to all Objects throughout all Worlds, he begets, and dwelleth in himself, he inhabits Eternity in a Blessed and more vigorous Manner, by establishing the Felicity of all his Creatures, and becomes their infinite and Eternal Glory. *Wherein* his particular Kindness and Love to us appeareth because he hath fitted us with Qualities and Powers adopted for so great an End, and as particularly appropriated all to us, as the Sun to the Eye of every Spectator. For our Bodies and our Souls are made to enjoy the Benefit of all, and his Desire is that we should attain the End for which we are created. On his side all is prepared; on ours nothing is wanting but Love to embrace and take pleasure in his Goodness, which shineth in all these Things, and created them on purpose, that being manifested by them, we might delight in it for ever.

HE that loveth not GOD with all his Heart, liveth a Life most contrary to Nature. For to Love is as natural for the Soul, as to shine for the Sun: and the more Lovely any thing is, the more prone we are to Delight in it: if any thing be infinitly Amiable, we are prone to Love it in an infinite measure, we prefer the Better above the worse, & cannot rest but in the best of all. Reason is the Essence of the Soul, and tends always to the utmost Perfection. The more Divine and Glorious any Thing is, the more high and Noble is the Love that we bear it: No Beauty less then the most Perfect, no Pleasure, no Wisdome, no Empire, no Learning, no Greatness, Wealth, or Honour, less then the most sublime can be our full Satisfaction: no little degree of Love, nothing less then the most Supreme and violent can content us: So that GOD being most truely perfect in all these, is the Adequate Object of all our Desires, and the only Person fit to be esteemed in an infinite manner. It is as natural for Man to Love him, as to desire and delight in any being, which supplies the ordinary and daily necessities of his Life.

TO Love him as we ought implies two things, that are agreable to the Nature of Love, yet very rarely to be found among the Sons of Men, a desire to please him, and a Desire to enjoy him. The Desire of *Pleasing* is a constant fruit and effect of Love. For he that Loves, is very desirous to approve himself, and to do whatsoever he thinks will be grateful to his Beloved. According to the Degree of Love, the desire is more or less. Where we Love Earnestly, we are extreamly Earnest and Careful to please: Where Love is remiss, there is little need or Regard of any thing: But *infinite* Love! It is impossible to declare what favour and Zeal it will produce. If we Love GOD, we shall keep his Commandements with a Tenderness and Desire so extreme, that no Joy will be so great as the Observation of his Laws; It will be with us, as it was with our Lord Jesus Christ, it will be

our Meat and Drink to do the Will of our Father which is in Heaven.
The measure of our Love will not infuse some slight and faint Endeavours of Pleasing, but put us on the most painful and costly Duties,
make us willing to forsake our own Ease, Goods, Friends, yea Life
it self, when we cannot keep them without offending our Creator.

THE desire of *Enjoying* is constantly seen in our Love to one another. If any man hath a friend whom he intirely loveth, he desires
his Conversation, Wishes to be always in his Company, and thinketh
the Time long till he and his friend be together. And thus will it
be in our Love to GOD, if as great and Hearty as it ought to be.
In this Life our Enjoyment of GOD is more imperfect, more compleat
and perfect in the Life to come. Here upon Earth we desire to converse
with him in his Ordinances, in Prayer, Meditation, hearing his Word,
in receiving the Sacrament, which are intended all for this purpose,
to bring us into a neerer Intimacy, and familiarity with GOD by speaking so to him, & hearing him speak, and shew himself to us. If we
love him indeed, we shall highly Value these Ways of Conversing with
him: it is all here upon Earth whereby we can enjoy him. It will
make us with *David* esteem *one Day in his Courts better than a thousand.* We shall delight in all the Means of approaching to him as often
as possible, and use them diligently, to the End of uniting us more
and more unto him, who is the Object of our Desire and the Life
of our Souls. And for as much as there is another Enjoyment of GOD
which is more compleat and perfect, we shall groan earnestly, *desire
to be dissolved and be with Christ,* where we may see no more in
a Glass, but Face to Face, and Know as we are Known. For Love
is strong as Death, many Waters cannot quench Love, neither can
the floods drown it. Affliction, Persecution, Sickness, any thing that
will bring us to Heaven, will be acceptable and Delightful.

IF you would know more fully, why GOD desires to be Beloved,
you may consider, that Love is not onely the Motive, and Incentive
to Vertue, the Cause of Obedience, but the form and Essence of every
Grace, and the fulfilling of the Law, We shall chuse him for our GOD,
and have no other GODS but him, no Delights, no Sovereign Enjoyment but him alone. We shall honour him with all our Souls, and
adore him with every Power of our Will and Understanding: We shall
not regard Images and shadows, but worship him immediately in Spirit
and in Truth. We shall not take his Name in vain, nor contentedly
stand by when others abuse it: But shall praise his Name, and desire
to see it glorified throughout the World. For Love desires the Honour,

and delights in the Glory and Advancement of its Beloved. We shall reverence his Sanctuary, and keep his Sabbaths, desiring Rest from other Avocations, that we may contemplate his Glory in all his Works. For his sake we shall observe the Laws of the second Table, and Love our Neighbour as our self. For to Love him is no Impediment, but a Strong Engagement, and incentive to the Love of all his Creatures. We shall honour our Parents for his sake, and preserve the Life of our Neighbour: We shall not rob him of his happiness in his Wife, nor wrong him in her Chastity and Fidelity towards him. We shall not steal from him, nor diminish his Possessions. We shall not defame him, nor hurt him by Lies; but vindicate and preserve his Reputation: it will be our joy and Satisfaction to see his honour clear and unblemished. We shall not injure him so much as in a thought, nor covet ought that is his, either for necessity or pleasure: but study to add to his Contentments.

WERE all the World as full of this Love as it ought to be, Paradice would still continue, and all Mankind would be the Joy and Glory of the whole Creation. The Love of GOD towards all would dwell and abide in every Soul, and the Felicity of all would be the particular Joy of every person. All the Earth would be full of Repose, and Peace, and Prosperity, nothing but Honour, and Kindness, and Contentment would replenish the World. Which leads me now to that other Branch of Love, which is Charity to our Neighbour.

Charity to our Neighbour most natural and Easie in the Estate of Innocency: Adams *Love to* Eve *and his children a great Examplar of our Love to all the World. The Sweetness of Loving. The Benefits of being Beloved. To Love all the World, and be beloved by all the World is perfect security and Felicity. Were the Law fulfilled all the World would be turned into Heaven.*

CHARITY to our Neighbour is Love expressed towards GOD in the Best of his Creatures. We are to Love GOD in all the Works of his Hands, but in those especially, that are most near unto him, chiefly those in which he manifesteth himself most clearly, and these are they that are most like him, most exalted by him, most loved of him, and most delightful to him.

ANGELS and Men, are so distinct from the residue of the Creation, that all the Works of GOD, as if they were Things of another Kind, are put in Subjection under their feet. They were made in his Image, and are often called *the Sons of GOD.* They are the Sovereign Objects of his Eternal Love, every one of them, considered apart, is so Glorious; as if he were the Sole individual friend of GOD, and King of the Universe, so that they are to be treated in another Manner, as High and Sacred Persons, elevated above the Race of ordinary Creatures, as a Progeny of Kings that are all of them friends to the King of Kings, Ambassadours representing his Person, in whom he is injured, or Obliged.

I confess there are many Disguises, that overcast the Face of Nature with a vail, and cloud these Sovereign Creatures: the Excellency, the

Absence, and Distance, and unknown Nature of Angels; the Perversness of Nature, the Ignorance, and Unkindness, and Disorders of Men Darken, and Eclipse this Glorious Duty, and make it uncouth and difficult to us: But all these Disorders came in by Sin, and it is expedient to remove the Confusions that blind us, in our miserable Estate, and to look upon this Vertue of Charity, in the Naked Beauty which appeareth to us in the Light of *Eden.*

IN the Purity of Nature, Men are Amiable Creatures and prone to Love, Two great Advantages; of which Sin and misery hath bereaved us, and to which we are restored but in Part, even then when we are Sanctified. Where the Beauty of the Object is intire, and perfect, and the Goodness of the Spectator clear and undefiled, to Love is as Natural and Easie as for fire to enflame when applied to convenient matter. For the Beauty of the Object is Oyl and Fuel to the affection of the Spectator. It is not more Easie to delight in what is pleasant, than it is to desire what is Good and Amiable. To be commanded to take pleasure in it is Liberty, not Constraint. To be forbidden would be hard. A Prohibition would be the Severest Law, and the most cruel Bondage. There was no Possitive Law in *Eden,* that required a Man to Love his Neighbour, it was a Law of Nature. The Nature of the Object required it, and our Nature prompted it self thereunto. The Service that Law required was perfect freedome. *Adam* was commanded to Love *Eve,* by a silent Law, Surprized by her Beauty and captivated by the Chains of Nature. He was amazed at so fair a Creature, her Presence was so Delightful that there was no need of a Law; an injunction had imported some Sluggishness in the zeal of his Affection. His Appetite and Reason were united together, and both invited him to lose himself in her Embraces: She was as acceptable a Present of the Love of GOD, as Wisdome and Goodness could invent for him. He was too apt to admire her, had not her Soul been as worthy; as her Symmetry was transcendent. He admired the Bounty of the *Donor* in so Great a Gift, and Great Part of his Life was to be spent in the Contemplation of his Treasure. He had a Noble Creature made in the Image of GOD for him alone! Her soul was far more excellent in Beauty then her Face, a Diviner and more Glorious Object than the whole world. Her Intelligence and Vivacity, Her Lofty and clear Apprehensions, Her Honour and Majesty, Her Freedome of Action, her Kindness of Behaviour, her Angelical Affections, Her fitness for Conversation, Her sweet and Tender Principles, a million of Graces and Endowments conspiring to enrich Her Person and Perfection, made all the World to serve *Adam* with one Degree of Pleasure more in serving and pleasing her. The Universe seemed to be Nothing but the Theatre of their mutual Love, as if all the World were made for nothing else, but to minister to her for his sake, and to make him happy in the Enjoyment of Her. While the fruition was sanctified by a Just acknowledgement and Thanksgiving to the Author.

WE produce *Eve* only for a President; this first sweetness is but a Pattern and Copy of what follows, fair Prologue to a more magnificent scene, and used by us as a meer Introduction. *Adam* was able to Love Millions more, and as *She* was taken out of his *side*, so were *they* to spring from his *Bowels:* All to be as Great, and fair, and Glorious as she, as full of Soul, and as full of Love. As the Woman was the Glory of man, so were their Off-springs the Glory of both: I mean they had been so, by the Law of Nature, had not the due course of it been disturbed. Which Accident is wholy to be fathered on *Adams* fondness to please his Wife, and to be mothered upon her Lightness and Credulity. But we being here to disclose the Felicity which is hid in the fulfilling of GODS Laws and to justifie his Love in commanding this *Charity* to our Neighbors, must not regard the Malevolence of Men, but look upon the pure Intention of the Law; and the success that would have followed, had it been, as it might have been, perfectly observed.

ALL *Adams* Children had been himself divided, and multiplied into millions, and every one a Greater Treasure to him than the whole world. The Stars had not been by a thousand Degrees so great an Ornament to the skies, as they to the Earth, an ofspring of Incarnate Angels, an assembly of corporeal Seraphims, a Race of Celestial Kings, every one loving and Honouring *Adam,* as the Fountain of their Being, and the Author of their Well being, of the one in begetting them, of the other by *standing* and abiding in his Integrity. They had all been so many Pledges of his Wives Affection; Monuments of love, New and Powerful Endearments, Enlargements of their Parents, Being Mirrors and Memorials of both their perfections; For all had been made for every one; and every one had been the Joy, nay and the Beauty of all. All had been every ones Objects, and every one the Spectator of all, every one would have delighted in the Beauty of all, and all had conspired and strived together in the love of every one, their concurrence in fulfilling the Law would have banished all sin and Oppression, Discontentment and sorrow, Wrong and Injury, Theft and Murder, and Adultery, and Lying out of the World, there had been no noise of War or Contention, or anger, or Envy, or Malice, or Revenge, this accursed *the Black Guard* had never appeared; but all would have been Delightful to one another: Affections, Honours, Benefits, and Services, Pleasures, Praises, and Prosperities, these alone had filled the World, with Beauty, Security, Peace, and Glory, Wisdome, Goodness, Love, and Felicity, Joy, and Gratitude had been all that had been Known, had Love been intirely and inviolably observed.

BUT where GODS Laws are broken there is confusion and every Evil Work. Which nevertheless does more highly commend the excellency of his Nature, and reflect a Praise upon that Authority, which must first be despised, before any Misery can come into the World. If the Duty which the Law requires be all sweetness, and Felicity, and Glory, Compleatly good, and on every side Advantageous and Profitable; we that fail in the Discharge of our Duty may be condemned, but GOD is to be admired, and still to be confessed most Glorious and Holy, because he delights in the welfare of his Creatures, and makes Religion so desireable a Mystery, and enjoynes such admirable Things, as would make all transcendently Blessed, and Good, and Perfect were they perfectly observed. He designes that all should be amiable, whom we are commanded to Love, and that we should be not only prone to Love, but actually full of it, and the reason why he constitutes Love, as the Sovereign Law; is, because, as our Saviour saith, *There is none other greater Commandement,* none more Blessed, or Divine, or Glorious, none more conducive to our Bliss, his pleasure, the perfection of his Kingdome. Removing the Law of Love, it is impossible to put another Law in its Place, which can answer the Designs of his Wisdome and Goodness, or comply with the Exigencies of our Estate and condition. It is as easie to change the Nature of GOD, and devise another deity as Good and convenient, as to invent a better Law then this, which is plainly of all other the most Divine and Holy.

If we ascend up into Heaven, and take a perfect account of all the Operations and Effects of Love as they appear in Glory; we may first give our selves the Liberty of Wishing, and consult, what of all Things possible is most fit to be desired. Had we a Power to chuse, what Kind of Creatures would our selves be made? Could we desire to be any thing more great and Perfect then the Image of GOD? In the full extent and utmost height of its Nature it is the Resemblance of all his Blessedness and Glory. To have Beings without Power, or power without Operations, will never make us like GOD, because by an infinite and Eternal Act of Power he is what he is. Actions are so necessary that all Felicity and Pleasure is continually founded in some act or other, and no Essence is of any value, but as it employs it self in a delightful manner. What Law then would we have to regulate our actions by? Since Actions are of different Kinds, some good, some Evil, some convenient, some Hurtful, some Honourable and some Delightful, some Base and Odious, some are Miserable, and some are Glorious; we would chuse such a Law to guid our Actions by, as might make them honourable and delightful, and good and Glorious. All these are with Wisdome and Blessedness shut up in Love. And by Love it is that we make our selves infinitly Beautiful, and Amiable, and Wise, and Blessed, while we extend that Delightful and Blessed Affection to all objects that are Good and Excellent, so that on this side we have all we can desire, Essences, Laws and Actions that most tend to our full and compleat perfection. If on the other side, we look after objects for this Affection, and desire to have some Creatures most Excellent, and fit for their Goodness to be Beloved, what Creatures can we wish above all other, that can be made to satisfie and please us? Can any thing be more high and perfect then the similitude of GOD? GOD is LOVE, and his Love the Life and Perfection of Goodness. There is no *Living Goodness* so sweet and amiable as that alone, none so Wise, none so Divine, none so Blessed. What Laws can we desire those Creatures to be guided by, but the Laws of Love? By Love they are made Amiable and delightful to us; by Love they are made Great and Blessed in themselves. All Honour and Praise, Benevolence and Good-will, Kindness and Bounty, Tenderness and Compassion, all Sweetness, and Courtesie, and Care, and Affabilitie, all Service and Complacency are shut up in Love: It is the Fountain of all Benefits and Pleasures whatsoever. All Admiration, Esteem and Gratitude, all Industry, Respect, and Courage are shut up in Love, and by Love alone doth any object of ours Sacrifice it self to our Desire and Satisfaction. So that on that side our Wishes are Compleated too: while the most High, and Blessed, and Glorious Creatures love us as themselves. For thereby they are as much our Felicity as their own, and as much take pleasure and Delight therein. *As for GOD his Way is perfect;* like curious needle work on either side, compleat and exquisite.

ALL that we can fear, or except against, is his Omission, in forbearing to compell his Creatures to love, whether they will or no. But in that Liberty which he gave them, his Love is manifested most of all. In giving us a Liberty it is most apparent: for without Liberty there can be no Delight, no Honour, no Ingenuity, or Goodness at all: No action can be Delightful that is not our Pleasure in the Doing. All Delight is free and voluntary by its Essence. Force and Aversion are inconsistent with its nature. Willingness in its operation is the Beauty of the Soul, and its Honour founded in the freedom of its Desire. Whatsoever it does not desire and delight in, tho the matter of the performance be never so excellent, the Manner is spoiled, and totally Blasted. Now can we compel another to desire or delight in any Thing? The Soul in it self hath an Inclination to, or an aversion from every object. The Ingenuity and Worth of the Soul is expressed in the Kindness of its own Intention, in the freedom of its Desire to do what is Excellent, in the delight it taketh to love, its Goodness is founded. Now tho GOD infinitely hated Sin, yet he gave us an irrevocable Power to do what we pleased, and adventured the Hazzard of that which he infinitely hated, that being free to do what we would, we might be Honourable and delightful in doing (freely, and of our own Accord) what is Great and Excellent. For without this Liberty there can be no Love, since Love is an active and free affection; that must spring from the Desire and pleasure of the Soul. It is the Pleasure of a Lover to promote the Felicity of his object. Whatsoever Services he is compelled to do, he is either meerly passive in them or Cross unto them, they are all void of the Principal Grace and Beauty that should adorn them, and make them pleasant and satisfactory: men may be Dead, and moved like stones; but in such causes there is no Love, neither do they act of themselves, when they are over-ruled, and forced by another. For this cause hath it pleased God, in order to our Perfection, to make the most Sublime and Sovereign Creatures all *Free*, wherein he hath expressed the greatest Love in the World. As we may see by all the Displeasures and Pains it hath cost him, through our Abuse of so illimited and great a perfection. But where his Love is most Highly and Transcendently expressed, there are we most prone to suspect it, Nature is so Cross and disorderly. There can be no Wisdom without a voluntary Act, for in all Wisdome there is Counsel and design. Where no consultation nor Election precedes, the best operation in all the World is Blind and Casual. Fortune and chance must have no hand in that which wisdom Effecteth: no more then Force and necessity must have in that Goodness, where all the kindness ought to be in the Intention of the Benefactor. There is something in it which I cannot explain. It is easily conceived, but will never (I think) in Words, be expressed. The *Will* has a mighty hand in all the Divinity of perfect Goodness. It is the *Mind* of the Doer that is the principal object of all our Desire and Expectation.

HAVING for these Causes made his Creatures free, he has forfeited their Choise, and secured their Determination, as far as was possible. He hath done all that can be devised to make them Love us, and left nothing undone but only that which was absolutely necessary that they might *Love*. They could not Love us, if they were not left to themselves to do it freely. And their *Ability* being provided for, nay an Inclination given to make them willing, he has strictly commanded & enjoyned them to Love, by Nature allured them, & ordered us so, that we might be fit to be Beloved, he hath made it sweet and rational to Love, given them his own Example, and solemnly protested that he will accept of no Love to himself, but what is accompanied with Love to his friends and servants, engaged them to Love, or be Eternally miserable. And if for all this they will not Love, the fault is none of his. All that he has done to let secure their Love to himself, he has done to secure their Love to us: and is as much or more concerned in their Love to us, then in that which himself requireth and Expecteth. Nay he hath made it impossible for them (truly) to Love themselves without doing of it: And if they will neither Love GOD nor themselves, we may well be despised for Company. He infinitely desires their Love, and would take infinite Pleasure in the Operation. There is no Way to make themselves Honourable and Delightful to GOD, but only by Loving us, as his soul requireth. And by all these Inducements and Causes, are we our selves stirred up to Love, freely to exert the Power of Love to others in like manner.

THAT which yet further commendeth this Vertue of Love unto us, is, that it is the only Soul of all Pleasure and Felicity *in all Estates.* It is like the Light of the Sun, in all the Kingdomes, and Houses, and Eyes, and Ages, in Heaven, in Earth, in the Sea, in Shops and Temples; in Schooles and Markets, in Labours and Recreations, in Theatres and Fable. It is *the Great Dæmon of the World,* and the Sole Cause of all Operations. It is evidently impossible for any Fancy, or Play, or Romance, or Fable to be composed well, and made Delightful, without a Mixture of Love in the Composure. In all Theatres, and Feasts, and Weddings, and Triumphs, and Coronations, Love is the Soul and Perfection of all, in all Persons, in all Occupations, in all Diversions, in all Labours, in all Vertues, in all Vices, in all Occasions, in all Families, in all Cities and Empires, in all our Devotions, and Religious Actions, Love is all in all. All the Sweetness of Society is seated in Love, the Life of Musick and Dancing is Love; the Happiness of Houses, the Enjoyment of Friends, the Amity of Relations, the Providence of Kings, the Allegiance of Subjects, the Glory of Empires, the Security, Peace and Welfare of the World is seated in Love. Without Love all is Discord and Confusion. All Blessings come upon us by Love, and by Love alone all Delights and Blessings are enjoyed. All happiness is established by Love, and by Love alone is all Glory attained. GOD Knoweth that Love uniteth Souls, maketh men of one Heart in a House, filles them with Liberallity and Kindness to each other, makes them Delightfull in presence, faithful in Absence, Tender of the Honour and Welfare of their Beloved, Apt to obey, ready to please, Constant in Trials, Patient in sufferings, Couragious in Assaults, Prudent in Difficulties, Victorious and Triumphant. All that I shall need to observe further, is, that *it compleated the Joys of Heaven.* Well therefore may Wisdome desire Love, well may the Goodness of GOD delight in Love. It is the form and the Glory of his Eternal Kingdome. And therefore it is that the Apostle saith, *Charity never faileth: but whether there be Prophesies, they shall fail; whether there be Tongues, They shall cease; whether there be Knowledge it shall vanish away. For we know in part, and we Prophesie in part, but when that which is perfect is come, then that which is in part shall be done away. For now we see through a Glass darkly, but then Face to Face; now I Know in part, but then shall I know, as also I am Known. And now abideth Faith, Hope and Charity, these three, but the Greatest of these is Charity.*

Of Prudence. Its Foundation is Charity, its End Tranquillity and Prosperity on Earth, its Office to reconcile Duty and Convenience, and to make Vertue subservient to Temporal Welfare. Of Prudence in Religion, Friendship, and Empire. The End of Prudence is perfect Charity.

CHARITY is that which entereth into every Vertue, as a main Ingredient of its Nature and Perfection. Love is the fountain and the End of all, without which there can be no Beauty nor Goodness in any of the Vertues. Love to one self, Love to GOD, Love to man, Love to Felicity, a clear and intelligent Love is the Life and Soul of every Vertue, without which Humility is but Baseness, Fortitude but Feirceness, Patience but Stupidity, Hope but Presumption, Modesty but Simpering, Devotion but Hypocrisie, Liberality is Profuseness, Knowledge vanity, Meekness but a sheepish Tameness, and Prudence it self but fraud and Cunning. For as all other Vertues, so is Prudence, founded on Charity. He that is not Good can never be Prudent: for he can never benefit himself, or others. For the Designes of Prudence are to secure one self in the Exercise of every Vertue, and so to order the Discharge of ones Duty, as neither to hurt a mans self in his Life, Estate, Honour, Health, or Contentment, nor yet to fail in the Attainment of that Worth and Beauty, which will make our Lives Delightful to others, and as Glorious to our selves, as Beneficial and Delightful.

PRUDENCE hath an eye to every Circumstance, and Emergence of our Lives. Its Designe is to make a mans self as Great and glorious as is possible, and in pleasing all the World, to order and improve all Advantages without incurring the least inconvenience: To reconcile our Devotion, Obedience and Religion, to our Interest and Prosperity in the World: To shun all extreams, to surmount all Difficulties, to overrule all Disadvantages, to discern all Opportunities, and lay hold on all Occasions of doing Good to our selves. Its Office is to consult, and contrive, and effect our own Welfare in every Occurrence that can befal us in the World, and so to mingle all Vertues in the Execution of our Duties, that they may relieve, and aid, and perfect each other, in such a manner as at once to be pleasing to GOD, profitable to his Creatures, and to our selves. To take heed that we do nothing out of Season, nor be guilty of any Defect, or Excess, or Miscarriage. All the Vertues are United by Prudence like several Pieces in a Compleat armour, and disposed all like Souldiers in an Army, that have their several Postes and Charges, or like the several Orders and Degrees in a Kingdom, where there are Variety of Trusts, & services to be done, and every Man has his Office assigned by the King, and knows his own work, and is fitted for the same.

FOR as no one man is sufficient for all; the same person cannot be chief Priest in the Temple, and General in the Army, and Admiral at Sea, &c. So neither can every Vertue serve for all purposes, but there must be several Vertues for several Ends.

AS the King ordereth and directeth all his Officers and subjects in their several Places; if they do their duty in their own sphere, the Great End is attained by *all*, which no *one* of them alone, was able to Effect: so here, one Vertue supplies the Defects of another, and tho every one of them moves in his own Precincts, and does not at all intermeddle with anothers charge, yet the Work is done as effectually as if any one Vertue did all alone.

WHILE all the Vertues conspire to supply what is wanting in each other, Prudence is the general Overseer, and Governour of all, which, while every single Vertue is ignorant of what the other are doing, fits and proportions the subservient Ends, to which every one of these Directeth its Care, and Labour, and Skill, to the Great and last End of all, the intire Perfection and Glory of the Kingdome. So that here upon Earth Prudence seemeth to be the King of Vertues, because we have such a Multiplicity of Concernes and Affairs to look after, that it is impossible for any one Vertue, but Prudence alone to attend them all.

THIS discovereth the Excellency of Vertue, & detecteth a very great Error to which we are liable, while we are prone imprudently to expect more from any Vertue than it is able to perform. We are apt to believe that in every Vertue there is an infinite Excellency. And this great Expectation of ours is a good opinion of Vertue, yet turneth (not seldome) to its Disgrace and Infamy. For when we look upon any single Vertue, and see it so Defective, that it scarce answereth one of many Ends, because we find our selves deceived in our expectation of its perfection, and the Service of that Vertue so Curt and narrow, which we thought to be infinite; we are distasted at its *Insufficiency,* and prone to slight it as a poor inconsiderable Business, infinitly short of our Hopes and expectations. Nay and to be discouraged from the practice of it, because we find it attended with many Difficulties and inconveniences, which it is not able to remedy or answer. Thus are we deterred from Liberality for fear of the Poverty to which it exposeth us; from Meekness, because it encourageth all People to trample us under feet; from Holiness, because it is scorned and hated in the World; from Fortitude and Courage, because of the Perils and Hazzards, that attend it; from self-Denial, because of the Displeasures we do to our selves in crossing our Appetite. Nay sometimes men are so wicked as to hate to be obliged, for fear of the Inconveniences of Gratitude, and are much Prejudiced against Fidelity, and Love, and Truth, and Constancy. For all these Vertues can answer but one exigence, for which they are prepared (especially in our Daily Conversation with men) and a mistake in one of them doth expose us to more Inconveniences, then its Benefit is worth.

THIS is the Offence: and the Truth is, no Vertue is of any Value as cut off from the rest. We may as well expect all Beauty in a Nose divided from the Face, or an eye pluckt out of the head, all Perfection in an Ear, or a tongue cut off, all serviceableness in a Hand, or Foot dismembred from the Body; as a full and perfect Security from any one Vertue whatsoever. If one were sufficient, the rest would be Superfluous. Mans Empire and Dominion would be a very narrow Thing, (at least a very *Empty* and *Shallow* thing) if any one Vertue were enough for his Felicity. As his Exigencies and Concerns are Innumerable, so are his Cares and Endowments, his Honors and Pleasures, his Offices and Employments, his Vertues and Graces. His Offices and his Vertues must be at least so many, as will serve to regulate all his Concerns. And if any be so comprehensive as to cure many Exigencies at the same time, his Vertues are the Greater in force and Extent, but the fewer in Number. Their perfect sufficiency is to be measured by the ends for which they are prepared: and their Beauty Consists, (like that of an Army with Banners) in the Proportion and Symmetry of the entire Body, the mutual Supplies and Succors they afford to one another, the Unity of such a Great Variety of things in order to the Attainment of the same great and ultimate end, the full and compleat Number of Offices and inferior Ends, and the Extream Providence wherewith they are reducible to one supream End, which is most High and Excellent. It is enough for the Ear if it can hear well, tho it is no more able to See, or Taste, than a Stone. It is enough for the eye to see well, tho it is no more sensible of Noise, then a Rock or a Tree. The Office of the Tongue is to Tast well, of the Nostril to smell well, &c. and there is no Defect in any of these, because they are every one sufficient for its own immediate end, and all so tempered and united together, that the rest are Supplies to make up the Defect of every single Sence and Organ, and altogether perfectly subservient to the whole Man, for whose sake they were prepared, that he might enjoy the benefit of them all. The eye sees for the Ear, and the Tongue, and all the rest of the Members of the Body: the foot supports and carries the eye, the hand defends and feeds the Eye, the Ear instructs and Counsels the Eye, the Nostrils smell for the eye, and the Tongue tasts and talks for the Eye, which the eye cannot do for it self, because it was made to need the assistance of the rest, the eye directs all these in Liew of their Services, and is of far greater Value, then if a man had no other Member, but an eye alone. For the Eye is the Light of all the members, and Great in its Relation to the whole man: It sees for the Ear, and the Hand, and for all, and is to all these after some manner Beneficial, but without these would be to no purpose. There is an infinite Excellency in every Vertue, but it is to be sought in its Relation to all the Rest. It is Good for nothing in its Place but for that Particular End to which it is assigned, in attaining that end it is subservient to all other Vertues; and while it serves all, is aided by all. The other Virtues remedie the inconveniences to which this doth expose us, and being all joyned together carry us safely and securely to our Last end: Because the Influence of every one passeth thorow all, every single Vertue is Pleasing to God, and a means in its place of our whole Felicity. The Beauty of all the Vertues is to be sought in Prudence, for there they meet in an intire Body: their Correspondence and convenience, their Symmetry and proportion, their Unity and Variety, their ful and perfect Harmony, makes up the features of the Soul, and compleats its Graces, just as the Diversity of Members perfects the Body. Knowledge gives Light to Love, but Love gives Warmth and Feeling to Knowledge. Love may perhaps, like a Separate Soul, dwell in Heaven, alone; and yet even then it must include all Knowledge, and Righteousness, and

Wisdome, and Holiness: for if Love know not how to guide it self, it will never attain its End, nor be a perfect Vertue. But here upon Earth tis like the Soul in the Body, it must Eat, and Drink, and see, and hear, has a thousand Works to do, and therefore standeth in need of many Vertues. Love without Goodness is perhaps a Thing impossible, because it always designs well. But Love without Wisdome is a Common Thing: for such is all that mistakes its End. Love without Discretion is a mischievious Thing, Love without Prudence an Helpless Thing, Love without Courage a feeble and Cowardly Thing; Love without Modesty an impudent and Troublesome Thing; Love without the Fear of GOD is Lust and Wantonness; and if the most Great and Glorious of all the Vertues stands in need of all its Companions, the less and inferior must needs be lame and maimed without the residue, especially without the Superior.

UPON this account it is, that so much Care and Study goes to the making up of a Vertuous man. All kind of Vertues must concur to Compleat his Perfection. The Want of any one Denominates a Vice, and makes him Vicious. Nay the Want of any one destroys the form and Essence of the rest. Vertue is not Vertue but in order to felicity. If it hath lost its force, it hath lost its Nature. As a little Poyson turnes the best Meat from Nourishment into Poyson so doth one Vice cherished and allowed corrupt and viciate all the Vertues in the whole World. Hence it is that the Phylosophers say, all the Vertues are linked together in the golden Chain of Prudence. And that a Thing is made Good by all its Causes, Evil by the least Defect. For as one Tooth wanting in a Clock, makes all the other wheels and Materials Useless; tho the frame be never so Elaberate and Curious; so doth the abscence of the smallest Vertue make void and frustrate all the residue. A man of a Kind and Bountiful Disposition, that is loose and intemperate, may ruine his Estate, and dye like a Prodigal and vain-glorious fool. A stout Couragious person that is proud and debauched will be little better then a *Souldierly Ruffian,* and Live if not like a Thief for Want of Honesty, yet like a Swaggering Hector for Want of Discreetion. A Man endued with all Kind of Learnning may be Morose and Covetous, and by one Vice lose all the Benefit of his Education. A Religious Votary that is Splenetick and Revengeful, brings a Disgrace upon his whole Profession. But he that is Wise, and Learned, and Holy, and Just, and Temperate, and Couragious, and Kind, and Liberal, and Meek, and Humble, and Affable, and Cheerful, and Prudent, and Industrious, shall be serviceable, and Honourable, and delightful

to others, profitable to himself, and alwayes Triumphant: Especially
if he be so discreet and Prudent, as to make all these Vertues move
like the Stars in their Courses, and knows how to apply and manage
their Excellencies in their due and proper places upon all occasions:
for they are so many different in nature that some of their Influences,
will hit every business, and all of them together pass a Grace and
Lustre upon each other, so Divine and Heavenly that they will make
their owner Venerable in the Eys of the World, and correct the Malignity of the most injurious and Censorious. Which moved our Saviour
to exhort us to be *Wise as Serpents, Innocent as Doves,* to joyn many
Vertues together: And occasioned that of the Apostle,* *He that will
love Life and see good Days, let him refrain his Tongue from Evil,
and his Lips that they speak no Guile: let him eschew Evil, and do
Good, let him seek Peace and ensue it, for the Eyes of the Lord are
over the Righteous: And who is he that will harm you, if ye be followers of that which is Good?* The only sure Way to live happily here
upon Earth, is to joyn all kind of Vertues together, and to let them
work in season according to their several Natures.

WHAT the efficacy of Prudence is may be seen in friendship, in
the Regiment of States and Kingdoms, in the Rule and government
of Private Famelies. He that is fitted for all these is an Excellent Person.

IT is the office of Prudence in all Estates, to find out the Temper
of those with whom we are to deal; and so to suit the Exercises of
all Vertues with their several Humours, as may make their Operation
consistent with our own Repose, and their Benefit, without infringing
our Duty.

IN Friendship it often falleth out by reason of the spiritual *Sickness*
of those to whom we relate, that we must either make shipwrack of
Fidelity and a good Conscience, or run the Hazzard of losing our
Friend by displeasing, that we may be Profitable to him. There is
no Duty so necessary, as that of free and faithful Reproof: no Duty
so nice as this. A Good man Knows it is incumbent upon him, and
yet is very Averse from the Discharge of it. It is as Troublesome to
himself as to the Person that needs it. Tis difficult to be done well,
and so unpleasant to both. Here Prudence comes in, and deviseth expedients for all Inconveniences, and with a strange facility scatters
all Doubts and Fears. Three Things it discovers to be necessary in
the foundation of the Business, Three in the Superstructure, and Three
in the Conclusion. He that reproves well, must shew a great respect

* 1 Pet. 3.10.

and Tenderness to the Person, a necessity of the Discharge of that Duty, his Aversness to it, and how Nothing but his Perfect Love could make him undertake it. The foundation of the Success is laid by these Provisions: In the Superstructure, he must consider whether it be best to be done merrily or severely; by a Brief Hint or a strong Enlargement, according to the Temper and Degree of the Person. He must chuse out the Best Opportunities, and consult the Honour of him he reproveth. And if he be displeased and grow angry at the Liberty, he must in the Close of all bear it patiently, surmount it with Courtesie, and pursue him with Kindness. He that rules his own Passion is Master of another mans: He must needs win him and Melt him: For no man thus dealt with, is so very a Beast, as to be angry long. Or the mischief is, when he that reproveth miscarrieth in some of these Rules, especially the last: for there are few so prudent as not to be exasperated with the Affront that is put upon their kindness and Fidelity, when they are injured for their Good Will: few so discreet as to consider which way their patience and Meakness are to be made the Instruments of Amity and Happiness.

IN the Management of Empires, and Kingdomes Prudence hath a vast and Mighty Province to reign in. A Good King when he designs the extirpation of Vice, and the Establishment of Righteousness and pure Religion, meets with many Rubs and Obstacles in his Way, all which are sweetly and easily by Prudence removed. His Great encouragement is the Beauty of Religion, and the Assistance of GOD. For he Knows very well that Equity and Piety are such Glorious Things, that tho few practice them as they ought to do, yet all admire them.

GODLINESS, and Honesty, need nothing but to be maintained and assented by the Prince, when they are once countenanced by authority all the Enemies of Religion are confounded, and dare not lift up their face against it. Wise and Holy men may easily be exalted, and are more capable of Exaltation then others. As they are more faithful when they are in power, they will be more Grateful to the Prince, and more Obliging to the people; and in all Respects more able to serve them both. The Good will secure the Throne and exalt the Kingdome. Prudence in such a work Knows where to begin and where to end, by what steps and Degrees to proceed, what Instruments to use, how to Oblige, and how to Awe; whom to Oblige, and Awe; where to remit the Rigor of the Law and where to be severe. The Truth is, Prudence consists most in attempting the Business, for it will go on, and is ever waited with success when undertaken. A King that is so Wise as to design and endeavor, the Refurmation of his Nation, must needs be Prudent. GOD has assured him, *The Throne is estab-lished by Righteousness. When it Goeth well with the Righteous the City rejoyceth, and when the wicked perish there is shouting. By the blessing of the upright the City is exalted, but it is overthrown by the Mouth of the Wicked.*

IN Families the force of Prudence is prodigious. Some men by the assistance of this Vertue live more happily upon a mean state, then others upon Thousands, they have more respect among their Servants, more honour among their Neighbors, more plenty at home, more Au-thority abroad, more peace & comfort every where, then Men forty times above themselves in State & Grandure. Its first care is to be Wary in the Choise of Servants: For they that are good act well by Nature, and have little need of Force and compulsion. Its next Business is to oblige them, which is done by a religious example which instilles a Reverence, a strict prohibition of all Debauchery, a sweet and affable Behaviour, a plentiful Provision for their comfortable Subsistence, a prudent connivance at smaller faults, a Distribution of Rewards as well as punishments for the Encouragement of their Vertues, a meek and Gentle reproof of their Faults, a kind acknowledgment of their Good deserts; which is a cheap and easie kind of payment, yet more Obliging then any Dry gift of Gold or Silver. A prudent man will so demean himself in his Family, as to make himself cordially beloved of all: so order his affairs, that the Services of those about him shall be like Preferments. By which Means it will first come to pass, that he shall have his choise of servants, because it will be esteemed a Bless-ing to be with him: and in the next place their service will be mingled with respect and Love. They will be faithful as well for his sake, as their own. In the Midst of all this, his Prudence will guid him to take a strict account, and to make all his Servants see, it is impossible to cheat him. Thus in all Affaires Prudence happily demeans it self; and of this Gift especially is that* of *Solomon* to be understood, *A gift is as a precious stone in the hand of him that hath it, whithersoever it turneth, it prospereth.*

FOR the Foundation of all kind of Prudence you must remember, that he that winneth Souls is Wise. Mens Hearts are the stars by whose Influences the affairs of the World are regulated: they are as our Saviour calleth them Good or Evil Treasures; out of which proceeds Murders, Adulteries, Thefts, Slanders, &c. Or Praises, Honours, Pre-

* Prov. 17.8.

ferments, Riches, Pleasures, all kind of Gifts, and Benefits: And the prudent mans main Business is to make himself intirely beloved by all the World, which can never be without great Fidelity, Courage, Goodness, Prudence and Dexterity. Flattery and Base compliances makes a man Odious.

THE Last End of Prudence is Eternal Happiness and Glory, to which it moveth by crooked Meanders and windings out as occasion requireth. It is a strange Vertue, for its Conversant amongst Terrene and inferior Objects, and yet a far more Difficult Vertue then Wisdom it self. Wisdome is a more High and Heavenly Vertue, but its Rules are always fixed, and its objects Stable, where as Prudence hath no set and Stated Rules, but in all occasions, is to mould and shape it selfe, it knows not which way, till it comes to Action. Its Paths are in the Deep and mighty Waters, among Storms and tempests.

Encouragements to Courage. Its Nature, Cause, and End. Its Greatness and Renown. Its Ornaments and Companions. Its Objects, Circumstances, Effects and Disadvantages; how Difficulties increase its Vertue. Its Victories and Triumphs. How subservient it is to Blessedness and Glory.

LOVE and Prudence are the Parents of Courage. A Feeble Hen, a Timerous Mother, will Sacrifice their Lives for their young ones. And he that forgetteth all his own Interests, divests himself (together with them) of his Fears, and despising Death first, easily slighteth all other Things. Even a Coward by Nature, is made more Bold and confident by Skill at his weapon. And he that is always assured of the Victory, can never be afraid of the Encounter, or the Enemy. He that is Dexterious at the use of all Vertues, and knows how to apply them so, as ever to come off more honourably, will laugh at the Trial of his own Innocence and make a Game of Difficulties and Terrors.

VALOUR is a right and strong Resolution of the Soul, whereby it dare encounter with any Difficulty and Trouble, for Vertues sake. It is the Armour of the Soul against all Impressions of Fear, its Effect is an Equal and uniform stayedness of Mind, against all Dangerous and Terrible Accidents. It containeth Magnanimitie, Patience, Constancy, Invincible Resolution, Boldness and Industry in its Nature. Its cause is the Love of Vertue, and the sence of Honour, Indignation against any thing that is Base and vile, a High Ambition and desire of Glory. Its End is the preservation of a Mans person and Honesty, the Conquest of all Opposition in the Way to Bliss, the Destruction or Subjection of Enemies, Triumph and Conquest, the Establishment of Peace, the Attainment of Liberty and Glory. Its Attendants are Prudence, Justice and Temperance, the principal Ornament and Grace of valour is Worth and Goodness. Its Aids and Encouragements are infinite, it groweth Great and High, by making use of all the Causes of Hope and Confidence. Conflicts and Dangers are the Element in which it lives. It owns its whole being to them; for without Causes of Fear, there could be no courage in all Nature. The Knowledge of GOD is the root of Divine Valour, and Fidelity to his Laws its Commendation. The Assurance of his Love, and all those Things that serve to beget and confirm it, are subservient to it. It draws in strength and Encouragements from all Obligations and Rewards, from all Great and Holy examples, from the Knowledge of its own Sublimity, from the Greatness of Felicity, from the Omnipotence, and Omnipresence, and Providence of the Deity, from his Truth and Goodness, and from all those Things wherein he has manifested his Love above the Heavens.

OF all the Vertues in greatest Estimation, this is most renowned. For its Prerogative is so great, that it is simply called VERTUE. Vertue being the Word to express and signifie Valour among the Latines; because the Force and Efficacy that is in it, is most visible and Apparent, and by that all other Vertues are secured, vindicated, Exercised, and made Useful. It is stiled *Manhood* among the English, with a peculiar Emphasis: As if the Essence of a man was founded in Courage, because his Vigor is emasculated, and his Dignity lost, that is Effeminate and Timerous; for he is scarce a Man that is a Coward.

WHAT a Glorious and incomparable Vertue this is, appeareth from the Baseness and Ineptitude of its Contrary. A Coward and an Honest Man can never be the same; a Coward and a constant Lover can never be the same; a Coward and a Brave Man can never be the same: Cowardice, and Wisdome are as incompatible forever, as Love and Wisdom were thought to be of Old. A Coward is always despicable and Wretched; because he dares not expose himself to any Hazzards, nor adventure upon any Great Attempt for fear of some little Pain and Damage, that is between him and an Excellent Atchievment. He is baffled from the Acquisition of the most Great and Beautiful Things, and nonplust with every Impediment. He is conquered before he begins to fight. The very sight of Danger makes him a Slave; He is undone, when he sees his Enemy a far off, and wounded, before the Point of the Sword can touch his shadow. He is all wayes a Terror and Burden to himself, a Dangerous Knave, and an useles Creature.

STRANGE is the Vigour in a Brave Mans Soul. The Strength of his Spirit and his irresistible Power, the Greatness of his Heart, and the Height of his Condition, his mighty Confiedence and Contempt of Dangers, his true Security and Repose in himself, his Liberty to dare and do what he pleaseth, his Alacrity in the midst of Fears, his invincible Temper, are advantages which make him Master of Fortune. His Courage fits him for all Attempts, renders him serviceable to GOD and MAN, and makes him the Bulwark and Defence of his King and Country.

LET those Debauched and unreasonable men, that deny the Existence of Vertue, contemplate the Reality of its Excellency here, and be confounded with shame at their Prodigious Blindness. Their Impiety designs the Abolishment of Religion, and the utter Extirpation of all Faith and Piety, while they pretend the Distinction between Vertue and Vice to be meerly feigned, for the Awing of the World; and that their Names have no foundation in Nature but the Craft of Politicians and the Tradition of their Nurses. Are there no Base fellows, nor Brave Men in the World? Is there no difference between a Lion and a Hare? a faint hearted Coward, and a Glorious Heroe! Is there Nothing Brave nor vile in the world? What is become of these *Rodomontadoes* wits! Where is the boasted Glory of their Personal Valour; if there be no Difference, but Courage and Cowardize be the same thing!

HOW empty these Self, but shallow-conceited Ranters are, is evident by their short and narrow measures. They place all Gallantry and Worth in Valour: all the Vertue of a man they think seated in this: They forget that Policy, and Learning, and Prudence, and Gratitude, and Fidelity, and Temperance, and Industry, and Compassion and Bounty, and Affability, and Courtesie, and Modesty, and Justice, and Honesty are Vertues, and that in every one of these there is something fitting a Man for the Benefit of the World. Nay they have lost the Notion of Vertue, and know not what it is. Those things by which a man is made serviceable to himself and the World, they think not to be Vertues, but imagine Chimeraes which they cannot see, & then deny they have any Existence. A Man is capable of far more Glorious Qualities then one of them: And his Courage it self may be raised to far higher Ends and purposes then Buffoons and Thrasonical Heroes can dream of.

IT is to be noted here, that any one of those Things that are called Vertue, being alone, is not a Vertue. It is so far from aiding and setting us forward in the Way to Happiness, that oftentimes it proveth a Great and intollerable Mischief, and is never safe, but when it is corrected and guided by the rest of its Companions. To stir no further then Courage alone: What is Courage in a Thief, or a Tyrant, or a Traytor, but like Zeal and Learning in a pernicious Heretick.

YOU may note further, that Goodness is a principal Ingredient in the excellency of this Vertue, tho it be distinct in its Nature from the Being of Courage. A brave man will expose his Life in an Honest cause, for the Benefit and preservation of others, tho not for the Dammage or Destruction of any. He will slight his own safety, and despise his Repose to make himself a Saviour, and a Benefactor. A true Courage holdeth Vertuous Actions at such a Price, that Death, Imprisonment, Famine, Dishonour, Poverty, Shame, Indignation, all Allurements and Temptations are nothing, compared to the Performance of Heroick Deeds. He exceedeth all constraint, and walketh in the Glorious Liberty of the Sons of GOD.

THE last note which I shall offer to your Observation on this Occasion, is this, (for the Illustration of the Reason and excellency, of GODS Dispensations:) The Great End for which GOD was pleased not to seat us immediately in the Throne, but to place us first in an estate of Trial, was the Multiplication of our Vertues. For had we been seated in the Glory of Heaven at the first, there had no such Vertues as Patience, and Courage, and Fidelity been seen, no Faith, or Hope, or Meekness, no Temparance, or Prudence, or self Denial, in the World. Which Vertues are the very clothes and Habits of the Soul in Glory. The Graces and Beauties of the Soul are founded in the exercise of them. Actions pass not away, but are fixed, by the permanent Continuance of all Eternity, and tho done never so long ago, shall appear before the Eye of the Soul for ever in their places, be the Glory of their Author, the Lineaments and Colours of his Beauty, seen by GOD and his holy Angels, and Delightful to all that love and delight in worthy things. Our Life upon Earth, being so diversified like a Sphere of Beauty, so variously adorned with all sorts of Excellent Actions, shall wholly and at once be seen as an intire Object, rarely and curiously wrought; a Lively Mirror of the Nature of the Soul, and all the Elements of which it is compounded, all the Parts that conspire in its Symetry, all the Qualities, Operations, and Perfections that contribute to its Glory, shall afford wonder and pleasure to all Spectators. While every Soul shall be concerned more in its Actions then in its Essence; indeed its Essence, (how ever considerable) is of little or no Value in Comparison of its Operations. Every Vertue being the Natural Off-spring and production of the Soul, in which its Vigor principally appeareth, an effect discovering the Nature of the cause, and the sole occasion of its shame or Glory. For if the Essence of the Soul be all Power and its power exerted in its operation, the Soul must needs enter into its Actions, and consequently be affected with all that befalls its Operation. All Acts are Immortal in their places, being *enbalmed* as it were by Eternity, till the Soul revive and be united to them. Then shall it appear in its own Age, and in eternity too, in its last life enjoying the Benefit of its *first*. And in that sence is that voice from Heaven to be understood, which commanded the Divine to write* *Blessed are they that die in the Lord, from henceforth, yea saith the Spirit, that they may rest from their Labours, and their Works do follow them.* For the Glory of the place is nothing to us, if we are not endued with those Glorious Habits, which will make our Souls *all Glorious within.* We must be Glorious and Illustrious our selves, and appear in Actions that will Beautifie the Throne to which we are exalted.

THAT these Actions may be Great and Amiable, manifold and Excellent, is the desire of every soul, the natural Wish and Expectation both of Reason it self and of self Love.

HOW Glorious the Counsel and Design of GOD is for the Atchieving of this Great End, for the making of all Vertues more compleat and Excellent, and for the Heightening of their Beauty and Perfection we will exemplifie here in the Perfection of Courage. For the Hieght, and depth, and Splendor of every Vertue is of great Concernment to the Perfection of the Soul, since the Glory of its Life is seated in the Accomplishment of its essence, in the Fruit it yeildeth in its Operations. Take it in Verse made long ago upon this occasion.

> *For Man to Act as if his Soul did see*
> *The very Brightness of Eternity;*
> *For Man to Act as if his Love did burn*
> *Above the Spheres, even while its in its* Urne;
> *For Man to Act even in the Wilderness,*
> *As if he did those Sovereign Joys possess,*
> *Which do at once confirm, stir up, enflame,*
> *And perfect Angels; having not the same!*
> *It doth increase the Value of his Deeds,*
> *In this a Man a Seraphim exceeds:*
> *To Act on Obligations yet unknown,*
> *To Act upon Rewards as yet unshewn,*

* Rev. 14.13.

To keep Commands whose Beauty's yet unseen,
To cherish and retain a Zeal between
Sleeping and Waking; shews a constant care;
And that a deeper Love, a Love so Rare,
That no Eye Service may with it compare.

   The Angels, who are faithful while they view
His Glory, know not what themselves would do,
Were they in our Estate! A Dimmer Light
Perhaps would make them erre as well as We;
And in the Coldness of a darker Night,
Forgetful and Lukewarm Themselves might be.
Our very Rust shall cover us with Gold,
Our Dust shall sprinkle while their Eyes behold
The Glory Springing from a feeble State,
Where meer Belief doth, if not conquer Fate,
Surmount, and pass what it doth Antedate.

THE Beatifick Vision is so sweet and Strong a Light, that it is impossible for any thing that Loves it self, (and sees the Face of GOD) to turn away to any vanity from so Divine and Strong a Blessedness. To Love GOD in the clear and perfect Light is a cheap and Easie Thing: The Love that is shewed in a more weak Estate to an absent Object, is more remiss perhaps, and Black in appearance; but far Deeper, if in the Lovers Weakness, and its Objects absence; it be Faithful to the Death; constantly Solicitous, and Careful to please, Laborious and Industrious, Wakeful and Circumspect, even and immutable, and freely springing from its own Desire, not out of bare pleasure; but humble Obedience to the Laws of its Benefactor. All the Courage which it shews in such Occasions is more full of Mystery and Divinity then is imaginable; far more Moving and full of Vertue, while it struggles with Impediments, Disadvantages, and Difficulties, then if without any such Occasion of shewing its Vertue, it did smoothly and Peaceably proceed in the Highest Rapture. Add to that the mysteriousness of its Beauty in all the varieties of its Operation, and the Different Sweetnesses that still appear in all its several Effects upon new occasions. The very Representation of Love upon the stage, in its Conflicts and Agonies, produces another kind of sence in the Spectator, then that of Embraces. It is more Tender and endearing, touches the Soul (of its Beloved especially) in a more Vigorous and lively manner, it makes all fruitions (afterward) more precious; by Fidelity, Courage, and Immoveable Perfection it maketh the Lover more Honourable, and Effects far more Serious Alterations in the Soul, solid Joys and tender Compassions, moving and Bleeding Resentments; all which, End in satisfactions heightened with more Perfect Complacencies.

THUS you see Courage in the Root made more Glorious by a Persons Exposure and Abasement. In the fruit and Exercise it is otherwise to be considered. Where there is no Evil to be endured, or no Strength to be resisted, there can be no Courage or Vertue at all. Where the conflict is more sharp the Victory is more pleasant, and the success of the fight is far more Honourable. Where a Giant is to fight with a Gnat, or a Dwarf, the Disproportion of his Strength takes away the Pleasure of its Trial, and a Glory of the Combate. There is no Room, or occasion for its Exercise. And tho it might without any Trial be known by him that sees all things in their hidden Essences, yet without its Exercise it remaineth unexerted, is wholly vain, especially when there is no occasion for it in Nature. The Pleasure of the Spectacle springeth from its Operation.

TO see a Seraphim surmount one of our Difficulties, in the midst of all his Strengths and Advantages, is no more then to see a Giant destroy a Gnat, or subdue a Grass hopper. But in Man there is a certain Degree of strength, that makes him *a fit Match* for the appointed Encounter. In the Estate of Innocency indeed his Enemies and Difficulties were very few, just as many as were needful for the trial of his Obedience, Gratitude, Fidelity. All the Hardship he was to undergo, was to cross his Appetite in an Apple, and tho he did not as yet see which way it was reserved for him, to be so Couragious as to hope well, so Grateful to GOD, as to dare to confide in him, rather let go the Knowledge he might gain by eating it, than break his Commandement. All other Duties were his Pleasure and Felicity: here lay his Trial, and his Obedience should have been crowned with infinite Reward. All which would in some Measure have risen out of the Duty discharged by him. For by this Resignation and Self-Denial he had manifested his Obedience, and acquitted himself, and shewed his Love, and his Prelation of his Makers Pleasure above all other Concernes, wherein he had been approved; and Wise, and Holy, and well pleasing to GOD, he would have put the Crown upon all Gods Works in accomplishing the End for which he was made, and been very Delightful to all the Angels: He had been crowned with Glory and Honour in all their Complacency. If that were too little, because he had then no enemy but his Appetite, the Dimness of his Sight maketh up the Mystery. If his Clarity was too Great, and there was no Proportion between his Strength and the Temptation; that proceeded of the Tenderness of GODS Love, which feared to adventure him too far, and had rather something of Honour should be endangered, then his Soul lost, or thrust upon the Hazzard of too great a Temptation. When the Angels fell, the Devil was let loose upon man, for the increase of his Honour and Dominion: Yet like a Dog in his Chain so far, and no further. He had but one Way, and that was to perswade our first Parents to do what was forbidden: Perswade he might, and try his Skill to deceive, but could not compell, nor otherwise afflict, or hurt him in the least. He had not Power so much as to diminish the least Hair of his Head: yet so Gracious was Almighty GOD, that upon this Trial of his Prudence and Courage, the Exercise of these Vertues had been infinitely pleasing to his Eternal Love, because he infinitely delighted in the Welfare and Preservation of what was so precious to himself, as a Soul is, that is infinitely Beloved. In that Complacency *Adam* had found little less then infinite Glory. It did not become the tenderness of GODS Love to expose him to any Severer Trial.

> *For there are certain Periods and fit Bounds,*
> *Which he that passeth, all his Work confounds.*

But when *Adam* fell, and brought more Hazzards and Difficulties on himself GOD might justly leave him to them, for his greater Trial and more perfect Glory. Now we are more blind and Weak by Nature, yet infinitely Beloved and more Precious: For the price of the Blood of the Eternal Son of GOD is laid upon the Soul as an Addition to its interior Value. We are even in our corruption to Grapple with Sin, and Hell, and Death, and Sickness, and Poverty, and Fear, and all the Devils, and Afflictions in the World; nay which is worse then all, with our own Errors, Lusts and Passions, more neer and Bitter Enemies: A poor Clod of Earth is to overcome all the World, to fight (as the Apostle speaks) *with Principallities and Powers, with the Rulers of the Darkness in this World, with spiritual Wickednesses in high places*. And to return laden with Victories and Trophies into the Kingdome of Heaven. Nor is the Combat so unequal, but that there is a mighty Hope and Assurance of triumphing, tho *Lucifer* and all his Angels are to be trampled under feet. For under the Disguise of this apparent Clod, there lies concealed a mighty Great and Cœlestial Personage, a Divine and Glorious Creature, Miraculous and Mysterious, even the Image of the Deity, that can derive Strengths and Succours from all eternity, and being aided by the Conduct of so great a Captain as our Lord *Jesus Christ* who has taught us by his example not to fear, because he has *overcome the World,* we may safely sing, *O Death where is thy sting? O Grave where is thy Victory!* And challenge all the powers of Heaven, Earth, and Hell to the combat, Which for one single person to do against all the Creation, is the most Glorious Spectacle which the universe affords. *Who shall separate us from the Love of Christ? shall Tribulation, or Distress, or Persecution, or Famine, or Nakedness, or Peril, or Sword? as it is writen, for thy sake we are Killed all the day long, we are accounted as Sheep to the slaughter. Nay in all these things we are more then Conquerors through him that loved us. For I am perswaded, that neither Death, nor Life, nor Angels, nor Principalities, nor Powers, nor things present, nor things to come, nor Height nor Depth, nor any other Creature shall be able to separate us, from the Love of GOD which is in Christ Jesus our Lord.*

A REMARK.

To be Couragious is the Easiest thing in the World, when we consider the certain success, which Courage founded on Goodness must needs attain. For he that makes his Fortitude subservient onely to the excess of his Love, has all the Powers of Heaven and earth on his side, and the Powers of Hell that are already subdued are the only foes that are to be vanquished by him. To dare to be Good, is the Office of true and Religious valour. And he that makes it his Business to oblige all the world, he whose design it is to be delightful to all mankind, has nothing to overcome, but their error & bitterness, which by meekness, and Kindness, and Prudence, and liberality will easily be accomplished. For they all love themselves, and cannot chuse but desire those that are kind and Serviceable to them, and must so far forth as they love themselves, honor & delight in their Benefactors. So that Courage thus guided by Prudence to the works of Charity and goodness must surely be safe and prosperous on earth, its Admirableness and its Beauty being a powerful Charm, an Invincible Armour.

Of Temperance *in Matters of Art, as Musick, Dancing, Painting, Cookery, Physick, &c. In the works of Nature; Eating, Drinking, Sports and Recreations: In occasions of Passion, in our Lives and Conversations. Its exercise in Self-denial, Measure, Mixture and Proportion. Its effects and atchievments.*

PRUDENCE giveth Counsel what Measure and Proportion ought to be held in our Actions, Fortitude inspires Boldness and Strength to undertake, and set upon the Work; but it is Temperance doth execute what both of them design. For Temperance is that Vertue, whereby the actions of Prudence and Power are moderated, when they come to be exerted.

IT is the Opinion of some, that as Patience respects Afflictions, so Temperance is wholy taken up in moderating our Pleasures, and hath no employment but in the midst of Prosperities. But since there are certain bounds which Fear and Sorrow ought not to exceed, Temperance hath its work in the midst of Calamities, and being needful to moderate all our Passions, hath a wider sphere to move in, than Prosperity alone; its Province is more large and comprehensive, including all estates and conditions of Life whatsoever.

OTHERS there are that admit of its use in all Conditions, but confine it to one particular employment, even that of enlarging or bounding the Measure of every Operation; but in real truth it has another Office, and that more deep perhaps, and more important than the former. For Actions are of two kinds, either Mixt, or Simple. Where the work is single and but one, it is exprest in nothing else but the Measure of the Action, that it be neither too short, nor too long;

too remiss, nor too violent; too slow, nor too quick; too great, nor too little: But where many things are mixt and meet together in the Action (as they generally do, in all the affairs of our Lives;) there its business is to consider what, and how many things are to enter the *Composition,* and to make their Proportion just and convenient. As in preparing Medicines, the skill whereby we know what is to be put in, and what left out is of one kind, and that of discerning how much of every *Ingredient* will serve the turn, of another. The skill of Mingling is like the vertue of Prudence, but the actual tempering of all together, exhibits the vertue of *Temperance* to the Life, because it reduces the Skill to its operation. Its End is the beauty and success of our Endeavours.

OF what use and value Temperance is in our Lives and Conversations, we may guess by its necessity, force and efficacy on all Occasions.

THE fit mixture and proportion of the four Elements in all Bodies, is that upon which their Nature, Form and Perfection dependeth. Too much of the Fire, too much of the Water, too much of the Air, too much of the Earth, are pernicious and destructive. There is an infinite wisdom exprest in the Mixture and Proportion in every Creature.

BEAUTY and Health, Agility, Repose, and Strength, depend upon the due Temperament of Humane Bodies. The four Humors of Choler, Melancholy, Flegm, and Blood are generally known: But there are many other Juyces talkt of besides, by the discreet and accurate mixture of which the Body of a Man, or Beast, is perfected. Some great inconvenience alwaies follows the excess or defect of these. Disorder and Disproportion go hand in hand, and are attended by Sickness, and Death it self.

IN matters of Art, the force of *Temperance* is undeniable. It relateth not only to our Meats and Drinks, but to all our Behaviours, Passions, and Desires.

> *All Musick, Sawces, Feasts, Delights and Pleasures,*
> *Games, Dancing, Arts consist in govern'd Measures;*
> *Much more do Words, and Passions of the Mind*
> *In Temperance their sacred Beauty find.*

A Musician might rash his finger over all his strings in a moment, but *Melody* is an effect of *Judgment* and *Order:* It springs from a variety of *Notes* to which *Skill* giveth *Time* and *Place* in their Union. A Painter may daub his Table *all over* in an instant, but a Picture is made by a regulated Hand, and by variety of Colours. A Cook may put a Tun of Sugar, or Pepper, or Salt in his Dishes: but Delicates are made by Mixture and Proportion. There is a Temperance also in the Gesture of the Body, the Air of the Face, the carriage of the Eye, the Smile, the Motion of the Feet and Hands, and by the Harmony of these is the best Beauty in the World either much commended, or disgraced. A Clown and a Courtier are known by their *Postures.* A Dancer might run into Extreams, but his Art is seen in the measure of his Paces, and adorned with a variety of sweet and suitable Behaviours. A Physician may kill a man with the best Ingredients, but good Medicines are those wherein every Simple hath its proper *Dose,* and every Composition a fit admixture of good Ingredients. A Poem, an Oration, a Play, a Sermon, may be too tedious, or too dull, or too feeble and impertinent; but all its faults are avoided by a fit Temperance of Words and Materials. Temperance every where yields the Pleasure: And *Excess* is as destructive as *Defect,* in any Accomplishment whatsoever; Vertue being seated in the Golden Mean; It is by an Artificial limiting of Power that every Thing is made as it ought to be, Compleat and Perfect. All kind of Excellence in every sort of Operation springs from Temperance. A curious Picture, a melodious Song, a delicious Harmony by little invisible motions of the Pen or Pencil, or by Ductures scarce perceivable in the throat, or fingers, finisheth the Work, where Art is the only power of performing.

WE know that upon Mens Actions far more does depend, than upon Dancing and Painting: their Wisdom and Vertue, their Honour, Life and Happiness. And therefore more Care ought to be exhibited in the Actions of which their Conversation is made up and accomplished. In their Meats and Drinks, and Recreations, it is apparent, that without Temperance there can be no Success or Order. The best Wine in the World makes him that is lavish in the use of it a *Sot.* The most wholsom and delicious Meat upon Earth by excess in eating, may turn to a *Surfeit.* If Sports and Recreations take up all a mans Time, his Life is *unprofitable:* their End is lost, and their Nature changed; for instead of recruiting, they consume ones Strength; and instead of fitting a Man for it, devour his Calling.

AN exact hand over all our Passions, and a diligent Eye to extravagant Actions, tend much to our Welfare, Repose, and Honour. Loose and impertinent Laughter, excessive Cost in Apparel, a Lascivious wandering of the Eyes, an ungoverned Boldness which turns into Impudence, an extremity of Fear which degenerates into Baseness, a Morose and sour Disposition, Anxiety and needless Care, immodest and violent strivings after Things we too eagerly desire, inordinate Love, too keen and bitter Resentments, a fierce and raging Anger, a blockish Stupidity, a predominant Humour of Melancholy, too much Sloth and too much Activity, too much Talk, and too much Silence: all these are diligently to be ordered and avoided: for upon the right Temperament of these we are made Acceptable and Amiable, and being so, are full of Authority, and can do within the compass of Vertue and Reason, all that we desire, among our Friends and Companions, for our own good, or the benefit of others. And by this means also we shall be admitted to the society and friendship of Great men, where a Nod or a Word is able to prevail more, than the strength of Oxen and Horses among the dregs of the People. But for lack of tempering these Ingredients aright, and as we ought, we become odious and insupportable, lose all Esteem and Interest, are rejected, and trampled under feet, as vicious and deformed.

HERE you may observe, that all the qualities and dispositions in Nature, are ingredients and materials in our Lives and Conversations, and for the most part it is their Excess or Defect that makes the miscarriage, when we erre in the Measure. There is a certain mixture of Gravity and Chearfulness, Remisness and Severity, Fear and Boldness, Anger and Complacency, Kindness and Displeasure, Care and Carelesness, Activity and Idleness, Joy and Sorrow, Forwardness and Reservedness; nay of Envy, Pride, and Revenge in every Mans life, as well as of Selfishness and flowing Courtesie, Plainness and Policy; at least the grounds of these things, which are neither Vertues nor Vices in themselves, yet make *Conversation* transcendently Vertuous, when they are wisely tempered and united together.

I do not look upon Ambition and Avarice, nay nor upon Envy and Revenge, as things that are evil in their root and fountain. If they be, Temperance has a strange vertue in its Nature, for as Chymists make Antidotes of Poysons, so doth this vertue turn the Matter of all these into a Quintessential perfection. Nay Selfishness and Pride it self escape not its influence. A little touch of something like Pride, is seated in the true sence of a mans own Greatness: without which his Humility and Modesty would be contemptible Vertues. In all baseness of Mind there is a kind of folly and Cowardice apparent; and more veneration follows an humble Man that is sensible of his Excellency. An aiery Humor without something of the Melancholy to ballast it a little, would be light and trifling: And a melancholy Humor without something of Air and Jovialness in it, too sour and disobliging.

Anger without Softness is like untemper'd Steel, brittle and destructive: and a plyant Humor without some degree of stiffness, too near to Flattery and Servility. Anger is the matter and fuel of Courage, and its appearance afar off puts a Majesty into Meekness, that makes it redoubted. A sorrowful Humor neatly allayed with a mixture of sweetness, begets a tenderness and compassion in the Spectator, that turns into a deeper and more serious Love: A little Selfishness puts our Companions in mind of our own Interest, and makes them perceive that we understand it: which adds a lustre to our Self-denial, and renders our Liberality more safe and precious. Plainness without Policy is downright Simplicity, and Policy without Plainness void of Honesty. The one makes us Crafty, and renders us suspected; the other exposes us, and makes us *Ridiculous;* but both united are venerable and prudent. By the appearance of Revenge in its shady Possibility, a man that never does other than Actually forgive, does oblige for what is past, yet threaten and discourage from the like Offences. All these are the Subjects of Temperance. A little spice of Jealousie and Emulation are advantagious, in the midst of our Security and Resignation. They give a relish to our Confidence in, and Prelation of others; and make our Security and Civility taste of our Love to the Person we prefer, and of our Love to Vertue. There is not one Humor, nor Inclination, nor Passion, nor Power in the Soul, that may not be admitted to act its part, when directed by Temperance.

NOR is it unlawful to alter the Natural Complexion by Care and Study. I know very well, that the Complexion of the Body can hardly be changed by the strongest Physick: and that Choler, and Phlegm, and abundance of Blood, will, where they are, have their Natural Course without any remedy. But the Humors of the Soul are more tractable things; they are all subject to the Will in their operations: and though they incline, yet they cannot act, but by consent and permission. I know furthermore that Custom and Habit is a Second Nature: what was difficult at first, becomes at last as easie in its Exercise as if it were *innate;* and that the Soul of a Vertuous man does in process of time act by a new *Disposition.* I know further that all vertuous Operations are free and voluntary; and that the office of Vertue is to correct and amend an Evil Nature. Let no man therefore be disgusted, because a *Made-up man* is Artificial, and not Natural: for when the Conversation is sincerely guided to a good End, the more free and voluntary it is, it is the more Noble: the more Industry and Desire a man expresses in attaining all these measures and perfections, they are the more Vertuous: and the Probity of his Will is to be the more accepted. For Vertues are not effects of Nature, but Choice. Which how free soever it may appear, is as stable as the Sun, when founded on Eternal principles: it secures any Friend in the good and amiable Qualities he desires in his Beloved, as much as Nature it self could do, though they depend upon the Will, which is capable of changing every moment. This of Temperance in the Government of our *Humors*.

I shall add but one Note more, and that is, That a Wise man discards the *Predominancy* of all Humors, and will not yield himself up to the Empire of any: for he is to live the life of *Reason;* not of *Humor*. Nor will he have any Humor of his own, but what he can put off and on, as he sees occasion. He will cleave eternally to the Rules of Vertue, but will comply in his Humor so far as to make his conversation sweet and agreeable to every Temper. Religion and Charity, as well as Courtesie and Civility, prompt to this; and where these concur with his Reason, and favour his Interest, he may well do what S. *Paul* taught him, *become all things to all men, that he might gain some.* And this encouragement he hath, A man by sacrificing his own, may comply with the satisfaction of all the World: and find his own far more great and honourable, and sweet and amiable in the End, far more high and blessed, in the Love and Esteem he shall obtain thereby, than if he had gratified his first inclination without any respect to the Prelation of others. It will bring him to the fruition of Pleasures, far greater than those he despised.

TEMPERANCE in the full composition and use of Vertues, is far more sublime, and more immediately approacheth the end of Vertue, than any Temperance in Meats and Drinks: It is resident nearer the Throne of Felicity, and seateth us by her. You may see its Task as it is prescribed in Prudence. But for Example sake we will instance it in Meekness, which of all the Vertues is the most weak and naked. A meek Spirit receiveth its Temper, its encouragement, strength, and facility, from the union and concurrence of all the Vertues. Knowledg is its light, and Love the principle of its life and motion. Wisdom guideth it to the highest End; Righteousness is a great incentive thereunto, while it teacheth us to esteem the favour of God, and the excellency of those Souls, whose value maketh us tender of their Repose, and prone to honour them with a due esteem, as well as to desire their peace and salvation. Holiness maketh us to delight in our Duty. Goodness inclines us to sacrifice our own, to the welfare of others.

Mercy leads us to pity their Infirmities, and more to compassionate their Misery, than to be provoked with their Distemper. Justice makes us to pay our Saviours Love and Merits, what we owe unto *him*. All these establish the habit of Meekness in our Souls. Fortitude does several waies conspire thereunto, for it makes us to adventure upon any Trouble that we can fall into thereby, and puts a lustre upon us in the act of Meekness. Patience habituates the Soul to Afflictions, and makes our sence of Injuries easie. Repentance minds us of other employments than Anger and Revenge, even a contrite Sorrow for our own Offences. Humility gives us a sence of our own Unworthiness; and a willingness to be yet more low than our Enemies can make us. It inclines us also to confess, that we have deserved far worse, and more bitter Evils; and to despise our selves; which when we truly do, no Injuries or Wrongs can move us. Faith carries us up to higher Enjoyments. Hope hath respect to the promised Reward. Our Love towards GOD enflames us with Desire to please him, Charity to our Neighbour is prone to forgive him. Prudence teacheth us to expect no Figs from Thorns, nor better entertainment from Briars and Brambles: but rather to right our selves by improving their Wrongs, and to turn their Vices into our Vertues. Magnanimity despiseth the Courtship of Worms, and scorneth to place its rest and felicity in Trifles. Liberality is industrious to find out occasions of Obliging and Conquering: Contentment is fed by higher Delights, and beautifies our Meekness with a chearful Behaviour. Magnificence carries us to the most high and illustrious Deeds, and by very great and expensive Methods to multiply favours and benefits on our Beloved: for all are our Beloved whether Friends or Enemies. Temperance it self takes off the stupidity and sluggishness of our Meekness; puts activity and vigour into it, that it may not be a Sleepish, but Heroick Vertue; nay, adorns, secures, and perfects it by the Addition and Exercise of all these; and by giving to every other Vertue its Form and Perfection, makes them more fit and able to aid and assist us here. It moderates our Passions, and puts a better dose of Life into our Consideration. If there be any other Virtue, it is not so remote, but that it may lend us its helping hand, and be subservient to the perfection of our Love and Meekness. Which, however simple it may appear in Solitude, is very strong and irresistable, amazing, as far from Contempt as the Sun is from Darkness, when it is animated with Courage, and made illustrious by Love, enriched with Liberality, and made bright by Knowledg, guided by Wisdom to the highest End, and by Prudence to well-known and advantagious, tho inferiour Purposes. When the Soul appeareth neither foolish, nor Cowardly, nor base, nor soft, but High and Magnanimous in its Operation, Meekness is redoubted.

IN the Throne of Glory all the acts of Faith, and Hope, and Repentance shall be for ever perfected, or swallowed up in fruition. The fruit of all occasional and transient Vertues shall remain, the Divine Vertues shall be so firmly united, that in their Act and Exercise they shall be *one* for ever. By Knowledg we shall see all that the light of Heaven and Eternity can reveal. By Love we shall embrace all that is amiable before GOD and his holy Angels. By Wisdom we shall use the most glorious Means for the attainment and enjoyment of the highest End; which is GOD in all his Joys and Treasures: in the use of those Means we must actually enjoy all Blessedness and Glory. Righteousness and Holiness, and Goodness and Charity shall with all the rest be the Lineaments and Colours of the Mind, the Graces and Beauties of the blessed Soul: They shall shine upon its face, and it self shall be glorious in the perfection of their Beauty, as GOD is. Its Goodness shall make it a fountain of Delights to all the other Creatures. It shall be all Humility, yet all Enjoyment: Amazed at its own Nothingness and Vileness, yet ravished with wonder and the height of its Felicity: For the lower it is in its own Eyes, the more Great doth the Goodness of GOD appear, and the more transcendently Sweet is its Adoration and Satisfaction. By its Gratitude it sacrifices it self Eternally to the Deity, and taketh more pleasure in his Glory than its own. It is all Godliness and Contentment. All these Vertues are exercised together in the state of Glory, not so much by our own Temperance, as by the Infusion of his most Heavenly Grace, who fills us with his own Fulness and Perfection by way of Reward, and causing us to enter into his Eternal Rest, maketh us *to cease from our own Works, as he also did from his,* by inspiring us with his own Wisdom, Life and Strength, and actuating all our Powers by his own for ever: That we, by vertue of his Grace infused, may live in the Image of his Eternal Moderation, and attain that extremity of Bliss and Glory, which he hath (exceeding his Almighty Power) by an exquisite and mysterious Temperance in all his Operations, Divinely attained.

So, righteousness, holiness, goodness and charity are Beauty

CHAP. XXIII.

Of Temperance in GOD. How the Moderation of Almighty Power guided in its Works by Wisdom, perfecteth the Creation. How it hath raised his own Glory and our Felicity beyond all that Simple Power could effect by its Infiniteness.

IF Moderation hath such happy effects in Men, where the Strength is small, the Wisdom little, the Matter base, the Occasion low, as in divers Instances it is manifest it hath: how glorious must this Vertue be, where the Power is Almighty, the Wisdom Infinite, the Subject-Matter Perfect, the End, and the Occasion most Divine and Glorious!

IT would seem a strange Paradox, to say, That Almighty Power could not exist without Infinite Wisdom: but it is infinitely true: For the Wisdom and Power of GOD are *one*. No Blind Power can be Almighty, because it cannot do all that is Excellent. That Power would without Wisdom be Blind, is as evident as the Sun, the want of that being as great an impediment to its Operations, as the lack of Eyes is to a Man upon Earth: which so Eclipseth and darkneth his Power, that he cannot perform those excellent Works, to which Light is necessary. There is no Blind Power in GOD, and therefore no Power distinct from his Understanding. *By his Wisdom he made the Heavens, by his Understanding he established the Earth. By his Knowledge the Depths are broken up, and the Clouds drop down the Dew.** Wisdom is the Tree of Life, which beareth all the fruits of Immortality and Honour. Inartificial Violence will never carry it: There is a Mark to be hit; and that is in every thing what is most fair and eligible. It may be miss'd as much by shooting over it, as by falling short of it. Naked Power cannot tell what to propose as its Aim and Object. Only that which is able to contrive, is able to effect its Desire, in the Work it conceiveth most fit and excellent for its Power to perform.

* Prov. 3.19, 20.

IT is a stranger Paradox yet, That Power limited is Greater and more Effectual, than Power let loose; for this importeth, that Power is more infinite when bounded, than Power in its utmost liberty. But that which solveth the Riddle, and removeth the Inconvenience, is our Assurance of this, That GOD can do nothing but what is Wise, and that his Wisdom therefore is all his Power. And of this it followeth, That nothing is possible with GOD, but what is infinitely Excellent: for to do any thing less than the Best is unwise; and being so, is contrary to the Nature of Wisdom which is his Power.

THE Will of GOD is his Wisdom: By the meer Motion of his Will he Created all things, and therefore it is his Power: his Power and his Wisdom meet in his Will and are both the same. By his Word he made the Worlds, and his Eternal Word is his Eternal Wisdom.

ALL this I speak because it is the Office of Wisdom to propose the most excellent End, and to pursue it by the most efficacious Means: And because the Wisdom of GOD will be found one with his Eternal *Moderation*.

THE utmost End of all that is aimed at, is indeed illimited: It is the Best and Greatest Thing that infinite and Eternal Wisdom could conceive: but being out of all measure High and Excellent, it includeth innumerable Varieties, that are shut up in bounds for their greater Perfection. Whereupon it followeth, that GOD hath attained a more excellent Effect, than if he had made any one Thing singly infinite.

HIS Love being Infinite and Eternal, in sacrificing it self in all its Works for its Objects welfare, became an infinite and eternal Act; which was not contented, unless in all its Works, it added Art unto Power, and exerted its Wisdom in all its Productions. Had it made one Infinite, some are of Opinion, it had exceeded it self; at least done all that was possible, both for it self, and for its Object, and that one Infinite, being so Created, must be its only Object. For more than Infinite what can be? We are apt to think that nothing can be beside. But to shew that GOD is infinitely more than what we conceive, while we think him infinite; and that we infinitely wrong him, while we limit his Essence to one single Infinity; Who is every way Infinite, in Himself, in all his Works, in all his Waies, in all his Counsels, in every one of his Perfections; He hath made every thing either Infinite, or better than so. For by variety of Effects he hath attained an End in the Beauty and Correspondence of all his Productions, far more Amiable and Divine than any one Effect is capable of being. All Things by a kind of Temperance are made and ordered in Number, Weight and Measure, so that they give and receive a Beauty and Perfection, every thing to and from all the residue, of inestimable value, in relation to the Goodness and Love of their Creator.

I doubt not but GOD (would his Wisdom have permitted such a thing) could have made an infinite Object. For whereever GOD is, he is able to Act; and his Omnipresence is infinite Wisdom and Power; which filling Infinity is able to exert it self beyond all the bounds of Space in an infinite Manner all at once. If it so do, it cannot rest in a less Attainment, than one that answers the measure of its Operation: if it did, that Attainment would be infinitely defective: For infinite Wisdom could certainly conceive one infinitely Better. But this I will aver, that GOD hath wrought abundantly more, than if he had made any one single Effect of his Power infinite. He hath wrought a Work that pleaseth him infinitely Better, and so will it please us, when we are Wise as he is.

HAD he made any one single Infinite, it must be either Corporeal, or Spiritual: Be it either, there is room enough in his Understanding and Omnipresence to receive it. Empty Space is an infinite Object in his understanding. But for the Glory of his Moderation, it is evident that he hath attained a far greater and more perfect End.

HAD he made an Infinite Object of a Spiritual Nature, it must be a Spirit endued with illimited Power, to see his Omnipresence and Eternity. And had he made no more but only this, it is to be feared that the Spectator would be displeased for want of Objects, in preparing which the Love of GOD should have glorified his Wisdom and Goodness for its fruition.

IF you say, the Omnipresence and Eternity of GOD had been filled with that Creature, it is evident that Spirits fill no Room, though they see all things: and that it had been much better if Objects had been prepared for its Enjoyment.

HAD he prepared any one Corporeal Object for the fruition of that Creature; any Corporeal Object if infinite in Dimensions, would be wholly useless: nay pernicious and destructive: for it would exclude all other Beings to which it might be serviceable, out of place, and have nothing whereto to be beneficial.

IF you say it would be Beneficial to GOD, or to that Spectator, or that Intelligible Power, that Spirit for whom it was made: It is apparent that no Corporeal Being can be serviceable to a Spirit, but only by the Beauty of those Services it performeth to other Corporeals, that are capable of receiving them: and that therefore all Corporeals must be limited and bounded for each others sake. And for this Cause it is, that a Philosophical Poet said;

> *As in a Clock, 'tis hinder'd-Force doth bring*
> *The Wheels to order'd Motion, by a Spring;*
> *Which order'd Motion guides a steddy Hand*
> *In useful sort at Figures just to stand;*
> *Which, were it not by Counter-ballance staid,*
> *The Fabrick quickly would aside be laid*
> *As wholly useless: So a Might too Great,*
> *But well proportion'd, makes the World compleat.*
> *Power well-bounded is more Great in Might,*
> *Than if let loose 'twere wholly Infinite.*
> *He could have made an endless Sea by this,*
> *But then it had not been a Sea of Bliss;*
> *A Sea that's bounded in a finite shore,*
> *Is better far because it is no more.*
> *Should Waters endlesly exceed the Skies,*
> *They'd drown the World, and all whate're we prize.*
> *Had the bright Sun been Infinite, its Flame*
> *Had burnt the World, and quite consum'd the same.*
> *That Flame would yield no splendor to the Sight,*
> *'Twould be but Darkness though 'twere Infinite.*
> *One Star made infinite would all exclude,*
> *An Earth made Infinite could ne're be view'd.*
> *But all being bounded for each others sake,*
> *He bounding all did all most useful make.*
> *And which is best, in Profit and Delight,*
> *Though not in Bulk, he made all Infinite.*
> *He in his Wisdom did their use extend,*
> *By all, to all the World from End to End.*
> *In all Things, all Things service do to all:*
> *And thus a Sand is Endless, though most small.*
> > *And every Thing is truly Infinite,*
> > *In its Relation deep and exquisite.*

THIS is the best way of accommodating things to the Service of each other, for the fruition of all Spectators.

MODERATION is not so called from Limiting and Restraining, but from Moderating and Ruling. If Reason require that a Thing should be Great, it is the part of Temperance to make it so. Where Reason requires, it is a point of Moderation to enlarge and extend

Power: Nay to stretch it out to the utmost of its Capacity if Wisdom order it, is but equal. To moderate Almighty Power is to limit or extend it, as Reason requires. Reason requires that it should be so limited and extended, as most tends to the perfection of the Universe.

IF it be more Wise, and more tends to the perfection of the Universe, that Millions of intelligible Spirits should be Created, and every one of them be made infinite in Understanding, it shall be done: If not, Temperance forbears. If Sands and Atoms tend more to the perfection of the World than Angels; there where they do so, Sands and Atoms shall be made, and Angels there where they tend more to the perfection of the World. So that every thing is best in its proper place. Were there no Sands or Atoms there would be no *Universe:* For the Earth, the Sea, the Skie, the Air, all Bodies consist of these, either united or divided. If they had been left unmade, and Angels had been created in their Places, there had been no visible World at all.

TO make Visible Objects useful it was necessary to enshrine some Spirits in Corporeal Bodies, and therefore to make such Creatures as *Men,* that might see, and feel, and smell, and taste, and hear, and eat and drink by their Bodies, and enjoy all the Pleasures of the World by their Souls: And by their Souls moreover know the Original and End of all, understand the design of all, and be able to celebrate the Praises of the Creator. For by this means pure Essences abstracted from all Corporeity might enjoy the World, while they delight in the glory of its Uses, and especially in those compleat and amiable Creatures, for whom it was prepared.

IT was expedient also to make their Bodies finite, that they might converse together: but their inward Intelligences of endless reach, that they might see the holy Angels, delight in them, and by their Love be delightful to them: that they might also be able to search into the depth of all Things, and enjoy Eternity; Nay, that they might be fit Recipients for the infinite Bounty and Goodness of GOD, which is infinite in its Communications.

THAT they should be subject to his Laws, and depend upon him, was necessary in like manner. For by that distinction an infinite difference was between him and them: that disparity being laid in the foundation, though the benefits they receive are altogether infinite, the distance is still the more infinite between them: for the greater the Bounty is, the deeper is the Obligation. The Love and Service they owe is infinite, and so is the Gratitude.

TO see all his Glory is to be able to admire it, and to adore it with infinite amazement and joy, which is to be compleatly just unto it, and perfectly blessed.

There is but one thing more, wherein Almighty Power was by Wisdom infinite to restrain it self for the perfection of his Kingdom: And that is to create them free, that were made to enjoy it. Not to determine their Wills by a fatal Necessity, but to make their esteem and fruition of GOD and his Works their duty, and to leave them to themselves for the more free and voluntary discharge of their duty. For by that means, it would make them capable of Rewards and Punishments, in the Righteous distribution of which the nature and the glory of a Righteous Kingdom consisteth.

THUS did GOD by infinite Moderation, and by a sublime and transcendent Temperance prepare his Kingdom, and make every Thing exquisite in his whole Dominion, to the praise of his Glory, and the satisfaction of his infinite and Eternal Reason. The similitude of which Reason being the Essence of the Soul, all these things fall out for our glory and satisfaction also.

NOW if GOD himself acquired all his Joyes by Temperance: and the glory of his Kingdom is wholly founded in his Moderation: We may hope that our Moderation and Temperance in its place, may accomplish Wonders, and lead us to the fruition of his, by certain steps and degrees, like those that are observed in the Womb towards Manhood, and in the School of our Childhood towards perfect Learning.

TOO much Rain, or too much Drought will produce a Famine: the Earth is made fertile by a seasonable mixture of Heat and Moisture. Excess of Power may overwhelm, but moderation is that which perfecteth and blesseth the Creation.

ALMIGHTY Power is carried far beyond it self, or really is made Almighty, by vertue of that Temperance, wherein Eternal Wisdom is eternally Glorified.

IF any thing be wanting to the full demonstration of the perfection of GODS Kingdom, it is the consideration of his Delay: for we are apt to think, he might have made it Eternally before he did. But to this no other Answer is necessary (though many might be made) then that all Things were from all Eternity before his Eyes, and he saw the fittest Moments wherein to produce them: and judged it fit in his Wisdom first to fill Eternity with his deliberations and Counsels, and then to beautifie Time with the execution of his Decrees. For were there no more to be said but this, his Empire is eternal, because all Possibilities, nay and all Impossibilities are subject to his Will. But if it be confessed that Eternity is an everlasting Moment, infinite in duration, but permanent in all its parts, all Things past, present, and to come, are at once before him, and eternally together. Which is the true Reason, why Eternity is a standing Object before the Eye of the Soul, and all its parts, being full of Beauty and Perfection, for ever to be enjoyed.

IF any man be disposed to cavil further, and to urge, that GOD might at the very first have placed Angels and Men in the state of Glory, the Reply is at hand: that GOD very well understandeth the beauty of Proportion, that Harmony and Symmetry springs from a variety of excellent Things in several places, fitly answering to, and perfecting each other: that the state of Trial, and the state of Glory are so mysterious in their Relation, that neither without the other could be absolutely perfect: Innumerable Beauties would be lost, and many transcendent Vertues and Perfections be abolished, with the estate of Trial, if that had been laid aside, the continual appearance and effect of which is to enrich and beautifie the Kingdom of GOD everlastingly: That GOD loveth Man far more than if he had placed him in the Throne at first, and designeth more Glory and Perfection for him, than in that dispensation he could have been capable of: all which springeth from the Restraint of his Power in some occasions, that it might more fully be exerted in the perfection of the whole, and of all things that were possible to be made, might end in the Supream, and most absolutely Blessed.

Therefore upon the whole Matter, we may conclude with *Solomon, Happy is the man that findeth Wisdom, and the man that getteth Understanding. For the Merchandize of it is better than the Merchandize of Silver, and the Gain thereof than of fine Gold. She is more precious than Rubies, and all the things thou canst desire are not to be compared with her. Length of Daies is in her right hand, and in her left hand Riches and Honour. Her Waies are waies of Pleasantness, and all her Paths are Peace. She is a Tree of Life to them that lay hold upon her, and happy is every one that retaineth her. The LORD by Wisdom hath founded the Earth, by Understanding hath he established the Heavens. My Son, let not them depart from thine Eyes: Keep sound Wisdom and Discretion.* Wisdom is the principal Thing: therefore get Wisdom, and with all thy Getting, get Understanding. For the same Wisdom which created the World, is the only Light wherein it is enjoyed.

CHAP. XXIV.

Of Patience. Its Original. How GOD was the first Patient Person in the World. The Nature, and the Glory, and the blessed Effects of his Eternal Patience. The Reason and Design of all Calamities. Of Patience in Martyrdom. The extraordinary Reward of ordinary Patience in its meanest obscurity.

PATIENCE is a Vertue of the Third estate; it belongs not to the estate of Innocence, because in it there was no Affliction; nor to the estate of Misery, because in it there is no Vertue: but to the estate of Grace it appertains, because it is an estate of Reconciliation, and an estate of Trial: wherein Affliction and Vertue meet together. In the estate of Glory there is no Patience.

THIS is one of those distasful Vertues, which GOD never intended. It received its bitterness from Sin, its life and beauty from GOD's Mercy. If we dislike this Vertue we may thank our selves, for we made GOD first to endure it. And if all things are rightly weighed, no Creature is equal to GOD in Sufferings. We made it necessary for the Eternal GOD-HEAD to be Incarnate, and to suffer all the Incommodities of Life, and the bitter Torments of a bloody Death, that he might bear the Penance of our Sins, and deliver us from eternal Perdition.

THE Corporeal Sufferings of our Saviour are not comparable to the Afflictions of his Spirit. Nor are there any Sufferings or Losses so great as those we cast upon the GOD-HEAD. He infinitely hateth Sin, more than Death: and had rather be Crucified a thousand times over, than that one Transgression should be brought into the World. Nothing is so quick and tender as Love, nothing so lively and sensible in resenting. No loss is comparable to that of Souls, nor any one so deeply concerned in the loss, as GOD Almighty: No Calamity more peircing, than to see the Glory of his Works made Vain, to be bereaved of his Desire, and frustrated of his End in the whole Creation. He had rather we should give him the Blood of *Dragons*, or the cruel Venom of *Asps*, to drink, than that we should pollute our selves, or his Kingdom with a Sin. Nay it were better (if without a Sin it could be done) that the whole World should be annihilated, than a Sin committed. For the World might be Created again with ease, and all that is in it be repaired with a word: but a Sin once committed, can never be undone; it will appear in its place throughout all Eternity: Yet is so odious, and so infinitely opposite to the Holiness of GOD, that no Gall or Wormwood is comparable thereunto. To see his Beloved blasted, his Love despised, and his Son rebellious; to see the most amiable Law in the World broken, his Kingdom laid waste, and his Image defaced; to see all his Labour marred and spoiled, his Benefits slighted, and his infinite Goodness abused and undervalued; all Obligations imposed, and all Rewards prepared, in vain: is worse than to see ones Palace on fire as soon as it is builded, or ones Wife smitten with Leprosie, and ones only beloved Son run mad. For a Child to trample on his Fathers Bowels is nothing in Comparison! He therefore that feels what he made GOD to endure, what Grapes of *Sodom*, and Clusters of *Gomorrah* he offered to his Teeth, how evil a thing and bitter it is, to forsake GOD, how the Scripture saith, *He was grieved at the Heart,* when he saw the Corruption and Impiety of the Earth; and how the Sorrow inflicted was so sore, as to make him *repent that he had made Man* in the World: he surely will be more concerned at the Evil he hath *done,* than at any Evil he can otherwise *suffer:* and his Godly Sorrow (as *Moses*'s Rod did eat up all the Rods of the *Egyptians*) will devour all other Sorrows whatsoever.

TO consider that GOD was the first *Patient* Person in the World, must needs sweeten the Bitterness of Patience, and make it acceptable unto us: to consider that we alone brought it upon our selves, and may thank our selves for the folly of its Introduction, must make us out of very Indignation against our selves contented to suffer, and in pure Justice, quietly to digest it: but to consider yet further, that *GOD,* by bearing our Offences with Patience, took off the trouble of them from us, and by refusing to ease himself of the greatness of his displeasure, in pouring it back again on our own heads, digested it so, as to turn our eternal Torments into transitory Woes, nay into his own Agonies and Pains on the Cross: this will help our Reason to rejoyce at *our light Afflictions which are but for a moment;* especially since they *work* out *for us a far more exceeding, and eternal weight of Glory.*

The first Impression of that abominable Mischief, which occasioned Patience in *GOD*, made it a Calamity, but not a Vertue. Detestation and Grief in themselves are but Sufferings, and meer Sufferings have no Vertue, nor so much almost as Action in them. If his detestation and grief had broken out in Impatience, we had all been destroyed: Anger and Fury had been poured down upon us. That which made it a Vertue was the great and mighty Continence, whereby it was kept in, and governed for all our Benefit. For it was full of Goodness, and Compassion, and Mercy, and Love; and that was indeed the vertue of Patience, in which so much Magnanimity and Government did appear, so much Wisdom, and Stedfastness, and Immutability; and upon this vertue of that Act whereby he retained his displeasure, the whole Kingdom of Grace, and the glory of his Mercy and Love, and the blessedness and exaltation of his Church is founded, it depended upon it, and from his Patience it proceeded.

PATIENCE then is that Vertue by which we behave our selves constantly and prudently in the midst of Misfortunes and Troubles: That Vertue whereby we do not only forbear to break out in Murmurings and Repinings, or support our selves from sinking under Afflictions, or suppress our Discontentments, and refrain from Anger and Disquiet; but whereby we retain our Wisdom, and the goodness of our Mind, notwithstanding all the Confusions and Disorders that would disturb us, and demean our selves in a serene and honourable manner, surmounting the Pains and Calamities that trouble us, and that would otherwise overwhelm us. While we move in a quick and vigorous manner under our Burthen; and by a true Courage improve our Afflictions, and turn them into the *Spoils* of Invincible Reason.

IT is an easie Observation, that Troublous Times are the Seasons of Honour, and that a Warlike-Field is the Seed-Plot of great and Heroical Actions. Men that live in quiet and peaceful Ages, pass through the World as insensibly as if they had all their daies been asleep. Hazards, and Calamities, and Battles, and Victories fill the Annals with Wonder, and raise Great Men to an eminent degree of Fame and Glory. It is Saint *Chrysostoms* opinion, That a Man shews far greater Bravery, that grapples with a Disease, or surmounts his evil Fortune, or behaves himself with Courage in distress, bears the burning of his House, or the loss of his Goods, or the death of his Children with an equal Spirit, in the midst of all Calamities retains his Integrity with Humility and Patience, and Blesses GOD, chearfully submitting with Resignation to his Will, and shews himself Constant in all Estates: then he that in the midst of a prosperous Condition, buildeth Hospitals and Temples, shineth in the exercise of Bounty and Magnificence, and obligeth all the World without any other Expence than that of his Monies. A *Pelican* that feeds her young ones with her Blood, is a more Noble Bird than an Eagle, that fills her Nest with *Ravine*, though taken from the Altar: For though that of a Sacrifice be the more Sacred food, that of ones own Blood is more near and costly.

TIMES of Affliction are Seed-times for a future Harvest. *We are made perfect through Sufferings:* though the Way be mysterious, and the Manner almost incomprehensible, whereby the Sufferings we endure conduce to our Perfection. *Consider the Patience of* Job, how great a spectacle his Sufferings made him *to GOD, Angels, and Men,* and how glorious he became by his Patience to all *Generations.*

THIS Vertue has an Appearance, by reason of its Objects and Materials, so cross to its disposition, that if any thing be difficult in all Nature to be understood, Patience is one, it being a thing of the most deep and obscure value. Its Nature and Effect seem contrary to each other. It raises a Man by depressing him, it elevates by overwhelming, it honours by debasing, it saves by killing him. By making a Man little and nothing, it magnifies and exalts him. No Act of Love is attended with such bleeding Circumstances as that of Cruel Resolution, in exposing our selves to all Calamities that can befal our Souls, for our Beloved's sake. It is the glory of the good Shepheard that *He laies down his life for the Sheep.* And for this very Cause is our Saviour honoured by GOD and Men, *because being in the form of GOD he made himself of no Reputation, but took on himself the form of a Servant,* and died the most cursed *Death of the Cross,* for the sake of the World: *Wherefore,* saith the Text (that is, *For which very Cause) GOD also hath highly exalted him, and given him a Name which is above every Name, that at the Name of* JESUS *every Knee should bow, of things in the Heaven, things in the Earth, and things under the Earth.* Nor is this Gift of *GOD* so purely Arbitrary, but that it has a foundation in Nature. Angels and Men do not bow their Knees only because they are commanded; but because they see Reason to incline them to bow their Knees. There is something in our Saviours

Nature, Action, and Merit, that deserves it at their Hands. The wonderful Love wherewith he loved us is the Root, the Soul, and Glory of his Passion. It is wonderful as it made him willing to become Death, and Sin, and a Curse for us. But the height of our Extasie is in the Reality of his Passion, and in the full accomplishment of all its Purposes.

IT is the Vertue of Love which is infused into Patience, and the chief Elixir of its Nature is founded in the Excellency of a Spirit, that Suffers for anothers sake. This therefore we ought ever to remember, That Patience when it is a Vertue springs from Love; and that this Love is chiefly towards *GOD*, and next that to our Neighbour. When we suffer any thing for *GOD*'s sake, or for our Neighbours good, we suffer in a Wise and Vertuous manner. And the Honour which follows such a Suffering is the Crown of Glory which it shall for ever wear. It is a vain and insipid thing to Suffer without loving *GOD* or Man. Love is a transcendent Excellence in every Duty, and must of necessity enter into the Nature of every Grace and Vertue. That which maketh the solid Benefit of Patience unknown, its Taste so bitter and comfortless to Men, is its *Death* in the separation and absence of its Soul. We Suffer, but Love not. Otherwise Love to the Person for whose sake we Suffer, is its own support and comfort; It makes the Action to be valuable; and infuses a sweetness into all the Affliction it can make us endure: A Sweetness answerable to the Welfare and Pleasure, which is either caused or secured, to our Object thereby. Our own growth in the approbation and esteem of the Person we love, is the desirable Greatness which we covet to attain, which can no way be confirmed, and increased so perfectly, as by Suffering for him. For our Fidelity, Sincerity, Reality, Vigour, Life and Industry, can never be made so fair and apparent, as when we pursue our love, and are carried by it to the utmost extremities of Death and Misery, and labour through all disasters, Persecutions, and Calamities, to obey, and honour, and please, and glorifie the Object which in times of quiet we pretend to love. In an easie and prosperous Estate there is little difference between Friendship and Flattery: but he that sticks firm in Calamity is a Friend indeed. The Trial of Love consists in the difficulties it endures for its Beloved.

AND for this Cause it is, that *GOD* will expose us to so severe a Trial: himself ordaining some Trials in the beginning; but permitting more, when we brought them upon our selves: Many also he suffereth to come, which we daily bring upon our own heads by our own folly.

Some he inflicteth perhaps himself, for the Chastisement of our Sins, or the Medicine of our Souls, to abate our Confidence, and to excite our Care; to awaken us out of our Lethargy, and to quicken our sence both of our Miserable Condition, and our need of his Favour: to humble our Rebellion, to heal and purge our Corruptions, to moderate our Passions, to heighten our Penitence, to abate our Pride, to increase our Ardour in Devotion and Prayer; to make our subjection to, and dependance on him Clear; to stir us up to a more strict Examination of our selves in our Thoughts, Words, and Deeds, least some *Jonas* or other should lie in the Ship, that continues the Tempest upon us; to enkindle our Compassion towards our afflicted Brethren, and to enflame us with more perfect Zeal, and Love towards *GOD;* It is like Wormwood that imbitters the Nipple, to wean us from the World, and augment our desire *to be dissolved and to be with Christ;* to make us groan after our *Eternal Rest,* and long for the *glorious Liberty of the Sons of GOD.* Sometimes he suffereth Tribulations and Trials to come upon us, by the Perverseness of Men, who being left at Liberty in their dominion over the World, are the principal Authors of all the Troubles and disorders in it. To know the several springs and sources of Affliction is very expedient; for our Patience and Contentment much dependeth upon it. A confused Apprehension makes us blind, but a clear Sight distinguisheth between the Will of *GOD,* and the Corruption of Nature; which in our selves and others is the principal Cause of all our disturbances.

BE it by which of all these Occasions it will, or for which of all these Ends it can befal us, it is evermore to increase our Conquest, and to make us like the King of Sufferings *pure* and *perfect.* And the Consideration of Gods over-ruling Power and Providence therein, which makes all these Things work too together for our good, begetteth a grateful Admiration in us as well as a sence of our dependance on his Goodness, which increaseth the Fear of *GOD* in our Souls, and animates us with great Wonder, that he should put his hand to touch the vile and evil Off-spring of our Sin, and turn all into Good, and make it to rest in our Exaltation and Glory by his Wisdom and Mercy.

Concerning *GOD*'s End in bringing, and permitting all these Evils, the Scripture is very frequent: It was one of *Job*'s Contemplations,* *What is Man that thou shouldest magnifie him, and that thou shouldst set thine Heart upon him; and that thou shouldst visit him every Morn-*

* Job. 7.17, 18.

ing, and try him every Moment? Man is magnified by his Trials. It was *David*'s Observation,* *The LORD is in his holy Temple, the Lords Throne is in Heaven: his Eyes behold, his Eye-lids try the Children of Men.* *The Lord trieth the Righteous; but the Wicked and him that loveth Violence his Soul hateth.* It was *Daniel*'s Prophesie,† *And some of them of Understanding shall fall, to try them, and to purge, and to make them White, even to the time of the End.* GOD himself expresseth his own Resolution,‡ *I will bring part of them through the fire, and will refine them as Silver is refined, and try them as Gold is tried: They shall call on my Name and I will hear them; I will say, It is my People, and they shall say, The LORD is my GOD.*

THE meaning of all which places is, not as if *GOD* did stand in need of all these Trials to know what is in us: for he knoweth what is in Man from all Eternity: before these Trials come he *searcheth the Heart, and trieth the Reins,* and discerneth the thoughts, and purposes of the Soul: He seeth every Inclination in the seed, every Grace in the secret habit of the Mind, and every Vertue in the Root. They lie in the Seed, but yet he seeth a mighty difference between quiet Habits, and effectual Operations: for they differ as much as the Root and the Blossom, or the Blossom and the Fruit. For Vertues to lie asleep in the Soul, and for Vertues to be actually and fully perfected, is as great a difference, as for a Vine to be of a generous kind, and prone to bear, but to remain without Fruit; or for a Vine to bring forth, and to be really laden with all the bunches of Grapes that beautifie it. The Excellency of its Nature is vain, if its Fruit be never brought to perfection. There is a Glory in the Work which the silent Habit is uncapable of. It is the Life and Vigour of the Exercise in which all the brightness consisteth. Even Diamonds in the Quarry are dull and dim, they receive not their full lustre and Price till they are cut and polished. *GOD* hath placed our Trial in sharp and bitter Atchievments, because the Love that is exprest in Agonies and Conflicts, acquires other kind of Beauties, that produce more violent and strong Effects in the Mind of the Spectator, and touch the Soul of the Beloved with more quick and feeling Compassions, than any Love expressed in Ease and Pleasure can pretend to. And since all our Felicity consists in the violence of Gods Love, his great and perfect Sence of our Beauty and Honour, his full and compleat delight and Complacency, all that which affecteth his Soul with more feeling and tender

---

* Psal. 11.4, 5.   † Dan. 11.35.   ‡ Zech. 13.9.

Resentment, must be very dear and precious to us, because it maketh us more dear and precious to him. We live in him more effectually, and feel our selves rooted in his Love, and crowned with his Complacency more abundantly, by how much the more his Affection bleedeth, and his Pity (which enbalms Love) is stirred up to receive us. And therefore it is that St. *Peter* saith,* *We are in Heaviness for a season through manifold Temptations, that the Trial of our Faith being much more precious than of Gold that perisheth, though it be tried with Fire, might be found unto Praise, and Honour, and Glory at the Appearing of Jesus Christ.* For as we have before observed, Love is more effeminate in a condition of Repose, where all is sweet and easie to our selves: there can be no Fidelity, no Patience, no Fortitude, no actual Sacrificing of all our Contentments and Joyes to our Beloved; no Victory over Death, and Hell, and the Grave; no Self denial, no Endearments springing from the same, no Prelation of our Object above our selves; no loss of Honours, Riches, Liberties, and Lives for our Objects sake; and the more of this is Actually done, the more of Necessity must be the following Joy of Glory. And for this Cause doth St. *Peter* further exhort us,† *Beloved, think it not strange concerning the fiery Trial which is to try you, as though some strange thing happened unto you: But rejoyce, in as much as ye are Partakers of Christs Sufferings: that when his Glory is revealed, you may be glad also with exceeding Joy. If ye be reproached for the Name of Christ happy are ye, for the Spirit of Glory and of God resteth upon you: on their part he is evil spoken of, but on your part he is glorified.*

THIS he speaketh I confess of the Persecutions, Imprisonments, and Flames of the Martyrs, that were Gods Friends, and the Champions of his Truth in the World, that in vindication of his Glory endured the Brunt, and received all the Arrows of his Enemies in their Bosom: but no Man has cause to be discouraged. For where the greatness of the Cause is wanting, and the apparent glory of the Consequence unseen, as for the most part it is in all our common and ordinary Afflictions; there to submit to the Will of GOD, where there is so much Baseness as in Poverty: in Sickness where there is so much Unprofitableness, in private Losses and Calamities where there is so much Obscurity; meerly because it is GODS pleasure, and because in other things he hath infinitely obliged us, and prepared infinite and eternal Joyes: this hath a peculiar Grace in its nature, that in ordinary occurrences makes our Patience more rare and extraordinary.

* 1 Pet. 1.6, 7.   † 1 Pet. 4.12, 13, 14.

THERE are a thousand things that may be said on this Theme, which for brevity I must pass: All I shall observe further is this, that as the Scriptures open the design of Patience, and unvail the face of its mysterious Nature, so doth Reason shew its invincible height and magnanimity. Patience is a Vertue whose element is in Miseries: it owes its being to Pains and Calamities: were there no Miseries there could be no Patience. Evils are its Play-fellows, it feeds upon Sorrows, thrives by Disadvantages, grows rich by Poverties, it must needs surmount all Opposition, for the more it endures the greater it is. It is impossible for Calamity to hurt Patience: it is made perfect by Sufferings. The more Patient a man is, his Patience is the greater: and the greater his Patience is, the more strong and mighty his Soul is. Nothing can quell him, or discourage, or overcome him, that is compleat in Patience. He dareth all things, because he can endure them. All his Martial and Heroical Vertues are knit together in Patience. Fortitude it self cannot win the field without it. The most valiant Souldier is but useless if he cannot endure Hunger and Cold, and Heat and Rain, the Incommodities of a March, and lying on the Ground. While he that endures all things marches on, and gets into the Field where Fidelity, Love, and Loyalty are tried, and cannot be hindered from the full and perfect exercise of all these, because he can bear any thing that is Evil, he can do any thing that is Good: He will fight the good fight with alacrity, and at last most certainly attain the Crown of Righteousness, and the Kings favour.

The Cause of Meekness is Love. It respects the future beauty and perfection of its Object. It is the most supernatural of all the Vertues. The Reasons and Grounds of this Vertue in the estate of Grace and Misery. Its manifold Effects and Excellencies. Of the Meekness of Moses *and* Joseph.

MEEKNESS is a Vertue of the Third estate, as well as Patience. Patience regards Calamities, Meekness Wrongs. The Injuries that we receive from others are its proper Objects. It springs from Love, and tends to its Continuance and Preservation. It hath something peculiar in its nature, because it gives Immutability to Goodness, and makes our Worth not to depend on other Mens Deservings, but our own Resolutions. It is fed by Charity, and like a grateful Off-spring of a Parent so amiable, helps in its greatest extremity to preserve it from its extinction. For all Love by Nature dies into Distaste, when its Object hath offended: because Approbation which is the first step to Esteem, and Esteem it self which is a degree to Love, have no other Object but something that is Amiable and fit to be beloved. And again every thing that is divested of all its excellence, is common, if not odious; and lost to our Affection, till Meekness comes in to rescue and save both our Love and it from its dismal Period. Its End is the Recovery of what has offended, Hope and Possibility are the foundation of its exercise, Prudence is the Guide by which it is conducted to the satisfaction of our desire in the restitution of Amity between us and our Adversary.

WHERE there is no hope that the Beauty of what we love may be regained, Meekness hath lost its *Vertue,* and with that its *Existence.* For if it be impossible that an evil Person should ever be reclaimed,

194

it is to no purpose to be Meek. He that can never be delightful more, is utterly useless: Meekness therefore which derives its solidity and Power from its End, is in such cases utterly abolished. For this cause it is that we are to esteem our Saviours Blood the ground on which it stands: since all Nature without his Incarnation, Death, and Passion, could never restore a Sinner to the possibility of becoming Just and Amiable. This Vertue of Meekness respects the future beauty and perfection of an Object that is now deformed; It must needs be of transcendent excellency, since the practice of Meekness is acquired by the price of our Saviours Blood, and the first step to its exercise did cost the death of the Eternal GOD.

IT is a transcendent Vertue, because the Means of introducing it are wholy Supernatural. It carries us above all the Rules of Nature, above all the Principles of Reason, and in that is Supernatural. For by Nature we are to be Just and Good towards all that are Innocent, and kind to all those to whom Kindness is due: but it is not by Nature either just or rational that we should love any Creature that is Evil: and how GOD came to do it first is an infinite Wonder. Though now since *he hath first loved us* who are so vile, nothing is more natural than that we should do as we are done unto, imitate him, and love those whom our Creatour loveth: With Pity and Benevolence at first, that we may hereafter do it, with full Complacency.

That Humane Nature is infinitely exalted by the Incarnation of the Son of GOD is confessed by all those, that believe the Article of our Saviours Incarnation: that the Earth how base soever it seem is the Bride of Heaven, its own quiet, and the embraces of the Skies, that make it the Centre of all their Revolutions, sufficiently demonstrate; though few have observed that the Sun, and Moon, and Stars dance attendance to it, and cherish it with their Influences, while the Earthly Globe is crowned with the fruits of all their secret Endeavours: That the Angels desire to look down into those things which are done upon Earth, the very Scriptures witness; and yet for all this, it would seem a New Doctrine, to affirm, that there are Works done here upon Earth, that are by Nature above the Heavens. Yet all the Operations of the Holy Ghost, and all the Good Works of Holy Men, especially the Meekness and Patience of the Saints, which are founded on the greatest Miracle in all Eternity, the Love of GOD to Sinners, and his stupendious Humiliation and Passion for them, are set upon a higher Basis than all Nature, except that of the Deity, can afford unto us. Which Note I make for our greater encouragement to the works of Meekness.

Meekness is Super-natural

They are all in Nature like the effects of our Saviours Love to the greatest Offendors. Reason it self is now exalted above all its former heights, and there is reason since our Saviours Death for the doing of that which no reason, before he designed to forgive, and Die for us, could lead us to do.

THAT GOD through the greatness of his Love may condescend to such Indignities as are infinitely unworthy of him, we see by the Examples of Kings and Queens, and other high and delicate Personages, that suffer their Children to play with their Beards, and the Tresses of their Hair; which other Persons dare not so much as approach, for the Reverence of their Majesty. I have oftentimes admired at the mean Offices to which Parents stoop, and the familiar boldness they permit to their little ones, to play with their Scepters, and Crowns, and Eyes, and Lips, with their Breasts and Jewels, and sometimes to pinch and hurt, nay and to defile them too, being unmindful of their State, and far from all Anger and Indignation. But the free Pardon, and desire of the Return of vicious and debauched Children, is a nearer instance and resemblance of GOD, in his gracious Dispensations, who suffers all Nature still to attend us, though we continually prophane his Name, and injure his eternal Goodness by our manifold Transgressions.

THIS Example of GOD, who died for Sinners, in the Person of his Son, and prayed for his Tormentors, in the very Act of their Cruelty and Rage against him, should prevail with us to esteem all those whom he owneth for his Children, as our own Bowels, and to be as Meek and Condescending to all Mankind, as Parents are to their Children. The Reasons of which Duty are thus variously offered to our Consideration.

TO labour after those Principles only that establish our repose in the estate of Bliss and Innocency, is utterly impertinent to our present Condition.—

> *Were all the World a Paradice of Ease*
> *'Twere easie then to live in Peace.*
> *Were all men Wise, Divine, and Innocent,*
> *Just, Holy, Peaceful, and Content,*
> *Kind, Loving, True, and alwaies Good,*
> *As in the Golden-Age they stood;*
> *'Twere easie then to live*
> *In all Delight and Glory, full of Love,*
> *Blest as the Angels are above.*

But we such Principles must now attain,
(If we true Blessedness would gain)
As those are, which will help to make us reign
Over Disorders, Injuries,
Ingratitudes, Calamities,
Affronts, Oppressions, Slanders, Wrongs,
Lies, Angers, bitter Tongues,
The reach of Malice must surmount, and quell
The very Rage, and Power of Hell.

NO Man but he that came down from Heaven, and gave his Apostles power to handle Vipers, and drink any deadly thing without harm, was able to reveal the way of Peace and Felicity to Sinners. He, and only he that made them able to trample Satan under feet, and taught them how to vanquish all the Powers of Darkness, was worthy to make known this glorious mystery of Patience and Meekness, by which in despite of all the Corruptions and Violences in the World, the holy Soul of a quiet Man is armed and prepared for all Assaults, and so invironed with its own repose, that in the midst of Provocations it is undisturbed, and dwells as it were in a Sanctuary of Peace within it self, in a Paradice of Bliss, while it is surrounded with the howlings of a terrible Wilderness. Nothing else can make us live happily in this World, for among so many Causes of Anger and Distaste, no man can live well, but he that carries about him perpetual *Antidotes* and *Victories*.

THERE are two things absolutely necessary to Felicity, outward *Security,* and inward *Contentment.* Meekness is as it were the *Bulwark* of *Security,* which though it be as soft as *Wool,* is able with more success to repel the violence of a Cannon-Bullet, than the rough temper of a *Stone-Wall.* *Contentment* springs from the satisfaction of Desire in the sight and fruition of all Treasures and Glories: And as the Sun is surrounded with its own Light, the felicity of the Enjoyment becomes its own fortress and security. For he that is throughly Happy, has so much work to do in Contemplation and Thanksgiving, that he cannot have while to be concerned with other mens disorders, he loves his Employment too well to be disturbed, and will not allow himself the thoughts of Revenge or Anger.

IN two things Meekness is greatly profitable to a Mans self, *Possession* and *Triumph.* He that permits the Tumult of the World to enter into his Soul, and suffers the Temple of the Holy Ghost to be defiled with Rage and Anger, makes it an *unfit* habitation for the Blessed

Spirit. Doves will not dwell in *Pigeon-Houses* disturbed, or haunted
with Vermin: nor can Felicity be enjoyed but by serene and quiet
Thoughts that are full of tranquillity. For *where Envying and Strife
is, there is Confusion and every evil Work. But the Wisdom that is
from above is first pure, then peaceable, gentle and easie to be intreated,
full of Mercy and good Fruits. And the fruit of Righteousness is sown
in Peace of them that make Peace.* Which must of necessity precede
fruition, as Triumph followeth.

WERE I for my life to interpret that Text of our Saviour, *The
Meek shall inherit the Earth,* I should in the first place say, that every
Knowing man may enjoy the beauty and glory of the whole World,
and by sweet Contemplations delight in all the abundance of Treasures
and pleasant Varieties that are here upon Earth, especially since by
the Ordinance of Nature all men are to be his peculiar Treasures.
This he might do, I say, did all men love him, and fill the World
with Glory and Vertue. But since all is confounded by their perverseness
and disorder, his Fruition is utterly lost, unless he will forgive all Injuries, and by the vertue of Meekness maintain the quiet of his own
Soul in the midst of their distempers. The Meek man is not fretted
nor disturbed, but may enjoy all Still: and the unspeakable Joy which
all the Glories of Gods Kingdom do afford him, shall make him more
meek, and able also to pacifie, and rule, and heal the minds of his
Enemies, and even by the love of Sinners to recover his Right, and
ancient Fruitions.

TO be able to live at quiet, and enjoy the felicity of Heaven and
Earth, notwithstanding all the attempts of our Enemies, makes them
mad when they see they cannot fret us, and so by Consequence a
greater Revenge is seated in Meekness than in Revenge it self. For
our Repose is their punishment and torment that hate us. Their vexation falleth on their own head, when they see they miss of their aim,
and cannot molest us: but it is a joy to see our selves seated in a
throne of Repose, clean out of their reach; it breeds a kind of triumph
and ovation in the Soul. The secret Conscience of its own Power is
a glory and satisfaction unimaginable.

HE that masters his own Passion is master of another mans, and
seldom falls into those Broils and Inconveniencies that are the destruction of ungoverned and hasty Spirits. Which made *Solomon* to say,
*He that is slow to Anger is better than the Mighty, and he that ruleth
his Spirit, than he that taketh a City.*

HE that troubleth his own house shall inherit the Wind; he that is nice and exquisite in exacting all Faults shall never be beloved. They are disobliging, angry, testy men that are hated; and the Revengful that do frequently fall into mischief. But to be kind to the Unthankful and the Evil, and to deal with all men better than they deserve, is the way to be beloved by the worst of men, and admired by the best.

MEEKNESS is the retreat of Goodness, and the only force in the rear of Liberality. He that does one Injury after forty Kindnesses, blots out the memory of all his Courtesies; and he that revenges an Injury seems to do one. For he that did the Wrong, seems innocent to himself, because he felt it not; and seeming innocent takes the Revenge as an undeserved Injury, and is lost for ever. Now some Injuries we must expect from our best Friends, which are alwaies lost for want of Meekness. So are all the Benefits we do, unless we will forgive as well as give. But an Injury forgiven is forgotten by him that did it, and the Friendship continues at the expence, and to the honour and comfort of the Pardoner, as if no Offence had ever been committed: Nay if afterwards he comes to see the Candor of his abused Friend, he that did the Injury loves him better than before, because he pardoned the Wrong.

MEEKNESS as it preserves Friendship between *two,* makes Goodness invincible and unalterable in *one.* He shall not be good long whose Goodness dependeth on others Merits. He is a miserable weak man, that is of an Exceptious humor; he is a trouble to his own flesh, and subject to the power of every Wasp, whether he shall be good or no. He is quickly stopt in his *Careir* of Vertue, and easily turned out of the way, that is apt to be infected with anothers Malice. He carries no Antidotes about him, and for want of a Preservative, is in danger of the Contagion. Meekness is a means of the health of the Soul: a Passionate man being all over *sore,* is covered with hot and angry Boils, which cannot be touched.

IT preventeth much mischief in Families. An occasion of Anger is like a spark of Fire, it is of great Consequence where it falleth. If it falls into barrels of *Gunpowder,* it blows up the World; if into green Wood or watery places, it does no harm. Penitent Tears, and the verdure of Humility prevent such flames, and extinguish the quarrel. If *Wild-fire* be thrown, I will put it out with my foot, and not by throwing it back, give my Enemy the advantage of retorting it upon me. *A soft Answer pacifieth much Wrath,* but virulent Speeches are a fireball tossed to and fro, of them that love Death.

BY Revenge a man at best can but preserve himself, by killing his Enemy: but Meekness well managed, destroys the Enmity, preserves the Person, and turns the Enemy into an excellent Friend.

MEEKNESS is not the way to Peace, and Repose, and Victory only, but to Honour and Glory. As it is the strength, *it is the Glory of a man to pass over a Transgression:* He that is lightly angered is quickly lost, and a fickle Friend is not worth a farthing. A straw and a feather shall forfeit all the Obligations in the World, in some Tempers. Nay he that is Revengful, is a dangerous Person: and *with an Angry man thou shalt not go:* He has the Plague upon him and is prohibited Company. All this is dishonourable. But a man that is a resolved and stable Friend, that cannot be alter'd, that will not change, though he be wronged, but forgive, and pity, and continue to serve and love his Friend, though he shews him some dirty Tricks; he that will surmount all by invincible Kindness, he is a solid and weighty Friend, a rare Treasure, and exceeding precious. Neither my Errors nor Misfortunes are able to change him that loveth me purely because he will love me. When his Excellency is found out, he will more highly be esteemed, not only by his Friend, but by all that see him, and note his Fidelity.

INJURIES well forgiven are the highest Obligations in the World: especially if a man has been injured after many Benefits. A Friend that will so oblige, is more to be preferred than the Gold of *Ophir.*

MEEKNESS brings a man into respect with his Servants, and into power with his Neighbours. *Anger resteth in the bosom of Fools,* but Meekness hath alwaies this advantage, it is attended with Wisdom, and other Vertues, as Goodness and Courage. A man that is prudent in Affairs, and zealous of Good Works, faithful in retaining Secrets, and so full of Love, that he is prone to do all manner of Good with industry, and is couragious to expose himself to any Hazard, for the benefit of his Neighbours, shall keep his Servants in awe, and yet be beloved of them: He shall be able to do among his Neighbours what he pleaseth: He shall when known well, become the Father of all their Families, they will entrust their Wives and Children in his hands, as I have often experienced; their Gold, their Bonds, their Souls, their Affairs, their Lives, their Secrets, Houses, Liberties, and Lands; and be glad of such a Friend in whom to be safe, and by whom to be assisted. But though you have all the Vertues in the World, the way

to the use of them is blockt up without Meekness: for your Neighbours
are few of them Wise, or Good; and if you will be provoked by Injuries,
you will upon forty occasions so distaste them, that they will never
trust you. You will look as like a Trifle, a Knave, or a Fool, as
one of them; and be as very a Mad man. He that will not do good
but to deserving Persons, shall find very few to do good to. For he
shall not be acquainted with Good men, and from doing good to others
he excludes himself. But if all his other Vertues are beautified by Meekness, such a man will be like an Angel, and live above all his Neighbours, as if he were in Heaven. So that Meekness is his real exaltation.
And this made our Saviour to cull out that Blessing for the Meek,
The Meek shall inherit the Earth. Even here upon Earth the Meek
are they that are most blessed.

TO do good to an innocent Person is Humane, but to be kind
and bountiful to a man, after he has been Injurious, is Divine. *Philanthus* gave Laws and Countries to the *Parthenians,* and was disgraced
and banished: But he did them good after the Injury, and was made
their God, as *Justine* recordeth.

THE very nature of the Work encourageth us to its exercise, because
it is GOD-like, and truly Blessed. But there are many other Considerations moving us unto it.

Mankind is sick, the World distemper'd lies,
Opprest with Sins and Miseries.
Their Sins are Woes; a long corrupted Train
Of Poyson, drawn from Adam's *vein,*
Stains all his Seed, and all his Kin
Are one Disease of Life within.
They all torment themselves!
The World's one Bedlam, *or a greater Cave*
Of Mad-men, that do alwaies rave.

The Wise and Good like kind Physicians are,
That strive to heal them by their Care.
They Physick and their Learning calmly use,
Although the Patient *them abuse.*
For since the Sickness is (they find)
A sad Distemper of the Mind;
All railings they impute,
All Injuries, unto the sore Disease,
They are expresly come to ease!

If we would to the Worlds distemper'd Mind
  Impute the Rage which there we find,
We might, even in the midst of all our Foes,
  Enjoy and feel a sweet Repose.
  Might pity all the Griefs we see,
  Anointing every Malady
   With precious Oyl and Balm;
And while our selves are Calm, our Art improve
  To rescue them, and shew our Love.

But let's not fondly our own selves beguile;
  If we Revile 'cause they Revile,
Our selves infected with their sore Disease,
  Need others Helps to give us ease.
  For we more Mad then they remain,
  Need to be cut, and need a Chain
   Far more than they. Our Brain
Is craz'd; and if we put our Wit to theirs,
  We may be justly made their Heirs.

But while with open eyes we clearly see
  The brightness of his Majesty;
While all the World, by Sin to Satan sold,
  In daily Wickedness grows old,
  Men in Chains of Darkness lye,
  In Bondage and Iniquity,
   And pierce and grieve themselves!
The dismal Woes wherein they crawl, enhance
  The Peace of our Inheritance.

We wonder to behold our selves so nigh
  To so much Sin and Misery,
And yet to see our selves so safe from harm!
  What Amulet, *what hidden Charm*
  Could fortifie and raise the Soul
  So far above them; and controul
   Such fierce Malignity!
The brightness and the glory which we see
  Is made a greater Mystery.

And while we feel how much our GOD *doth love*
  The Peace of Sinners, how much move,
And sue, and thirst, intreat, lament and grieve,
  For all the Crimes in which they live,

And seek and wait, and call again,
And long to save them from the pain
Of Sin, from all their Woe!
With greater thirst, as well as grief we try,
How to relieve their Misery.

The life and splendour of Felicity,
Whose floods so overflowing be,
The streams of Joy which round about his Throne,
Enrich and fill each Holy One,
Are so abundant, that we can
Spare all, even all to any Man!
And have it all our selves!
Nay have the more! We long to make them see
The sweetness of Felicity.

While we contemplate their Distresses, how,
Blind Wretches, they in bondage bow,
And tear and wound themselves, and vex and groan,
And chafe and fret so near his Throne,
And know not what they ail, but lye
Tormented in their Misery
(Like Mad-men that are blind)
In works of darkness nigh such full Delight:
That they might find and see the sight,

What would we give! that they might likewise see
The Glory of his Majesty!
The joy and fulness of that high delight,
Whose Blessedness is infinite!
We would even cease to live, to gain
Them from their misery and pain,
And make them with us reign.
For they themselves would be our greatest Treasures
When sav'd, our own most Heavenly Pleasures.

O holy JESUS *who didst for us die,*
And on the Altar bleeding lie,
Bearing all Torment, pain, reproach and shame,
That we by vertue of the same,
Though enemies to GOD, *might be*
Redeem'd, and set at liberty.
As thou didst us forgive,

So meekly let us Love to others shew,
And live in Heaven on Earth below!

Let's prize their Souls, and let them be our Gems,
Our Temples and our Diadems,
Our Brides, our Friends, our fellow-Members, Eyes
Hands, Hearts and Souls, our Victories,
And Spoils and Trophies, our own Joyes!
Compar'd to Souls all else are Toyes!
O JESUS *let them be*
Such unto us, as they are unto thee
Vessels of Glory and Felicitie!

How will they love us, when they find our Care
Brought them all thither where they are!
When they conceive, what terrour 'tis to dwell
In all the punishments of Hell:
And in a lively manner see,
O Christ, eternal Joyes in thee!
How will they all delight
In praising thee for us, with all their might,
How sweet a Grace, how infinite!

WHEN we understand the perfection of the Love of GOD, the
excellency of immortal Souls, the price and value of our Saviours Blood,
the misery of Sin, and the malady of distemper'd Nature, the danger
of Hell, and the Joyes of which our sorest Enemies are capable, the
Obligations that lie on our selves, and the peace and blessedness of
so sweet a Duty, Compassion it self will melt us into Meekness, and
the wisdom of knowing these great things will make it as natural to
us as Enjoyment it self, as sweet and easie, as it is to live and breath.
It will seem the harshest and most unnatural thing in the World to
forbear so fair, so just, so reasonable, so divine a Duty.

NOR is it a small comfort, that the more vile our Enemies are,
the more price and lustre is set upon our Actions. Our Goodness is
made by their Evil, the more eminent and conspicuous: we improve
their Injuries and turn them into Benefits, we make a Vertue of Necessity, and turn their Vices into Graces, make them appear more abominable and vile if they continue obstinate; and the greater their Perversness is, the more great and honourable is our Vertue. It was the praise
of *Moses,* that *the Man Moses was the Meekest man upon all the*
Earth, yet one passionate expression lost him so much in the esteem

of GOD, that it hindered his entrance into the Land of *Canaan*. How
great an Instrument he was nevertheless in the Conduct and Felicity
of the *Jews,* and how much he profited the whole Nation by his Meekness Sacred story does record. How *Joseph* also dealt with his Brethren,
how he saved all the Family of *Israel* in the Root by his Meekness,
and by Meekness purchased an everlasting Name of Glory and Renown, all Christian Ages and Nations understand, where his Praises
are celebrated to this day: And the benefit thereof is spread abroad,
and propagated throughout all Generations for evermore.

Humility is the basis of all Vertue and Felicity, in all Estates, and for ever to be exercised. As Pride does alienate the Soul from GOD, Humility unites it to him in Adoration and Amity. It maketh infinite Blessedness infinitely greater, is agreeable to the Truth of our Condition, and leads us through a dark and mysterious way to Glory.

MEEKNESS respecteth others faults; Humility and Penitence our own. But Humility is more large than Penitence, and is a distinct Affection of another nature. Penitence is an exercise of the Affection of Sorrow, and that only for Sin. Humility is an acknowledgment of all our Vileness; it respects our Original out of nothing as well as our Guilt, our Weakness and Unworthiness, our dependance upon anothers Will, our Debt and Obligation, the duty of Obedience and Allegiance which we owe, and all the naked Truth of our Condition. It confesseth our homage, and is sensible of our Smallness and Subjection. All that a man hath received it distinguisheth from what he is of himself: And its Fruits or Effects are suitable to its Nature. It is the Vertue by which we think basely of our selves, and behave our selves in a lowly and submissive manner. It makes us soft and pliant as Wax, susceptible of any form that shall be imposed on us by our Benefactour, and prone to Gratitude. It is accompanied with a high and mighty sence of Benefits received, and made Noble by the honour which it inclines us to return to GOD and Man for all the goodness which they shew unto us. It is of incomparable use in our Felicity, because it magnifies our esteem of all our happiness and glory.

IT is not through Ignorance, or want of good Will, that we speak nothing of Vices, the woful deformity of which being exposed to view, near the excellence of Vertue, would put a greater lustre on all their brightness: but the abundance of matter which Vertue it self doth afford, forbids us to waste our Time and Paper in the description of their Contraries. The glory of their nature being so full and perfect in it self, that it needeth not the aid of those additional Arts, which labour to set off the dignity of imperfect things by borrowed Commendations. And besides this, the mischief and inconveniency of every Vice is so great and manifold, that it would require a distinct and intire Volume to unfold the deformity of their destructive nature, so fully as their baseness and demerit requires. It is sufficient therefore here to observe, that Pride is of all other things most odious to GOD; because it puffeth up the Soul with Self-conceit, is forgetful of its Original, void of all Gratitude, and prone to Rebellion. Is it not an odious and abominable thing, for a Creature that is nothing in himself to flie in his Creators face, and to usurp a dominion over it self to the apparent wrong of its Soveraign Lord, to rob its Benefactor of all the glory of his Bounty, to renounce and deny all dependance on him, and to forswear its homage and allegiance, to ascribe all its Glories to it self, and abhor all sence of honour and gratitude, to look upon it self as the sole original and author of all its Greatness, and to be dazled so with the brightness of its condition, as to forget the true fountain of it, the goodness and the love of him that first raised him to all that Treasure and Dominion: to dote on its own Perfections without any reflexion on the Bounty of him that gave them! All this is to act a *Lie,* and to be guilty of apparent Falshood: It is as full of *Fraud* and *Injustice* as is possible: and as full of *Folly* as it is of *Impiety.* For Pride aimeth at the utmost height of Esteem and Honour; and is fed by its own beauty and glory: yet foolishly undermineth and blasteth the Person it would advance with the greatest baseness and shame imaginable, it devours the Beauty which ought to feed it, and destroies the Glory in which it delighteth. The higher, the greater, the more perfectly glorious and blessed the Person is that is exalted, his Ingratitude (which is the dregs of Baseness) is the more black and horrid, and provokes the greater detestation. It forfeits and renounces all the Delight which the goodness of its Lord and Benefactor affordeth, it cuts off the Soul like a branch from the root that gave it life and verdure, it tends all to division, alienation and enmity, it turns that Complacency, which is its only bliss, into wrath and indignation: And whereas it delights in nothing more than appearing highly amiable in the eyes of all Spectators, it falleth into contempt and extream disgrace before all the Creatures in Heaven and Earth, that look upon it, and behold its Unworthiness. No Toad has so much deformity, or poyson, or malignity as Pride, in its nature. It is the ruine of all that is great, and turns the brightest of the Seraphims into the most abominable of Devils.

NOW if Pride be so pernicious, and be by nature (though a meer *Phantasie*) so destructive: what shall Humility be which is full of truth and reality! How forcible, how divine, how amiable, how full of truth, how bright and glorious, how solid and real, how agreeable to all Objects, how void of errour and disparity, how just and reasonable, how wise and holy, how deep, how righteous, how good and profitable, how mightily prone to exalt us in the esteem of GOD and Man! How agreeable to all its Causes and Ends, how fit and suitable to all the circumstances of Mans Condition! I need not say more: It bears its own evidence, and carries Causes in it that will justifie our Saviours words, *He that humbleth himself shall be exalted.* He that is puffed up has but a counterfeit glory, but Humility is full of solid glory. Its beauty is so amiable that there is no end of counting its proportions and excellencies. The Wise man that saw into the nature of all things very clearly, said long before our Saviour was born, *Pride goeth before a fall, but before Honour is Humility.* He that exalteth himself must needs be humbled, because the Colours are envenomed wherewith he painteth his face, which in a little time is discerned, and at the very first instant the Painting begins to turn into a Canker.

THE *Amiableness* of Humility appeareth by its *Excellency*; on these two the greatness of its beauty and success is founded. It is so agreeable to all the principles of Nature, and Grace, and Glory, to all the desires of Angels and Men, to all the designs of GOD himself, and to all the interests and concerns of the Soul, that it cannot but be the most advantagious Vertue in the whole World. It is strange that a man should look with the same Eye upon two Objects so infinitely distant and different from each other. But at the same time he seeth GOD and Nothing, Heaven and Earth, eternal Love and Dust to be his Original. Self-love and Justice, Wisdom and Goodness, Joy and Gratitude have the same Objects, but look upon them in a several manner: and are very differently affected with them. Humility regards all Objects high and low, Good and Evil: but with a peculiar remark and notice of its own. It takes them in in another light, and discerns them all with another kind of sence. It is in some manner the taste of the Soul. Their Truth appeareth to the eye of Knowledge, their Goodness

is apprehended by the life of Love, the perfection of their serviceableness to the most perfect End is discerned by Wisdom, the benefit which
all Spectators receive is the delight of Goodness, the incomprehensible
depth and mysterious intricacy of their frame and nature is the peculiar
Object of our Wonder and Curiosity: they help our Faith as they
shew a Deity, and the truth of all Religion and Blessedness. As they
are the gifts of GOD they are the provocations of Gratitude, and as
they are aggravations of Sin they are respected by Repentance. As
they are the means of our Glory, and our proper Treasures, they are
the Objects of Contentment; but Humility looks upon them in relation
to its Unworthiness, compares them with it self and its own deserts,
and admires the disproportion that is between them. It useth them
all as grounds of a deeper and profounder Lowness in the esteem which
it ought to have of it self, and as the incentives to Love and Gratitude;
which it paies in the depth of a more profound Acknowledgment
and Adoration.

THIS habit or affection of the Soul is not inconsistent with its Joy
and Glory (as by some foolish people, that are by Ignorance and Errors
far from GOD, is generally supposed) but highly conducive and subservient to its perfection. It gives us the tenderest and greatest sence;
it passeth *thorow* all things, embraceth the *Poles,* and toucheth all
Extreams together. The *Centre* it self is but the middle of its profun-
dity: it hath a *Nadir* beneath it, a lower point in another Heaven,
on the other side opposite to its Zenith. In its own depth it containeth
all the height of Felicity and Glory, and doubles all by a mystery
in Nature. It is like a Mirror lying on the ground with its face upwards:
All the height above increaseth the depth of its Beauty within, nay
turneth into a new depth, an inferiour Heaven is in the glass it self;
at the bottom of which we see the Skie, though it be not transplanted,
removed thither. Humility is the fittest Glass of the Divine Greatness,
and the fittest Womb for the conception of all Felicity; for it hath
a double Heaven. It is the way to full and perfect Sublimity. A man
would little think, that by sinking into the Earth he should come to
Heaven. He doth not, but is buried, that fixeth and abideth there.
But if he pierceth through all the Rocks and Minerals of the inferiour
World, and passeth on to the end of his Journey in a strait line downward, in the middle of his way he will find the Centre of Nature,
and by going downward still begin to ascend, when he is past the
Centre; through many Obstacles full of gross and subterraneous Darkness, which seem to affright and stifle the Soul, he will arrive at last

to a new Light and Glory, room and liberty, breathing-place and fresh-air among the *Antipodes,* and by passing on still through those inferiour Regions that are under his feet, but over the head of those that are beneath him, finally come to another Skie, penetrate that, and leaving it behind him sink down into the depth of all Immensity. This he cannot do in his Body, because it is gross and dull, and heavy and confined: but by a Thought in his Soul he may, because it is subtile, quick, aiery, free, and infinite; Nothing can stop or exclude it, oppress or stifle it. This local descent through all the inferiour Space and Immensity, though it brings us to GOD, and his Throne, and another Heaven full of Joyes and Angels, on the other side the World; yet is it but a real Emblem of the more spiritual and mysterious flight of Humility in the mind. We all know that the way to Heaven is through Death and the Grave, beyond which we come to another Life, in Eternity: but how to accommodate this to the business of Humility, few understand. By this Vertue we are inclined to despise our selves, and to leave all the garish Ornaments of Earthly bliss, to divest our selves of the splendors of Temporal prosperity, and to submit to all Afflictions, Contempts and Miseries, that a good Cause can bring upon us. In the eyes of other men we are beneath their feet, and so we are in our own, till we are gone a little further: but on the other side of all this Baseness, we find a better Life in Communion with the Deity. *Forasmuch then,* saith St. *Peter,** as Christ hath suffered for us in the flesh, arm your selves likewise with the same mind: for he that hath suffered in the flesh hath ceased from sin: That he no longer should live the rest of his time in the flesh, to the lusts of Men, but to the will of GOD. For the time past of our life may suffice us to have wrought the will of the Gentiles, when we walked in Lasciviousness, Lusts, Excess of Wine, Revellings, Banquettings, and abominable Idolatries; wherein they think it strange that ye run not with them to the same excess of Riot.* There is a motion from Vice to Vertue, and from one degree of Grace to another: by which we leave the phantastick World, with all its Shews and Gauderies; and through many Afflictions and Persecutions, come to the real and solid World of Bliss and Glory.

WHAT hand Humility has in leading us through all Afflictions, and in facilitating the way of Pressure and Calamity, I need not observe; I shall note the Errour which men incur, by their Weariness

---

* 1 Pet. 4.1, 2, 3, 4.

and Haste; who because they do not immediately see the Bliss of Humility and Patience, if they do not curse, yet they boggle at all Calamity. These men ought to be informed, that the middle of the Way is not the place of Rest and Perfection. They must pass thorow all these things to the further Regions of Clarity and Glory. Men are not to stick in Calamities themselves: but if Humility lead them to suffer all Indignities with Patience, it must lead them further to the bottom of their estate and condition; to the true light, and to the clear and perfect sight of their own Vileness: In which they shall see their Original, their Misery, their Sin, their Glory; their GOD and themselves, their Bliss and their Forfeiture, their Recovery and their Saviour, their Hope and Despair, their Obligations in the height of eternal Love and Bounty, and their shame and confusion in the depth of their Apostasie and Ingratitude; their infinite demerit, and GODS infinite Mercy; the riches of free Grace, and their own Unworthiness: And in all these, *the length, and breadth, and depth, and height of the Love of GOD which passeth Knowledge, that they might be filled with all the Fulness of GOD.*

HUMILITY makes men capable of all Felicity. All deep Apprehensions and great Resentments, all extents and distances of things, all degrees of Grace and Vertue, all Circumstances that increase the guilt of Sin, all Adorations, Prostrations, Admirations, Debasements, Thanksgivings, Praises, Exaltations, are founded in Humility. All the Fulness of all Estates, all Honour and Obedience, all Devotion and Worship, all the beauty of Innocence, all the deformity of Sin, all the danger of Hell, all the cost of our Redemption, all the hatred of our Stupidity and Perverseness, all the hope of Heaven, all our Penitence and Grief, all our Fear and Expectation, all our Love and all our Joy are contained in Humility: there they are expressed, there they are exercised: There they are enlarged, and beautified in like manner: There they grow deep, and serious, and infinite: there they become vigorous and strong; there they are made substantial and eternal. All the Powers of the Soul are employed, extended and made perfect in this depth of Abysses. It is the basis and foundation of all Vertue and Gratitude whatsoever. It is in some sort the very fountain of Life and Felicity it self. For as nothing is great but in comparison of somewhat less; so nothing is sweet but what is New and Eternal. All Life consists in Motion and Change. The pleasure of Acquiring is oftentimes as great, and perhaps alwaies greater than that of Enjoying. The long possession of that which we have alwaies had, takes away the sence, and maketh us dull: Old and Common things are less esteemed, unless we rub up our Memories with some helps, to renew them and our sences together. Gifts are alwaies sweeter in the coming, than in the abiding with us. And if what I observe in the course of nature be of any force, there is no possibility of enjoyment, at least no perfection in fruition, without some relation to the first Acquisition. Old things are apt to grow stale, and their value to be neglected, by their continuance with us. I have noted it often in the joy that young Heirs have, when they first come to their Estates, and the great felicity which Lovers promise to themselves, and taste also when they meet together in the Marriage-bed. The pleasures of all which pass off by degrees, not solely by reason of our dulness and stupidity, but far more from a secret in the nature of things. For all Delight springs from the satisfaction of violent Desire: when the desire is forgotten, the delight is abated. All Pleasure consists in Activity and Motion: While the Object stands still, it seemeth dead and idle. The sence of our want must be quick upon us to make the sence of our enjoyment perfect. The rapture proceeds from the convenience between us, the marvellous fitness that is in such Objects to satisfie our Capacities and Inclinations. The misery and vacuity must needs be remembred to make that Convenience *live*, and to inspire a sence of it perpetually into us. The coming of a Crown, and the joy of a Kingdom is far more quick and powerful in the *surprize* and novelty of the Glory, than in the length of its Continuance. We perceive it by the delight which Lovers taste in recounting their Adventures. The Nature of the thing makes the *memory* of their first Amours more pleasant, than the *possession* of the last. There is an instinct that carries us to the beginning of our Lives. How do Old men even dote into lavish discourses of the beginning of their lives? The delight in telling their old Stories is as great to themselves as wearisom to others. Even Kings themselves, would they give themselves the liberty of looking back, might enjoy their Dominions with double lustre, and see and feel their former Resentments, and enrich their present Security with them. All a mans Life put together contributes a perfection to every part of it, and the Memory of things past is the most advantagious light of our present Condition. Now all these sparkles of Joy, these accidental hints of Nature, and little raies of Wisdom, meet together in Humility. For an Humble man condescendeth to look into his Wants, to reflect upon all his Vices, and all his Beginnings, with far deeper designs than is ordinarily done.

WE recount these ordinary discoveries of the inclination of Nature, because Humility is (if I may so speak) the Rendezvous of their perfection. All the stirrings of Grace and Nature, all the acts of GOD and the Soul, all his Condescensions, and beginnings to advance us, all his Gifts at their first coming, all the depths and changes of our Condition, all our Desires, all our primitive and virgin Joyes, the whole story of our Creation, and Life, and Fall, and Redemption, in all the newness of its first appearance, all our Wants and Dangers, Exigencies and Extremities, all our Satisfactions and Delights are present together in our Humility; and are so infinitely near and present thereunto, so sweet and vigorous in their mixture, so strangely powerful in their influence, that they inspire our Hearts, enter our Thoughts, and incorporate with our Souls, and are as near and sweet, as our present condition, be it never so blessed: All put together is far more sweet than our present Condition, a great part of our felicity and glory is in it, while we take it in by our Conceptions here, and apply it to our Souls, in an humble manner; but it will be much more our felicity in Heaven. It is of so much concernment, that a Great Divine* in our *English* Zion said, *The greater part of our eternal happiness will consist in a grateful Recognition* (not of our Joyes to come, but) *of Benefits already received*.

NOW look into the office and work of Humility. I will not tell you how here upon Earth it shunneth all strife and contention about Places; and all the Mischiefs consequent thereto; nor of the Unity, and Peace, and Honour it produceth. These are all but Temporal Benefits. It has ten thousand other Walks and Circuits, and periods of Revolution. I will tell you how it behaves it self in Paradice and in Heaven.

HUMILITY by leading us to the bottom of our Condition, sets our Original before our eyes, considers that eternal abyss of Idleness and Vacuity out of which we were taken, that miracle by which we were made of Nothing. How destitute we should have been in our selves had not GOD created the World, had he not been pleased to communicate himself and his Glory to us. How weak and unable we were to devise or desire any Felicity, yet how infinitely necessary the preparation of it after we were created. How great our desires and expectations were, how sore and urgent our wants and necessities: how much we needed infinite Wisdom, and almighty Power to fill Immensity with the omnipresence of their Glory, and to fill their omnipresence

* Dr. *Hammond*.

with Effects and Treasures: How gracious and good GOD was to do all this for us, without our asking: and how justly *Davids* rapture* may be taken up by the Soul, *The King shall joy in thy strength, O Lord, and in thy Salvation how greatly shall he rejoyce! Thou preventest him with the blessings of Goodness, thou settest a Crown of pure Gold on his head! His glory is great in thy Salvation, Honour and Majesty hast thou laid upon him. For thou hast made him most Blessed for ever; thou hast made him exceeding glad with thy Countenance!* We might have been made, and put, in the condition of Toads; who are now created in the Image of GOD, have dominion over all his Works, and are made capable of all Eternity. The infinite condescention of GOD is the amazement of the Soul: The depth of its low estate increaseth the height of its exaltation. All that it wanted in it self it findeth in the goodness of its Benefactour, and the joy of being so Beloved, is greater than that of having all these things of our selves for ever. For the Love of GOD alone, and his goodness in Giving, is our last, and best, and proper Felicity. Hereupon follows the extinction of all Envy, Regret, and Discontentment; the sacrificing of our selves, the annihilating of our selves, the lowliness of our selves; And the Exaltation of GOD, and the Adoration of GOD, and the Joy of adoring the Greatest of all other, The Amity and Friendship between GOD and his Creature, the Unity of both, and their happiness for ever. Without this Humility of looking into the *bottom* of our first Condition, all this is impossible: And for this cause is Humility an eternal Vertue, in all estates for ever to be enjoyed; (I might have said) exercised.

THUS in the estate of Sin and Misery, all the odiousness of our Guilt, all our despair and deformity, all our shame and misery, all the necessity of Hating GOD and being hated of him, comes before the eyes of an humble Soul, with all the mercies and condescentions of eternal Love in the work of Redemption.

AND in the state of Glory it self all the particular Sins, Neglects, Rebellions, Apostasies, and Villanies we committed against GOD after all his mercy and goodness in the Death of his Son; how infinitely base we were in despising all his Bounties and Glories; how infinitely those Offences made us unworthy of Heaven, and the eternal Glory we now enjoy; how marvellous and incomparable his Love was, in pursuing us with so much Long-suffering and Patience; how amiable he is, and how vile and unworthy we are in all this, it is the office

* Psal. 21.

of Humility to feel and ponder. Thus you see its work, and you may easily conjecture at its eternal Reward. All things are in it, in the utmost height and depth of Resignation and Contentment, enjoyed.

I need not observe that sweetness of Conversation, that Civility, and Courtesie, that springs from Humility. The Meek and Lowly are the same men: the Kind, and the Charitable, and the Affable and the good are all of them Humble, and so are all they that prefer others above themselves, and render themselves amiable by honouring their Inferiours, and giving place to their Equals. At least they imitate Humility as Complemental Courtiers do, for their advantage. And it is no small token of its excellency, that the greatest enemies of Humility and Vertue, are forced sometimes to flie to it for succour: as those that well know they can never thrive, nor prosper in the World without Esteem, nor gain Esteem without covering their Vices under the mask of Vertue. All the advantages and effects of this will be enjoyed eternally.

That Contentment is a Vertue. Its Causes and
its Ends: Its Impediments, Effects, and Advantages.
The way to attain and secure Contentment.

THOUGH we have not named it, in our first distribution of Vertue into its several kinds, yet the commendation which Contentment hath in Scripture, imports it to be a Vertue: so does the difficulty of attaining it, and the great and mighty force it is of in our Lives and Conversations. *Having Food and Rayment,* saith the Apostle, *let us therewith be content: For Godliness with Contentment is great Gain.* Where he fitly noteth, that Godliness is the original of true Contentment, and that the Gain of so great a Vertue is inestimable. The truth is, it is impossible to be happy, or grateful without it. A discontented Mind is exceeding prone to be peevish and fretful, and throws a man into all the indecencies of Avarice, Ambition, Envy, Treason, Murther, Contention, Turbulency, Murmuring, Repining, Melancholy and Sowrness, Anger, Baseness and Folly, into all the Malevolence and Misery which can disorder the Soul, or disturb the World. Suspicion, Unbelief, Enmity against GOD, Fear and Cowardice, Barrenness in good and praise-worthy Employments, Weariness and Complaint, hatred of Retirement, Spiritual Idleness and Ignorance are its Companions, followed by Debaucheries, and all the sorts of vile and wicked Diversions. For Man is an unwelcome Creature to himself till he can delight in his Condition, and while he hates to be alone, exposeth himself to all kind of Mischiefs and Temptations, because he is an active Creature, and must be doing something, either Good, or Evil.

TRUE Contentment is the full satisfaction of a Knowing Mind. It is not a vain and empty Contentment, which is falsely so called, springing from some one particular little satisfaction, that however Momentany it be, does for the present delight our Humour: but a long habit of solid Repose, after much study and serious Consideration. It is not the slavish and forced Contentment, which the Philosophers among the *Heathen* did force upon themselves; but a free and easie

Mind attended with pleasure, and naturally rising from ones present Condition. It is not a morose and sullen Contempt of all that is Good. That Negative Contentment, which past of Old for so great a Vertue, is not at all conducive to Felicity, but is a real Vice: for to be Content without cause, is to sit down in our Imperfection: and to seek all ones Blis in ones self alone, is to scorn all other Objects, even GOD himself and all the Creation. It is a high piece of Pride and stiffness in a man, that renders him good for nothing, but makes him Arrogant and Presumptuous in the midst of his blindness, his own slave and his own Idol, a Tyrant over himself, and yet his only Deity. It makes a man to live without GOD in the World, and cuts him off from the Universe. It makes him incapable either of Obligation or Gratitude, his own Prison and his own Tormentour. It shuts up the Soul in a Grave, and makes it to lead a living Death, and robs it of all its Objects. It mingles Nature and Vice in a confusion, and makes a man fight against Appetite and Reason. Certainly that Philosopher has a hard task, that must fight against Reason, and trample under foot the essence of his Soul, to establish his Felicity!

Contentment is a sleepy thing!
If it in Death alone must die;
A quiet Mind is worse than Poverty!
Unless it from Enjoyment spring!
That's Blessedness alone that makes a King!
Wherein the Joyes and Treasures are so great,
They all the powers of the Soul employ,
And fill it with a Work compleat,
While it doth all enjoy.
True Joyes alone Contentment do inspire,
Enrich Content, and make our Courage higher.
Content alone's a dead and silent Stone:
The real life of Bliss
Is Glory reigning in a Throne,
Where all Enjoyment is.
The Soul of Man is so inclin'd to see,
Without his Treasures no mans Soul can be,
Nor rest content Uncrown'd!
Desire and Love
Must in the height of all their Rapture move,
Where there is true Felicity.
Employment is the very life and ground
Of Life it self: whose pleasant Motion is

The form of Bliss:
All Blessedness a life with Glory Crown'd.
Life! Life is all: in its most full extent
Stretcht out to all things, and with all Content!

The only reason why a Wise and Holy man is satisfied with Food and Rayment, is because he sees himself made possessour of all Felicity, the image of the Deity, the great Object of his eternal Love, and in another way far more Divine and perfect, the Heir of the World, and of all Eternity. He knows very well, that if his honour be so great, as to live in Communion with GOD in the fruition of all his Joyes, he may very well spare the foul and feeble Delights of men: And though the Law be not so severe, as to command him to be Content without Food and Rayment: yet if for GOD's sake he should by the wickedness of Men be bereaved of both, he may well be Patient, nay and die with glory. And this indeed is that which maketh Contentment so great a Vertue. It hath a powerful influence upon us in all Estates; to take off our Perplexity, Sollicitude and Care, and to adorn our lives with Liberty and Chearfulness, by which we become acceptable and admirable to the Sons of Men. It makes us prone to be Kind and Liberal, whereby we become Obliging and full of good Works. For it delivers us from all servile Fear, and gives us Courage and Confidence in GOD. For well may we dare to trust him in such little Matters, who has manifested his Friendship and Bounty in such infinite good things, and made it impossible for us to be Miserable, if we are pleasing to him. An intelligent and full Contentment elevates the Soul above all the World, and makes it Angelical: it instills a Divine and Heavenly Nature, enflames the Soul with the love of GOD, and moves it to delight in Devotion and Prayer. The sweetness of his Thoughts, and the beauty of his Object draws a Lover often into Solitudes. And a Royal Man in a strange Country (especially when he has heard tidings of his Fathers Death, and the devolving of his Crown and Throne on himself) desires to be alone, that he may digest these Affairs in his Thoughts a little: He delights in being retired, because he can find nothing worthy of himself in Company. Magnanimous Souls are above Garlands and Shepherds: And there is no greatness of Soul like that which perfect Contentment inspires.

BUT that which above all other things makes me to note the Vertue of Contentment, is its great influence, efficacy, and power in confirming our Faith. For when I see the *Beauty* of Religion I know it to be *true.* For such is its excellency, that if you remove it out of the World, all the things in Heaven and Earth will be to no purpose. The business of Religion is the Love of GOD, the Love of Angels and Men, and the due esteem we owe to inferiour Creatures. Remove this Love, this Charity, this Due Esteem, this delight that we should take in all amiable Objects; Life and Pleasure are extinguished. I see Nature it self teaching me Religion: And by the admirable Contexture of the Powers of my Soul, and their fitness for all Objects and Ends, by the incomparable Excellency of the Laws prescribed, and the worthiness and Beauty of all the Objects for which my powers are prepared, see plainly, that I am infinitely Beloved: and that all the cross and disorderly things, that are now upon Earth, are meer Corruptions and depravations of Nature, which free Agents have let in upon themselves. All which since they are reducible to the Government of Reason, and may by Wisdom be improved to my higher happiness, I am sure I am redeemed, and that there is some eternal Power that governs the World with so much Goodness for my felicity, since I my self was not able to do it. That all Ages are beautified by his Wisdom for my enjoyment I hope in like manner: nay I see it plainly. And of all these Joyes the Cross of Christ is the Root and Centre.

I confess it is difficult to gain this high and divine Contentment, because its measure and value is infinite: Nay there are other causes both Temporal and Eternal that may seem to be impediments. One was a business which David did experience, *The prosperity of the Wicked.* They live in so much Splendour, Pomp, and Grandeur, have so much Respect and Reverence paid unto them, and reign as it were in the high Esteem of all that are round about them in such a manner, that a Poor good man is hardly lookt upon among them. His condition seemeth Servile, and he is little regarded. *David* carried the Temptation far higher, yet triumphed over it, *Psal.* 73.1, &c. *Truly GOD is good to* Israel, *even to such as are of a clean heart. But as for me my feet were almost gone, my steps had well nigh slipt. For I was envious at the foolish, when I saw the prosperity of the Wicked. For all the day long have I been plagued, and chastened every morning.* Whether it be through Nature, or its Corruption, I cannot tell (at least I will not stand to dispute it) but it is somewhat grievous, to see men of the same mould with our selves so highly magnified, and our selves slighted, and unable to appear with Equality among them: because the true Greatness of our Souls is hidden, oppressed, and buried as it were in the Meanness of our Condition. But yet we have excellent

Company, *David* and the Prophets, *Christ* and his Apostles, and all
the Martyrs, that are now so glorious. And if you please you may
consider, what these Great men do when the *shew* is over: We when
we come *abroad* are weak and despised, and they when they are *alone*.
A Vertuous man is Great within, and glorious in his Retirements, is
honoured also among men in Truth and *Reality;* the rest make an
outward shew, and are honoured in *Ceremony.* We are accepted in
the eyes of GOD and his holy Angels, and they are condemned: Their
Life is a Dream, and ours is Eternal: We expatiate over all the World
with infinite Joy and Pleasure in our Solitudes, and they are nothing
when they return to themselves. That wherein the greatest difficulty
of all doth consist, is the boundless desire and ambition of the Soul,
whereby we are tempted to envy any thing that is above us, and for
ever to be displeased unless our glory and blessedness be Eternal; I
do not mean Immortal only, but of everlasting Extent, and infinite
Beauty. We soar to the Best and highest of all that is possible: And
unless in all Ages and Kingdoms our Satisfaction be compleat, and
our Pleasure exquisite; we are prone to be tormented with the perfection of our Desires. But GOD having given himself, and all his Kingdom and Glory to us, there is no room for Complaint. All his Power
being glorified by his Wisdom and Goodness for our advancement,
we need nothing but a clear sight of the face of Truth, and a lively
sence of our Condition, to ravish and transport us into Extasies, and
Praises.

THE happiness of a Contented Spirit consists not alone in the fruitions of its Bliss, but in the fruits and effects it produceth in our Lives.
It gives us many advantages over Sin, Temptation, Fear, Affliction,
Poverty, Sickness, Death, and all other Casualties to which we are
obnoxious, by reason of our frail and fickle condition. But all these
I shall pass over, and only mention two, which are worth our care
and desire; *Security* and *Power.*

AS there is a vain and empty Contentment, so there is a rash and
foolish Security. For a man to wink at all Hazards to which he is
exposed, and without any consideration of what may befal him, to
give himself up to his ease and pleasure, is as great a madness, as
it is for a *General* environed with Enemies to sleep without his *Guards,*
or be totally negligent of his *Camp,* and his *Army.* But when he has
Conquered all his Enemies, then to be filled with *Melancholy* fears,
and *Pannick* terrours, is as great a weakness, as a man of Worth can
be capable of. Even in the midst of them, when he has surveyed all

their strengths, and made full provision for their incursions; he may take his rest with liberty: provided he be moderate and wary in his proceedings. This last is our Condition. We must not live as if there were no Sickness and Death in the World. We must remember there are Calamities of every kind, and fortifie our selves with Principles and Resolutions against them all, *put on the whole Armour of GOD,* which is called sometimes *the Armour of Light,* and stand prepared for all Assaults whatsoever. When we have so done, as it is a terrible thing to be surprized, so it is a glorious thing with open eyes to see and know all the Evil that is in Death, Imprisonment, Persecution, Shame and Poverty, Famine, Banishment, Pain and Torment; and yet to be secure in the midst of our fruitions. There is a worthless, and there is a divine Security: It is a poor business for a man to be secure, that has nothing to lose. A Beggar sings upon the Road without any fear of Thieves. But to be full of Gold and Jewels, yet safe from danger; to be secure in a Palace of Delights; in the midst of a Kingdom, and in the possession of all its glory to rest with safety, this is a valuable and sweet Security, a safety enriched with solid Enjoyments, much more is it here upon Earth to have the bliss and security of Angels. Among Wolves, and Tygers, and Bears and Dragons; among Thieves and Murtherers, Bloody Men and Devils; among Dead-mens Bones, and Graves and Sepulchres, when showers of Arrows fall round about us, and Hell is beneath us; this is something more than to be secure where no danger is near, no Calamity possible. It is a kind of triumph in Security, and hath a peculiar glory in it which the very security of Heaven is incapable of. And yet poor frail Man obnoxious and liable to all these destructions is safe among them all, when he is once gotten into the heart of GOD's Kingdom, and surrounded with Felicity. Its very Beauties are its Strengths. He knows himself beloved of the eternal GOD, and that the King of Terrors is but a disguised Bug-Bear, a dark and doleful passage to the Ignorant, but to him a bright and transparent way to the King of Glory. This Blessedness is of a stable, incorruptible nature, which nothing can destroy. It digesteth all kind of Evils, and turneth them into nourishment. There is a Wisdom above us, and a Wisdom within us, that maketh *all things to work together for good to them that love GOD,* and nothing is able to hurt us but our selves.

Now for Power which Felicity giveth: There is an intrinsick power in the enjoyment it self, for which Felicity is to be admired: in comparison of which all other Powers are but poor and feeble. To speak with the tongue of Men and Angels, to move Mountains, or turn them into Gold, to raise the Dead, to command the Sun, are common things: The power of creating Worlds is but vain, without the power of enjoying them. All Honour, Pleasure and Glory are shut up in Felicity. Had we a power of Creating and enjoying all Worlds, it were infinitely short of the power of enjoying GOD, because he is infinitely greater and higher than all. The Creating Power is superfluous to us, because all is most exquisite and perfect already. The fools Wishing Cap, and the Philosophers Stone are but trifles: All things (that are not gold) are better than gold. Felicity giveth us the power of enjoying all, even GOD himself, all Angels and Men, and all Worlds, nay all their Riches, Splendors and Pomps in their places, which is the most amiable and desirable, the most sweet and profitable Power of all other.

BUT when we are Contented, there is another Power worth the having, which Felicity giveth us. It enables us to despise the Menaces and Angers of Men, it setteth us above their reach, and inspires us with a comely boldness to dare to do any thing that is good, as well as with ability to dare to suffer any thing that is evil. He that is secure, and he that hath enough, is independant, and *bold as a Lion:* And besides all this he has a certain lustre in his Actions, that gives him authority and power over others, to intercede and prevail in his requests, to live in honour and good esteem, and to make many subservient to his best occasions. He is great in Heaven, and whatever he asks of his eternal Father in his Sons Name, with Wisdom and Piety, shall not be denied him. He can touch the hearts of millions by his Fathers Mediation: *For the hearts of Kings are in the hands of the Lord, to turn them as the Rivers of water.* He made his people to be pitied of all them that carried them away Captive, and gave them favour in the sight of the *Egyptians.* And this secret alone is of more value then we can well describe.

To receive power from Heaven to be Vertuous, to delight in Vertue, to be irresistible and invincible in the practice of it, is a very divine and glorious Priviledge. Felicity it self is the fountain of this Power, and the knowledge of its greatness that which enflames us with the love of it. Felicity is excellent not only as it is the end of Vertue, but the encouragement of it. He that is Content has a great advantage above all other men, because he moves with greater ease, and passeth through all difficulties with greater pleasure. A general of an Army, that works with the Common Souldiers in the Trenches, does the same work, but with more honour and less labour. He is not servile in it as the rest are, but his pleasure is to do it for all their encouragement. He does it in the quality of a Prince, and with less molestation; he has higher Incentives, and more sublime Rewards. Yet he does it too with greater merit and acceptance. A man that sees and knows the glory of his high and heavenly Estate, does all things triumphantly. The sweetness of his Bliss alters the very nature of his Fights and Battles. He does all things in the light, without groaning and reluctancy: He marches on with dancing and melody, and chearful looks, and smiles, and thanksgivings: whereas they that know not the glory of Felicity groap in the dark; they that are discontented move heavily, and are in all their proceedings lame and maimed.

THE way to attain the felicity of Contentment, is to attain Felicity that we may be contented. True Felicity is the source of Contentment, and of all Vertue. It is never to be gotten but by digging after Knowledge as for hidden Treasures. Praying for it is a good way, but Prayer without Industry is a meer mockery. Industry on the other side without Prayer is loose Presumption. For a man to pray to GOD to make his Field fruitful without ploughing and sowing, is madness, and to expect all from his own labour, without GOD's Blessing, impiety. But GOD never yet said to any of the seed of *Jacob, Seek ye my face in vain.*

WHEN Contentment is gotten, it must be secured by the same means by which it was obtained. Care in fencing is as necessary as Care in ploughing, and there is Labour too but sweet and delightful even in reaping in the Harvest. But all the work is reduced into narrow room: Thou hast no charge over any other than thine own *Vineyard.* When thou hast gotten the knowledge of Felicity and thy self, the grand means of Contentment is continually to enjoy it. With all thy getting get Wisdom, and with all thy keeping keep thy Heart; *For out of it are the Issues of Life and Death.* Nothing can waste thy Conscience but Sin, and nothing trouble thy Repose, but what disturbs thy Conscience. Let Vertue and Felicity be thy only good, and believe firmly that nothing can hurt thee but SIN alone. One evil action done by thy self, is more mischievous to thee, then all the Calamities and Sufferings in the World.

Of Magnanimity, or Greatness of Soul. Its Nature. Its Foundation in the vast Capacity of the Understanding. Its Desire. Its Objects are infinite and eternal. Its Enquiries are most profound and earnest. It disdaineth all feeble Honours, Pleasures and Treasures. A Magnanimous Man is the only Great and undaunted Creature.

MAGNANIMITY and Contentment are very near allyed, like Brothers and Sisters they spring from the same Parents, but are of several Features. Fortitude and Patience are Kindred too to this incomparable Vertue. Moralists distinguish Magnanimity and Modesty, by making the one the desire of greater, the other of less and inferiour Honours. But in my apprehension there is more in Magnanimity. It includes all that belongs to *a Great Soul:* A high and mighty Courage, an invincible Patience, an immoveable Grandeur which is above the reach of Injuries, a contempt of all little and feeble Enjoyments, and a certain kind of Majesty that is conversant only with Great things; a high and lofty frame of Spirit, allayed with the sweetness of Courtesie and Respect; a deep and stable Resolution founded on Humility without any baseness; an infinite Hope; and a vast Desire; a Divine, profound, uncontrolable sence of ones own Capacity, a generous Confidence, and a great inclination to Heroical deeds; all these conspire to compleat it, with a severe and mighty expectation of Bliss incomprehensible. It soars up to Heaven, and looks down upon all the dominion of Fortune with pity and disdain. Its aims and designs are transcendent to all the Concerns of this little World. Its Objects and its Ends are worthy of a Soul that is like GOD in Nature; and nothing less than the Kingdom of GOD, his Life and Image; nothing beneath the Friendship and Communion with him, can be its satisfaction. The Terrours, Allurements and Censures of men are the dust of its feet: their Avarice and Ambition are but feebleness before it. Their Riches and Contentions, and Interests and Honours, but insignificant and empty trifles. All the World is but a little Bubble; Infinity and Eternity the only great and soveraign things wherewith it converseth. A Magnanimous Soul is alwaies awake. The whole globe of the Earth is but a Nutshell in comparison of its enjoyments. The Sun is its Lamp, the Sea its Fishpond, the Stars its Jewels, Men, Angels its Attendance, and GOD alone its soveraign Delight and supream Complacency. The Earth is its Garden, all Palaces its Summer houses, Cities are its Cottages, Empires its more spacious Courts, all Ages and Kingdoms its Demeans, Monarchs its Ministers and publick Agents, the whole Catholick Church its Family, the eternal Son of GOD its Pattern and Example. Nothing is great if compared to a *Magnanimous Soul,* but the Soveraign Lord of all Worlds.

Mistake not these things for arbitrary flourishes of Luxuriant fancy: I speak as I am inspired by Felicity. GOD is the Cause, but the knowledge of a Mans self the Foundation of Magnanimity. *Trismegistus* counteth thus, *First GOD, secondly the World, thirdly Man: the World for Man, and Man for GOD. Of the Soul that which is sensible is Mortal, but that which is reasonable Immortal. The Father of all things being full of Life and Light, brought forth Man like unto himself, whom he loved as his proper Off-spring: for he was all Beauteous having the Image of his Father.* This in his *Poemander.* Again he saith, *Man is a divine and living thing, not to be compared to any Beast that lives upon the Earth, but to them that are above (in the highest Heavens) that are called Gods. Nay rather if we shall be bold to speak the truth, he that is a MAN INDEED is above them!* He is infinitely greater than the gods of the Heathen: And a God like unto himself (as the Wise Man observes) he cannot make. *At least,* saith *Trismegistus, they are equal in Power: For none of the things in Heaven will come down upon Earth, and leave the limits of Heaven: but a Man ascends up into Heaven, and measures it. He knoweth what things are on high, and what below. And that which is the greatest of all, he leaveth not the Earth, and yet is above: so mighty and vast is the greatness of his Nature! Wherefore we must be bold to say, that an Earthly Man is a Mortal God, and the Heavenly GOD is an Immortal MAN.*

THIS is the Philosophy of the ancient Heathen: wherein though there be some Errors, yet was he guided to it by a mighty sence of the interiour Excellency of the Soul of Man, and the boldness he assumes is not so profane, but that it is countenanced here and there in the Holy Scripture. GOD himself said unto *Moses, Lo, I have made thee a God to* Pharoah. Again he telleth him concerning *Aaron, He shall be to thee instead of a Mouth, and thou shalt be to him instead of God.* And again concerning all the Great men of the World in general, *I have said ye are Gods, but ye shall die like Men.* But let us see the Reason of the Heathen a little, on which he foundeth his great Opinions. In one place he maketh his Son *Tatius* to say, *I conceive and understand, not by the sight of mine Eyes, but by the intellectual Operation,* &c. *I am in Heaven, in the Earth, in the Water, in the Air: I am in the living Creatures, in Plants, in the Womb: every where.* Whereupon he asketh him, *Dost thou not know (O my Son) that thou art born a God, and the Son of The One as I am?* And the ground of this Question he unfoldeth in another place thus; *Consider him that contains all things, and understand, that nothing is more Capacious than that which is* Incorporeal, *nothing more swift, nothing more powerful: but (of all other things) it is most Capacious, most swift, and most strong. And judge of this by thy self. Command thy Soul to go into* India, *and sooner than thou canst bid it, it will be there. Bid it pass over the Ocean, and suddenly it will be there: not as passing from place to place, but suddenly it will be there. Command it to flie into Heaven, and it will need no wings, neither shall any thing hinder it; not the fire of the Sun, nor the Æther, nor the turning of the Sphears, nor the bodies of any of the Stars, but cutting through all it will flie up to the last and furthest Body. And if thou wilt even break through the Whole, and see those things that are without the World (if there be any thing without)* [i.e. if the World be confined,] *thou maist. Behold how great Power, how great swiftness thou hast! Canst thou do all these things, and cannot GOD? After this manner therefore contemplate GOD to have all the whole World in himself, as it were all Thoughts or Intellections. If therefore thou wilt not equal thy self to GOD, thou canst not understand GOD. For the like is intelligible by the like. Increase thy self to an immeasurable Greatness, leaping beyond every Body, and transcending all Time, become* ETERNITY; *And thou shalt understand GOD. If thou believe in thy self that nothing is impossible, but accountest thy self Immortal, and that thou canst understand all things, every Art, every*

*Science, and the manner and custom of every living thing, become
higher than all Height, and lower than all Depth, comprehend in thy
self the qualities of all the Creatures, of the Fire, the Water, the Dry,
and the Moist, and conceive likewise that thou canst at once be every
where, in the Sea, in the Earth; at once understand thy self not yet
begotten, in the Womb, Young, Old, Dead, the things after Death,
and all these together; as also all Times, Places, Deeds, Qualities,
Quantities, thou maist, or else thou canst not yet understand GOD.
But if thou shut up thy Soul in thy Body, and abuse it; and say,
I understand nothing, I am afraid of the Sea, I cannot climb up into
Heaven, I know not who I am, I cannot tell what I shall be; what
hast thou to do with GOD? For thou canst understand none of those
fair and good things, but must be a lover of the Body and Evil. For
it is the greatest evil not to know GOD. But to be able to Know,
and to Will, and to Hope, is the strait Way, and the divine Way
proper to the Good. It will every where meet thee, and every where
be seen of thee plain and easie, when thou dost not expect, or look
for it. It will meet thee Waking, Sleeping, Sailing, Travelling, by Night,
by Day, when thou speakest, and when thou keepest silence. For it
is nothing, which is not the Image of GOD.* His Close is most divine;
*And yet thou sayest, GOD is Invisible; but be advised: for who is
more manifest than he? For therefore he made all things, that thou
by all things mightst see him. This is the Good of GOD, his Vertue
is this, to appear, and be seen in all Things.* This is the bottom of
all other Greatnesses whatsoever: GOD is infinitely communicative,
infinitely prone to reveal himself, infinitely Wise, and able to do it.
He hath made the Soul on purpose that it might see him: And if
the Eye that was made for the World, being so little a ball of Earth
and Water, can take in all, and see all that is visible, if the sight
of the Eye be present with all it beholdeth; much more is the Soul
both able to see, and to be present with all, that is Divine and Eternal.

I know very well that a Man divided from GOD is a weak inconsiderable Creature, as the Eye is, if divided from the Body, and without
the Soul: but united to GOD a Man is a transcendent and Celestial
thing. GOD is his Life, his Greatness, his Power, his Blessedness and
Perfection. And as the Apostle saith, *He that is joyned to the Lord
is one SPIRIT.* His Omnipresence and Eternity fill the Soul, and make
it able to contain all Heights and Depths, and Lengths and Breadths
whatsoever. And it is the desire of the Soul *to be filled with all the
fulness of GOD.*

Magnanimous desires are the natural results of a Magnanimous Capacity. The desire of being *like Gods, knowing Good and Evil,* was the destruction of the World. Not as if it were unlawful to desire to be *Like GOD:* but to aspire to the Perfection in a forbidden way, was unlawful. By Disobedience, and by following our own Inventions, by seeking to the Creature, to the stock of a Tree, to make us *Like GOD;* that is erroneous, and poor, and despicable: but to know our selves, and in *the strait and divine Way* to come immediately to GOD, to contemplate him in his Eternity and Glory, is a right and safe Way: for the Soul will by that means be the Sphere of his Omnipresence, and the Temple of the God-head: It will become ETERNITY, as *Trismegistus* speaketh, or ONE SPIRIT with God, as the Apostle. And then it must needs be present with all things *in Heaven, and in the Earth, and in the Sea,* as GOD is: for all things will be in it, as it were *by Thoughts and Intellections.*

A Magnanimous Soul then, if we respect its Capacity, is an immovable sphere of Power and Knowledge, far greater than all Worlds, by its Vertue and Power passing through all things, through the Centre of the Earth, and through all Existencies. And shall such a Creature as this be contented with Vanities and Trifles, Straws and Feathers, painted Butterflies, Hobby-horses and Rattles. These are the Treasures of little Children! but you will say a Man delighteth in Purses of Gold, and Cabinets of Jewels, in Houses and Palaces, in Crowns and Scepters: Add Kingly Delights, and say he delighteth in Armies and Victories, and Triumphs and Coronations. These are great in respect of *Play-things.* But all these are feeble and pusillanimous to a great Soul. As *Scipio* was going up to Heaven,* the Earth it self seemed but a Nutshel, and he was ashamed of all his Victories and Triumphs, amazed at his madness in Quarrelling, and fighting about Territories and Kingdoms contracted to a Star, and lost into nothing. The whole Earth is but one invisible Point, when a man soareth to the height of all Immensity, and beholdeth and compasseth its everlasting Circumference, which is infinite every way beyond the Heavens. It is the true and proper Immensity of the Soul: Which can no more be contented with the narrow confinement of this World, no more rest in the Childishness of all the noise and Interests of Men, be no more satisfied with its Earthly Glories, than the SUN can be shut up in a *Dark-Lanthorn.* It is true indeed it would desire to see, as the Angels do, the least and lowest of all the Creatures full of the Glory and

* *Tully* in *Somn. Scipion.*

Blessedness of GOD, all Wisdom and Goodness in every thing, and is apt to complain for want of some eternal and Celestial Light wherein to behold them: but if all the expansions of Time and Eternity should be void, and all the extents and out-goings of Infinity empty round about them; though things upon Earth, nay and things in the Heavens, should be never so Rich, and divine, and beautiful, yet such is the Magnanimity of a Great Soul, that it would hugely be displeased: its loss and its distaste would be alike Infinite. Infinite Honours, infinite Treasures, infinite Enjoyments, things endless in number, value, and excellency are the Objects of its Care and Desire; the greatness of its Spirit leads it to consider and enquire, whether all the spaces above the Heavens, and all the parts of GOD's everlasting Kingdom be full of Joyes, whether there be any end or bound of his Kingdom; whether there be any defect or miscarriage, any blemish or disorder in it, any vile and common thing, any remissness or neglect, any cause of complaint or deformity? As also whether all the Ages of the World are Divine and Sacred; whether after they are gone, they abide in their places; whether there be any thing in them to entertain the Powers of the Soul with delight, and feed them with satisfaction? What end, what use, what excellency there is in Men? Whether all the waies of GOD are full of beauty and perfection; all Wisdom, Justice, Holiness, Goodness, Love and Power? What Regions eternal Blessedness is seated in? What Glory, what Reason, what Agreeableness and Harmony is in all his Counsels? Whether those durations of Eternity before the World is made, are full or empty, full of bright and amiable Objects, or dark and obscure? Whether the government of the World be perfect; whether the Soul be Divine in it self; whether it be conducive to its own felicity, or to the happiness of all those in whom it is concerned? Whether the World shall end? If it shall, after what manner; whether by Design or Accident? Whether all Ages and Nations shall rise from the Dead? Whether there shall be a general Doom, or a day of Judgment? Whether I am concerned in all the transactions and passages at that day? Whether all Mankind shall be united into one, to make up one compleat and perfect Body, whereof they all are the fellow-Members? What shall be after the End of the World? Whether we shall live for ever? Whether we shall see GOD, and know one another? Whether we shall reign in eternal Glory? Whether in the Confusions of Hell there be any Beauty, and whether in the Torments of the damned we shall find any joy or satisfaction? Whether all the Riches, Customs and Pleasures of this World shall be seen?

Whether in the World to come any fruit shall appear and arise from them, for which they shall be esteemed to have been not in vain, but profitable in relation to all Eternity? What kind of Life we shall lead, and what kind of Communion and fellowship Angels and Men shall have with each other? Whether the Works of GOD were unworthy of his Choice, or the best of all that were possible? What his Laws are as to their nature and excellency? Whether his Love be really sincere and infinite? Whether there be any such thing as infinite Wisdom, Goodness and Bounty, Blessedness and Glory? Such things as these are the Concerns and Inquiries of a Magnanimous Soul. And if its expectations and desires are absolutely satisfied, it will easily appear, and break forth upon all Occasions, into the most high and Magnanimous Actions.

Trismegistus (or whoever else was the Author of that Book) saw the deep Capacity of his own Soul, but if a Conjecture may be made by the residue of the discourse, did not understand the end (at least not clearly) for which it was implanted. Some knowledge he had, that all the things in Eternity were the Objects of that Power, by reason of which he calls them *Fair and Good:* but that they were to be the *Treasures and Enjoyments* of the Soul I do not find him affirming. He that knows this must needs be of our Saviours mind, who when all the Kingdoms of the World, and the Glory of them were shewed him by Satan in a moment of time, despised them all. For the divine and Celestial Kingdom is infinitely greater, and in a far more perfect manner to be enjoyed.

HE that knoweth the Honour which cometh from above, will despise the Honour which men can pay, and in comparison of that Honour which cometh from GOD only, esteem all the Honour of this World but false and feeble. Not as if Men were in the truth of Nature vile and despicable Creatures; a Magnanimous man knows all others to be by Nature like himself, and is apt to reverence all of his kind as sublime and Celestial Creatures. But he is a Man of a clear and discerning Spirit, and the Corruption of Nature makes him to slight all that is defiled. He sees that Men are generally Evil, deformed and blind, erroneous, perverse and foolish, poor and miserable: And that all the Honour which they generally give is irrational and feigned. A little colour in the face, a gay Coat, a fine Horse, a Palace and a Coach, an Exchequer full of Gold, or some such light and superficial Causes, are all the grounds of the respect that they pay us.

And if the Glory and Esteem I have,
Be nothing else than what my Silver gave;
If for no other ground
I am with Love or Praises crown'd,
'Tis such a shame, such vile, such base Repute,
'Tis better starve, than eat such empty Fruit.

IF a King be dejected from his Throne, it is but a poor comfort that he is admired by Persons condemned to die, and praised by Beggars. The dignity and power of the Persons that admire us, is of great consideration, in the love and delight which they take in us. They all must vanish and perish as a Dream: no Honour is truly great, but that which is continual and endless too. A great and mighty Soul can care for no Honour but that which comes from wise and amiable Persons, that are themselves great and honourable, most rich and powerful, holy, just, blessed and glorious. Honour from GOD and his holy Angels, from the eternal Son of GOD and all his Saints, is marvellous and substantial. That Honour which is paid upon great and solid causes; because a Man is well-pleasing to GOD, and exalted to his Throne; because he is the very true Image of GOD, and has dominion over all the Creatures; because he is infinitely beloved of GOD, and all Angels and Men are commanded to love him; because he is redeemed by the Blood of Christ, and made a Temple of the Holy Ghost; because he is a Priest and King to his eternal Creatour, because he is full of Goodness and Wisdom, adorned with all kind of Vertue, and made an Heir of eternal Glory; because he is Faithful and True, and Just and Holy; because he hath conquered Death, and Hell, and Sin, and the Grave, and triumpheth over them, this is being paid by such Persons, Honour indeed: and to desire this Honour is the Property and the Vertue of a Magnanimous Soul.

An Eagle cannot stoop at Flies. An *Alexander,* or a *Cæsar* cannot debase or confine their Souls to the pleasures of a Cottage in a Wilderness. Infinite Hopes and infinite Desires, infinite Fears, and Despairs, and Sorrows, infinite Joyes, and Delights, and Glories, infinite Adorations, Praises and Thanksgivings, infinite and eternal Objects are the only fit and proper Concerns for the Affections of a Great and *Magnanimous* Soul. The very signification of the word is *Greatness of Soul,* or if you please, *of Mind:* For a distinction may be made between the *Soul,* and *Mind.* The Soul of Man is the immutable essence, or form of his Nature, unimployed. His power of Reasoning is alive, even

then when it is quiet and unactive; and this is his Soul. It is one
and the same in all men, and of it self equally inclined to all great
and transcendent things: but in the most it is misguided, baffled and
suppressed, and though it be never so great it is to no purpose. This
greatness implanted by Nature is not *Magnanimity:* It is a Natural
disposition, not an acquired habit, as all Vertue is. A Man is then
said to be of such a *Mind,* when he determines, or thinks in such
a manner. His mind is Good that intendeth well, his mind is Evil
that designeth mischief. So that the Mind is the Soul exerting its power
in such an act: and the greatest Soul in all the World is but *Pusillanimous* that mindeth little things. A great Soul is Magnanimous in
Effect, a *Mind* applyed to mighty Objects. Some men have a Magnanimity infused by the power of Education, and are led by Custome
to Great things, and in a manner by Necessity, for such is their Place
and Calling, that they are frequently led to greater Objects than other
men. Of this sort are the most eminent rank of Grandees, and Princes:
Kingdoms, and Thrones, and Privy Councils, and Queens, and Armies
are their natural Dialect. This is no Vertue, for though it be not innate
by *Nature,* yet they are *born* to it, and it is given by *Fortune.* Others
consider what they have to do, and make an election, and though
they are born in a poor and despicable estate, are not Magnanimous
by Nature, or Fortune, but by *Choice* and voluntary Election. Not
to satisfie the humour of a high Blood, choler and fire, nor to answer
the necessities of a higher Calling; but to discharge the office of Vertue
and Wisdom. And this is the Off-spring of the *Will,* the true and
genuine *Vertue.* Which as it is far more worthy than any of the rest,
is guided to far better and more glorious Objects, and more diffusively
given by the Bounty of GOD to all kind of Men in all Conditions.
In the Poor it is more marvellous than in the Great and Rich: It
has such an undaunted property in its Nature, that though the disproportion between them and their Assurance, or Hope, or Desire seem
infinite, and the end which they aim at by their Magnanimity is judged
impossible: though their attempt appear a ridiculous madness to them
to whom the Verities of Religion appear incredible, yet they are no
whit discouraged or disheartened at the matter, but stoutly march on,
being animated by the alarum of such a Trumpet, such a Drum as
Magnanimity is. His Faith is more Divine by conquering the discouragements of the World, than if he met with no censure or opposition.

IF you would have the Character of a Magnanimous Soul, he is
the Son of eternal Power, and the Friend of infinite Goodness, a Tem-

ple of divine and heavenly Wisdom, that is not imposed upon by the foul and ragged disguises of Nature, but acquainted with her great Capacities and Principles, more than commonly sensible of her interests, and depths, and desires. He is one that has gone in unto Felicity, and enjoyed her beauties, and comes out again her perfect Lover and Champion: a Man whose inward stature is miraculous; and his Complexion so divine, that he is King of as many Kingdoms as he will look on: One that scorns the smutty way of enjoying things like a Slave, because he delights in the Celestial way, and the Image of GOD. He knows that all the World lies in Wickedness; and admires not at all, that things palpable and near, and natural, are unseen, though most powerful and glorious; because men are blind and stupid. He pities poor vicious Kings that are oppressed with heavy Crowns of Vanity and Gold, and admires how they can content themselves with such narrow Territories: yet delights in their Regiment of the World, and paies them the Honour that is due unto them. The glorious Exaltation of good Kings he more abundantly extols, because so many thousand Magnanimous Creatures are committed to their Trust, and they that govern them understand their Value. But he sees well enough that the Kings glory and true repose consists in the Catholick and eternal Kingdom. As for himself he *is come unto Mount Sion, and to the City of the living GOD, the Heavenly Jerusalem, and to an innumerable Company of Angels, to the General Assembly and Church of the First-born, which are written in Heaven, and to GOD the Judge of all, and to the Spirits of Just men made perfect, and to JESUS the Mediatour of the New Covenant:* And therefore receiving a Kingdom which cannot be moved, he desires to serve GOD acceptably with reverence and godly fear: And the truth is he can fear nothing else, for GOD alone is a consuming fire. He very well understands what the Apostle saith, and dares believe him: *I cease not to give thanks for you, making mention of you in my Prayers, that the GOD of our Lord Jesus Christ, the Father of Glory, may give unto you the Spirit of Wisdom and Revelation in the knowledge of him, the eyes of your Understanding being enlightened, that ye may know what is the HOPE of his Calling, and what the RICHES of the GLORY of his INHERITANCE in the Saints. And what is the EXCEEDING GREATNESS of his POWER to us-ward who believe, according to the WORKING of his Mighty Power: which he wrought in Christ when he raised him from the dead, and set him at his own RIGHT HAND in the HEAVENLY places: far above all Principality, and*

Power, and Might, and Dominion, and every Name that is named, not only in this WORLD, but in that also which is to come: And hath put ALL THINGS under his feet, and he gave him to be HEAD over all Things to the CHURCH which is his BODY, THE FULNESS OF HIM THAT FILLETH ALL IN ALL. *Now to him that is able to do exceeding abundantly above all that we ask or think, according to the Power that WORKETH in us, Unto him be Glory in the Church by Christ Jesus, throughout all AGES, World without end.* Amen.

A great and a clear Soul knoweth that all these intimations must needs be true, for it is an amazing Miracle that they should be otherwise. *Infinite Love* and *Eternal Blessedness* are near allyed; and that these should cease, is contrary to all Nature, in GOD, in the Soul of Man, in Heaven, in Earth, in the order of the Universe, and contrary to all that VISIBLE GLORY which in the World appeareth.

Of Modesty. Its Nature. Its Original.
Its Effects and Consequences.

MODESTY is a comely Grace in the Behaviour of a Man, by which he piously dissembleth his own Perfections, and blusheth at his Praises. It springeth from a certain fear and sence of his Imperfection. 'Tis the shadow of Guilt, and a beautiful cover of Original Corruption. It is sometimes Natural, and, which is contrary to all other Vertues, more truly vertuous for being so. For then it is Simple, Genuine, and Real; but studied Modesty is affected and artificial: yet where Nature has not been so obliging as to give the endowment, 'tis not altogether to be condemned, since it is agreeable to the best of our conditions in this World, and supplies a defect in his Nature, that is born without it.

IT is akin to Shame, yet increases the honour of him that wears it; it is the shade of Vertue, yet makes it brighter: It is a tincture of Humility, visible in a vermilion and deeper die; and the more natural and easie, the more sweet and delightful.

IT charms the Envy of those that admire us, and by seeming to extinguish our worth gives it a double beauty. It reconciles a man to the Enemies of his Grace and Vertue, and by a softness irresistible wins a Compassion in all Spectators. It is a Vertue which by refusing the honour that is due unto it, acquireth more; a real Counterfeit, and the only honest and true dissimulation. It is an effeminate, yet a laudable quality; a spice of Cowardice, more prevalent than Courage; a Vertue by which we despise all meaner Honours, while we are ambitiously carried to the highest Glory. It seemeth inconsistent with Magnanimity, yet is her youngest Sister.

IT hath not many Objects, nor are its Aims apparent, nor its Ends conspicuous. It is the Mother of fine and delicate Resentments; its strength consisteth in tenderness and fear. He that is Magnanimous in one respect, may be modest in another. Praises and Commendations are the fuel of its Nature, it feedeth upon them, while it grows by rejecting them. It delights in what it feareth; and is full of discords, but more full of harmonies. It is pleased in its displeasure, and alwaies fighteth with its own Repugnancies. It is a Vertue mixt of Sence and Reason; its region is in the Body more than in the Soul, and in all its Spiritual motions it is attended with Corporeal impressions. The Blood and Spirits dance in the Veins, as if Nature were delighted with its own Confusions. By captivating the favour of Men upon Earth, it affecteth the very Angels in Heaven, with much of pleasure. It putteth us in mind of Guilt and Innocency at the same time, and by confession of the one adds lustre to the other. By making way for the acceptance of a mans Person, it giveth more esteem, success, and efficacy to his other Vertues. And by this means it hath much of excellency in a little.

HE that hath it not, must needs acquire something like it; and if he be elaborate in expressing it, must hide his Art under the vail of Nature. Though it be remote from the highest End, it may be guided to it, and when so directed, is alwaies innocent. It is very just, for while other Vertues make it a Vertue, it is a Grace unto them all. You may look upon it as a tangible flame and see it in others, but must feel it in your self before you can understand it. It is old in Children, young in middle Aged men, at last an Infant. It is greatest in the beginning of our life, it decayeth in Youth, in Old Age it vanisheth; at least changeth its dwelling, for it ceaseth to be in the Body of an Aged man, and turneth into Courtesie or Civility, in the Conversation. When it dieth, it is buried in Humility, and liveth in its Tomb, being empaled in as it were with Meekness, and waiting daily for its Resurrection. Much cannot be said of it precisely: but it is best commended, when left to your Practice. It is the only tender Infant of all the Vertues: like *Cupid* among the gods: it appeareth frequently, and is much exercised, in the School of *Venus:* but is capable of more high and more noble uses.

MODESTY in Apparel is commended in the Scriptures. It implies Moderation and Chastity together. It is sometimes opposed to Lasciviousness, sometimes to Excess, sometimes to Impudence: And is a great Vertue, if for nothing else, but the exclusion of these abominable Vices.

THE other Vertues seem to be the Members, and substantial parts of the Body of worth: Modesty like the Air, and Meen of them all. It is the guard of the Soul against Loosness and Pride, a Vertue repressing the fumes of Self-conceit, and a kind of silent restraint of all that Arrogance, that delights in pomps and superfluities.

THOUGH it be a little Vertue, its Reality is apparent: for unless it be made up with some other supplies, the want of Modesty is pernicious and destructive.

IT is exercised in small things, but is of long extent in the vertue of its influence; and because of the multiplicity of its uses and occasions, amounts to a considerable degree of *Goodness*. It hath something like Love in its nature, for it preferreth another above it self, and in that its magnetical and obliging quality much consisteth. *In honour preferring one another*. It fulfils that Law, wherein our most near and tender Interest is concerned. In preferring one another there is a lovely contest, more sweet and happy than the best Agreement. It is of all other the most friendly strife, and kind Contention.

CHAP. XXX.

*The excellent Nature of Liberality. Rules to be
observed in the practice of it. Regard to our
Servants, Relations, Friends and Neighbours
must be had in our Liberality, as well as to the
Poor and Needy. How our external acts of Charity
ought to be improved for the benefit of mens Souls.
Liberality maketh Religion real and substantial.*

LIBERALITY, in the common use and acceptation of the Word,
differs from Magnificence, as Modesty from Magnanimity. There is
much of liberty and freedom in its Nature. For Avarice is a strict
and sour Vice, and they that are guilty of it are called *Misers;* but
a Bountiful man hath a good eye, and is as free from Anxiety, as
he is free in disbursing. His Communicative humor is much his enlargement: he knows little of Confinement, Care or Bondage.

THERE are two Vertues that endanger a Mans welfare in this
World; and they have all the *Temporal Promises.* Meekness seems
to encourage our Enemies to trample us under feet, because it promiseth
Impunity: And it is directly said *The Meek shall inherit the Earth:*
nay be so far from having Enemies, that *the Meek shall inherit the
abundance of Peace.* And concerning Liberality which makes a man
a Beggar, at least threatens to make him so, by wasting his Estate,
the Scripture saith, *The Liberal Soul shall be made fat. The Liberal
Heart deviseth liberal things, and by liberal things shall he stand.*

MEN are almost in all things contrary to GOD. For since they
tumbled out of *Eden,* they have lost their wits, and their heads are
downwards: They think it wisdom to keep their Mony *against a rainy
day:* and to lay it up for fear of Poverty. But *Solomon* adviseth them
to the direct contrary, and maketh it an Argument why they should

be Liberal, *Because they know not what evil may come upon the Earth.* We cannot put our Treasures into safer hands, than into GOD Almighty's: Nor can we make any use of Gold and Silver, comparable to that of Charitable uses. By this it is that we *lay up a good foundation against the time to come;* and oblige others to receive us into Mansions here, into everlasting habitations hereafter.

MY Lord *Bridgeman,* late Lord Keeper, confessed himself in his Will to be but a Steward of his Estate, and prayed GOD to forgive him all his offences, *in Getting, Mispending, or not Spending it as he ought to do:* And that after many Charitable and Pious works, perhaps surmounting his Estate, though concealed from the notice and knowledge of the World.

I have heard of a smart obliging Calumny fastned on a Great Man of *France,* by one that had largely tasted of his Bounty: for having been in his House honourably entertained for some space of time, and observing how much the Palace was frequented by all kind of Learned Men: and how Liberal the Master of it was, especially to men of Worth and Vertue; he charges the Man with the greatest Covetousness in the World: *because he turned all his Riches into Obligations:* As if he had put all his Estate and Monies to Use: But to covet affections, and be rich in hearts is no deformity.

THE truth is, when the waies whereby Love is begotten in the Soul are well examined, and the happiness of being truly beloved, and delighted in, is known; no man is so wise as the Liberal man. He is his own end, while he thinks not of it. For nothing is more conducive to his ease and honour, than the bounty of Munificence which enriches his Soul. There are three things which beget Love, *Beauty, Benefits* and *Praises:* They are all three shut up in Goodness, which is the fountain of Liberality. The beauty of the face is a silent Oratory, a high stile of Commendation without an Epistle: yet by doing Benefits it prevaileth more, than by any of its Charms; and maketh it self great by enriching others. Love inspires it with an amiable Soul; and if others are delighted with their own Praises, he that is liberal in the acknowledgment of mens Vertues, and giveth Honour to the Worthy, is full of musick in his words, of a sweet and pleasing behaviour, agreeable in his deeds, and fraught with the Honour which he imparteth so freely. A Liberal man is cloathed like the Sun with the Raies of his own glory, and establishes himself in the hearts of his Neighbours, and reigns like a King by the sole interest of Vertue and Goodness. *Every man is a Friend to him that giveth many Gifts.*

He may be as holy, and as temperate, and as wise as an Angel, no man will be offended at him, because he beautifies his Religion with so much goodness. He enjoys himself, and his Riches, and his Friends, and may do what he will (with perfect liberty) because he delights in the felicity of all that accost him. He puts embroideries on Religion by the chearfulness of his Spirit, and carries a light wherever he goes, that makes men to reverence his Person, and esteem his Censures. He moves in a sphere of Wonders, his life is a continual stream of Miracles, because he is alwaies sacrificing himself and his Possessions, to the benefit of the World, and the comfort of others. Benefits and Blessings are his Life-guard, like his guardian Angels alwaies attendant on him. His House is the habitation of joy and felicity, and yields a spectacle of Contentment to every beholder. His Neighbours are his Security, not his Suspicion; and other mens Houses the forts and ram-parts about his own. No man will hurt him, because they extinguish their own contentment and benefit in him. They tender him as the apple of their eye, because he is a greater comfort and advantage than that unto them. The ancient custome of *Paradice,* so long since lost and forgotten in the World revives in its Family, where all men are entertained as Brothers and Sisters, at the expences of GOD and Nature. He taketh care, because Thrift is the fuel of Liberality; and is Frugal, that he may be Bountiful. All his aim and labour is, that he may *maintain Good Works;* and *make* his *light so shine before men, that they seeing his good works may glorifie his Father which is in Heaven.* There is a generous Confidence discovered in all his Actions, and a little glimpse of Heaven in his Behaviour; for he lives as if he were among a company of Angels. All mens Estates are his, and his is theirs: If he had them all he would impart them, and restore them to supply their Wants: perhaps not with so much wisdom as GOD hath done, but with as much pleasure and contentment, as his goodness can inspire, in the exercise of power so kindly and well em-ployed. But because the designs of GOD are infinitely deeper than he can well apprehend, and laid all in eternal Wisdom, he is pleased and delighted, that his Care is prevented; and that GOD hath done that for other men, to which his own inclination would readily prompt him were it left undone. If it were permitted him to wish whatsoever he listed, of all other things he would chiefly desire to be a Blessing to the whole World; and that he is not so, is his only discontentment. But for that too there are remedies in Felicity: when he knows *all,* his desire is granted. For a Life beautified with all Vertue is the greatest gift that can be presented to GOD, Angels and Men. And when all Secrets shall be revealed, all hidden things brought to light, his life shall be seen in all its perfection, and his Desires themselves be the enjoyments and pleasures of all the Creatures. There is a certain kind of sympathy that runs through the Universe, by vertue of which all men are fed in the feeding of one: even the Angels are cloathed in the Poor and Needy. All are touched and concerned in every one. Like the Brazen Pillars in the Temple of *Minerva,* if one be smitten all resound the blow throughout the Temple: or like the strings of several Lutes skrewed up to *Unisones,* the one is made to quaver by the others motions. If Christ himself be fed in the Poor, much more may Angels and Men. At the last day we find no other scrutiny about Religion, but what we have done or neglected in Liberality. *Come ye blessed of my Father, inherit the Kingdom prepared for you from the foundations of the World, for I was hungry and ye gave me meat, thirsty and ye gave me drink, naked and ye cloathed me, a Stranger and ye took me in; I was sick and ye visited me, I was in Prison and ye came unto me. Inasmuch as ye have done it to the least of these my Brethren, ye have done it unto me.* LOVE it seems will sit in Judgment on the World: and the Rule of Trial shall be the fulfilling of its Laws. *Love* shall be the glory too of all the *Assessors.* And every act of Cruelty and Oppression infinitely odious in all their eyes.

THERE was a certain King which would take account of his Servants: and when he had begun to reckon, one was brought unto him, that ought him 10000 *Talents. But forasmuch as he had not to pay, his Lord commanded him to be sold, and all that he had, and payment to be made. The Servant therefore fell down and worshipped him, saying, Lord have patience with me, and I will pay thee all. Then the Lord of that Servant was moved with Compassion, and loosed him, and forgave him the Debt. But the same Servant went out, and found one of his fellow-Servants which ought him* 100 *pence, and he laid hold on him and took him by the throat, saying, Pay me that thou owest. And his fellow-Servant fell down at his feet and besought him, Have patience with me and I will pay thee all. And he would not, but went and cast him into Prison till he should pay the Debt. So when his fellow-Servants saw what was done, they were very sorry, and came and told to their Lord all that was done.* Every neglect and contempt of our fellow-Brethren is injurious and grievous to GOD, Angels and Men: for there is one common Principle in all Nature, to hate evil Deeds, and especially those of Rigour and Severity, when we our selves stand in need of Mercy, and have received Favour. This common principle of Sympathy and Compassion intitles us to all the good, that is done to any Man in the World. The love of Equity and Reason, and the natural inclination that carries us to delight in excellent Deeds, gives us an interest in all that are performed. The beauty of the one is as sweet and blessed as the deformity of the other is odious and distastful. And if we our selves are infinitely obliged, and live by the bounty and goodness of another, after we have forfeited the Kings favour, have received it again with pardon and forgiveness, nay and with more and greater benefits; if we shall not be liberal to one another, it is a strange inequality. But the discharge of our duty will make us amiable and delightful.

That the King of Glory is so concerned in the welfare of his Subjects, were there nothing else in the Duty but that consideration, is an infinite encouragement. *He that receiveth you, receiveth me,* is such an obligation, that as it is all Goodness in it self, so is it all Motive unto us. Eternity will scarce be sufficient to fathom its depth. Do we feed GOD himself in feeding the Poor, and his eternal Son Jesus Christ? Are these Needy persons the Representatives of the GODHEAD, in whom we are to shew all our affection, love and gratitude to the fountain of all Life and Happiness? How infinite ought our Liberality to be, when we consider the excellency of our Bliss and Benefactour? Are they beloved, are they all his Sons, the very express image of himself; all disguised and concealed Kings; all Temples of eternal Glory? What measure can confine or shut up our bowels? Are the Spectators so innumerable, so divine, so blessed, so nearly allyed to our selves, so rich, and great, and beautiful, are they so deeply concerned in the welfare of others, and does every act of Charity extend to all; shall we appear in the very act it self eternally before them? What a vast ambition of pleasing all these glorious Persons, should be exprest in every operation of the Soul? As every Thought is seen throughout all eternity, and every Word (that is spoken here on Earth) heard in the utmost extents of immensity; so is there a kind of Omnipresent greatness in the smallest action, for it is vertually extended through all the omnipresence of Almighty GOD: even as every Centre, wherein it can be done is eternally near, nay and within him in the remotest part of his omnipresence. 'Tis dilated in a moment, and fills the immensity of GOD with its nature. According to its kind it affecteth all his Essence in all spaces whatsoever.

YET is there a Rule for the bounding of all external acts of Charity, and another for improving it. Intelligence is the light wherein Almsdeeds ought to shine, and attain their glory: Love is the soul of Compassion, and Zeal the fervour of Perfection: without which *though a man bestow all his Goods to feed the Poor, and give his Body to be burned, it profiteth nothing.* Where this great abyss of goodness is, Prudence may dispence it, as it seeth occasion. All other Vertues attending upon it, it is impossible to destroy it self here on earth, unless the case be so urgent, that it is better die, than to live in the World. *For a good man sheweth favour and lendeth;* but it is added, *He will guide his affairs with discretion.*

The first Rule is, to secure the life and growth of the tree, by causing it so to bear one year, that it may bring forth fruit another. It is no good husbandry to cut it down: nor any charity to make it wither and expire. And on this very account a Charitable man must preserve himself, that he may do more good, by continuing longer able to do it.

HE that will examine the proportions and measures of his Liberality may take this Rule for the second: Let thy Superfluities give place to other mens Conveniencies, thy Conveniencies to their Necessities, thy Necessities to their Extremities.

A third Rule is this; Our Riches must be expended according to the several Circumstances and occasions of our lives. A Liberal man will not pinch and starve his Servants. For it is contrary to the nature of Bounty to oppress any, to hurt any, to trample upon any. He will be good to all, and to those most, that are near unto him. GOD hateth robbery for burnt Offering, or that Strangers should eat the Childrens meat, or that Beggars or Riotous persons should devour the right of a mans Servants. He that does brave acts abroad, but is a Niggard within doors, has a glorious train spread abroad like a Peacock, but stands upon black feet; and may bear that unlucky bird for his Crest, which is the emblem of Pride and Vain-glory. So is it with young Prodigals that oppress poor Tradesmen, by defrauding them of their Debts, yet are lavish enough to the Poor and Needy. This is a defect with which Goodness is inconsistent, and it blasteth their Charity. It is better take off 100 pound a year from ones benevolence to the poor, than wrong a Servant or Creditour of a shilling. The Rule therefore is this, First secure the works of Necessity; have food and rayment for thy self: keep out of debt. Next render to every man his due in point of Justice, and employ no man thou canst not pay; rather perish

thy self than oppress another. If thou art able, and hast any thing
to spare, then let the miseries of the Needy be supplied in the works
of Compassion and Charity: but let not all be swallowed up here,
thy Neighbours, and Acquaintance, and Friends, and Kindred claim
a share; and thou must secure something for the works of Courtesie
and Hospitality. So order all both in thy Estate and Life, that the
kindness of GOD may shine in all. So doing thy Stewardship shall
be acceptable to the whole World, and thy Memory blessed among
men and Angels.

Our Saviour when he wrought his Miracles, as he opened the eyes
of the blind, healed the sick, cast out Devils, raised the dead, gave
food to the hungry, tongues to the dumb, ears to the deaf, and legs
to the lame: so did he give advice to the ignorant, and interpret all
his design, by those Parables and Sermons which attended his Cures.
Good Counsel is oftentimes a greater gift than a Trunk of Mony.
While the Iron is hot it is time to strike. Good Counsel is like a bitter
Pill, that must be gilded with Liberality. If the Word of GOD be
like *good seed,* the heart in which it is sown is softened by Sorrow,
and ploughed up by affliction, and prepared to receive it by the husbandry of Providence. And the properest Season that can be chosen
for Instruction is the time of Obliging. He that intendeth the welfare
of the Soul by all the good works he doth to the Body, is deep and
perfect in Charity. A wise man will improve his advantages, and enrich
his Gifts with pious discourses. A Benefactour has authority to talk
what he listeth, and bribes his Auditor to patience by his Bounty.
Since *He that winneth Souls is wise,* a profound Liberality will not
let slip a golden Opportunity, nor suffer his Gift to be dark and insignificant. He will make mention of the glory of GOD, and the Love
of Christ, the guilt of Sin, the danger of Hell, and the hope of Heaven,
and alwaies endeavour to make his Love apparent to that GOD, for
whose sake he pities the Poor, and is kind towards all. Forasmuch
as man hath two parts, and his Body is without the Soul but a putrid
Carkass; he will put life into his Mony, and inspire his Munificence
with all his Reasons, that his Bounty may consist of two parts in like
manner, and have a Soul for its Interpreter. Liberality to the Soul
is the Soul of Liberality. Paradice and Heaven are better to be given
than Gold and Silver. And every Good man will imitate the Apostle,
who was ready not to impart the Gospel of GOD only, but his own
Soul to the benefit of those for whom Christ died.

THIS one thing further I desire you to note,* *He that soweth sparingly shall reap sparingly, but he which soweth bountifully shall reap also bountifully.* In the Kingdom of Heaven every man receiveth his Penny: because all their Joyes are common and equal. Their *Treasures* shall be the same, but they will differ in *Glory.* The same GOD, the same Angels, the same Men, all the same Objects shall be round about every man. Every man shall see and enjoy all the Glory of his eternal Kingdom, because every ones life and felicity shall be perfect. But yet their works follow them; and every man shall be cloathed in the beauty of his own actions, Vertues and Graces. There may be twenty Children in the same family, yet all of several Features. There may be a thousand Trees in the same Orchard, yet all of different kinds. The same brightness and glory may be round about them, the same skie cover them, the same Earth support them, the same Stars serve them, the same Sun shine upon them, the same Sea, the same Dew, the same Air and Nourishment feed them, and yet the one be more fair, and honourable, and excellent than the other. All the World does know that a Tree laden with Fruits and Blossoms is far more beautiful than a Tree that is barren and unfruitful. And the degrees of Beauty are according as the Fruits are, more or less. And as the Fruits they bring forth adorn them, so do their own works praise them in the Gates. Heaven as it is a Kingdom of Light and Knowledge, is a Kingdom of Perfection; Righteousness and Justice flourish there in their fulness: and every several degree of excellence is entertained with an answerable degree of esteem: according to the number and greatness of their Vertues every one is honoured by Saints and Angels.

NOW least these Fruits should receive any impediment by the Vices and Corruptions of men, order is taken, *that we should love our Enemies, bless them that curse us, do good to them that hate us, pray for them that despightfully use, and persecute us.* By which means it is that a Liberal man surmounts all obstacles whatsoever, lives among Dragons as if he were surrounded with Doves, and though he be environed with Devils, is as if he were conversant with Angels: Because he takes no notice of any Vice in any man, to stop him, but is as Liberal as if all were full of worth and vertue. Nay he is more good and more miraculous. Their Vices, their Provocations, their Disorders cannot stain or imbitter his Nature: but he will be alwaies chearful, and bright, and fair, and free and perfect. To love the amiable, and

* 2 Cor. 9.6.

be kind to the beautiful is natural and easie. It is not given to the Angels but to visit the Faithful and the Penitent. But to love the Evil, to be kind, and good and serviceable to the Deformed and the Odious, to the Injurious and Ungrateful, is somewhat more than Angelical. We learn it not of them but of GOD, and of his eternal Son: who hath commanded us *to be the Children of our Father which is in Heaven; for he maketh his Sun to rise on the Evil and on the Good, and sendeth rain on the Just and on the Unjust.* Even Publicans and Sinners do in some manner as much as Angels, love them that love them. In Heaven they have no malignity, or malice, or wrong to over-come, all that they love is Beauty and Goodness: unless they learn of Jesus Christ, and imitate him here on Earth towards us Sinners. But our duty is far greater, and our opposition more. Which is inti-mated also in our Saviours words: *For if ye love them which love you, what reward have you? Do not even the Publicans the same? And if ye salute your Brethren only, what do ye more than others? Do not even the Publicans so? Be ye therefore perfect even as your Father which is in Heaven is perfect.*

In the Close of all, I beseech you to consider this one most cogent and weighty expostulation. It is the beloved Disciples,* *If a man say, I love GOD, and hateth his Brother, he is a Liar: for he that loveth not his Brother whom he hath seen, how can he love God whom he hath not seen?* Our Neighbours are not only the representatives of GOD, but they are here upon Earth, are visible, are present with us, are Corporeal as we are, and alwaies near us, our actions among them are palpable, and our Conversation with them real. GOD is invisible, and absent from us, he is afar off in the highest Heavens, Incorporeal, and Incomprehensible: If we are remiss and careless in our duty towards our Neighbour, all our devotion towards GOD will be but imaginary, our Religion will degenerate into an idle and vain *Chimera,* become a weak and feeble shadow, be seated in the fancy, and dwindle away into an aiery Speculation. The reality of Religion consists in the solid practice of it among the Sons of men that are daily with us. The difficult and serious actions of our Lives abroad, feed our Meditation in all our retirements, and infuse a reality and strength into our Devotions, which make them solid and substantial.

* 1 Joh. 4.20.

Of Magnificence in GOD. Its resemblance in Man.
The chief Magnificence of the Soul is Spiritual.
It is perfectly expressed in the outward Life, when
the whole is made perfect, and presented to GOD.
GOD gives all his Life to us: and we should give
ours all to him. How fair and glorious it may be.

GOD being proposed as the Pattern of our Liberality and Kindness by our Saviour, the nature of his Bounty is fit to be considered for our Information: which is great, and publick, and advantagious to many. In some of his private dispensations it walks under the notion and form of Liberality, as it giveth food and Rayment, Gold and Silver, Houses and Lands to particular persons: But in other effects of his eternal love, which are great and publick, its nature is changed into the highest Magnificence.

MAGNIFICENCE is a Vertue scarcely to be found, but in Kings and Emperours. It is busied in erecting Temples and Triumphal arches, Magnificent Theatres, Colledges and Universities, Aquæducts and Palaces, Royal Monuments and Pyramids, Marts, Havens, Exchanges, and all those other great and mighty things wherein the glory of Imperial Power is made conspicuous, and whereby whole Nations are benefited, and Kingdoms adorned.

GREAT Power, Riches, Wisdom and Goodness must concur in the effect which is truly Magnificent. It must be of great lustre and glory, as well as of publick use and benefit; and as it is wrought with great labour and expence, be imparted by a great Soul, and freely given to the good of the People. For Magnificence implies Greatness and Bounty united.

THE Creation of the Universe was a great and Magnificent work, because the lustre and beauty of the WORLD is a sublime and wonder-

ful Gift imparted to millions. The bounty of GOD in adorning all
ages with Cities and Empires, for the benefit and enjoyment of all
the World is another piece of his Royal Magnificence. The infusion
of a Soul so divine and everlasting into the Body of a Man is an
act of love transcendently greater than all the Aquæducts and Trophies
in the World. For such a Celestial presence, such a sublime and illimited power, such a vast and noble Workmanship, as that is, which
can see and comprehend all Eternity and Time together, extend to
all Objects in all Worlds, and fill Immensity with life and joy, and
love and knowledge, with light, and beauty, and glory, with adorations
and praises; though its essence be invisible, and all its splendour within,
is next under GOD the highest Object of all the admiration of Men
and Angels: It is a being as publick as the Sun, the great occasion
of all the extasies of the Seraphims, the wonder and the rapture of
all the Cherubims, the glory of GOD communicated to the World
in so divine a Creature; a miraculous effect of his eternal Power, and
the resemblance of his Godhead among all the Creatures.

THE Incarnation of his Eternal Son, and the giving of the Holy
Ghost was another Magnificent effect of his almighty Power: so was
the preparation of his Word, with the Gifts he gave unto Men in
the Patriarchs, Prophets and Apostles, adorned with all the varieties
of their Labours and Vertues, Wisdom, Courage and Patience, Lives
and Examples, Deaths and Sufferings, Oppositions and Successes,
Miracles and Revelations. The *Jewish* Nation alone is a Magnificent
gift to the whole World. The Apostle phraseth the Regiment of it
as a matter of Bounty:* *Now if the Fall of them be the Riches of
the World, and the diminishing of them the Riches of the* Gentiles,
how much more their Fulness! And again, *When he ascended up on
high, and led Captivity captive, he gave Gifts unto Men, some Apostles,
and some Prophets,* &c. When he presented all Nations and Kingdoms
as a token of his love to the Angels; when he gave all those glorious
Hosts in the Heavens to the vision, service and pleasure of Men; much
more when he gave all these in their marvellous order and amity united,
to every Soul: When he filled the Heaven of Heavens with Joyes;
and gave all the glory of his Kingdom to one (and that one to every
one) he manifested the glory of his Magnificent power, in that of
his great and transcendent goodness. And in relation to this we may
cry out with the Apostle (more than for the mysterious Regiment of
a little Nation, as he doth upon the account of GODS dealing with

* Rom. 11.12.

the *Jews*) *O the depth of the riches** *both of the Wisdom and Knowl-edge of GOD! How unsearchable are his judgments, and his waies past finding out!* For all things are yours,† *Whether* Paul, *or* Apollos, *or* Cephas, *or the* World, *or Life or Death, or things present, or things to come, all are yours, and ye are CHRISTS, and CHRIST is GODS.* Wherefore he saith,‡ *My Thoughts are not your Thoughts, nor your Waies my Waies. For as the Heavens are higher than the Earth, so are my Waies higher than your Waies, and my Thoughts than your Thoughts.* You give triflles, and give them but to one, I give Worlds and give them to every one. You divide and disperse your Gifts, and lessen by dispersing them, I communicate and unite my Gifts, and aug-ment by giving them: You think it impossible for one man to enjoy all things, I think it possible for innumerable Millions. You think your interest is abated, and your fruition endangered by the communication of your Treasures to many, I know they are increased and multiplied by the number of the Enjoyers. You think Gold and Silver to be the greatest Gifts, and that nothing is yours but what is shut up within such Shores, and Walls, and Hedges, I know that Men are the greatest Treasures, and that your interest is extended through all Worlds, and your Possessions illimited. For according to the tenour of these words, and a little before he saith,§ *Thou shalt break forth on the right hand and on the left, and thy seed shall inherit the Gentiles, and make the desolate Cities to be inhabited. Fear not, for thou shalt not be ashamed: neither be thou confounded, for thou shalt not be put to shame: for thou shalt forget the shame of thy Youth, and shalt not remember the reproach of thy Widowhood any more. For thy Maker is thy husband, the Lord of Hosts is his Name, &c.* And a little after he saith,‖ *Thou shalt also be a Crown of Glory in the hand of the Lord, and a royal DIADEM in the hand of thy GOD. Thou shalt no more be termed* Forsaken, *neither shall thy land any more be termed* Desolate, *but thou shalt be called* Hephzibah, *and thy land* Beulah: *for the Lord delighteth in thee, and thy Land shall be married. For as a young Man marrieth a Virgin, so shall thy Sons marry thee: and as the Bridegroom rejoyceth over the Bride, so shall thy GOD rejoyce over thee.* For a Son to marry with his Mother is Incest: it is Confusion also for a Child to go in unto his Fathers Wife: And yet the Church of GOD shall be the lawful Bride of every one of all her Sons. Here is Magnificence! GOD giveth himself, and his eternal

---

* Rom. 11.33. † 1 Cor. 3.21, 22. ‡ Isai. 55.8, 9.
§ Isai. 54.3,4,5. ‖ Isai. 62.3,4,5.

Son, and his Holy Spirit, and his Bride, and his Apostles and Prophets, and all the Universe to every Soul! Which justifieth that saying of St. *Chrysostome, GOD loveth every one with all the Love wherewith he loveth the whole World.* His Magnificence exceedeth all Limits, Laws, Imaginations, Wishes, Possibilities, and he maketh every one * *Heir of the World,* † *Coheir with Christ,* ‡ *to inherit all things;* every one more than the sole end of all his Kingdom. For all the Ornaments and Riches of a Bride are given with her Person: her Palace and Attendants are her Lovers upon the Marriage, as well as she: and all things that magnifie, or make her amiable, are subservient to his enjoyment, and really his that is her Husband. So that GOD giving us his Church to be our Mother and our Bride, hath intended us in all the things whereby he benefited her in all kingdoms and ages: and hath loved us in all the Love which he hath exercised towards her: and all the fruit of all his Love to the whole World resteth in our Exaltation. This is the Magnificence of Almighty GOD to every Soul in his Kingdom. And for this it is that the Church is called, *The Assembly of the First-born,* because all her Children are the perfect Heirs, and Kings, and Bridegrooms, every one compleatly, and more to his satisfaction, than if he were so alone. For as GOD is wholly every where, and the more here for being in other places; and infinitely here because he is Omnipresent: So does he wholly see and intend every one, as if him alone; and love him far the more, by loving every one; for his Love being infinite, it is expressed towards him in all the parts of his Kingdom: and the more rich and glorious he maketh all things, the more great and happy he maketh *Him,* according to the immeasurable All-sufficiency of his infinite Wisdom.

THERE is in the Goodness of GOD an infinite Greatness that makes it Magnificent: for he gives *Himself.* When a Queen gives her self, whether it be to a Beggar, or to one of her Courtiers, or to another King, if it proceed from an ardent Love the Gift is full of sweetness within; but it is alwaies attended with great Magnificence without: together with her self she gives him her Palace, her Exchequer, Gardens of Pleasure, her Crown and Throne, her Soveraignty, her Nobles, Attendants, and all her Kingdom. GOD doth infinitely more. He gives himself by Loving, and with himself gives us all his Wisdom, Goodness and Power, by making them full objects of Complacency: by doing with them for us, all that we could devise, or desire, or effect with them, had they been our own and seated in our selves. His bounty

* Rom. 4.13.   † Ro. 8.17.   ‡ Rev. 21.7.

in giving himself is attended with infinite advantages, innumerable wonders of love and goodness; a care to make himself (as a Bridegroom
does) exceeding amiable and glorious, a care to purifie and fit his
Queen for himself with all kind of greatness and beauty: a care to
adorn his Palace with all kind of delectable things, Riches, Pleasures,
magnificent Furnitures, Perfumes, Musicians, Pictures, Jewels, Dainties,
Feasts, Attendants, Nobles, &c. In all which he infinitely exceedeth
all the Monarchs of the World. His Kingdom is celebrated by *David*
with great Exultation, *Psal.* 145.·

NOW if we would be Magnificent as GOD is, we must have a
love within our Souls, that is willing to impart all these incomprehensible Treasures and Glories to every Soul, and to all his Hosts; and
if it be possible, to out-do all this, to give all these Worlds, nay GOD
himself, and every Soul to all with greater ardour, and joy and gratitude: Angels and Men, our selves to all, and all to every one. For
that Love which is the fountain of all is greater than all, a greater
Gift, and a greater Treasure. And that love which imitates the first
is in its place the only desirable and excellent thing that is possible.
GODS love in its place is infinitely better then all. Removing it you
shake and abolish all. But in such a Creature he desires to be beloved.
He made him free, that he might be capable of Loving, for it is impossible to love by constraint or necessity: and having made him free and
left him to himself, infinitely desires to be beloved of him. All his
own love unto him, and all the glories of Heaven and Earth which
are prepared for him, are means for the obtaining of that end, Obligations, Motives, Allurements, Incentives of that Love which GOD desires. If he will not return Love, all are imbittered and made distastful.
Infinite Love infinitely desires to be beloved, and is infinitely displeased
if it be neglected. GOD desires to take Complacency in all, to see
the beauty of his Bride, and the accomplishment of his design, in the
Love of his Beloved. And nothing in all Worlds but the love of that
Person can be his satisfaction. For nothing can supply the absence
or denial of that Love which is his end. For in its place it is the
only needful and proper thing, far more desired than all that went
before: All that went before was but the Means, this is the thing designed and endeavoured by them. For upon this Return all the sweetness of the rest dependeth. All is made sweet and compleat, and delightful, if this Soul doth love GOD in all these things; if not, they are
all made vain, and his love is turned into sour displeasure. All the
other things are so far from *alleviating* that they increase his displea-

sure; the glory and abundance of them is so far from making him to despise this Love, that in respect of these things he the more desires it; because he would not have his labour vain; and his own infinite Love makes him more to esteem the love of this Creature, which is (in its place) his Soveraign object; and for that very cause so beloved and admired by all Angels and Men. Is not then the Love which a man returneth a Magnificent thing! Certainly if it answers all these preparations and obligations as their end, and be lookt upon as that without which all the Creation is vain and frustrate, it is the most great and marvellous thing in all the World, and is *in its own place* of all other things most highly desired by all Angels and Men; and is the greatest Gift which (in, and by that Soul) can possibly be given. It is esteem of, honour paid to, and delight in, all these great and most glorious things. It contains in it self a *desire* to see GOD pleased with more than the fruition of all Worlds, and of becoming it self the greatest Treasure to his eternal essence of all that is possible. And if this *desire* be not satisfied, all the grandeurs of his eternal Kingdom are to no purpose. But *the desire satisfied is a Tree of Life*. What the Sun is to the Eye, that is Love to the Desire. GODS infinite desire of our Love makes it infinitely delightful to him. *Davids* purpose to build the *Temple* was more accepted than *Solomons* performance. And if one Contrite groan be better than all Sacrifices, to love GOD with all the Soul and Understanding is better than to give him all Worlds. We sacrifice all by Loving him as we ought. We see the Beauty and Glory of all, and offer it all up to him, with infinite Desire, our selves also with infinite Gratitude. Could we make millions of Worlds, infinitely greater and more perfect than this, they should all be his. No delight, no joy, no pleasure can be greater to us, than to see him reigning. He gives all to us, that we might give it all to him: In our Affection and with our Love it is most delightful. Our Affections are the flames and perfumes that enrich the Sacrifice. He is a Spirit to be served in a Spiritual manner: all that we *would* do, we do. Infinite desires and intentions of Pleasing him are real objects to his Eye. The Goodness of the Soul, and the Greatness of his Goodness consisteth in them. A Will enlarged with an infinite Fancy is a prodigious depth of goodness when it is all Love. It would do millions of things for its Object! But GOD is incapable of more Worlds: and all that are possible he can make himself: our Magnificence must be shewn in something he cannot do, unless he were in our Circumstance, and which of all things in the World he knows most fit to be done, were he in our places. He cannot be the Soul of any of his Creatures: but would be the Soul of that Soul: the joy and delight of that Soul; the life and glory of that Soul: and that he cannot be, unless that Soul will delight in him, and love and honour him. It is not he must honour himself: but that Soul: His desire is, that that Soul would freely turn, and delight in him freely, of its own accord, would incline it self to consider his Excellencies, and dedicate it self to love and honour him. This is one way for the Soul to be Magnificent towards Men too: who by Nature delight to see GOD beloved, and satisfied in a point of such infinite importance.

IT is true indeed, that GOD can be full of Indignation and punish: but for love to turn into anger is no compensation for the pleasure it lost by our miscarriage: and to punish is a strange and troublesome work, in which Love is extinguished, or else afflicted. Infinite Love puts an infinite value on the Gift. And I think it is Magnificence to give a Gift of infinite value.

OUR Magnificence towards Men must be laid on a deep and eternal foundation. We must be willing to give our selves to their comfort and satisfaction. And that we cannot do, but by imitating GOD in all his Goodness, studying their felicity, and desiring their love with the same earnestness to the utmost of our power: doing in all places, in all things, in all Worlds, the things they desire: supposing them to be what they ought to be, like Gods themselves.

THE best Principle whereby a man can stear his course in this World, is that which being well prosecuted will make his Life at once honourable and happy: Which is to love every man in the whole World as GOD doth. For this will make a man the Image of GOD, and fill him with the mind and spirit of Christ, it will make every man that is, the Representative of GOD and of all the World unto him. It will make a man to reverence GOD in all Mankind, and lift him up above all Temptations, Discouragements and Fears. It will make him to meet the love of GOD, Angels, and Men, in every Person. It will make a man truly glorious, by making him pleasing to GOD, and universally good to every one; diffusive like the Sun, to give himself to all, and wise to enjoy their compleat Felicity. If there were but one, the Case is evident: supposing more than one, his duty is to love every one the more for all their sakes. For since he must love all, and they are all to love one, and every one, he must please them all by gratifying their love to one, and by doing so to every one, they are all concerned in the welfare of one, and pleased in the love that is

born to every one. This in the state of Glory will be clear, where
every one like the Sun shall be clearly seen extending his love to all;
though here upon Earth, where our estate is imperfect, by reason of
the imperfection of our Knowledge it doth not appear. Our actions
are limited: for being finite in our outward demeanour, they must needs
be regulated by Justice and Wisdom. But two things come in here
to the assistance of Magnificence, whereof the first is the interiour
perfection of our Love to all, the second is the universal Satisfaction
which the beauty of our outward life will afford at last. Concerning
the last, two things are fit to be considered. First, that as GOD has
communicated the Sun, by making it visible, to all; and there is not
a Star but is seen by all Nations and Kingdoms: so has he communicated the Soul, by making it visible, to all; and there is not a Thought
that shall remain uncovered; nor an action, but it shall be seen by
all for ever. Secondly, that as GOD himself is admired for his *Inward
Love,* so is he for the operations of his *Outward Life,* I mean for
his *Works* and *Judgments.* When they saw his *Works* finished,* *The
Morning Stars sang together, and all the Sons of GOD shouted for
joy.* The Elders are represented before his Throne, casting down their
Crowns, and saying,† *Thou art worthy, O Lord, to receive Glory,
and Honour, and Power, for thou hast created all these things, and
for thy pleasure they are, and were created.* Where the perfection of
GODS Pleasure in the GLORY of the *Creation* is evidently discovered,
to be one of the *Joyes of Heaven;* a great matter of their Contemplation, an eternal cause of their Praises. His infinite and eternal Love
is that by which he is *All Glorious within:* all the sweetness of his
Essence, and all the perfection of the Soul is there: but yet his Saints
in the Church Triumphant, sing the Song of *Moses,* and the Song
of the *Lamb,* saying,†† *Great and Marvellous are thy WORKS, Lord
GOD Almighty, Just and True are thy WAYES thou King of Saints!*
His Works are the substantial Creatures in Heaven and in Earth: his
Waies are his proceedings and dispensations among them in all ages.
For all shall appear together for ever, the one being *Great* and *Marvel-
lous,* the other beautified with *Truth* and *Justice.* So that neither of
these doth swallow up the other, but both are distinct and perfect.
Our Love may be infinite on the Inside, and yet our Life be diversified
with many limited and particular actions. Now if our Life be like
GODS, eternally to be seen; and our Actions in passing pass not away,
but in the sphere of our life abide for ever, *our Life all at once is*

* Job.   † Rev. 4.11.   †† Rev. 15.3, 4, 5.

a mysterious Object, interwoven with many Thoughts, Occurrences, and Transactions; and if it be to be presented to GOD like a Ring, or a Garland, we had need to be very choice in the mixture of our Flowers, and very curious in the Enammel of so *rare a Token*. Perhaps it is his Crown, nay our own; His and our Royal Diadem. It shall shine like a glory about our Souls for ever. That there should be any dirt or blemish in it, is inconsistent with our Felicity: but it is a Magnificent Present if it be enchased with Jewels, well chosen and curiously set, I mean with the most pure and fit elections, the most Wise, and Just, and excellent Actions, the most bright and clear Apprehensions, the most divine and ardent Affections. The last are like Gold, the ground work of the Crown: but the work it self is a mixture of elaborate Distinctions that sparkle in their lustre like Gems of several cuts and colours. An imperial Crown is a Magnificent Present from a King to a King: But a Life like GODS in a sphere, for which Time was lent that it might be well wrought, and presented before him when made perfect, as far surpasseth the most glorious Crown that did ever sit upon Monarchs brows, as that can be supposed to excel a dull *Clod* of *Earth,* or a piece of *Rusty Iron.* There all Obligations, and Laws, and Duties, and Occasions are interwoven, all our Vertues, and Graces, and Vices, all our Tears, and Devotions, and Prayers, our Servants, the Poor, the Rich, our Relations, Parents, Friends, Magistrates and Ministers are set, and exhibited in their proper places; they appear to the life with all our Behaviors towards them: and though we did deny a Poor mans Request for the sake of another, and this and that, and the other particular action did not at present extend to all: but the Soul was feign to use much wisdom in contracting its operation for the greater advantage, in finding out its Duty, in moderating its Behaviour, in ballancing its occasions and accounts; yet in the result of all, it will be found full of Bounty and Goodness to all, by taking care to be just and pleasing to all in the beauty of its Conversation. When two things it desires to do, are incompatible to each other; it studies which of the two was more just, and fit, and necessary; which tends most to the full and final perfection of its Life; the interest of a Child sometimes carries it from another man, a debt of Necessity is paid with that we would give, for a work of Charity: yet when all is Obedience, Duty, and Love, that life is a most Magnificent Gift. A Wife, a Sister must be respected in her place, a Son, a Servant, a Friend, before a Stranger; if the case be such that one of them only can be relieved. All in the Family, being made

in the Image of GOD, as well as the Beggars without doors, are Objects
of our Charity. But so much *Goodness* being in the bottom of the
design, and so much *Prudence* and *Justice* in the denial: Where his
Gold and Silver faileth, his affection may be infinite, and the restraints
he sets upon his Actions, be the several cuts and distinctions in the
Work, the very true Engravings that make the Jewel, or the Crown
Glorious. Its *Matter* is *Life* it self, yet the *Workmanship* far excels
the *Matter,* when it is as *Accurate* and *Divine* as it ought to be. This
great and deep Thought makes every little act of Life magnificent
and glorious, a better Gift to GOD in its place, than the Creation
of all Worlds before him. While a mans Love is really infinite towards
all, and he is ready to sacrifice himself with *Moses,* and St. *Paul,*
for the good of the World: but is fain to set a restraint upon himself
for the sake of others. The very grief which true *Goodness* conceives
at the deficiency of its power, and the force that lies upon it in so
ungrateful a Necessity, where it must be an Umpire and a Judge between its Bowels and its Children, is a molestation which he endures
in the midst of his duty, filling all Spectators with as much pleasure
as him with pain. All shall be remembered, and all these things which
are now so grievous, shall themselves become a part of our future
Glory.

REMEMBER alwaies thou art about a Magnificent work: and as
long as thou dwellest here upon Earth lay every action right in its
place. *Let* not *Patience* only, but every Vertue *have her perfect work.*
Let Wisdom shine in its proper sphere: let Love *within* be infinite
and eternal, in the light of true Knowledge it is impossible to exceed:
be right in all thy Conceptions, and wise in all thine Elections, and
righteous in all thy Affections, and just in all thy Actions; let the
habits of Compassion and Mercy appear and break out fitly upon
all occasions: and the severity of Justice too for the preservation of
the World! Let all be underlaid with solid Goodness, and guided with
Prudence, and governed with Temperance, ordered with Care, and
carried on with Courage: lay hold on thy Incentives by a lively Faith,
and on all the strengths of Eternity by a glorious Hope, let all be
sweetened with a gracious Charity, fortified and secured with invincible
Meekness, and profitably concealed, and vail'd over with Humility;
let thy Contentment put a lustre and grace upon all: let Magnanimity
and Modesty appear in thy actions, Magnificence and Liberality act
their part; let Resignation to the Divine Will, and Gratitude, come
in to compleat all these, and thy Life be beautified with the sweet

intermixture of Obedience and Devotion: Thy GODLINESS will be so divine, that all Angels and Men will be perfectly pleased, especially when thou hast wiped out the Miscarriages by the bloud of the Lamb, which in a little chrystal Vial pure and clear thou ought'st alwaies to carry about with thee, when thou hast washed away the defilements contracted in the work, with the Tears of Repentance: Those Tears too he putteth in his Bottles, and they will turn into Jewels. There is not one drop so small, but it shall turn into a Precious Stone, and continue for ever as it were frozen into a Gem. *Many, O Lord my GOD, are thy wonderful Works which thou hast done, and thy Thoughts which are to us-ward: they cannot be reckoned up in order unto thee: If I would declare and speak of them, they are more than can be numbered:* how precious also are thy Thoughts O GOD; how great is the sum of them! If I should count them they are more in number than the Sand! When I awake I am still with thee!†* And with whom else can I be! for thou only art infinite in Beauty and Perfection: O my GOD, I give my self for ever unto thee!

* Psal. 40.5.   † Psal. 183.17, 18.

CHAP. XXXII.

*Of Gratitude. It feeds upon Benefits, and is in height
and fervour answerable to their Greatness. The
Question stated, Whether we are able to love
GOD more than our selves. It is impossible to
be grateful to GOD without it. A hint of
the glorious Consequences of so doing.*

WHAT GOD has made us able to do by way of *Gratitude,* you must
see in the Chapter of *Magnificence.* The Love wherewith all these
things ought to be done, shall be so great in the estate of Perfection,
our Charity and Wisdom so directly intend all Angels and Men, and
especially GOD above all blessed for ever, our Gratitude and Goodness
make us so zealous for their satisfaction, that no pleasure in the whole
World shall be comparable to that of being Delightful to them. To
receive all is sweet, but to communicate all (adorned thus within the
sphere of our own lives) is infinitely beyond all that can be sweet
in the reception, both for our glory and satisfaction. There is ever
upon us some pressing want in this World, and will be till we are
infinitely satisfied with varieties and degrees of Glory. Of that which
we feel at present we are sensible: when that want is satisfied and
removed, another appeareth, of which before we were not aware.
Till we are satisfied we are so clamorous and greedy, as if there were
no pleasure but in receiving all: When we have it we are so full,
that we know not what to do with it, we are in danger of bursting,
till we can communicate all to some fit and amiable Recipient, and
more delight in the Communication than we did in the Reception.
This is the foundation of real Gratitude, and the bottom of all that
Goodness which is seated in the bent and inclination of Nature. It
is a Principle so strong, that Fire does not burn with more certain

violence, than Nature study to use all, when it hath gotten it, and to improve its *Treasures* to the acquisition of its *Glory*.

THE Holiness of all the work consists in the Fervour wherewith it is done, and if our Love shall in Heaven answer all its Causes, it will be equal to all its Obligations and Rewards, and as infinite in a manner as the excellencies of its objects, the very love of GOD towards all things will be in it, our Love shall be in all his, and his in ours. And if we love GOD, Angels and Men, all Vertue, Grace and Felicity as they deserve; we shall so delight in excellent actions, and in appearing amiable and glorious before them, that we would not for all Worlds miscarry in a tittle: And therefore every defect (even after pardon) will be an infinite *disaster* as well as *blemish*. This is one effect of *Gratitude* in Nature. And if it were not for the Satisfaction of *Jesus Christ,* and the efficacy of Faith and Repentance in his Blood, the least Sinner in all Nature would be eternally miserable, notwithstanding the advantages of *Christs* blood. It is the desire of the Soul to be spotless in it self. And if it be so prophane as to build upon these advantages, without taking care to be as excellent as it is able, it is the most ungrateful Creature in the World, and is too base and dirty, to appear in Glory.

TO talk of overflowing in the disbursments and effusions of Love and Goodness, till our emptiness and capacity be full within, is as impertinent and unseasonable, as to advise a Beggar to give away a Kingdom, or a dead man to breath, or one that is starving to give Wine and Banquets to the Poor and Needy. But when a man is full of blessedness and glory, nothing is so easie as to overflow unto others: to forbid, or hinder him, is to stifle and destroy him. Breath with the same necessity must be let out, as it is taken in. A man dies as certainly by the confinement, as the want of it. To shut it up and deny it are in effect the same. When a man hath the glory of all Worlds, he is willing to impart the delights wherewith he is surrounded, to give away himself to some amiable Object, to beautifie his Life, and dedicate it to the use and enjoyment of Spectators, and to put life into all his Treasures by their Communication. To love, and admire, and adore, and praise, in such a case are not only pleasant, but natural, and free, and inevitable operations. It is then his supream and only joy to be amiable and delightful. For the actions of Love and Honour belong in a peculiar manner to a plentiful estate: Wants and Necessities when they pinch, and grind us in a low condition, disturb all those easie and delicate Resentments, which find their element in the midst of Pleasures and Superfluities. Hence it is, that high-born Souls in Courts and Palaces are addicted more to sweet and honourable excesses, than Clowns and Peasants. The one spend their life in Toil and Labour, the other in Caresses and soft Embraces. Amities and Bounties, Obligations and Respects, Complements and Visits are the life of Nobles: Industry and Care is that of the meaner People. Honours and Adorations are fit for the Temple, not for the Market. Soft and tender Affections are more in the *Court*, than in the *Shop* or *Barn*. There is some difference in this respect even between the City and Country. But *Heaven* is the Metropolis of all Perfection. GOD is a mighty King, and all his Subjects are his Peers and Nobles. Their life is more sublime, and pleasant, and free, because more blessed and glorious. Their very Palaces and Treasures are infinite Incentives to the works of honour and delight, and they cannot rest either day or night, but continually cry, *Holy, Holy, Holy, Lord GOD of Hosts, Heaven and Earth are full of the Majesty of thy Glory*. Their Beauties and Perfections enflame one another. Their very Joyes inspire them with eternal Love: and as all Care and Labour are removed, so are all delights and extasies established. Ravishments and Caresses, Adorations and Complacencies, all the force and violence of Love, Charms, Allurements, high Satisfactions, all the delicacies and riches of sweet Affection, Honours and Beauties are their Conversation. Towards GOD, towards themselves, towards each other, they are all Harmony, and Joy, and Peace, and Love: they flie upon Angels wings, and trample upon Spices. *Aromatick* Odours and Flowers are under feet; the very ground upon which they stand is beset with Jewels. Such you know were the foundations of the Walls of the *New Jerusalem,* and the pavement of the Street was beaten Gold. GOD and the Lamb were the Light, and the Temple of it.

THAT we are to *Enjoy* all Angels and Men by communicating our selves unto them, is a little *mysterious*: but may more easily be understood, than a thing so obscure as *The Enjoyment of GOD by way of Gratitude*. That we are to love GOD more than our selves is apparently sure, at least we ought to do it, but whether it be possible, is a question of importance. That we gain infinitely by his Love, is certain; but that we gain more by our own, is prodigious! It is our duty to love him more than our selves, but whether it be our Nature, or no, is doubtful. It is impossible to ascend at the first step to the top of the Ladder. Even *Jacobs* Ladder will not bring us to Heaven, unless we begin at the bottom. Self-love is the first round, and they that remove it, had as good take away all: For he that has no love for himself can never be obliged. He that cannot be obliged cannot delight in GOD: He that cannot delight in him cannot enjoy him: He that cannot⁵ enjoy him, cannot love him: He that cannot love him cannot take pleasure in him, nor be Grateful to him. Self-love is so far from being the impediment, that it is the cause of our Gratitude, and the only principle that gives us power to do what we ought. For the more we love our selves, the more we love those that are our Benefactors. It is a great mistake in that arrogant *Leviathan,* so far to imprison our love to our selves, as to make it inconsistent with Charity towards others. It is easie to manifest, that it is impossible to love our selves, without loving other things: Nature is crippled (or if it has her feet, has her head cut off) if Self-preservation be made her only concern: We desire to live that we may do something else; without doing which life would be a burden. There are other principles of Ambition, Appetite, and Avarice in the Soul: And there are Honours, and Pleasures, and Riches in the World. These are the end of Self-preservation. And it is impossible for us to love our selves without loving these. Without loving these we cannot desire them, without desiring canot enjoy them. We are carried to them with greater ardour and desire by the love of our selves. Preservation is the first, but the weakest and the low'st principle in nature. We feel it first, and must preserve our selves, that we may continue to enjoy other things: but at the bottom it is the love of other things that is the ground of this principle of Self-preservation. And if you divide the last from the first, it is the poorest Principle in the World.

TO love another more than ones self is absurd and impossible. In Nature it is so, till we are obliged; or perhaps till we see it our interest, and find it our pleasure: It is a surprize to an Atheistical fool; That it should be ones interest to love another better than ones self: yet Bears, Dogs, Hens, Bees, Lions, Ants do it: they die for their young-ones. Nurses, Fathers, Mothers do it. Brides and Bridegrooms frequently do it; and so do Friends. All valiant Hero's love their Country better than themselves: *Moses* would have his Name blotted out of the Book of Life rather than the *Israelites* destroyed. St. *Paul* could wish himself accursed from Christ for his Brethren the *Jews:* and they both learnt it of their *Master, who made himself a Curse,* and even Sin *for us.* And it was his interest to do it! If we are immortal, and cannot but be blessed, it must needs be our interest to love him that is more blessed than we, better than our selves; because by that love we enjoy his blessedness, which is more than our own, and by that Love it is made ours and more than ours. Is not all our Glory, and Vertue, and Goodness seated in the excess of this perfect love! Do not all brave and heroical deeds depend upon it? And does not the man deserve to be burnt as an enemy to all the World, that would turn all men into Knaves and Cowards, and destroy that only principle which delivers them from being Mercenary Slaves and Villains; which is *the Love of others!* That alone which renders a man useful to the World is *the Love of others.* He that destroyeth this would pluck up all Gratitude by the roots: all Worth, Goodness, and Honour! No wonder therefore he should be an Atheist, since Nature is so base and abominable before him. But its Principles are oftentimes so generous, in Truth, that they are too great for themselves. Nothing is so ordinary in the false way, as that of loving others better than our selves. Even Dogs have starved themselves to death upon the absence of their Masters. How many Fathers have gone down with sorrow to their Graves, and lost all the comfort of their lives in the death of their Sons! How many Mothers have broken their hearts for the death of their Children! How many Widows have buried themselves alive for the loss of their Husbands; I mean, by sequestring themselves from all the delights and pleasures of the World! How many Lovers dote, and wax pale, and forget their Meat, Sleep, and Employment, and run mad for their Mistresses! Are there no such Examples; or is there no strength in such Examples as these? But to love GOD better than ones self seemeth more unnatural. Ah vile! the more base, and more wicked we! How we should love GOD better than our selves is easie to unfold by the principles of Self love, and Self exaltation. Take it in the manner following: (and when you have seen its possibility, consider the glory of doing it, the benefit, and felicity, and honour that is in it. For it is all worth and pleasure, goodness and beauty, Gratitude and Vertue, wisdom and security, perfection and excellency. We love our selves more in doing it, than it is possible to do without it.)

IT is natural to all them that love themselves, to love their Benefactors, and all those things that are conducive to their welfare, pleasure, satisfaction: And the more they love themselves, the more apprehensive they are of the benefit they receive, and the more prone to love that which occasions it. The more goodness we find in any thing, the more we are prone to love it; and the more we love it, the more to take pleasure in it. And if we find it highly convenient, and extreamly delightful, we had (not seldom) rather die than part with it: we love our selves only that we might live to enjoy that glory, or delight, or beauty, or convenience that we find so agreeable. It often falls out, for want of acquaintance with delightful things, that we think nothing so powerfully sweet, as to engage our Soul, beyond the possibility of retrieving it self: and that nothing can cleave so strangely to our minds, as to be nearer and dearer than Life it self. Yet oftentimes we find men of this opinion changing their minds, when they have chanced to taste some sweetness in Nature, they were not aware of, and then to become such miraculous Converts, that they love not themselves but for the sake of that delight which they have found in the World. I make it a great Question, would men sink into the depth of the business, Whether all Self-love be not founded on the love of other things? And whether it be not utterly impossible without it? Only the love of those things is so near and close to the love of our selves, that we cannot distinguish them, but mistake them for one and the same. If the Sun were extinguished, and all the World turned into a Chaos; I suppose there are few that love themselves so, but they would die, which plainly shews that the love of the World is inseparably annexed with the love of our selves, and if the one were gone, the other would be extinguished: especially if the sweetness of the Air, and its freedom and ease, were changed into fire and torment. For then we would surely desire to die, rather than endure it: which shews that the love of ease and repose is greater than the love of our very Beings, though not so perceivable, till we have examined the business. But if there be any pleasure, or goodness, or beauty truly infinite, we are apt to cleave unto it with adhæsion so firm, that we forget our selves, and are taken up only with the sence and contemplation, of it. The ravishment is so great, that we are turned all into extasie, transportation and desire, and live intirely to the object of our fruition. The power of infinite delight and sweetness is as irresistible, as it is ineffable. And if GOD be all beauty and delight, all amiable and lovely, truly infinite in goodness and bounty, when we see him, and taste the grace of his excellency, the blessedness and glory wherewith we are amazed, possesseth us intirely and becometh our sole and adæquate concern. After that sight it is better perish and be annihilated, than live and be bereaved of it. The fall from so great a height would fill the Soul with a cruel remembrance, and the want of its former glory and bliss be an infinite torment. Now if it loved nothing but it self, it could endure all this; rather than forsake it self, or lose, or be bereaved of its essence, it would endure any misery whatsoever.

Or to speak more correct and accurate sence, it would be incapable of any Passion, Patience or Misery, but only that which flow'd from its abolition. Nothing could prejudice it but the change of its Being.

THAT is not likely to love it self after the way which some conceive proper to Self-love, which is willing to forsake it self upon any Misery, and apt to forget it self upon any great felicity. It loves it self that it might enjoy such a pleasure, but loves that pleasure so much beyond it self that it is ready to go out of it self, and is almost beside it self for the fruition of it. Loving it self only for that end, and that chiefly and for its own sake, it loves that far more than it loves it self. And there is no limit nor bound, when it once begins to love any thing more than it self, it may proceed eternally: and provided its Object be infinitely more excellent, it will easily and greedily love it infinitely more than it can it self, and value the continuance of its own life only for the sake of that which it so infinitely esteems and delights in. It is true indeed it presupposes its Capacity: but what would that capacity be worth, were it not for Objects.

WERE there no SUN it were impossible for so fair an *Idea* to be conceived in a Mirror, as is sometimes in a Glass, when it is exposed to the skie. The Mirror is in it self a dark piece of Glass; and how so much fire, and flame, and splendor should come from it while it is a cold Flint or piece of Steel, how it should be advanced by any Art whatsoever to so much beauty and glory, as to have a Sun within it self, and to dart out such bright and celestial beams no man could devise. Yet now there is a Sun, the Matter is easie, 'tis but to apply it to the face of the Sun, and the Glass is transformed. And if GOD dwelleth in the Soul as the Sun in a Mirror, while it looketh upon him, the love of GOD must needs issue from that Soul, for *GOD is love,* and his love is in it. The impression of all his Beauty swallows up the Being of the Soul, and changes it wholly into another nature. The Eye is far more sensible of the Day, and of the beauty of the Universe, than it is of it self, and is more affected with that light it beholds, than with its own essence. Even so the Soul when it sees GOD is sensible only of the glory of that eternal Object: All it sees is GOD, it is unmindful of it self. It infinitely feels him, but forgets it self in the Rapture of its Pleasure.

BUT we leave Illustrations, and come to the reason of the thing in particular. The Soul loving it self is naturally concerned in its own happiness, and readily confesseth it oweth as much love to any Benefactour, as its bounty deserveth. And if the value of the Benefit be the

true reason of the esteem, and Reason it self the ground of the return,
A little Kindness deserveth a little love, and much deserveth more.
Reason it self is adapted to the measure of the good it receiveth, and
for a shilling-worth of Service, a shilling-worth of Gratitude is naturally
paid. For a Crown or a Kingdom the Soul is enflamed with a degree
of affection that is not usual. Now GOD created and gave me my
self; for my Soul and my Body therefore I owe him as much as my Soul
and Body are worth: and at the first dash am to love him as
much as my self. Heaven and Earth being the gifts of his Love superadded to the former, I am to Love him upon that account as much
more as the World is worth; and so much more than I love my self.
If he hath given all Angels and Men to my fruition, every one of
these is as great as my self, and for every one of those I am to love
him as much as that Angel or Man is worth. But he has given me
his Eternity, his Almighty Power, his Omnipresence, his Wisdom, his
Goodness, his Blessedness, his Glory. Where am I? Am I not lost and
swallow'd up as a Centre in all these Abysses? While I love him as
much as all these are worth, to which my Reason, which is the essence
of my Soul, does naturally carry me, I love him infinitely more than
my self; unless perhaps the possibility of enjoying all these things makes
me more to esteem my self, and increases my Self-love for their sake
more than for my own. Thus when I see my self infinitely beloved,
I conceive a Gratitude as infinite in me, as all its Causes. Self-preservation is made so natural and close a Principle, by all the hopes and
possibilities to which I am created. Those Hopes and Possibilities are
my tender concern: and I live for the sake of my infinite Blessedness.
Now that is GOD: And for his sake it is that I love my self, and
for the glory and joy of delighting in him, I desire my continuance;
and the more I delight in him, my Continuance is so much the more
dear and precious to my self. Thus is GOD infinitely preferred by
Nature above my self, and my Love to my self, being thoroughly satisfied, turns into the Love of GOD, and dies like a grain of Corn in
the Earth to spring up in a new and better form, more glorious and
honourable, more great and verdant, more fair and delightful: more
free, and generous, and noble; more grateful and perfect. The Love
of GOD is the sole and immediate Principle upon which I am to
act in all my Operations.

NOW if you enquire what Advantages accrue by this Love, to the
Soul of the Lover, we are lost again in Oceans of infinite Abundance.
The strength, and brightness, and glory of the Soul, all its Wisdom,

Goodness and Pleasure are acquired by it, founded in it, derived and spring from it: as we have before declared upon the Nature of Love. The solution of that one Question will open the mystery, Whether we gain more by his Love, or our own? All that we gain by his Love amounts to the *Power* of Loving, the *Act* of Loving we gain by our own, and all that depends upon it.

BY his Love he existeth eternally for our Enjoyment, as the Father of GLORY which is begotten by it self: but we do not gain all this by his Love; but by our own. Some man would say, We gain our Souls and Bodies by the Love of GOD, all Ages and Kingdoms, Heaven and Earth, Angels and Men, infinite and eternal Joyes, because all these were without our care or power prepared by him, and his love alone. They were prepared indeed by *his* Love, but are not acquired, or enjoyed by it. *He so loved the World that he gave his only begotten Son,* and with him all the Laws and Beauties of his Kingdom: but unless we love him, unless we are sensible of his Love in all these, and esteem it, we do not enjoy our Souls or Bodies, Angels or Men, Heaven or Earth, Jesus Christ or his Kingdom: Rather we trample upon all, and despise all, and make our selves deformed. All these do but serve to increase our Damnation, and aggravate our Guilt, unless we love and delight in their Author, and his Love it self will eternally confound us. So that we gain and enjoy the Love of GOD by ours. Now Love returned for Love is the Soul of Gratitude. In that act, and by it alone, we gain all that is excellent: And beside all these become illustrious Creatures. It is more to our avail to be Divine and Beautiful, than to see all the World full of Delights and Treasures. They would all be nothing to us, without our Love. Nothing does so much alienate and estrange the Soul from any Object, as want of Affection. All the Kingdom of Heaven is appropriated and made ours by Love alone. The inferiour perfections of our own Essence are gained by Love, and by it we accomplish the end of our Creation. We receive and enjoy all the benevolence of GODS former Love by ours; are made excellent in our selves, and delightful to GOD, which can never be brought to pass any other way, but by our Love alone. By Loving him as we ought to do, we enable him to take pleasure in us! And this is of all other the greatest benefit. We cloath our selves with the similitude of all his Attributes, and shine in his Image by Love alone. Our Love, as it acquires, crowns our Perfections with his infinite Complacency. *This is my beloved Son in whom I am well pleased,* is a voice that can be directed to none, but him only that loveth GOD with an eternal Love. He cannot rest satisfied in any that hate, or despise him. The eternal complacency and delight of GOD, whereby we are crowned with eternal Glory is acquired, and receives its Being in a manner by Love alone.

NOW to love GOD is to desire Him and his Glory, to esteem him and his Essence, to long for him and his Appearance, to be pleased with him in all his Qualities and Dispositions, or (more properly) in all his Attributes and Perfections, to delight in all his Thoughts and Waies. It is to love him in all his Excellencies. And he that is not resolved to love every Excellency in him, as much as it deserveth, does not love GOD at all: for he has no design to please him. But he that purposes to do it, must of necessity love GOD more than himself, because he finds more Objects for his Love in GOD, than in himself; GOD being infinitely more excellent than he. But if this seem a grievous task, it is not a matter of *Severity,* but *Kindness.* We mistake its nature, the Duty does not spring from any disorder in GOD, not from any unreasonable or arrogant *Selfishness,* as base and foolish men are apt to imagine, but from his Excellency: it *naturally* springeth from the greatness of his *Worth:* And it is our *freedom,* when we see his infinite Beauty, to love it as it *deserveth.* When we so do, we shall infinitely love it *more* than our selves: because it is infinitely *better:* And indeed, shall find it so conveniently seated in the Deity for us, that could it be transposed or remov'd, it would no where else be fit for our fruition. It is that eternal act of Love and Goodness that made all the Kingdom of Glory for us: that Care and Providence that governs all Worlds for our Perfection, that infinite and eternal Act that gave us our Being. That Beauty is it self the Deity, and wherever it appeareth there GOD is. The GOD-HEAD is the Beauty in which we are all made perfect. And because we *were* nothing, we must be infinitely pleased that he *is* Eternal; because it is his eternal Act that gives us a Being: and the Act, Oh how Divine! It is his Beauty and Glory. Can we chuse but love that Act, which is all Goodness and Bounty! Which prepares for, and gives to, us, infinite felicity! If we love our selves we must needs love it, for we cannot forbear to love the fountain of all our delights, and the more we love it, the more ardently we delight in it, the sweeter and more transporting will all our Raptures be, the more feeling and lively, the more divine and perfect will our Souls and our Joyes be: When we know GOD, we cannot but love him more than our selves: and when we do so, his Blessedness and Glory will be more than ours; we shall be more than Deified, because in him we shall find all our Perfection, and be eternally Crowned. We must of necessity sit in his Throne, when we see him enjoying all his Glory, because his Glory is his Goodness to us, and his Blessedness our Felicity: Because in the acts of our Understanding we shall eternally be with him, and infinitely be satisfied in all his Fruitions. That Excellency which obliges us, will enable us to love him more than our selves: and while we delight in him for our own sakes, we shall steal insensibly into a more divine and deeper Delight, we shall love him for his. And even in point of Gratitude adore his Glory.

TO *Adore* and *Maligne* are opposite things: to *Envy* and *Adore* are inconsistent. Self-love is apt to leap at all advantages, and the more we love our selves, the more prone we are to covet and wish whatsoever we see Great and Excellent in another. But he hath conquered our Envy by his infinite Bounty: and made us *able* to adore him by the Perfection of his Essence. To covet the Perfections of him we adore, is impossible. It is impossible to adore him whom we would spoil, and rob of his Perfections. For Adoration is a joyful acknowledgment of the infinite Perfections of an *Adorable* Object, resting sweetly in them with acquiescence and rejoycing. It is prone to add and to offer more. An adoring Soul is in the act of sacrificing it self to the Deity, and with infinite Complacency admiring and adoring all his Glories.

HIS Glories will be inspired into the Soul it self, for the healing of that Envy to which it is otherwise addicted. And instead of Robbery, and Discontentment, and Blasphemy, and Covetousness, the Soul shall be full of Honour and Gratitude, and Complacency: and be glad to see its GOD the full and eternal act of Perfection and Beauty. It was from all eternity impossible there should be any other but he; and he from all eternity has so infinitely obliged us, that were it possible for any other to have been, it would not be desirable. He hath obliged us, and we love him better than any other. Should we fancy or conceive another, a Power from all Eternity acting, should we suppose it possible that a Power besides him might have bin; it must be just such a Power as this is, and act just in such a manner as this hath done: or it would be displeasing. This hath done all that we can desire, all that all Powers infinite and eternal can do *well:* and therefore all possible Powers are conceived in him. He is the full and adæquate object of all Desire; because the Fountain of all the most Glorious things, and the sole perfect cause of all Enjoyment whatsoever.

CHAP. XXXIII.

The Beauty of Gratitude. Its principal Causes. Amity and Communion are the great effect of its Nature. The true Character of a Grateful Person. GOD's Incommunicable Attributes enjoyed by Gratitude. All Angels and Men are a Grateful Person's Treasures, as they assist him in Praises. He sacrifices all Worlds to the Deity, and supreamly delighteth to see him sitting in the Throne of Glory.

GOD having prepared the way to Gratitude by infusing generous and noble Principles into the Soul, beautified the Exercise of it by divers other provisions, that conspire to make it amiable and delightful. By the one he made it *Possible,* by the other desirable.

ONE of the greatest ornaments of this *Vertue,* is the *Grateful Sence* of Benefits received: For in it the Felicity of the Receiver consisteth; on it his Grateful Behaviour dependeth; by it he is made *Grateful,* or *Acceptable;* and it is one of the great Ends intended in the Gift bestowed by the Donor, whose Satisfaction ought to be regarded highly by every honest and worthy Receiver. That Grateful Sence is the crown of the Gift, the Light wherein its Beauty appears, the Temple of its Honour as it were, the Womb wherein it is conceived, and findeth its life and value perfected.

SHOULD we stand upon the Explication of these, we should have little room for the Fruits and Effects of Gratitude, which are the principal things intended in this Chapter. But in short you may take this account. The greatest Benefits we can receive, are but *Abortive,* or rather turned into *Curses,* without a Grateful acknowledgment of them: All Gifts are but *Carkasses* devoid of Life, unless inspired with that

Sence, which maketh them *Delightful.* For as Causes without Effects
are not Causes; so Blessings, if they Bless not, are falsely reputed Blessings. No Benefits can be Blessings, unless they are *crowned* with our
Complacency. They must be conceived in the Mind before they can
be transformed into Joy, and be transformed into Joyes before they
can produce those Praises which are the musick of the Benefactors
Soul, as well as of the Receivers. They are not *conceived,* unless they
are *quickened* with the *Life* of the Receiver, nor are they reputed
Blessings, till they are had in *Reputation.* An *interior Sence* is the
Life and Soul of every Blessing: without which a whole World of
Delights would be but a *Chaos,* the very Kingdom of Heaven but
a Confusion to him for whom it is prepared, and a Soul among the
Angels but a *Fool* in Paradice. An Ungrateful Person bereaves himself
of the Pleasure, that should spring from his Enjoyment, for he stifles
the enjoyment of the Gift he receiveth. He *Eclipses* and extinguishes
his own blessedness by the *dulness* of his Soul, and the perverseness
of his Behaviour. He may be surrounded with *Causes* of Delight, but
is not blessed, that is not full of the *Joyes* wherewith he is surrounded.
When he is full of Joyes he must needs overflow with Complacencies;
which are the very element of Thanksgiving, the matter and fuel, as
well as the Soul of Praises. Were there nothing in a Grateful Sence
but this, Gratitude were an incomparable Vertue, because all the effects
of infinite and eternal Bounty are by vertue of that Grace applyed
to the Soul, and enjoyed thereby, but are lost without it. That certainly
must be a great Vertue, by force of which we inherit all things.

AS for the Beauty of the Receiver, it is evident that a *dull* and
heavy Complexion is the disgrace of his Nature. His Stupidity makes
him a worthless piece of *Clay,* that cannot be improved to any advantage. A carelessness and contempt of Benefits springeth from his
Sottishness, which maketh him *Ingrateful,* that is, *Odious:* because
he cannot be won by Kindness, nor wrought upon by Gifts. But he
is more deformed, because he acts in a bruitish manner, *against Reason;*
while he faileth to do what is fit and proper on such occasions. It
is a base and dirty Temper that cannot be enflamed with the Love
of a Benefactor. It is incapable of high and generous *Sentiments;* is
dull and dry, insipid and untractable, as dead as a Log of Wood,
a crabbed and knotty piece of matter, that cannot be wrought, and
only fit for the fire! But a quick and lively Perceiver, a tender Sence,
and sprightly Intelligence, is all honour and delight upon the Reception,
all activity, life, and vigour, Angelical in his nature, sweet and

heavenly; apt to come up to the Benefactor, and answer his desires: He is rich and abundant in amiable Resentments, and prone to make Returns suitable to the Kindness wherewith he is affected. He has a strange kind of Beauty lodged in his Soul; there is a sweet Correspondence, and a delicate Convenience between his Nature and his Benefactors. All his Inclinations are Purity and Praise, he is a great encouragement to the Love of his Benefactor, an ornament to his Person, an admirer of his Worth, an appendix of his Honour, and a pleasure to his Disposition; all Life and Goodness. He is capable of Amity in the heights of its exercise.

A wise and worthy Benefactor designs the felicity and contentment of the Person, to whom he imparteth his Bounties: and if he were able, would do that for him, which above all other things is most to be desired; not *compel* him to be Grateful, whether he would or no; for that would but spoil the beauty of his Return, but make him capable of the best and highest Resentments; that he might have the Joy of seeing his Benefits work kindly. All which are lost and thrown away upon an ungrateful Person. This GOD hath done. He has put brave Principles and Inclinations into the Soul of Man, and left him freely to exert them, with infinite desire to see him act freely, but generously and nobly. For by this means only, is he made capable of Honour, and the essence of Gratitude consists in the freedom of its operation. Having so made him, and desiring nothing more than a lovely Behaviour, his Joy is as great as his Goodness can inspire, when he sees that sweetness which attends the Operation and the work of Reason, in a Grateful Person; and the Joy which he occasions is his own Joy, in the Soul of his Creature. Of which to rob GOD is a kind of *Spiritual Sacriledge,* and a cruel Murther committed on our selves. For we have an inclination to delight in the Joyes, of which we are the Authors, and by a kind of Eccho, or reflection, find the Pleasure doubled which we take, and which is taken in the communication of our Bounties. And in this there is founded a certain sympathy of Delight, which carries us to feel and be affected with anothers Joy, and makes *it* an Object, and a Cause of ours, nay almost the very Form and Essence of ours, when we are the Authors of it. A Grateful Soul holds Intelligence with GOD; as it receives his *Bounties,* it delights in his *Complacencies.*

THE great effect of Obligation and Gratitude, is Amity and Communion. A Grateful Soul is deeply concerned in the Honour of his Benefactor; in his Benefactors Pleasure, Life, and Safety, in all his

Successes, Prosperities, Advancements; in all his Felicity and Glory! He is afflicted in all his Afflictions, he is delighted in all his Enjoyments, he is crowned in all his Promotions, he is wronged and injured in all his Affronts, he is touched with the least Displeasure that can befal him: Nay he is more tender of his Benefactors Repose than his own: The apple of his Eye is the tenderest part in himself, yet he had rather have it touched, than the Person of his Benefactor. No wounds can wound him more than those which his Benefactor receiveth, and he in him. His own wounds may kill his Body, but these destroy his Contentment. A thousand Injuries and Calumnies against himself he can forgive, and is never provoked but when his Friend is offended. He slights himself, and prefers his Benefactor: He would make his Face a Stepping stone to his Benefactors Glory. He exposes his body to Swords, and Spears, and Arrows, for his Benefactors safety: He would rather be torn to pieces, and suffer a thousand Deaths, than permit his Benefactor to be slain or dishonoured. Now all this in time of Trial and distress, would seem disadvantagious. But besides the Obligation, there is a Sence of Honour that compels a man thereunto; and a certain beauty in the act of Gratitude, distinct from the goodness of the Benefit, that is so naturally sweet to the goodness of the Soul, that it is better to die than renounce it. And a certain Baseness on the other side, an odiousness in *Ingratitude* (in the very act) so abominable, that it blasts any Safety and Repose that can be gotten by it.

WHERE the Benefits are small, the Vertue of Gratitude is less powerful and perfect: for its strength depends upon its food and nourishment. A thin and spare diet is not very healthful for it. Though all the benefits that are done upon the Earth by Men to Men are infinitely mean, if compared to those which the Godhead does to the least of his Creatures; yet the World is full of the praise of this Vertue, and an Ingrateful man is the most hateful Object living. Former Ages afford us many rare and glorious Examples of the power of Gratitude, and its sacred Zeal for, and tenderness of its Object. The union between the Body and the Soul is nothing comparable to the union of Love and its Beloved, though the Causes are but slight upon which it is founded. The Soul will often forsake its mansion to dwell with its beloved. It esteems all its beauties and Members only for its Beloveds sake. Yet Colours and Features, a little red and white, a sparkling Eye, a brisk Conversation, and a delectable Humor, are all that breed it, all that produce this mighty effect, this prodigy of Nature. There is something more, where the Life and Honour of a man has been saved, by the kindness of a Benefactor: especially if he be rich and amiable that has delivered us. If he be great and honourable that was the Author of the benefit, the obligation is the greater. For the Worth of the Person enters into the nature of the act, and enhances its value. Yet all this put together is exceeded by the Gratitude of a worthy Soul, because his own Worth inclines him to be more *Generous* than the Cause requires, and to magnifie the benefit, by the mighty addition of his own goodness. It is the natural property of Goodness to communicate it self, any occasion of doing it, is instead of a Cause. But when there is a Cause, it is like a spark to Powder, it enkindles a flame in his *Inclination*. All acts of Gratitude have a great deal of sweetness in their own nature, and for the sake of that beauty which is seated in themselves will not be rigorous and exact in their proportions, since it is a beautiful thing to exceed in Goodness. Its own disposition prompts it to do more than is deserved by the Kindness it receives, and if not to conceive it self more obliged than it is, yet to be more honourable in its Returns, than the meer goodness of its Benefactor can exact; because it conceives it self by its own Vertue obliged to be Noble and Munificent, in all its acknowledgments.

BUT however slow Gratitude may be in the Returns which it maketh for smaller benefits, it is infinitely prone to exceed all measure, when it is *infinitely* obliged. Praises are not fed by mean Contentments, but by sublime ones. The acknowledgment is cool, where the benefits are small; and the Contentments imperfect, where they are limited and restrained. Full Satisfaction hath another kind of influence on the Soul of Man, than single Kindnesses, or some few particular Supplies. An infinite Bliss produces more vigorous and joyful efforts, than bare Acknowledgments. Here upon Earth there are disquiets, and desires, and expectations, and Complaints, and defects, and imperfections, fears and interests to be still secured, that lame and darken our Contentment and Gratitude. But in Heaven all these admixtures of alloy are remov'd. The glory of the light in which our Gratitude appeareth, adds lustre and beauty to the increase of its Perfection. In the utmost height of our Satisfaction there is such an infinite and eternal *force,* that our Gratitude breaks out in exulting and triumphing Effusions; all our Capacities, Inclinations, and Desires being fully satisfied, we have nothing else to do, but to Love and be Grateful. An infinite and eternal Kingdom given to him that was taken out of Nothing, by a King that is infinite in greatness and beauty; all his Joyes, and all his Treasures! It makes the Soul a fountain of Delights, whose nature is to receive no more, but overflow for ever. When the Soul cometh once to love GOD so infinitely above it self, as the cause requireth, its only delight is to magnifie him and to see him blessed. The beauty and sweetness of its own Gratitude is as rich and divine as all *his* Gifts. It is tempted here infinitely more to exceed its Causes than ever before. Amazements, Admirations, Affections, Praises, Hallelujahs, Raptures, Extasies, and Blessings are all its delights: The pleasure of Loving is its only business; it is turned all into flame, and brightness, and transportation, and excess. It infinitely passes Light and Fire in quickness and motion: all Impediments are devoured, and GOD alone is its Life and Glory. The more Great, the more high, the more excellent he is; the more blessed is it self, the more joyful, and the more contented. Its Nature is to shine, and burn, and admire; to offer, and to sacrifice up it self to its Joyes: And GOD is its soveraign Joy, its perfect happiness. To suspend its beams were to act against Nature. All overtures of Pleasure, Beauty, Glory, Power, Exaltation and Honour it would have added to its happiness. The more Great, the more Good, the Wiser GOD is, the greater is its Happiness. The more he is admired and praised, the greater is its Happiness. The more he is magnified and pleased, the greater is its Happiness. All the Excellencies and Perfections in its Objective bliss, though they are not locally removed, are removed into the Soul of him that enjoyes it; and there express themselves far more powerfully and effectually, than if they were there alone. No joy can be like that of seeing its Creatour adored, no Service like that of magnifying its Beloved, no pleasure like that of delighting its Beloved, no melody like that of praising its Benefactor, no honour like that of obeying its Preserver. All Worlds are its Treasures, because they manifest his Power and Glory; all Angels and Men its Delights, because they see and acknowledge the beauty of its Soveraign, and eternal *Perfection;* all Creatures the Instruments of its Joy, that celebrate his Praises! In him it enjoyes the glory of all Eternity, the infinite beauty of all Immensity, the innumerable riches of all Worlds, the pleasures and adorations of all the Angels, the state and magnificence of all Empires, the splendour and perfection of all Ages; all which it has in it self, by his infinite Bounty, as its own immediate and proper Possessions; but far more divinely and sweetly enjoyes them, by vertue of its Gratitude and Love, to him, whose they originally are, and from whom they proceeded. For the very true reason why it enjoyes *it self,* and all its *own* Treasures, is because it loves *it self:* And the more it loves *him,* the more it will be delighted with *his* fruitions. It is more concerned, it feels more, it sees more, it tastes more, it possesses more, it rejoyces more in its Object than it self. The imagination and fancy that is in Love frames all the thoughts of its Beloved, in it self; it has an exquisite and tender sence of every change and motion in the mind of its Beloved. *Stir not up, nor awake my Love, till he please,* is the song of a feeling and affectionate Soul. Every prick with a Needles point in its Object, is a stab with a Dagger to it self. Its heart bleeds in every drop of its Objects finger. It loves his Beloved ten thousand times more than it self: and is infinitely more pleased with its exaltation, than its own. The happiness of its Object is most its own. True Gratitude is crowned in its Benefactor, enthroned in its benefactor, admired in its benefactor, adored in its benefactor. Nothing in all the World is so easily ravished as Love, nothing is so lively as Love, nothing so lovely! Nothing so violent in its grief or joy, nothing so capable of pain or pleasure: All the Victories and Triumphs of its Saviour are its own. My Joy, my Life, my Crown, my Glory; my exceeding great Reward, my Love, my Soul, my Idol, nay the GOD of my Soul! My All in all! This is the language of Love in its Rapture. Seraphick Love! It is Altar, Heart and Sacrifice, Angelical Love! It is Priest and Temple: All Service, Freedom, Duty, Reward, Desire, Enjoyment, Honour, Praise, Adoration, Thanksgiving, Extasie, Pleasure, Bliss and Happiness. It is all Goodness and Beauty, Paradice, Heaven; the life and Soul of Heaven! All that is incommunicable in GOD, Eternity, almighty Power, supream Dominion, independent Majesty, infinite Immensity, with all the adorations and praises of all the Creatures, are by such a Love and Gratitude enjoyed. Loving GOD more than it self, it is more happy in GOD, than if it were a GOD. Could his Deity be taken away, and seated in it self, the Soul of a Grateful Creature would be grieved at the exchange. Even GOD in his place is perfectly enjoyed. All Envy is by perfect Gratitude removed: All Discontentment at any thing in its Object, especially at its Objects Blessedness is abolished. It is carried above all Thrones, Dominions and Powers, and still ascends eternally higher, the higher its Object is exalted. Could it be miserable in it self, it would be happy in its Object: but the higher it is exalted, the more is its Creatour delighted. If the resentment be wholly Spiritual, the Soul perhaps may be transformed to Gratitude, as Gratitude is to Contentment, and Praise, and Thanksgiving. But it will have no Body, no frail and corruptible Flesh, no bones or members to look after. All its operations are of one kind, all its works and concernments are the same. It has no Fear, or Care to divert it; no impediment, or danger, or distraction. Pure Gratitude is so divine a thing, that the Soul may safely wish to be turned *all* into Gratitude. Its Employment and Nature are all one, acknowledgment and benevolence united together. It sacrifices all Worlds to the Deity, and with infinite delight desires to offer all Honour and Glory to him. It is very sensible, that it can never pay so much Honour to GOD as is his due, unless it be assisted with all the Tongues of Men and Angels. It goes along with their Joyes, and consents to their Praises. In them it adores, and by them it admires, with them it conspires, and takes in all their powers and divine affections. It sees with all their Eyes, hears with all their Ears, speaks with all their Mouths, and useth all their Hearts in loving and adoring. All the tendencies and operations of Universal Nature are subservient to its desires. It surmounts the Songs of *David,* and yet we know how earnestly he exhorted all Creatures to praise him. *Praise ye the Lord: Praise him in the Sanctuary; Praise him in the Firmament of his Power; Praise him in his mighty Acts; Praise him according to his excellent Greatness. Praise him in the Heights; Praise him all ye Angels; Praise him all his Hosts: Praise him Sun and Moon, Praise him all ye Stars of light. Praise him ye Heaven of Heavens!* And when all is done, it still confesseth, that *his Name is exalted far above all Blessing and Praise.*

HE that praiseth GOD only for his Health, and Food, and Rayment, and for his blessing on his Calling (as too many only do) either is very ignorant, or upon a strict scrutiny, will be detected for upbraiding GOD, for the meanest of his bounty. For his Love must infinitely be defective, that is able to bestow Gifts infinitely more, yet giveth us none but these. He that sees not more Causes of Joy than these, is blind and cannot see afar off: The very truth of Religion is obscure to him, and the cause of Adoration unknown. He wanteth ten thousand demonstrations of the Love of GOD, and as many Incentives to enflame his Soul in the Return of Love, that is unacquainted with these high and mighty bounties. No man can return more Blessings than he receiveth: nor can his Praises exceed the number (and greatness) of his Joyes. A House is too little, a Kingdom is too narrow for a Soul to move in. The World is a confinement to the power, that is able to see Eternity, and conceive the Immensity of Almighty GOD! He that can look into infinite Spaces, must see them all full of delights, or be infinitely displeased. How like an Angel doth he soar aloft, how divine is his life, how glorious and heavenly; that doth converse with infinite and eternal Wisdom, intermeddle with all the delights of GOD, assume the similitude of his knowledge and goodness, make all his Works his Riches, his Laws his Delights, his Counsels his Contemplations, his Wayes his Joyes, and his Attributes his Perfections! He that appropriates all the World, and makes it his own peculiar is like unto GOD, meet to be his Son, and fit to live in Communion with him. The Kingdom of GOD is made visible to him to whom all Kingdoms are so many Mansions of Joy, and all Ages but the streets of his own City. The man that sees all Angels and Men his Fellow-members, and the whole Family of GOD in Heaven and Earth, his own Domesticks, is fit for Heaven. As he hath more encouragements to believe in GOD, and to delight in him, so hath he more concerns to engage his fear, more allurements to provoke his desire, more incentives to enflame his love, and more obligations to compel his obedience: More arguments to strengthen his Hope, more materials to feed his Praises, more Causes to make him Humble, more fuel for Charity to others, more grounds of Contentment in himself, more helps to inspire him with Fortitude, more rewards to quicken his Industry, more engagements to Circumspection and Prudence, more ballast to make him Stable, more lights to assist his Knowledge, more sails to forward his Motion, more employments in which to spend his Time, more attractives to Meditation, and more entertainments to enrich his Solitude. He hath more aids to confirm his Patience, more avocations from Injuries to Meekness, more wings to carry him above the World, and more Gates to let him into Heaven. He hath more *Withholders* to keep him from Sin, more aggravations to increase his Guilt, more odious deformities in every Vice, more waters to augment his Tears, more motives to Repentance, and more Consolations upon his Reconciliation: More hopes to relieve his Prayer, more bounds to secure his Prosperity, more comforts in Adversity, and more Hallelujah's in all Estates: More delights to entertain his Friends, more sweetness in his Conversation, more arts to conquer his Enemies, more Feasts in abstemious Fasts, more and better sawce than other at his Feasts, innumerable Companions night and day, in Health, in Sickness, in Death, in Prison; at his Table, in his Bed, in his Grove, in his Garden, in the City, in the Field, in his Journy, in his Walk, at all times, and in all places. He hath more antidotes against Temptation, more weapons in his Spiritual Warfare, more balsom for his Wounds, and more preservatives against the contagion of Worldly Customs. From this Spring of *Universal Fruition* all the streams of Living Waters flow that refresh the Soul. Upon this Hing all a mans Interests turn, and in this Centre all his Spiritual Occasions meet. It is the great Mystery of Blessedness and Glory, the Sphere of all Wisdom, Holiness and Piety, the great and ineffable Circumstance of all Grace and Vertue, the Magazine and Store-house of all Perfection.

An APPENDIX.

Of Enmity and Triumph: Of Schism and Heresie, Fidelity, Devotion, Godliness. Wherein is declared, how Gratitude and Felicity inspire and perfect all the Vertues.

I Should here have ended all my discourse on Vertue, had it not been necessary to speak something of our Enemies. Since there was never any man so Wise but he had some, it is not to be expected that the most Vertuous Man living should be altogether without them. *Moses,* and *David,* and *Elijah,* and *Daniel* had Enemies, so had our Lord Jesus Christ himself. *Joseph* had some in his younger daies, and *Solomon* some in his Old age: Of all the Prophets I find *Samuel* the most clear and exempted from them. But this I observe, that Men of great and transcendent Principles, of staid and well-govern'd Passions, of meek and condescending Behaviours, highly kind and serviceable in their Age, free from the spots and blemishes of the World, have frequently arrived to an universal Applause and Honour, and moved in a sphere so high above the Nation in which they lived, that as if they had been Creatures of another World, they have enjoyed a Veneration above their Degree, and been surrounded with a repose, that makes them look like Angels in a kind of Heaven; that that Heaven which they enjoyed upon Earth, was the Work, and the Reward, and the Crown of Vertue. Thus *Moses* after his long Meekness, and invincible Fidelity to the *Jewish* Nation, was in the close of his life most exceedingly honour'd by all the People, and lamented after his death by a million of Persons, that felt the disastre of so great a loss. *Joseph* suffered much by the Envy of his Brethren in the beginning, and the Lust and Slander of his Mistress. But after he had once been the Saviour of the Land of *Egypt,* and of his Fathers Family, his Vertue being known, he enjoyed a long life of Glory and Honour, and of the abundance of his own peace and tranquility, communicated a repose and prosperity to his Nation. *Joshua* did run the hazard of being stoned for crossing the perverse humour of the *Jews,* when he returned from searching the Land of *Canaan:* but from *Moses*'s death, throughout all his life afterwards was an absolute Prince among his own People, and a glorious Victor over all their Enemies. *Samuel* was from his Infancy chosen of GOD, and from *Dan* even to *Beersheba* they knew he was established to be a Prophet of the Lord. The honour of his Communion with Heaven joyned with his great Integrity and Gravity on Earth, gave him a Reputation that made him Greater than all the Elders in the Land. And it is very apparent, that the eminent Holiness, and Goodness, and great Wisdom of these Men made them to prevail, with GODS blessing on their Vertues, and to reign like Benefactors, and magnificent Patriots of their Country. *Solomon* was by his Wisdom exceeding glorious, till he revolted from GOD: and those Mischiefs which befel *David* after he came to the Throne did spring from his Fall in the matter of *Urias.* These things I note to encourage Men to Vertue. For though our Lord Jesus Christ, and his Apostles, were persecuted to the Death, yet two things are very considerable: First, that their Glory surmounted the Rage of all their Enemies, and continues immortally shining throughout all Kingdoms and Ages: Next, That they were born to troublesome Times, and were to break the Ice for all their Followers. For their business was extraordinary, to change the state and condition of Kingdoms, to alter the publick Rites of Religion both among *Jews* and *Gentiles,* and therein to shake and dissettle the Secular Interests of Millions, as well as to touch and offend the Conscience, in defaming that for which so many Ages had so great a Veneration. This created all the difficulty in their Lives. But where the publick Rites of Religion are approved, and a Man is born in peaceable and quiet Times, I do not see but the most Vertuous Men inherit all the Honour and Esteem of the People, and whatever estate and degree they are of, reign in the fullest and freest Prosperity. Nor has the Death of Christ so little prevailed upon Earth, but that all the World does now take notice of the Glory of his Doctrine, and far better understand the excellency of Vertue than they did before: They feel and admire its influences. Insomuch that as some Vertuous Men grow contemptible by their Vices; so do the most debauched and vicious Men, find a Necessity of appearing Vertuous, if they mean to be Honourable; for as all Errours receive their strengths from some Truths professed by Hereticks, so do all Vices and vicious Persons owe their supports to the powerful strengths of those Vertues on which

they lean, and which they use (though in a wicked manner) for their
own security. For they cannot rise and thrive in the World without
some Vertue, or shew of Vertue at least, to cover and help out their
Vices. Three things I desire you to note seriously, when you have first
observed, that it is a very hard matter to hate an Excellent Man,
or contemn him, when he is known. The one is, that Enmities and
Disgraces are like the pangs and throws of the New-Birth, they fall
like Storms and Showers upon budding Vertues in their spring and
greeness: When a Man first begins to be Vertuous he is despised, suspected, unknown; he may be censured and hated: But when he has
made himself eminent and conspicuous, is a man of tried and approved
Vertue, well known for a Person of Honour and Worth; the first Envies
and Censures abate; and if he constantly exercise all Honesty and
Goodness with great activity, courage, and prudence, he shall conquer
all his Enemies, and inherit the benefit of his own Vertues in the peace
and tranquility of his happy Condition. Note also, that it is not so
much the Malignity of the World, as some Vice of the Proficient,
or some occasion that Religious men give the World to blaspheme
Religion by some Infirmity or other, that makes them to be hated.
And this I note, because I would have you not cry out of other Mens
Corruptions, so much as of your own. There is a little Pride, or Covetousness, or Laziness, or Scorn, or Anger, or Revenge, some one Deformity or other, that gives Men advantage against us, when they deride
at our Profession: but under the Name and Notion of Vertue no Man
was ever yet upbraided. As a Fool perhaps, and a Coward (but not
as a Wise and gallant Man) he may be scorned. Thirdly, Some Secular
Interest may put People together by the Ears, but no Man is hated
for being perfectly Vertuous. Misapprehensions, Slanders, Injuries,
Quarrels about Estates and Possessions may arise; but where the Land
is at peace, and the True Religion established, no Man is hated for
being Wise, and Good, and Holy, and Chaste, and Just, and Liberal,
and Honest, and Merciful, and Meek, and Couragious, but the more
admired for being Holy and Blessed, when he joyns all GODS Vertues
together. A man may be perverse and turbulent, a Schismatick* and
a Heretick, and by a rash and erroneous Zeal bring many Enemies
and Penalties on himself, while he rails against the Magistrates, and
reviles the Bishops and Pastours of the Church, breaks the Laws, and
disturbs the Kingdom, prophanes and blasphemes GODS publick Worship, and endeavours to overthrow the established Religion and Disci-

* *Of Hereticks and Schismaticks.*

pline among us. But all the Troubles which a man brings on himself by any such means as these, are not to be fathered on Vertue, but rightly to be ascribed to their proper Causes. Had he that suffered them been more Vertuous, he had been less miserable. And truly this I may say for the glory of Christianity, Where it is freely and purely Professed in any Nation or Kingdom (as at present in Ours) a Man may be as divine and heavenly as an Angel. And if he be Liberal, and Kind, and Humble, and Cheerful, especially if withal he be Undaunted and Couragious, most exceedingly Honest and Faithful in his dealings; the more Holy and Divine he is, the more he is commended and valued in the Land: but if he have any *flaw,* the greater stir he makes in Religion, the more he is hated. He loses his Credit, and undergoes the Censure of a supercilious Hypocrite.

AS for all the Enemies which Strife and Contention about Worldly Goods occasion to a Vertuous Man, he is no more liable to them than other persons: And yet when he meets them, he has far more advantages over his Enemies than other Men. For being full of Courage, he dares do any thing that is fit against them, and that sparkle of the Lion makes them to dread him: whereas a Coward is baffled and run over in a moment. Being full of Temper and Humility, he is not apt to exasperate them, and make them mad, as hot and angry Spirits are apt to do. By Kindness he obliges, and wins, and softens them: By Prudence he knows how to manage them, and all his other Vertues come in as so many strengths against them. Being Just he never quarrels but in a *Good Cause;* being Good and Merciful, he is not apt to make an Enemy: Being Wise and Holy his Soul is in another World, and it is no trivial Injury that can make him *contend:* Being Liberal and Magnanimous he is prone to do Heroical things, and to make himself Venerable to his very Adversary: And above all to tender and to love his Soul, and to steer all the Contention to both their benefit. We rail on the World when the fault is in our selves. The most of Men professing Vertue are but Children in Worth; very weak, and very defective: And too timorous too, GOD knows. They neither trust GOD enough, nor carry Vertue to the height. Vertue is base and not Vertue, while it is remiss: It never shineth gloriously and irresistibly, till it be acted almost in a *desperate* manner. He only is the *Great* Man, that contemns Danger, Life, and Death, and all the World, that he may be supreamly and compleatly Vertuous.

ENEMIES may sometimes spring from Envy. And indeed there alone lies the Core of the Matter: when some Men imperfectly Vertuous, abhor others for being more Excellent than themselves; at least for being more Honoured, and more Prosperous. Here again Temporal Interest is the ground of the Enmity. For thus our Saviour was hated by the Scribes and Pharisees. *Pilate* knew that they delivered him for Envy. But the main pretext and Cause of his Condemnation, was the Testimony of those that heard him say, *He would destroy the Temple.* Without which, and his imputed *Blasphemy* they could hardly have killed him. But he came to die, and was the less solicitous. Where these publick Cases are away: They that envy Vertuous Men are generally Men of equal rank and degree with themselves; but a Man truly Vertuous will out-strip them, as far as a Swallow will a Snail; all his Inferiours, and all his Superiours that understand him, and the most also of his Equals, and all they too, if he invents wayes and methods to oblige them, will at last be won to confess and acknowledge him. But in the mean time he grows, and thrives, and enjoyes their very Enmity. He never speaks ill of them behind their backs. He is not a jot discouraged, nor exasperated, he pities *their* Weakness, and is humble under the sence perhaps of his *own:* He is careful to give them no advantage against him: He confides in GOD, and strengthens himself in hope of Divine assistance: He rejoyces exceedingly that he has the opportunity of Forgiving, and considers how many Vertues he has to exercise upon that Occasion. It makes him to exult, when he considers that these Enemies are the Instruments and Materials of his greater Glory. He foresees the Victory, and delights in the Triumph. And besides all this, He is obliged by Jesus Christ to forgive greater Wrongs than these, and gladly yields some Trials of his Obedience: He has an infinite felicity in daily View, and remembers he is a Pilgrim in a strange Country. He is dead to the World, and alive unto GOD. The Moon is beneath his feet, and so are all fickle and transitory things. He is cloathed with the Sun, and walketh in the Light, environed with the beams of his own Enjoyments. If his Enemy be able to do him a Mischief; (which to a man perfectly Vertuous seldome happens) he turns it into Good, which a Foolish and a Vicious Man cannot do: He sinks not under it, but plunges out again, and surmounts it altogether: immediately forgives it, and can after cheerfully serve his Enemy. For his part he will be an Enemy to no man in the World. He knows his Duty and his Master: the value of Souls, and the excellency of Vertue: His very Gratitude to GOD and Jesus Christ is enough to make him go through a thousand greater and more terrible brunts than these.

I would not have Men ingrateful to Jesus Christ; nor blind to themselves. I know very well that the Age is full of Faults, and lament it: but withal I know, it is full of Advantages. As Sin abounds, so does Grace also super-abound. Never so much clear Knowledge in any Age: Learned Ministers, multitudes of Sermons, excellent Books, translated Bibles, studious Gentlemen, multitudes of Schollers, publick Liberty, Peace and Safety: all great and eminent Blessings. There were many disorders in the Church of *Corinth,* and yet the Apostle tells them of their *Reigning,* and wishes, Would to GOD he did reign with them! after their City had a little flourished in peace, and received Religion: and makes his Comparison between them and himself after such a manner, that when it is considered, it would make one apt to think the Reigning of the Saints, which is spoken of in the Book of the *Revelations,* were either now *present* or already *past. Now ye are full* (saith he*) *now ye are rich, ye have reigned as Kings without us, and I would to GOD ye did reign, that we also might reign with you. For I think GOD hath set forth us the Apostles last, as it were appointed to Death: for we are made a spectacle to the World, and to Angels, and to Men: We are fools for Christs sake, but ye are wise in Christ; we are weak, but ye are strong: Ye are honourable, but we are despised. Even to this present hour we both hunger and thirst, and are naked, and are buffeted, and have no certain dwelling place.* A small matter will make a Saint to Reign, by reason of the greatness of his interior Bliss. If he be not buffetted and cast out of doors; having Food and Rayment, with his Godliness it is *Great Gain.* Especially when Kings and Princes *yield a professed Subjection to the Gospel of Christ.* For then *all the Kingdoms of the World become the Kingdoms of the Lord, and of his Christ:* When the Cross is exalted above the Crown, and the Kings Palaces surmounted by the magnificence of our Saviours Temple, and there is no Idolatry nor Poyson in the Church, but a pure publick worship, when the very Laws and Magistrates countenance Religion, and those Apostles that were once persecuted and cast out as Vile, are now glorified and admired for their Sanctity. Men may be Christians publickly and in the face of the Sun, it is horrible ingratitude to be unsensible of the advantage, to calumniate, and reproach, and disturb the Church, as if it were a sink of *Paganisme.* Rather we should admire and adore GOD Almighty, *that other men laboured, and we are entered upon their Labours.* We inherit the blood, and toyl, and sweat of the Martyrs,

* 1 Cor. 4.

they bore the burthen and heat of the day, and we enjoy the victory
and the peace they acquired. This is one, but not one of the least
of GODS Mercies for which we should be Grateful.

THAT all the business of Religion on GODS part is Bounty, Gratitude on ours, and that this Gratitude is the sphere of all Vertue and
Felicity, easily is discerned after the first intimation. Gratitude is all
that is to be expressed here upon Earth, and above in Heaven. All
our Complacencies in his infinite Highness, all our Delights in his eternal Praises, all our Adorations, Extasies, and Offerings, all our Joyes
and Thanksgivings, are but the Feathers and the Wings of that
Seraphim in Glory. All the Acknowledgment, and Faith, and Hope,
and Repentance, all the Obedience and Resignation of a Sinner upon
Earth, all his Care and fear to offend, all his Desire and Endeavour
to please, all his Worship and Charity, all his Courage, and Perseverance, and Patience, all his Fidelity, Devotion, and Godliness, are but
Gratitude in several dresses, as Time, Place, and Occasion require.
Sermons are to inform and assist our Gratitude, Sacraments to revive
and exercise its vertue. Vertues themselves are our Aids to bring us
thereunto. Upon Sabbaths it enjoyes a Rest, that hath something in
it of Heaven; and it is a hard matter to be wicked in the Sanctuary.
But in ordinary Conversation, in Shops and Taverns, in the Camp,
in the Navy, at a Feast, or in a Journey, to retain the Sence of all
Mercies, and to carry all these Vertues and Graces about a Man,
is not ordinary for a Common Christian. But that which does realize
our Gratitude, and make it perfect, is a true Fidelity to GOD and
our selves, which is an acquired habit, or a Grace infused, by vertue
of which we keep all those Promises which we made to GOD in our
holy Meditations, and all those holy Resolves which in our best Retirements we put upon our selves to do his Will, even in the midst of
all Assaults and Temptations. It is a Vertue by which we remain Constant in all Persecutions and Allurements; not warping, or moving
aside on any Consideration; neither melting with Pleasures, not flinch-
ing at Distresses; but continuing *faithful to the death, that we may
obtain the Crown of Life.* He certainly that sees himself a King of
all Worlds, and Brother to our Lord JESUS CHRIST (who hath
said, *He that doth the will of my Father, is my Mother, Sister, and
Brother:*) will not be wrought on to forsake or hazard so great a
Bliss. His knowledge of its Perfection will animate his Soul with all
Fidelity.

IT will draw him from the World too, and make him desire to

be much alone, that he may be much with GOD. A Covetous man will be telling his Monies, an Ambitious man aspires to be alwaies near the Kings Person, an Epicure is for his Wine, or Women, or Feasts continually. A Vertuous man is more Covetous, more Ambitious, more prone to Celestial Epicurisme, if I may so speak, than all the World besides: And so art thou, if thou art really engaged in the study of Felicity. A Pious man has greater Treasures, higher Honours, more pure Pleasures, sincerer and truer Delights, a more glorious Friend than all the Earth beside. Why should we not enjoy him, why should we not retire to adore him, why not delight in Devotion and Communion with him? There a Man is to feed by sweet Contemplation on all his Felicities: He is there to pray for open Eyes, and a pure Heart, that he may see GOD. There thou art to exercise thy strengths, and acquaint thy self with him, to look into all Ages and Kingdoms, to consider and know thy self, to expaciate in the Eternity and Immensity of GOD, and to gain that GODLINESS, which with real Contentment is *Great Gain.* There thou art to stir up thy self, *by way of pure Remembrance,* to recollect thy scattered and broken Thoughts, and to cloath thy self with all thy necessary Perfections.

FOR Godliness is a kind of *GOD-LIKENESS,* a divine habit, or frame of Soul, that may fitly be accounted *The fulness of the stature of the Inward Man.* In its least degree, it is an Inclination to be Like GOD, to Please him, and to Enjoy him. He is *GOD-LIKE* that is high and serious in all his Thoughts, humble and condescending in all his Actions, full of love and good-will to all the Creatures, and bright in the knowledge of all their Natures. He delights in all the Works of GOD, and walks in all the Wayes of GOD, and meditates on all the Commandements of GOD, and covets all the Treasures of GOD, and breaths after all his Joyes! He that hates all that *GOD* hates, and desires all that *GOD* desires, and loves all that *GOD* loves, and delights in all his delights, is *GODLY:* He that aspires to the same End, by the same Means, and forms himself willingly to the same Nature. Every Like in Nature draweth to its Like, the Beautiful, and the Wise, and the Good, and the Aged; but especially the *GOD-Like.* There is more reason why they should delight in each other. They have more Attractives and Incentives. *GODLINESS,* or *GOD-LIKENESS* is the cement of Amity between *GOD* and *MAN.* Eternity and Immensity are the sphere of his Activity, and are often frequented, and filled with his Thoughts. Nothing less than the Wisdom of *GOD* will please the *GOD-LIKE Man:* Nothing less content him, than the

Blessedness and Glory of his Great Creatour. He must enjoy GOD, or he cannot enjoy himself. That is, he must rest satisfied in him, as the Creatour, the Lawgiver, the Lord and Governour of the World; and for that end must be compleatly satisfied with the Glory and Perfection of all his Works, and Laws, and Wayes. He must delight in all his Counsels, that he may enjoy him as the Great Counsellour of all Nature; and see the Beauty of his Mind, that he may take pleasure in him as the Blessedness of the Angels, the Redeemer of Men, the Sanctifier of his Elect People, and the Soveraign End of all things. He must enjoy him as his own supream and eternal Object, his King, his Father, Bridegroom, Friend, Benefactour, All in all. Which he can never do, till he sees *GOD* to be the best Father, the best King, the best Benefactour, Bridegroom and Friend in all the World: Nor that, till he sees the Beauty of the whole Creation, the great and wonderful things of his Law, the marvellous glory of his All-wise dispensations, the Sacred perfection of his Decrees, and the nature of his Essence: And all these must be as sweet and satisfactory to himself, as they are to the Deity. To be GOD-Like is a very sublime and most glorious Perfection: which no man can attain, that is not either *curiously* satisfied in all these things, or *humbly* confident of their Beauty and Perfection. And for this Cause have we thus written upon all the Vertues, that all that need it, and read the Book may be elevated a little higher than the ordinary Rate, have something more erect and Angelical in their Souls, be brought to the Gates (at least) of GODS Kingdom, and be endued with GODLINESS a little more compleatly by their Care, than hitherto they have been; because they know, both *that GOD is, and is a Rewarder of them that diligently seek him.*

FINIS.

Textual Notes

[The page and line numbers before entries refer to pages and lines in the present text.]

P. 7:30. attaineth the best] Compare the similar emendation (of *"attaineth best"* to *"attaineth the best"*) made in the corresponding chapter summary on p. 65.

P. 8:16. Of what Nature] The phrase ("Of Nature") has been brought into line with the better reading appearing in the corresponding chapter summary on p. 106.

P. 27:24. Vertuous] The uncorrected Cambridge copy reads "Virtuous". Up to this point (sig. D1), Compositor B had spelled "Virtue", "Virtues", and "Virtuous" with an "i" 40% of the time. From this point on (D—Z8^v), he spelled these words with an "i" only 6% of the time. Other spelling tests indicate that a new compositor had not taken over at D1; perhaps the increased frequency of "e" forms in Compositor B's work from this point on indicates a conscious attempt to bring the spelling of these words into line with either the manuscript or Compositor A's spelling (if Compositor A was setting his portion concurrently or had already finished it). Compositor A spelled the words with an "i" only .4% of the time.

P. 38:36. Dammage] The catchword on sig. E5 is "Dam-", but the first unit of letters on sig. E5^v is "mage". A combination of the two yields "Dammage", an acceptable seventeenth-century spelling of "Damage" (*OED*).

P. 47:14. Goodness, and Holiness, and that] The uncorrected British Museum and Cambridge copies read "Goodness, and Bounty, and Holiness, and that"; the sentence just previous to this one contains a similar series: "Beauty and his Holiness, his Bounty and his Godhead". It is possible that the compositor's eye strayed for a moment to that sentence and that he erroneously added "and Bounty," to the second sentence. The eventual deletion of "and Bounty," would seem to indicate, however, a carefulness on the part of a proofreader that most of the rest of the book does not bear out.

P. 48:5. familiarly] The 1675 edition reads "familiary", but the *OED* records the word only once, with the meaning "pertaining to the control of a family" (Milton), a meaning not here pertinent.

P. 54:20. in the Spirit] The 1675 reading ("in Spirit") has been emended to bring it into line with Rev. 1:10, which reads, "I was in the Spirit on the Lord's day, and heard behind me a great voice. . . ."

P. 60:3. want] The phrase "for want of Conversation" is obviously parallel to the earlier phrase "for want of Education"; the reading ("for wont of Conversation") of the 1675 edition has therefore been emended.

P. 65:2. *attaineth the best*] Compare the similar emendation (of "attaineth best" to "attaineth the best") made in the corresponding chapter summary on p. 7.

P. 85:19. one] It is possible that the word was "own" in the manuscript. Even so, "one" is a possible seventeenth-century spelling of "own". Probably "one" is correct, the word meaning, however, not "own" but "unique" or "singular." In either case, emendation is not necessary.

P. 90:1. Ruler] The 1675 reading ("Ruled") has been emended to "Ruler". Another possible emendation of "Ruled" would be "Rule".

P. 104:27. a] It is barely possible that *"a"* (the 1675 reading) is correct, that the word was italicized in the manuscript for emphasis. No instance quite like this one appears elsewhere in the book, however; and perhaps the compositor's tendency to set initial italic capitals was here carried over to the lower case.

P. 109:25. Credible] The *OED* cites this as the latest use of the form to mean "ready, willing, or inclined to believe."

P. 113:36. *Volumne*] The *OED* lists one example of "Volumen" being used to mean "a volume, a book"; Bellenden (1536) wrote of "ane compendius volumen." But *"Volumen"* (in the 1675 edition of *Christian Ethicks*) is probably a misprint for *"Volumne"*. For similar phrasing, see Ps. 40:7–8: "Then said I, Lo, I come: in the volume of the book it is written of me, I delight to do thy will, O my God. . . ." Cf. also Heb. 10:7.

P. 119:27. adapts] The meaning is "fits" or "suits" ("adapts"), not "chooses" ("adopts", as in the 1675 edition). Compare p. 141, l. 3, where "adopted" means "chosen."

P. 119:40. altogether] Typical Traherne spelling of "all together". Cf. the Church's Year-Book, f. 53: "they [the angels] & thou & altogether . . . shall liv in Heavenly Joys." The *OED* cites similar examples in other writers of the sixteenth and seventeenth centuries.

P. 128:39. sweat and Labour] Compare the *OED* (Rogers, 1642): "All well affected Christians would be loth to lose their labour and sweat. . . ." That the reading ("sweat Labour") of the 1675 edition means "sweet Labour" is unlikely; the *OED* does not list "sweat" as a form of "sweet".

P. 141:1. becomes their] The compositor misplaced the "s" in the 1675 edition. Since "he" is the subject of the verb in question, the phrase should be "becomes their", rather than "become theirs".

P. 141:33. Degree] The 1675 reading ("Decree") has been brought into line with the reading in Traherne's source, *The Whole Duty of Man* (I.33).

P. 144:9. *into*] The 1675 reading (*"in"*) has been altered to *"into"*, a reading similar to the one appearing in *"The Contents"* (p. 9).

P. 145:9. Two] It is possible that the 1675 reading ("To") is correct; however, "Two" is more congruous with Traherne's characteristic pairing in this passage.

P. 151:23. *then*] The 1675 reading (*"when"*) has been emended to *"then"*; 1 Cor. 13:12 reads in part, "then shall I know even as also I am known."

P. 155:11. altogether] See the textual note for p. 119, l. 40.

P. 157:6. pass] Although the 1675 reading ("past") may be correct (meaning "paste"), "past" is more likely a compositor's error for "pass". Less likely is "put", but cf. *C* I.44: "His Wants put a Lustre upon His Enjoyments. . . ."

P. 161:6. *Victories*] The obviously incomplete 1675 reading (*"Ver-"*) has been emended to *"Victories"*. See *"The Contents"* (p. 9) for a similar reading (*"Victories"*).

P. 162:28. to] The version ("tos") of the word appearing in the sheets (Bodleian and Yale) which underwent two stages of "correction" was the result of an accident. After the sheets (Z, outer forme) of the Union and Illinois copies were printed, the proofreader noted that the page number on Z8^v was incorrect. The press was stopped and the page number was corrected. The British Museum and Cambridge sheets were then printed without incident. But before the Bodleian and the Yale sheets were printed, the "s" of "thatis" (sig. Z1, l. 28) worked loose and lodged at the end of "to" (sig. Z1, l. 22), resulting in the second stage of "correction."

P. 163:31. imagine] The passage is obscure. The subject of the verb in question ("imagines") is presumably "they"; "imagines" (of the 1675 edition) should probably, therefore, be emended to read "imagine". Another possible emendation would be "imagined".

P. 165:38. *unknown,*] Margoliouth (*Centuries, Poems, and Thanksgivings,* II, 185) silently emended *"unknown."* of the 1675 edition to read "unknown,".

P. 166:13. *sprinkle*] In a note on this poem Margoliouth wrote, "I accept Dobell's suggested emendation ['sparkle'] of 'sprinkle', surely a misprint" (II, 398). This emendation is not, however, necessary; the *OED* lists "sprinkle" as a synonym of "sparkle" (see George R. Guffey, "Margoliouth's Emendation of a Line in Traherne's 'For Man to Act,'" *AN&Q*, V[1967], 162–163).

P. 168:19. *confounds.*] The "corrected" reading (appearing on sig. Z7^v of the Bodleian, Union, Illinois, and Yale copies) is *"confouds."*. Actually *"confounds."* (British Museum and Cambridge copies) was not intentionally changed to *"confouds."*. The latter reading is the result of an accident. The sequence of events resulting in this change was probably as follows. The British Museum and Cambridge sheets were printed reading *"confounds."*. But the page numbers on Z7^v and Z8 were reversed in those sheets, Z7^v being numbered "351" and Z8 "350". The press was stopped and the page numbers were corrected. In the process, however, the types used to print *"confounds."* at the end of the second line in the British Museum and Cambridge sheets were disturbed, and consequently the "n" dropped out of the word altogether. Sig. Z7^v of the Illinois sheet was printed reading *"confouds"*. The period which had appeared after *"confouds"* in the British Museum and Cambridge sheets did not here print at all. The "d" in "blind" at the end of the seventh line on Z7ᵛ of the Illinois sheet was also disturbed. Sometime after the printing of this sheet of the Illinois copy, the press was stopped again, the types were tightened up, and the Bodleian, Union, and Yale sheets were printed. The Bodleian, Union, and Yale sheets then read *"confouds.".* When Margoliouth printed the lines in his edition (see his notes, [II, 398]), he misread the form *"confouds."* as *"confonds.".* A comparison of the form in the Cambridge copy with the form in the Illinois copy leaves no doubt that the letter remaining is a "u" rather than an "n".

P. 181:19. *whate're*] Margoliouth (II, 186) silently emended the word to "whate'er".

P. 217:41. *it self:*] Margoliouth (II, 192) silently altered the colon to a semicolon.

P. 221:35. maketh *all things to work together for good*] In the first stage of correction, someone changed "maketh *all things work together for good"* (the reading of the Authorized Version [cf. *C* III.30 and SM II.14]) to "maketh *all things work too together for good".* Someone then became aware that the passage was incorrect (and perhaps consulted the manuscript); the passage was then corrected a second time to read "maketh *all things to work together for good".* It is barely possible that the manuscript read "maketh *all things work too together for good"*; sig. Cc8ᵛ (p. 190, l. 29, of this edition) contains a passage reading "makes all these Things work to[o] together for our good".

P. 223:20. *ye my face in*] The Authorized Version reads "ye me in", but *"ye my face in"* probably reflects Traherne's manuscript. Compare "sees the Face of GOD" on p. 166 (l. 18) and "see the face of God" in *C* II.17.

P. 225:24. *Life and Light*] In this case the manuscript was almost certainly consulted before *"Light and Life"* of the Bodleian, Cambridge, and Yale copies was corrected (in the British Museum, Union, and Illinois copies) to read *"Life and Light".* Both Dr. Everard's translation (1650, 1657) of *The Divine Pymander* (II.18) and Traherne's Commonplace Book (*s.v.* "Man") read "Life and Light". It is not likely that a proofreader would have been familiar enough with Everard's translation to spot the rearrangement of these words without checking the manuscript of *Christian Ethicks.*

P. 227:11. *cannot tell what*] This (the corrected state) is the reading of Dr. Everard's translation (X.131), and Traherne's Commonplace Book (*s.v.* "Capacity").

P. 227:17. *dost not expect*] Compare Dr. Everard's translation (X.133) and Traherne's Commonplace Book (*s.v.* "Capacity"), which read ("dost not expect") as the corrected state of this forme does.

P. 254:7. interiour] Although Traherne's obscure comparison seems to be between an inward ("interiour") condition and "outward life," the 1675 reading ("inferiour") is, although unlikely, possible.

P. 280:10. he] It is barely possible that the passage is correct as it stands in the 1675 edition, "it may be" meaning "perhaps."

Corrections of the Text

[The page and line numbers before entries refer to pages and lines in the present text. Collated copies of the 1675 edition are distinguished as follows: *Bod* (Bodleian Library), *BM* (British Museum), *Cam* (Cambridge University Library), *U* (Union Theological Seminary Library), *UI* (University of Illinois Library), and *Y* (Yale University Library). An erroneous reading appearing in all six collated copies is followed by *all*. In entries involving press-variants, copies with readings identical to readings of the present edition are not listed.]

P. 7:30.   attaineth the best] attaineth best   *all.*
P. 8:16.   Of what Nature] Of Nature   *all.*
P. 9:36.   excellencies.] excellenlencies.   *all.*
P. 13:9.   Means] Mean   *all.*
P. 13:10. Acquisition] Acquisiton   *all.*
P. 14:29. under the Notion] under Notion   (*u*) *Bod, BM, Cam, UI, Y.*
P. 16:7.   and] an   *all.*
P. 16:12. unknown,] ~∧   *all.*
P. 16:24. puts] put   *all.*
P. 16:25. cannot∧] ~,   *all.*
P. 19:8.   impossible] impossiable   *all.*
P. 20:22. Lovely,] Louely,   (*u*) *BM.*
P. 21:5.   thorow,] ~∧   *all.*
P. 22:5.   *patience,*] ~∧   *all.*
P. 22:6.   *kindness,*] ~∧   *all.*
P. 23:4.   BEFORE] BEfore   *all.*
P. 23:25. we are making] we making   *all.*
P. 24:1.   has] have   *all.*
P. 25:7.   *Soul*] Soul   *all.*
P. 25:9.   *Soul*] Soul   *all.*
P. 26:30. order'd Habits alone] orderd Habits alone   *all.*

P. 26:35.   inuring] in uring   *all.*
P. 26:38.   created.]] created.$_\wedge$ *all.*
P. 27:1.   vertuous$_\wedge$] ~,   *all.*
P. 27:24.   Vertuous,] Virtuous,   (*u*) *Cam.*
P. 27:25.   Beginning.] Begnining.   *all.*
P. 27:25.   Vertues] Vertue   (*u*) *Cam.*
P. 27:27.   vertuous] virtuous   (*u*) *Cam.*
P. 28:2.   Whether]   Wether   *all.*
P. 29:10.   *Fear,]*   ~$_\wedge$ *all.*
P. 31:36.   Idle] ldle   *all.*
P. 32:10.   also, in relation] also, in in relation   *all.*
P. 34:7.   Incarnation;] ~,   *all.*
P. 34:28.   *Atheism*$_\wedge$] ~,   *all.*
P. 36:17.   in the Soul,] in Soul,   *all.*
P. 36:32.   appeareth] appeaeth   *all.*
P. 38:36.   Dammage,] mage,   *all.*
P. 39:40.   Col. 1.9,] Col. 1:9,   (*u*) *Bod, BM, UI, Y.*
P. 43:13.   infinitely] in finitely   *all.*
P. 46:24.   conformable] comformable   *all.*
P. 47:14.   Goodness, and Holiness, and that]   Goodness, and Bounty, and
             Holiness, and that   (*u*) *BM, Cam.*
P. 48:5.   familiarly] familiary   *all.*
P. 48:7.   *Eden,]* ~$_\wedge$ *all.*
P. 49:21.   Objects;] ~,   *all.*
P. 49:23.   Perfection] Perfeon   (*u*) *Bod.*
P. 50:31.   Col. 1.16.] *C*ol. 116..   *all.*
P. 51:30.   is it onely in] is onely it in   (*u*) *Bod.*
P. 51:34.   embrace] embraces   *all.*
P. 52:21.   Services,] Service,   *all.*
P. 52:32.   awaken] a waken   *all.*
P. 53:18.   one;] ~,   *all.*
P. 54:20.   in the Spirit] in Spirit   *all.*
P. 54:26.   commanded] commaned   *all.*
P. 54:29.   one place,] one-place,   *all.*
P. 54:29.   *hath,]* ~$_\wedge$ *all.*
P. 56:31.   finds,] ~$_\wedge$ *all.*
P. 57:18.   Gifts),] Gifts)$_\wedge$ *all.*
P. 59:18.   Right] Righ   *all.*
P. 59:27.   Actors$_\wedge$] ~,   *all.*
P. 60:1.   Knowledge,] ~$_\wedge$ *all.*
P. 60:3.   want] wont   *all.*
P. 60:34.   Felicity,] ~;   *all.*
P. 61:14.   Number] Nunber   *all.*
P. 61:31.   Actions$_\wedge$).] Actions;)$_\wedge$ *all.*
P. 61:37.   Thought$_\wedge$] ~,   *all.*
P. 62:17.   Apprehensions] Apprenhensions   *all.*
P. 62:18.   Conscience and please] Conscience and and please   *all.*

P. 62:36.　　of the fall,] of fall,　　*all.*
P. 63:3.　　Neighbours,] ～ₐ　*all.*
P. 65:2.　　*attaineth the best*] *attaineth best*　　*all.*
P. 65:6.　　whetherₐ] ～,　*all.*
P. 67:25.　　every] very　*all.*
P. 67:27.　　Willing, Decreeing,] Willingₐ Decreeingₐ　*all.*
P. 68:19.　　becomethₐ] ～,　*all.*
P. 68:21.　　inward;] in ward;　*all.*
P. 68:37.　　Creatures] Greatures　　(*u*) *UI.*
P. 69:12.　　Wisdom,] ～ₐ　*all.*
P. 69:21.　　Beautiful] Beatutiful　*all.*
P. 71:6.　　Wisdome] Wisnome　*all.*
P. 71:14.　　Righteousness of Esteem,] Rightteousness of Esteem,　*all.*
P. 72:14.　　akin] a kin.　*all.*
P. 74:28.　　infinite] nfinite　*all.*
P. 74:35.　　Expectation] Expectations　*all.*
P. 75:10.　　contentment;] ～,　*all.*
P. 75:30.　　Amiable and Delightful] Amiable and and Delightful　*all.*
P. 76:7.　　work;] ～ₐ　*all.*
P. 76:27.　　Goodness.] Godness.　*all.*
P. 77:23.　　1 Cor. 4.5.] *omitted*　(*u*) *Cam, UI.*
P. 78:12.　　it is profitable.] it it profitable.　*all.*
P. 79:2.　　Understanding.] Understaudingₐ　*all.*
P. 80:38.　　theₐ Wonder] the, Wonder　*all.*
P. 81:28.　　ever.] ～ₐ　*all.*
P. 82:28.　　selves;] ～.　*all.*
P. 82:40.　　them,] ～!　*all.*
P. 83:27.　　all, as he] all, as as he　*all.*
P. 84:3.　　also that they] also that, that they　*all.*
P. 84:11.　　Sence and feeling,] Sence and and feeling,　*all.*
P. 85:13.　　Consentₐ)] Consent.)　*all.*
P. 85:15.　　much as is] much as as is　*all.*
P. 85:20.　　are possible,] are, possible　(*u*) *Bod, Cam, U, UI.*
P. 86:39.　　Greater.] ～,　*all.*
P. 87:12.　　apprehend,] ～ₐ　*all.*
P. 87:31.　　Object.] ～ₐ　*all.*
P. 88:26.　　and is the real] and the is real　*all.*
P. 89:40.　　Stain.] Srain.　*all.*
P. 90:1.　　Ruler] Ruled　*all.*
P. 90:15.　　understand,] vnderstand,　*all.*
P. 91:17.　　the right use] the right right use　*all.*
P. 95:12.　　*for he that Loveth another hath fulfilled the Law.*] *for the he that Loveth another hath fulfilled Law.*　*all.*
P. 95:39.　　Justice;] ～,　*all.*
P. 96:1.　　flourisheth;] ～,　*all.*
P. 96:10.　　Tradesmen,] ～ₐ　*all.*
P. 96:13.　　Affections] Affection*s*　*all.*

P. 96:22.   is a Severe] is a a Severe   *all.*
P. 98:5.   feel the] feel. The   *all.*
P. 98:15.   *Servants.*] *Seruants.*   *all.*
P. 99:24.   Holiness of God,] Holiness God,   *all.*
P. 100:15.   be] he   *all.*
P. 100:23.   Amen.] ~,   *all.*
P. 100:27.   it,ᴧ *that*] it,; *that*   *all.*
P. 100:40.   Gal. 3.21.] Gal. 3.21ᴧ   *all.*
P. 101:35.   Account] Atcount   *all.*
P. 102:7.   continuedᴧ] ~,   *all.*
P. 103:1.   by the Coming] by Coming   *all.*
P. 103:6.   adorning] adornig   *all.*
P. 104:27.   a] *a*   *all.*
P. 105:34.   Sanctification,] Sanctificaton,   *all.*
P. 107:29.   Innocency,] ~ᴧ   *all.*
P. 110:19.   enrich] enriched   *all.*
P. 110:22.   it was prepared:] it was was prepared: *all.*
P. 111:38.   Delightful] Delighful   *all.*
P. 113:12.   sweeter] sweet   *all.*
P. 113:36.   *Volumne*] *Volumen*   *all.*
P. 115:35.   *And*] *and*   *all.*
P. 116:7.   eternalᴧ] ~,   *all.*
P. 117:13.   past,] ~ᴧ   *all.*
P. 119:17.   For] for   *all.*
P. 119:27.   adapts] adopts   *all.*
P. 119:28.   things] thing   *all.*
P. 119:39.   sweetness] sweetnees   *all.*
P. 121:18.   *and*] *and*   *all.*
P. 121:40.   Rom. 15.4.] Rom. 15.4ᴧ   *all.*
P. 122:4.   Possible] Possibles   *all.*
P. 122:20.   touchingᴧ the] touching. The   *all.*
P. 123:1.   theseᴧ] ~,   *all.*
P. 123:18.   GOD,] ~ᴧ   *all.*
P. 123:19.   Bridegroomᴧ] ~,   *all.*
P. 123:22.   Eternities,] Eterternities,   *all.*
P. 123:26.   Superior] Supeperior   *all.*
P. 123:38.   some] so me   *all.*
P. 124:1.   abominable,] ~ᴧ   *all.*
P. 126:26.   must] musts   *all.*
P. 128:35.   righteousness] rightteousness   *all.*
P. 128:39.   sweat and Labour] sweat Labour   *all.*
P. 129:17.   at the Incense] at the the Incense   *all.*
P. 129:38.   Saviours] Saviour   *all.*
P. 130:11.   made] make   *all.*
P. 131:40.   misery,] ~ᴧ   *all.*
P. 132:1.   Estate,] ~ᴧ   *all.*
P. 132:7.   Yet] yet   *all.*

P. 133:18.   corrected,] correctd,   *all.*
P. 133:20.   Delights,] Delighs,   *all.*
P. 134:11.   them;] ∼ₐ   *all.*
P. 134:11.   delights] delighs   *all.*
P. 134:14.   perfection] pefection   *all.*
P. 135:25.   *is*] *it*   *all.*
P. 135:40.   13.1.] 13ₐ1.   *all.*
P. 136:34.   in a distasteful] in distasteful   *all.*
P. 136:35.   Honour,] ∼ₐ   *all.*
P. 137:11.   or is as distinct] or distinct   *all.*
P. 138:3.   *acceptable.*] ∼?   *all.*
P. 138:3.   Wills] Wilis   *all.*
P. 139:5.   Him;] ∼,   *all.*
P. 140:6.   Faculties,] ∼ₐ   *all.*
P. 140:17.   Perfection,] Pefection   *all.*
P. 140:23.   Goodness and Excellency] Goodness and and Excellency   *all.*
P. 140:26.   Ocean.] Oeean.   *all.*
P. 140:28.   it is no] it no   *all.*
P. 140:40.   all his Creatures,] all his his Creatures,   *all.*
P. 141:1.   becomes their] become theirs   *all.*
P. 141:3.   adopted] adapted   (*u*) *Bod, Cam, U, Y.*
P. 141:14.   we are] weare   *all.*
P. 141:33.   Degree] Decree   *all.*
P. 142:24.   *desire*] *desired*   *all.*
P. 142:33.   fulfilling] fufilling   *all.*
P. 143:17.   the Joy and Glory] the a Joy and Glory   (*c*) *UI;*   the a Joy nd Glory   (*u*) *Cam.*
P. 144:2.   *and*] *an*   *all.*
P. 144:9.   *into*] *in*   *all.*
P. 144:20.   apart,] a part,   *all.*
P. 144:23.   above] aabove   *all.*
P. 145:9.   Two] To   *all.*
P. 146:32.   Parents,] Parent,   (*u*) *Bod.*
P. 146:38.   in fulfilling] infulfilling   *all.*
P. 147:6.   beenₐ all] been, all   *all.*
P. 147:33.   Operations] Opperations   *all.*
P. 147:36.   Could] could   *all.*
P. 149:9.   Inclination] Inclnation   *all.*
P. 149:9.   aversion] a version   *all.*
P. 150:6.   wasₐ] ∼,   *all.*
P. 150:7.   They] The   *all.*
P. 150:7.   were not left] were no left   *all.*
P. 150:9.   willing,] ∼ₐ   *all.*
P. 150:35.   In] in   (*u*) *Cam, U, UI.*
P. 150:36.   Coronations,] Goronations,   *all.*
P. 150:37.   in all Persons,] n all Persons,   (*u*) *Cam, U, UI.*
P. 151:23.   *then*] *when*   *all.*

P. 152:16.   Prudence] *Prudenee*   *all.*
P. 153:22.   Vertue] Vertues   *all.*
P. 153:36.   detecteth] detected   *all.*
P. 154:12.   feet;] ~,   *all.*
P. 154:22.   Truth is,] Truth is∧   *all.*
P. 155:5.   It] it   *all.*
P. 155:9.   all so] also   *all.*
P. 156:4.   has] as   *all.*
P. 156:12.   Companions, the] Companions. The   *all.*
P. 157:6.   pass] past   *all.*
P. 158:30.   and] an   *all.*
P. 158:39.   is,] ~∧   *all.*
P. 159:16.   prohibition] prohibitation   *all.*
P. 159:24.   order] ordered   *all.*
P. 159:38.   Saviour] Savour   *all.*
P. 160:3.   World,] ~.   *all.*
P. 161:2.   *Nature,*] ~∧   *all.*
P. 161:6.   *Victories*] *Ver-*   *all.*
P. 162:1.   Its] its   *all.*
P. 162:4.   lives.] ~,   *all.*
P. 162:9.   from] form   *all.*
P. 162:28.   to] tos   (*c*) *Bod, Y.*
P. 162:31.   that is] thati   (*c*) *Bod, Y;*   thatis   (*u*) *BM, Cam, U, UI.*
P. 162:37.   himself,] ~-   *all.*
P. 162:37.   useles∧] ~,   *all.*
P. 162:38.   a] as   *all.*
P. 163:17.   Is] Its   *all.*
P. 163:20.   Difference,] Defference,   *all.*
P. 163:31.   imagine] imagines   *all.*
P. 165:18.   is] as   *all.*
P. 165:38.   *unknown,*] ~.   *all.*
P. 166:30.   Impediments,] Impediment,   *all.*
P. 167:23.   Apple, and tho∧] Apple, and and tho,   *all.*
P. 168:19.   *confounds.*] *confouds.*   (*c*) *Bod, U, UI, Y.*
P. 168:32.   *places.*] *plaees.*   *all.*
P. 169:10.   *more*] *nore*   *all.*
P. 175:17.   Interest,] Interest,   *all.*
P. 180:2.   Perfection, every thing to∧] Perfection∧ every thing to,   *all.*
P. 181:41.   requires,] ~∧   *all.*
P. 184:38.   Getting,] ~∧   *all.*
P. 190:29.   too] to   *all.*
P. 198:35.   another] anothers   *all.*
P. 201:18.   recordeth.] recorderh.   *all.*
P. 204:26.   Duty,] ~.   *all.*
P. 219:10.   powers] power   *all.*
P. 221:33.   of a stable,] of stable,   (*u*) *Bod, Cam, Y.*

P. 221:36.   *things to work together*] *things work too together* (*c*) *U, UI;*
            things work together (*u*) *Bod, Cam, Y.*

P. 222:7.   The] the   (*u*) *Bod, Cam, Y.*

P. 222:38.   difficulties] difflculties   *all.*

P. 223:15.   Prayer] Prayers   (*u*) *Bod, Cam, Y.*

P. 223:18.   sowing,] $\sim_\wedge$ (*u*) *Bod, Cam, Y.*

P. 223:20.   *ye my face in*] *ye me in*   (*c*) *BM, U, UI.*

P. 225:3.   Censures] Ceusures   (*u*) *Bod, Cam, Y.*

P. 225:6.   Bubble;] $\sim$,   (*u*) *Bod, Cam, Y.*

P. 225:13.   Courts,] Conrts,   (*u*) *Bod, Cam, Y.*

P. 225:24.   *Life and Light,*] *Light and Life,*   (*u*) *Bod, Cam, Y.*

P. 225:35.   *but*] *bur*   (*u*) *Bod, Cam, Y.*

P. 226:30.   [i.e.] $_\wedge$i.e.   (*u*) *Bod, Cam, Y.*

P. 226:39.   *believe*] *belive*   (*u*) *Bod, Cam, Y.*

P. 227:3.   *Dry,*] $\sim_\wedge$ (*u*) *Bod, Cam, Y.*

P. 227:11.   *cannot tell what*] *cannot what*   (*u*) *Bod, Cam, Y.*

P. 227:17.   *dost not expect,*] *dost expect,*   (*u*) *Bod, Cam, Y.*

P. 228:20.   Trifles,] Trlfles,   (*u*) *Bod, Cam, Y.*

P. 228:24.   Scepters:] $\sim$.   (*u*) *Bod, Cam, Y.*

P. 228:28.   Triumphs,] Triumhs,   (*u*) *Bod, Cam, Y.*

P. 228:30.   The] the   (*u*) *Bod, Cam, Y.*

P. 228:32.   of all Immensity,] of Immensity,   (*u*) *Bod, Cam, Y.*

P. 228:36.   noise and Interests] noise of the Interests   (*u*) *Bod, Cam, Y.*

P. 244:14.   attended] artended   *all.*

P. 245:39.   9.6.] 9.6$_\wedge$ *all.*

P. 247:19.   Monuments] Momuments   *all.*

P. 249:30.   *more be termed*] *more termed*   *all.*

P. 249:32.   *delighteth*] *deligheth*   *all.*

P. 249:39.   55.8, 9.] 55.8$_\wedge$9$_\wedge$ *all.*

P. 249:40.   62.3, 4, 5.] 62.3-4, 5.   *all.*

P. 254:7.   interiour] inferiour   *all.*

P. 262:3.   And] and   *all.*

P. 268:5.   and infinitely be] and infinitely more than Infinitely be   (*u*) *Cam.*

P. 268:28.   other] ther   (*u*) *Cam.*

P. 272:17.   Obligation,] $\sim_\wedge$ (*u*) *Cam.*

P. 272:21.   better to die than renounce it.] better die than renounce it.
            (*u*) *Cam.*

P. 272:36.   Beloveds] Beloloveds   *all.*

P. 273:27.   efforts,] effors,   (*u*) *Cam.*

P. 273:40.   It] it   *all.*

P. 275:17.   My] my   *all.*

P. 280:10.   he] it   *all.*

P. 280:29.   Possessions] Possessessions   *all.*

P. 282:11.   Snail;] $\sim$,   *all.*

P. 286:21.   for this Cause] for Cause   *all.*

Press-Variants by Formes

SHEET B (*outer forme*)

Corrected: U.
Uncorrected: Bod, BM, Cam, UI, Y.

Sig. B2 verso.
  ll. 27–28. under the Notion] under Notion

SHEET C (*outer forme*)

Corrected: Bod, Cam, U, UI, Y.
Uncorrected: BM.

Sig. C1 recto.
  l. 30. Lovely,] Louely,

SHEET D (*outer forme*)

Corrected: Bod, BM, U, UI, Y.
Uncorrected: Cam.

Sig. D1 recto.
  ll. 18–19. Vertuous,] Virtuous,
  l. 21. Vertues] Vertue
  ll. 24–25. vertuous] virtuous

SHEET E (*inner forme*)

Corrected: Cam, U.
Uncorrected: Bod, BM, UI, Y.

Sig. E6 recto.
  marginal note. Col. 1.9,] Col. 1:9,

SHEET F (*outer forme*)

Corrected: Bod, U, UI, Y.
Uncorrected: BM, Cam.

Sig. F6 verso.
   ll. 16–17. Goodness, and Holiness, and that] Goodness, and Bounty, and
   Holiness, and that

SHEET G (*outer forme*)

Corrected: BM, Cam, U, UI, Y.
Uncorrected: Bod.

Sig. G1 recto.
   l. 24. Perfection] Perfeon
Sig. G2 verso.
   page number. 84] 49
Sig. G3 recto.
   l. 14. is it onely in] is onely it in
Sig. G4 verso.
   running-title. 𝕷𝖔𝖇𝖊.] 𝕷𝖔𝖝𝖊.
Sig. G5 recto.
   page number. 89] 99
Sig. G8 verso.
   running-title. 𝕰𝖙𝖊𝖗𝖓𝖆𝖑] 𝕰𝖙𝖔𝖗𝖓𝖆𝖑

SHEET I (*inner forme*)

Corrected: Bod, BM, Cam, U, Y.
Uncorrected: UI.

Sig. I6 recto.
   l. 2. Creatures] Greatures

SHEET K (*inner forme*)

Corrected: Bod, BM, U, Y.
Uncorrected: Cam, UI.

Sig. K7 verso.
   marginal note. 1 Cor. 4.5.] *omitted*

SHEET L (*outer forme*)

Corrected: BM, Y.
Uncorrected: Bod, Cam, U, UI.

Sig. L8 verso.
   l. 24. are possible,] are, possible

SHEET R (*inner forme*)

Corrected: Bod, Cam, U.
Uncorrected: BM, UI, Y.

Sig. R2 recto.
   page number. 243] *omitted*

SHEET V (*outer forme*)

> *1st stage corrected:* BM, Cam, U, UI, Y.
> *Uncorrected:* Bod.

Sig. V7 recto.
  l. 16. Parents,] Parent,

> *2nd stage corrected:* BM, UI.
> *Uncorrected:* Bod, Cam, U, Y.

Sig. V1 recto.
  l. 6. adopted] adapted

SHEET V (*inner forme*)

> *1st stage corrected:* UI.
> *Uncorrected:* Cam.

Sig. V3 verso.
  l. 26. the a Joy and Glory] the a Joy nd Glory

> *2nd stage corrected:* Bod, BM, U, Y.

Sig. V3 verso.
  l. 26. the Joy and Glory] the a Joy and Glory

SHEET X (*inner forme*)

> *Corrected:* Bod, BM, Y.
> *Uncorrected:* Cam, U, UI.

Sig. X4 recto.
  l. 25. In] in
  l. 28. in all Persons,] n all Persons,

SHEET Z (*outer forme*)

> *1st stage corrected:* Bod, BM, Cam, Y.
> *Uncorrected:* U, UI.

Sig. Z8 verso.
  page number. 352] 350

> *2nd stage corrected:* Bod, Y.
> *Uncorrected:* BM, Cam, U, UI.

Sig. Z1 recto.
  l. 22. tos] to
  l. 28. thati] thatis

SHEET Z (*inner forme*)

> *Corrected:* Bod, U, UI, Y.
> *Uncorrected:* BM, Cam.

Sig. Z7 verso.
  page number. 350] 351
  l. 2. confouds.] confounds.
Sig. Z8 recto.
  page number. 351] 350

SHEET Hh (*outer forme*)

1st stage corrected: U, UI.
Uncorrected: Bod, Cam, Y.

Sig. Hh1 recto.
    l. 3. of a stable,] of stable,
    l. 8. things work too together] *things work together*
    l. 29. The] the
Sig. Hh2 verso.
    l. 28. Prayer] Prayers
Sig. Hh3 recto.
    l. 4. sowing,] sowing
    l. 8. ye me in] *ye my face in*
Sig. Hh4 verso.
    l. 2. Censures] Ceusures
    l. 7. Bubble;] Bubble,
    l. 20. Courts,] Conrts,
Sig. Hh5 recto.
    ll. 11–12. Life and Light,] *Light and Life,*
    l. 29. but] *bur*
Sig. Hh6 verso.
    l. 2. [i.e.] i.e.
    l. 15. believe] *belive*
    l. 23. Dry,] *Dry*
Sig. Hh7 recto.
    l. 6. cannot tell what] *cannot what*
    l. 16. dost not expect,] *dost expect,*
Sig. Hh8 verso.
    l. 2. Trifles,] Trlfles,
    l. 8. Scepters:] Scepters.
    l. 16. Triumphs,] Triumhs,
    l. 20. The] the
    l. 22. of all Immensity,] of Immensity,
    l. 29. noise and In-] noise of the In-

                    2nd stage corrected: BM.
                    Uncorrected: U, UI.

Sig. Hh1 recto.
    l. 8. things to work together] *things work too together*

SHEET Oo (*outer forme*)

Corrected: Bod, BM, U, UI, Y.
Uncorrected: Cam.

Sig. Oo3 recto.
    ll. 5–6. and infinitely be] and infinitely more than Infinitely be
Sig. Oo8 verso.
    l. 29. efforts,] effors,

SHEET Oo (*inner forme*)

Corrected: Bod, BM, U, UI, Y.
Uncorrected: Cam.

Sig. Oo3 verso.
 l. 15. other] ther
Sig. Oo7 verso.
 ll. 4–5. Obligation,] Obligation
 l. 10. better to die than renounce it.] better die than renonnce it.

Commentary

[Passages being annotated in the Commentary are printed in italics, regardless of the kind of type used in the text of *Christian Ethicks*. Otherwise, quotations follow exactly the text of the present edition. Cross-references to notes in the Commentary are keyed to page and line of the present edition, thus: *CE*, p. 23:6 n. See Preface, pp. vi–vii, for the short forms used for references to Traherne's works. See Selected Bibliography, p. 377, for an explanation of the abbreviated forms of other works cited in the Commentary.]

P. 3:4. *Conversation.* Social intercourse; also used in this sense *CE*, p. 173.

P. 3:10. *Author of The whole Duty of Man.* This anonymous work, first published in 1658, is most commonly attributed to Richard Allestree, Regius Professor of Divinity at Oxford. The eminent theologian Henry Hammond contributed a prefatory letter to the bookseller, observing, "The subject matter of it is indeed what the title undertakes, *The Whole Duty of Man*, set down in all the branches, with those advantages of brevity and partitions, to invite, and support, and engage the reader; that condescension to the meanest capacities, but withal, that weight of spiritual arguments, wherein the best proficients will be glad to be assisted" (ed. 1731, sig. A2). A model of common sense and conventionality, *The Whole Duty* eschewed doctrinal controversy and became the most popular religious work of the latter seventeenth century, its fame extending well into the eighteenth. Traherne, despite his disclaimer here, borrowed without acknowledgment from *The Whole Duty* in *CE*, pp. 140–142; see Commentary on those pages.

P. 3:13. *the French Charron of Wisdom.* Traherne refers to the treatise *De la sagesse* (1601) by the French Neo-Stoic Pierre Charron (1541–1603), who drew upon Seneca, Plutarch, Guillaume du Vair, Justus Lipsius, and above all upon his close friend Montaigne. *De la sagesse* was translated into English by Samson Lennard (*Of Wisdome Three Bookes,* 1612). Charron described his plan: "There are three Bookes: The first is wholly in the knowledge of our selves and humane condition, as a preparative unto wisdome. . . . The second Booke containeth in it the treatises, offices, and generall and principall rules of wisdome. The third, the particular rules and instructions of wisdome, and that by the order and discourse of the foure principall and morall vertues" (1640 ed., sigs. A5–A5^v). Traherne alludes, therefore, to the third part, from which (again *pace* his disclaimer) he borrowed in *CE*, pp. 161–162.

Because of its scepticism, *De la sagesse* upon its first publication incurred charges of atheism; Charron made changes for the second (posthumous) edition of 1604. Joseph Glanvill wrote approvingly of "wise Monsieur *Charron*" and declared: "I cannot quarrel with his *Motto* [on the English as well as French title-page]: in a sense *Je ne scay,* is a justifiable *Scepticism,* and not mis-becoming a Candidate of *wisdom*" (*The Vanity of Dogmatizing* [1661], p. 234). It seems unlikely that Traherne would have endorsed Charron so strongly. In temperament he and Charron were poles apart, scepticism leading Charron not to the earnest search for knowledge which impelled Glanvill and other Fellows of the Royal Society, but rather to a pessimism which harks back to the medieval *contemptus mundi.* "Our present life," Charron wrote, "is but . . . a web of unhappy adventures, a pursuit of diverse miseries inchained together on all sides" (p. 121); and man he considered an "uncleane seed in his beginning, a sponge of ordures, a sacke of miseries in his middle age, a stench and meat for wormes in his end; and to conclude, the most miserable and wretched thing in the world" (p. 123). On Charron see Richard H. Popkin, *The History of Skepticism from Erasmus to Descartes* (Assen, Neth., 1960), pp. 56–63 *et passim.*

P. 3:15–17. *knowledge . . . study.* It is Traherne's personal experience of felicity which makes *Christian Ethicks* the unique work it is; in the *Centuries* (III.46) he described his youthful resolution to devote his life to the "Search of Happiness" and the "Study of Felicity." Cf. *C* IV.11, 12, and *CE,* p. 225: "I speak as I am inspired by Felicity."

P. 3:33. *I do not speak much of Vice.* Traherne returns to this point, *CE,* pp. 206–207. Cf. also his advocacy in *CE,* p. 34, of fuller recognition of the "Original and Primitive Vertues" now viewed through a *"Mask* or *Vizor* of Ordinances and new Duties." The metaphor of the straight and crooked line derives ultimately from Aristotle (*De Anima* I.5.411^{a}4): "By means of the straight line we know both itself and the curved. . . ."

P. 4:1–7. *the very Glory . . . Contrary.* Cf. SM IV.23, and John Smith: "As there would need nothing else to deterr and affright men from *Sin* but its own ugliness and deformity, were it presented to a naked view and seen as it is: so nothing would more effectually commend Religion to the Minds of men, then the displaying and unfolding the Excellencies of its Nature, then the true Native beauty and inward lustre of Religion it self" (*Select Discourses* [1660], p. 450). For the jewel-dirt metaphor, cf. *CE,* p. 31, and *C* I.82, *C* IV.45, and *C* IV.52.

P. 4:14. *Were there nothing in the World.* With this utopian yearning cf. *CE,* pp. 33–34, 143, and 146–147. Note as well the more realistic assessment in the poem in *CE,* pp. 196–197.

P. 4:36. *Original.* Origin, as frequently hereafter: a common form in the seventeenth century. Cf. Traherne's source in the Commonplace Book, Thomas Jackson's *Treatise Containing the Originall of Unbeliefe* (1625).

P. 4:37–38. *Estate of Innocency . . . Glory.* The distinction is basic to *Christian Ethicks;* see General Introduction, p. xxxv, and *CE,* pp. 30–35, 92, 105, 164, and 194. For an explanation of the concept, see *C* III.43 (Margoliouth in a note on this passage points to *CE,* p. 185, to which he also makes reference in a note on *C* II.89). The four estates are mentioned also in the *Thanksgivings* (II, 307); in CYB, f. 48ᵛ; and in SM III.37, 53. The classification occurs in other writers of the period. The nonconformist divine John Bartlet advised his reader "to meditate on the Four-fold Estate of Man: his blessed state by Creation, cursed state by Transgression, gracious state by Regeneration, and happy estate by Glorification" (*The Practical Christian* [1670], p. 133). The usual arrangement was tripartite. Henry Scougal discussed man in the "State of Innocence," "his lapsed Estate," and "his renewed State" (*An Account of the Beginnings and Advances of a Spiritual Life,* pp. 2–3, in *The Life of God in the Soul of Man* [Newcastle, 1742]).

P. 5:12. *he hopes.* Traherne, that is.

P. 5:14–16. *not the least tittle . . . Councels.* Traherne manifested his knowledge of early Church councils in both *Roman Forgeries* and the Church's Year-Book. In the latter work he urged upon the Church of England a return to ceremonial orthodoxy. "Save us from Novelty," he prayed in the Year-Book, calling upon his audience "to follow Holy Antiquity in their Purest & Virgin Piety" (f. 16). He complained that after Cromwell's overthrow "Primitive Devotion" continued to be rare: "it hath Scarce room to be rememberd . . . To do it is branded with Superstition & Hypocrisie" (f. 20). "Nevertheless," he added (protecting himself against charges of popery), "the H. Church retains commends & Commemorats" such devotion as "a Glorious Duty, ubraided by none without the Guilt of Horrid Iniquity" (f. 20). Cf. also SM III.24–25 and CYB, f. 23, quoting Edward Sparke's *Scintilla Altaris* (4th ed., 1666, p. 19), and f. 104, quoting William Austin's *Devotionis Augustinianae Flamma. Or Certayne . . . Meditations* (1635, p. 215).

P. 5:24. *casting . . . Exchequer.* A reference to the story of the widow's mite told in Luke 21:2–4 and Mark 12:42–44.

P. 5:32. *concurrent Actions.* An allusion to, but hardly an enunciation of the theological doctrine of concurrence, which "suggests that divine activity runs parallel with the activity of things and creatures" (Dagobert D. Runes, *Dictionary of Philosophy,* 15th ed. [New York, 1960], *s.v.* "Concursus dei"). Cf. Traherne's poem "The City" (II, 145): "I must see other Things to be / For my Felicity / Concurrent Instruments. . . ." In a passage copied by Traherne in EN (pp. 11–12), Eustache de Saint-Paul discussed the question of divine concurrence; the section Traherne quoted begins: "Sic igitur actio libera, tota immediate pendet tum a voluntate cum à concursu Dei; ita ut concursus ille non sit influxus quo Deus primo per se moveat voluntatem ad operandum, sed quo cum ipsa voluntate concurrat ad actum liberum eliciendum" (*Ethica* [1658], p. 48). Note that Traherne withdraws his proposed third category—actions in the creatures—almost as soon as he suggests it. The thought of this paragraph is part of his treatment of moderation, elaborated in Chaps. XXII–XXIII.

P. 6:5. *under feet*. In this phrase Traherne favored the plural usage, now obsolete; see *CE*, pp. 154, 168, and 173; and also CYB, ff. 96, 101.

P. 6:8. *inestimable Gifts . . . common*. Traherne's stress on the glory of the "common" things of the world pervades the *Centuries* and the *Poems*. He studied "the most Obvious and Common Things. . . . I saw clearly, that there was a Real Valuableness in all the Common things; in the Scarce, a feigned" (*C* III.53); sinful men are blind to "the Truth and Commonness of thy [God's] Glorious Works" ("Thanksgivings for the Wisdom of his WORD," II, 300). In CYB (f. 89) he wrote: "It is Natural to the Infinit Goodness of God to make those Things which are most Excellent, most Common; & only those Things Rare, that are less Serviceable." He would have concurred with the statement translated by Henry Hammond from the pseudo-Aristotelian *Mechanics:* "The every-day wonders are the greatest, the perfectest miracles those that by their commonness have lost all their veneration" (*Thirty-one Sermons*, I [Oxford, 1849], 173).

P. 6:26. *For to feel . . . Glory*. "It hath been long since observ'd," wrote John Flavell, "That the world below, is a Glass to discover the World above; *Seculum est speculum*" (*Husbandry Spiritualized*, 3d ed. [1674], sig. A2). Few of the many who made the observation felt its truth with Traherne's intensity. Some of the Cambridge Platonists shared his fervor. Cf. John Smith: "Every created Excellency is a Beam descending from the Father of lights. . . . We should love all things in God, and God in all things" (*Discourses*, p. 432). Nathanael Culverwel resorted to the bakery to express the beauty of creation: "All the Motions and Operations of Nature are mix'd and season'd with sweetnesse; Every Entity 'tis sugared with some delight; Every being 'tis roll'd up in some pleasure" (*An Elegant Discourse of the Light of Nature* [1652], sig. Aa3^v).

P. 13:7–12. *THE End . . . attained by them*. The opening phrase of this paragraph (for a variant form see *CE*, p. 5) was proverbial (Morris Palmer Tilley, *A Dictionary of the Proverbs in England in the Sixteenth and Seventeenth Centuries* [Ann Arbor, Mich., 1950], E 116, p. 185); Eustache provided the scholastic formula—"finis vero, Id cujus gratia caetera fiunt" (p. 15; paraphrased in EN, p. 8)—which comes ultimately from Aristotle (*Rhetoric* 1.7.1363^{b}17; cf. *Nic. Eth.* I.7.1097^{a}19). For a likeness to the phraseology of the following sentence, cf. Traherne's quotation of Eusebius in *C* IV.79: "Man is the End, and therfore the Perfection of all the Creatures. but as Eusebius Pamphilus saith . . . He was first in the Intention, tho last in the Execution." CYB shows that Traherne knew Meredith Hanmer's translation, *The Auncient Ecclesiasticall Histories* (1577), but perhaps the source is Aquinas: "Although the end is last in the order of execution, yet it is first in the order of the agent's intention" (*ST* I–II, 1, a. 1 *ad* 1). In a scholastic discussion of the end and the means, Benjamin Whichcote wrote: "In moral agents, their actions are specified and distinguished by their ends; for in morals the end is the cause of all causes. . . . Also that which was last in action, is first in intention" (*Works*, II [Aberdeen, 1751], 163–164).

Traherne follows Aristotle's *Nicomachean Ethics* in beginning with a discussion of the end of virtue, a procedure observed by most moralists of the period. Dealing early with the question "Utrum omnia agant propter finem," Eustache concluded that in an absolute sense "omnia agunt propter finem," but in a stricter sense only intellectual creatures act according to an end, for only they can perceive their ends (pp. 16–17; paraphrased in EN, p. 8). The end, Traherne said in "The Anticipation," is "the very Spring, / Of evry Glorious Thing" (II, 160); cf. "The Vision," II, 28; and SM II.84.

P. 13:13–15. *IT is the Office . . . Efficacy.* Eustache explained (in a passage borrowed by Traherne) that the subject of moral philosophy is human action as it may be directed to good behavior (p. 4; EN, p. 7). Traherne stated in the *Centuries* (III.45): "Ethicks teach us the Mysteries of Moralitie, and the Nature of Affections Virtues and Maners, as by them we may be Guided to our Highest Happiness." In this vein is Henry More's definition of ethics as *"the Art of Living well and happily"* (*An Account of Virtue,* tr. Edward Southwell [1690], p. 1). William Colvill defined moral philosophy in scholastic terms as *"Habitus practicus directivus actionum humanarum ad honestatem"* (*Philosophia Moralis Christiana* [Edinburgh, 1670], sig. B2). One could find definitions as restricted as Colvill's was inclusive. Robert Ferguson noted that "practical Divines" commonly understand "morality" to mean "the observation of the precepts of the Second table of the decalogue. . . . But this acceptation [is] much too narrow"; Ferguson arrived at the conclusion that "Morality then consists in an observance of the precepts of the law of our creation, & that by the alone strength and improvement of our natural abilities, whether the particular duties we are under the sanction of by the foresaid law, be discoverable by and in the *light* of *Reason,* yea or not" (*Moral Virtue* [1673], pp. 27–28, 30).

P. 13:28–29. *Reason . . . Beast.* A commonplace; see St. Thomas, *ST* I, 79, a. 8 (and the quotation there of Augustine). Cf. Sir Matthew Hale: "The propounding of an End to what we do, is one thing that gives us Reasonable Creatures a priviledg above the Beasts" (*Contemplations Moral and Divine* [1676], Pt. II, "Of the Chief End of Man," p. 19). Hale noted elsewhere, however, that "Many Learned Men . . . have therefore declined to define a Man by his *Reason,* because of that analogical ratiocination which they find in brutes, but define a man by his *Religion, Homo est animal religiosum . . .* : for man is the only visible creature that expresseth any inclination to Religion or the sense of a Deity" (*Contemplations,* I, "Of Wisdom and the Fear of God," 30; Hale made the same point in *Of the Nature of True Religion* [1684], p. 1). This was the argument of Marsilio Ficino in his *Theologica Platonica* (1482); and John Smith observed similarly, citing Plutarch and Cicero, "that Reason in relation to the capacitating of Man for converse with God was thought by some to be the *Formal Difference* of Man" (*Discourses,* p. 388). On reason, see also *CE,* p. 14:7 n., 109:1 n., and 112:29 n.

P. 14:1. *THE Heathens . . . Ethicks.* "The name τα ἐθικά is derived from ἦθος, character, which again is closely connected with ἔθος, signifying custom. Ethics, therefore, according to Aristotle is the science of character, character being understood to mean . . . customs or habits of conduct." Ethics also includes "that which gives to custom its value, viz., the sources of action, the motives, and especially the ends which guide a man in the conduct of life" (Archibald B. D. Alexander, *Christianity and Ethics* [New York, 1914], p. 10). Cf. Epicurus: "By *Ethicks,* or *Morals,* we understand that part of Philosophy, which hath for its proper Object the End, or Finall and main scope of Mans Life; containing certain Directions and Precepts, for the right information of his Understanding, and (consequently) the conduct of his Will, in the Election of real Good, and Avoidance of Evill, in order to his attaining the true End of life, the Supream Good, or Felicity" (*Epicurus's Morals,* tr. Walter Charleton [1659], p. 2).

P. 14:7–11. *REASON . . . Rule of Right Reason.* Cf. *CE,* p. 141: "Reason is the Essence of the Soul"; this is the accepted formula. The "similitude" of God's "infinite and Eternal Reason" is "the Essence of the Soul," as Traherne explains later (p. 183). See St. Thomas, *ST* I–II, 94, a. 3: "The rational soul is the proper form of man . . ."; and also Robert Hoopes, *Right Reason in the English Renaissance* (Cambridge, Mass., 1962), especially pp. 174–175 on the Cambridge Platonists.

Eustache defined right reason as "bonam mentem ab omni opinionum fumo liberatam, Dei naturaeque leges pernoscentem, ac de quaque re agenda ex praescripta lege sapienter ac prudenter judicantem" (p. 63; quoted EN, p. 14). Antoine Le Grand's definition sounds like a translation of Eustache: "By Right Reason I understand, here *a true Judgment of every thing, free from the Paint or Fucus of any Opinions,* whereby the *Laws* of *GOD* and *Nature* are understood, and every thing rightly and prudently discerned, according to the Prescript of the *Law*" (*Body of Philosophy,* tr. Richard Blome [1694], X. 21, p. 379).

The "Rule of Right Reason" which Traherne cites goes back to Aristotle: "Of goods the greater is always more desirable" (*Nic. Eth.* I.7.1097^{b}20; cf. *Rhetoric* I.7); Hooker regarded it as one of the "main principles of Reason . . . 'that the greater good is to be chosen before the less' " (*Laws of Ecclesiastical Polity,* I.viii.5; Everyman ed., I, 177). George Herbert included a jaunty version in his *Outlandish Proverbs* (no. 454): "Good is good, but better carries it" (*Works,* ed. F. E. Hutchinson [Oxford, 1941], p. 337). Cf. also *CE,* pp. 15, 74, and 141.

P. 14:12–14. *WHATEVER Varieties . . . perfect Happiness.* A similar statement occurs in *Nic. Eth.* I.4.1095^{a}16–20. Traherne dilates upon this topic in *C* II.99; there he cites Varro's calculation of "288 Opinions of Philosophers concerning Happiness," a tabulation made famous by Augustine's citation of it in *De civitate dei* XIX.1.

P. 14:40–p. 15:2. *the more Eager . . . presumed.* Traherne makes a similar observation later in *CE,* p. 111: "The great Moment of what" the unorthodox "took for granted made the strife the more Eager."

P. 15:6. *The lip of the Cup.* Cf. the reference to Circe's cup, *CE,* p. 37.

P. 15:10–14. *IT is as natural . . . capable.* Cf. *C* III.56: "It was the infinit Wisdom of God, that did implant by Instinct so strong a Desire of felicity in the Soul. . . ." Man's instinctive desire of happiness was a subject dear in particular to the Cambridge Platonists. "The whole work of this World is nothing but a perpetuall contention for True *Happiness,*" wrote John Smith, "and men are scatter'd up and down the world, moving to and fro therein, to seek it" (*Discourses,* pp. 136–137). Thomas Jackson, an earlier Platonist, spoke too of *"our inbred desire of happinesse"* (*Treatise,* p. 464; quoted CB, *s.v.* "Desire," f. 34ᵛ.1). The idea was commonplace outside Platonic circles as well; John Scott, for example, noted the "unquenchable thirst and desire of happiness which God hath implanted in our nature" and observed that reason guides our passions and instincts which naturally desire moral good (*Works* [Oxford, 1826], I, 445–448).

P. 16:19–20. *the Maxime . . . the Eye.* Traherne paraphrases this common Latin adage with an equally common English saying (see Tilley, L 501, p. 396) which goes back at least to Aristotle (*Nic. Eth.* IX.5.1167ᵃ4). He gives more of a literal translation in the *Centuries,* where he says it is "a Maxime in the Scholes, That there is no Lov of a thing unknown" (*C* I.2). In both cases Traherne cited the maxim only to deny it: "I hav found, that Things unknown have a Secret Influence on the Soul" (*C* I.2). Most writers approved the saying—for example, two authors of books we know Traherne read: Edward Reynolds (*A Treatise of the Passions and Faculties of the Soule of Man* [1640], p. 179) and Thomas Jackson (*Treatise,* p. 452). John Norris explained that "every man has a restless Principle of Love implanted in his Nature, a certain *Magnetism* of Passion, whereby (according to the *Platonic* and true notion of Love) he continually aspires to somthing more excellent than himself, either really or apparently, with a design and inclination to perfect his Being. This affection and disposition of Mind *all* Men have, and at *all* times" ("A Discourse Concerning Heroic Piety," in *A Collection of Miscellanies* [Oxford, 1687], pp. 286–287). With reference to *C* I.2, K. W. Salter explains that this is "a re-state-ment . . . of one of the dominant ideas of medieval scholasticism, that like causes beget like effects. The very desire for Felicity argues that there is a Felicity" (*Thomas Traherne* [1964], pp. 33–34).

P. 16:21. *touched with an unknown Beauty.* Cf. *CE,* p. 166: "To keep Commands whose Beauty's yet unseen. . . ."

P. 17:1–3. *Stoical . . . Liberty.* Two of the main challenges to Christian ethics in the seventeenth century came from Neo-Stoicism and libertarianism. On Traherne's rejection of the Stoic doctrine of contentment, see *CE,* p. 60:36 n.; and on his scorn of libertinage, see *CE,* p. 163:8 n.

P. 17:8. *Goods of fortune.* Traherne discusses this topic in the following two paragraphs.

P. 17:30. *as Mariners in a storm.* This example was common in moral philosophy. Aristotle (*Nic. Eth.* III.1.1110ᵃ9) and Eustache after him (p. 62; quoted EN, p. 14) used it to illustrate a discussion of voluntary and involuntary actions, as did Jean Buridan in his *Quaestiones* on the *Nicomachean Ethics* ([Oxford, 1637], p. 184) and Thomas Hobbes in *Humane Nature* (in *Hobbs's Tripos,* 3d ed. [1684], p. 80).

P. 18:4–6. *THE Peripateticks . . . perfect Happiness.* Aristotle's followers, the Peripatetics, observed the distinction he made in *Nic. Eth.* I.8.1098ᵇ12–13, where Aristotle was himself repeating Plato (Ross's note refers to *Euthydemus*

279ab, *Philebus* 48e, *Laws* 743e). See Traherne's censure of the Stoic view of these "goods," *CE*, p. 60. Like Traherne, Henry More observed the usefulness of *"external Comforts,"* which—he said—"do much conduce to the making happiness complete" (*Account*, p. 4).

P. 18:11–13. *Distinction . . . Journey.* Cf. *CE*, p. 211: ". . . the middle of the Way is not the place of Rest and Perfection."

P. 18:21. *Goods of the Body.* Charron's list ran: "Health, Beauty, Cheerefulnes, Strength, Vigor, a prompt readinesse and disposition" (*Of Wisdome,* p. 17). Henry More included *"Strength, Agility, Comliness, and Health"* (*Account,* p. 161).

P. 19:12–13. *FELICITY . . . Virtue.* Traherne acknowledges Aristotle as the source immediately below. Cf. *C* III.68: "Aristotle . . . saith Felicity is the Perfect Exercise of Perfect Virtu in a Perfect Life." Aristotle did not express himself so concisely; see *Nic. Eth.* I.7.1098^{a}17–18; I.13.1102^{a}5–6; and X.7.1177^{a}12–13. Theophilus Gale's translation of *Nic. Eth.* I.7, compressing Aristotle, comes close to Traherne's formula: *"Beatitude is the operation of the rational Soul, according to the best virtue in a perfect life"* (*The Court of the Gentiles,* Pt. II [Oxford, 1670], p. 386; quoted CB, f. 21.2; cf. Gale's alternate translation, p. 388, quoted CB, f. 21^v.2). Traherne copied the entirety of Gale's account of Aristotelian ethics (pp. 383–389) into his Commonplace Book (*s.v.* "Beatitude," ff. 21.1–21^v.2). The real source of the present quotation is such Aristotelian epitomes as that by Eustache, who wrote that Aristotle teaches "felicitatem esse *actionem virtutis in vita perfecta"* (p. 25). Traherne expanded Eustache thus: "felicitas formalis est operatio animae rationalis secundum virtutem perfecticissimam in vitâ perfectâ" (EN, p. 9).

P. 19:20. *our present Estate.* See above, p. 4:37 n.

P. 19:23. *Appointed Seed Time.* See Eccles. 3:2, a well as Jesus' parable of the mustard seed (Mark 4:30–32). For another example of the conventional imagery of this paragraph, see *CE*, p. 188, as well as the poem "The Inference: II," l. 16: "Seed-plots of activ Piety" (II, 142).

P. 19:37–40. *OBJECTIVE . . . Perfections.* In EN, "Felicitas objectiva" is defined as the "summum bonum absolutè perfectum" and "Felicitas formalis" is said to consist "in perfectissimâ . . . contemplatione et summâ dilectione" of objective felicity (pp. 8–9; derived from Eustache, pp. 20, 23–24). Gale (p. 383, quoted CB, *s.v.* "Beatitude," f. 21.1) attributed the distinction to Aristotle; see *Nic. Eth.* I.6–7. Thomas Aquinas said that "perfect happiness" (by which he seems to have meant "formal") "includes the aggregate of all good things, by being united to the universal source of all good" (*ST* I-II, 3, a. 3 *ad* 2). Benjamin Whichcote explained that according to scholastic moralists formal happiness "is that act of ours, whether it be intellection, or dilectation, or both, whereby we ourselves are united to God [and] God is the objective happiness, because he is the object that makes them happy who do enjoy him" (*Works,* IV, 301).

P. 19:40. *Complacency.* Pleasure or delight, as frequently hereafter. Antoine Le Grand defined "complacency" as "another *Species* of *Love,* whereby the *Soul* is carried out in *desire* towards *Beautiful Objects,* being greatly taken, and charmed with their aspect" (*Body of Philosophy,* X.15, p. 370).

P. 21:21–23. *the children . . . together.* Rom. 8:16–17. The concept of man as God's heir is prominent in Traherne's work; Margoliouth observed that "if Traherne had given [the *Centuries*] a title, he might very well have called it 'The Heir of the World'" (*C* I.3.5 n.). See *CE,* pp. 61 and 250:6 n.

P. 21:24–25. *our light . . . Glory.* 2 Cor. 4:17.

P. 21:25–28. *beholding . . . the Lord.* 2 Cor. 3:18. Here, as frequently, Traherne departs from the wording of the Authorized Version; most of his variations go without comment in this edition, being relatively minor.

P. 21:28–30. *They are . . . pleasure therein.* Ps. 111:4, 2. As Margoliouth noted with reference to the *Thanksgivings* (II, 409), Traherne used the A.V. translation of the Psalms, not the Prayer Book Psalter.

P. 21:37–p. 22:8. *He hath given . . . Jesus Christ.* 2 Pet. 1:3–7, 11.

P. 22:9–17. *bow our Knees . . . fulness of GOD.* Eph. 3:14–19; the speaker is, of course, Paul, not Peter.

P. 23:6. *VERTUE is a comprehensive Word.* Socrates posed the question "whether virtue is one whole, of which justice and temperance and holiness are parts; or whether all these are only the names of one and the same thing" (*Protagoras* 329C). Included in Ficino's epitome of the *Meno* was the statement that virtue is one, though differentiated into species (Ficino, *Opera,* II [Paris, 1641], 106; FN, f. 12). Gale quoted the *Republic* IV: *". . . to me the face of Virtue seems to be one;* whence virtue is stiled by [Plato] *Concent, and . . . symmetrie* and . . . *harmonie.* Whence also the *Stoicks* held . . . all virtues are equal, or alike" (*Court,* p. 412; quoted *CB, s.v.* "Virtue," f. 96.2). One of the topics treated by Eustache was "Utrum virtutes morales sint inter se connexae" (p. 111; quoted EN, p. 17). This question, a philosophical cliché, was answered affirmatively by Traherne and most other authors, including Whichcote: "All moral virtues are conjoined amongst themselves inseparably. The reason is, because the exercise of one virtue requires that temper which is productive of all the rest" (*Works,* IV, 389). This belief "occasion'd the Philosophers to terme this noble alliance, the *golden chain of Vertue,* each being linkt with, and depending upon it's fellow" (Sir George Mackenzie, *A Moral Paradox* [Edinburgh, 1667], p. 33).

P. 23:13–14. *Predicament . . . Dispositions or Habits.* "Predicament" is a scholastic word for Aristotle's term "category." Aristotle explained: "By 'quality' I mean that in virtue of which people are said to be such and such. . . . One sort of quality let us call 'habit' or 'disposition.' Habit differs from disposition in being more lasting and more firmly established. The various kinds of knowledge and of virtue are habits" (*Categories* VIII.8^{b}25–29). Traherne distinguished more sharply than Aristotle between habits and dispositions; see *CE,* p. 25.

P. 23:18–26. *THE Theological Vertues . . . Godliness.* The Pauline triad (1 Cor. 13:13) was endorsed by St. Thomas (*ST* I–II, 62, a. 3), who explained that they are called "theological . . . first, because their object is God, because they direct us rightly to God; secondly, because they are infused in us by God alone; thirdly, because these virtues are not made known to us except by Divine revelation, contained in Holy Writ" (*ST* I–II, 62, a. 1). With Traherne's additions compare the proposal of Francesco Piccolomini that the theological virtues be augmented by three others: piety, corresponding to hope; religious observance, corresponding to faith; and holiness, corresponding to charity (*Universa philo-sophia*, rev. ed. [Venice, 1594], p. 182). Cf. Traherne's list of the theological virtues in SM IV.62: "Faith Righteousness Holiness & Humility."

P. 23:27–28. *THE Intellectual Vertues . . . Art.* The traditional list, deriv-ing from Aristotle (*Nic. Eth.* VI.3.1139ᵇ15–17); see also St. Thomas, *ST* I–II, 57. Intelligence, wisdom, and science (or knowledge) were "speculative" virtues; art and prudence, "practical" virtues. The conventionality of Traherne's defini-tions in the following paragraph may be seen by comparison with Christoph Scheibler's: intelligence "cognoscit principia scientiarum & demonstrationum"; science "est habitus demonstrativus ex necessariis"; wisdom "est habitus ex scientia & intelligentia rerum praestantissimarum constans" (*Philosophia com-pendiosa*, 7th ed. [Oxford, 1647], VII.18.2–5, p. 105).

Note that prudence fits in two categories; St. Thomas elucidated: "Prudence is essentially an intellectual virtue. But considered on the part of its matter, it has something in common with the moral virtues, for it is right reason about things to be done. . . . It is in this sense that it is numbered among the moral virtues" (*ST* I–II, 58, a. 3). Traherne's chapter on prudence treats it as a cardinal (moral) virtue. He subsumed art under temperance (Chap. XXII).

P. 23:33–p. 24:1. *Wisdom . . . explained.* See *CE*, Chap. IX, for Tra-herne's elucidation.

P. 24:14–20. *The Principal . . . compounded.* The distinction of the four cardinal virtues goes back at least as far as Plato, who listed them as wisdom (prudence), courage (fortitude), temperance, and justice (*Republic* IV.428a–430d; Ficino's epitome of this passage is quoted in FN, f. 42ᵛ; see also Traherne's quotation of Ficino's epitome of the *Meno*, FN, f. 12ᵛ). St. Ambrose in *De officiis ministrorum* brought the quartet into the mainstream of Christian ethics, under the name of principal virtues. As for the term "cardi-nal," Jean Buridan offered this account: ". . . secundum Albertum, virtutes ex eo dicuntur cardinales, quia in eis, veluti in cardinibus, tota volvitur humana conversatio" (*Quaestiones*, p. 225). Defining the cardinal virtues, Eustache noted that prudence pertains to the reason, justice to the will, temperance to the concupiscible appetite, and fortitude to the irascible appetite; he also gave the (by then standard) etymological explanation and observed that all the other moral virtues may be reduced to these four (p. 109; quoted EN, p. 17). Note that in *CE*, p. 94, Traherne reclassified justice among the divine virtues; Chaps. XX–XXIII treat the other three cardinal virtues.

P. 24:21–23. *THE less Principal . . . Urbanitie.* These virtues are approxi-mately the same as the list (not derived from Eustache) following the cardinal virtues in EN (pp. 20–21): *liberalitas, magnificentia, modestia, magnanamitas, honor* (not discussed as such in *CE*), *mansuetudo* ("Gentleness of behaviour"), *comitas* ("Affability, Courtesie"), *urbanitas, veritas,* and *taciturnitas* (not men-tioned in *CE*). The treatment of the "less principal" virtues in EN is schemati-cally Aristotelian; for example: "Quid est Magnificentia? Magnificentia est virtus in magnis sumptibus erogandis, mediocritatem servens. ejus excessus est Luxus inepta Splendoris affectatio, defectus est sordes" (p. 20). Chaps. XXVIII–XXXI of *CE* are devoted to the less principal virtues; Traherne singled out for extensive discussion the first four of the list, alluding to several of the remainder on p.

215. These are all virtues treated by Aristotle (*Nic. Eth.* II.7; IV.1–7; cf. St. Thomas, *ST* I–II, 60, a. 5), though the Aristotelian emphases vary markedly from Traherne's. Aside from the omission of honor, Christoph Scheibler's list is identical with Traherne's in EN (*Philosophia compendiosa,* VII.9–13, pp. 100–103). The lesser "less principal" virtues were termed *"the Virtues of Common Conversation"* by Richard Cumberland, who identified them as gravity, courteousness, taciturnity, veracity, fidelity, and urbanity (*A Treatise of the Laws of Nature,* tr. John Maxwell [1727], pp. 333–335).

P. 24:28–29. *DIVINE Vertues . . . Heroical.* Many Christian moralists used the pagan term. John Norris defined heroic virtue as "such a vehement and intense pursuance of a mans last and best end, as engages him upon such excellent and highly commendable actions, which advance him much above the ordinary level of human Nature, and which he might wholly omit, and yet still maintain the Character of a good man. *Aristotle* in his *Ethics l. 7 c.* 1. [1145ª20–24] calls it . . . that Vertue that is above us." This means, said Norris, "that it is above our obligation, and that when it is attain'd, it will elevate us above our selves" ("A Discourse Concerning Heroic Piety," in *Collection,* pp. 278–279). The Platonists, according to William Colvill, classified the virtues as civil, purgatorial, and exemplary or heroic; true heroic virtue, Colvill asserted, had appeared only in the great men of Judaeo-Christian history (*Philosophia,* pp. 31–32; see also *CE,* p. 126:14 n.). Since heroic virtue was a heightening of all the virtues combined, few authorities provided lists such as Traherne's (which he augmented with justice, *CE,* p. 94). Henry More said that charity, humility, and purity are called *"Divine Vertues . . .* because they are such as are proper to a Creature to whom God communicates his own nature" (*The Grand Mystery of Godliness* [1660], p. 53).

P. 24:37–38. *some Vertues . . . called Christian.* John Hartcliffe listed charity, meekness, patience, and humility as "the distinguishing Graces of the *Gospel*" (*A Treatise of Moral and Intellectual Virtues* [1691], p. 1).

P. 24:40. *Manners . . . derived.* St. Thomas defined "mos" (in its etymological relationship to "moral") as "a natural or quasi-natural inclination to do some particular action" (*ST* I–II, 58, a. 1). As he remarked (I–II, 58, a. 2), the distinction between intellectual and moral virtues goes back to Aristotle (*Nic. Eth.* I.13.1103ª3–6). Note that the Greek term equivalent to *mores* is ἦθος, from which derives ἠθικά or "ethics." In Latin and then English usage, however, the term "moral philosophy" came to include "economics" and "politics" as well as personal ethics; see Eustache, p. 5 (EN, p. 7).

On the marginal notes in the 1675 edition, see Textual Introduction, p. lxi.

P. 25:7–10. *VERTUE . . . Blessedness.* Cf. Gale's paraphrase of Plato's *Meno:* "Virtue is an habit of the Soul, by the concurrence of the natural power, working that which is best, according to reason, and tending to the best End" (*Court,* p. 412; quoted CB, *s.v.* "Virtue," f. 96.2; cf. *Meno* 88c–89a). Traherne quoted Ficino's epitome of the *Meno* in FN: "Est autem hominis virtus affectio siue habitus animae, quo potentia naturalis eius quàm optime suum opus exercet" (Ficino, *Opera,* II, 106; FN, f. 12). Gale also translated Aristotle's definition: "Virtue is an Elective habit consisting in mediocritie of things relating to us, defined by reason, and so as a wise man defines" (*Court,* p 411; quoted CB, *s.v.* "Virtue," f. 96.2; *Nic. Eth.* II.6.1107ª1–2). Eustache's definition is identical with Aristotle's (pp. 104–105; EN, p. 16).

P. 25:11–25. *All Habits . . . Heaven.* In both Greek philosophy and in Christian theology there was some controversy regarding the infusion of habits. Thomas Aquinas maintained "that some virtues are infused into us by God" and "in this respect we cannot differentiate gifts [i.e., graces] from virtues"; but he went on to observe "that the gifts [graces] perfect man for acts which are higher than acts of virtue" (*ST* I–II, 68, a. 1). Eustache discussed in technical terms the meaning of habit (pp. 41–46; EN, p. 11). Traherne agreed with Benjamin Whichcote that "all habits are acquired, and men attain them by particular acts" (*Works,* I, 158). Habits are therefore generically different from natural (infused) dispositions or graces. On the different scholastic definitions of grace, see Robert Ferguson, *Moral Virtue,* pp. 35–45; Ferguson defined "*Gratia habitualis,* habitual Grace" as "a quality impressed on the minds and souls of men, whereby they become habitually disposed for God" (pp. 40–41). Ferguson observed that if one believed with Plato that virtue is infused, then one could not logically conclude with "all the Stoicks . . . *that Vertue was teachable*" (pp. 15–16).

P. 25:37–39. *GOD . . . perish.* On God's "Election of perticular persons," see *CE,* p. 74.

P. 26:32. *A Mind in Frame.* One of Traherne's favorite phrases; see *C* I.10, I.13, and III.60.

P. 26:35. *inuring.* Habituating.

P. 28:3. *Grateful.* Pleasing or agreeable, as frequently hereafter.

P. 28:6. *conceit.* Think.

P. 29:5. *Glory and Treasure.* Cf. the entries in CB under "Treasure" (f. 94.2) and "Preparation" (f. 77.2). That under "Preparation" begins: "In order to Felicity there is a twofold Preparation the one of Treasures, the other of Enjoyers" (from an unidentified source). This pair is related to Traherne's distinction here of treasure (the end) and glory (our actions in achieving the end). "Preparation" includes a passage which Traherne incorporated into *CE* (see *CE,* p. 126:31 n.).

P. 29:6. *the Faculties of the soul.* The following discussion refers not only to the faculties (understanding, will, reason) but to the passions as well. The passions were variously numbered by seventeenth-century psychologists and moralists, the most popular account remaining that of St. Thomas (*ST* I–II, 23, a. 4). Traherne here lists the eleven Thomistic passions (he adds "*Appetite*"), as did Eustache (pp. 84–85; EN, pp. 15–16). The Early Notebook shows (pp. 140, 143, 154) that Traherne had read Edward Reynolds's *Treatise of the Passions and Faculties of the Soule of Man* (1640). The principal passions Reynolds discussed are love, hatred, desire, joy, sorrow, hope, boldness, fear, and anger; he treated the faculties in dealing with reason, understanding, and will: in short, Reynolds's passions and faculties are approximately the same as Traherne's. Unlike many moral philosophers, Traherne did not consider the psychology of the passions but dealt with them only as they relate to the virtues. In some cases, of course, one man's passion was another man's virtue (e.g., love, hatred, hope, boldness). For further information on the passions, see *CE,* p. 96:10 n.

P. 29:27–28. *THE Inclinations . . . towards Objects.* Cf. Thomas Wright: "Passions, are not only, not wholly to be extinguished (as the Stoicks seemed to affirme) but sometimes to be moved, & stirred up for the service of vertue, as learnedly *Plutarch* teacheth" (*The Passions of the Minde*, rev. ed. [1620], p. 17). Henry More insisted against Stoic "autarchy" (see *CE*, p. 60:36 n.) that "the *Passions* of the Body are not to be quite extinguished, but regulated, that there may be the greater plenitude of life in the whole man. . . . For the Divine Life as it is to take into it self the humane nature in general, so it is not abhorrent from any of the complexions thereof" (*The Defense of the Moral Cabbala*, in *A Collection of Several Philosophical Writings* [1662], p. 158). For the Neo-Stoic viewpoint, see (for example) Antoine Le Grand, *Man Without Passion: Or, The Wise Stoick, According to the Sentiments of Seneca,* tr. G. R. (1675). On "defect" and "excess" in Aristotelian philosophy, see *CE*, p. 172:15 n.

P. 30:21. *SOME Vertues are necessary.* With this and the following paragraphs cf. Traherne's early version in his Select Meditations. Some virtues belong "to the State of Innocency, & Some to the Estate of Misery and Grace. Goodness & wisdom & Temperance & justice haue immediatly their original in the Divine Essence. And Fortitude also to Adventure upon Great Things Not withstanding infinit hazard. which is fed by Lov Encouraged by Goodness Sustained by Power Aided by wisdom. & Deriveth strength From the Magazines of Hope, & Certain Prospect of what will Follow. . . . And these continue throughout all Ages. upon mans Sin & Redemption by the Bloud of Jesus there rose up a new mine & offspring of vertues. which are properly Conversant in that State. Forgivness Penitence & patience Faith Meekness &c. of all which Penitence and patience seem hardest. But if they be hard, Remember that we First made God Endure them. It repented God that He had mad[e] man. & till we sinned there Could be no Patience. But how Infinitly [*sic*] is His Glory who could rais such children out of [the] Horrid Womb of such a Monster" (SM III.53).

P. 31:8. *GOD gave us Liberty.* No theological tenet is more central to Traherne's thought than belief in free will; see General Introduction, p. xliv; *CE*, pp. 85, 90–93, 148–150, 183, and 271; *C* IV.42, 46, and the quotation of Pico in *C* IV.74–78. Note also that one of the books he quoted in CB was Thomas Jackson's *Treatise of the Divine Essence and Attributes* (2 parts, 1628, 1629), which favored free will against a virulent Calvinist opposition.

P. 31:26. *preventing.* Predisposing (i.e., by prevenient grace, which predisposes "the heart to seek God, previously to any desire or motion on the part of the recipient": *OED, s.v.* "prevenient"). In the *Meditations* Traherne prayed to God that "my *habitual Care* co-operating with thy *preventing Grace,* may preserve me from all *Relapses*" into sin (p. 23). Cf. *CE*, p. 47:3 n., for the less technical seventeenth-century meaning.

P. 32:3. *obnoxious.* Liable, as again, *CE*, pp. 104, 220, and 221 (where the phrase is "obnoxious and liable"). See *CE*, p. 128:3 n.

P. 32:13. *denounced.* Proclaimed (cf. *CE*, p. 101: "the Denunciation of the Sentence").

P. 32:14. *nice.* Intricate, delicate, requiring fine discrimination.

P. 32:30. *Admiration.* Wonder.

P. 33:1. *WHEN we fell into Sin.* Some students of Traherne have considered him heretical with regard to the Anglican doctrine of Original Sin; but as this paragraph shows, he held the orthodox position (see also *CE*, pp. 99–102; his orthodoxy is demonstrated by William H. Marshall, "Thomas Traherne and the Doctrine of Original Sin," *Modern Language Notes*, LXXIII [1958], 161–165; cf. Louis L. Martz, *The Paradise Within* [New Haven and London, 1964], pp. 84–87; see, for a variant view, A. L. Clements, "On the Mode and Meaning of Traherne's Mystical Poetry: 'The Preparative,'" *Studies in Philology*, LXI [1964], 515). It is true, however, that Traherne had a presumably unconscious heretical inclination and placed much more emphasis than was then usual upon innocence. Thus conscious orthodoxy underlies his statement later in *CE*, pp. 58–59, that natural man (if uncorrupted) could understand all truths "by the Light of Nature"; but his stress is not so much on the effects of original corruption as on the beauty and glory of the world, so obvious to Traherne that he marveled that "the Heathens did miss the fruition of it." Cf. also his development, *CE*, pp. 33–34, of the utopian conditions which would have prevailed had Adam not sinned.

P. 33:30. *commutative Justice.* See *CE*, p. 95:22 n.

P. 34:7–8. *no Ceremonial Law . . . Typified.* See *CE*, p. 110:2 n.

P. 34:30–31. *an Idea . . . Wise and Good.* The word "idea," used here in its Platonic sense, was still regarded by seventeenth-century printers as a foreign word; hence the italics. Like all Platonists, Traherne endorsed the theory of innate ideas, which was opposed by the Aristotelian championship of the mind as a *tabula rasa* (cf. the scholastic formula: "Nihil est in intellectu quod non prius fuerit in sensu"). See Sterling Lamprecht, "Innate Ideas in the Cambridge Platonists," *Philosophical Review*, XXXV (1926), 553–573. The belief that God is by his nature good so preoccupied the Cambridge Platonists that an opponent complained in 1666 that "these mens minds are so excessively possessed with thoughts of Gods goodness, as to neglect all his other Attributes" (Samuel Parker, *An Account of . . . the Divine Dominion & Goodnesse* [Oxford, 1666], p. 27). Note Traherne's statement: "I was guided by an Implicit Faith in Gods Goodness" (*C* III.53).

P. 35:11. *Eligible.* Worthy of choice (cf. Latin *eligere*, to choose); used in this sense *CE*, p. 66.

P. 35:31. *Sweeter then . . . Hony Comb.* Ps. 19:10.

P. 35:32. *thousands of Gold and Silver.* Ps. 119:72.

P. 36:2. *the Necessity . . . of Knowledge.* Traherne included in CYB an extended encomium of knowledge: "The Soul of Man cannot lie under a Thicker Cloud then Ignorance: nor have stronger Desires after any Thing then Knowledg. . . . This Ardent Inclination in the Soul of Man, is a Rare Ingredient & Caus of Glory. . . . never did any constantly & Sincerely Study it, but he was recompenced with Such a Fruition of it, as to be Happy here, & Glorious herafter" (ff. 56ᵛ–57). His exaltation of knowledge may be paralleled in two works he quoted in CB. According to Hermes Trismegistus, "the wickednesse of a Soul, is ignorance. . . . On the contrary, the vertue of the Soul is Knowledge" (*His Divine Pymander*, tr. John Everard [1657], IV.27–28). Thomas Jackson's *Treatise of Unbeliefe* dilates upon the innate human desire for knowledge;

Traherne quoted some of his words on this subject under "Joy" (f. 60ᵛ.1) and "Desire" (f. 34ᵛ.1). Jackson's Platonism and his affinity with Traherne appear in this extract: "So that knowledge properly is but our naturall desire, or implanted blind love restored to sight: and nature doth as it were first grope after that, which at length she comes to see, and having seene desires to embrace or kisse" (p. 462; CB, f. 34ᵛ.1).

P. 36:10. *GOD is Light . . . at all.* 1 John 1:5.

P. 36:17–20. *THE understanding . . . its Object.* Traherne uses the word "understanding" in the scholastic sense of "the power of knowing" (Bernard Wuellner, *Dictionary of Scholastic Philosophy* [Milwaukee, 1956], *s.v.* "understanding"). By "Matter" he means material cause: "that out of which something arises" (Runes, *Dictionary, s.v.* "cause"), "an intrinsic capacity for perfection" (Wuellner, *Dictionary, s.v.* "matter"). By "form" he means essence. The gist of this arid cento of scholasticism is that knowledge is made possible by the understanding. Cf. Charron: "The actions come after and follow the faculties, and so there are three degrees, according to the doctrine of Great S. *Denis* followed of all, that is, we must consider in spirituall creatures three things; *Essence, Facultie, Operation:* By the latter, which is the action, we know the facultie, and by it the essence" (*Of Wisdome,* pp. 26–27). Among the followers of the *Angelic Hierarchy* of the Pseudo-Dionysius, to whom Charron refers, was St. Thomas (who quoted the passage to which Charron alludes: *ST* I, 75; 77, a. 1).

P. 36:22–26. *For all Powers . . . Power exerted.* Cf. *CE,* p. 68:15 n. Note also that God, being "all Act, . . . Himself is Power Exerted" (*C* III.64).

P. 36:33. *be perfect . . . perfect.* Matt. 5:48.

P. 37:8–9. *Seraphim . . . Highest Order.* See *CE,* p. 275:18 n.

P. 37:14–16. *Vertues . . . Error.* A reference to Aristotle's doctrine of the mean; cf. *CE,* p. 172:15 n. Ignorance Traherne describes as the defect of knowledge; error he appears rather oddly to consider the excess. Thomas Aquinas classified knowledge as a gift, not a virtue, and therefore did not define it in terms of the mean (*ST* II–II, 9, a. 1); he considered the "vices opposed to knowledge and understanding" to be "ignorance . . . blindness of mind and dulness of sense" (*ST* II–II, 15).

P. 38:20. *THE Existence of many Souls.* One of the most fundamental tenets of Traherne's philosophy is the paradox that the greater the number of souls enjoying God's gifts, the greater will be the enjoyment of each individual soul. See *CE,* pp. 55, 83:36 n., 203, and 250:6 n.; *C* I.68, *C* II.61, 70. "One Soul in the Immensity of its Intelligence, is Greater and more Excellent then the whole World. . . . And yet the fruition of it is but Solitary. We need Spectators" (*C* II.70).

P. 39:1–2. *nothing Useless . . . usefulness.* The criterion of utility—conceived in a spiritual sense (cf. *C* I.26)—is prominent in Traherne's thought and, indeed, in the thought of most of his contemporaries. "A signal characteristic of the [seventeenth-century] revolution in thought," says Meyrick H. Carré, "was its practical intention. . . . The association of natural truth with utility exhibits a change of theological and moral beliefs" (*Phases of Thought in England* [Oxford, 1949], pp. 272–273). Cf. Traherne's statement in *CE:* "By Vertue the Creation is made *useful*" (p. 5); his explanation of "the Beauty and Service-ableness" (*C* I.18), the "use and Excellency" (*C* I.35) of the world; and his assertion in CYB (f. 92): "Things by their Ministery alone are Advanced. Nothing is Glorious but by Doing Service. Had the Sun been useless it would never hav been valued."

P. 39:35. *THE Sun is a glorious Creature.* The utility and magnificence of the sun are among Traherne's favorite subjects. See *CE*, pp. 48:33 n., 83, 140:30 n., and 263:16 n.; "The Dialogue," II, 137; and *C* II.7–11. In his *Meditations* he devoted pp. 39–46 to solar wonders, calling the sun "an universal Blessing which irradiates all things here below, infinitely more glorious to the Eye of the Understanding than to the Eye of the Body" (p. 40); cf. a similar passage in SM II.87. Note also that he quoted from Gale's account of pagan sun worship (*Court,* pp. 53–54, 69–70; CB, *s.v.* "Sun," f. 91).

P. 39:40. The note should read Col. 1:9–13.

P. 40:11–12. *The Sphere of its Activity is illimited.* Another of Traherne's central themes is the power of the human intellect, its ability to penetrate the "Boundless Habitations" of eternity (CYB, f. 53), to "see before and after its Existence into Endless Spaces" (*C* I.55). He dwelt upon this subject particularly in his poems; see "My Spirit," "Sight," "Insatiableness," "Consummation," and the four poems entitled "Thoughts." See also *CE*, pp. 48, 108–109, and the quotations from Hermes Trismegistus on pp. 225–227. Traherne must have agreed with Charron's list of the characteristics of the human soul (though not with his conclusion that these traits constitute "a great disposition and propension unto folly and madnesse"): (1) activity: "Motion and agitation is the true life and grace of the *Spirit*"; (2) universality: the soul "medleth and mingleth it selfe with all"; (3) speed: the soul "is prompt and speedy, running in a moment from the one end of the world to the other, without stay or rest, stirring it selfe and penetrating through every thing" (*Of Wisdome,* p. 59).

P. 40:35–37. *In his Presence . . . evermore.* Ps. 16:11.

P. 40:39. *Throne of GOD.* A phrase used in Matt. 23:22; Heb. 12:2; Rev. 7:15, 14:5, 22:1, 22:3.

P. 41:1. *be filled . . . GOD.* Eph. 3:19.

P. 41:4–5. *Nature never . . . vain.* A version of the scholastic cliché, *Natura nil frustra fecit,* which the Venerable Bede attributed to Aristotle, *De Caelo,* Book III, and *De Anima,* Book I (Bede, *Axiomata philosophica. Ex Aristotele* [n.p., 1608], p. 55). It does not seem to be in either work.

P. 41:18–24. *Plato . . . to conceive it.* The reference is to the *Republic,* Book VI, 507e–509a, of which Traherne had earlier made a much longer version (SM III.16). Cf. the reference to Plato, *CE,* p. 95.

P. 41:25–26. *In thy Light . . . Light.* Ps. 36:9.

P. 41:28. *Knowledge . . . Eternal.* A reference to the words of Jesus to God in John 17:3: "And this is life eternal, that they might know thee the only true God." Cf. *C* I.17: "To know GOD is Life Eternal."

P. 41:38–p. 42:1. *HE that would . . . Possessor of all.* This is an idea which Traherne develops in Chaps. XXXII–XXXIII on gratitude. Note his stylistic agility in the triple variation "a stranger to the Universe, an Alien to Felicity, and a foreiner to himself."

P. 42:17. *the Knowing . . . GOD.* Abraham "was called the Friend of God" (James 2:23); the phrase "the Knowing Man" is not in the A.V.

P. 42:31. *indeficient.* Inexhaustible; as also *CE,* pp. 48 and 79.

P. 42:34–35. *miserable Contentment . . . Cottage.* An attack on Stoic "autarchy"; cf. *CE,* pp. 14, 60, 71, and 231. Traherne evidently had a low opinion of cottage happiness. On Stoic apathy, see p. 60:36 n.

P. 44:10–14. *THERE is no Creature . . . bereaved of them.* Traherne brings in love among the beasts again, *CE,* p. 261. Instinctive love was sometimes denominated by the Greek term στοργὴ, to which William Pemble assigned the epithet "the Empresse of Nature." Pemble described the empress thus: "Birds build their neasts, and spare their owne crawes to fill their young ones: the Partridge flags before the Faukner, and ventures the taking, that her young ones may escape. The most timorous creatures grow most resolute in these combats: In the worst natures are some sparkles of love: As in Gold-mines amongst much earth shines a luster, and in beasts are rude lines of mans naturall affection" (*A Summe of Moral Philosophy* [1635], IX, pp. 13–14).

P. 44:19–24. *For to be Pleased . . . All is Love.* This is John Howe's distinction between desire and delight, quoted *CE,* p. 212:14 n. For Traherne's main discussion of love, see Chap. XVIII.

P. 45:2–4. *little Cupids . . . Daughter of GOD.* Gladys I. Wade (*Thomas Traherne* [Princeton, 1944], p. 217) suggests that this passage paraphrases Plotinus, *Enneads* III.v.2: "Heavenly Aphrodite, daughter of Kronos (Saturn)— who is no other than the Intellectual Principle—must be the Soul at its divinest. . . ." *Enneads* III.v is a commentary on Plato's *Symposium;* in the latter work, as Robert Burton recounts and translates, Pausanias "makes two Veneres and two loves. 'One Venus is ancient without a mother, and descended from heaven, whom we call celestial; the younger, begotten of Jupiter and Dione, whom commonly we call Venus'" (*Anatomy of Melancholy,* 3, 1, 1, 2, Everyman ed. [1932], III, 13; *Symposium* 180d–e). The concept of the celestial Venus was in the air; Peter Sterry found it attractive (*A Discourse of the Freedom of the Will* [1675], pp. 6–7, 32). Traherne's reference, *CE,* p. 236, to Cupid and Venus is to the better-known personages.

P. 45:33. *self-Love.* Traherne expands his views on self-love in connection with his attack on Hobbes (*CE,* pp. 261 ff.). See also *CE,* p. 28.

P. 45:35–36. *AS Love . . . Passions.* A commonplace; Thomas Aquinas quotes Augustine (*De civitate dei* XIV.7) as his authority (*ST,* I–II, 25, a. 2); cf. Ralph Venning: "Love is the root and spring of all other affections and passions" (*Things Worth Thinking On,* II.88 [1665], p. 52). Cf. SM II.64: love "is the Spring of all our affections, the Secret Mine of all our pleasures, the Rule of our Affayrs." Walter Montague explained: "Love in humane nature, is both the source and center of all passions, for not only Hope, Feare and Joy, but even Anger and Hatred, rise first out of the spring of Love; and the courses of these passions which seem to runne away from it, do by a winding resolution returne backe to rest againe in Love; for there could be no aversion if the last end of it were not some affection which our Love pursueth through opposition, with which our Anger and Hate combate, but in order to the conquest of our first Love; so that all the powers of a rationall Nature seeme to be ministeriall to this soveraigne power of Love, since even in Grace also, Love is both the way and the end of Beatitude, for *God himself is Love* [1 John 4:8, 16], and none end in God that do not go by Love" (*Miscellania Spiritualia or Devout Essayes* [1648], p. 149). Noting that love is "the very root or matter" of all the passions, Henry More concluded "that if we know what we chiefly love, and for whose cause man is to be loved, we shall find it not impossible to have our Souls work according to this Principle of *Love,* upon what **Object** soever: So that we may without contradiction fulfil these *Duties* in the Text, of *Universal* and *Perpetual Love*" (*Discourses on Several Texts of Scripture* [1692], pp. 479, 483–484). See also *CE*, p. 51:18 n.

P. 46:9–14. *Harmony of Complexions . . . mystery in nature.* On "Complexions," see *CE*, p. 174:25 n. Robert Fludd, the occultist, defined sympathy as "a consent, union, or concord, between two spirits, shining forth, or having their radical emanation from the self-same or the like divine property" (*Mosaicall Philosophy* [1659], p. 170). Kenelm Digby explained: "The little corporeities which issue from the one [creature] have such a conformity with the temper of the other, that it is therby moved to joyn it self to the body from whence they flow, and affects union with it in that way, as it receives the impression" (*Of Bodies* [1669], p. 423).

P. 46:14. *grateful Transpiration.* Pleasant emanation or effluence; this passage is one of two cited in the *OED* for this meaning of "transpiration." For the concept, see preceding note and Donne, "The Extasie," ll. 15–16: "Our soules, (which to advance their state, / Were gone out,) hung 'twixt her, and mee." Cf. CYB (f. 12ᵛ): "Nor is there one Atom [of our body] that flies away by Transpiration, but God Knows exactly where it is, & can Bring it to its Place again."

P. 46:16. *THE Consideration of Beauty.* Cf. Sir Thomas More: "Those pleasures that be receaved by the eares, the eyes, and the nose, . . . nature willeth to be proper and peculiar to man . . . for no other livinge creature doth behold the fairnes and the bewtie of the worlde" (*Utopia,* tr. Ralphe Robynson, ed. George Sampson, intro. A. Guthkelch [Bohn's Standard Library, 1910], p. 134). Cicero observed that "*only Man* is affected with the *Beauty,* the *Gracefulness,* and the *Symmetry* of *Visible Objects*" (*Tully's Offices,* tr. Sir Roger L'Estrange [1680], p. 8).

P. 47:3–4. *to prevent . . . Existence.* "Prevent" means "anticipate," as frequently hereafter. Traherne's logic seems somewhat at fault in this phrase; "Existence" obviously must precede "Beauty" in order of time and, one would assume, of verbal logic. It is possible that Traherne meant to write "Excellence" rather than "Existence," since in this paragraph he is discussing the qualities of being rather than being itself ("Felicity . . . Goodness . . . Beauty").

P. 48:3–4. *But man . . . in the World.* This is one of Traherne's favorite ideas; cf. his description of the soul as "a Power inspired into the Body of Man by Almighty God, whereby he is able to see Eternity, to enjoy infinity, to contain his Omnipresence, to apprehend his Omniscience, to behold his Omnipotence, and to be his Temple. . . . Hence comes it to pass, that all Ages and Kingdoms, Heaven and Earth, Time and Eternity, Angels and Seraphins [*sic*], the infinite Heights and Excellencies of God, are, after a sort, in the

Soul of Man" (*Mediations*, pp. 80–81). For a sampling of similar expressions in other of Traherne's works, see *C* I.55, 85; II.73; III.24; IV.67; SM III.72; IV.5; in CYB Traherne urged his "Redeemed Soul" to "enter . . . into all the Folds & Circuits of Eternity. All Ages are open unto Thee" (f. 1ᵛ) and asserted the existence of "a Spirit which enableth a Man . . . to Enquire into the Counsels that were in God before the World began: & like the H. Angels to look down into Ages & Generations to com for ever" (f. 53). Cf. Stephen Charnock, who—after quoting Culverwel and More on the soul—declared: "The mists of the Air that hinder the Sight of the Eye, cannot hinder the flights of the Soul; it can pass in a moment from one end of the World to the other, and think of things, a thousand miles distant" (*Several Discourses upon the Existence and Attributes of God* [1682], p. 32). Cf. *CE*, p. 226:18 n. Cf. also Henry More's "Psychathanasia, Or, The Immortality of the Soul," II.iii.26: "She [the soul] multitudes can close constrain / Into one nature. Things that be fluent, / As flitting time, by her be straight retent / Unto one point; she joyns future and past, / And makes them steddy stand as if present: / Things distant she can into one place cast" (in *The Complete Poems,* ed. Alexander B. Grosart [Edinburgh, 1878], p. 65).

P. 48:9. *Six Dayes Works.* Traherne made such a survey in his *Meditations on the Six Days of the Creation.* Cf. Thomas Aquinas's "Treatise on the Work of the Six Days," *ST* I, 65–74. On the older tradition, see F. E. Robbins, *The Hexaemeral Literature* (Chicago, 1912) and Maury Thibaut de Maisières, *Les Poèmes inspirés du début de la Genèse à l'époque de la Renaissance* (Louvain, 1931). The best-known Renaissance hexaemeral work was Du Bartas's *Divine Weeks and Works* (tr. Joshua Sylvester, 1605).

P. 48:19. *The capacity of Love.* Here is another of Traherne's cardinal ideas; cf. *CE,* Chap. XVIII, and *C* I.11: "Love is Deeper then at first it can be thought. It never ceaseth but in Endless Things. It ever Multiplies. Its benefits and its Designes are always Infinit."

P. 48:33–38. *The very Sun . . . after his similitude.* A frequent analogy in Traherne; cf. *CE,* p. 140:30 n.; *C* II.56 and 71 (paralleling the soul and the sun); and *C* II.65: "You are as Prone to lov, as the Sun is to shine." Cf. also the treatise on the soul in the Osborn MS. (p. 256): "The Sun is not more prone to Shine, then God is to Communicate Himself."

P. 48:38–39. *For as all Life . . . Action.* Cf. *CE,* p. 211: "All Life consists in Motion and Change"; also, p. 212: "All Pleasure consists in Activity and Motion. . . ." Note *C* II.22: "Life is the Root of Activity and Motion." Peter Sterry wrote along similar lines: "Motion is the chiefest part of Beauty, in as much as it is the most proper *expression* of Life, and the spring of Variety" (*Discourse,* p. 46).

P. 49:9–11. *Medea's faction . . . Sequor.* The lines are from Ovid's *Metamorphoses* VII.20–21, and were among the most popular poetic clichés of the English Renaissance; see R. M. Ogilvie, *Latin and Greek: A History of the Influence of the Classics on English Life from 1600 to 1918* (1964), ch. 1, "Ovid and the Seventeenth Century," pp. 1–33, especially pp. 10, 12. Sterry translated the lines thus: "Better things I see, approve; / The evil yet I choose and love" (*Discourse,* p. 186). In the midst of Traherne's quotations in EN

from Bacon's *De augmentis scientiarum* occurs this passage (source unidentified):
"Its a common Maxim, *Voluntas sequitur ultimum Dictamen Intellectus:* but
fouly falsified by those of Medeas faction: video meliora proboque, deteriora
sequor" (p. 153).

P. 50:9. *GOD is Love.* 1 John 4:8, 16.

P. 50:19–20. *the Brightness . . . Glory.* Heb. 1:3. The previous phrase
is not in the A.V.

P. 50:20–21. *by whom . . . Worlds.* Heb. 1:2.

P. 51:5. *had he never desired.* On God's "wants," see *CE*, p. 258:18 n.

P. 51:18–25. *Love, in several formes . . . it is glory.* Frances L. Colby
("Traherne and the Cambridge Platonists," Johns Hopkins diss. [1947], p. 232)
suggests that Traherne's source in this sentence is the following passage from
More's *Divine Dialogues:* "For as the various Superficies of Bodies naturally
causes such a diversification of pure Light, and changes it into the form of
this or that Colour; so the variety of Objects the Divine Goodness looks upon
does rightfully require a certain modification and figuration of her self into
sundry forms and shapes, . . . of Vengeance, of Severity, of Justice, or Mercy,
and the like" (2d Dialogue [1668], p. 300). Miss Colby comments: "It is impossible not to suspect that Traherne was echoing and in a sense answering More."
One may still refrain from suspicion, despite Traherne's now proven acquaintance
with the *Dialogues,* for the notion that God's attributes are all variant forms
of love was common at the times and derives from Augustine (cf. Martz, *The
Paradise Within,* pp. 40, 74–76). See *CE,* p. 45:35 n., and CYB, ff. 53ᵛ–54,
where Traherne again sees love as a center unifying all the virtues.

P. 52:3. *Grace . . . Gift.* The power to love ("To be able to Love") is
infused or "implanted" by God; its realization or transformation into act ("Actually to love") is cultivated by man with God's concurrence (grace) into what
Traherne would call a "habit."

P. 52:24. *resent.* Feel, as frequently hereafter.

P. 53:10. *IF by our voluntary Remissness.* With this paragraph cf. these
passages in the *Centuries:* "That Violence wherwith som times a man doteh
upon one Creature, is but a little spark of that lov, even towards all, which
lurketh in His nature" (*C* II.66). "Suppose a Curious and fair Woman. Som
have seen the Beauties of Heaven, in such a Person. . . . They lov her perhaps,
but do not lov God more: nor Men as much: nor Heaven and Earth at all.
And so being Defectiv to other Things, perish by a seeming Excess to that.
We should be all Life and Mettle and Vigor and Lov to evry Thing" (*C*
II.68). "To lov one Person with a Private Lov, is poor and miserable: to
lov all is Glorious" (*C* IV.69).

P. 53:30. *Hector.* Swaggering fellow, braggart ("Frequent in the second
half of the 17th c.; applied *spec.* to a set of disorderly young men who infested
the streets of London": *OED*). Traherne uses the word again in *CE,* p. 156.

P. 53:33. *I will not deny.* Traherne uses this rhetorical device again in
his Appendix, p. 283: "I know very well that the Age is full of Faults, and
lament it: but withal I know, it is full of Advantages."

P. 53:39–40. *the works of GOD, and the works of men.* Traherne explained
this point in the *Centuries:* "Truly there are two Worlds. One was made by

God, the other by Men. That made by GOD, was Great and Beautifull. . . . That made by men is a Babel of Confusions" (*C* I.7). Cf. Samuel Shaw in *The True Christians Test* (1682), p. 6: "The World is taken either in a *Physical* Sense, or in a *Theological*: In a *Physical* Sense, it signifies that vast Globe, that makes up Heaven, and Earth, and Sea, and all things contained in them. But in a *Theological* Sense; it is put in opposition to God . . . and so signifies all that which is contrary to the Spiritual Kingdom of Christ, and Warreth against it, and true Religion. . . ." See also Pierre La Primaudaye, *The French Academie* (1618), IV.7.3, p. 898. Henry Hammond gave this explanation in his *Practical Catechism*: "The 'world' signifies, either, first, the 'company;' or secondly, the 'customs;' or thirdly, the 'wealth;' or fourthly, 'power;' or fifthly, the 'glory' which is in the world: and 'the wicked world' is as much of these as hath any sinfulness or contrariety to the law of God in them, and so restrains the word 'world' to the two former of these, the three latter being in themselves lawful blessings of God, which though they may be either sought or used unlawfully, yet are not here to be styled wicked, or such as a Christian in his baptism is to renounce; but if he be lawfully possessed of them, he may very Christianly continue the use and enjoyment of them" (in *Miscellaneous Theological Works,* 3d ed., I[Oxford, 1847], 362).

P. 54:10–11. *the Greatest Evils Objects of Joy and Glory.* See *CE*, pp. 74:3 n., 98:4 n., and 229:38 n.; and *C* III.30. Cf. Traherne's praise of *"Jesus Christ,* who hath . . . taught us a Way to increase our own Goodness by other mens Evils" (*CE*, p. 103). In the *Meditations* he says God can "change Sorrow into Joy, Vice into Virtue, Afflictions into Consolations" (p. 31). He must have agreed with Thomas Jackson's statement in his *Treatise of the Divine Essence,* Part I: "Yet so essentiall it is unto this infinite Fountaine of Goodnesse [i.e., God] . . . to send forth onely streames of life; and such is the vertue of the streames which issue from him, that as well the evill and miseries which miscreants procure unto themselves, as their mischievous intentions towards others, infallibly occasion increase of joy and happinesse unto all that give free passage unto their current. . . . All the good which one refuseth or putteth from them, returnes in full measure to the other" (p. 145).

P. 54:21–25. *every Creature . . . for evermore.* Rev. 5:13.

P. 54:26–27. *enter . . . Lord.* Matt. 25:21, 23.

P. 54:28–29. *Lord will . . . his Goods.* Matt. 24:47.

P. 54:29. *over all that he hath.* Luke 12:44.

P. 54:30. *TO see beyond all Seas.* The soul is, as Traherne says on the next page, "a Temple of GODS Omnipresence." Cf. *CE*, p. 48:3 n.

P. 54:37. *IT is the Glory of man.* Traherne's purposefully hyperbolic use of "Avarice" and "Ambition" occurs again in his assertion below that hope contains "All that Ambition or Avarice can desire" (p. 122); see also *CE*, pp. 173, 212:14 n., and the second note on 258:18. Note also *C* I.22: "*It is of the Nobility of Mans Soul that He is Insatiable.*" *C* III.17 describes Traherne's curiosity as a child. Among his many poetic expressions of this idea, see "Insatiableness" (II, 145) and "Desire" (II, 177). Peter Sterry again offers an analogue: "The *Desires* of man are *Infiniteness* budding forth from its *Seed* in the Soul. These *Desires* are ever in Motion, and Restless, till they put forth into *Infiniteness* itself" (*The Rise, Race, and Royalty of the Kingdom of God* [1683], p. 139).

P. 55:10–11. *neither Eye . . . conceive.* 1 Cor. 2:9.

P. 55:14. *no Epicures Sence.* See *CE*, p. 285:5 n.

P. 55:24–25. *every one is the Sovereign Object.* In the *Centuries* Traherne dwelt ecstatically upon his paradoxical doctrine that God "maketh evry one the end of the World" (*C* I.15); every person is "the Sole Heir of the whole World," yet the world belongs to all, all being "evry one Sole Heirs, as well as you" (*C* I.29); cf. "Thanksgivings for the Blessedness of his LAWS," II, 272–273; and *CE*, p. 38:20 n. In CYB, Traherne exclaimed: "Thou hast made all for me, & Me for All" (f. 42ᵛ; cf. ff. 83–83ᵛ). He named three "infinitly Glorious" ways of God in SM IV.31: "1 He giueth unto one all Things, wholy to be enjoyd 2 He giveth one Thing to all, by each wholy to be enjoyed 3 He maketh the Enjoyers to enrich the Enjoyment." All three, he went on, "haue an infinit Influence upon all the Things in Heaven and Earth," and all were forgotten at the Fall; see also SM IV.32 and II.89.

The Biblical foundation for Traherne's paradox is explained in the *Meditations:* "In those Words, *God created Man in his own Image* [Gen. 1:26], we may understand that all his Care and Counsel was spent about the Creation of him; and not of many but of one, intimating that every one is so great, as if all the Care of God were about him alone" (pp. 72–73).

P. 56:10–11. *his Goodness . . . communicate it self.* See *C* IV.45: "To Giv is the Happiness of GOD; to Receiv, of Man." Cf. Peter Sterry: "Goodness is properly and formally the principle of *communication*. The more there is of the nature of good in any thing, so much the more *communicative* and diffusive it is" (*Discourse*, p. 20). Instancing the sun, the air, a fountain, Nathanael Culverwel asserted: "It is the very nature of goodnesse to diffuse it self abroad in a spreading and liberal manner; for it do's not thus lose any thing, but augments, and increases its being by communicating it self" ("Mount Ebal," in *Light of Nature*, p. 86). Traherne quoted Thomas Jackson's explanation of God's "goodnesse communicative" (*Treatise of the Divine Essence*, I, 189) in CB, *s.v.* "Libertie," f. 62ᵛ.1.

Throughout his works, Traherne stressed the corollary: man, bearing in himself the "*Similitude*" of God's goodness (*CE*, p. 82), must also "communicate" his goodness, must participate in the circulation of love (see following note). As he wrote in CYB (f. 51): ". . . all the Joy even of Living in Heaven, is the Two fold Joy of Communicating & Receiving. Without which the most Excellent Creature might pine away. Because Narcissus like, none can Enjoy Himself in Himself, unless He hath a fountain. Nor can any Enjoy themselvs in a fountain; tho they see the Reflexion of themselvs, but in a Shady manner; Compared to that, wherby Solid Objects, & Diviner Creatures enjoy each other." See as well *C* III.59, IV.18; and cf. Plotinus, *Enneads* II.9.3.

P. 57:5–6. *all is given . . . received from him.* The notion of a "circulation" of love between God and man occurs in all of Traherne's works; see, for example, *CE*, pp. 47, 81, 135–136, 251–252, and Chap. XXXII; note as well the circulation metaphor in the passage in *CE* (p. 140) taken from *The Whole Duty of Man.* The poem "The Circulation" expresses the idea fully: "All things do first receiv, that giv" (II, 154). "Silence" affords an example of the watery metaphors common in Traherne's poetry: "He [God] was an Ocean of Delights from Whom / The Living Springs and Golden Streams did com: / My Bosom was an Ocean into which / They all did run" (II, 48). A statement in the *Meditations* is also apposite: "We can never rest till we see all things from God to God, proceeding from him, and ending in him" (p. 82).

P. 57:21. *empty.* Pour out. Part of the doctrine of "circulation." We expend ("empty") God's gifts and in so doing replenish the supply ("offer up all these things unto him *again*").

P. 58:2. *Of the Excellency of Truth.* Observe that the truths Traherne discusses in this chapter are ones which he considers truisms but which, as he points out, are not perceived by the majority of men.

P. 58:8–9. *Aristotle . . . temporal Felicity.* Aristotle said that man exercises virtue in order to gain pleasure and avoid pain (*Nic. Eth.* II.3.1104^{b}9). He also maintained, more emphatically, that the end of virtue was happiness, which lay in "life according to reason" (*Nic. Eth.* X.6–7). Traherne termed Aristotle's account of happiness in *Nic. Eth.* I "a lucky Hit" (*CE*, p. 19).

P. 58:18–19. *Deus . . . soli.* Traherne translates immediately. He quoted this sentence in *C* I.15, where he also attributed it to Seneca. Dr. Margoliouth gives no reference, nor have I been able to find the quotation in Seneca's works. In *De beneficiis* (IV.5–8) Seneca dilated upon God's gift to man of the world, but he did not make the remark Traherne quotes (a remark which sums up a central tenet of Traherne's philosophy). Robert Ellrodt discusses parallels between Traherne's thought and Seneca's in *L'Inspiration personelle et l'esprit du temps chez les poètes métaphysiques anglais*, Pt. I, vol. II (Paris, 1960), 276–277.

P. 58:30. *Natural Man . . . Light of Nature.* The law of nature, "as *Aquinas* does very well tell us, . . . is nothing but . . . the copying out of the eternal Law, and the imprinting of it upon the breast of a Rational being" (Culverwel, *Light of Nature,* p. 29). In the seventeenth century, according to Norman Sykes, it "became an open, and certainly much-debated question not only whether natural religion without revelation might not be all-sufficient for salvation, but even whether revelation had merely confused the simple truths of natural religion by elaboration and mystery" (*From Sheldon to Secker* [Cambridge, Eng., 1959], p. 159). The usual liberal account explained that "the great *materials of natural light*, are first in reason, and then reinforced in scripture" (Whichcote, *Works*, I, 380); the Bible was necessary to supplement postlapsarian natural light. Traherne's attitude towards the heathens in *Christian Ethicks* is more cautious and less commendatory than in other writings which he did not intend for publication. In the Commonplace Book he termed Pythagoras "this great Example among the Heathens, [whom] I here represent as a Myrror for Christians" (f. 80^v.1). He asserted in the *Centuries* that "those Barbarous People that go naked, com nearer to Adam God, and Angels in the Simplicity of their Wealth, tho not in Knowledg" (*C* III.12). In general he copied in his works the advice from Thomas Jackson's *Treatise of Unbeliefe* which he copied into his notebook: Jackson recommended "*Trismegist, Plato* with his followers, *Plotine* specially, and amongst the Romanes *Seneca*. . . .

Their consonancies to Christian truth are . . . worthy to be lookt into by the most eagle-sighted Divines of our times" (*Treatise*, p. 438; CB, *s.v.* "Preparation of Objects," f. 77.1). On wise heathens, see Don Cameron Allen, *Doubt's Boundless Sea* (Baltimore, 1964), ch. 4. On natural truths, see *CE*, pp. 117 ff.

P. 59:7. *For the Earth is really better.* On Traherne's sense of a fit "place" for all parts of creation, see *CE*, p. 69:20 n.; on the related topic of God's moderation in distributing the parts of creation, see *CE*, pp. 179–182. With this particular passage, cf. the *Centuries:* "The Earth it self is Better then Gold becaus it produceth fruit and flowers" (*C* I.14). "Were all the Earth filthy Mires, or Devouring Quicksands; firm land would be an unspeakable Treasure. Were it all Beaten Gold it would be of no value. It is a Treasure therfore of far Greater valu to a noble Spirit, then if the Globe of the Earth were all Gold. . . . The Air is Better, being a living Miracle as it now is, then if it were Cramd and fild with Crowns and Scepters The Mountains are better then solid Diamonds, and those Things which Scarcity maketh Jewels (when you enjoy these) are yours in their Places" (*C* II.12). Cf. also *C* I.10; SM II.30; and "Right Apprehension": "A Globe of Gold must Barren be" (II, 124).

P. 59:17. *Inadvertency.* Heedlessness.

P. 59:19. *Arcanum.* Traherne translates immediately. He uses the word again, *CE*, p. 138, in a Latin phrase.

P. 59:29. *Were all other men removed.* The "Thanksgivings for the Body" contain a similar passage: "The sons of men thou hast made my treasures. . . . Were I alone, / Briars and thorns would devour me; / Wild beasts annoy me; / My Guilt terrifie me; / The World it self be a Desart to me; / The Skies a Dungeon, / But mine Ignorance more. / The Earth a Wilderness; / All things desolate" (II, 221–222).

P. 60:36. ʼΑυτάρκεια. Traherne translates immediately. The Greek word —associated with pagan Stoicism and used by St. Paul as well (e.g., 1 Tim. 6:6, where the A.V. translates it as "contentment")—was in common learned use in seventeenth-century England; it appeared in two passages in Gale's *Court of the Gentiles* (pp. 149, 135) which Traherne himself copied in CB, *s.v.* "Pythagoras," f. 80ᵛ.1, 2. See Thomas Watson's *ΑΥΤΑΡΚΕΙΑ, or the Art of Divine* (*Contemplations,* I, "Of Afflictions," 84). William Shelton remarked that he "this ἀυτάρκεια, or Contentment" as "a sweet temper of spirit whereby a Christian carries himselfe in an equal poize in every condition" (in *Three Treatises,* 6th ed. [1660], p. 190). More often than not, Englishmen did not follow Watson in adapting the term to Christianity, but rather concluded firmly with Sir Matthew Hale that "this is not that temper that becomes a Christian" (*Contemplations,* I, "Of Afflictions," 84). William Shelton remarked that he could endorse "that ἀυτάρκεια, that self-sufficiency" of the heathens, if it meant only "that a man in the exercise of Vertue can furnish himself with Joy and Comfort, without the external additaments of Fame and Honour": but unfortunately the Stoics "truly were blame-worthy in shutting God out" (*Moral Vertues Baptized Christian* [1667], p. 129). See Henry W. Sams, "Anti-Stoicism in Seventeenth- and Early Eighteenth-Century England," *Studies in Philology,* XLI (1944), 65–78.

For Traherne's other allusions to Stoic doctrine, see *CE*, pp. 14, 17, 71, 231, and Chap. XXVII, which argues "That Contentment is a Vertue" (see especially p. 216:32 n.). In *C* II.100 he roundly attacked the Stoics' "inward unnatural mistaken Self sufficiency and Contentment." His amanuensis copied the entirety of Gale's chapter on Stoicism into the Commonplace Book ("Stoicisme," ff. 88–89ʳ; Gale, *Court*, pp. 424–434). In the "Vita Socratis" copied into the Ficino Notebook the author wrote "putet enim Deos ἀυταρκεs esse; & nullius rei indigere" (ff. 51–51ᵛ; Traherne drew upon this passage in *C* I.40); Traherne wrote "Socratis ἀυ   " in the margin beside another passage in the "Vita" (f. 49).

On the goods of body, soul, and fortune mentioned just below, see *CE*, p. 18:4 n.

P. 61:25. *Mechanick.* Workman.

P. 61:26–27. *Heirs of the World.* Rom. 4:13. See *CE*, p. 21:21 n.

P. 61:35. *Dead Works.* Heb. 6:1, 9:14.

P. 61:37. *Inspired.* In the root sense of the Latin *inspirare,* to breathe into.

P. 61:39. *informes.* Gives the will its essential quality (a usage deriving from the scholastic *informare*).

P. 61:40. *series.* Continuous state.

P. 63:12. *a Work of Darkness.* Rom. 13:12; Eph. 5:11.

P. 63:39. *the Key of Knowledge.* Luke 11:52.

P. 64:3. *the Eye of the Soul.* Traherne dwells upon the inward eye in his poems. See "An Infant-Ey" and, especially, "Sight"; in the latter poem Traherne separates the insightful from the physical eye, postulating an extra visionary organ equipped to see the invisible, a third eye which "did lurk within, / Beneath my Skin" and "was of greater Worth than both the other" (II, 133). Furthermore, God's "Essence also is the Sight of Things" (*C* II.84). See also *Poems,* II, 20 ff., 52 ff., 58, 90 ff. Hermes Trismegistus, too, contrasted physical and spiritual sight; see the passage Traherne quotes in *CE*, p. 226. Cf. Anthony Horneck, who in his felicitously entitled *Happy Ascetick* (1681) advised his readers to make "greater use of the Eyes of our Minds, than those of our Bodies, *Matth.* 6.22. . . . The intellectual Eye looks beyond the Clouds, transcends the Sky, and sees through all the Mists and Foggs of this present World, into Eternity" (3d ed., 1693, pp. 150–151). See *CE*, p. 155:21 n.

P. 65:1. To the chapter on wisdom Traherne's early meditations in the Osborn MS. may have contributed; see the treatise on the soul there, p. 255.

P. 65:20–21. *not a meer Speculation . . . Habit.* Traherne's definition of wisdom, stressing its practical aspect, comes close to the Thomistic description of the intellectual virtue of prudence (*ST* I–II, 57, a. 5) and is somewhat removed from Aristotle's description of wisdom as "a science that investigates the first principles and causes" (*Metaphysics* I.2.982ᵇ9)—a definition endorsed by St. Thomas in his discussion of the "gift of wisdom" (*ST* II–II, 45, a. 1). In *C* III.42 Traherne defined wisdom as "a Knowledg Exercised in finding out the Way to Perfect Happiness, by discerning Mans real Wan[t]s and Soveraign desires. We com morover to Know Gods Goodness, in seeing into the Causes, wherfore He implanted such faculties and Inclinations in us, and the Objects, and Ends prepared for them." Cf. William Colvill's conventional listing of the three principal parts of Christian prudence, which consists "1. In proponendo fine bono & aequo. 2. In deliberando de mediis in ordine ad finem. 3. In prosequendo finem per ista media post deliberationem & electionem" (*Philosophia,* p. 353).

P. 66:13–14. *By himself . . . to be explained.* In *CE,* Chaps. XXXII–XXXIII, on gratitude; see also *CE,* p. 57:5 n.

P. 67:15. *Nature and extent of space.* Traherne and Henry More were among the first English writers to respond imaginatively to the new ideas of space, More making a contribution to the metaphysics of space (see Max Jammer, *Concepts of Space* [Cambridge, Mass., 1954], pp. 39–46). Traherne considered space "the Eternal and Incomprehensible Essence of the Deitie" (*C* V.3) and so followed More (as did Newton) in correlating space with deity. He drew the theological deduction that "As sure as there is a Space infinit, there is a Power, a Bounty, a Goodness, a Wisdom infinit, a Treasure, a Blessedness, a Glory" (*C* V.4). "The true exemplar of GODs infinity is that of your Understanding" (*C* II.24); furthermore, "Infinit is the first Thing which is naturaly Known . . . and we cannot unsuppose or Annihilat that do what we can" (*C* II.81)—a point Traherne had already made in his treatise of the soul in the Osborn MS. (p. 258; see also the conclusion of this treatise, pp. 262–264).

P. 67:29. *his Essence is his Act.* Cf. "The Anticipation," II, 162: "His Essence is all Act. . . ." Traherne explained in *C* III.63 that "GOD is not a Being compounded of Body and Soul, or Substance and Accident, or Power and Act but is All Act, Pure Act, a Simple Being." As Ellrodt observes, the definition comes from Thomas Aquinas, *ST* I, 3, a. 2 (*Poètes métaphysiques,* Pt. I, vol. II, 328). In CB, in response to a passage from Henry More's *Divine Dialogues,* Traherne argued that "Almighty Power therfore endued with Choise, & acting from all Eternity in the most wise & glorious Manner is the Deitie. a more pure Incomprehensible Eternal Act, that is never Desolate nor idle, but the fountain & the End of all Things, ordering all, & enjoying all, that is God" (*s.v.* "Deitie," f. 33ᵛ.1). Cf. also *C* III.64–65 and *C* II.39, as well as *CE,* pp. 36–37 and 76.

P. 67:38–39. *Eternity is . . . Stable manner.* Traherne paraphrases himself, *CE,* p. 184: "Eternity is an everlasting Moment, infinite in duration, but permanent in all its parts. . . ." Cf. also *CE,* pp. 111:22 n. and 242:32 n. Traherne's definition appears close to that of Boethius in *De consolatione philosophia,* V.6 (Chaucer's translation): "Eternite . . . is parfit possessioun and altogidre of lif interminable." The nature of eternity, because it is "all . . . at one Time," is a great "Mystery," as Traherne observes, *CE,* pp. 68–69. For his more metaphysical explanation of eternity, see *C* V.6–8. See Plotinus, *Enneads* III.7.5.

P. 67:39–40. *To fill . . . not Wise.* Cf. *C* V.5: "It would be an Absurditie to leave [infinity of space] unfinished, or not to fill it."

P. 68:14–15. *For of him . . . all things.* Rom. 11:36.

P. 68:15–18. *Matter is the Dreg . . . fulness of Power.* The stress on activity in this paragraph informs all of Traherne's writings, both metaphysical and ethical, both poetry and prose. See General Introduction, pp. xlv–xlvii. Note that in his Commonplace Book Traherne copied a number of Hermes's sayings about activity; for example: God's "Operation or Act, is his Will and his Essence" (*Pymander,* IV.4, p. 48; CB, f. 50.1). The present discussion is illuminated by Peter Sterry's explanations of the three kinds of power: 1. Active power "is a *Spirit* or a spiritual form . . . an *eminent* and universal Act . . . containing and sending forth from it self variety of Acts or forms, as a Spring doth streams. This Power is more *excellent* than the *Act* which is produced by it.

"2. The *Passive Power,* is that of *matter,* . . . comprehending or hiding variety of Acts or forms in it. . . . This *Power* is inferior to the *Act,* which . . . is the exaltation of this *Passive Power* to an higher degree of Being. . . .

"3. Power *in Act.* All Power *purely* Active is *ever* in Act. Such Power is alwayes abstracted from matter and a spiritual essence or form, eminent above all things in matter, an universal comprehending variety of Acts or spiritual forms in it self.

"Every Active Power, in matter is compounded, being partly Active, and partly Passive. This Power is never brought into Act, but as it is excited and awakened, from *without,* by its *Object,* from *above,* by power abstractive and purely active, shedding its beams upon it. . . .

"*Power* and *Act* are distinguished, not as two several Beings, but as the same Being in several *states,* modifications, or degrees of Being. When Power, as it is a spiritual and universal *Act,* comprehending all its own *Acts* formally and eminently in it self, being all at once in *Act* within it self, brings forth it self into any particular or single *Act* in matter. This is the same Power contracted, and so in a less degree of perfection. When a Passive Power in matter springs up into *Act,* This *Act* is the perfection of the Power. The Power and the *Act* are here the same form, sleeping and awakened, in the seed and in the flower" (*Discourse,* p. 19).

P. 68:39–40. *the Learned constantly affirm.* Two of the works we know Traherne read contain discussions of eternity. In the first of Henry More's *Divine Dialogues,* Hylobares states the common definition of eternity: "That it is an essential presence of all things with God, as well of things past, present, as to come; and that the Duration of God is all of it, as it were, *in one steddy and permanent . . . Instant at once.*" Philotheus stigmatizes this description as a "Notion of Eternity that some have rashly pitched upon," and he offers another account, postulating "That the whole Evolution of Times and Ages from everlasting to everlasting is so collectedly and presentifickly represented to God at once, as if all things and Actions which ever were, are, or shall be, were at this very Instant, and so always, really present and existent before him. . ." (pp. 58–60). Thomas Jackson in his *Treatise of the Divine Essence and Attributes,* Pt. I, cited a number of definitions of eternity. Referring to Tertullian and Augustine, he called eternity "the inexhaustible fountain or infinit Ocean, from which time or duration successive . . . doe perpetually flow" (p. 62). Praising St. Thomas's definition (*ST* I, 10, a. 1) as "very artificial," Jackson considered that "*Plotin* . . . gives a more deepe and full apprehension of it in fewer tearmes; . . . *Eternitie is infinitie of life.* And such we gather it to bee, because it is the university or totality of life, and can lose nothing, in that nothing of it is past, nothing to come" (p. 70). He quoted also the definition given by Ficino in his commentary on Plotinus: eternity "is a fixed instant or permanent Center, which needs no succession for supply" (p. 73). "And *Trismegists* description of the Deity, *commutatis commutandis,* as well exemplifies the Eternity, as the immensity of his nature. Eternity is a circular duration, whose *instants* are, *alwaies,* whose *terminations* or *extremities* never *were,* never *shall be:* It is coexistent to every parcell of time, but not circumscriptible by any: succession infinite cannot be coequall to it" (p. 75). Cf. as well the poetic Neoplatonism of Peter Sterry: "Time is the Shadow of Eternity, in which Eternity itself is sown. Eternity in its Season springs up, and drinks up its Shadow into itself, into its own Original Light, as the Seed is spread by the Spirit and Virtue of the growing Plant into its Flower, which first brought it forth in its Bosom, and contracted itself into it, obscuring itself within it" (*The Appearance of God to Man In the Gospel* [1710], p. 204).

P. 69:19. *stand.* Stop.

P. 69:20–27. *No single Part . . . Time, and Eternity.* One of Traherne's recurrent themes. Cf. *C* III.55: "That any thing may be found to be an infinit Treasure, its Place must be found in Eternity, and in Gods Esteem. For as there is a Time, so there is a Place for all Things. Evry thing in its Place is Admirable Deep and Glorious: out of its Place like a Wandering Bird, is Desolat and Good for Nothing. How therfore it relateth to God and all Creatures must be seen before it can be Enjoyed." See also *C* I.14; *C* II.12; *C* III.60, 62; *C* IV.16; SM IV.30, 32; and cf. Peter Sterry: "Being it self, . . . by beautiful, harmonious, just degrees and steps, *descendeth* into every Being. . . . Every part is tyed to the whole, and to all the other parts, by mutual and essential *Relations*" (*Discourse,* p. 30).

P. 71:14–15. *Righteousness of Apprehension . . . of Action.* A passage in Traherne's treatise on the soul in the Osborn MS. (p. 254) may well have served as the germ of the treatment of righteousness in *CE*; omitting righteousness of apprehension, he explained: "There is a Righteousness of Chois, a Righteousness of Esteem, and a Righteousness of Action. To prefer the Better before the wors, is a Righteousness of Chois, To render to all Things a Due Esteem, Righteousness of Esteem, & to do the Best things we are able, a Righteousness of Action. The Best of all Possible Effects being From all Eternity before the Face of God, when He Considered what to make, & what to Forbear; He must of Necessity chuse to make the Best, or be unrighteous in His Chois. which being made will be infinit: becaus the Best of all possible Effects are adaequate to the Greatness of Allmighty Power. which being made He Esteemeth infinitly (For whatsoever GOD doth He infinitly doth it) & in so doing is Righteous in Esteem, as He is Righteous in Action by Effecting His Chois in the Production of all. He therin is Righteous to us, For He exalteth to the Bosom & the Throne of God." The paragraph on righteousness in SM (IV.63) is not directly relevant to *CE*.

P. 71:20–21. *He that mistakes his Hand for his Meat.* Cf. *C* IV.15: "He that mistakes . . . his Hand to be his Meat, confounds him self by misapplications." The point at issue is identical.

P. 71:29. *low Cottage and course diet.* Cf. *CE,* p. 42:34 n.

P. 72:3–4. *RIGHTEOUSNESS in esteem . . . Merit requires.* Cf. *C* I.12: "Can you then be Righteous, unless you be Just in rendering to Things their

Due Esteem?" In the *Meditations* Traherne praised God "for the Justice that is implanted in my Nature, wherby I desire to render all their Due, and to thee thy deserved Praise, and to all Creatures, in thee and for thee, their due Esteem" (p. 86). Cf. also a passage in the *Meditations* (pp. 37–38) in the style of the *Thanksgivings:*

> "Therefore to prize every thing according to its Value
> "Is our bounden Duty to God,
> "The fulfilling of the Law of Justice,
> "The Answer of our Obligations,
> "The only Expression we can make of our Gratitude to God;
> "Its the way to all Rewards,
> "Its the very Fruition of all Mercies,
> "It makes us capable of eternal Glory."

P. 72:16–17. *A thing . . . attains its End.* A scholastic axiom. See *CE*, p. 13:7 n. Cf. Gale: "So the *Scholes* tell us, that every *Forme* is perfected by its *Act*" (*Court*, p. 387; quoted CB, *s.v.* "Beatitude," f. 21ᵛ.1). The ultimate source is Aristotle; cf. *Nic. Eth.* III.7.1115ᵇ23: "Each thing is defined by its end." In *Rhetoric* I.7.1363ᵇ17, Aristotle defines end as "that for the sake of which all else is done."

P. 72:21–23. *Application of Actives . . . Cures, and Productions.* Henry Cornelius Agrippa explained that some elements "are heavy, as Earth and Water, and others are light, as Aire and Fire. Wherefore the Stoicks called the former passives, but the latter actives" (*Occult Philosophy,* I.3, tr. J. F[reake], [1651], p. 6). On the four elements, see *CE*, p. 171:15 n. The active-passive theory was an integral part of the Galenic medicine still dominating medical studies in Traherne's day. According to Arturo Castiglioni, "The basic concept of the therapy of Galen is contained in the formula *contraria contrariis,* for instance, the application of heat for the diseases that come from cold, and vice versa" (*A History of Medicine,* tr. E. B. Krumbhaar, 2d ed. [New York, 1947], p. 224). In CYB (f. 91ᵛ) Traherne wrote that the angels (and Satan) manipulate the natural order "by a Neat Application of Actives to Passives." According to D. P. Walker, Campanella (and other Neoplatonists) spoke of "good, natural magic, which applies 'active to passive, and celestial to terrestrial' " (*Spiritual and Demonic Magic from Ficino to Campanella* [1958], p. 221).

P. 72:23–24. *All satisfactions . . . Objects well united.* A cliché of the time; witness three Cambridge Platonists. John Smith: "True *Delight* and *Joy* is begotten by the conjunction of some discerning Faculty with its proper Object" (*Discourses,* p. 416), a *dictum* which was borrowed *verbatim* (and without acknowledgment) by Benjamin Whichcote (*Works,* IV, 313). Nathanael Culverwel: "The Nobler any Being is, the purer pleasure it hath proportion'd to it. . . . all pleasure consisting in that Harmonious Conformity and Correspondency, that a faculty hath with its object" (*Light of Nature,* sigs. 2A4–2A4ᵛ).

Francis Bacon intended to write "The History of the Sympathy and Antipathy of Things," but never got beyond the Introduction, in which he stated: "Strife and friendship in nature are the spurs of motions and the keys of works. Hence are derived the union and repulsion of bodies, the mixture and separation of parts, the deep and intimate impressions of virtues, and that which is termed the junction of actives with passives; in a word, the *magnalia naturae*. But this part of philosophy concerning the sympathy and antipathy of things, which is also called Natural Magic, is very corrupt; and . . . there being too little diligence, there has been too much hope" (*Works,* ed. James Spedding, Robert Leslie Ellis, and Douglas Denon Heath, IX [Boston, 1864], 470).

P. 72:28. *Quadrat.* Harmonize, correspond.

P. 72:30–31. *it becometh . . . Righteousness.* Matt. 3:15.

P. 73:16. *Indwelling of GOD.* See *CE,* p. 226:11 n.

P. 73:17. *The Spiritual Room of the Mind.* Instinct told Traherne as a child that "there was endless Space / Within my Soul" ("Felicity," II, 90); the mature Traherne considered the "great Capacity" of the soul the trait "wherein (in my Opinion) it is most like God" (*Meditations,* p. 83). The soul's infinite capacity was a frequent topic of the Cambridge Platonists. Sterry called the soul "an indivisible Unity, yet *spacious,* enriched with a Variety of Powers and Forms, far *beyond* the compass or glory of this *visible World*" (*Discourse,* p. 92). Ralph Cudworth wrote: "Nay, the soul conceives extended things themselves, unextendedly and indivisibly; for as the distance of a whole hemisphere is contracted into a narrow compass in the pupil of the eye, so are all distances yet more contracted in the soul itself, and there understood indistantly" (*The True Intellectual System of the Universe,* ed. Thomas Birch, IV [1820], 70).

P. 74:1. *To prefer the Better above the worse.* This is that "Eternal Property in Reason" which Traherne noted at the outset; see *CE,* p. 14:7 n.

P. 74:3. *The Election of GOD.* Traherne distinguishes here between God's postlapsarian management of the universe and his original choice and disposition of creation. The discussion of primitive election in the present paragraph shows that Traherne stopped short of the most thoroughgoing exponents of plenitude, who argued that (as Peter Sterry put it) God created everything possible, not only harmony but its possible opposite, so that "Contrariety it self . . . is a part of the Variety of things in the Unity of the whole," and man's Fall was "in the Universal Design; was comprehended in it, and part of it" (*Discourse,* pp. 118–119). Vivian da Sola Pinto traces this view back to the Jewish Cabbala (*Peter Sterry* [Cambridge, Eng., 1934], p. 107). Cf. *CE,* p. 54:10 n. The "Select Meditations" show Traherne's early effort to work out a theodicy (see, e.g., III.52, IV.80).

P. 75:22. *several.* Different, distinct.

P. 75:31–32. *his soul . . . Ideas of GOD.* The purest Christian Platonism. Gale's *Court* (p. 316) explained that "*Plato* distinguisheth the *Intelligible world,* which he calls the exemplar subsisting in the Divine mind, from the sensible, which is but the *imitate* of the former." Traherne's amanuensis copied the material contiguous to this quotation in CB, *s.v.* "Creation," f. 30.1; he also copied a more involved and muddy explanation (p. 182), *s.v.* "Idea," f. 55.1–2. In CYB (f. 90) Traherne said that angels are "rightly called *Intelligible Spheres,* in which all Objects appear for ever."

P. 76:34. *to Act and to Be.* Cf. *CE,* p. 67: "We must take heed of conceiving GOD to be one Thing, and his Act another. . . ." See *CE,* p. 68:15 n.

P. 76:40. The marginal note should read more specifically "Wis. 7:24–27."

P. 77:4–5. *perfect . . . perfect.* Matt. 5:48.

P. 77:5–6. *we shall see . . . Known.* 1 Cor. 13:12 paraphrased; the first phrase departs widely from the A.V.

P. 78:11. *Convenience.* Agreement, correspondence (for this sense, cf. *CE*, pp. 79, 112, 125; on p. 271 "Correspondence" and "Convenience" appear synonymously). As used in the next paragraph, "Convenience" has a connotation of natural fitness (cf. *CE*, pp. 80, 145, and 212). The word—and the thought of this paragraph—is further explained by the following passage from Traherne's treatise on the soul in the Osborn MS. (pp. 255–256): "Goodness is ad Alium. Infinit Goodness is infinitly Communicativ, & Cannot be Goodness while it is Sullen & reserved. Bonem est Quod Alteri Conveniens. infinit Goodness is infinitly Convenient . . . It infinitly desireth the Exaltation of others, & must be satisfied or Cannot rest. It infinitly Delighteth in a nothers Exaltation, & is the more Blessed, the more it is enjoyed. . . ."

P. 78:13. *Natural Goodness . . . Divine.* John Scott described "natural good" as "consisting in the perfection and satisfaction of [the] bodily senses and appetites, and in those means which conduce thereunto" and "moral good" as consisting "in the perfection and satisfaction of [man's] rational facultys, and in those means which tend thereunto" (*Works*, I, 431). On God's goodness, see *CE*, p. 34:30 n.

P. 78:23. *Fatal Necessity.* Margoliouth cites this passage to illustrate the use of "fatal" to mean "destined" (*C* V.2, n. on l. 29). The phrase "fatal Necessity" appears again in *CE*, p. 183. Antoine Le Grand said that believers in "fatal necessity" "suppose *Men* to act from an imprest instinct, and [maintain] that nothing is done by them which is not necessarily determined" (*Body of Philosophy*, X.19, p. 376). Thomas Jackson discussed the heathen concept of fate in chs. 19–22 of his *Treatise of the Divine Essence and Attributes*, Pt. II.

P. 78:29. *Ingenuity.* Sincerity, honesty (an obsolete use confusing "ingenious" with "ingenuous"). Cf. *CE*, pp. 125 and 149.

P. 78:33–34. *measured more . . . Benefit.* Cf. Traherne's remarks comparing heathen and Christian morality, *CE*, pp. 60–63.

P. 80:3. *intends.* Is devoted to.

P. 81:31. *Original.* Origin (i.e., a noun, not an adjective; see p. 4:36 n.); God's goodness is both the first and the final cause of our gratitude.

P. 82:5. *its Similitude in our selves.* Cf. Traherne's *Meditations* (pp. 85–87), where he praises God for implanting in man the "Similitude" of (among other things) his infinity, eternity, greatness, life, essence, omnipresence, omniscience, and compassion. He thanks God as well "for that Principle of Goodness thou hast implanted in Man" (p. 86).

P. 82:14. *congratulates.* Rejoices in.

P. 82:19–20. *Inasmuch . . . done it to me.* Matt. 25:40.

P. 82:39. *Beams and influences.* See *CE*, p. 157:5 n.

P. 83:36–37. *WE Love . . . natural Desire.* Cf. *C* II.61: "We are all Naturaly Ambitious of being Magnified in others, and of seeming Great in others. Which Inclination was implanted in us that our Happiness might be Enlarged by the Multitud of Spectators." Cf. also *C* II.70 and *CE*, p. 38:20 n.

P. 84:5. *Into his Eternal Glory.* 1 Pet. 5:10.

P. 84:28. *It builds a Palace.* A reference perhaps to Cant. 8:9: "If she be a wall, we will build upon her a palace of silver. . . ." Cf. Traherne's *Meditations,* p. 72: "As a King having builded his Palace, and furnish'd it with Provisions, bringeth in his Bride, even so God having finish'd the World brought in Man, to the Possession of it."

P. 84:35–36. *THE Liberal Soul . . . stand.* Isa. 32:8.

P. 84:38. *no Excess in Goodness.* Neither the divine virtues (of which goodness is one) nor the theological accord with the Aristotelian definition of moral virtue as a just mean between excess and defect. See Jacques Maritain, *Moral Philosophy,* tr. Marshall Suther *et al.,* ed. Joseph W. Evans (New York, 1964), p. 80.

P. 85:15–16. *he has endeavoured . . . to secure their Duty.* On Traherne's advocacy of free will see *CE,* p. 31:8 n. On this particular point, see especially *CE,* pp. 90–93 and 148–150.

P. 86:4. *TO shew that there is such a Goodness.* This paragraph sums up Traherne's earlier work, the *Meditations on the Six Days of the Creation,* where of course he goes into greater detail: "all the Birds, with all their Inclinations, are ordain'd for the Use and Pleasure of Man"—including "their Fat, Skins, Quills, Beaks, Spurs, Claws, Entrails" (p. 60).

P. 86:31. *GOD is Good . . . Works.* Ps. 145:9 (the Prayer Book version of the second clause).

P. 87:1. In his discussion of holiness Traherne seems almost certainly to have drawn upon the treatise on the soul in the Osborn MS. (pp. 254–255). Cf. also SM IV.64: "Holiness is more then Righteousness is. It is the Zeal wherewith we render unto Things their Sacred value. . . . And this I[n]tension & vehemency of Lov . . . is . . . the onely thing that Sanctifieth our Duty. the onely Grace that maketh it Acceptable. The very Holiness of God is the infinit Intension & Greatness of his Lov. which maketh all Things Easy. Himselfe infinitly Delightfull unto us, & us unto Him."

P. 87:10. *the Beauty of Holiness.* 1 Chron. 16:29, 2 Chron. 20:21; Ps. 29:2, 96:9.

P. 87:25–31. *HOLINESS . . . Holiness of the Object.* Traherne is primarily concerned with holiness of the affections, above all with the affection of love. The extent to which his philosophy centers on love may be seen by comparing this paragraph with Benjamin Whichcote's account of holiness: "Holiness, as attributed to God, doth denote God's peerless majesty, together with infinite power and wisdom, as it is in conjunction with righteousness and goodness. . . . Holiness in angels and men doth import their deiformity, that is, their conformity to God according to their measure and capacity; in their being, in their measure and degree and proportion, what God is in his height, excellency and fulness" (*Works,* IV, 57, 58). Most writers dwelt on man's holiness, rather than upon God's.

P. 88:17–18. *The Beauty of Holiness.* See *CE,* p. 87:10 n.

P. 88:28. *Holy . . . Hosts.* Isa. 6:3 and Rev. 4:8 fused.

P. 89:26. *substraction.* Obsolete form of subtraction.

P. 89:35–39. *The least flaw . . . Wisdome and Honour.* This passage is akin to SM III.68: "Dead Flies Corrupt the Apothecaries oyntment, so doth a Little Folly Him that is in Reputation for wisdom & Honor, A little Flaw in a Precious Diamond maketh it Base. a small stain is Insufferable in the Finest Lawn. a Little Poyson spoyleth the Expence of the Curious Dish. And a Light mistake rendereth the most Pleasing Person['s] Discours Ingratefull. O my God How many Thousand Imperfections weaknesses & Errors hav I committed!" The Biblical quotation is from Eccles. 10:1, the first pharse much altered (in the same manner in both cases). Traherne used the example of the tooth in the clock again, *CE*, p. 156; see also *CE*, p. 181.

P. 90:11. *Accidental Cause.* "Some attribute of the cause or some feature accompanying the effect which however has no influence in the causal process nor in the origin of the effect; something incidental to the cause or effect or coincidental" (Wuellner, *Dictionary, s.v.* "Cause").

P. 90:15. *TO read these Riddles aright.* An example of Traherne's enjoyment of paradox: impossible things can be imagined though not actualized; we can conceive of a sin in God, but God by his nature cannot sin: "The least offence would be an infinite Blot in him" (*CE*, p. 75). This view is based on the Platonic trust in an immutable and eternal morality established by God—a trust unshared by believers in a God of absolute omnipotence. Speaking for the latter group, Jeremy Taylor held that morality did not exist eternally and of itself but was created by and dependent upon divine decree and hence capable of alteration: whatever God "wills or does is therefore just because he wills and does it" (*Ductor Dubitantium,* II.i.1.52, I [1660], 240). The opposite position, held by Traherne, was explained by Thomas Jackson: "When it is said [Things are good because God wils] then this *illative* infers only the cause of our knowledge, not of the goodness which we know: and the logicall resolution of this vulgar Dialect, would be this, *We know this or that to be good, because Gods will revealed commends it for such.* But his will revealed commends it for such, because it was in it[s] nature good; for unless such it had bin, he had not willed it" (*Treatise of the Divine Essence,* I, 148–149).

P. 91:3–4. *There is no Kingdome . . . Angels.* Cf. *CE*, p. 149 ("men may be Dead, and moved like stones"), and Christopher Nesse, *A Christians Walk and Work on Earth* (1678), p. 3: "Stones have a being, but not life: Plants have a being and life, but not sense: Beasts have a being, life, and sense, but they want understanding. Now Man . . . doth participate of a being with stones, of life with plants, of sense with beasts, of understanding with Angels. . . ."

P. 92:22. *mean.* Intermediate.

P. 94:9. *upon second Thoughts.* Traherne apparently did not make any thoroughgoing revision of *Christian Ethicks.* He made another change in his original plan by including Chap. XXVII, on contentment (see *CE,* p. 216). In his Select Meditations (IV.59, 61) Traherne had put justice among the cardinal virtues.

P. 94:12. *discover.* Reveal, unfold.

P. 94:15–18. *THE Universal Justice . . . whole World.* In traditional ethical theory the two main divisions of justice were (1) universal or general—here described—and (2) particular, which Traherne takes up two paragraphs later. Cf. the epitome of Eustache: "Iustitia (in genere) est vel generalis (quae item legalis dicitur) quae est universalis obedientia erga omnes leges societatis politicae, quâ quis probè affectus est alios, publici boni gratiâ: vel particularis et privata"

(EN, p. 17; Eustache, p. 122). See Aristotle, *Nic. Eth.* V.1.1129^{a-b}. The definition of universal justice which Traherne gives in the next paragraph is frequently found during this period in the Latin formulation; cf. Henry More: *"Justice is well defin'd by the Lawyers, to be, Constans & perpetua Voluntas suum cuique tribuendi, A constant and perpetual Will to give every man his own"* (*Account,* p. 111). This version was offered by Eustache (p. 121; EN, p. 17). In SM IV.59 Traherne defined justice as "that vertue by which we render unto all Their Due." His account in SM is markedly less severe than the later analysis in *CE.*

P. 95:8–13. *For this Cause . . . Law.* Rom. 13:6–8.

P. 95:22–31. *PARTICULAR Justice . . . Market.* Distributive justice—that "conversant in the Distribution of Rewards and Punishments"—is "used in Courts of Judicature." Commutative justice—concerned with "Buying and Selling"—is used "in the Market." Cf. the definitions in EN (p. 18; Eustache, p. 124): "Iustitia Distributiva est justitia particularis, quae in Distributione praemiorum et poenarum, proportionem servat Geometricam. . . . Iustitia Commutativa est quae in Contractibus et rerum permutationibus, proportionem servat Arithmeticam." See Aristotle, *Nic. Eth.* V.3 (1131^b) and V.4 (1132^a).

P. 95:28. *being to be.* Since it is: the use of "being" for "since" is frequent in Traherne's prose (cf. Margoliouth, *C* III.33 n.) and common at the time (the first citation in the *OED* is Sir Thomas More, 1528).

P. 95:32–38. *Observation of Plato . . . his own Soul.* *Republic* II.368d. This passage, in an adaptation of Ficino's translation, occurs in Traherne's Ficino Notebook (f. 37^v). The same illustration was used in another book we know Traherne read, though without reference to Plato as the source (see Reynolds's *Treatise of the Passions,* pp. 465–466). Cf. the previous reference to Plato, *CE,* p. 41.

P. 96:1. *Rampart.* This passage is cited in *OED.*

P. 96:6–9. *But where Tradesmen . . . such a State.* Probably a reflection of Traherne's youthful experience of the Civil War; for another similar passage, see *CE,* pp. 280–281. See Miss Wade's description of Herefordshire during Traherne's childhood, *Traherne,* pp. 18–26). For a similar metaphor, see *CE,* p. 153:9 n.

P. 96:10–13. *Irascible passions . . . Concupiscible Affections.* The distinction between the irascible and concupiscible passions was popularized by Thomas Aquinas, who attributed the concept to Gregory of Nyssa and Damascene; the concupiscible passions (from which the irascible spring) incline the soul "to seek what is suitable, according to the senses, and to fly from what is hurtful," whereas the irascible passions inspire the soul to resist "those attacks that hinder what is suitable, and inflict harm" (*ST* I, 81, a. 2; similarly in Eustache, pp. 78–79, quoted in EN, p. 15). Eustache (pp. 84–85; EN, pp. 15–16) followed St. Thomas in numbering six concupiscible passions (love, hatred, desire, aversion, joy, sadness) and five irascible (hope, despair, fear, daring, anger) (*ST* I–II, 23, a. 4). See also *CE,* p. 29:6 n.

P. 96:33. *He that is . . . over much.* Luke 16:10; Matt. 24:47.

P. 96:34–38. *Who then . . . in much.* Matt. 24:45–46; Luke 16:10.

P. 97:5–12. *Blessed . . . Teeth.* Matt. 24:46–51.

P. 97:17. *such as the King is, such is the people.* A proverb: Tilley, K 70, p. 356.

P. 98:4. *The Devils chiefest Hell is in the Conscience.* Cf. *C* I.36, IV.37; on hell, see *CE,* p. 229:38 n. The conception of hell in moral rather than physical terms occurs frequently among the Cambridge Platonists. Cf. John Smith: *"Hell* is *rather a Nature* then *a Place:* and *Heaven* cannot be so truly defined by any thing *without* us, as by something that is *within* us" (*Discourses,* pp. 446–447). Benjamin Whichcote explained: "Both *Heaven* and *Hell* have their Foundation *within Us. Heaven* primarily lies in a refined *Temper;* in an internal Reconciliation to the Nature of God, and to the Rule of Righteousness. The Guilt of Conscience, and Enmity to Righteousness, is the *inward* state of *Hell.* The Guilt of Conscience is the *Fewel of Hell"* (*Moral and Religious Aphorisms,* intro. W. R. Inge [1930], no. 100, p. 13).

P. 98:10. *his Punitive Justice springs from his Goodness.* Justice, said John Smith, "cannot delight to punish; it aimes at nothing more then the maintaining and promoting *the Laws of Goodness"* (*Discourses,* p. 153). The final section of Thomas Jackson's *Treatise of the Divine Essence and Attributes,* Pt. I, discusses the just punishment inflicted by divine anger for man's abuse of his liberty; under the headings "Punishment," "Fury," "Banishment," and "Passion," Traherne copied into his Commonplace Book various of Jackson's ruminations on wrath. Jackson, and Traherne with him, decided that God's infinite mercy overcomes his justifiably infinite anger. On God's patience, see *CE,* pp. 186–187.

P. 98:14–15. *beating . . . Servants.* Matt. 24:49.

P. 98:19. *tenders.* Cherishes.

P. 98:25. *other Discourses.* The subject of Henry More's *Divine Dialogues,* from which Traherne quoted in his Commonplace Book, was set by Philopolis in the First Dialogue (pp. 14–15): "First, *What the Kingdome of God is.* Secondly, *When it began, and where it has been or is now to be found.* Thirdly, *What Progress it hath made hitherto in the world.* Lastly, *What Success it is likely to have to the End of all things."* The first three Dialogues are a prolegomenon to the last two, which discuss directly the kingdom of God.

P. 99:21. *Exceeding sinful.* Rom. 7:13.

P. 100:7. *no Law of Works can justifie Sinners.* For a fuller explanation of the Protestant view on faith and works, see *CE,* pp. 106–107.

P. 100:12. *made a Curse and Sin for us.* Gal. 3:13 and 2 Cor. 5:21 fused, as again *CE,* p. 261.

P. 100:13. *from the Curse of the Law.* Gal. 3:13.

P. 100:15. *Devils can not be saved.* There was some contemporary debate as to eternal damnation, George Rust and Peter Sterry being among the minority who refused to admit the doctrine (see Vivian da Sola Pinto, *Peter Sterry,* pp. 103–104; and Rust, *A Letter of Resolution,* facsimile ed. [New York, 1933], pp. 79–82). Henry More discussed the matter and concluded for an eternity of damnation (*Annotations upon Lux Orientalis,* in Joseph Glanvill and Rust, *Two Choice and Useful Treatises* [1682], p. 76).

P. 100:16–17. *took not . . . Abraham.* Heb. 2:16.

P. 101:15–16. *In the Day . . . Death.* Gen. 2:17.

P. 101:20. *Denunciation.* Proclamation.

P. 101:29–30. *his Condition . . . better than before.* The old doctrine of the *felix culpa;* see Arthur O. Lovejoy's essay, "Milton and the Paradox of the Fortunate Fall," first published in *ELH,* IV (1937), subsequently in *Essays in the History of Ideas* (Baltimore, 1948).

P. 102:18–20. *the Love of GOD . . . Spectator.* On the trinity of love, see *C* II.39–46; *SM* II.72, IV.43; and Martz, *The Paradise Within,* pp. 74–76. In *SM* II.72 Traherne wrote: "The H. Ghost is the Lov of the Father and the Son Dwelling in us. or to Speak plainly seene by us."

P. 103:13–15. *our Father . . . Wicked.* Matt. 5:45, altered; the phrase "the righteous and the wicked" is found, not in Matthew, but in Eze. 21:3, 4 and Mal. 3:18.

P. 103:17–19. *As the Blood . . . our Enjoyments.* See Heb. 9:21–28 and *CE,* p. 129:13 n.

P. 103:21–22. *the Heavens . . . Handy work.* Ps. 19:1.

P. 103:33–35. *GOD so Loved . . . Life.* John 3:16.

P. 104:10. *the Nature of Angels.* Traherne discussed the nature of angels in CYB, ff. 89 ff., terming them "Pure & Simple Beings" (f. 90ᵛ). He also asserted in CYB (f. 12): "Without the Body of Man, the World would be in vain. . . ." For a further explanation of the necessity of bodies, see *CE,* p. 182; cf. CYB, f. 92, and *SM* III.95. Traherne's respect for the human body is familiar to readers of his *Centuries* (I.66), poems (see "The Salutation," "The Estate," "The Enquirie," and "The Person"), *Meditations* (see pp. 73–80 and 88–89), and "Thanksgivings for the Body." For a similar metaphor, cf. the *Meditations* (p. 73): "as we put fair and curious Pictures, which we much value, into rich and costly Cases, so God implanted his Image in this Body. . . ." In his Early Notebook he manifested interest in the relationship between body and soul, commenting that a passage from Reynolds's *Treatise of the Passions* "argues the great dependance the soule hath upon the body" (EN, p. 143). His view of the superiority of men to angels (cf. also *CE,* p. 195, and *C* II.33) finds a parallel in the *Soliloquia* of St. Augustine, in a volume from which he borrowed a poem (see Margoliouth, II, 401): "Man is not somewhat lesse then the Angells: nay, he is not onely equall to the Angells, but superior to them, because man is God, and God is a man, & not an Angell" (ch. 8, in *The Meditations, Soliloquia, and Manuall of the Glorious Doctour S. Augustine,* 2d ed. [Paris, 1655], pp. 221–222).

P. 104:14. *unspeakable.* The *OED,* which cites this passage, explains: "Incapable of being expressed in words; inexpressible, indescribable, ineffable." Note also "unspeakable different," *CE,* p. 140: the adjectival form served likewise as an adverb in the seventeenth century; *OED* cites two passages, dated 1635 and 1657.

P. 104:19–25. *Man seems . . . works are United.* In CYB, Traherne used verbatim the first metaphor of this passage, which, based on Col. 1:16, 18, is one of the great images of Renaissance humanism: man is "the Head of all Things visible & Invisible, since in His Body all visible, in his Soul all Invisible Things are Contained" (f. 94; cf. f. 24ᵛ). He quoted Pico della Mirandola's famous expression of the concept in *C* IV.74 and in the *Meditations* wrote: "All the rest of the Creatures were without a Head till he [man] was made, in him all were united, and made great in value. . . . So Man is the supreme Head of all visible and invisible things, the very Heaven and the Angels being created for him, the Sun and Moon being inferior to him, the four Elements comprehended in him, and all the Creatures upon Earth serving him" (pp. 82, 84). Charron called man "the tie and ligament of Angels and beasts, things heavenly and earthly, spirituall and corporall" (*Of Wisdome,* pp. 8–9). Henry More noted that "we acknowledg[e] Man to dwell as it were in the borders of the Spiritual and Material world (for he is *utriusque mundi nexus,* as *Scaliger* truly calls him)" (*Antidote to Athesim,* in *Collection,* p. 84). Cf. Sir Thomas Browne's well-known version: "Thus is Man that great and true *Amphibium,* whose nature is disposed to live . . . in divided and distinguished worlds" (*Religio Medici,* Everyman ed. [1951], p. 39). For another expression of homocentricity, see *CE,* p. 86; and, among many similar passages in the poems, "Hosanna," II, 149–151, and "Goodnesse," II, 182–184. On the body as God's temple, cf. the *Meditations* (p. 75): "The Temple of God, saith *Lactantius,* is not *Lime, Stone, Sand, and Timber, but Man bearing the Image of God. And this Temple is not adorn'd with Gold or Silver, but with divine Virtues and Graces."*

P. 104:26–27. *a little lower . . . Glory and Honour.* Ps. 8:5: one of Traherne's favorite quotations: cf. *C* I.65; *C* III.71; and the *Thanksgivings,* II, 244, 322.

P. 105:12–18. *For the same Mind . . . might bow.* Philip. 2:5–10.

P. 106:11. *without Faith . . . please GOD.* Heb. 11:6.

P. 106:15–16. *For as long . . . please him.* Cf. this similar passage in SM IV.62: "As Long as we Apprehend God implacable in His Hatred towards us, we must of Necessity hate Him. Before we can Love Him, we must belieu He Loveth us. That Jesus Christ is the Redeemer of the world we must needs belieue before we Can enjoy Him."

P. 106:31. *imputeth . . . Righteousness.* Paraphrase of Rom. 4:5–6. With this paragraph cf. *CE,* pp. 100 and 223.

P. 107:14. *OBJECTS of Faith.* Cf. Joseph Glanvill: "There are but three things from whence the *existence* of any *being* can be concluded, *viz. Sense, Revelation,* or *Reason"* (ΛΟΓΟΥ ΘΡΗΣΚΕΙΑ: *or, a Seasonable Recommendation, and Defence of Reason* [1670], p. 8). With the present paragraph—which embodies oft-reiterated arguments of the period—cf. this speech put into the mouth of "Firmianus" by Traherne's friend (see Margoliouth, I, xxviii) Thomas Good: "That there were such persons in the world as Christ and his Apostles, that they wrought those Miracles which are mentioned in the History of them, both Jews and Gentiles, (sworn enemies to Christianity), acknowledg, but besides their Testimony (which being from adversaryes is very cogent) we have the tradition of the Catholick Church in all ages, and most places of the world, for 1600 years and upwards; and . . . he that shall ascend through the several Centuries of the Church, . . . may be farr more certain, of the birth, and life, and works, and sufferings of this our blessed Saviour, of the writings of the Holy Evangelists, and Apostles, then that there have been such men in the world as *Alexander* the great, *Julius Caesar, Pompey, Scipio, Hannibal,* of the Warrs, and noble Acheivements managed by them, of *William* the Conquerour, the Barons warrs, and yet none but a fool or a mad man, or one that has vowed to believe no farther then what he can see with his own eyes, will doubt of these" (*Firmianus and Dubitantius* [Oxford, 1674], pp. 47–48). John Sergeant observed how "incomparably and in a manner infinitely greater must the Obligation be to believe Christ's Doctrin than *Alexander*'s or *William* the Conquerors Victories" (*Sure-Footing in Christianity* [1665], p. 228). Cf. *CE*, pp. 117:27 n. and 120:14 n.; "Thanksgivings for the Beauty of his Providence," II, 292–293; and CYB, f. 98, where Traherne comments that the "Truth" of the writings of "Eusebius & other Ancient Authors . . . , being Historicall, Obligeth us to a Moral Belief, tho not to a Divine & Infallible faith." See Henry G. Van Leeuwen, *The Problem of Certainty in English Thought* (The Hague, 1963), p. 63 *et passim*.

P. 108:6. *Jury*. I.e., Jewry, the Jewish people.

P. 108:17. *Mathematical Demonstration*. Traherne's contemporaries were fond of using mathematical metaphors to assert nonquantitative truths. One example of many occurs in the first of More's *Divine Dialogues* (p. 6): "For the chief Points of *Morality* are no less demonstrable then *Mathematicks;* nor is the Subtilty greater in *Moral* Theorems then in *Mathematicall*."

P. 108:34. *by Faith . . . understanding*. Traherne subsumed the faculty of faith under the intellect rather than the will. As Henry Hammond explained, "the seat or subject" of faith had never been "clearly set down,—some confining it to the understanding, others to the will,—till at last it pitched upon the whole soul, the intellective nature" (*Thirty-one Sermons*, II, 396).

P. 108:39. *Try . . . Good*. 1 Thes. 5:21.

P. 109:1. *For Reason is a transcendent faculty*. Cf. Henry More: reason is "a *Middle life* or *Facultie* of the Soul of Man betwixt the *Divine* and *Animal . . . whereby either from her Innate Ideas or Common Notions, or else from the assurance of her own Senses, or upon the Relation or Tradition of another, she unravels a further clew of Knowledge, enlarging her sphere of Intellectual light, by laying open to her self the close connexion and cohesion of the Conceptions she has of things, whereby inferring one thing from another she is able to deduce multifarious Conclusions as well for the pleasure of Speculation as the necessity of Practice*" (*The Grand Mystery of Godliness*, p. 51).

P. 110:2. *Types and Ceremonies*. John T. McNeill annotates Calvin's term *typus ille:* "The word *typus* has for its basic meaning a representative figure, or image, on a wall. In general, it is a mark or sign to indicate something not present. For Calvin, the ceremonies enjoined in the law were 'types,' or 'foreshadowings,' of the full and clear revelation of the Gospel in which the ceremonies cease. . . . This typology became a more or less constant feature of Reformed theology" (*Institutes of the Christian Religion*, ed. John T. McNeill, tr. Ford Lewis Battles, I [Philadelphia, 1960], 349 n.2). See *CE*, pp. 34, 113, and 129–130 (an exercise in typology). Three of Thomas Jackson's multivolume *Commentaries on the Creed—The Knowledge of Christ Jesus* (1634), *The Humiliation of the Sonne of God* (1635), and *A Treatise of the Consecration of the Sonne of God* (1638)—are typological studies.

P. 110:27. *NOW of all the Things*. Another thoroughly commonplace exposition. Cf. the passage from Good's *Firmianus and Dubitantius* quoted *CE*, p. 107:14 n.

P. 111:13–14. *The great Moment . . . more Eager.* Cf. *CE,* p. 15.

P. 111:22. *AMONG other Objects.* Margoliouth compares the first sentence of this passage with *C* I.17. Close parallels with other phrases in this paragraph occur in the Fifth Century. "The Everlasting Duration of infinit Space is another Region and Room of Joys. Wherein all Ages appear together, all Occurrences stand up at once, and the innumerable and Endless Myriads of yeers that were before the Creation, and will be after the World is ended are Objected as a Clear and Stable Object, whose several Parts extended out at length, giv an inward Infinity to this Moment, and compose an Eternitie that is seen by all Comprehensors and Enjoyers" (*C* V.6). "For as there is an immovable Space wherin all finit Spaces are enclosed, and all Motions carried on, and performed: so is there an Immovable Duration, that contains and measures all moving Durations" (*C* V.7).

On God's creation of a plenitude of being, see General Introduction, p. xlv. Traherne believed with "the *ROYAL SOCIETY,* and those of that *Genius*" that "There is an *inexhaustible variety* of *Treasure* which *Providence* hath lodged in Things" (Joseph Glanvill, *Plus Ultra,* facsimile ed. [Gainesville, Fla., 1958], pp. 6–7).

P. 111:27. *Objected.* Presented.

P. 112:17. *stooping down to the abyss of Nothing.* Cf. "The Design" (II, 70): "When first Eternity Stoopd down to Nought . . ."

P. 112:23. *Through faith . . . made.* Heb. 11:3 (the A.V. reads "framed" for "made").

P. 112:29–30. *Faith is . . . Perfected.* Gladys Wade suggests that Thomas Aquinas is the source for this statement ("St. Thomas Aquinas and Thomas Traherne," *Blackfriars,* XII [1931], 667); actually it was a commonplace in controversies of the time. Joseph Glanvill, in his essay "The Agreement of Reason, and Religion," wrote: *"The belief of our Reason is an Exercise of Faith; and Faith is an Act of Reason"* (*Essays on Several Important Subjects in Philosophy and Religion* [1676], p. 21). Nathanael Culverwel in his *Light of Nature* endeavored "to give unto *Reason* the things that are *Reasons,* and unto *Faith* the things that are *Faiths;* to give *Faith* her full scope and latitude, and to give *Reason* also her just bounds and limits," to steer between those fundamentalists who look upon reason "not as *the Candle of the Lord,* but as on some blazing Comet that portends present ruine to the Church" and the Socinians who "by their meer pretences to *Reason* have made shipwrack of *Faith*" (pp. 1–2). Culverwel argued: "One light does not oppose another; *Lumen fidei & Lumen rationis,* may shine both together though with farre different brightnesse . . . by their mutual supplies and intercourse they may produce most noble and generous fruit" (pp. 167–168). See Richard S. Westfall, *Science and Religion in Seventeenth-Century England* (New Haven, 1958), ch. 7.

P. 113:16–17. *the fulness of Time.* Gal. 4:4.

P. 113:35–36. *the Volumne . . . written of him.* Ps. 40:7; Heb. 10:7.

P. 114:4–5. *a Nation's being born at once.* Isa. 66:8.

P. 114:26. *the end of the Law.* Rom. 10:4.

P. 114:38–39. *that Jesus Christ might be Known.* Cf. Jer. 28:9.

P. 115:39. The marginal reference, more specifically, would be Heb. 11:4–5, 7–17, 24–29, 32–38 (summarized and paraphrased, except for verses 32–38).

P. 116:9–10. *more then conquerors . . . for us.* Rom. 8:37, modified by Gal. 2:20.

P. 117:5–7. *Janus . . . Eternity to come.* "The oldest of the Latin Gods," Janus "became god of the months, seasons of the year and of eternity. Thus he was represented as looking to the past and to the future" (Arnold Whittick, *Symbols, Signs, and their Meaning* [Newton, Mass., 1960], p. 143). Like Traherne, "Ficino occasionally compares the Soul to the head of Janus" (P. O. Kristeller, *The Philosophy of Marsilio Ficino,* tr. Virginia Conant [New York, 1943], p. 197). Pico della Mirandola, another Florentine Neoplatonist whom Traherne read, similarly declared Janus to symbolize the perfect soul able to look upon body and mind with proper balance (*A Platonick Discourse upon Love,* tr. Thomas Stanley, in Stanley's *Poems and Translations,* ed. Galbraith Miller Crump [Oxford, 1962], 2.XXI, p. 216).

P. 117:20. *HOPE presupposes . . . desire.* Traherne interprets hope in terms of Christian theology; he evidently agreed with Culverwel: "There's a vast difference between the Moralists hope, and that which is the Theological grace. . . ." Moral philosophers, according to Culverwel, "require these ingredients into the object of hope: that it must be (1.) *bonum,* (2.) *futurum,* (3.) *incertum;* but Christian hope is certain & infallible, it looks upon good as to come, and as certain to come" ("The White Stone," in *Light of Nature,* pp. 107–108).

P. 117:27. *THE Objects of Divine Faith.* Cf. Henry More: "The *Moral* and *Humane Certainty* of Faith is grounded upon the Certainty of *Universal Tradition, Prophecy, History,* and *the Nature of the things delivered,* Reason and Sense assisting the Minde in her Disquisitions touching these matters. . . . By *Universal Tradition* I understand such a Tradition as has been from the Apostles. . . . By *Prophecy* I understand as well those Divine Predictions of the coming of *Christ,* as those touching the Church after he had come. By *History* I mean not onely that of the Bible, and particularly the New Testament, but other History as well Ecclesiastick as Prophane" (*A Brief Discourse of the True Grounds of the Certainty of Faith,* annexed to *Divine Dialogues . . . The Two Last Dialogues,* pp. 478–479). On natural religion, see *CE,* p. 58:30 n.

P. 120:14. *How shall we know.* This passage is a continuation of the discussion of faith and historical truth begun on p. 107. Traherne repeats himself somewhat: "Turks acknowledge the Historical Part" of the Bible (p. 111); "The History of the Bible is confest by Turks" (p. 120). See p. 107:14 n. and as well *C* III.34 and "Thanksgivings for the Wisdom of his WORD" (II, 305–310).

The example of the antipodes—which Sir Thomas Browne defined as "points of the Globe diametrically opposed" (*Pseudodoxia Epidemica,* VI.7, 6th ed. [1672], p. 354)—was timely, since until recently "the *Antipodes,* and the *Circumvolution of the Earth* . . . were held wholly unreasonable and Phantasticall" (Walter Charleton, *The Immortality of the Human Soul* [1657], p. 133). S[imon] P[atrick], defending the use of reason in religion, made the same point (*A Brief*

Account of the New Sect of Latitude-men [1662], p. 20). See also Owen Feltham's *Resolves,* I.27: "St. *Augustine* would by no means endure the *Antipodes:* we are now of nothing more certain. Every *Age* both *confutes* old *Errors,* and begets *new*" (8th ed., 1661, p. 53). Thomas Jackson complained: "It was a great oversight . . . in *Lactantius* . . . not onely to deny there were any Antipodes, but to censure the Philosophers . . . of grosse ignorance or infatuation, for avouching this truth, now manifested to meaner Scholars, or more illiterate Christians" (*Treatise of the Divine Essence,* I, 77). Cf. *C* II.9 and III.17.

P. 121:37. *HOPE is for its Extent.* On "Ambition or Avarice" see *CE,* p. 54:37 n., and with the emotional concept of this paragraph cf. Peter Sterry's obstetrical metaphors: "*Hope* is the *Springing of the Soul towards good, or God. . . . Hope* is the *Conception* [i.e., generation] of Blessedness. *Desire* is the *Teeming,* the Breeding, Bearing, and Growing big with it, till it be brought forth. . . . The *Revelation* of God in Man is the Foundation of *Hope: Hope* the Foundation of *Desires,* which grow into great Streams, and so pour forth themselves into their Sea, into God again" (*Rise, Race, and Royalty,* p. 27).

P. 122:4–5. *more . . . think.* Eph. 3:20.

P. 122:22. *Love . . . in Romances.* Traherne speaks again in *CE* of love in fiction (p. 150) and of love on the stage (p. 166).

P. 123:8. *Anchor of our Souls.* Heb. 6:19. These words of St. Paul made the anchor a Christian symbol of hope.

P. 123:28–29. *like to . . . himself.* Philip. 3:21.

P. 123:35–36. *Presumption . . . Extreams of Hope.* Treating hope as a theological virtue, Thomas Aquinas considered its "contrary vices" to be presumption and despair (*ST* II–II, 20); again this is the framework of the Aristotelian mean. Thomas also treated hope as one of the irascible passions (*ST* I–II, 40). Henry More, following Descartes, described hope as a passion disposing the soul "*to believe the Event which it desires*"; fear, on the other hand, inclines the soul "*to believe, that what it desires, will not happen*"; and hope devoid of fear is "*Security, or Presumption,*" whereas fear devoid of hope is despair (*Account,* p. 49; cf. Descartes, *Passions of the Soul,* II.58).

P. 125:15. *ingrateful.* Displeasing.

P. 125:27–p. 126:5. *THE Efficient Cause . . . last Salvation.* This eruption of scholastic terminology suggests that Traherne here borrowed from some conventional treatise of moral philosophy, for he could well have produced his definition without this causal prelude. Runes (*Dictionary, s.v.* "Cause") explains: "Aristotle distinguished among (1) the material cause, or that out of which something arises; (2) the formal cause, that is, the pattern or essence determining the creation of a thing; (3) the efficient cause, or the force or agent producing an effect; and (4) the final cause, or purpose."

P. 126:7. *Grace, or Christian Vertue.* On the terms, see *CE,* pp. 24:37 n. and 25:11 n. Repentance is a Christian rather than a moral virtue because God concurs in it (as the remote efficient cause). "Repentance," said the Earl of Clarendon, "is the greatest business we have to do in this world, and . . . the only token we can carry [to heaven] of our being Christians. . . . Repentance then is a godly sorrow for having done or committed somewhat that God hath forbidden them to do, or for having omitted to do somewhat that he hath commanded us to do, one which was in our power to have done" (*Essays* [1815], I, 158, 160).

P. 126:14. *Purgative . . . Perfective.* A Neoplatonic distinction given wide circulation through Plotinus (*Enneads* I.ii.3–5), Macrobius (*Commentary on the Dream of Scipio,* I.viii.4, 8–9), and St. Thomas (*ST* I–II, 61, a. 5). In his Commonplace Book under the headings "Perfection" (f. 75ᵛ) and "Purgative" (f. 79ᵛ.2) Traherne quoted from Gale's section on Platonism (pp. 332–334, 216–217). Cf. William Shelton: "Faith and Repentance are but purgative Vertues (as the *Platonists* speak) but Charity, *&c.* are paradeigmatical; that is, by Faith and Repentance we are purg'd from Sin, and so prepared for Communion with God; but by the other we do properly resemble God" (*Moral Vertues,* p. 14).

P. 126:31–37. *Nor was there . . . their mysteries.* This passage is a modified version of a quotation from an unknown source in the Commonplace Book, under the heading "Preparation" (f. 77.2); the notebook reads: "Nor was there any Temple or Religion in the world, which pretended not som thing to diviner Mysteries, & had their Washings, Humiliations, Watchings, Retirements, shavings Sprinklings Sacrifices, or some such Ceremonies of Preparation for their votaries therunto." Traherne also included in CB (*s.v.* "Idolatrie," f. 56.1) Gale's translation of Diogenes Laertius: "*Pythagoras . . . held . . . That honors are to be performed to the Gods according to their own appointment, with a white garment, and chaste bodie, and soul, which purification is acquired by expurgations, washings, sprinklings, and separation from what ever is unclean*" (*Court,* p. 185).

P. 126:38. *sensible.* Apparent to the senses; the *OED* quotes John Norris's *Essay Toward the Theory of the Ideal or Intelligible World,* II (1704), 271: "By sensible objects, I mean those objects which the understanding has a perception of by the mediation of the senses."

P. 127:4. *the name of Pænitentia.* That is, the word "penitence" existed in heathen languages, though the heathens did not understand its true significance.

P. 127:40. The marginal reference, more specifically, is to Luke 15:7.

P. 128:3. *Obnoxious.* Exposed, as on next page. See *CE,* p. 32:3 n.

P. 128:20. *Verdure.* See *CE,* p. 199:37 n.

P. 129:7. *Dereliction.* Abandonment; the *OED* cites Jeremy Taylor's *Great Exemplar* (from which Traherne borrowed in CYB), I.viii.5: "Repentance and dereliction of sins."

P. 129:13–14. *It was fitly Typified.* This passage illustrates the then common typological approach to the Old Testament. Most of the customs alluded to are described in Ex. 25–39; on the sprinkling of blood on lintels, see Ex. 12:21–23; on the cherubim and palm trees painted on the walls, see 1 Kings 6:29; and on the sprinkling of blood and oil on priests and lepers, see Lev. 4:5–7, 14:14–18, 25–29. On typology, see *CE,* p. 110:2 n. St. Paul was the first to practice typology on these particular passages; see Heb. 9–10.

Typological analyses were standard fare in seventeenth-century Biblical scholarship. See, for example, *Annotations Upon all the Books of the Old and New Testament,* produced by J. Ley and others (1645), and Matthew Poole's *Annota-*

tions, 2 vols. (1688). In CYB (ff. 49ᵛ–50) Traherne made typological use of the candlesticks, incense altar, "Angels, Palm trees & Cherubims which we see in the Tabernacle," noting in a canceled passage that "the Levites were Types & Figures" of the "Members of the Church Invisible" (f. 49ᵛ). On f. 91 he wrote: "An Host [of angles] is about us at all times. And therfore were the Cherubims Engraven in Gold upon the Walls of the Tabernacle, among the Palm Trees; to intimat their Familiarity & Conversation with Us. The Palm Trees which are Strait and Victorious, being Saints, Growing upon Earth: & the Cherubims Angels flying in Heaven. In the midst of all which the H. Ghost figured by the Golden Candlestick with Seven Branches, continualy Shineth with equal Beams, on the Cherubims to Inlighten them. On the Palm Trees to make them flourish." See also SM III.60.

There is some likeness between these pages in *Christian Ethicks* and an unidentified source transcribed in CB (*s.v.* "Preparation," f. 77.2). The source lists as preparations for felicity to be made by one in the "Estate of Sin & misery": "Humiliation for Sin, washing away of Guilt, cutting off Superfluity of Naughtiness, Clarifying the Understanding, Purifying the Will, subduing the Appetite, ordering the Affections, self Denial, abstaining from pleasures, Mortifying the Deeds of the Body, &c. All which of old were shadowed forth in the Cleansing of the Leper, Consecrating the Priests, & the way of entering into the Tabernacle."

P. 130:29–30. *who of GOD . . . Redemption.* 1 Cor. 1:30.

P. 131:14. *Sensible.* Aware.

P. 131:32. *kindly.* Pleasant.

P. 133:22. *Bleeding, Resentments.* The phrase is used in *CE* again, p. 167. As usual, "resentments" means "feelings." See Textual Notes for a comment on the punctuation.

P. 133:24. *the falling out . . . Love.* Cf. *C* III.83: "The Falling out of Lovers is the Beginning of Lov. . . ." Margoliouth annotates: "a verbose translation of Terence's five words Amantium irae amoris integratio est (*Andria,* 555)." Erasmus (*Adagia,* III.i.89) cites this line as a proverb.

P. 134:32. *Love Life . . . Good Days.* Adapted from 1 Pet. 3:10.

P. 134:39–40. *another sort of Love . . . Charity.* The distinction is based upon the discrimination between *amor* and *caritas,* or (roughly) earthly and divine love. The more restricted meaning of charity as benevolence to one's neighbor was coming into increasing use in Traherne's day, but the broader sense was still current, as Traherne's definition shows. Henry More defined charity as "an Intellectual Love, by which we are enamoured of the *Divine Perfections*"; this "is the truest and highest kind of *Adoration,*" and by it we love not only God "but descend also in very full and free streams of dearest Affection to our fellow-Creatures" (*The Grand Mystery of Godliness,* pp. 53–54). All men agreed with Walter Kirkham Blount (and St. Augustine) that "the Spirit of Christianity consists only in Charity" (*The Spirit of Christianity* [1686], p. 3); not all would have concurred with Blount's opinion that the quintessential feature of Christian love "is to desire the good of those that wish us nothing but ill" (p. 26).

P. 135:19–21. *He that . . . to the Father.* John 14:12.

P. 135:25–26. *The End . . . Faith unfeigned.* 1 Tim. 1:5.

P. 135:30. *Oeconomy.* Dispensation, system of divine government.

P. 135:40. The marginal references, more correctly, are to 1 Cor. 13:1–3 and to Mark 12:29–31.

P. 135:39–p. 136:3. *the Love of Benevolence . . . of Complacency.* Peter Sterry explained more fully: "There is a *Twofold Love* in God; a *Love* of *Complacency*, or Delight; a *Love* of *Benevolence*, or good Will. The *first* is that, by which he taketh pleasure in thee, as a Bridegroom in his beautiful Bride. The second is that, by which his Will is set on work to make thee beautiful, and a Bride to himself. The love of Complacency is the first, and the last love. The love of benevolence is a middle-love, which ariseth out of this, and endeth in it; as Springs, and Rivers come from the Sea, and run into it" (*Rise,* p. 317).

P. 136:19–20. *Love . . . Law.* Rom. 13:10.

P. 136:20. *the Bond of Perfectness.* Col. 3:14.

P. 136:37. *not Mercenary or self ended.* Cf. this phrase in Traherne's discussion of love in the *Centuries:* "To be Self Ended is Mercenary" (IV.63).

P. 136:40. The marginal reference, more specifically, is 1 Cor. 13:4–8.

P. 138:2–3. *Holy, Good, and acceptable.* Combines Rom. 12:1 and 12:2.

P. 138:4. *nice Emergencies.* Unexpected occurrences which are difficult to handle.

P. 138:22–23. *Magnalia . . . Benevolentiæ.* Traherne paraphrases immediately. The source has proved elusive; the language is Late Latin.

P. 138:25. *Externals of Friendship.* Traherne's stress on the emotion over the "Offices" of friendship is noteworthy, since the reverse emphasis was characteristic of contemporary moralists. "The first and principal obligation" of friendship, said Clarendon, "is, to assist each other with their counsel and advice" (*Essays,* I, 113). On "the greatest Secret" in the nature of friendship, see *CE,* p. 46:9 n. On friendship in adversity, see *CE,* p. 189; on meekness in friendship, *CE,* pp. 199–200; on the duty of chastising one's friends, pp. 157–158.

P. 138:33. *proper Element and Refrigerium.* By "proper Element" Traherne means the completely appropriate sphere of operation (with an echo of the four elements of ancient science). "Refrigerium" is a Late Latin word; Traherne uses it in the Vulgate sense of comfort or consolation.

P. 138:39. *aims.* Guesses, conjectures.

P. 139:18–20. *tho we give . . . profiteth nothing.* A paraphrase of St. Paul's words in 1 Cor. 13:3.

P. 140:20–30. *THERE are two . . . all the Creatures.* From *The Whole Duty of Man* (I.28–29, pp. 13–14). On this work, see *CE,* p. 3:10 n. Gladys Wade was the first to observe Traherne's borrowings from *The Whole Duty* (*Traherne,* p. 142 n. 67). In this quotation, as in those following, Traherne departed somewhat from the phrasing of his source, a practice he followed in his quotations from other authors in the Commonplace Book and the Church's Year-Book; in general, his alterations render the passages quoted more akin to his own style.

P. 140:30. *The Sun is a lively Mirror.* For other evidences of Traherne's devotion to the sun, see *CE,* p. 39:35 n. See also "The Anticipation," II, 161. In the *Meditations* he observed (p. 45): "Now see, my Soul, how this glorious

Light resembles thy Creator, and is the greatest Sign and Symbol of Divinity in all Nature, by which thou art more clearly, O Lord, known unto Men, than by any other Creature, being the very shadow of the Divinity." Joseph Glanvill, like Traherne inclined to Platonism, said that "the most congruous apprehension that we can entertain of the *Infinite* and *eternal Deity,* is to conceive him as an *immense* and all *glorious Sun,* that is continually *communicating* and sending abroad its *beams* and *brightness*" (*Lux Orientalis,* in *Two Choice and Useful Treatises,* p. 96).

P. 141:3. *adopted.* Chosen.

P. 141:15–17. *we prefer . . . Essence of the Soul.* Cf. *CE,* pp. 13:28 n. and 14:7 n.

P. 141:30–35. *a desire to please . . . Careful to please.* From *The Whole Duty of Man* (I.33, pp. 16–17).

P. 142:1. *our Meat . . . Heaven.* Cf. John 4:34, Matt. 7:21, and Rom. 14:17.

P. 142:2–5. *some slight . . . our Creator.* From *The Whole Duty of Man* (I.34, pp. 17–18).

P. 142:6–22. *THE desire . . . more unto him.* From *The Whole Duty of Man* (I.36–38, pp. 18–19); Traherne diverges widely from his text in these extracts. The Biblical quotation is Ps. 84:10.

P. 142:23–24. *there is another . . . perfect.* From *The Whole Duty of Man* (I.40, p. 20).

P. 142:24–25. *desire . . . with Christ.* Philip. 1:23. A. V. reads "depart," not "be dissolved"; Traherne makes the same misquotation again, *CE,* p. 190.

P. 142:25–26. *see no more . . . are Known.* 1 Cor. 13:12, altered.

P. 142:26–28. *For Love . . . drown it.* Cant. 8:6–7.

P. 142:30. *IF you would know.* This paragraph is a gloss on the Ten Commandments; such commentaries were standard fare in the expositions of the Catechism so popular at the time.

P. 144:10. *CHARITY to our Neighbour.* Traherne's Commonplace Book contains two excerpts on this topic from Isaac Barrow's sermon *On the Duty and Reward of Bounty to the Poor* (1671), "Preached at the *Spittal* Upon *Wednesday* in *Easter* Week," 1671, as the title-page says (Traherne could therefore have heard it): "Charitie" (f. 26.1) and "Neighbor" (f. 70ᵛ.2). The latter entry contains an eloquent expression of the truism that every man "is our near Kinsman, is our Brother, is by indissoluble bands of cognation in blood, and agreement in Nature knit and united to us" (p. 131).

P. 145:21–22. *The Service . . . freedome.* The Second Collect of the Morning Prayer in the Book of Common Prayer invokes God, "whose service is perfect freedom." The paradox was very popular in Traherne's day; he himself quoted it also in SM IV.51.

P. 146:7. *President.* I.e., precedent; cf. "Thanksgivings for the Wisdom of his WORD" (II, 307, l. 293), where Margoliouth notes that the "*OED* quotes Cromwell for the spelling."

P. 147:2. *the Black Guard.* A term of doubtful origin and multiple meanings in the seventeenth century; the general connotation was loafer, vagabond, rogue. The typography and grammar here suggest that Traherne may have been thinking of some more specific use. The term was usually spelled in two words during the seventeenth century.

P. 147:23. *There is . . . Commandement.* Mark 12:31.

P. 148:35. *As for GOD . . . perfect.* 2 Sam. 22:31; with the following phrase, cf. Judges 5:30 ("divers colours of needlework on both sides").

P. 149:18. *Love is an active and free affection.* Cf. Tilley, L 499, p. 395: "Love cannot be compelled (forced)."

P. 149:32. *Cross.* Perverse.

P. 149:34. *no consultation nor Election.* Theophilus Gale explained these terms in his exposition of Aristotle, quoted by Traherne in his Commonplace Book under "consultation" (f. 29^v) and "Election" (f. 39^v). According to Gale (*Court,* pp. 393, 395), the best definition of consultation is Neoplatonic: "*a consideration of things future, so far as expedient,* i.e., for our end. For a wise man first proposeth, and wils his end, and then makes use of *Consultation,* as an instrument to find out *means* expedient for this end. . . . The main *effect* of Consultation, is *Election,*" for a definition of which Gale turned (p. 397) to Aristotle (*Nic. Eth.* III.5): "Election is a consulted, or judicious appetition of things in our power."

P. 150:32. *the Great Dæmon of the World.* Cf. *C* IV.67: love is "the Great Dæmon of the World, the End of all Things." Margoliouth gives no source. Diotima, in the *Symposium* (202e), calls love a Δαίμον μέγας, or "great spirit," possessing the power of "interpreting and transporting human things to the gods and divine things to men . . . : being midway between, it makes each to supplement the other, so that the whole is combined in one" (W. R. M. Lamb's translation in the Loeb ed.). In SM II.64 Traherne calls love a "Strange Dæmon."

P. 150:34. *Play, or Romance, or Fable.* Traherne asserts the necessary infusion of love into literature elsewhere in *CE,* pp. 122 and 166.

P. 151:17–25. *Charity never . . . Charity.* 1 Cor. 13:8–10, 12–13.

P. 152:13–17. *without which . . . Cunning.* Without love the virtues lead to their extremes: in the Aristotelian or post-Aristotelian scheme baseness is the "defect" of humility, presumption and profuseness the "excess" respectively of hope and liberality, and so on.

P. 152:25. *Emergence.* Unforeseen occurrence; cf. the title of Donne's *Devotions upon Emergent Occasions.*

P. 152:26. *Its Designe.* R. B. Schlatter comments on this description: "The most worldly and least religious definition of prudence came from an Anglican mystic, Thomas Traherne. . . . To Puritan ears, Traherne's definition must have aroused suspicions of the mystery of Jesuitism. For [to Puritans] business and religion were not antagonists to be reconciled: religion embraced the whole of life" (*The Social Ideas of Religious Leaders, 1660–1688* [1940], pp. 193–194). But Schlatter misreads; the sentiment he attributes to the Puritans and denies to Traherne is central to *Christian Ethicks.* As John Norris pointed out, "if one were to live in . . . a *Platonic* Commonwealth, where Men are just as they should be, there would be no need of Prudence . . . ; but considering what the World is, and what our Ingagements are in it, I think a Man were as good put out to Sea without a Compass, as to pretend to live in the World without Prudence" (*A Treatise Concerning Christian Prudence* [1710], p. 23). There is some likeness between Traherne's description of prudence in *CE* and his earlier summary in SM IV.57: "Prudence is a choys Selection of the means: wisdom Exercised in Particular Things, Removing obstacles, Improving Evils, Laying Hold of opportunities, finding Advantages, Shunning Extreams, Attaining the mean, & walking warily in it when it is found."

P. 153:9–14. *All the Vertues . . . for the same.* On this concept, see *CE*, p. 156:23 n. For other military metaphors, see *CE*, pp. 193, 220–223, and 232; and for another social metaphor, see *CE*, p. 96:6 n.

P. 153:32. *the King of Vertues.* Prudence traditionally sat on the throne. According to Charron "the generall Queene, superintendent, and guide of all other vertues," prudence consists of three things: "to consult and deliberate well, to judge and resolve well, to conduct and execute well" (*Of Wisdome*, p. 370). Eustache gives the same account (p. 117; EN, p. 17), as does John Hartcliffe, *A Treatise of Moral and Intellectual Virtues*, p. 265. See *CE*, p. 65:20 n.

P. 154:4. *Curt.* Short; this passage is cited in the *OED.*

P. 154:5. *distasted.* Disgusted.

P. 154:22–27. *no Vertue . . . Vertue whatsoever.* Cf. Plato, *Protagoras* 330a, and Plotinus, *Enneads* III.ii.3: "We have no right to demand equal powers in the unequal: the finger is not to be asked to see; there is the eye for that; a finger has its own business—to be finger and have finger power."

P. 155:11. *altogether.* I.e., "all together." See Textural Notes.

P. 155:21. *the Eye is the Light of all the members.* Cf. *CE*, p. 64:3 n., on Traherne's fondness for sight imagery; and also Matt. 6:22 (and Luke 11:34): "The light of the body is the eye."

P. 156:17. *Denominates.* Constitutes.

P. 156:23–24. *the Phylosophers . . . Chain of Prudence.* Aristotle (*Nic. Eth.* VI.13) was generally given as the authority for this philosophical cliché, though he did not make so clear-cut a statement. Francesco Piccolomini cited Aristotle, Pythagoras, Plato, and Christian theologians as agreeing on the concatenation of the virtues (*Universa philosophia*, IV.39, p. 185). Eustache drew his account of prudence from Aristotle (pp. 113–119; EN, p. 17). John Norris explained carefully Aristotle's meaning: "Whoever has true Prudence has all Vertues. Not that Prudence is in a formal Sense all Vertue, or that there is no other Vertue but Prudence, . . . but that Prudence contains them all radically or seminally . . . and so is a kind of *universal Vertue*. . . . This is what the Moralists mean, when speaking of the connection of the Vertues, they say they are all connected in *Prudence*, that is, as in the common Head or Principle" (*Christian Prudence*, p. 56). The metaphor of the golden chain derives ultimately from the *Iliad* VIII.18–26.

P. 157:5. *Influences.* A continuation of the simile likening well-regulated virtues to "the stars in their Courses." Cf. *CE*, pp. 159 and 195:28 n.; and *C* I.21. In astrology, says the *OED*, "influence" meant "the supposed flowing or streaming from the stars or heaven of an etherial fluid acting upon the character and destiny of men, and affecting sublunary things generally. In later times gradually viewed less literally, as an exercise of power or 'virute', or of an occult force. . . ."

P. 157:10. *Wise . . . Doves.* Matt. 10:16.

P. 157:20. *Regiment.* Government.

P. 157:37. *Three Things.* Traherne fails to carry out his outline fully. On friendship, see *CE*, pp. 138:25 n., 189, and 199–200.

P. 157:40. The marginal reference, more specifically, is 1 Pet. 3:10–13.

P. 158:28. *assented.* Sanctioned. This passage is cited in *OED*.

P. 159:2–3. *The Throne . . . Righteousness.* Prov. 16:12.

P. 159:3–6. *When it Goeth . . . Wicked.* Prov. 11:10–11.

P. 159:18. *connivance.* Overlooking, winking at.

P. 159:36. *he that winneth Souls is Wise.* Prov. 11:30.

P. 159:38. *Good or Evil Treasures.* Matt. 12:35, paraphrased.

P. 160:11–14. *Prudence hath no . . . tempests.* Cf. Charron: "Prudence then is a sea without either bottome or brinke, and which cannot bee limited and prescribed by precepts and advisements" (*Of Wisdome,* p. 371).

P. 161:18–23. *VALOUR is . . . Invincible Resolution.* Adapted from Charron, *Of Wisdome* (p. 534): "Valour . . . is a right and strong resolution, an equall and uniforme staiednesse of the mind against all dangerous difficult, an dolorous accidents . . . it containeth magnanimity, patience, constancy, and invincible resolution. . . ." On Charron, see *CE*, p. 3:13 n.

P. 161:30. *Prudence, Justice and Temperance.* These with valor (fortitude) are the quartet of cardinal virtues.

P. 162:14. *OF all the Vertues.* The first two sentences of this paragraph come from Charron, *Of Wisdome* (p. 534): "Of all the vertues in greatest estimation and honour, this is most renowned, who for the prerogative thereof is simply called a vertue." This sentence occurs between the first and second parts of the quotation borrowed in the previous paragraph.

P. 162:19. *It is stiled Manhood.* Francis Gouldman (*A Copious Dictionary in Three Parts,* 2d ed. [Cambridge, 1669]) gives as the basic meanings of "virtus": *"Vertue, strength, swiftness . . . puissance, manliness, power, help, perfection, merit, desert, authority . . . ."* William Colvill explained: "dicitur Latinis *virtus,* quod sit actio viro maxime digna" (*Philosophia,* p. 29).

P. 163:8. *Debauched and unreasonable men.* Probably a reference to Continental *libertins,* exemplified perhaps by the notorious Giulio Cesare Vanini, burned at the stake in 1619 for "atheism." Vanini's reputation was far worse than his reality. A pantheist, he was said to blaspheme all Christian beliefs, deny the existence of God and of human souls, and adore nature as his god. In his *De Admirandis* (1616) he expressed the opinion that while some moral laws are universal truths, most are impositions of opportunistic governors upon the ignorant governed. Vanini's fame reached England: Jeremy Collier and Bishop Samuel Parker attacked him. See J. S. Spink, *French Free-Thought from Gassendi to Voltaire* (1960), pp. 28–33. Vanini's contemporary, the French poet Théophile de Viau, contributed (along with other poets in his circle) to the evil repute of the *libertins* (Spink, pp. 42–45). On the brighter side of Renaissance *libertins* (the *libertins érudits*) see Richard H. Popkin, *The History of Skepticism from Erasmus to Descartes.*

P. 163:18. *Rodomontadoes wits.* I.e., the wits of these braggarts, these utterers of rodomontades.

P. 163:31. *imagine Chimeraes.* A pleonasm, chimeras being by definition unreal. Traherne uses the term "vain *Chimera*" in *CE,* p. 246.

P. 163:34. *Thrasonical.* Boastful; from Thraso, a braggart soldier in Terence's play *Eunuchus.* Cf. Charron, *Of Wisdome* (p. 536): "Now valour is not a quality of the body, but of the mind. . . . Moreover they are deceived, which disquiet themselves, and make account of those vaine Thrasonicall brags of such swaggering Braggadochios, who by their lofty lookes, and brave words, would win credit of those that are valiant and hardy, if a man would do them so much favour to beleeve them."

P. 164:17–19. *The Great End . . . Vertues.* Cf. Whichcote: "It is fit that virtue should be exposed to some difficulty, for this is a probation state" (*Works,* I, 323); earlier in the same paragraph Whichcote used the phrase "state of trial." See *CE,* pp. 189–192; and, for the four estates, *CE,* p. 4:37 n.

P. 165:14. *all Glorious within.* Ps. 45:13.

P. 165:27. *Verse made long ago.* The reader of Traherne's *Centuries* will be familiar with his practice of illustrating prose with poetry written at some other time (see *C* III.18–21). This poem is printed by Margoliouth, II, 185; see his notes, II, 397–398.

P. 166:35. *Love upon the stage.* For other allusions to love in drama or fiction, see *CE,* pp. 122 and 150.

P. 167:32. *Prelation.* Exaltation.

P. 168:18. *For there are certain Periods.* Printed by Margoliouth (II, 185) and, as he observes, "obviously from the 'Poem upon Moderation' (*C* III.18)," parts of which appear in *C* III.19, 21, and in *CE,* p. 181. Neither Dobell nor Miss Wade printed this poem. See Textual Notes of the present edition.

P. 168:30–32. *Principallities . . . high places.* Eph. 6:12 (A. V. reads "against," not "with").

P. 168:35–36. *this apparent Clod.* With this paean to man cf. *CE,* p. 104:19 n. In the *Meditations* Traherne comments on the wonder of the human body: "All this existing miraculously in a Clod, and being a lively Portraiture of the divine Wisdom, representing God as the Cause, in the Effect" (p. 76).

P. 169:2. *overcome the World.* John 16:33.

P. 169:2–3. *O Death . . . Victory.* 1 Cor. 15:55.

P. 169:6–15. *Who shall . . . our Lord.* Rom. 8:35–39.

P. 169:16. *A REMARK.* Possibly an insertion from some other writing, such as a sermon.

P. 169:22. *To dare to be Good.* Cf. *CE,* p. 281, where Traherne asserts that virtue "never shineth gloriously and irresistibly, till it be acted almost in a *desperate* manner."

P. 170:15. *the Opinion of some.* Cardinal Bona expressed the majority view: "The pleasures that arise from the Taste and Touch, are under the Government of Temperance" (*A Guide to Eternity,* 2d ed. [1680], p. 171).

P. 170:23. *OTHERS there are.* Cf. John Scott: moderation "consists in proportioning our concupiscible affections to the just worth and value of things, so as neither to set our affections too prodigally upon trifles, nor yet be oversparing or niggardly of them to real and substantial goods" (*Works,* I, 51–52).

P. 171:15. *the four Elements*. The belief that all matter is composed of fire, water, air, and earth goes back to ancient Greek science. Cf. Hermes's use of the doctrine, quoted *CE*, p. 227. On the four humors discussed in the following paragraph, see *CE*, p. 174:25 n.

P. 171:31. *All Musick*. Printed by Margoliouth (II, 186), who suggests that it was derived from the poem on moderation which served as a source for the poems in *CE* on pp. 168 and 181, as well as *C* III.19, 21. This hypothesis is now put in doubt by the discovery that the poem exists, in exactly this form, in SM IV.60.

P. 171:35. *rash*. To draw hastily; this passage is the only illustration for this definition in the *OED*.

P. 171:38. *Table*. Board, canvas.

P. 172:1. *Tun*. Cask.

P. 172:1. *Delicates*. Choice foods.

P. 172:10. *Simple*. A medicine consisting of one ingredient, a plant or herb used medicinally; hence something uncompounded with other substances.

P. 172:15–16. *Excess . . . Golden Mean*. The basis of Aristotle's ethical classifications; see *Nic. Eth.* II.6.1106^{a}28: virtue is "intermediate between excess and defect." Eustache explained the doctrine of the mean (pp. 105–106; EN, p. 16). Cf. *C* III.20: "Moderation is a Vertu observing the Golden Mean," a statement which introduces an earlier version (*C* III.21) of the poem on moderation in *CE*, p. 181.

P. 172:17. *Artificial*. Skilful.

P. 172:21. *Ductures*. "Extension or movement in some direction" (*OED*; this is one of two passages cited for this meaning). Traherne used the more common meaning of "duct" or "passage" in the *Meditations:* "This Clay [the human body] is form'd into Muscles, Sinews, Veins and Fibres, being curiously divided into many Ductures, and fill'd with Passages on the inside" (pp. 76–77).

P. 173:16. *HERE you may observe*. With this paragraph cf. the wordly wisdom of the Earl of Clarendon: "As long as the world lasts, and honour and virtue and industry have reputation in the world, there will be ambition and emulation and appetite in the best and most accomplished men who live in it" (*Essays*, I, 19–20).

P. 173:30–32. *as Chymists . . . Quintessential perfection*. Cf. Tilley, P 457 (p. 548): "One Poison expels another." Abel Boyer translated a contemporary French aphorism: "Some *Vices* are mingled with *Virtue*, just as poisonous Ingredients are put sometimes into the best *Medicines*" (*Characters of the Virtues & Vices of the Age* [1695], sig. N3ᵛ). There is an echo as well of medieval chemistry, one of the principal aims of which was to extract the "quintessence" or fifth essence believed to be the substance of heavenly bodies and latent in all matter. Thomas Jackson wrote: "Out of mixt bodies are drawne by art *Quintessences*, whose substances (though subtile and homogeneall) vertually containe the force or efficacy of many ingredients" (*Treatise*, p. 94). Charron observed that the quintessence is "the harmony" of the four qualities (hot, cold, dry, moist) (*Of Wisdome*, p. 49).

P. 174:19. *Prelation*. Preferment; used in this sense on the next page.

P. 174:25–27. *the Complexion . . . abundance of Blood*. According to medieval medicine, the "complexion" of the body consisted of the combination of the four "humors" Traherne listed in *CE*, p. 171, as well as in the present passage. Charron explained the physiology: *"Bloud, Choler,* which worketh, provoketh, penetrateth, hindereth obstructions, casteth forth the excrements, bringeth cheerefulnesse; *Melancholy,* which provoketh an appetite to every thing, moderateth sudden motions; *Fleame,* which sweetneth the force of the two *Cholers,* and all other heats" (*Of Wisdome,* p. 13).

P. 174:37. *Artificial.* The basic sense is "skilfully put together," i.e., of virtues; but the modern pejorative sense—which first appeared about 1650—is also present.

P. 174:38. *Conversation.* Behavior.

P. 175:7. *This of Temperance.* A carry-over of the phrase used in Latin moral treatises to demarcate subdivisions: "Haec de . . ." or "hactenus de. . . ." Cf. EN, p. 11 (Eustache, p. 46): "Haec de principijs internis."

P. 175:18. *become all . . . gain some.* 1 Cor. 9:22 (altered by transferal to the third person and the substitution of words taken from verses 19–22: "become" instead of "am made";"gain" instead of "save").

P. 176:18–19. *Figs . . . Brambles.* Cf. Luke 6:44.

P. 176:29. *Sleepish.* Somewhat sleepy; this passage is the latest citation in the *OED.*

P. 177:29–30. *to cease . . . from his.* Heb. 4:10.

P. 178:21–22. *By his Wisdom . . . the Earth.* Prov. 3:19 reads: "The Lord by wisdom hath founded the earth; by understanding hath he established the heavens." Traherne quotes the verse correctly later in *CE,* p. 184.

P. 179:1–2. *Power limited . . . let loose.* Traherne's concern with the seeming contradiction of curbed omnipotency was shared by Thomas Jackson, who began Part II of his *Treatise of the Divine Essence and Attributes* (1629) with a consideration of the problem. Jackson used a human analogy to prove the paradox: "Unlesse mans will be a law to his power, and goodnesse a law unto his will, how absolute and illimited soever his power may bee in respect of other men, or of any coactive law which they can make to restraine it, it may quickly come to make an end of it selfe" (p. 13; copied by Traherne, CB, *s.v.* "Impossibilitie," f. 57.1; see also "Omnipotencie," f. 71ᵛ.1, which copies pp. 8–9).

P. 181:3. *a Philosophical Poet.* Traherne himself, as Margoliouth points out (II, 398). See Textual Notes of the present edition. See Margoliouth's notes on this poem, which he prints in II, 186–187, and also his notes on the earlier version in *C* III. 21. Margoliouth observes (II, 410) that "the indented last couplet [of "As in a Clock"] suggests the editorial hand," as it does in the poem inserted in the "Thanksgivings for the Body" (ll. 339–340). In the Introduction to her edition of Traherne's *Poems, Centuries, and Three Thanksgivings* (London, 1966; p. xvi) Anne Ridler notes that the opening lines of "As in a Clock" carry "a direct echo of Quarles's *Job Militant,* Meditatio Secunda," lines 21–24:

> *As in a Clocke, one motion doth conuay,*
> *And carry diuers wheeles a seuerall way:*
> *Yet all together, by the great wheele's force,*
> *Direct the Hand vnto his proper course. . . .*

See *The Complete Works . . . of Francis Quarles,* ed. Alexander B. Grosart, II (Edinburgh, 1880), 75. On the thought of the poem, see the passages quoted in *CE,* pp. 59:7 n. and 69:20 n. For other clock metaphors, see *CE,* pp. 89 and 156, and this passage from the *Meditations:* all things "were worthless before, because they serv'd nothing, and were to no Purpose; even as a Clock is nothing till the Weight be put on, tho' the Wheels be in order; but the Weight being once on, it is suddenly put into Motion" (p. 82). With the antepenultimate line of the poem, cf. *C* I.27: "You never Enjoy the World aright, till you see how a Sand Exhibiteth the Wisdom and Power of God. . . ."

P. 184:27–37. *Happy . . . Discretion.* Prov. 3:13–19, 21.

P. 186:24–27. *He was . . . Heart; repent . . . Man.* Gen. 6:6, altered.

P. 186:29–30. *Moses's Rod . . . Egyptians.* It was Aaron's rod, not Moses'; see Ex. 7:12.

P. 187:2–4. *our light . . . for a moment; work . . . Glory.* 2 Cor. 4:17.

P. 187:8–11. *If his detestation . . . mighty Continence.* See *CE,* p. 98: 10 n.

P. 187:16. *retained.* Restrained.

P. 187:20–31. *PATIENCE then . . . Invincible Reason.* The Earl of Clarendon distinguished between patience as a "moral virtue, a temper of mind that controuls or resists all the brutish effects of choler, anger, and rage"; and patience as a "Christian virtue, a habit of mind, that doth not only bear and suffer contumelies, reproach, and oppression, but extracts all the venom out of them, and compounds a cordial out of the ingredients, that preserves the health" (*Essays,* I, 155–156).

P. 187:38–p. 188:8. *Saint Chrysostoms opinion . . . his Monies.* This is the sense of the first part of St. John Chrysostom's *Godly Exhortation . . . Touching Patience and Suffering Affliction,* tr. Robert Rowse (1597; earlier translations by Thomas Lupset, 1542, and T. Sampson, 1550). Cf. also Chrysostom's *Homilies on Matthew,* no. 85: "Tunc splendidissima victoria est, cum patiendo nocentes vincimus. Hinc ostenditur a Deo esse victoriam, quae naturam habet contrariam externae illi victoriae: idque maxime fortitundinis argumentum est" (tr. from Greek in J. P. Migne, ed., *Patrologia Graeca,* LVIII [Paris, 1862], col. 756). Traherne quotes Chrysostom again in *CE,* p. 250. He also appears to quote him twice in CYB, but in fact one reference (f. 20) was borrowed from Sparke's *Scintilla* and the other (f. 72) is a mistake caused by misreading a marginal note in Jeremy Taylor's *Great Exemplar.*

P. 188:8–9. *Pelican . . . Blood.* The old belief that the pelican nourishes its young with its own blood gave rise to the symbolic equation of the pelican with Christ the redeemer. Traherne would have been familiar with the sixteenth-century pillar statue of a pelican feeding its young in the first quadrangle of Corpus Christi College, Oxford. See Whittick, *Symbols,* p. 236.

P. 188:13–14. *We are . . . Sufferings.* Heb. 2:10.

P. 188:16. *Consider the Patience of Job.* Cf. James 5:11.

P. 188:20. *cross.* Contrary.

P. 188:28–29. *He laies . . . Sheep.* John 10:15.

P. 188:30–37. *being . . . Servant; Death . . . Cross; Wherefore . . . Earth.* Philip. 2:6–8(telescoped), 9–10.

P. 189:15. *insipid.* Foolish.

P. 189:33. *pretend.* Profess, claim.

P. 189:34–35. *he that sticks . . . Friend indeed.* Tilley (F 694, p. 243) under "A Friend is never known till a man have need" lists first Erasmus, *Adagia,* 1055A: "Amicus certus in re incerta cernitur." On friendship, see *CE,* pp. 157–158 and 199–200.

P. 190:10–11. *Jonas . . . Tempest upon us.* See Jonah 1:2.

P. 190:14. *to be dissolved . . . Christ.* Philip. 1:23. See *CE,* p. 142:24 n.

P. 190:15–16. *glorious . . . Sons of GOD.* Rom. 8:21.

P. 190:29. *all . . . good.* Rom. 8:28.

P. 191:15–16. *searcheth . . . Reins.* Jer. 17:10.

P. 191:31. *GOD hath placed our Trial.* Cf. *CE,* p. 164:17 n.

P. 195:19. *he hath first loved us.* 1 John 4:19.

P. 195:26–27. *the Skies . . . Revolutions.* A preference for Ptolemaic over Copernican astronomy (the latter by this period accepted by educated Englishmen) is all the more astonishing coming from a man who manifested an interest in contemporary science (e.g., his embrace of new ideas on space and the entry on the nature of cold in the Commonplace Book, f. 27.1).

P. 195:28–29. *the Sun . . . Influences.* Cf. Traherne's statement in the *Meditations* that the sun has power "to cause such Influences, as do quicken and make the Plants, and other living things, to grow, helping all things both in their Life and Conversation" (p. 40). He added that the sun and stars caused the four qualities of "Heat, Coldness, Dryness, and Moisture, as they are near or remote in their Influences and Approximation; for so accordingly are they weak or strong in their Influences" (p. 48). Cf. also *CE,* p. 82: "GOD by giving Beams and influences to [the stars] made our Treasures more rich and fair. . . ." On "influences," see *CE,* p. 157:5 n.

P. 195:33. *a New Doctrine.* A doctrine which accords with Traherne's elevation of man above the angels; see *CE,* p. 104:10 n.

P. 196:11. *admired.* Wondered.

P. 196:30. *impertinent.* Irrelevant, inappropriate.

P. 196:32. *Were all the World.* Margoliouth prints the poem, II, 187; see his notes. With the first stanza, cf. Traherne's account of the "Paradice of Ease" in *CE,* pp. 33–34.

P. 197:26. *Security . . . Contentment.* On this subject, see *CE,* p. 220.

P. 197:34. *while.* Time, leisure.

P. 198:3–7. *where Envying . . . Peace.* James 3:16–18.

P. 198:9–10. *The Meek . . . Earth.* Matt. 5:5; cf. Ps. 37:11.

P. 198:38–39. *He that is slow . . . City.* Prov. 16:32.

P. 199:1. *HE that troubleth . . . Wind.* Prov. 11:29.

P. 199:2. *nice and exquisite.* Precise and exact.

P. 199:25. *Exceptious.* Peevish.

P. 199:27. *Careir.* I.e., career. The *OED* cites this passage and quotes Dr. Johnson for the definition: "Rapid and continuous 'course of action, uninterrupted procedure' (J.); formerly also, The height, 'full swing' of a person's activity."

P. 199:37. *verdure.* This figurative usage is cited in *OED,* as is the similar use in *CE,* p. 207; cf. p. 128.

P. 199:38. *Wild-fire.* Inflammable substance used in war.

P. 200:1. *A soft Answer . . . Wrath.* Prov. 15:1.

P. 200:2. *fireball.* A ball filled with combustible matter used as a projectile in war; Traherne's figurative usage is cited in the *OED*.

P. 200:7–8. *it is the Glory . . . Transgression.* Prov. 19:11.

P. 200:9. *a fickle Friend is not worth a farthing.* See *CE*, p. 189:34 n.

P. 200:11–12. *with an Angry man thou shalt not go.* Prov. 22:24.

P. 200:25. *the Gold of Ophir.* 1 Chron. 29:4; Job 22:24, 28:16; Ps. 45:9.

P. 200:27. *Anger resteth in the bosom of Fools.* Eccles. 7:9.

P. 201:3. *distaste.* Displease, offend.

P. 201:4. *Trifle.* A worthless person, trifler; the *OED* cites this passage.

P. 201:5. *very.* Veritable, thorough.

P. 201:12. *The Meek . . . Earth.* Matt. 5:5; cf. Ps. 37:11.

P. 201:15–18. *Philanthus . . . Justine recordeth.* Marcus Junianus Justinus's third-century abridgment of Pompeius Trogus's *Historiae Philippicae* was a popular university history textbook; it was translated into English by Arthur Golding (1570), G. W[ilkins] (1606: little more than a reissue of Golding's work), and Robert Codrington (1654). Traherne's Early Notebook contains (pp. 47–55) a "Compendium Historicum ex Justino excerptum," which summarizes in Latin the first eighteen of Justin's forty-four chapters. Traherne did not take notes on the anecdote mentioned in *Christian Ethicks,* which is recounted in Justin's third chapter. Leader of the Parthenians for many years, Philantus (alternate form: Phalantus) was driven into banishment by sedition; he remained faithful to his people's interests, and his dying message gave them possession of the city of Tarentum. "In memory of which benefit," says Codrington's translation, "divine honours were decreed to *Phalantus*" (*The History of Justin,* 2d ed. [1664], p. 54).

P. 201:22. *Mankind is sick.* This poem is printed by Margoliouth, II, 187–191; see his notes. The metaphor of the world as a hospital is an old one; in his Ficino Notebook (f. 44ᵛ) Traherne quotes Ficino's commentary on the *Republic* V.459c, where Socrates says the "rulers will often have to practise upon the body corporate with medicines." Cf. John Worthington: "This World is a great Hospital or Pest-house, a Place for diseased and infected Souls; and Afflictions are [God's] Physick" (*Select Discourses,* ed. John Worthington, Jr. [1725], p. 57). Closer to Traherne's metaphor is Henry More's: "We see, the Bulk of Mankind are like those; who, falling sick of a Disease and not knowing how to cure themselves, ought to be visited by others that are in Health, and from them take Remedies and Advice. So the Generality, that see little of themselves, while they are dazled by false Lights and the bare Apparitions of Good, can never discover, What is the Ultimate Good, and what the most Excellent Object of Human Life" (*Account,* pp. 184–185). Note, however, that Traherne announces early ("*The World's one* Bedlam") that his is a *mental* hospital. Cf. *C* IV.20: "To think the World therfore a General Bedlam, or Place of Madmen, and one self a Physician, is the most necessary Point of present Wisdom: an important Imagination, and the Way to Happiness."

P. 203:10–12. *we can / Spare all . . . our selves.* For an explanation of the paradox, see *CE*, p. 38:20 n.

P. 204:3–4. *Let's prize . . . Diadems.* Cf. "The Enquirie": "Mens Sences are indeed the Gems, . . . Their Souls the Diadems" (II, 84); and "On News" (in *C* III.26): "The Glorious Soul" is "The Gem, / The Diadem. . . ." Jewel imagery is frequent in Traherne's poems.

P. 204:34. *make a Vertue of Necessity.* Tilley's first listing of this phrase is 1576 (V 73, p. 699). It occurs in Chaucer: *The Knight's Tale,* l. 3042; and *The Squire's Tale,* l. 593.

P. 204:38–39. *the Man . . . Earth.* Num. 12:3, altered.

P. 205:4–5. *How Joseph . . . Family of Israel.* Gen. 37–50.

P. 207:10–11. *It is sufficient . . . to observe, that Pride.* As Traherne might have explained, in traditional moral theology pride was the vice opposed to humility; cf. Bona: "Next to Vertues Theological and Intellectual, it [humility] holds the first place; for it overthrows Pride, which is the fountain of all evil" (*Guide,* p. 182).

P. 207:37. *verdure.* This figurative use is cited in *OED*; cf. *CE,* p. 199:37 n.

P. 208:2–5. *No Toad . . . Devils.* Possibly an allusion to Milton's Lucifer, "th' Arch-Enemy . . . who in the happy Realms of Light / Cloth'd with transcendent brightness didst outshine / Myriads" (*P.L.,* I.81, 85–87); and who was discovered, "Squat like a Toad, close at the Ear of *Eve*" (*P.L.,* IV.800). Toads were proverbially associated with poison; cf. Tilley (T 360, p. 672): "Full as a Toad of poison." See *CE,* p. 214, for another metaphor of a toad.

P. 208:7. *what shall Humility be.* With Traherne's enthusiasm cf. Henry More's: a man "is surrounded with the beams of Divine Wisdome, as the low depressed Earth with the raies of the Stars; his deeply and profoundly *humbled* Soul being as it were the Centre of all heavenly illuminations, as this little globe of the Earth is of those celestial influences. I professe I stand amazed while I consider the ineffable advantages of a Mind thus submitted to the Divine Will, how calm, how comprehensive, how quick and sensible . . . she is in all things" (*Enthusiasmus Triumphatus,* in *Collection,* pp. 37–38).

P. 208:16. *He that humbleth . . . exalted.* Luke 14:11, 18:4.

P. 208:20–21. *Pride goeth . . . Humility.* Prov. 16:18 (altered), 15:33, and 18:12.

P. 208:22–24. *the Colours are envenomed . . . Canker.* Cosmetics were sometimes physically harmful to the wearer; cf. John Downame's polemic: "Againe, whilest they labour to attaine unto this counterfeit complexion, they lose that true beauty which they have by nature; for with their medicines, and minerals which they use to this purpose, they make their colour pale and wan, they wrinckle the face, yea, oftentimes poyson the skin" (*The Christian Warfare Against the Devill World and Flesh* [1634], II.i.14, p. 412).

P. 208:39–40. *the taste of the Soul.* In SM IV.66 Traherne says that humility "giue[s] a Relish, & Diviner Tast to all our Joys." The entirety of this Meditation bears a strong likeness to the present chapter on humility.

P. 209:17–18. *not inconsistent with its Joy and Glory.* Cf. Anthony Horneck: "And though [humility] be look'd upon by the Frantick World, as baseness of Spirit, Cowardice, and a low-bred Mind; yet . . . [it] leads to the highest joys, to the richest content, to the greatest satisfaction, and he is happier that sees his own Sins, than he that sees an Angel, for an Ass can see a Spirit, but none but a Favourite of Heaven beholds his Sins with Humility, or Self-abhorrency" (*Happy Ascetick*, pp. 85, 88).

P. 209:21. *it passeth thorow all things*. The following passage may derive its concept and some of its vocabulary from SM III.78: "Mans Humility & Gods Highness are wedded objects to each other. Let me See the Nothing out of which I was taken & I shall See the Glory to which I am exalted. . . . For as the Heavens a boue are in a Mirror Seen, as far beneath them, as they are a boue, & both Conjoyned make an Intire Sphere, Seeming Divers but the very Same; So doth God & my Nothing, both Apprehended. . . . while I Contemplat the Nothing out of which I was made in the Bottom of my being I See his Glory. And at once possess the Zenith & the Nadir of his Eternal Sphere, the Heights and Depths of His Infinit fullness."

P. 209:23. *Nadir.* "The point of the heavens diametrically opposite to the zenith; the point directly under the observer" (*OED*); Traherne's figurative use, which is cited in the *OED,* is scientifically exact.

P. 209:26. *like a Mirror . . . face upwards*. Mirror images were far more than Platonic clichés for Traherne; cf. his striking poems "Shadows in the Water" and "On Leaping over the Moon," as well as other poems on pp. 38, 58, 152, 156, 169, 182; "Thanksgivings for God's Attributes," II, 315; *C* I.31, 87; *C* II.17, 78, 84, 97; *C* III.10; *C* IV.84–86; SM II.72, III.78.

P. 209:38. *by going downward still begin to ascend*. Traherne's image of a spiritual journey has analogues, but none of such power. Cf. Ralph Cudworth: "The way to obtain a good assurance indeed of our title to heaven, is . . . to dig as low as hell by humility. . . . We must . . . as the Greek Epigramme speaks, *ascend downward, & descend upward*" (*A Sermon Preached before the House of Commons, March 31, 1647,* facsimile ed. [New York, 1930], pp. 10–11). Cf. also Peter Sterry: "He that will pass from the dismal Depths of sin and Woe, to those Heights of Strength, Holiness and Sweetness in God, must make his *first Motion* a *Conversion,* a *Change* from a *Descent* to an *Ascent;* from going *Outward* to the *Circle,* to go *Inward* towards the *Center* of things, which comprehends and casts forth all the *Circles*" (*Rise,* p. 2). The Christian source of the metaphor is explained by John Spencer: "We say in our *Creed,* that Christ descended into hell, *descendit ut ascendit*: He took his *rising* from the *lowest place,* to *ascend* into the *highest*" (ΚΑΙΝΑ ΚΑΙΠΑΛΛΑΙΑ. *Things New and Old* [1658], p. 195).

P. 210:2. *Antipodes.* See *CE,* p. 120:14 n., and also the poem "Shadows in the Water": "I plainly saw by these / A new *Antipodes*" (II, 128).

P. 210:7. *by a Thought in his Soul he may.* See *CE,* p. 40:11 n. Henry More—who called the soul "subtiler than the silken air," "quick . . . Hot, sparkling, active" ("Psychathanasia, Or, The Immortality of the Soul," I.ii.48, II.ii.9, in *Poems,* ed. Grosart, pp. 50, 60)—explained how the soul may in an ecstasy leave the body (*The Immortality of the Soul,* in *Collection,* pp. 124–126). With Traherne's adjectives, cf. also Agrippa, who described the spirit as "the subtile, pure[,] lucid, airy, and unctuous vapour of the blood" (*Occult Philosophy,* I.45, p. 90).

P. 210:33. *phantastick.* Imaginary, in the Platonic sense that the material world is but an imperfect reflection of the eternally existing archetypal ideas.

P. 211:3–4. *the middle . . . Perfection.* Cf. Traherne's earlier observation in *CE,* p. 18, that "it is necessary, to make a Distinction between the way to Felicity, and the Rest which we attain in the end of our Journey."

P. 211:16–18. *the length . . . Fulness of GOD.* Eph. 3:18–19.

P. 211:34. *foundation of all Vertue.* This point is treated at greater length in SM IV.68.

P. 212:14–15. *Delight . . . Desire.* See *CE,* pp. 44–45, 54:37 n., and the second note on 258:18. Note the distinction made by John Howe: "Desire and Delight are but two acts of *Love,* diversified only by the distance, or presence of the same Object. . . . *Desire,* is therefore, *love in motion; Delight,* is *love in rest*" (*The Blessedness of the Righteous,* in *Works,* ed. Edmund Calamy, I [1724], 475).

P. 213:2. *Humility . . . perfection. The Whole Duty of Man* explained (VI.2, p. 139) that humility takes "the prime place" among our duties to ourselves, "not only in respect of the excellency of the virtue, but also of its usefulness towards the obtaining of all the rest; this being the foundation on which all the others must be built." Sir Matthew Hale remarked in a similar vein that all the virtues are interconnected and necessary to one another, "but especially this Virtue of Humility, when it is genuine and true, is ever accompanied with all those excellent Habits and Graces, that perfect the soul" (*Contemplations,* I, "Of Humility," 310–311).

P. 213:2. *Rendezvous.* The word came into use in England about 1590.

P. 213:6. *primitive and virgin Joyes.* Joys such as Traherne described in his poems; see especially II, 4–24, 64–70, 86–92. The phrase is characteristic of him ("joy" occurs in profusion in his writings); cf. *C* III.1, 4: "those Pure and Virgin Apprehensions"; and "The World": "My virgin-thoughts in Childhood were / Full of Content" (II, 93).

P. 213:18. *a Great Divine.* A thorough search has failed to locate this quotation in the works of Henry Hammond, whose most popular productions were his *Practical Catechism* and his *Paraphrase and Annotations Upon . . . the New Testament.* Possibly the marginal identification is the printer's contribution and not Traherne's.

P. 213:26–27. *Walks and Circuits, and periods of Revolution.* An astronomical metaphor. Cf. Job 22:14: God "walketh in the circuit of heaven." In CYB (f. 1ᵛ) Traherne wrote: "Enter, O my Redeemed Soul, into all the Folds & Circuits of Eternity."

P. 214:40. The marginal reference, more precisely, is Ps. 21:1, 3, 5, 6.

P. 215:4–5. *that sweetness . . . Courtesie.* These are among the "less Principal Vertues" which Traherne omitted: "*Gentleness of behaviour, Affability, Courtesie, . . . Urbanitie*" (p. 26).

P. 216:5. *THOUGH we have not named it.* This is the second time Traherne revised his initial plan. See *CE,* p. 94:9 n.

P. 216:9–10. *Having Food . . . Gain.* 1 Tim. 6:8, 6.

P. 216:30. *Momentany.* Momentary; this form was common in the sixteenth and seventeenth centuries.

P. 216:32.   *slavish and forced Contentment.*   Another attack on Stoic "autarchy" and pride; see *CE*, p. 60:36 n. Traherne agreed with John Smith that the highest happiness "does not so much consist, *in Quiete,* as *in Actu & vigore*" (*Discourses,* p. 445; plagiarized by Samuel Shaw in *Immanuel* [1669], p. 156) and with Peter Sterry that *"Peace is not Rest without Motion; but Rest in Motion"* (*Appearance,* p. 281). Cf. Smith's vigorous affirmation that "Religion is no sullen *Stoicisme* or oppressing *Melancholie,* it is no enthralling tyranny exercised over those noble and vivacious affections of Love and Delight, . . . but it is full of a vigorous and masculine delight and joy, & such as advanceth and ennobles the Soul, and does not weaken or disspirit the life and power of it" (*Discourses,* pp. 416–417).

P. 217:19.   *Contentment is a sleepy thing.*   This poem is printed by Margoliouth, II, 191–192.

P. 218:30–32.   *a Royal Man . . . be alone.*   Presumably a reference to Charles II. On 31 January 1649 Prince Charles was in The Hague, where (according to Clarendon) the news of his father's death struck him into "all the confusion imaginable," but the exigencies of his position forced him to shoulder "the burden of his grief" and "to resume so much courage as was necessary for his present state" (*History of the Rebellion,* XII.1 [pp. 1–2 vol. V of W. Dunn Macray's ed., Oxford, 1888]). Clarendon reported nothing specifically of any desire by Charles for solitude on this occasion; Traherne could have heard such a story while chaplain to Charles's chief minister. For evidence of Traherne's royalism, manifest also later in *CE* (pp. 280, 283), see *CE*, p. 96:6 n.; "Thanksgivings for the Beauty of his Providence," II, 296; *C* I.61 (referring to "King Charles the Martyr"); and SM III.11, 23, and 25.

P. 219:20.   *the Cross of Christ is the Root and Centre.*   Cf. *C* I.58: "The Cross is the Abyss of Wonders, the Centre of Desires, the Schole of Virtues, the Hous of Wisdom, the Throne of Lov, the Theatre of Joys and the Place of Sorrows; It is the Root of Happiness, and the Gate of Heaven."

P. 219:24–25.   *The prosperity of the Wicked.*   Ps. 73:3.

P. 219:30.   *Psal. 73.1, &c.*   The verses quoted are 1–3 and 14.

P. 220:32–33.   *Contentment . . . Security.*   Cf. *CE*, p. 197.

P. 221:6.   *put on . . . GOD.*   Eph. 6:11.

P. 221:7.   *the Armour of Light.*   Rom. 13:12.

P. 221:36.   *all things . . . love GOD.*   Rom. 8:28.

P. 221:40–p. 222:1.   *To speak . . . Angels.*   1 Cor. 13:1.

P. 222:19.   *bold as a Lion.*   Prov. 28:1.

P. 222:26–27.   *For the hearts . . . water.*   Prov. 21:1.

P. 223:8.   *He marches on.*   Magnanimous men, too, "stoutly march on" (*CE*, p. 232).

P. 223:15–17.   *Praying for it . . . Presumption.*   On faith and works, see *CE*, pp. 106–107.

P. 223:20–21.   *the seed of Jacob . . . in vain.*   Isa. 45:19.

P. 223:29–30.   *For out of it . . . Death.*   Prov. 4:23, with an addition from Ps. 68:20 ("issues from death").

P. 224:12.   *Moralists . . . Modesty.*   Cf. Richard Cumberland: "Modesty . . . may be defin'd, *Justice toward our-selves, consisting in a pursuit of Honours subordinate to the Common Good.* The same *Modesty, . . .* as it raises the Mind to the Pursuit of the greatest Honours subservient to this End, is true *Magnanimity" (Treatise,* p. 339).

P. 225:14. *Catholick.* Universal: i.e., all Christians.

P. 225:18–19. *Mistake not . . . inspired by Felicity.* Cf. *C* IV.78, speaking of Pico: "He permitteth his fancy to wander a little Wantonly after the maner of a Poet: but most deep and serious things are secretly hidden under his free and luxuriant Language." On Traherne's personal knowledge of felicity, see *CE,* p. 3:15 n.

P. 225:21–23. *First GOD . . . Immortal.* On the *Divine Pymander* of Hermes Trismegistus, see General Introduction, p. xxxviii. Traherne used the second ed. of John Everard's translation (1657). The passage here is Book I, verses 25–27, p. 6; quoted CB, f. 65.1, *s.v.* "Man," in the hand of Traherne's amanuensis. Traherne included in *Christian Ethicks* all of the entries from Hermes under "Man" in CB except for VII.16 and VII.60, and in the order they occur in the manuscript.

P. 225:23–26. *The Father . . . his Father. Pymander,* II.18, p. 22; quoted CB, f. 65.1, *s.v.* "Man," in the hand of the amanuensis.

P. 225:27–30. *Man is a divine . . . above them. Pymander,* IV.89–90, p. 70; quoted CB, f. 65.1, *s.v.* "Man," in the hand of the amanuensis.

P. 225:32–40. *At least . . . Immortal MAN. Pymander,* IV.90–93, pp. 70–71; quoted CB, f. 65.1, *s.v.* "Man," in the hand of the amanuensis.

P. 226:5–6. *Lo . . . Pharaoh.* Ex. 7:1.

P. 226:6–8. *He shall . . . God.* Ex. 4:16.

P. 226:9. *I have said . . . like Men.* Ps. 82:6–7.

P. 226:11–15. *I conceive . . . every where. Pymander,* VII.47, pp. 103–104; quoted CB, f. 65.1, *s.v.* "Man," in Traherne's own hand, with the introductory phrase: "Tris. maketh his Son Tat: to speak thus. . . ." After the MS. citation Traherne wrote: "Refer this to Indwelling"; there is no such entry in the Commonplace Book, but in the *Meditations* Traherne explained the "In-dwelling" of God's omnipresence in man's soul, in CYB (f. 49ᵛ) remarked that "the Indwelling of the H. Ghost is Invisible," and in the *Centuries* referred to "In-being"; cf. *CE,* p. 73, and *C* IV.100.

Books I, IV, V, VII, XI, XII, and XIV–XVI of the *Pymander* are cast as either addresses from Hermes to his son Tat, or as dialogues between the two; Book II contains a vision of Hermes in which he converses with "Poemander [also called "Pimander"], the minde of the great Lord, the most Mighty and absolute Emperor" (II.2, p. 16). Books III, VI, IX, XIII, and XVII are directed to Asclepius, participant also in the dialogue known as *Asclepius;* Book VIII is addressed to mankind in general; Book X is directed from *"The Minde to* Hermes."

P. 226:15–16. *Dost thou . . . I am. Pymander,* VII.57, p. 106; quoted CB, f. 65.1, *s.v.* "Man," in Traherne's own hand, and prefaced by the words "Tris. asketh his Son, . . ."

P. 226:18–p. 227:24. *Consider him . . . in all Things. Pymander,* X.119–137, pp. 153–158; quoted CB, f. 23ᵛ.1, *s.v.* "Capacity": Traherne has here included the entirety of the entry, which is in the hand of his amanuensis.

With verse 120 (p. 308:8)—"*Command thy Soul to go into* India"—cf. Traherne's assertion in CYB that man's soul may "by a Thought appear in the very Indies, & mov in an Instant from East to West" (f. 90); and his statement in SM III.72 that "the Swiftness of my Soul that can Flie in an Instant from East to West is my joy & Felicity." With Hermes's exaltation of man's spiritual powers—which is Traherne's as well—cf. Nathanael Culverwel: "The workings of the soul are *quick and nimble.* . . . What quicker then a Thought? what nimbler then the twinkling of an intellectual Eye?" Culverwel characterizes the soul as "*vigorous and indefatigable . . . Vast and comprehensive.* . . . Large and spacious. . . . Nay, it won't be bounded with reall objects; it will set up Beings of its own. . . ." He comments ungracefully on the soul's capacity: "The soul can quickly open its mouth so wide, as that the whole world can't fill it" ("The Worth of Souls," in *Light of Nature,* pp. 200–201).

P. 227:36–37. *He that . . . SPIRIT.* 1 Cor. 6:17 (quoted again in the following paragraph).

P. 227:39–40. *to be filled . . . GOD.* Eph. 3:19.

P. 228:2. *being like God's, knowing Good and Evil.* Gen. 3:5.

P. 228:8. *the strait and divine Way.* Cf. Matt. 3:3 (and Mark 1:3, Luke 3:4, John 1:23).

P. 228:11. *become ETERNITY.* *Pymander,* X.128, p. 155 (see *CE,* p. 226).

P. 228:18–19. *passing through . . . Centre of the Earth.* Like the humble soul (see *CE,* pp. 209–210), the magnanimous soul goes on a spiritual voyage. See also the travels proposed by Hermes in the passage quoted above, p. 226.

P. 228:20–26. *Vanities . . . Play-things.* Vocabulary and meiosis typical of Traherne. Cf. *C* III.9, where he speaks of "the Tinsild Ware upon a Hobby hors . . . a Ribban or a Feather . . . A Purs of Gold . . . Gold Silver Houses Lands Clothes. . . ." For one example of several in the poems, take "The Apostacy": "All Bliss / Consists in this . . . not to know . . . Those little new-invented Things, / Fine Lace and Silks, such Childish Toys / As Ribbans are and Rings, / Or worldly Pelf that Us destroys . . . Baubles . . . Pence and Toys . . . Hobby-horses . . . Som Tinsel thing whose Glittering did amaze" (II, 96–97). See also *C* I.34, III.31. A close parallel with Traherne's phraseology occurs rather oddly in an early treatise by Thomas Jackson, where he says that Roman Catholic methods of argumentation remind him "how craftie companions cosen children of what they love, or stay their crying at what they dislike, by promising them some *Gallant, Fine, Gaudie, Trimme, Goodly, Brave, Golden, New Nothing.* Such brave epethites so ravish a childs thoughts, as at the first hearing he parts with any thing hee hath, or forbeares to seeke what otherwise he would have. . . . With like bombast outsides doe moderne Priests and Jesuites terrifie silly soules" (*How Farre the Ministerie of Man Is Necessarie For Planting the True Christian Faith* [1613], p. 466).

P. 228:27–30. *As Scipio . . . lost into nothing.* In Traherne's day the only known fragment of Cicero's (Tully's) *De re publica* was the closing portion, known as the *Somnium Scipionis,* a poetic vision closely imitating the Vision of Er in Book X of Plato's *Republic. Scipio's Dream* had been preserved in manuscripts containing the much longer, exceedingly popular *Commentary* upon it by the Late Latin encyclopedist Macrobius; both works retained their fame well into the seventeenth century (there were thirty-seven Continental editions of the *Commentary*-cum-*Dream* by 1700, one London printing in 1694; William Harris Stahl, intro., ed., and tr., Macrobius, *Commentary on the Dream of Scipio* [New York, 1952], pp. 60–61). Traherne refers to the concluding sentence of ch. 3 of the *Dream,* where Scipio Africanus the Younger reflects (still in his dream) upon the sights being shown him from a vantage point in the Milky Way by his adoptive grandfather, the elder Scipio: "From here the earth appeared so small that I was ashamed of our empire which is, so to speak, but a point on its surface" (tr. Stahl, p. 72; see also Stahl's valuable Introduction, especially pp. 10–11; Cicero's text may also be found in the Loeb Classical Library [London and New York, 1928], pp. 260–283, with a translation of *De re publica* by Clinton Walker Keyes). Macrobius commented on this passage: "Astronomers have shown us that the earth occupies the space of a point in comparison with the size of the orbit in which the sun revolves" (ch. 16, tr. Stahl, p. 154).

One of Cicero's phrases in the *Dream* was a philosophical cliché among Neoplatonists: "mens cuiusque is est quisque" ("the spirit is the true self") (Loeb ed., pp. 278, 279); cf. *Conway Letters,* ed. Marjorie Hope Nicolson (New Haven, 1930): Henry More wrote Lady Conway (3 Sept., 1660) that she was "so good a Platonist as not to deny that famous maxim of their Schoole: *Animus cuiusque is est quisque*" (p. 164). Miss Nicolson in her note on this passage points not only to Cicero but to Plotinus, *Enneads* IV.vii.1.

P. 229:38–39. *whether in the Torments . . . satisfaction.* See *CE,* p. 54:10 n. Traherne answered unequivocally in the affirmative: "Hell it self is a Part of GODs Kingdom, to wit His Prison. It is fitly mentioned in the Enjoyment of the World: And is it self by the Happy Enjoyed, as a Part of the world" (*C* I.48). Cf. also *C* III.30, IV.67; and "The Vision": "Mens Woes shall be but foyls unto thy Bliss" (II, 26). With the questions posed in this paragraph, cf. Traherne's inquiries as a child, *C* III.17–18. See D. P. Walker, *The Decline of Hell* (1964), pp. 29–32.

P. 230:14. *Trismegistus . . . Author of that Book.* On Traherne's doubts as to the authorship of the *Pymander,* see Introduction, p. xxxviii. The philologist Isaac Casaubon first perceived the textual inconsistencies in the *Pymander* in his *Exercitiones* (1614). Edward Stillingfleet termed the hermetic books "that *Cento* or confused mixture of *Christian, Platonick,* and *Ægyptian doctrine*" (*Origines Sacrae* [1662], p. 35). See also Ralph Cudworth's *True Intellectual System of the Universe* (1678), pp. 321–333.

P. 231:1. *And if the Glory.* Printed by Margoliouth, II, 192.

P. 231:7. *dejected.* Deposed.

P. 231:9 *dignity . . . admire us.* Cf. *CE,* p. 273, where Traherne says that "the Worth of the Person [who benefits us] enters into the nature of the act, and enhances its value." Cf. also the milder statement *CE,* p. 137, regarding the necessity of "a good opinion of the Nature and Intention of the Person with whom we are united." Traherne had developed the point in *C* II.85.

P. 231:30. *An Eagle . . . Alexander.* Tilley (E 1, p. 178): "The Eagle does not catch flies." Tilley lists Erasmus, *Adagia,* 761E: "Aquila non captat muscas"; the first citation of an English version is 1578. Like Traherne, Joseph Glanvill conjoined the Erasmian adage and an Alexandrian *exemplum:* "Aquila non captat muscas, The Royal Eagle flyes not but at noble Game; and a young *Alexander* will not play but with Monarchs" (*Vanity of Dogmatizing*, p. 243).

P. 231:32–36. *Infinite Hopes . . . Magnanimous Soul.* Margoliouth compares this sentence with *C* I.72.

P. 231:36. *signification . . . Greatness of Soul.* I.e., Latin *magna anima;* this is in turn a version of the Greek μεγαλόψυχία (see Aristotle's use in *Nic. Eth.* IV.3).

P. 231:38. *the Soul, and Mind.* A. C. Clements comments on this passage: "Traherne's distinction between mind and soul follows the traditional distinction between ego and Self, *nefesh* and *ruach, psyche* and *pneuma,* between the first Adam who is a living soul and the last Adam who is a quickening spirit" ("On the Mode and Meaning of Traherne's Mystical Poetry: 'The Preparative,'" *Studies in Philology*, LXI [1964], 504, n. 6).

P. 232:11. *mindeth.* Pays attention to.

P. 232:39. *the Character of a Magnanimous Soul.* Traherne writes "characters" to illustrate the "less Principal Vertues"; cf. the "characters" of the liberal man (*CE*, pp. 239–241), of the grateful soul (*CE*, pp. 273–276), and of the virtuous man (*CE*, pp. 281–282). His discussions of the other virtues occasionally take the form of "characters," as in the description of knowledge (*CE*, p. 39) and the meditation on love in CYB, ff. 53ᵛ–54, quoted by Marks, "Traherne's Church's Year-Book," *PBSA*, LX (1966), 70–71.

P. 233:10. *admires.* Wonders.

P. 233:16. *the Honour that is due unto them.* Traherne demonstrates the respect for monarchy characteristic of a good Church-of-England man; this is the temper of the Cambridge Platonists with regard to kingship.

P. 233:21–26. *is come . . . New Covenant.* Heb. 12:22–24.

P. 233:30–p. 234:8. *I cease not . . . Amen.* Eph. 1:16–23, 3:20–21.

P. 235:8–9. *sometimes Natural . . . truly vertuous.* According to Traherne, virtues are acquired rather than natural (or infused): see *CE*, p. 25:11 n.

P. 235:25. *prevalent.* Powerful.

P. 236:26. *empaled.* Impaled, placed side by side.

P. 236:33–34. *sometimes opposed . . . Impudence.* "Opposed" in the sense of an Aristotelian excess.

P. 237:8–9. *In honour preferring one another.* Rom. 12:10.

P. 238:9–10. *LIBERALITY . . . differs from Magnificence.* For the distinction, see the quotation from Cardinal Bona, *CE*, p. 247:11 n.

P. 238:19–21. *The Meek . . . Earth; the Meek . . . Peace.* Ps. 37:11; Matt. 5:5.

P. 238:23. *The Liberal Soul shall be made fat.* Prov. 11:25.

P. 238:23–24. *The Liberal Heart . . . stand.* Isa. 32:8.

P. 238:27–28. *against a rainy day.* Tilley, D 89, p. 142: "Lay up for a rainy Day." The first citation, c. 1565, is "agaynst a raynye day."

P. 239:1. *Because they . . . Earth.* Eccles. 11:2.

P. 239:2–4. *We cannot put our Treasures . . . Charitable uses.* Two of the six extracts Traherne made from Isaac Barrow's sermon *On the Duty and*

Reward of Bounty to the Poor concern the usefulness of wealth, which Barrow says is its sole justification: "'tis the power it affords of benefiting men, which only can season, and ingratiate it to the relish" of a wise man (pp. 179–180; quoted in CB, *s.v.* "Bounty," f. 23.2). "The poor man's Pocket," Barrow explained in businessmen's metaphors, "is a Bank for our Money, which never can disappoint or deceive us" (p. 181; quoted in CB, *s.v.* "Liberalitie," f. 62.1). The idea was a commonplace; cf. Cardinal Bona: "If we would secure [our possessions], and make them our own, we must bestow them. *For he that gives to the poor, lends to the Lord* [Prov. 19:17]; and . . . secures himself of a blessed Eternity in Exchange" (*Guide*, p. 151).

P. 239:4–5. *lay up . . . time to come.* 1 Tim. 6:19.

P. 239:7–10. *MY Lord Bridgeman . . . ought to do.* This reference proves that the latter part of *CE* was written between Bridgeman's death on 25 June, 1674, and Traherne's own death three and a half months later (buried 10 October); SM IV.21 proves that Traherne had etablished his criteria for the good, liberal man long before he entered Bridgeman's service. On Bridgeman, see General Introduction, pp. xxvi–xxxi. Bridgeman's bipartite will, on file in Somerset House (Will Register, P.C.C., Bunce f. 83), was made 19 February, 1674, and delivered into the safekeeping of his former chaplain, Hezekiah Burton, on 1 May, 1674; a codicil was added on 1 May (witnessed by Burton) and a "Memorandum" on 4 June; the will was proved in the Prerogative Court of Canterbury on 10 July, 1674, by Bridgeman's son John. Traherne was among the five witnesses of both parts of the February will; of the other witnesses John Berdo was shortly to be the recorder of Traherne's own will, and Phillipp Landman (apparently a Bridgeman family servant) received in Traherne's will 5*s.* and any old clothes rejected by Philip Traherne (see Traherne's will in Margoliouth, I, xxvi). Traherne also was "in the room" when the "Memorandum" was made. The will opens with instructions for a funeral "without Pompe"; before detailing the disposition of his property, Bridgeman says that he makes his will "as touching that worldly Estate whe[re]with it hath pleased God to intrust mee beseeching him for Jesus Christs sake to pardon all my sinnes in the acquiring mispending or not spending it or any part of it as I ought and to blesse what I haue giuen or left to my Children in giving them Grace to vse it aright for his service and Glory Amen." These words are conventional, but according to Traherne, his patron fulfilled "The Account of the Good Servant" written—no doubt autobiographically—by Bridgeman's friend and fellow lawyer, Sir Matthew Hale: "I esteemed all the Wealth and Honour that I had, but intrusted to me by the Great Master of the world. . . . I thought it no more mine, than the Lords Baily, or the Merchants Cash-keeper thinks his Masters Rents or Money his" (*Contemplations*, I, 61–62).

P. 239:13–14. *a Great Man of France.* Evidently a wealthy virtuoso and patron of learning such as Pierre Gassendi described in *The Mirrour of True Nobility & Gentility. Being the Life of the Renowned Nicolaus Claudius Fabricius Lord of Peiresk, Senator of the Parliament of Aix,* tr. William Rand (1657). Peiresc was an exemplar of Traherne's liberal man. "Doubtless there was never man gave more chearfully, liberally, or frequently" (sig. 2L1).

P. 239:20. *Use.* Gain interest.

P. 239:40. *Every man . . . many Gifts.* Prov. 19:6.

P. 240:23. *maintain Good Works.* Titus 3:8, 14.

P. 240:23–25. *light so shine . . . in Heaven.* Matt. 5:16.

P. 240:34. *prevented.* Anticipated.

P. 241:8. *Brazen Pillars in the Temple of Minerva.* The temple of Athena of the Brazen House was located in Sparta; it had walls of brass, but the pillars have eluded scholarly search.

P. 241:10. *Unisones.* "A sound or note of the same pitch as another" (*OED*). About the time of Traherne's writing (1673 *et seq.*), William Noble, Thomas Pigot, and John Wallis were conducting experiments "On the Trembling of Consonant Strings," to quote the title of Wallis's paper of 1677 in the *Philosophical Transactions* of the Royal Society (see *Grove's Dictionary of Music and Musicians,* ed. Eric Blom, 5th ed., VII [New York, 1959], 978; and Claude V. Palisca, "Science and Music," in *Seventeenth Century Science and the Arts* [Princeton, 1961], pp. 97–100). Traherne may be thinking also of the "sympathetic strings" employed in such instruments as the viola d'amore; these strings are not played upon but vibrate by resonance in unison with the strings which are played. The phenomenon of sympathetic strings, whether on a viola d'amore or on several lutes tuned to the same pitch, provides metaphors consonant with the musical analogies frequent among Platonists. Cf. Peter Sterry: "When *Two Lutes* are rightly tuned one to another; touch a String upon One Lute, and the same String upon the other Lute will answer it with a like Sound. *Jesus Christ,* and a *Saint* are thus tuned by a mutuall Love, each to other" (*The Comings Forth of Christ* [1650], p. 18). Cf. also John Scott: the Church Triumphant "being all composed of consenting hearts, that like perfect unisons are tuned up to the same key, when any one is touched, every one echoes and resounds the same note; and whilst they thus mutually strike upon each other, and all are affected with every one's joys, it is impossible but that in a state where there is nothing but joy, there should be a continual consort of ravishing harmony among them" (*Works,* I, 139). See Leo Spitzer, *Classical and Christian Ideas of World Harmony,* ed. Anna Granville Hatcher (Baltimore, 1963), pp. 127–128, 135–136, *et passim;* and John Hollander, *The Untuning of the Sky* (Princeton, 1961), pp. 137–138, on sympathetic strings, and also Hollander's reproduction of Jacob Cats's emblem in which two lutes in sympathetic vibration symbolize love.

P. 241:13–19. *Come ye blessed . . . unto me.* Matt. 25:34–36, 40.

P. 241:24–38. *THERE was . . . that was done.* Matt. 18:23–31.

P. 241:26. *ought.* A.V. reads "Owed." The form "ought," which occurs in Wyclif's translation of this verse (1382), was largely out of use by Traherne's day; see *Wyclif: Select English Writings,* ed. Herbert E. Winn (1929), p. 9.

P. 242:16. *He that receiveth you, receiveth me.* Matt. 10:40.

P. 242:26. *bowels.* Compassion.

P. 242:32–38. *As every Thought . . . his omnipresence.* Cf. *C* V.8: "The Swiftest Thought is present with him [God] Eternaly. . . . The smallest Thing by the Influence of Eternity, is made infinit and Eternal." On God's omnipresence, see *C* V.9–10. Cf. also *CE,* p. 184: "Eternity is an everlasting Moment . . . all Things past, present, and to come, are at once before him [God] and eternally together." On eternity, see *CE,* p. 68:39 n.

P. 243:4–6. *though a man . . . profiteth nothing.* 1 Cor. 13:3.

P. 243:9–11. *For a good . . . with discretion.* Ps. 112:5.

P. 243:26–27. *GOD hateth . . . burnt Offering.* Isa. 61:8.

P. 243:30–32. *glorious train . . . Vain-glory.* Cf. Robert Cawdray: "As the Peacocke beholding his gay and goodly feathers, waxeth forthwith very proud thereof, but as soone as he casteth downe his eyes, and looketh upon his feete, which are farre different in beautie, his Pride is quickly abated" (*A Treasurie or Store-house of Similies* [1609], p. 600; cf. pp. 32–33). Sir Thomas Browne exploded this common myth in *Pseudodoxia Epidemica,* III.27.2. Cf. Tilley, P 157, p. 528: "As proud as a Peacock."

P. 243:37–38. *The Rule therefore is this.* "Who gives to all, denies all," according to George Herbert's *Outlandish Proverbs* (no. 38, in *Works,* ed. Hutchinson, p. 322). Cicero warned that we must keep "our Bounty within *Compass;* and not . . . *give* beyond our *Ability;* for they that extend their Kindnesses beyond this Measure, wrong their Relations, by transferring those Bounties to *Strangers,* which they should rather have communicated, or left to their *Friends"* (*Tully's Offices,* p. 25). Traherne discusses the need for setting up an order of precedence in beneficence in *CE,* pp. 255–256.

P. 244:4–5. *thy Neighbors . . . claim a share.* Cf. Walter Kirkham Blount: "What we owe to our Kindred is of a more strict obligation then that which is due to an unknown Person and a Stranger" (*Spirit of Christianity,* p. 63).

P. 244:16. *While the Iron is hot it is time to strike.* Tilley, I 94, p. 342: "It is good to strike while the Iron is hot." The earliest listing is *c.* 1500.

P. 244:16–17. *Good Counsel is like a bitter Pill.* Tilley (P 326, p. 539) gives many variant citations under the general heading: "To swallow (digest) a bitter Pill." On the duties of proffering advice, cf. Walter Kirkham Blount: "The care a Christian takes to teach and instruct a poor body is more meritorious before God, then what is bestowed to deliver him from misery" (*Spirit of Christianity,* p. 61). "The best Charity." Traherne said (SM III.56), "is in Giving Counsels."

P. 244:18. *good seed.* Matt. 13:24.

P. 244:26. *He that winneth Souls is wise.* Prov. 11:30.

P. 244:35–36. *Liberality . . . Liberality.* An example of the rhetorical device known as antimetabole. Traherne is sparing of puns; cf., however, the pun on "pitch" in "The City": "The Musick in the Churches, which / Were Angels Joys (tho Pitch / Defil'd me afterwards) did then me crown" (II, 143).

P. 245:28–30. *that we should . . . persecute us.* Matt. 5:44.

P. 246:6–8. *to be . . . Unjust.* Matt. 5:45.

P. 246:14–18. *For if ye love . . . perfect.* Matt. 5:46–48.

P. 246:32–34. *The reality of Religion . . . daily with us.* Cf. Isaac Barrow in the sermon Traherne quoted in his Commonplace Book: "It is indeed the special grace and glory of our Religion, that it consisteth . . . in really producing sensible fruits of goodness" (*On the Duty and Reward of Bounty to the Poor,* p. 199; this passage does not appear in CB). Traherne's predecessor in Bridgeman's service, Hezekiah Burton, wrote "that a good Life is the best and only Religion; and that the best Worship we can give to God, is to do good to Men" (*Several Discourses,* ed. John Tillotson [1684], p. 8). Stress on an active, practical religion was one of the gifts of the Cambridge philosophers to the Church of the Restoration. Henry More rounded off the fifth of his *Divine Dialogues* with a rejection of the contemplative life; Philotheus says: "God forbid, *Philopolis,* that the Sweet of Contemplation should ever put your mouth out of tast with the savoury Usefulness of Secular Negotiations. To doe good to men, to assist the injured, to relieve the necessitous, to advise the ignorant in his necessary affairs, to bring up a Family in the fear of God and a chearful hope of everlasting Happiness after this Life, does as much transcend our manner of living [in rustic seclusion], if it ended in a mere pleasing our selves in the delicacy of select Notions, as solid Goodness does empty Phantastry, or sincere Charity the most childish Sophistry that is." Philopolis, chastened, answers that he is "fully convinced that all Speculation is vain that tends not to the Duty of Practice" (pp. 462–463). Cf. Traherne's statement in the *Centuries* (IV.2): "Philosophers are not those that speak, but Do great Things." He explains why God desires good works in SM III. 38, 40–42. See General Introduction pp. xlvi–xlvii.

P. 247:11–15. *notion and form of Liberality . . . Magnificence.* Cardinal Bona explained: "Where the expence is moderate, we call it Liberality; where it is high and splendid, Magnificence; . . . for Magnificence lies properly in the glory of the work. . . . Under this Head are comprehended all works of great expence, which relate to Divine Worship, common Utility, publick Exercises and Entertainments" (*Guide* pp. 151–152).

P. 248:28–30. *When he ascended . . . Prophets.* Eph. 4:8, 11.

P. 249:35–36. *For a Son . . . Fathers Wife.* A reference to Lev. 7–8, 23.

P. 249:39. The marginal reference to 1 Cor. should be extended to include verse 23.

P. 250:2–4. *saying of St. Chrysostome . . . whole World.* As in the case of Traherne's previous quotation of St. Chrysostom, the location has proved elusive (see *CE,* p. 187:38 n.). But cf. this passage from an anonymous translation of Chrysostom's *Exposition Upon the Epistle of S. Paule the Apostle to the Ephesians:* "The love of God, hath ioined the earth to the Heaven. The love of God, hath set man upon the princely throne. The love of God, hath shewed God upon the earth" (1581, p. 129).

P. 250:6. *Coheir with Christ.* A.V. reads "joint-heirs"; the Rheims version has "co-heires." On the importance of the concept in Traherne's work, see *CE,* p. 21:21 n. Cf. CYB (f. 53): "The Spirit beareth Witness with our Spirit that we are the Children of God, & if Children then Heirs & Coheirs with Christ. . . . There is a Spirit which raiseth a Man abov all the Riches of this World, that Enableth Him to Enjoy Heaven & Earth; Ages; & the Souls of Men: Eternity also & the Beauties of that Kingdom which is Divine & Infinit. Where evry Man will be so full, that evry Man will hav all: being Heir of all the Joys of Heaven & Earth." Cf. *CE,* pp. 38:20 n. and 48:3 n.

P. 250:18. *The Assembly of the First-born.* Heb. 12:23.

P. 252:18. *the desire satisfied is a Tree of Life.* The identical maxim appears in *C* I.43 and in *Thanksgivings,* II, 286. Cf. Thomas Jackson: "And knowledge againe *relying* upon the internall desire of happinesse, which is the stemme or branch, whence these fruits of loue preceede, doth season and sweeten the very nature or propertie of it, and in a sort transforme from a wilde plant to a tree of life" (*Treatise,* p. 464; quoted in CB, *s.v.* "Desire," f. 34ᵛ.1).

P. 252:20–21. *Davids purpose . . . Solomons performance.* See 1 Chron. 22; 1 Kings 5–6; 1 Kings 8:17–19; 2 Chron. 6:7–9; and Acts 7:45–47. The Bible does not make Traherne's point, which he also proposed in "Thoughts: II": "That Temple David did intend, / Was but a Thought, and yet it did transcend / King Solomons" (II, 173). Cf. also "The Inference: II": *"David* a Temple in his Mind conceiv'd; / And that Intention was so well receiv'd / By God, that all the Sacred Palaces / That ever were did less His Glory pleas" (II, 141). For Traherne's admiration of David, see *C* III.69; on the general point, see *C* IV.88.

P. 254:26. *All Glorious within.* Ps. 45:13.

P. 254:40. The references, more accurately, are to Job 38:7 and Rev. 15:3.

P. 255:4. *curious.* Careful in details, precise, skilled; used *CE,* p. 148, to describe needlework.

P. 255:32. *Conversation.* Behavior.

P. 256:1. *without doors.* Outdoors.

P. 256:16. *ungrateful.* Unpleasant.

P. 256:17. *Bowels.* Compassion.

P. 256:24. *Let . . . work.* James 1:4.

P. 257:6–7. *Tears . . . Bottles.* Cf. Ps. 56:8: "Put thou my tears into thy bottle. . . ." The image is common in Renaissance English poetry; cf. Spenser, *Faerie Queene,* VI.viii.24: "Here in this bottle . . . I put the teares of my contrition. . . ." In the *Meditations* Traherne prayed: "O cast away these *evil Tears,* and drown them in thy Son's *Blood,* and *bottle up* all my *penitential Tears,* for my Good" (p. 23); he explained, or rather interpreted, the image in SM I.93.

P. 257:18 *183.* An obvious mistake, since the last Psalm is numbered 150; the reference here is to Ps. 139.

P. 258:18. *some pressing want.* See *CE,* pp. 54:37 n. and 212:14 n., on desire. This Augustinian concept of "wants," discussed by Martz in *The Paradise Within* (p. 40), is central to Traherne's philosophy, pervading the *Centuries* in particular: "Felicitie [is] composed of Wants and Supplies. . . . It is very Strange; Want itself is a Treasure in Heaven" (*C* I.41). "Wants are the Bands and Cements between God and us" (*C* I.51). In the First Century Traherne plays upon the paradox "that GOD should Want. for in Him is the Fulness of all Blessedness. . . . It is Incredible, yet very Plain: Want is the Fountain of all His Fulness" (*C* I.42). See the *Meditations*: "I praise thee for thine infinite Wisdom in creating all Things so by degrees, that thereby we may see our Wants, and better praise thee for our Supplies" (p. 13). The topic is expounded in SM III.79 and appears as well in the poems; see "The Anticipation" (II, 159). In *Christian Ethicks* the idea has been shorn of the peculiar and unorthodox aspects which make it so striking in Traherne's private prose and poetry. There is even a surface likeness here to Hobbes's famous statement that "the Felicity of this life, consisteth not in the repose of a mind satisfied. . . . Nor can a man any more live, whose Desires are at an end, than he, whose Senses and Imaginations are at a stand. Felicity is a continuall progresse of the desire, from one object to another" (*Leviathan*, I.11, p. 79 of the American Everyman ed. [New York, 1950]). Cf. also John Smith: "There is an insatiable appetite in the Soul of man. . . . There are Two principall faculties [desire and love] in the Soul which, like the two daughters of the Horsleach, are always crying, *Give, Give*" (*Discourses*, p. 420; plagiarized by Samuel Shaw in *Immanuel* [1669], p. 128). (On the "daughters of the Horsleach," see Prov. 30:15.)

P. 258:26. *more delight in the Communication.* See *CE*, p. 56:10 n.

P. 260:15–16. *Holy . . . thy Glory.* Isa. 6:3 (altered through Isa. 2:10, 19, 21).

P. 260:27. *New Jerusalem.* Rev. 21. For Traherne's conception of the New Jerusalem in his childhood, see "Christendom" (II, 106–110) and "The City" (II, 142–145).

P. 260:35–36. *That we gain infinitely . . . prodigious.* Cf. *CE*, p. 135: God's love "is the End of ours, ours of his."

P. 260:40. *Self-love is the first round.* Cf. *C* IV.49, 53, 55, 60; and Salter, *Traherne*, pp. 51–53, 97–103, 125. Self-love, said a French moralist, is "a natural Inclination . . . most Divine in its Original: We love our selves for this very Reason, because God has loved us" (Jacques Abbadie, *The Art of Knowing One-Self: or, An Enquiry into the Sources of Morality*, tr. T. W. [Oxford, 1695], p. 44). Conventional optimists like the Scottish lawyer Sir George Mackenzie wished not "to root out Self-love, but rather to direct and improve it. For certainly God has grafted Self-love in every Man's Heart, to the end, Man might thereby be the more oblig'd to love him, to whom he owes all those Excellencies which he loves in himself, and that he may be thereby oblig'd to preserve himself" (*Reason: An Essay* [1690], p. 99). (On the connection between self-love and self-preservation, see the following note.) Using a circular rather than the vertical metaphor Traherne employs, Henry More called self-love "the hinge or centre upon which we turn from God to the Creature; and upon which we *begin* to circle from the Creature to God again" (*Discourses*, p. 182). Traherne alludes to the self-love of the damned above, p. 58.

P. 261:9. *a great mistake in that arrogant Leviathan.* "The finall Cause, End, or Designe of men" in forming commonwealths, said Hobbes, "is the foresight of their own preservation" (*Leviathan*, II.17, p. 139). Self-preservation being the dominant passion, man outside society falls naturally into a state of war and his life is—in the famous phrase (which Traherne adapted in his *Thanksgivings*, II, 222)—"solitary, poore, nasty, brutish, and short" (*Leviathan*, I.13, p. 104). On the contemporary hostility to Hobbes, see Samuel I. Mintz, *The Hunting of Leviathan* (Cambridge, Eng., 1962), *passim*, and on this particular issue, pp. 144–145. Hobbes, said Shaftesbury in his Preface to Benjamin Whichcote's sermons (1698), "has done but very ill service in the moral world. And however other parts of philosophy may be obliged to him, *ethicks* will appear to have no great share in the obligation. He has, indeed with great zeal and learning, been opposed by all the eminent and worthy divines of the church of *England*" (in Whichcote, *Works*, III, iv). With Traherne's statement that "Nature is crippled . . . if Self-preservation be made her only concern," cf. this assertion in Spinoza's *Ethics*, completed (but not published) in the year of Traherne's death: "The effort for self-preservation is the first and only foundation of virtue" (IV.22, in *The Chief Works of Benedict de Spinoza*, tr. R. H. M. Elwes [New York, 1955], II, 203–204).

P. 261:27. *TO love . . . impossible.* This is the "Atheistical fool" mentioned in the next sentence speaking. On the loving animals Traherne instances, see *CE*, p. 44:10 n. On the main point of this paragraph, see *C* IV.56.

P. 261:34. *Moses would have . . . Book.* Ex. 32:32.

P. 261:35–36. *St. Paul . . . his Brethren.* Rom. 9:3.

P. 261:37. *who made . . . for us.* Gal. 3:13 and 2 Cor. 5:21 fused, as earlier, *CE*, p. 100.

P. 262:24–25. *But to love . . . unnatural.* Again the "Atheistical fool" speaks.

P. 262:35. *apprehensive.* Aware.

P. 263:16. *If the Sun were extinguished.* The possibility had occurred to Traherne before: "Suppose the Sun were Extinguished" (*C* I.46); "Suppose the Sun were absent" (*C* II.7). The continuation of the thought in *CE* (p. 264) is thoroughly Platonic. See *CE*, p. 39:35 n.

P. 265:8. *at the first dash.* Immediately.

P. 266:14–15. *He so loved . . . Son.* John 3:16.

P. 266:39–40. *This is . . . well pleased.* Matt. 3:17, 17:5; 2 Pet. 1:17.

P. 269:14–15. *the Grateful Sence of Benefits received.* Cf. the remark attributed (*CE*, p. 213) to Henry Hammond: "*The greater part of our eternal happiness will consist in a grateful Recognition . . . of Benefits already received.*" Traherne's analysis of gratitude is predicated upon his concept of a "circulation" of love in the universe and more particularly between God and man. In his view love and gratitude are "natural, and free, and inevitable operations" (p. 259); his depiction of a spontaneous gratitude differs markedly from the almost prudential morality of other writers—for example, Robert Boyle, who urged that gratitude to God is a duty which we are "oblieged" by divine law to perform (Boyle, *The Excellency of Theology, Compared with Natural Philosophy* [1674], p. 75). Everyone would have agreed with Sir Matthew Hale that God's "ultimate and more universal End" in creating the universe "was, that by this Communication of the Divine Goodness unto something without himself, the Glory, and Honour, and Praise thereof might return unto himself" (*Contemplations*, II, "Of Prayer and Thanksgiving," 214). Traherne's own *Thanksgivings* are a notable contribution to the literature of gratitude.

P. 271:17. *kindly.* In accordance with nature, pleasantly.

P. 273:1–2. *kindness of a Benefactor . . . rich and amiable.* See *CE*, p. 231:9 n.

P. 273:37–38. *An infinite and eternal Kingdom.* Another "character" begins here, heralded by the inclusion in the chapter heading (p. 269) of "The true Character of a Grateful Person."

P. 275:4. *Stir not . . . till he please.* Cant. 2:7, 3:5, 8:4.

P. 275:18. *Seraphick Love.* The identification of the seraphim with love derives from the *Celestial Hierarchies* (*c.* 500) of Dionysius the Pseudo-Areopagite, who makes them the highest of the nine ranks of angels. According to Thomas Heywood, "The *Seraphim* doth in the word imply, / A *Fervent*

Love and *Zeale to the Most-High*" (*The Hierarchie of the Blessed Angells*, IV [1635], p. 194). In the *Meditations* Traherne thanks God for the "Seraphins [*sic*] Charity" and prays for "a Seraph's ardent inflamed affection to love" God (pp. 8, 9).

P. 276:13–18. *Praise ye . . . Heaven of Heavens.* Ps. 150:1–2, 148:1–4.

P. 276:19. *his Name . . . Blessing and Praise.* Neh. 9:5.

P. 276:30–31. *No man can return more Blessings than he receiveth.* Cf. *CE*, p. 265: reason dictates that "for a shilling-worth of Service, a shilling-worth of Gratitude is naturally paid."

P. 276:36. *How like an Angel.* Cf. the opening of the poem "Wonder" (II, 6): "How like an Angel came I down!"

P. 277:1. *peculiar.* Possession.

P. 277:19. *avocations.* Diversions, ability to withdraw.

P. 278:9–12. *Moses . . . Old age.* On Moses, see Ex. 5–19; on David, 1 Sam. 18:29, 26:8; on Elijah, 1 Kings 21:20; on Daniel, Dan. 2:13; on Joseph, next note; on Solomon, 1 Kings 11:14–40.

P. 278:27–28. *Joseph . . . Mistress.* Gen. 37, 39.

P. 279:1–3. *Joshua . . . Moses's death.* Cf. Num. 13:2, 14:10; Deut. 34:9; Joshua 1:1–2.

P. 279:5–6. *Samuel . . . chosen of GOD.* 1 Sam. 10:24.

P. 279:6–7. *from Dan . . . Prophet of the Lord.* 1 Sam. 3:20.

P. 279:13–14. *Solomon . . . revolted from GOD.* See 1 Kings 11.

P. 279:16. *the matter of Urias.* 1 Kings 15:5; see 2 Sam. 11.

P. 280:17. *Proficient.* One who is making progress (in the study of religion) but is not yet perfect; cf. More, *Dialogues*, I, p. 118: "You are an excellent Proficient, . . . that can thus vary, emprove and maintain things from so few and slender hints."

P. 280:34–35. *a Schismatick and a Heretick.* The following passage is further evidence of Traherne's royalism; see *CE*, pp. 96:6 n. and 218:30 n.

P. 281:14. *AS for all the Enemies.* Here begins an extended "character" of the virtuous man, interrupted formally from time to time.

P. 281:36. *almost in a desperate manner.* Cf. *CE*, p. 169: "To dare to be Good, is the Office of true and Religious valour."

P. 282:6. *heard him say . . . Temple.* Mark 14:58.

P. 283:2–7. *I know very well . . . Blessings.* With this "character" of the age, cf. Henry Hammond: "I will hope . . . that as all Europe hath not more moderation and purity of religion than this kingdom, so it never had a more learned clergy; never more encouragement for learning from religion; never more advantages to religion from learning" (*Thirty-one Sermons*, pp. 470–471). But such cheerfulness was unusual in considerations of the age. More ordinary were accounts such as this by Walter Kirkham Blount: "The Luxury, Self-interest, Ambition, and general Irregularities of the Manners of this Age, have they not spread every where the Spirit of Division? and what judgment ought one to make of the Christianity of these later Times, wherein Animosities, Jealousies, Law-Suits, Quarrels, Envies, Calumnies, Repinings, Injustices, and Revenge, reign with so much heat?" (*Spirit of Christianity*, pp. 124–125). Rom.

5:20 is the slightly modified source of Traherne's assertion: "As Sin abounds, so does Grace also super-abound."

P. 283:13. *Reigning of the Saints.* Rev. 5:10, 20:4, 20:6, and 22:5.

P. 283:25. *having Food . . . Great Gain.* 1 Tim. 6:8, 6.

P. 283:26–27. *professed Subjection to the Gospel of Christ.* 2 Cor. 9:13.

P. 283:27–28. *all the Kingdoms . . . Christ.* Rev. 11:15.

P. 283:31. *pure publick worship.* This passage reflects Traherne's support of the Restoration version of the Laudian party in the Church of England. See *CE*, p. 5:14 n.

P. 283:38–39. *other men . . . their Labours.* John 4:38.

P. 283:40. The reference is to 1 Cor. 4:8–11.

P. 284:33–34. *faithful to . . . Life.* Rev. 2:10.

P. 284:36–37. *He that doth . . . Brother.* Matt. 12:50; Mark 3:35.

P. 285:5. *Celestial Epicurisme.* A sort of oxymoron, versions of which were not uncommon in the seventeenth century. Cf. Isaac Barrow's assertion that "a man may be vertuously voluptuous, and a laudable Epicure by doing much good" (*On the Duty and Reward of Bounty to the Poor*, pp. 142–143; quoted in CB, *s.v.* "Charitie," f. 26.1). Nathanael Culverwel exhorted the students of Emmanuel College: "Do you devour with a golden Epicurisme, the Arts and Sciences . . . let not an Epicure take more pleasure in his garden then you can do in your studies" (*Light of Nature*, p. 198). Traherne speaks of his "Heavenly Avarice" in "Desire" (II, 177).

P. 285:15. *expaciate.* Move freely in space.

P. 285:16–17. *GODLINESS . . . Great Gain.* 1 Tim. 6:6.

P. 285:17–18. *stir up . . . Remembrance.* 2 Pet. 1:13.

P. 285:21–22. *The fulness . . . Inward Man.* Cf. Eph. 4:13: "the measure of the stature of the fulness of Christ." The phrase "the inward man" occurs in Rom. 7:22 and 2 Cor. 4:16.

P. 285:33–35. *Every Like in Nature . . . GOD-Like.* Possibly a reflection of the saying of Plotinus (*Enneads* I.vi.9) so popular among the Cambridge Platonists: "Nothing but a sun-like eye perceives the sun; nothing but a God-like soul perceives God" (Whichcote's paraphrase in *Works*, IV, 314; cf. John Smith, *Discourses*, pp. 2–3). Traherne quoted this passage in Thomas Jackson's clumsy translation in CB, *s.v.* "Preparation of Objects," f. 77.1 (Jackson, *Treatise*, p. 439). One of the dicta of Hermes which Traherne quoted *CE*, p. 226, is similar: "For the like is intelligible by the like"; this is also akin to a Thomistic maxim frequently cited by religious writers of the time: "Quidquid recipitur ad modum recipientis recipitur."

P. 286:19. *curiously.* Minutely.

P. 286:26–27. *that GOD is . . . seek him.* Heb. 11:6.

Selected Bibliography

[The following list does not attempt to be exhaustive. It includes works which have been cited more than once in the introductions or the Commentary; the abbreviated forms used in the annotations are given in brackets preceding the full bibliographical citation. Unless otherwise observed, place of publication is London.]

[Agrippa, *Occult Philosophy*.] Agrippa, Henry Cornelius of Nettlesheim. *Three Books of Occult Philosophy*, tr. J. F[reake]. 1651.

Allestree, Richard. See *The Whole Duty of Man*.

Arber, Edward, ed. *The Term Catalogues, 1668–1709 A.D.; with a Number for Easter Term, 1711 A.D.* 3 vols. 1903, 1905, 1906.

[Aristotle, *Nic. Eth.*] Aristotle. *Nicomachean Ethics*, in *The Basic Works*, ed. Richard McKeon. New York, 1941. References to Aristotle's other works are also to this edition.

Augustine. *The Meditations, Soliloquia, and Manuall of the Glorious Doctour S. Augustine.* 2d ed. Paris, 1655.

Bacon, Francis. *Works*, ed. James Spedding, Robert Leslie Ellis, and Douglas Denon Heath. 15 vols. Boston, 1860–1864.

Barrow, Isaac. *On the Duty and Reward of Bounty to the Poor.* 1671.

Baxter, Richard. *Reliquiae Baxterianae*, ed. Matthew Sylvester. 1696.

Blount, Walter Kirkham. *The Spirit of Christianity.* 1686.

[Bona, *Guide*.] Bona, Giovanni. *A Guide to Eternity: Extracted out of the Writings of the Holy Fathers, and Ancient Philosophers*, tr. Roger L'Estrange. 2d ed. 1680.

Browne, Sir Thomas. *Pseudodoxia Epidemica: or, Enquiries into Very Many Received Tenets and Commonly Received Truths.* 6th ed. 1672.

Browne, Sir Thomas. *Religio Medici and Other Writings*, intro. by Frank L. Huntley. New York and London, 1951.

Buridan, Jean. *Quaestiones in decem libros Aristotelis ad Nicomachum.* Oxford, 1637.

Burnet, Gilbert. *History of My Own Time: The Reign of Charles the Second,* ed. Osmund Airy. Vol. I. Oxford, 1897.

Campbell, Lord John. *Lives of the Lord Chancellors and Keepers of the Great Seal of England, from the Earliest Times Till the Reign of King George IV.* 5th ed. 1868. Vol. IV.

Carré, Meyrick H. *Phases of Thought in England.* Oxford, 1949.

[Charron, *Of Wisdome.*] Charron, Pierre. *Of Wisdome Three Bookes,* tr. Samson Lennard. 1640.

Clarendon, Edward Hyde, Earl of. *Essays Moral and Entertaining.* 2 vols. 1815.

Colby, Frances L.   "Traherne and the Cambridge Platonists: An Analytical Comparison." Unpublished Johns Hopkins diss., 1947.

Collier, Jeremy. *Miscellanies upon Moral Subjects.* Part II. 1695.

[Colvill, *Philosophia.*]   Colvill, William. *Philosophia Moralis Christiana.* Edinburgh, 1670.

[*Conway Letters.*]   *Conway Letters,* ed. Marjorie Hope Nicolson.   New Haven, 1930.

Costello, William T.   *The Scholastic Curriculum in Early Seventeenth-Century Cambridge.* Cambridge, Mass., 1958.

Cragg, Gerald R.   *From Puritanism to the Age of Reason.* Cambridge, Eng., 1950.

Cudworth, Ralph. *The True Intellectual System of the Universe.* 1678. Also ed. Thomas Birch, 4 vols., 1820.

[Culverwel, *Light of Nature.*] Culverwel, Nathanael. *An Elegant and Learned Discourse of the Light of Nature, With Several Other Treatises,* ed. William Dillingham.   1652.

[Cumberland, *Treatise.*] Cumberland, Richard. *A Treatise of the Laws of Nature,* tr. John Maxwell.   1727.

[Curtis.] Curtis, Mark H. *Oxford and Cambridge in Transition, 1558–1640.* Oxford, 1959.

Ellrodt, Robert. *L'Inspiration personnelle et l'esprit du temps chez les poètes métaphysiques anglais.* Part I: *L'Inspiration personnelle.* Vol. II: *Poètes de transition, poètes mystiques.* Paris, 1960.

[Eustache.] Eustache de Saint-Paul (Eustachius à Sancto Paulo). *Ethica, Sive Summa Moralis Disciplinae, in tres partes divisa.* 1658.

Eyre, G. E. Briscoe, and Charles Robert Rivington, eds. *A Transcript of the Registers of the Worshipful Company of Stationers; from 1640–1708 A.D.* 3 vols. 1913–1914.

[Ferguson, *Moral Virtue.*] Ferguson, Robert. *A Sober Enquiry into the Nature, Measure, and Principle of Moral Virtue.* 1673.

Ficino, Marsilio. *Opera.* Paris, 1641. Vol. II (containing the commentaries on Plato).

[Gale, *Court.*] Gale, Theophilus. *The Court of the Gentiles,* Part II. Oxford, 1670. Quotations are from the Oxford, 1671, reissue.

Glanvill, Joseph. *Lux Orientalis, in Two Choice and Useful Treatises: The One Lux Orientalis . . . The Other, A Discourse of Truth, By . . .* [George] *Rust . . . With Annotations on them both* [by Henry More]. 1682.

[Glanvill, *Vanity of Dogmatizing.*] Glanvill, Joseph. *The Vanity of Dogmatizing.* Reproduced from the edition of 1661. With a Bibliographical Note by Moody E. Prior. New York, 1931.

Good, Thomas. *Firmianus and Dubitantius, or Certain Dialogues Concerning Atheism, Infidelity, Popery, and other Heresies and Schismes.* Oxford, 1674.

[Hale, *Contemplations.*] Hale, Sir Matthew. *Contemplations Moral and Divine.* 1676. Parts I and II.

Hammond, Henry. *Miscellaneous Theological Works.* 3d ed. 2 vols. Oxford, 1847–1849.

[Hammond, *Thirty-one Sermons.*] Hammond, Henry. *Thirty-one Sermons Preached on Several Occasions.* Parts I and II. Oxford, 1849–1850.

Hartcliffe, John. *A Treatise of Moral and Intellectual Virtues.* 1691.

Herbert, George. *Works,* ed. F. E. Hutchinson. Oxford, 1941.

[Hermes, *Pymander.*] Hermes Trismegistus. *His Divine Pymander, in Seventeen Books. Together with his Second Book Called Asclepius,* tr. John Everard. 1657.

Hinman, Charlton. *The Printing and Proofreading of the First Folio of Shakespeare.* 2 vols. Oxford, 1963.

Hobbes, Thomas. *Hobbs's Tripos, In Three Discourses: The First, Humane Nature, . . . The Second, De Corpore Politico. . . . The Third, Of Liberty and Necessity.* 3d ed. 1684.

Hobbes, Thomas. *Leviathan,* intro. by A. D. Lindsay. New York, 1950.

Hoopes, Robert. *Right Reason in the English Renaissance.* Cambridge, Mass., 1962.

Horneck, Anthony. *The Happy Ascetick: or, the Best Exercise.* 3d ed. 1693.

[Jackson, *Treatise.*] Jackson, Thomas. *A Treatise Containing the Originall of Unbeliefe.* 1625.

Jackson, Thomas. *A Treatise of the Divine Essence and Attributes.* Part I, 1628. Part II, 1629.

[Le Grand, *Body of Philosophy.*] Le Grand, Antoine. *An Entire Body of Philosophy, According to the Principles of the Famous Renat Des Cartes,* tr. Richard Blome. 1694.

'A Library for Younger Schollers' Compiled by an English Scholar-Priest about 1655, ed. Alma DeJordy and Harris Francis Fletcher. ("Illinois Studies in Language and Literature," Vol. XLVIII.) Urbana, 1961.

Locke, John. *On Politics and Education,* ed. Howard Penniman. New York, 1947.

Macrobius, Ambrosius Aurelius Theodosius. *Commentary on the Dream of Scipio,* tr., ed., and with intro. by William Harris Stahl. New York, 1952.

Martz, Louis L. *The Paradise Within: Studies in Vaughan, Traherne, and Milton.* New Haven and London, 1964.

Mintz, Samuel I. *The Hunting of Leviathan: Seventeenth-Century Reactions to the Materialism and Moral Philosophy of Thomas Hobbes.* Cambridge, Eng., 1962.

[More, *Account.*] More, Henry. *An Account of Virtue: or, Dr. Henry More's Abridgment of Morals Put into English,* tr. Edward Southwell. 1690.

[More, *Collection.*] More, Henry. *A Collection of Several Philosophical Writings . . . Antidote against Atheism* [1653]. *Appendix to the said Antidote. Enthusiasmus Triumphatus* [1656]. *Letters to Des-Cartes, &c. Immortality of the Soul* [1659]. *Conjectura Cabbalistica* [1653]. 1662. These treatises were first published on the bracketed dates.

[More, *Discourses.*] More, Henry. *Discourses on Several Texts of Scripture,* ed. John Worthington, Jr. 1692.

[More, *Divine Dialogues.*] More, Henry. *Divine Dialogues . . . The Three First Dialogues.* 1668. *Divine Dialogues . . . The Two Last Dialogues.* 1668. The latter volume was actually published a few months before the first.

[More, *Grand Mystery of Godliness.*] More, Henry. *An Explanation of the Grand Mystery of Godliness; or, A True and Faithfull Representation of the Everlasting Gospel of our Lord and Saviour Jesus Christ.* 1660.

[More, *Poems.*] More, Henry. *The Complete Poems,* ed. and with intro. by Alexander B. Grosart. Edinburgh, 1878.

[Norris, *Christian Prudence.*] Norris, John. *A Treatise Concerning Christian Prudence: or the Principles of Practical Wisdom.* 1710.

[Norris, *Collection.*] Norris, John. *A Collection of Miscellanies.* Oxford, 1687.

North, Roger. *The Lives of the Right Hon. Francis North, Baron Guilford . . . the Hon. Sir Dudley North . . . and the Hon. and Dr. John North.* New ed. 1826. Vol. I.

Parker, Samuel. *An Account of the Nature and Extent of the Divine Dominion & Goodnesse, Especially as they refer to the Origenian Hypothesis Concerning the Preexistence of Souls.* Oxford, 1666.

[Pemble, *Summe.*] Pemble, William. *A Summe of Moral Philosophy.* 1635.

Piccolomini, Francesco. *Universa philosophia de moribus.* Rev. ed. Venice, 1594.

[Pinto, *Sterry.*] Pinto, Vivian de Sola. *Peter Sterry, Platonist and Puritan.* Cambridge, Eng., 1934.

Plato. *Dialogues,* tr. Benjamin Jowett. 4th ed. 4 vols. Oxford, 1953.

Plomer, Henry R. *A Dictionary of the Printers and Booksellers Who Were at Work in England, Scotland and Ireland from 1641 to 1667.* 1907.

Plomer, Henry R. *A Dictionary of the Printers and Booksellers Who Were at Work in England, Scotland and Ireland from 1668 to 1725.* Oxford, 1922.

Plotinus. *The Enneads,* tr. Stephen MacKenna, ed. B. S. Page. 3d ed. 1962.

Popkin, Richard H. *The History of Skepticism from Erasmus to Descartes.* Assen, Neth., 1960.

Pufendorf, Samuel. *The Whole Duty of Man According to the Law of Nature,* tr. Andrew Tooke. 4th ed. 1716.

[*Pymander.*] See above, Hermes.

[Reynolds, *Passions.*] Reynolds, Edward. *A Treatise of the Passions and Faculties of the Soule of Man.* 1640.

[Runes, *Dictionary.*] Runes, Dagobert D. *Dictionary of Philosophy.* 15th ed. New York, 1960.

Salter, K. W. *Thomas Traherne: Mystic and Poet.* 1964.

[Scheibler, *Philosophia compendiosa*.] Scheibler, Christopher. *Philosophia compendiosa, Exhibens 1. logicae, 2. metaphysicae, 3. physicae, 4. geometriae, 5. astronomiae, 6. opticae, 7. ethicae, 8. politicae, 9. oeconomicae, compendium methodicum.* 7th ed. Oxford, 1647.

Scott, John. *Works.* 6 vols. Oxford, 1826.

[Shelton, *Moral Vertues*.] Shelton, William. *Moral Vertues Baptized Christian: Or the Necessity of Morality Among Christians.* 1667.

Sidgwick, Henry. *Outlines of the History of Ethics for English Readers.* 1922.

[Smith, *Discourses*.] Smith, John. *Select Discourses*, ed. John Worthington. 1660.

[Sterry, *Appearance*.] Sterry, Peter. *The Appearance of God to Man In the Gospel, and the Gospel Change. Together with Several Other Discourses from Scripture.* 1710.

[Sterry, *Discourse*.] Sterry, Peter. *A Discourse of the Freedom of the Will.* 1675.

[Sterry, *Rise*.] Sterry, Peter. *The Rise, Race, and Royalty of the Kingdom of God in the Soul of Man.* 1683.

Sykes, Norman. *From Sheldon to Secker: Aspects of English Church History, 1660–1768.* Cambridge, Eng., 1959.

[Thomas Aquinas, *ST*.] Thomas Aquinas. *Summa Theologica*, tr. Fathers of the English Dominican Province, rev. by Daniel J. Sullivan. 2 vols. Chicago, London, Toronto, 1952.

[Tilley.] Tilley, Morris Palmer. *A Dictionary of the Proverbs in England in the Sixteenth and Seventeenth Centuries.* Ann Arbor, Mich., 1950.

Traherne, Thomas.

    Centuries Bodleian MS. Eng. th. e. 50.

    Centuries, Poems, and Thanksgivings, ed. H. M. Margoliouth. 2 vols. Oxford, 1958. The abbreviated forms used for citations from this edition are listed in the Preface, pp. vi–vii.

    Christian Ethicks. 1675.

    [CYB.] Church's Year-Book Bodleian MS. Eng. th. e. 51.

    [CB.] Commonplace Book, Bodleian MS. Eng. poet. c. 42.

    [EN.] Early Notebook, Bodleian MS. Lat. misc. f. 45.

    [FN.] Ficino Notebook, British Museum MS. Burney 126.

    [*Meditations*.] *Meditations on the Six Days of the Creation* (1717), intro. by George Robert Guffey. Los Angeles, 1966.

    Of Magnanimity and Charity, ed. John Rothwell Slater. New York, 1942.

    Roman Forgeries. 1673.

    [SM.] Select Meditations, Osborn MS.

Tulloch, John. *Rational Theology and Christian Philosophy in England in the Seventeenth Century.* 2 vols. 2d ed. 1874.

Venning, Ralph. *Things Worth Thinking On; or, Helps to Piety.* 2d ed. 1665.

[Wade.] Wade, Gladys I. *Thomas Traherne.* Princeton, 1944.

[Whichcote, *Aphorisms*.] Whichcote, Benjamin. *Moral and Religious Aphorisms.* intro. by W. R. Inge. 1930.

[Whichcote, *Works*.] Whichcote, Benjamin. *Works.* 4 vols. Aberdeen, 1751.

Whittick, Arnold. *Symbols, Signs, and Their Meaning.* Newton, Mass., 1960.

The Whole Duty of Man, attrib. to Richard Allestree. 1731.

[Wing.] Wing, Donald. *Short-title Catalogue of Books Printed in England, Scotland, Ireland, Wales, and British America and of English Books Printed in Other Countries, 1641–1700.* 3 vols. New York, 1945–1951.

Wood, Anthony. *Athenae Oxonienses,* ed. Philip Bliss. 4 vols. 1813–1820.

Wood, Anthony. *The History and Antiquities of the University of Oxford,* ed. John Gutch. 3 vols. Oxford, 1786–1796.

[Wuellner, *Dictionary.*] Wuellner, Bernard. *Dictionary of Scholastic Philosophy.* Milwaukee, 1956.

Zöckler, Otto. *Die Tugundlehre des Christentums geschichtlich dargestellt in der Entwicklung ihrer Lehrformen, mit besonderer Rücksicht auf deren zahlensymbolische Einkleidung.* Gütersloh, Ger., 1904.

Index

[Modern scholarly authorities cited in this volume are not included in the Index; they are, however, listed in the Selected Bibliography.]